BATMAN THE LONG HALLOWEEN

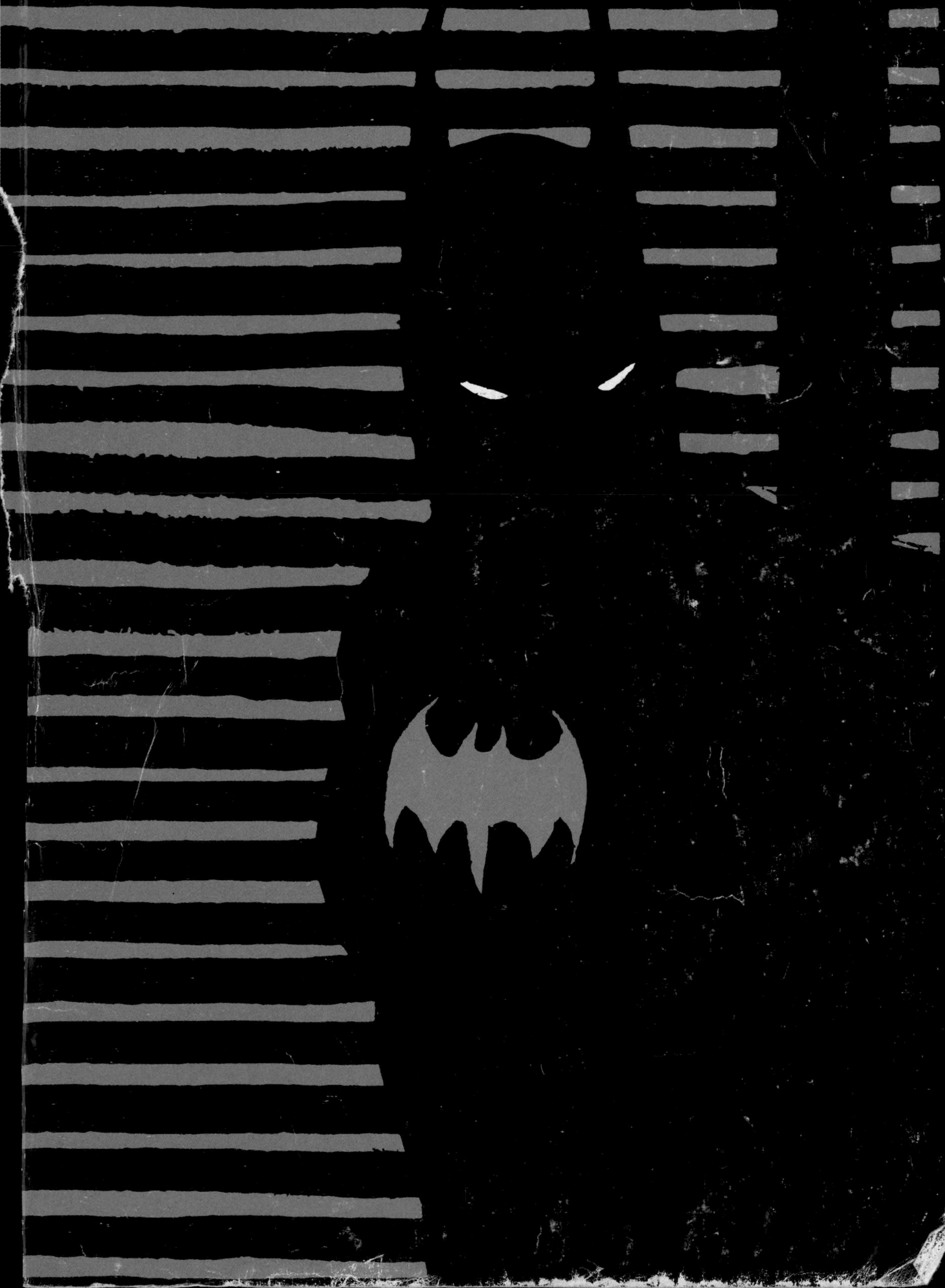

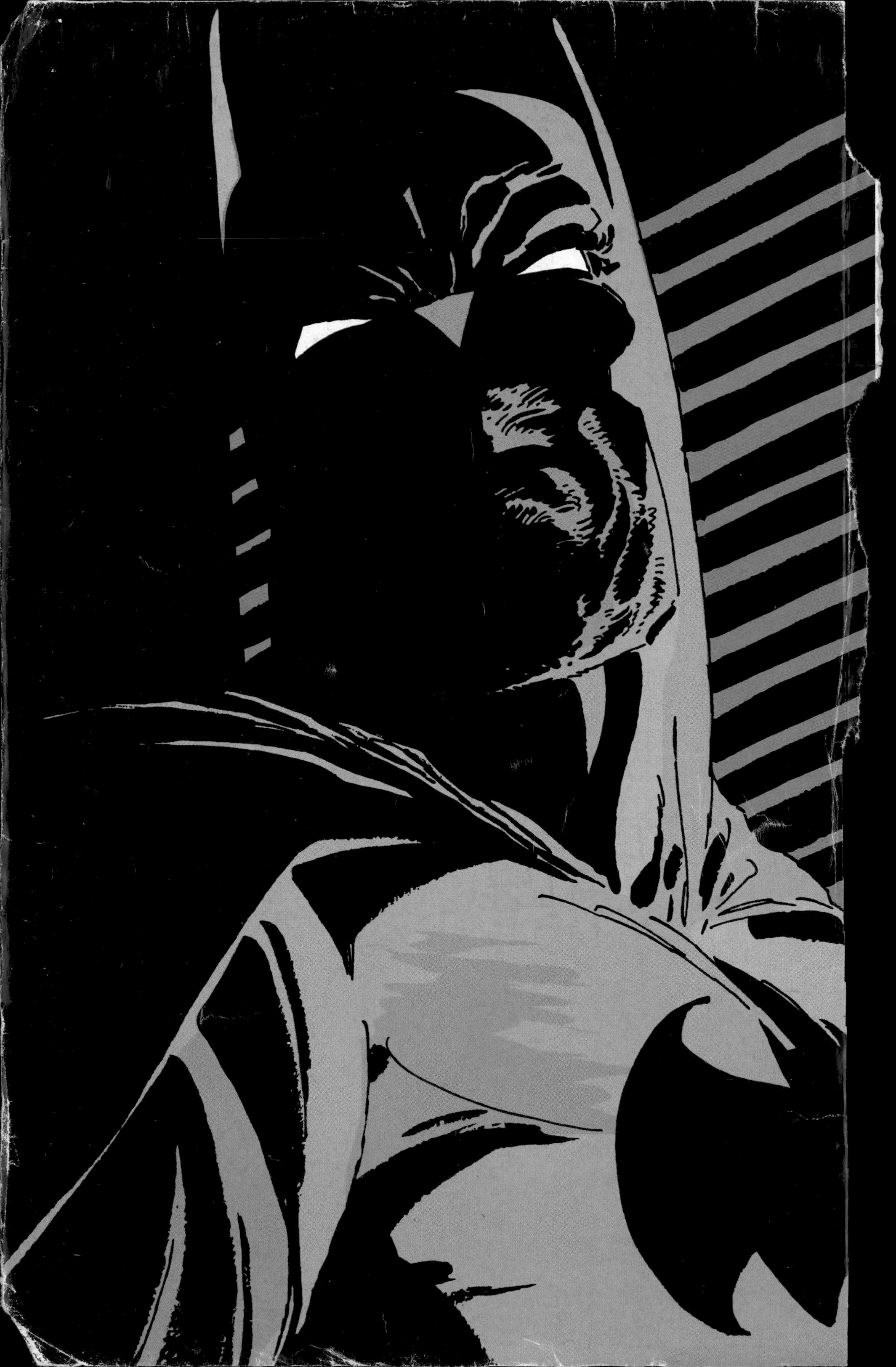

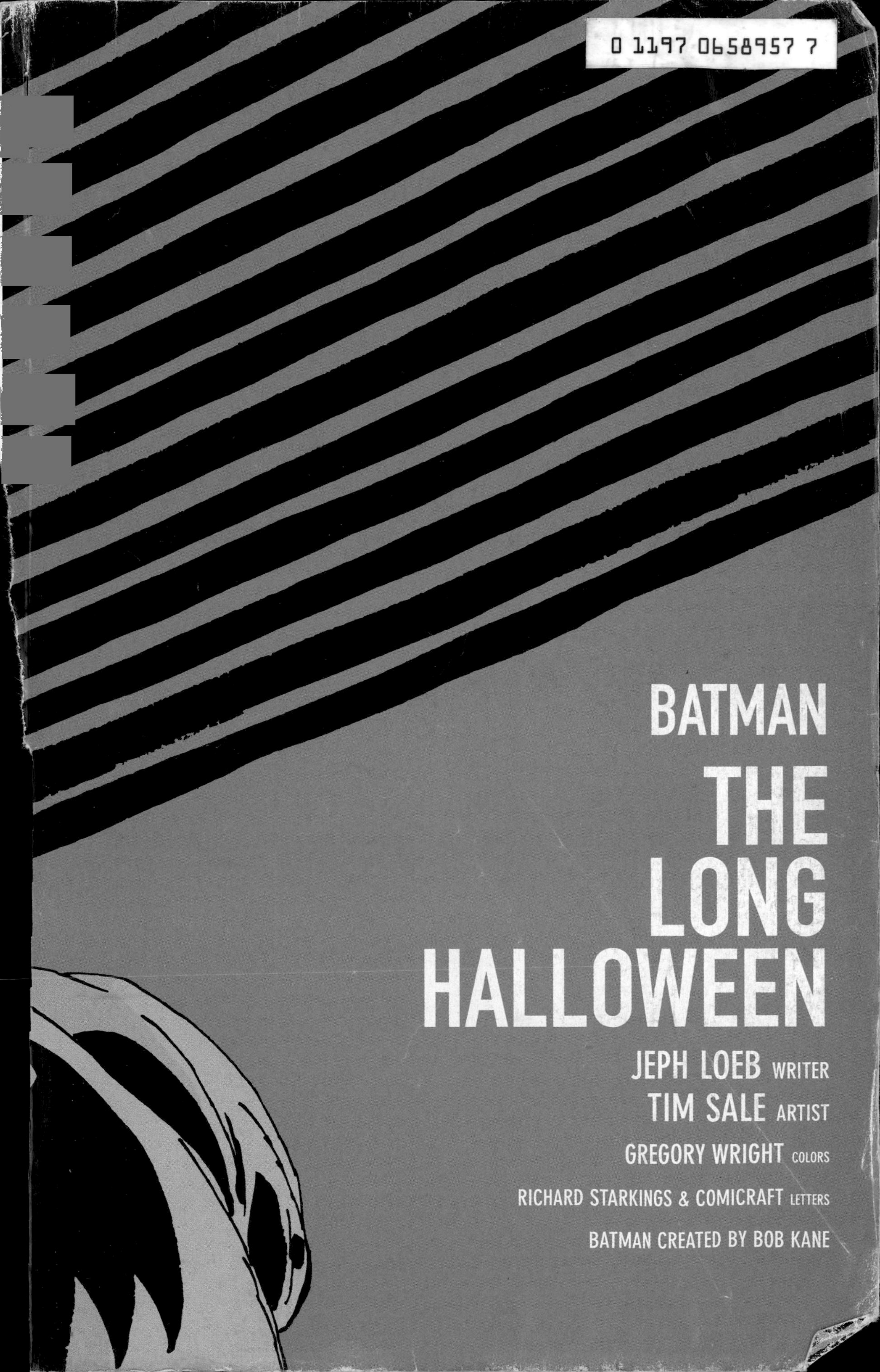

BATMAN
THE LONG HALLOWEEN

JEPH LOEB WRITER
TIM SALE ARTIST
GREGORY WRIGHT COLORS
RICHARD STARKINGS & COMICRAFT LETTERS
BATMAN CREATED BY BOB KANE

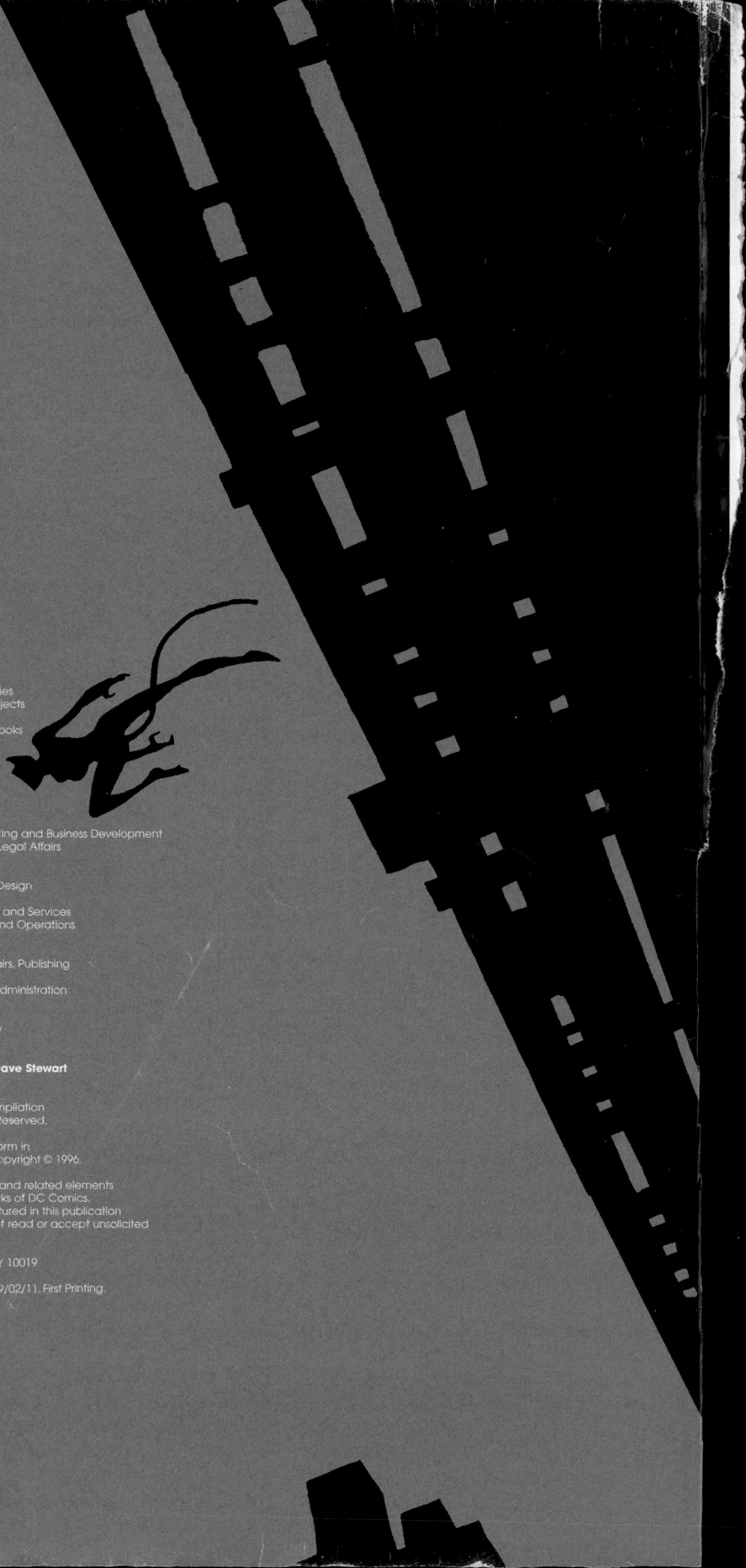

Archie Goodwin Editor – original series
Chuck Kim Assistant Editor – original series
Ian Sattler Director Editorial, Special Projects and Archival Editions
Robbin Brosterman Design Director – Books

Eddie Berganza Executive Editor
Bob Harras VP – Editor in Chief

Diane Nelson President
Dan DiDio and **Jim Lee** Co-Publishers
Geoff Johns Chief Creative Officer
John Rood Executive VP – Sales, Marketing and Business Development
Amy Genkins Senior VP – Business and Legal Affairs
Nairi Gardiner Senior VP – Finance
Jeff Boison VP – Publishing Operations
Mark Chiarello VP – Art Direction and Design
John Cunningham VP – Marketing
Terri Cunningham VP – Talent Relations and Services
Alison Gill Senior VP – Manufacturing and Operations
David Hyde VP – Publicity
Hank Kanalz Senior VP – Digital
Jay Kogan VP – Business and Legal Affairs, Publishing
Jack Mahan VP – Business Affairs, Talent
Nick Napolitano VP – Manufacturing Administration
Ron Perazza VP – Online
Sue Pohja VP – Book Sales
Courtney Simmons Senior VP – Publicity
Bob Wayne Senior VP – Sales

Coloring on pages 127-128, 366-367 by **Dave Stewart**

BATMAN THE LONG HALLOWEEN
Published by DC Comics. Cover and compilation

DC Comics, 1700 Broadway, New York, NY 10019
A Warner Bros. Entertainment Company
Printed by RR Donnelley, Salem, VA, USA. 9/02/11. First Printing.
ISBN: 978-1-4012-3259-7

SUSTAINABLE FORESTRY INITIATIVE
Certified Chain of Custody

Fiber used in this product line meets the sourcing requirements of the SFI program.
www.sfiprogram.org SGS-SFI/COC-US10/81072

INTRODUCTION A Conversation with Christopher Nolan and David S. Goyer

CN: When you're putting together a Batman film, people always ask, "Are you looking at this comic book or that comic book?" And the truth is you look at all of them. As a filmmaker, though, THE LONG HALLOWEEN was one Batman story that really drew me in in terms of cinematic potential.

DG: It is cinematic. I think that THE LONG HALLOWEEN stands out as probably the most ambitious Batman story that's been told. It certainly feels like the most densely plotted.

CN: It's a crime epic. Jeph Loeb did this incredible job of taking the more exotic elements of the Batman universe and grounding them in a believable world. He took supporting characters and gave them real lives and real emotions. And real consequences to their actions. This has tremendous impact on the reader. THE LONG HALLOWEEN is more than a comic book. It's an epic tragedy.

DG: Right. And Tim Sale's artwork accentuates that by relying on a restricted color palette and a strong usage of shadow. It creates this stylistic balance between being expressionistic but also feeling somewhat realistic. It reminds me of Fritz Lang's *M.* Most of the time people want to make these things look more like *Metropolis*, but I think it looks and feels more like *M.*

CN: Exactly. The artwork is fantastically noirish. It portrays this massive American city and the underworld that threatens to envelop it in striking detail and remarkable scope.

DG: In so many of the previous depictions of Batman, he was running around, fighting bad guys in a vacuum. The machinations of the police, the corruption within the force, how Batman, and Gordon, and Dent negotiate all of that — none of that has been examined prior to THE LONG HALLOWEEN.

CN: Well, we co-opted THE LONG HALLOWEEN's idea of the triumvirate for *Batman Begins* to some extent, showing Batman function as one point of a strong triangle with the police and the D.A. by acting as a force that can crack things open and provide a wedge against all the corruption.

DG: That scene on the rooftop between Gordon, Dent, and Batman in THE LONG HALLOWEEN — in which you realize Batman can obviously bring criminals to justice, but he needs the police to arrest them and the D.A.'s office to prosecute them — that was something new that Jeph Loeb introduced into the lore. For *Batman Begins*, we used Rachel instead of Dent as the pinnacle of the triangle, but she still served the same function.

CN: Same function exactly. THE LONG HALLOWEEN suggested a very strong utility for Batman in Gotham, which helped us because when you try to adapt the character into a movie in a realistic manner, you're left with that question, "Okay, what's Batman's purpose?" He can't be everywhere at once. He's not superhuman. He's just a regular guy. So how will he be most effective? How can he leverage his skills to transform the whole city? THE LONG HALLOWEEN answered that question, positioning Batman and Bruce Wayne as part of a greater mechanism in Gotham. Along those lines, I was impressed with how seamlessly Loeb and Sale were able to integrate the more fantastical elements of Batman, most notably the villains, within the context of the real world, striking a balance that felt credible. It was a great inspiration to us in terms of tonality.

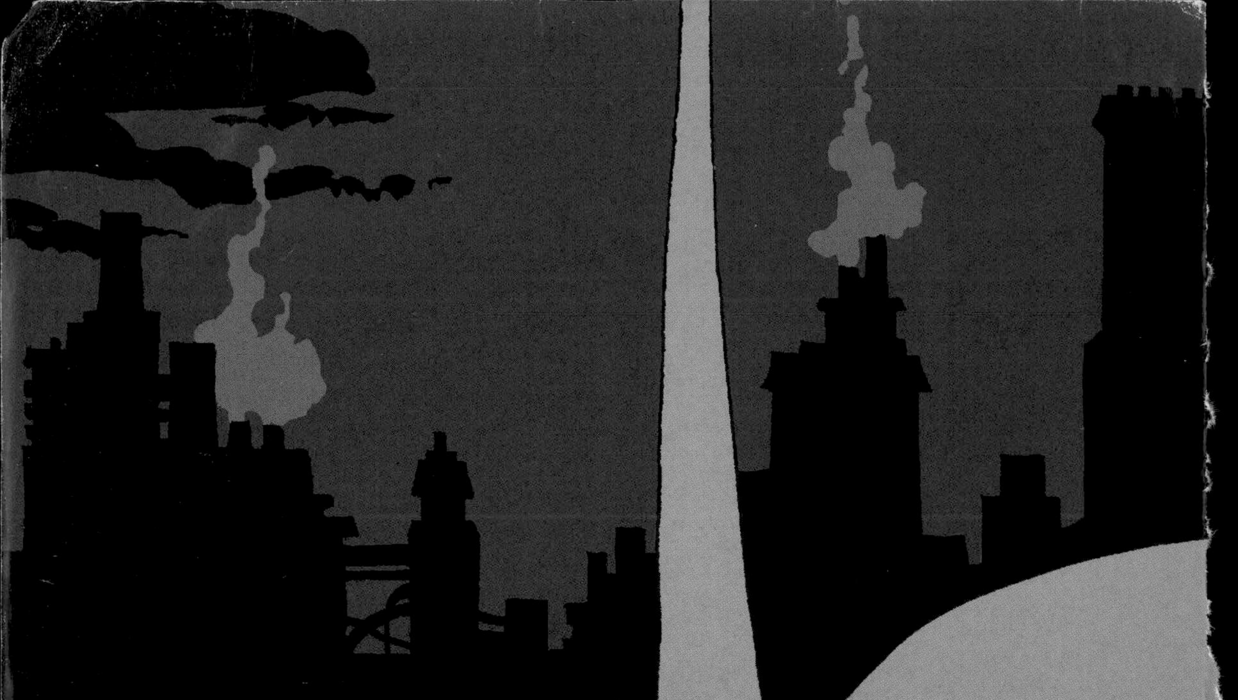

DG: That's certainly the case with Jim Gordon. THE LONG HALLOWEEN really ran with what YEAR ONE started, giving us an entirely different depiction of Gordon. Previously in the comic books, in the movies, and in the TV show, Gordon was this kind of bumbling, avuncular character, whereas in these stories, he is depicted as this beleaguered, mid-level sergeant in this rampantly corrupt police force, which is the Gordon we meet in *Batman Begins.*

CN: Yes. And I think as we get on with *The Dark Knight*, THE LONG HALLOWEEN is becoming more influential in terms of Harvey Dent. Throughout writing *Batman Begins,* we had always talked a lot about dealing with Harvey Dent, whether or not to feature him in some way in the movie. I think we had him in there in the very earliest stages of conception.

DG: Yeah, we did. Briefly.

CN: And then we realized we couldn't do him justice.

DG: For me, there are three major comic book influences within the Batman lore. There's YEAR ONE, the Neal Adams stuff, and there is THE LONG HALLOWEEN. But by the time *The Dark Knight* comes out, it will become apparent that LONG HALLOWEEN is the preeminent influence on both movies.

CN: Yeah, I think that could be right.

Christopher Nolan and David S. Goyer spoke about THE LONG HALLOWEEN on November 15, 2006, a few weeks before principal photography began on THE DARK KNIGHT.

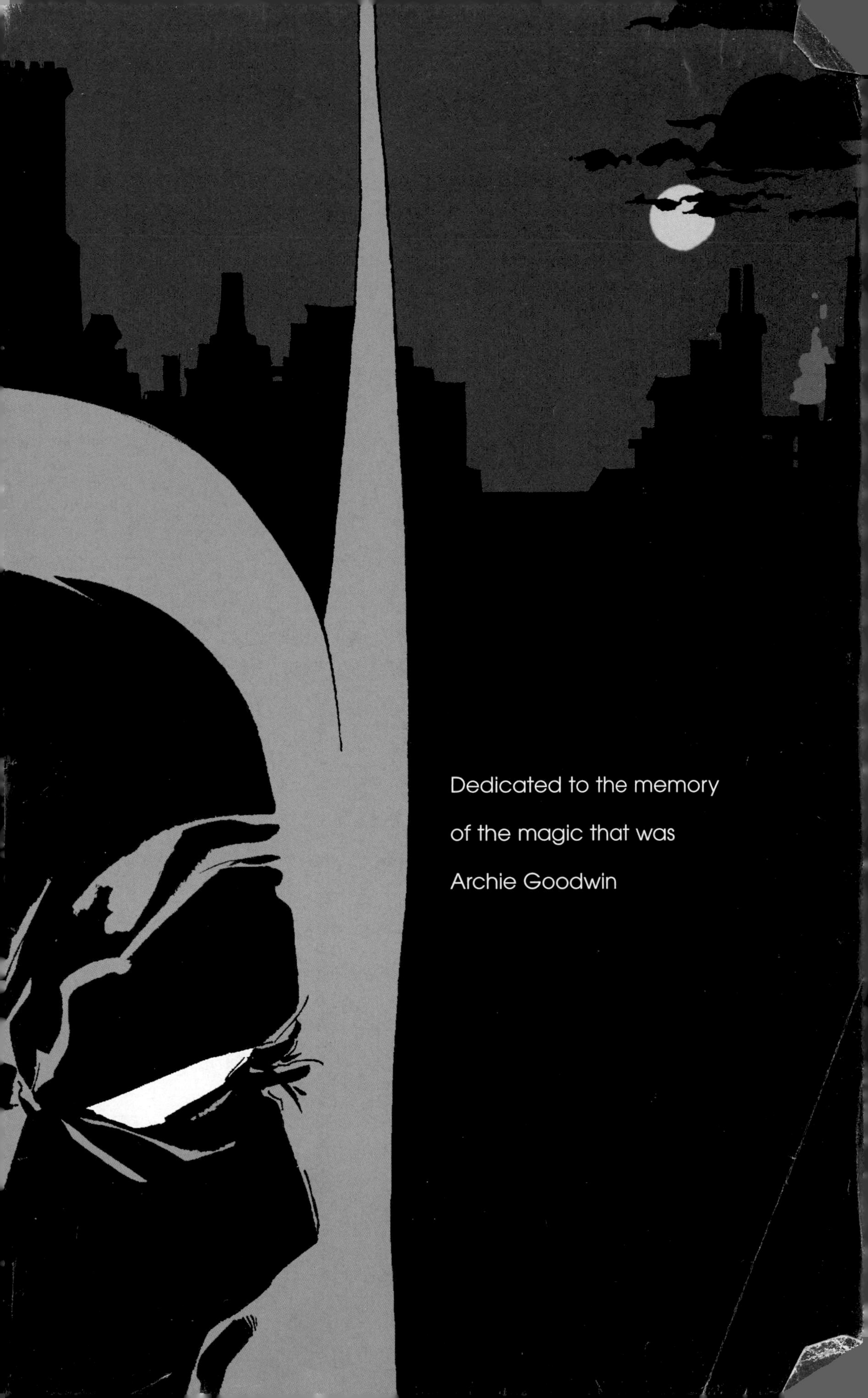

Dedicated to the memory
of the magic that was
Archie Goodwin

CHAPTER ONE
CRIME

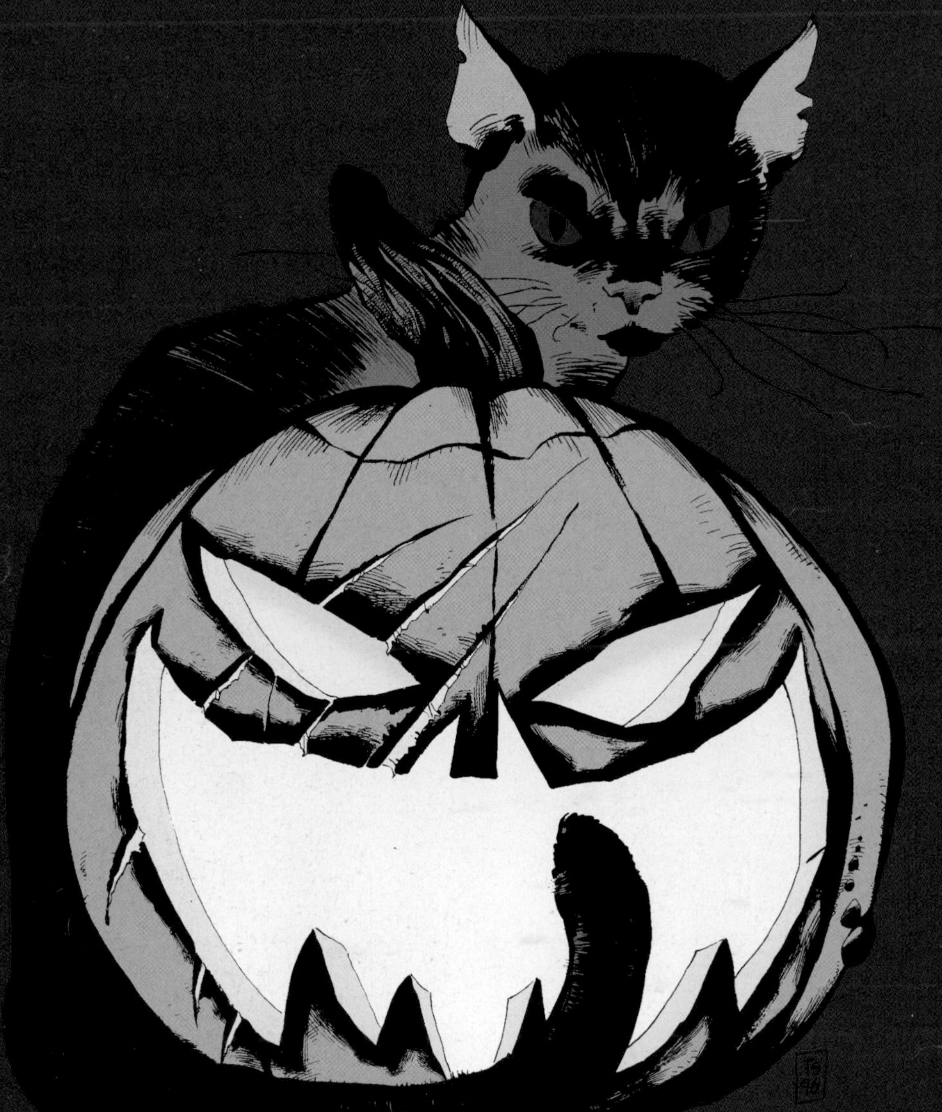

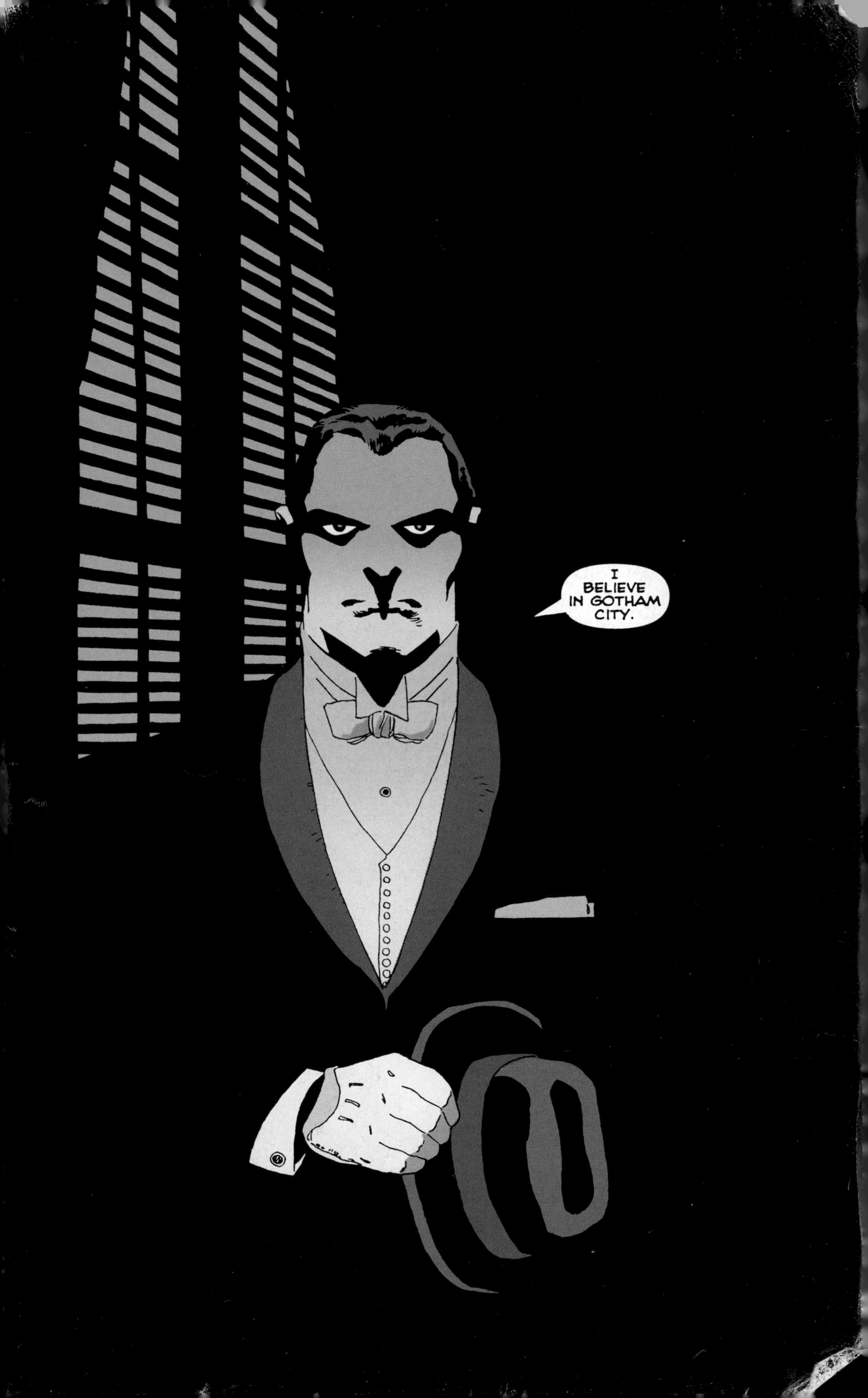
I BELIEVE IN GOTHAM CITY.

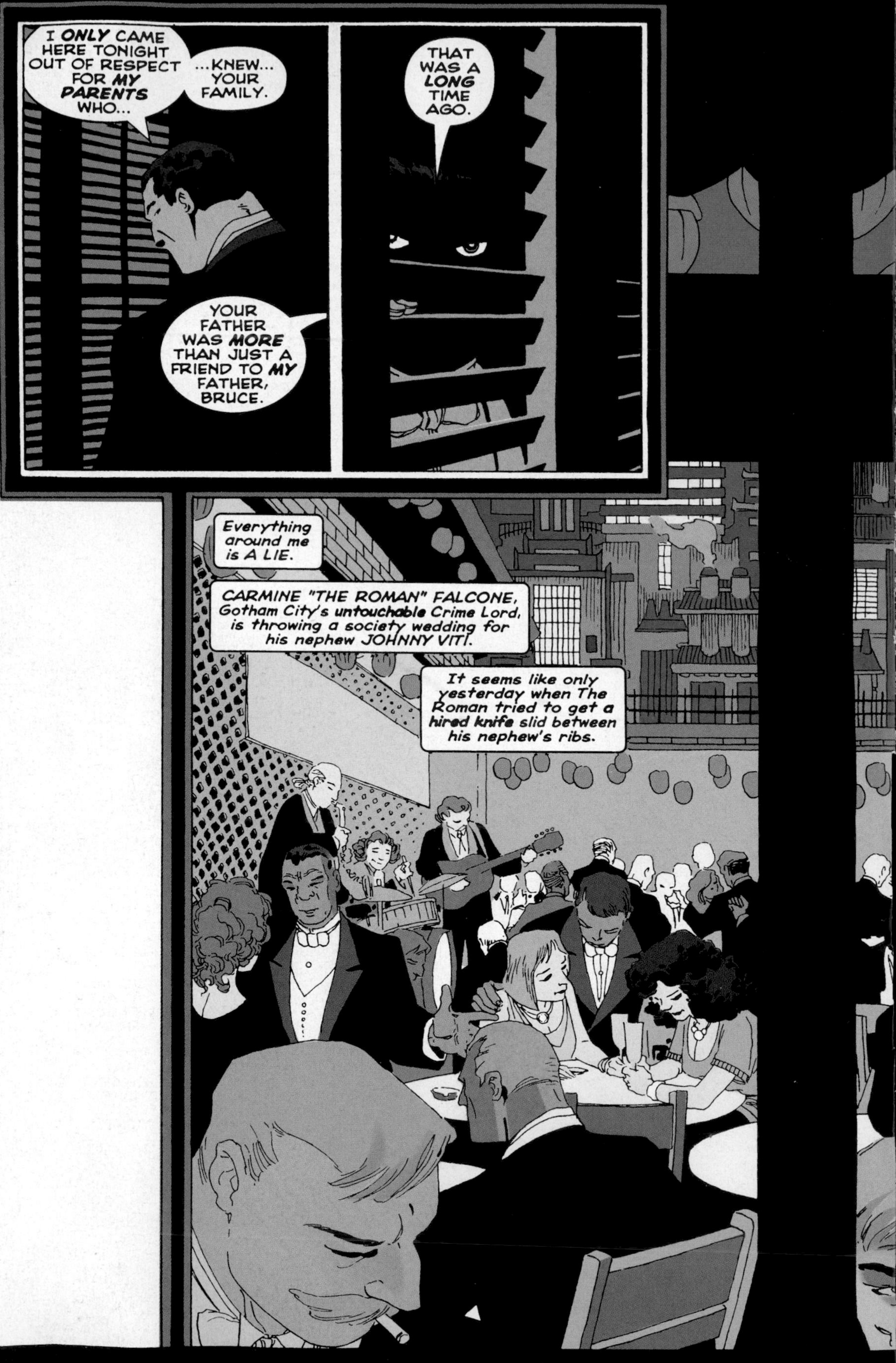
I ONLY CAME HERE TONIGHT OUT OF RESPECT FOR MY PARENTS WHO...
...KNEW... YOUR FAMILY.
YOUR FATHER WAS MORE THAN JUST A FRIEND TO MY FATHER, BRUCE.
THAT WAS A LONG TIME AGO.
Everything around me is A LIE.
CARMINE "THE ROMAN" FALCONE, Gotham City's untouchable Crime Lord, is throwing a society wedding for his nephew JOHNNY VITI.
It seems like only yesterday when The Roman tried to get a hired knife slid between his nephew's ribs.

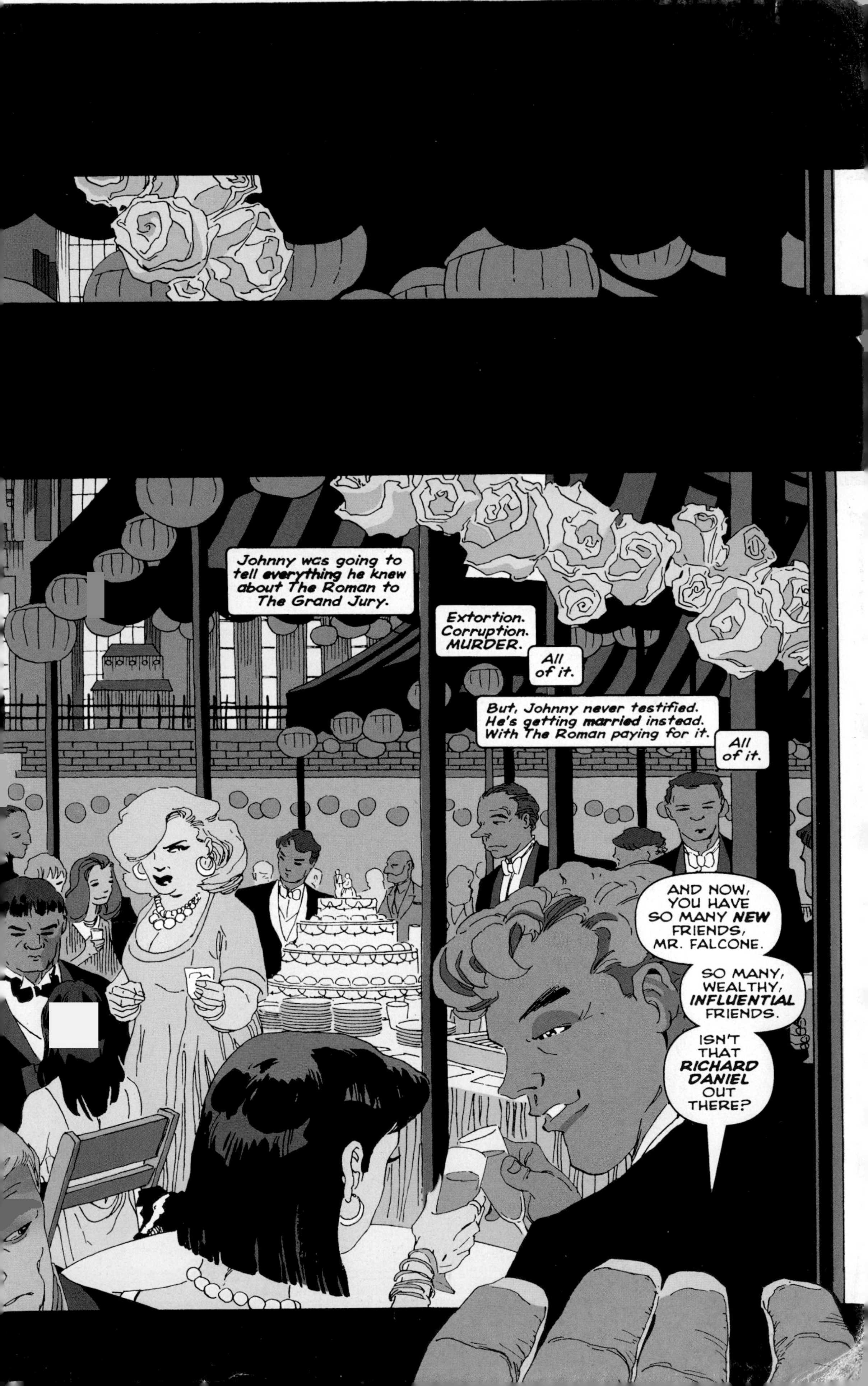
Johnny was going to tell everything he knew about The Roman to The Grand Jury.
Extortion. Corruption. MURDER.
All of it.
But, Johnny never testified. He's getting married instead. With The Roman paying for it.
All of it.
AND NOW, YOU HAVE SO MANY NEW FRIENDS, MR. FALCONE.
SO MANY, WEALTHY, INFLUENTIAL FRIENDS.
ISN'T THAT RICHARD DANIEL OUT THERE?

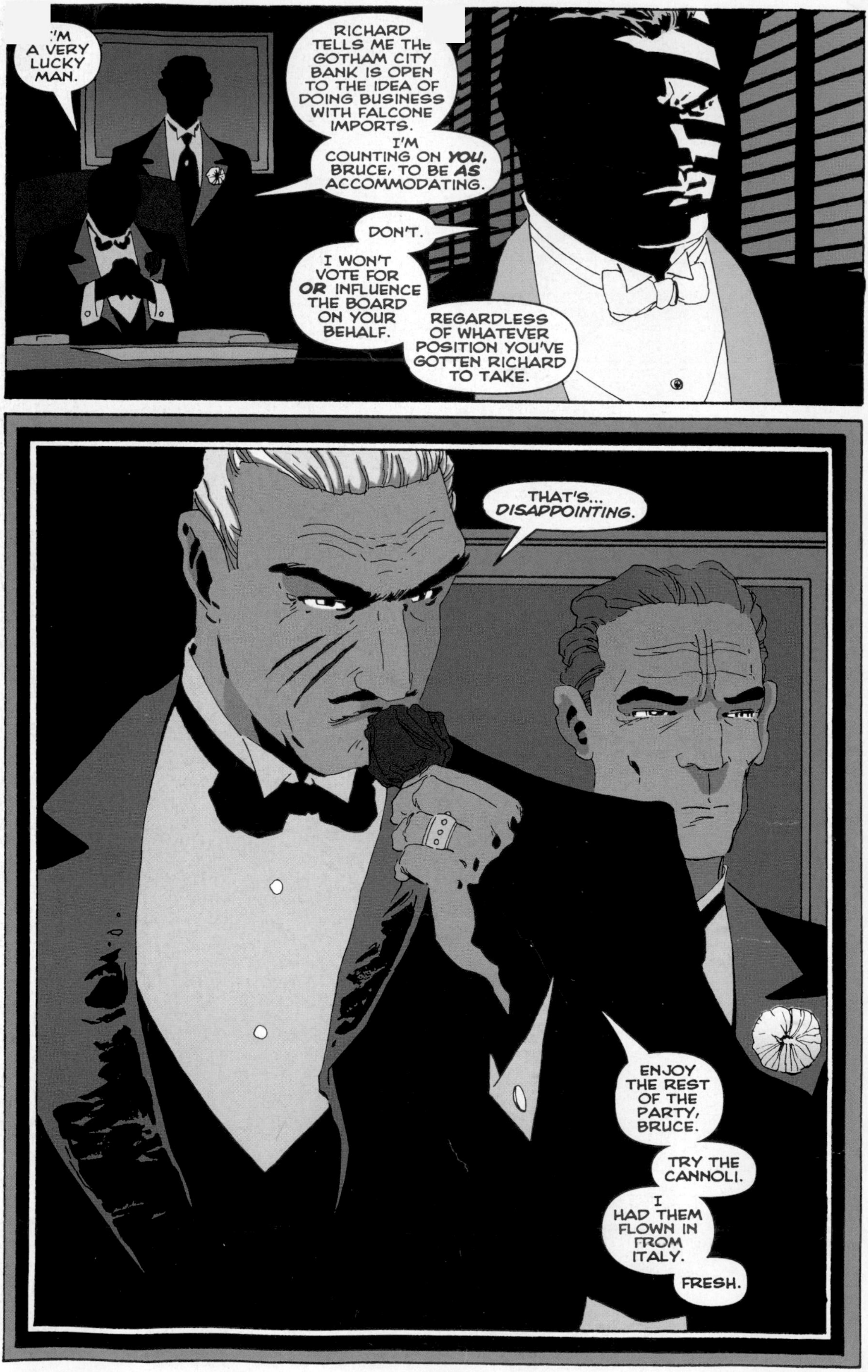
'M A VERY LUCKY MAN.
RICHARD TELLS ME THE GOTHAM CITY BANK IS OPEN TO THE IDEA OF DOING BUSINESS WITH FALCONE IMPORTS.
I'M COUNTING ON YOU, BRUCE, TO BE AS ACCOMMODATING.
DON'T.
I WON'T VOTE FOR OR INFLUENCE THE BOARD ON YOUR BEHALF.
REGARDLESS OF WHATEVER POSITION YOU'VE GOTTEN RICHARD TO TAKE.
THAT'S... DISAPPOINTING.
ENJOY THE REST OF THE PARTY, BRUCE.
TRY THE CANNOLI.
I HAD THEM FLOWN IN FROM ITALY.
FRESH.

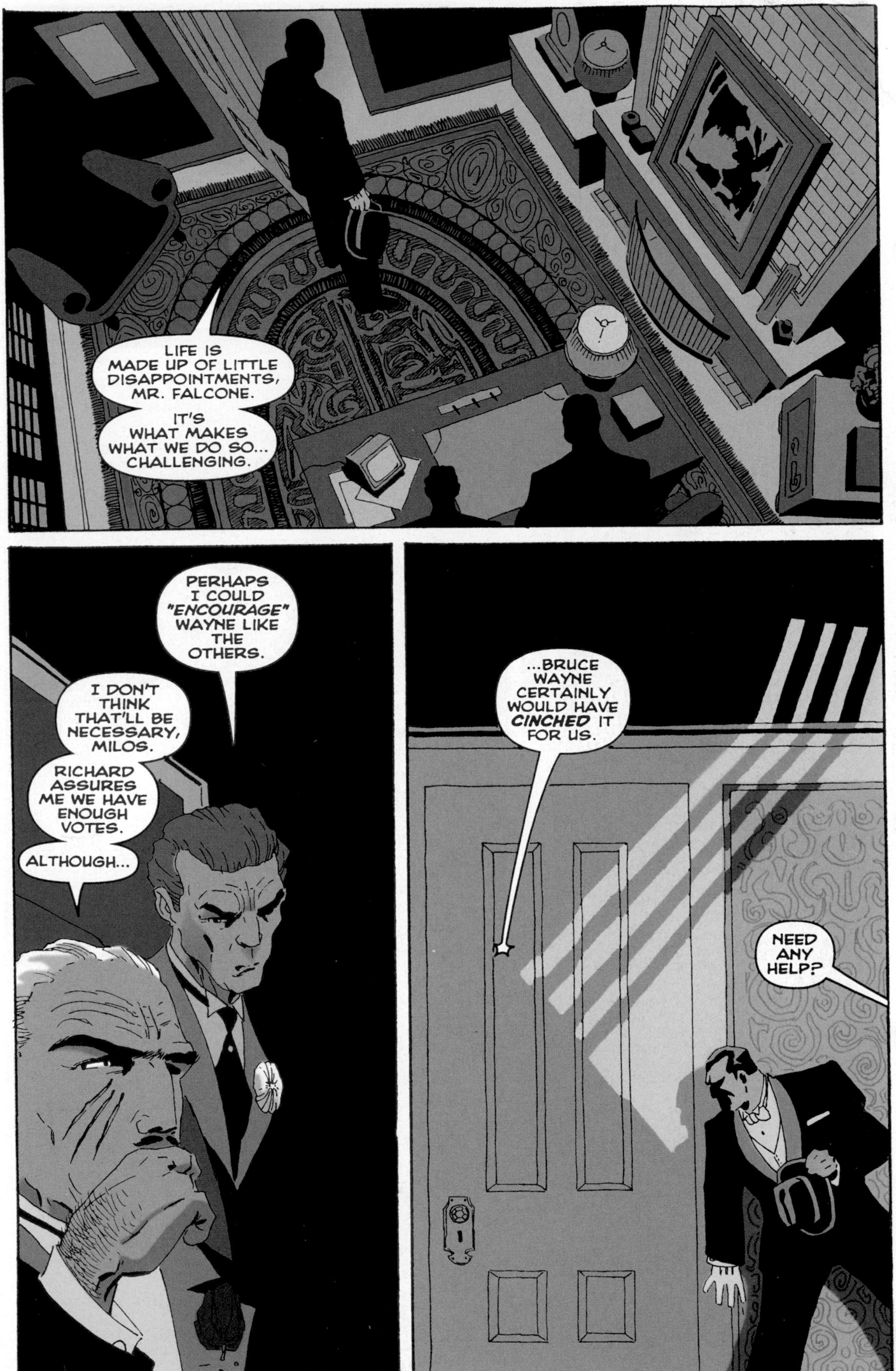

LIFE IS MADE UP OF LITTLE DISAPPOINTMENTS, MR. FALCONE.
IT'S WHAT MAKES WHAT WE DO SO... CHALLENGING.
PERHAPS I COULD "ENCOURAGE" WAYNE LIKE THE OTHERS.
I DON'T THINK THAT'LL BE NECESSARY, MILOS.
RICHARD ASSURES ME WE HAVE ENOUGH VOTES.
ALTHOUGH...
...BRUCE WAYNE CERTAINLY WOULD HAVE CINCHED IT FOR US.
NEED ANY HELP?

I WENT LOOKING FOR THE WASHROOM --

-- AND I GUESS I GOT TURNED AROUND.

TOO MUCH CHAMPAGNE WILL DO THAT, YOU KNOW.

ALBERTO FALCONE. *Harvard M.B.A. Oxford Rhodes Scholar.*

The good son.

DOWN THE HALL TO YOUR RIGHT.

MISTER WAYNE.

VERY SPECIAL NIGHT.

PARTICULARLY THE CANNOLI.

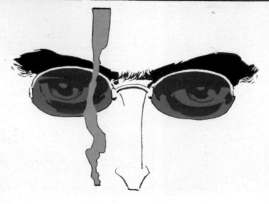

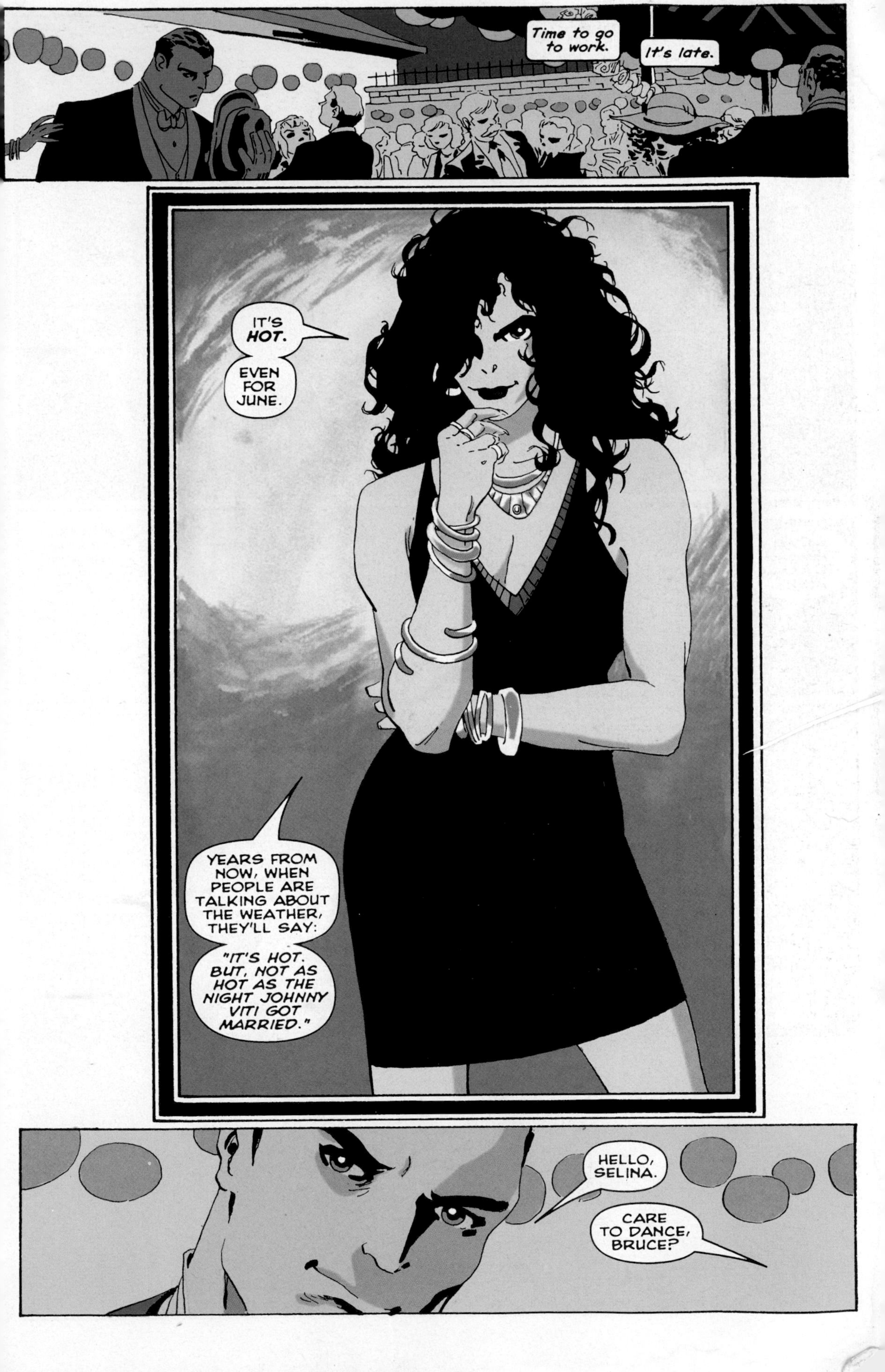
Time to go to work.
It's late.
IT'S HOT.
EVEN FOR JUNE.
YEARS FROM NOW, WHEN PEOPLE ARE TALKING ABOUT THE WEATHER, THEY'LL SAY:
"IT'S HOT. BUT, NOT AS HOT AS THE NIGHT JOHNNY VITI GOT MARRIED."
HELLO, SELINA.
CARE TO DANCE, BRUCE?

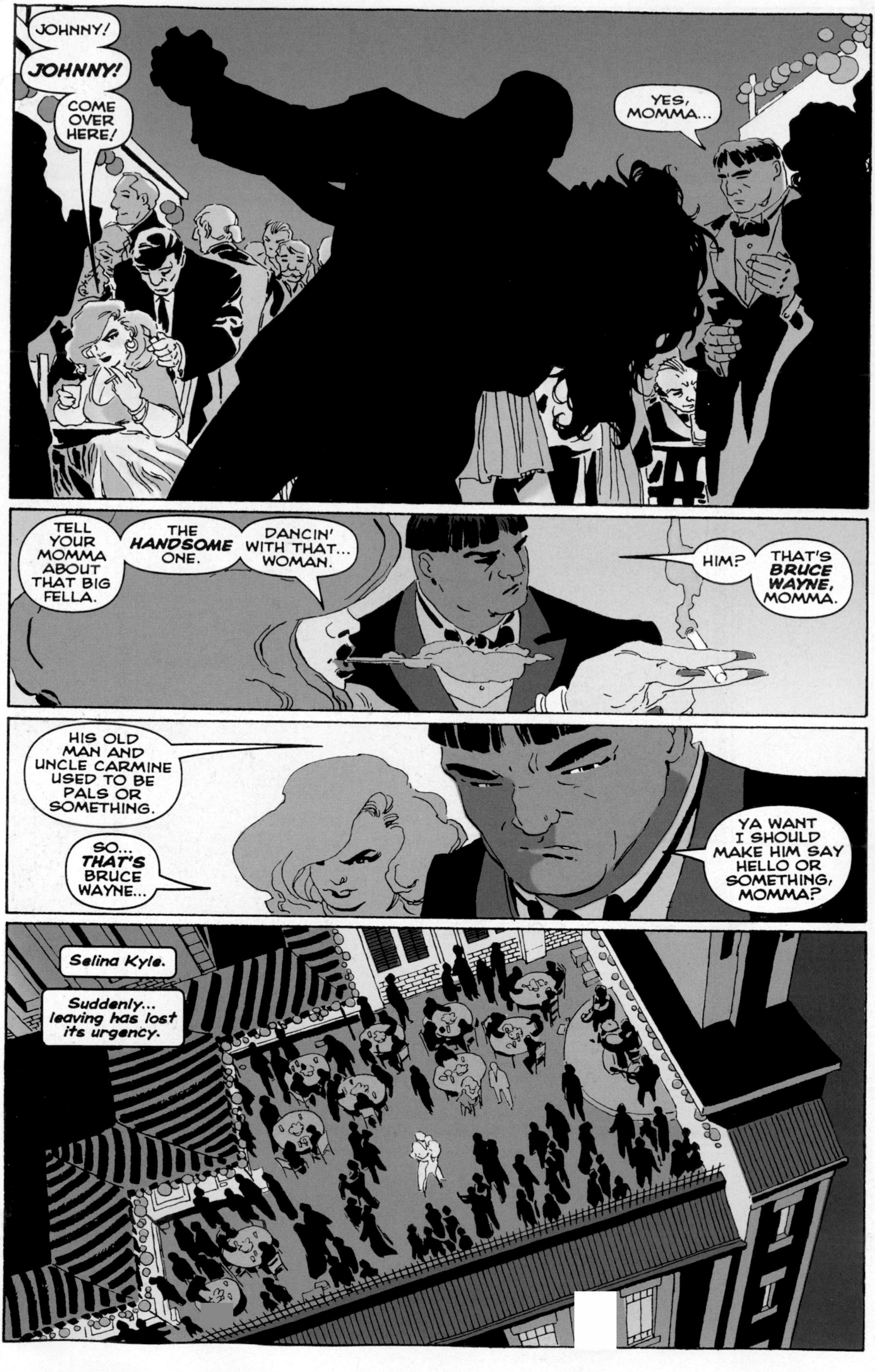
JOHNNY!
JOHNNY!
COME OVER HERE!
YES, MOMMA...
TELL YOUR MOMMA ABOUT THAT BIG FELLA.
THE HANDSOME ONE.
DANCIN' WITH THAT... WOMAN.
HIM?
THAT'S BRUCE WAYNE, MOMMA.
HIS OLD MAN AND UNCLE CARMINE USED TO BE PALS OR SOMETHING.
SO... THAT'S BRUCE WAYNE...
YA WANT I SHOULD MAKE HIM SAY HELLO OR SOMETHING, MOMMA?
Selina Kyle.
Suddenly... leaving has lost its urgency.

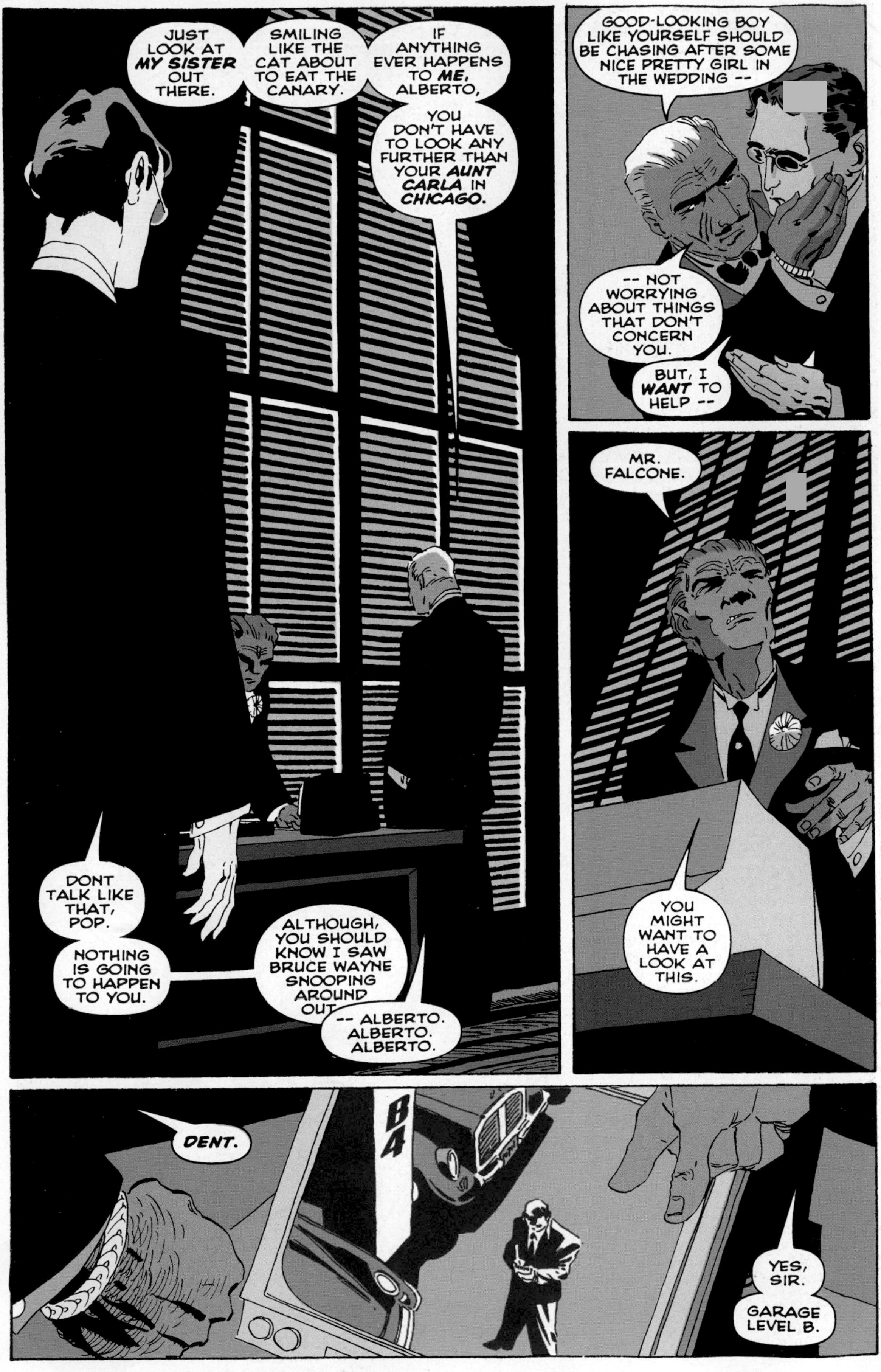
JUST LOOK AT MY SISTER OUT THERE.
SMILING LIKE THE CAT ABOUT TO EAT THE CANARY.
IF ANYTHING EVER HAPPENS TO ME, ALBERTO,
YOU DON'T HAVE TO LOOK ANY FURTHER THAN YOUR AUNT CARLA IN CHICAGO.
DONT TALK LIKE THAT, POP.
NOTHING IS GOING TO HAPPEN TO YOU.
ALTHOUGH, YOU SHOULD KNOW I SAW BRUCE WAYNE SNOOPING AROUND OUT--
-- ALBERTO. ALBERTO. ALBERTO.
GOOD-LOOKING BOY LIKE YOURSELF SHOULD BE CHASING AFTER SOME NICE PRETTY GIRL IN THE WEDDING --
-- NOT WORRYING ABOUT THINGS THAT DON'T CONCERN YOU.
BUT, I WANT TO HELP --
MR. FALCONE.
YOU MIGHT WANT TO HAVE A LOOK AT THIS.
DENT.
B4
YES, SIR.
GARAGE LEVEL B.

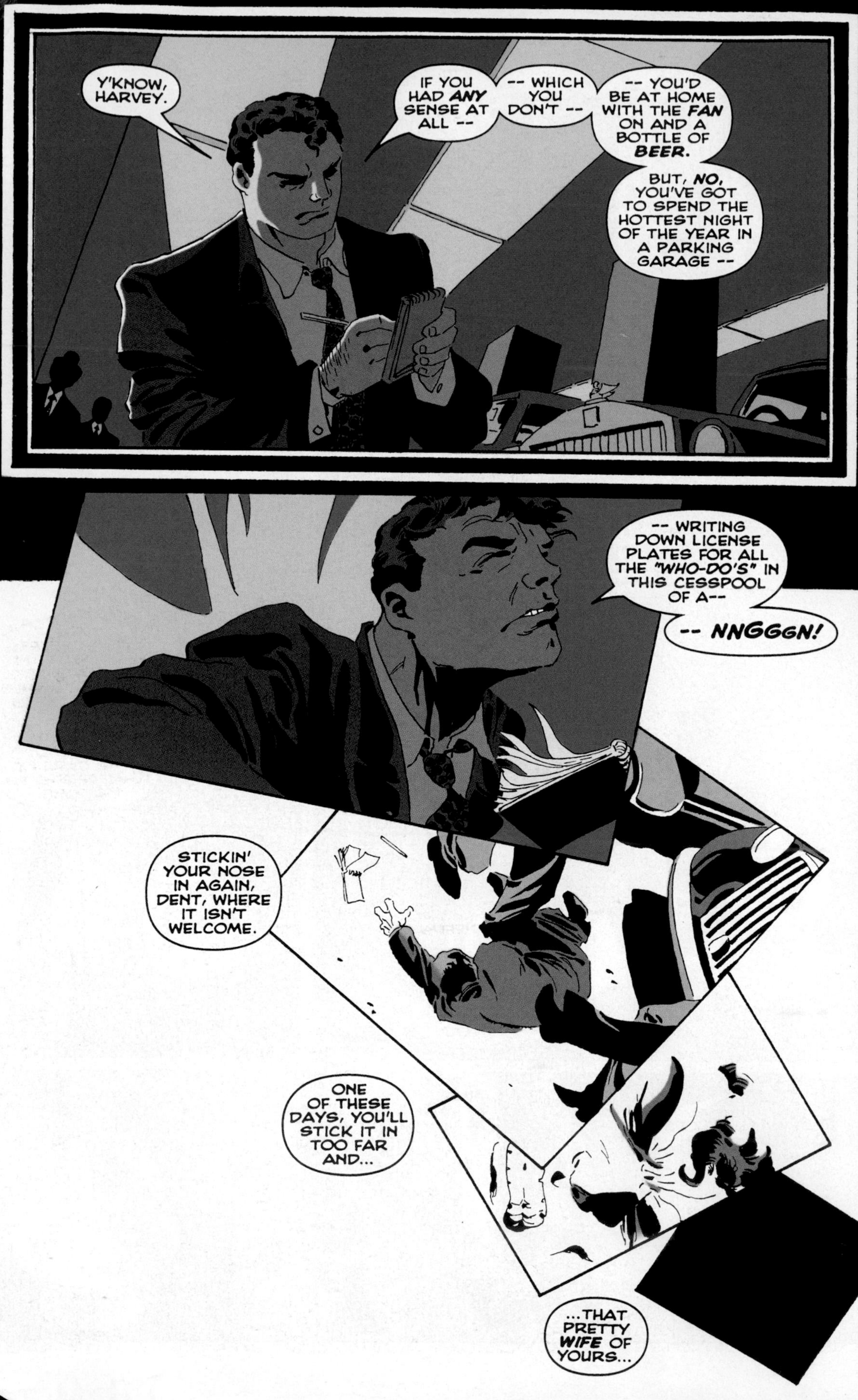
Y'KNOW, HARVEY.
IF YOU HAD *ANY* SENSE AT ALL --
-- WHICH YOU DON'T --
-- YOU'D BE AT HOME WITH THE *FAN* ON AND A BOTTLE OF *BEER*.
BUT, *NO*, YOU'VE GOT TO SPEND THE HOTTEST NIGHT OF THE YEAR IN A PARKING GARAGE --
-- WRITING DOWN LICENSE PLATES FOR ALL THE *"WHO-DO'S"* IN THIS CESSPOOL OF A--
-- *NNGGGGN!*
STICKIN' YOUR NOSE IN AGAIN, DENT, WHERE IT ISN'T WELCOME.
ONE OF THESE DAYS, YOU'LL STICK IT IN TOO FAR AND...
...THAT PRETTY *WIFE* OF YOURS...

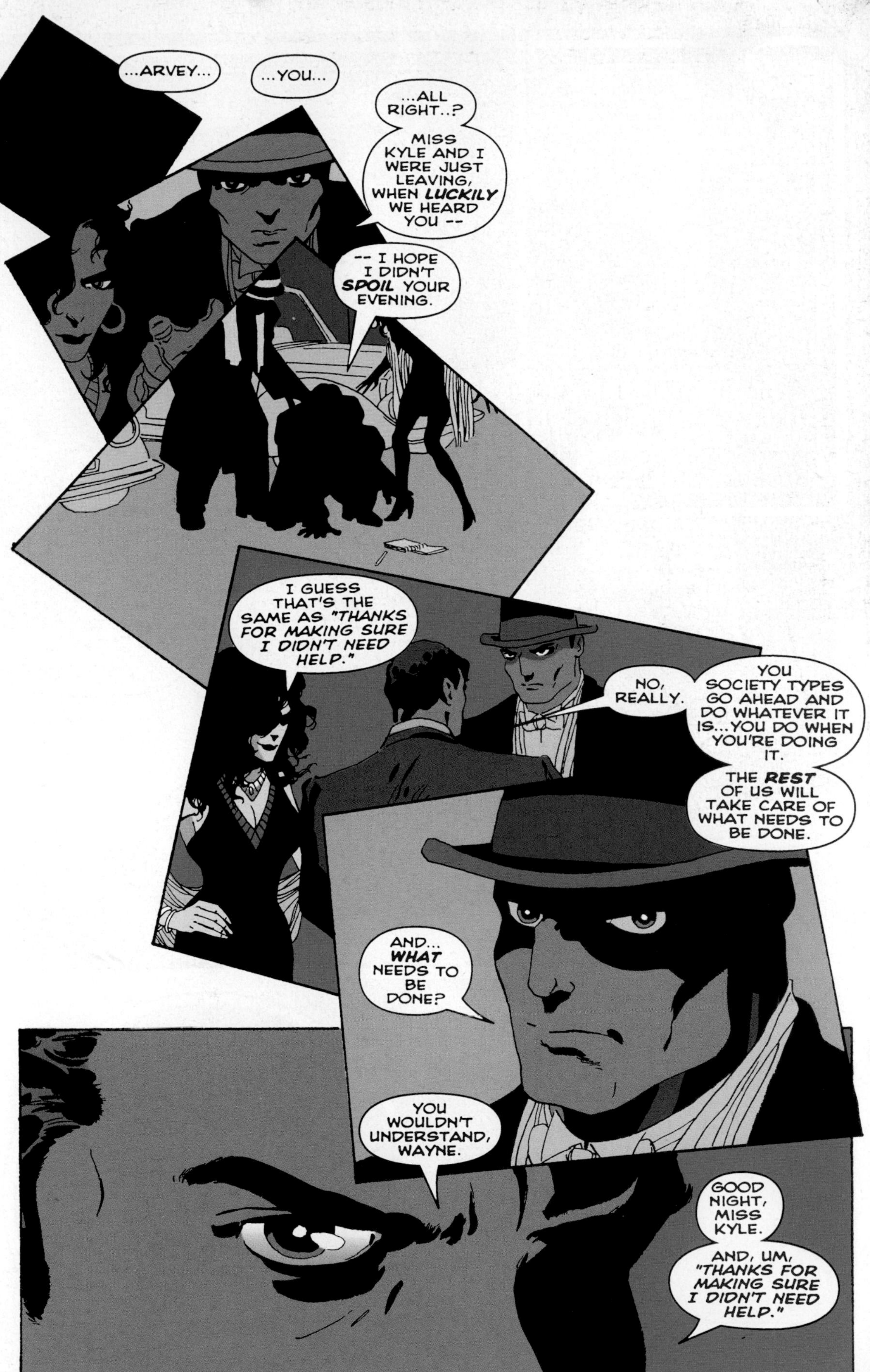
...ARVEY...
...YOU...
...ALL RIGHT..?
MISS KYLE AND I WERE JUST LEAVING, WHEN LUCKILY WE HEARD YOU --
-- I HOPE I DIDN'T SPOIL YOUR EVENING.
I GUESS THAT'S THE SAME AS "THANKS FOR MAKING SURE I DIDN'T NEED HELP."
NO, REALLY.
YOU SOCIETY TYPES GO AHEAD AND DO WHATEVER IT IS...YOU DO WHEN YOU'RE DOING IT.
THE REST OF US WILL TAKE CARE OF WHAT NEEDS TO BE DONE.
AND... WHAT NEEDS TO BE DONE?
YOU WOULDN'T UNDERSTAND, WAYNE.
GOOD NIGHT, MISS KYLE.
AND, UM, "THANKS FOR MAKING SURE I DIDN'T NEED HELP."

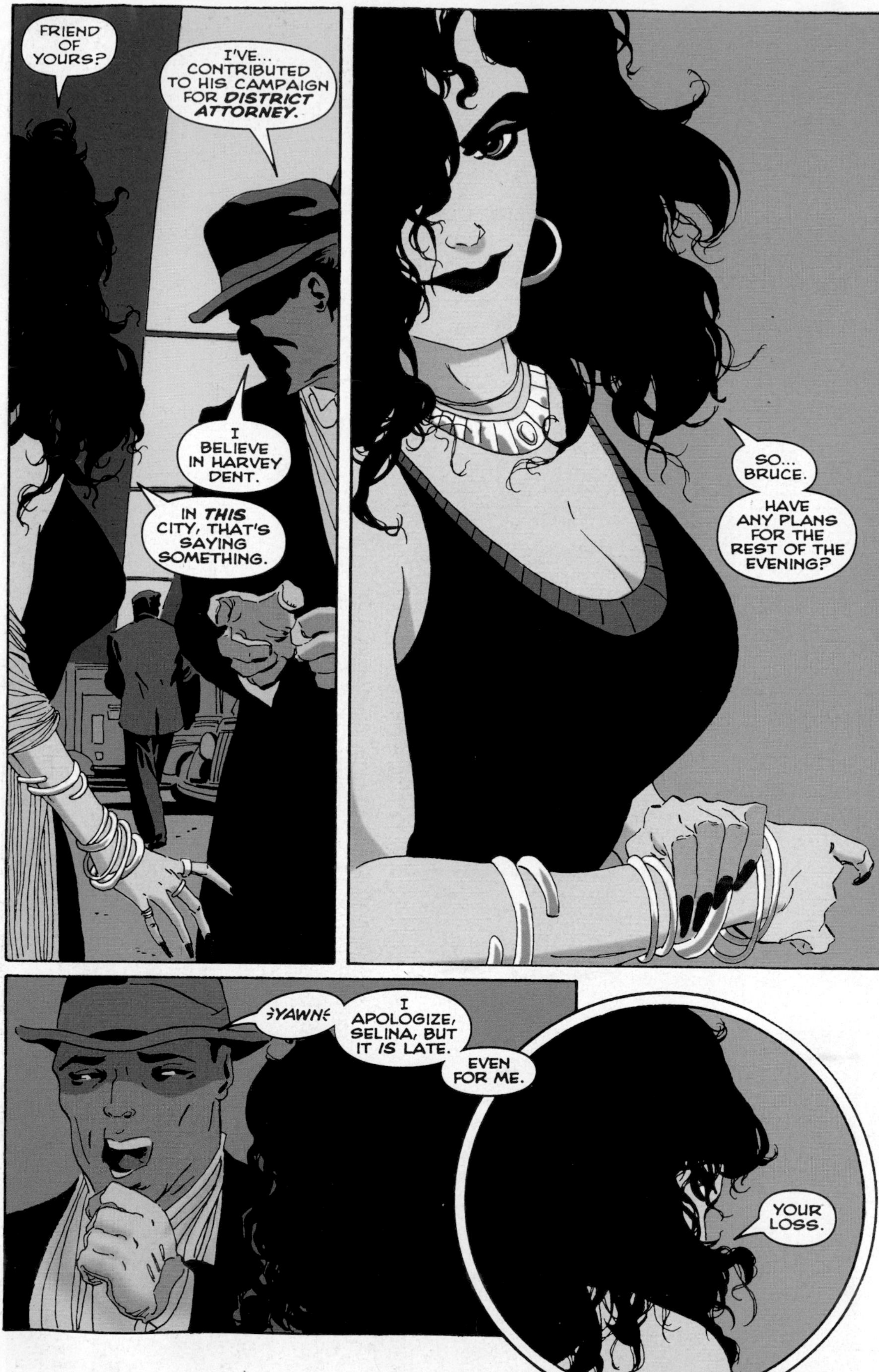
FRIEND OF YOURS?
I'VE... CONTRIBUTED TO HIS CAMPAIGN FOR DISTRICT ATTORNEY.
I BELIEVE IN HARVEY DENT.
IN THIS CITY, THAT'S SAYING SOMETHING.
SO... BRUCE.
HAVE ANY PLANS FOR THE REST OF THE EVENING?
YAWN
I APOLOGIZE, SELINA, BUT IT IS LATE.
EVEN FOR ME.
YOUR LOSS.

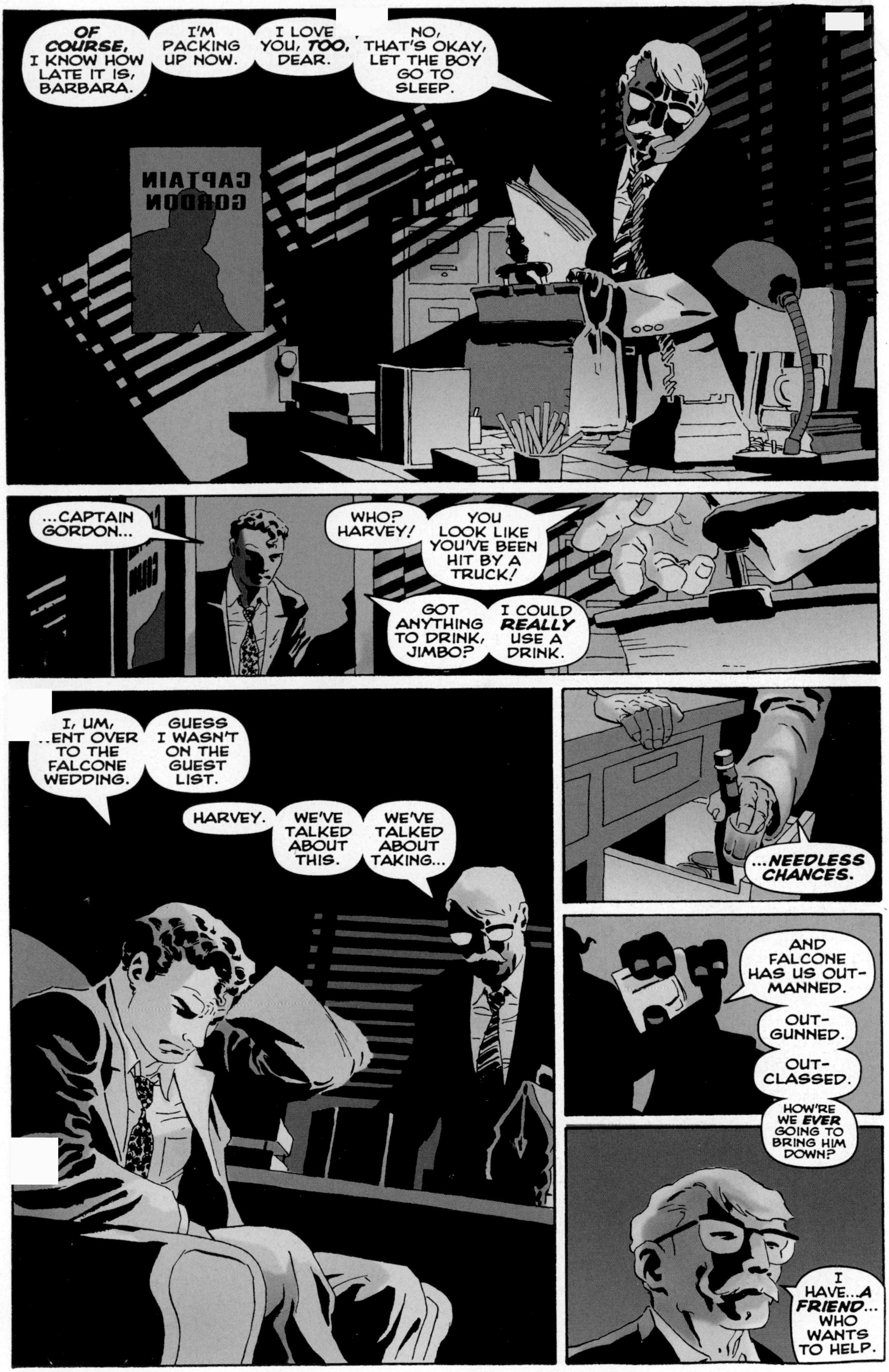
OF COURSE, I KNOW HOW LATE IT IS, BARBARA.
I'M PACKING UP NOW.
I LOVE YOU, TOO, DEAR.
NO, THAT'S OKAY, LET THE BOY GO TO SLEEP.
...CAPTAIN GORDON...
WHO? HARVEY!
YOU LOOK LIKE YOU'VE BEEN HIT BY A TRUCK!
GOT ANYTHING TO DRINK, JIMBO?
I COULD REALLY USE A DRINK.
I, UM, ..ENT OVER TO THE FALCONE WEDDING.
GUESS I WASN'T ON THE GUEST LIST.
HARVEY.
WE'VE TALKED ABOUT THIS.
WE'VE TALKED ABOUT TAKING...
...NEEDLESS CHANCES.
AND FALCONE HAS US OUT-MANNED.
OUT-GUNNED.
OUT-CLASSED.
HOW'RE WE EVER GOING TO BRING HIM DOWN?
I HAVE...A FRIEND... WHO WANTS TO HELP.

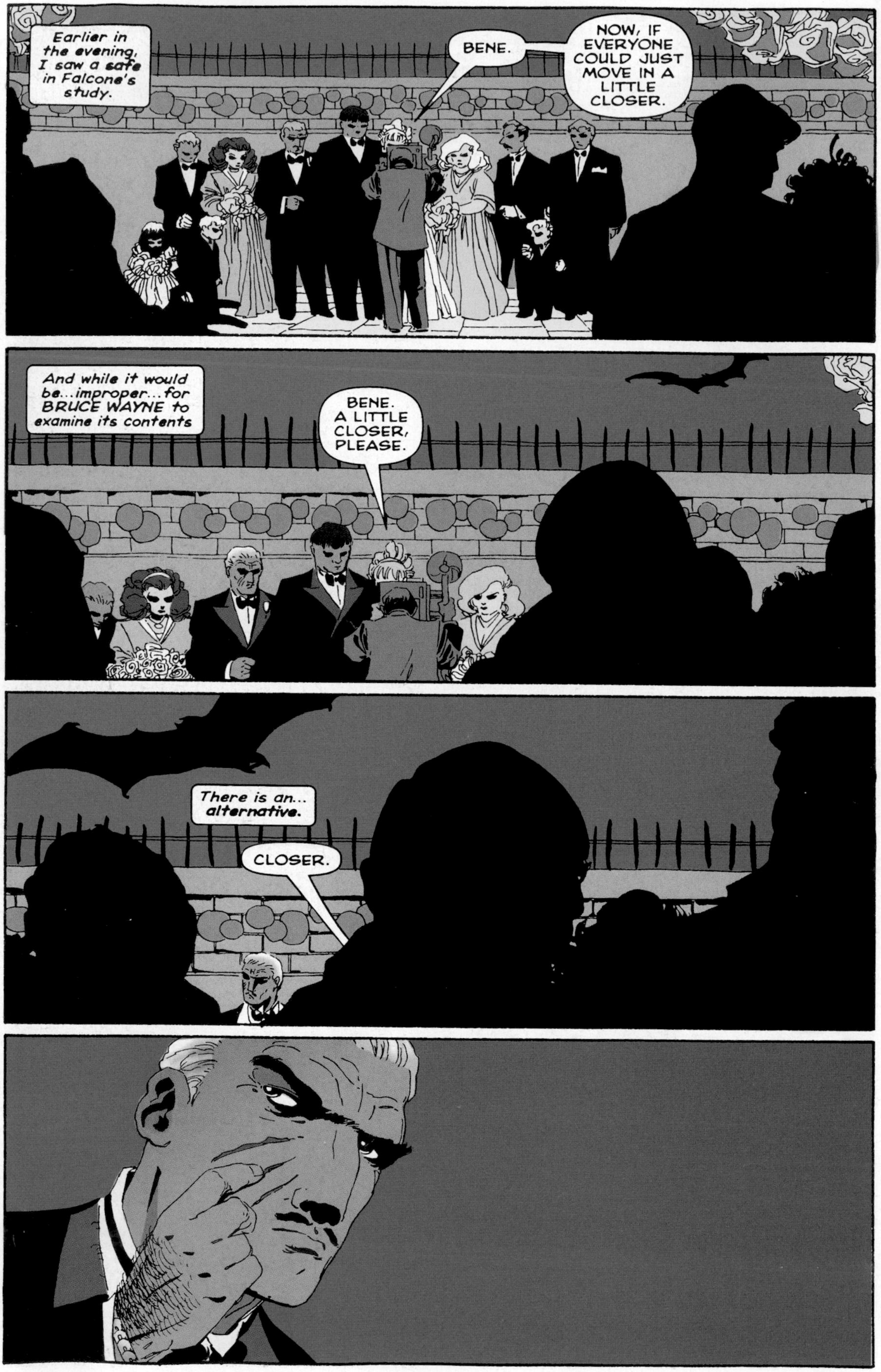
Earlier in the evening, I saw a safe in Falcone's study.
BENE.
NOW, IF EVERYONE COULD JUST MOVE IN A LITTLE CLOSER.
And while it would be...improper...for BRUCE WAYNE to examine its contents
BENE. A LITTLE CLOSER, PLEASE.
There is an... alternative.
CLOSER.

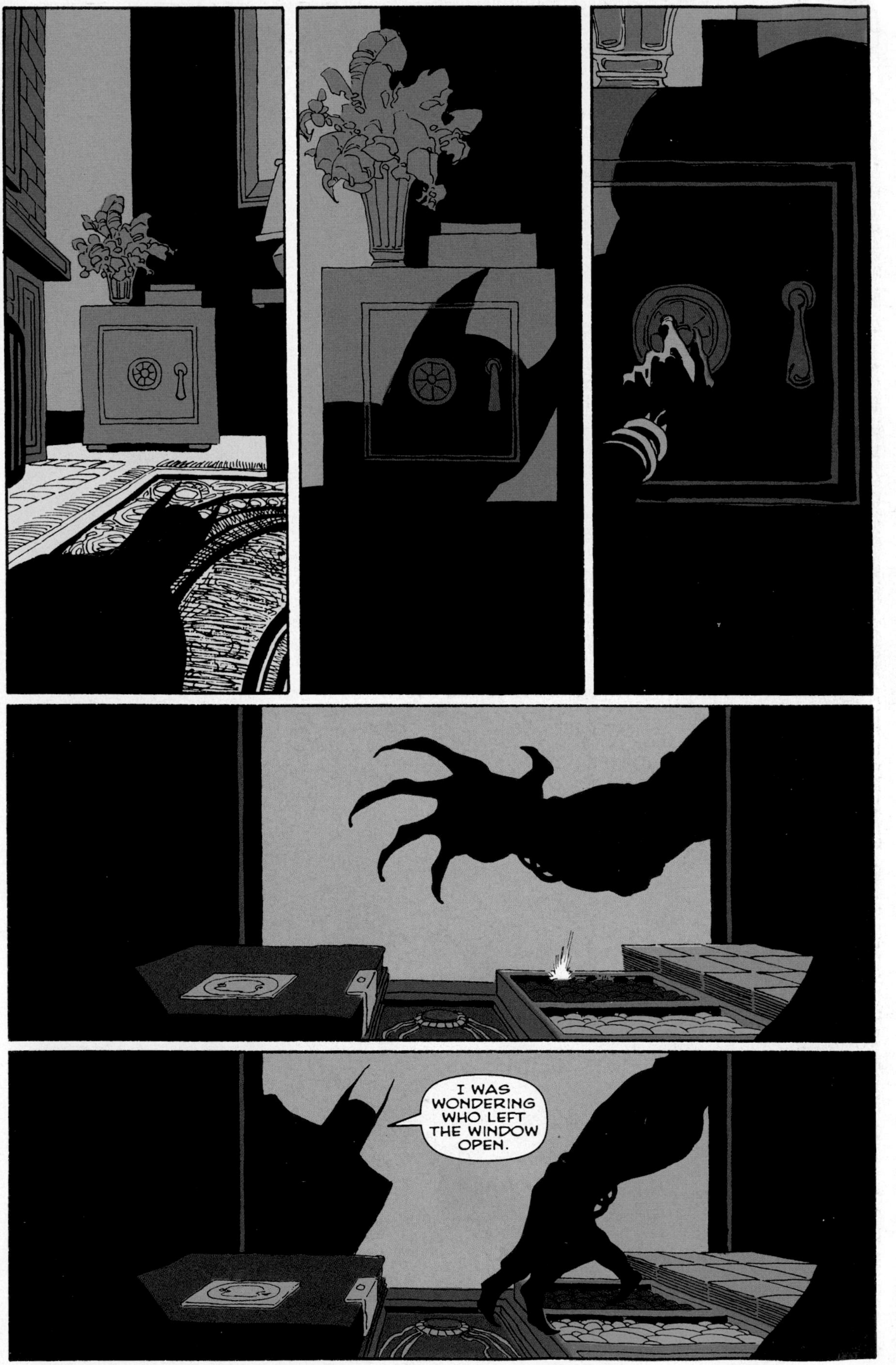
I WAS WONDERING WHO LEFT THE WINDOW OPEN.

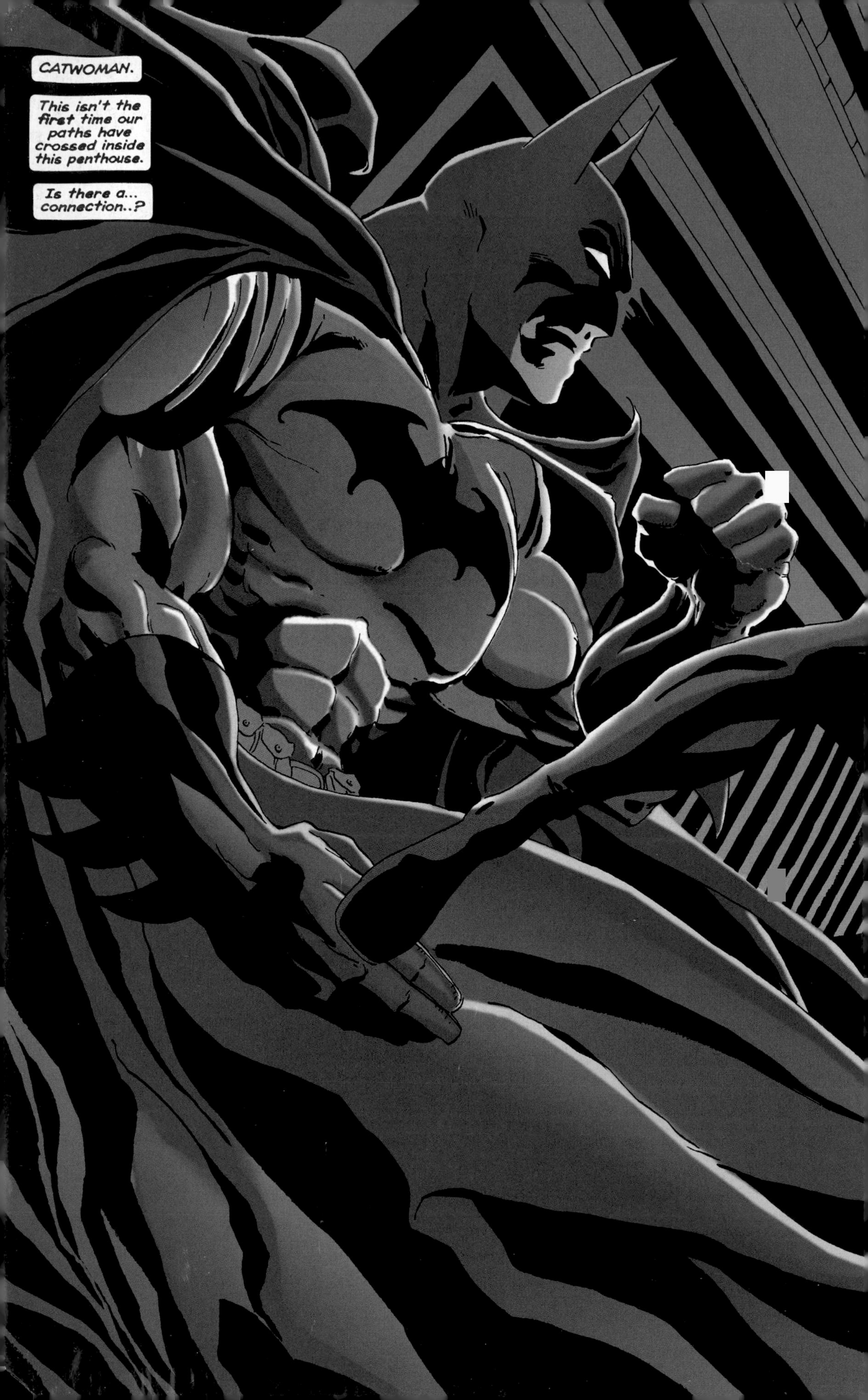
CATWOMAN.
This isn't the first time our paths have crossed inside this penthouse.
Is there a... connection..?

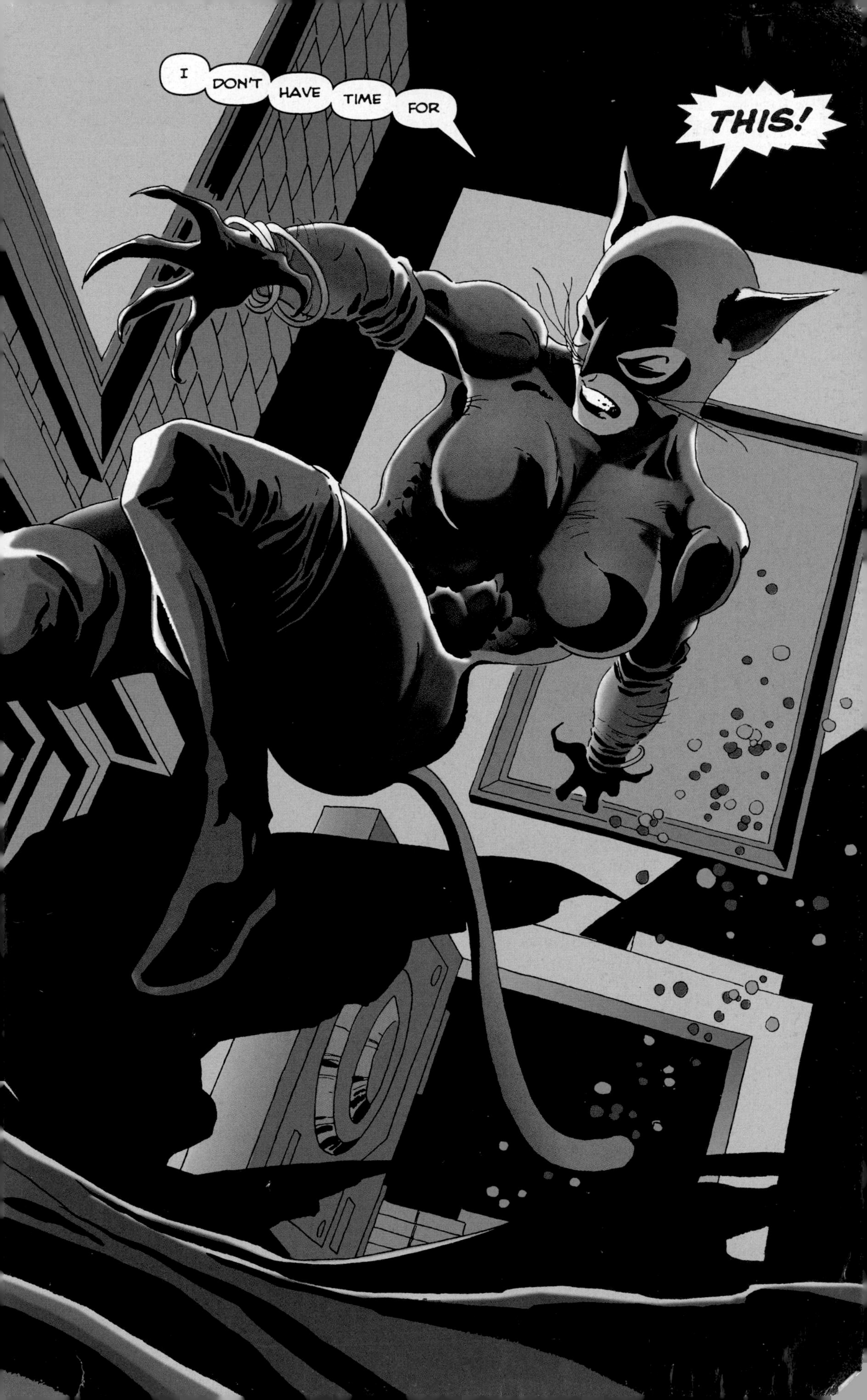
I DON'T HAVE TIME FOR
THIS!

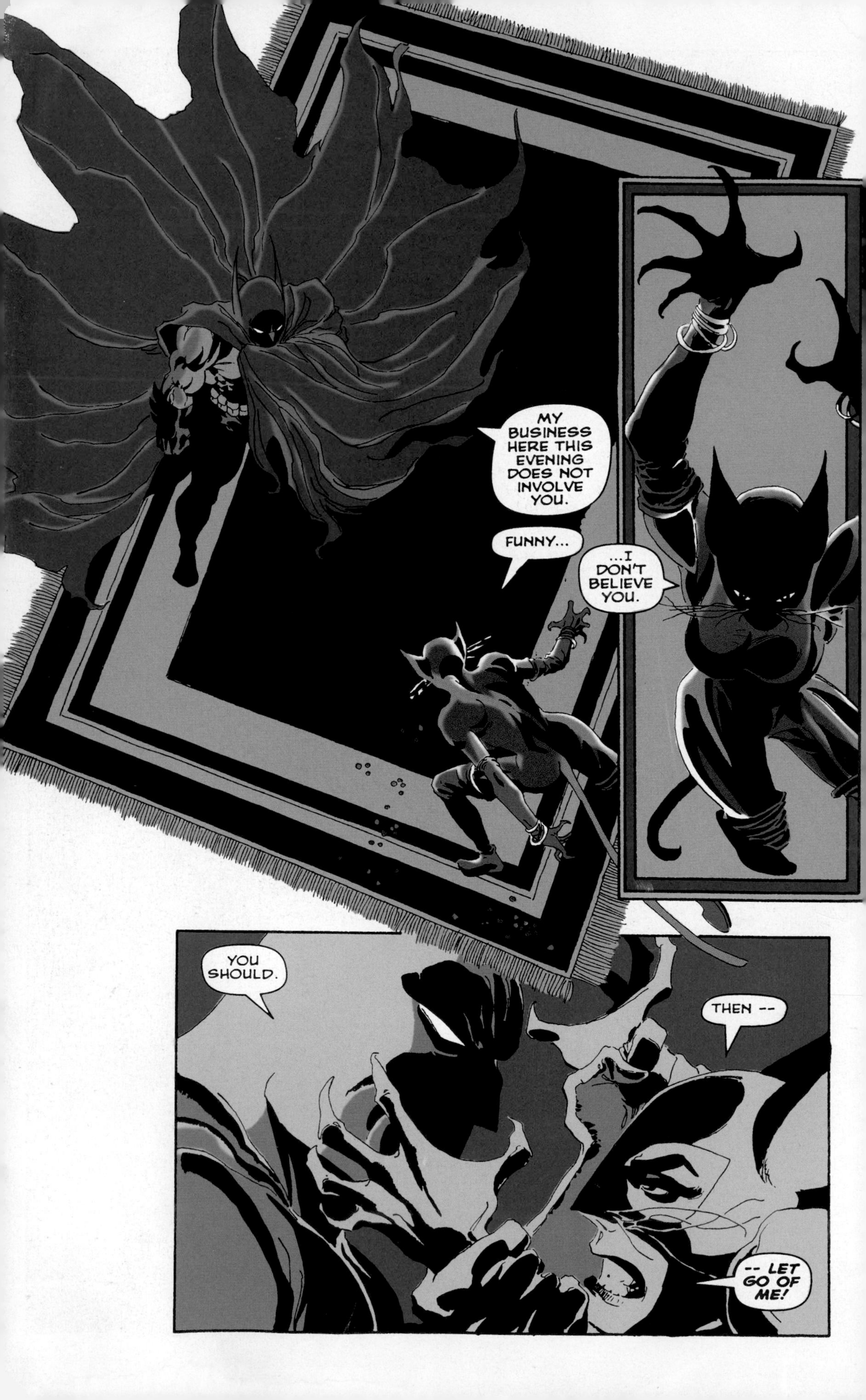
MY BUSINESS HERE THIS EVENING DOES NOT INVOLVE YOU.
FUNNY...
...I DON'T BELIEVE YOU.
YOU SHOULD.
THEN --
-- LET GO OF ME!

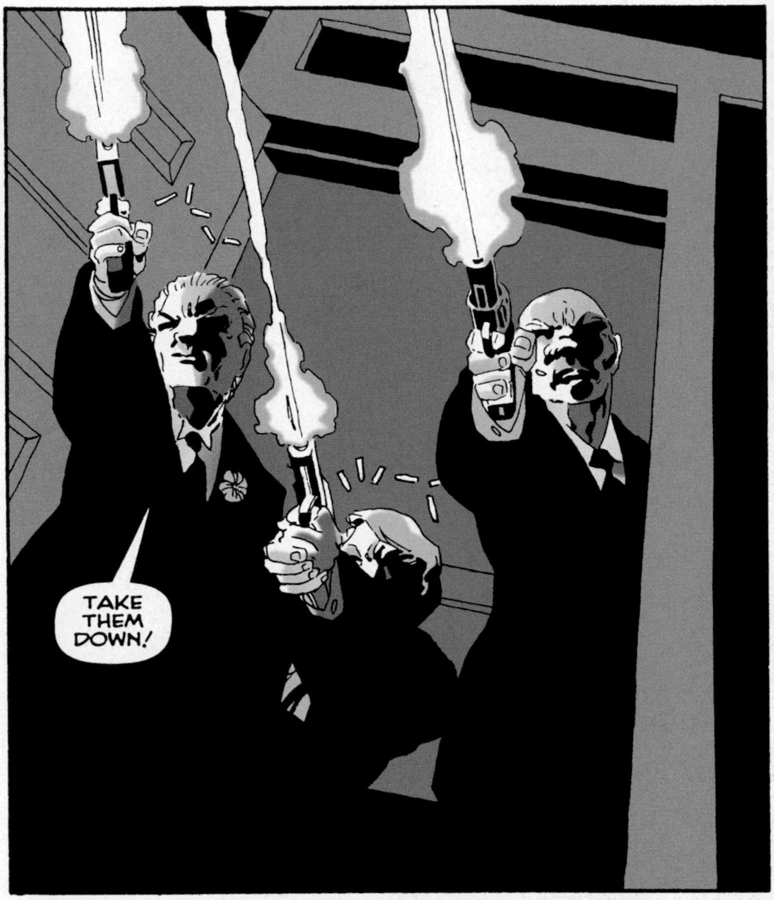
TAKE THEM DOWN!
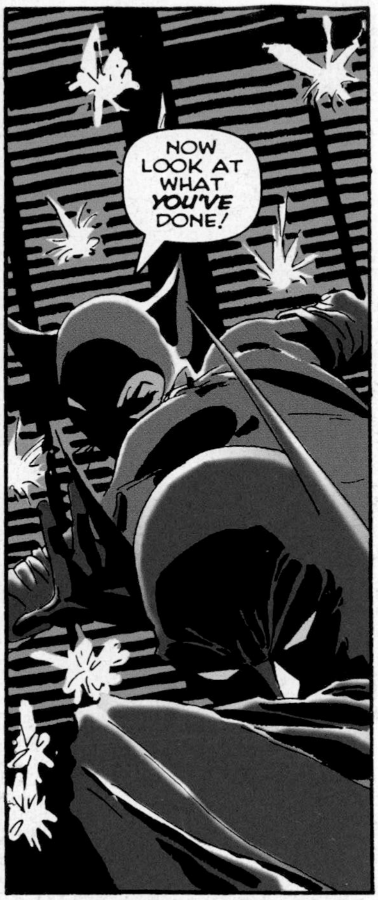
NOW LOOK AT WHAT YOU'VE DONE!
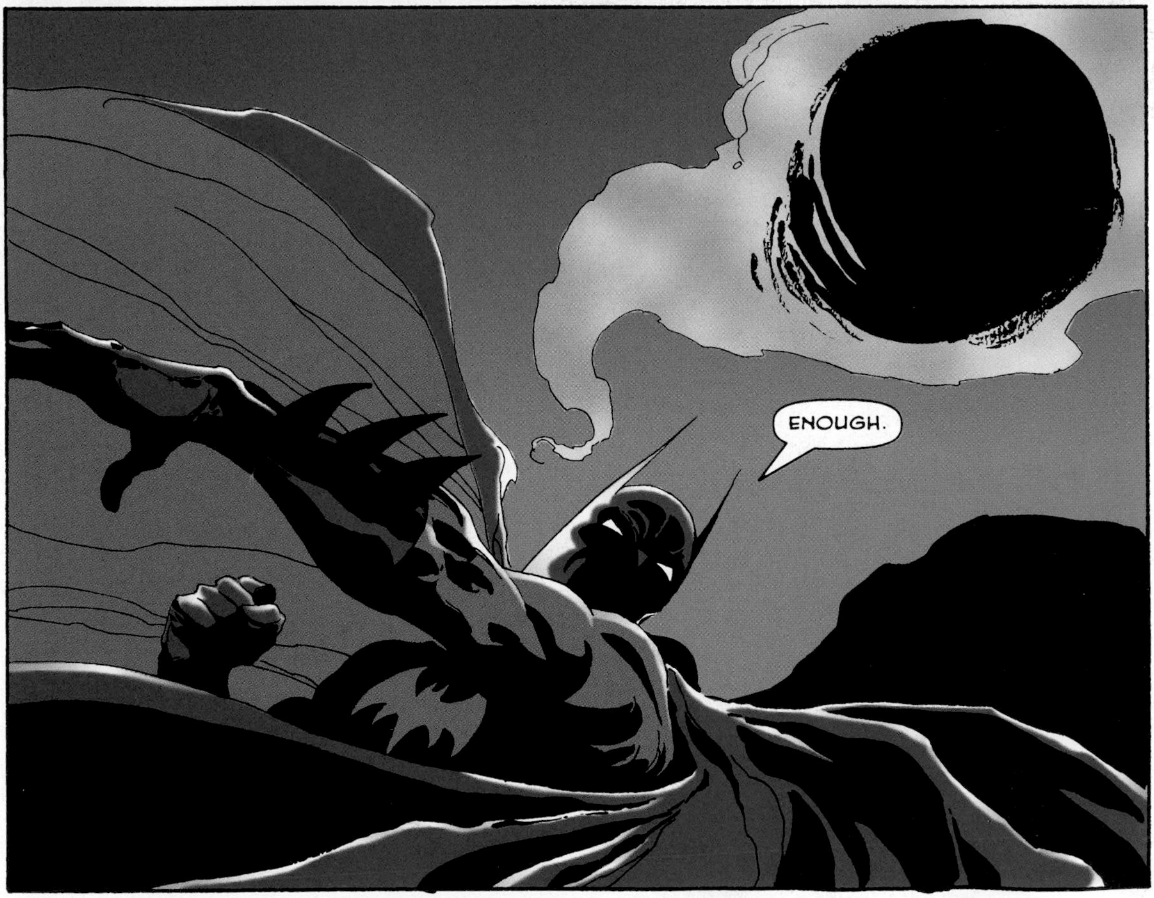
ENOUGH.

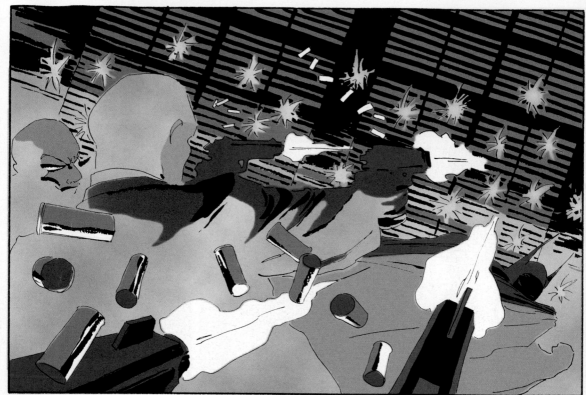

IN MY OWN HOME.

WHERE MY CHILDREN SLEEP.

ON MY NEPHEW'S WEDDING DAY!

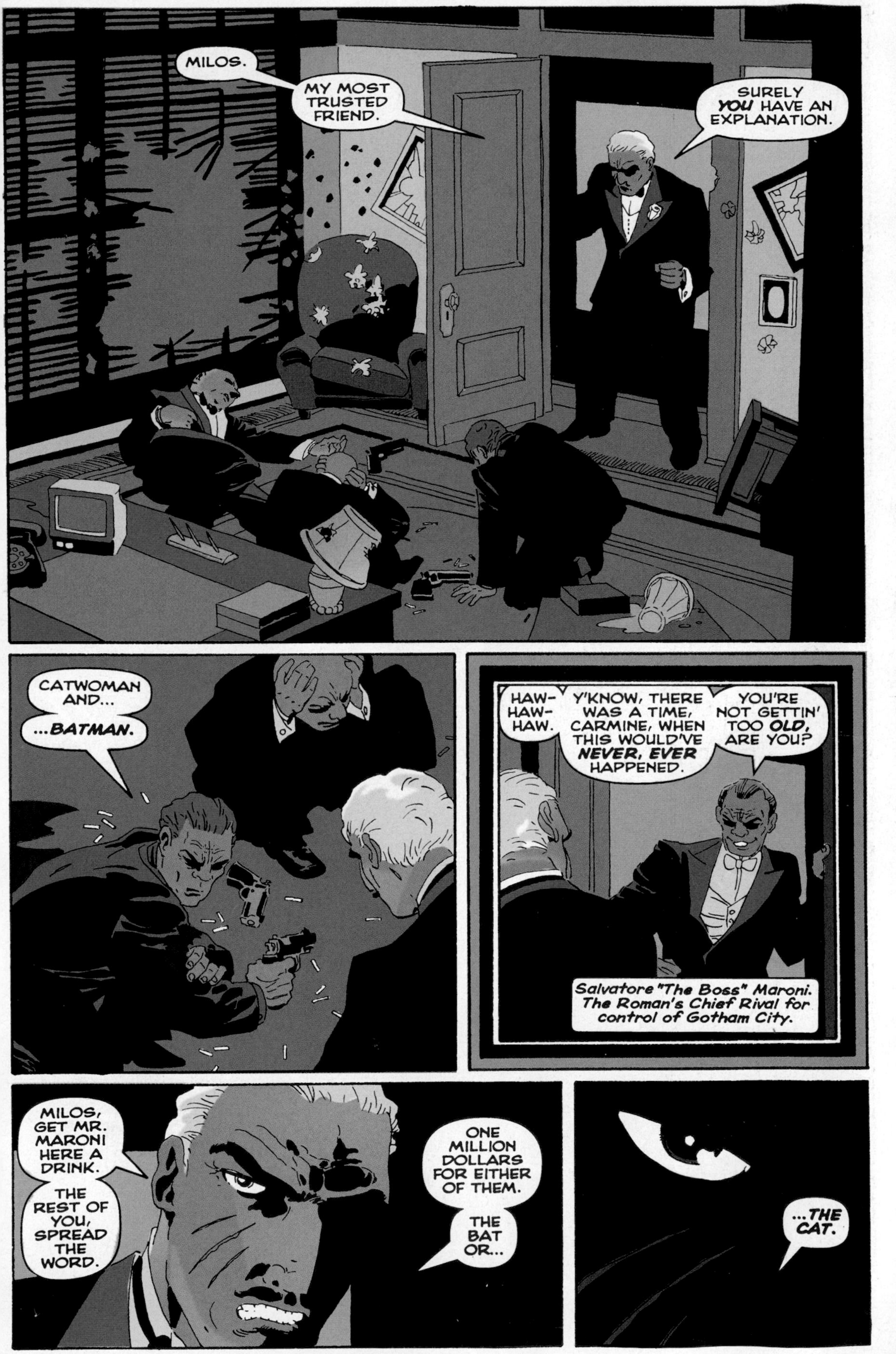
MILOS.
MY MOST TRUSTED FRIEND.
SURELY *YOU* HAVE AN EXPLANATION.
CATWOMAN AND...
...*BATMAN.*
HAW-HAW-HAW.
Y'KNOW, THERE WAS A TIME, CARMINE, WHEN THIS WOULD'VE *NEVER, EVER* HAPPENED.
YOU'RE NOT GETTIN' TOO *OLD,* ARE YOU?
Salvatore "The Boss" Maroni. The Roman's Chief Rival for control of Gotham City.
MILOS, GET MR. MARONI HERE A DRINK.
THE REST OF YOU, SPREAD THE WORD.
ONE MILLION DOLLARS FOR EITHER OF THEM.
THE BAT OR...
...*THE CAT.*

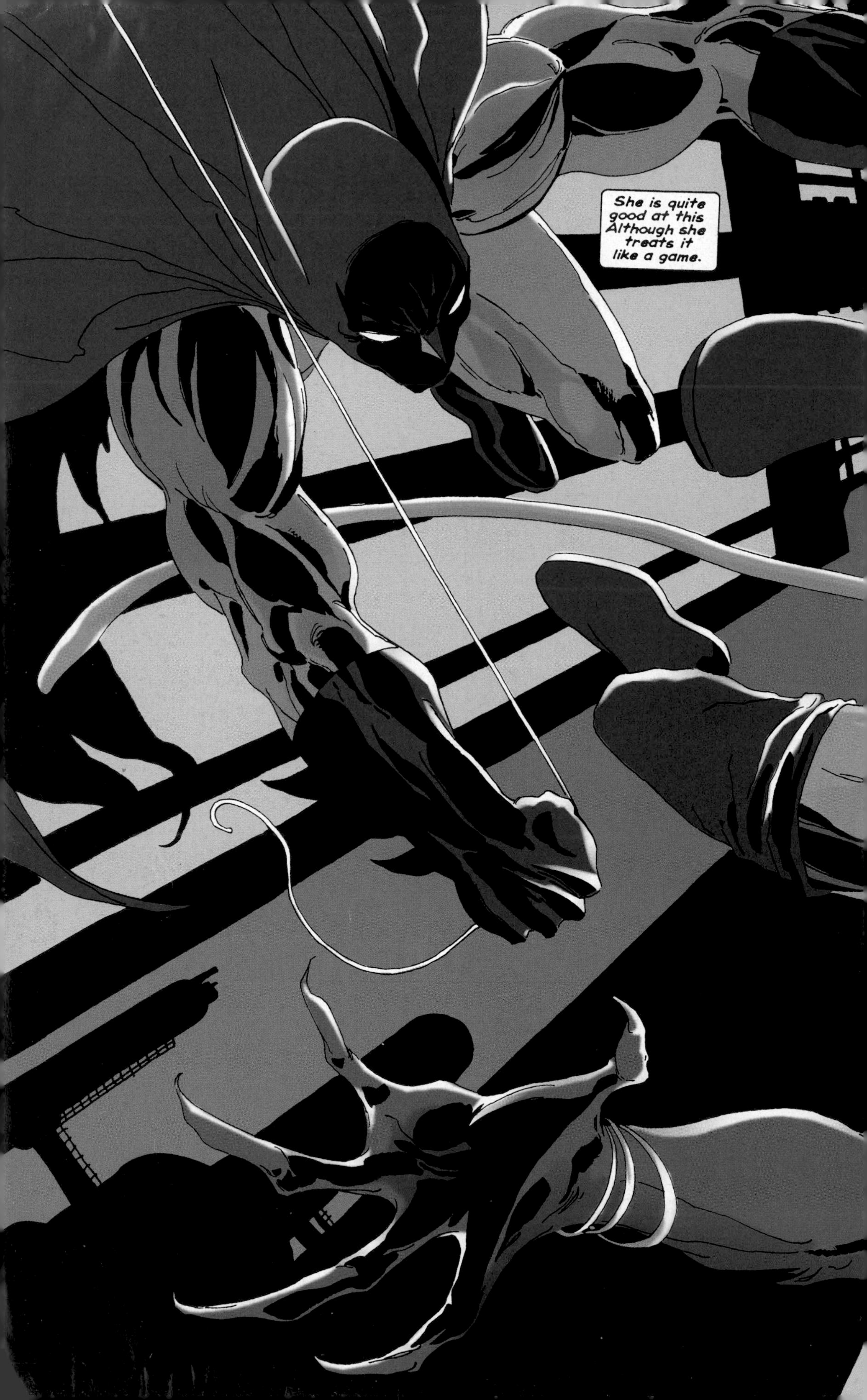
She is quite good at this Although she treats it like a game.

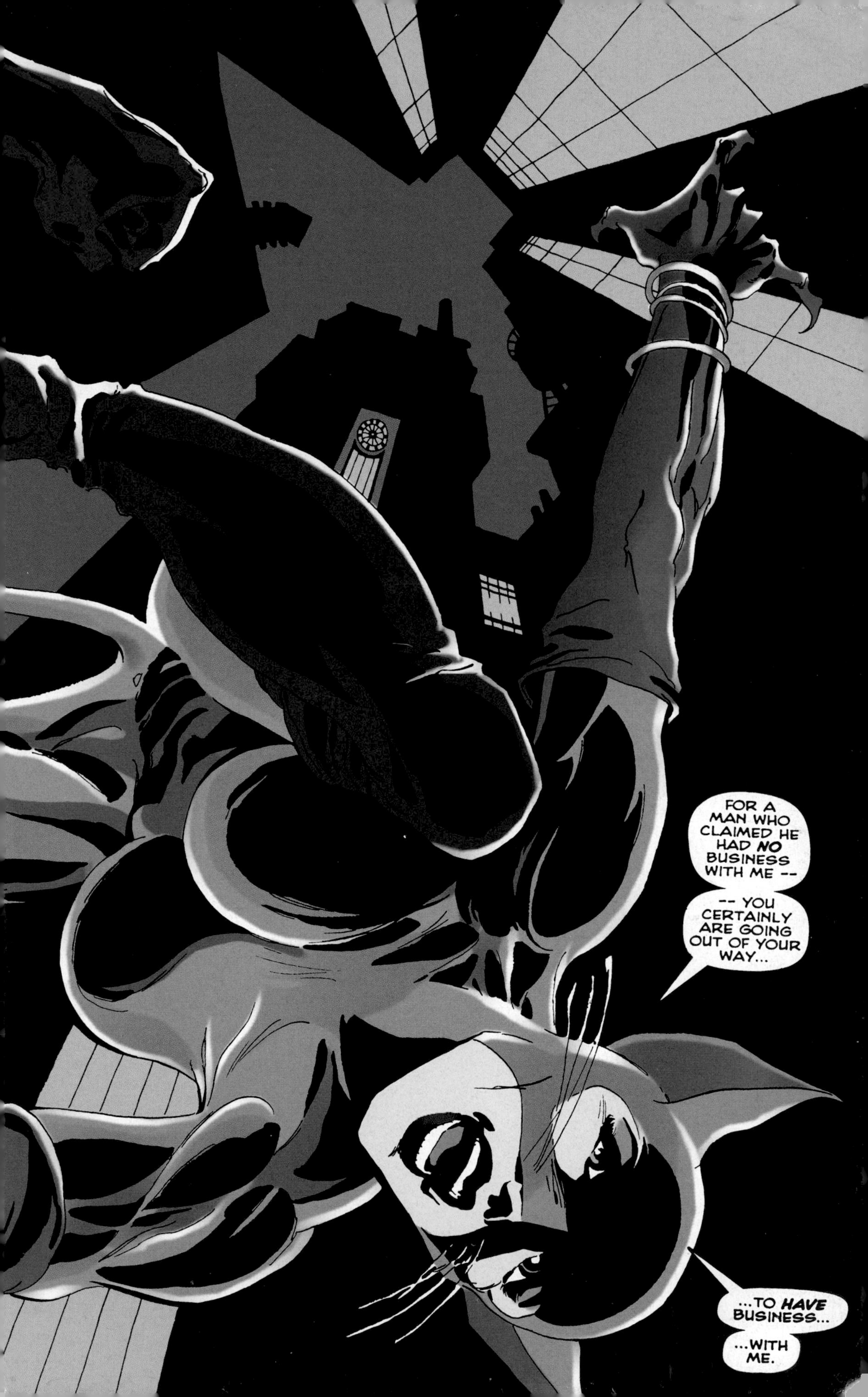
FOR A MAN WHO CLAIMED HE HAD NO BUSINESS WITH ME --
-- YOU CERTAINLY ARE GOING OUT OF YOUR WAY...
...TO HAVE BUSINESS...
...WITH ME.

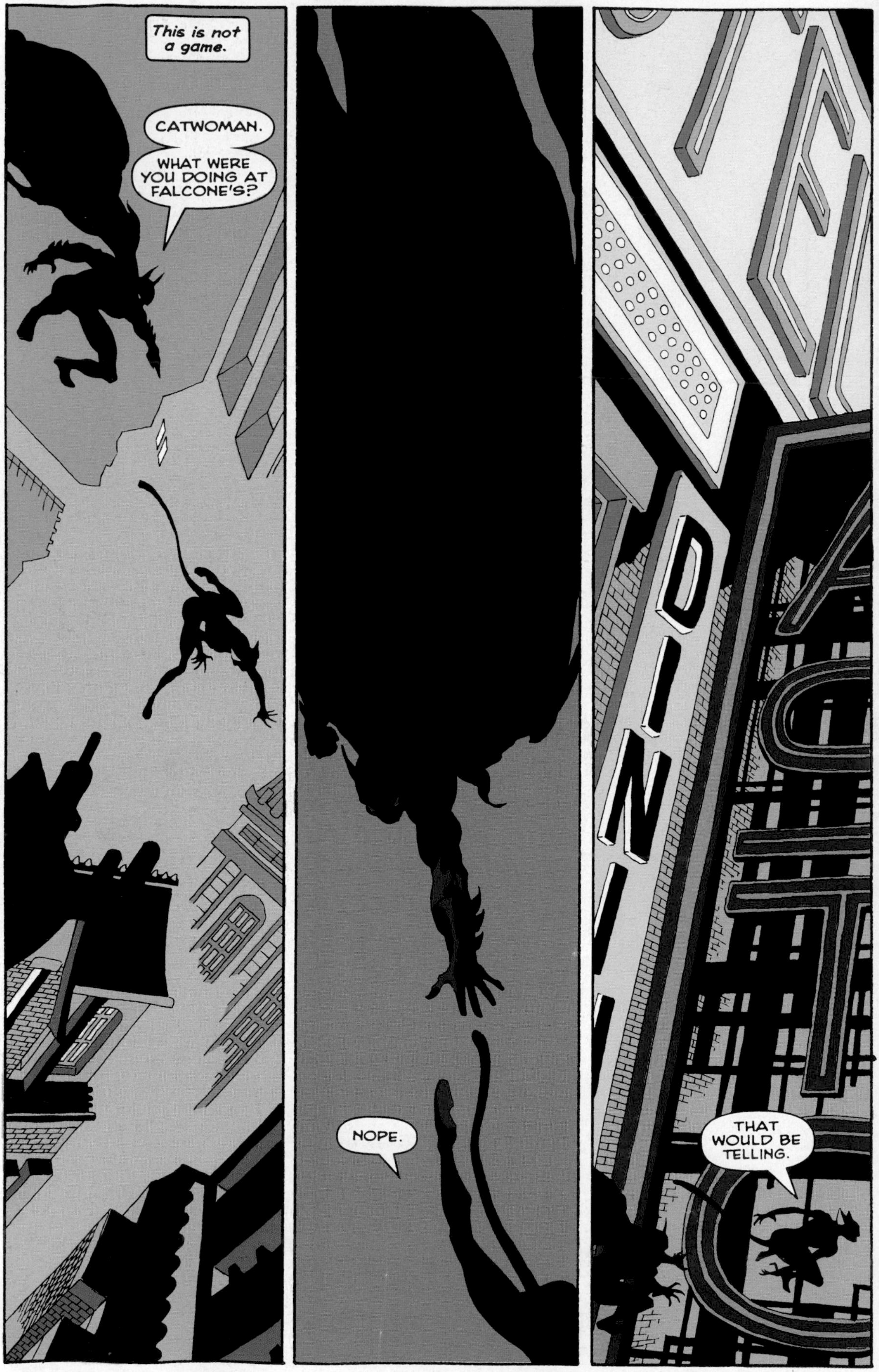
This is not a game.
CATWOMAN.
WHAT WERE YOU DOING AT FALCONE'S?
NOPE.
THAT WOULD BE TELLING.

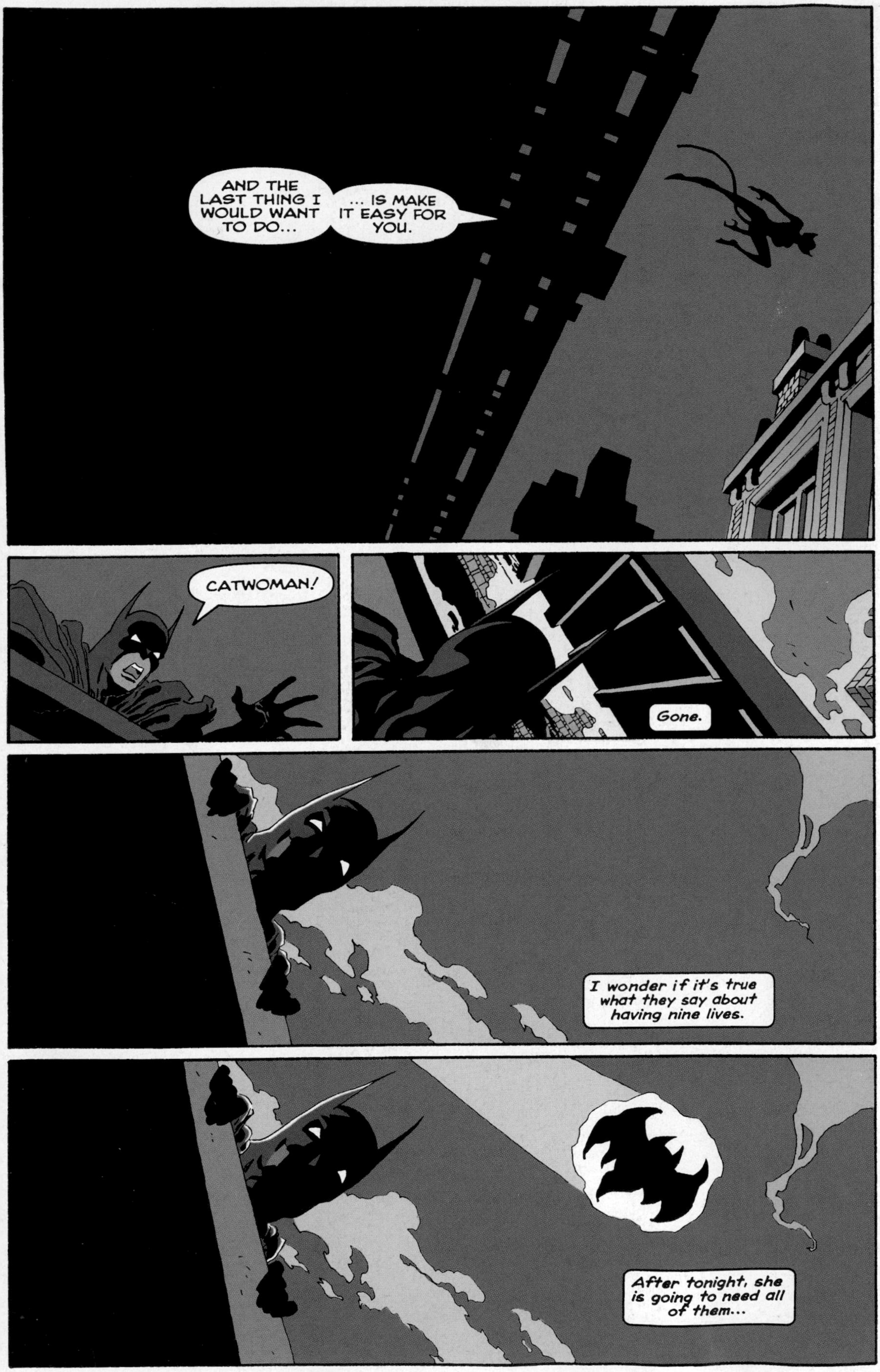

AND THE LAST THING I WOULD WANT TO DO...
... IS MAKE IT EASY FOR YOU.
CATWOMAN!
Gone.
I wonder if it's true what they say about having nine lives.
After tonight, she is going to need all of them...

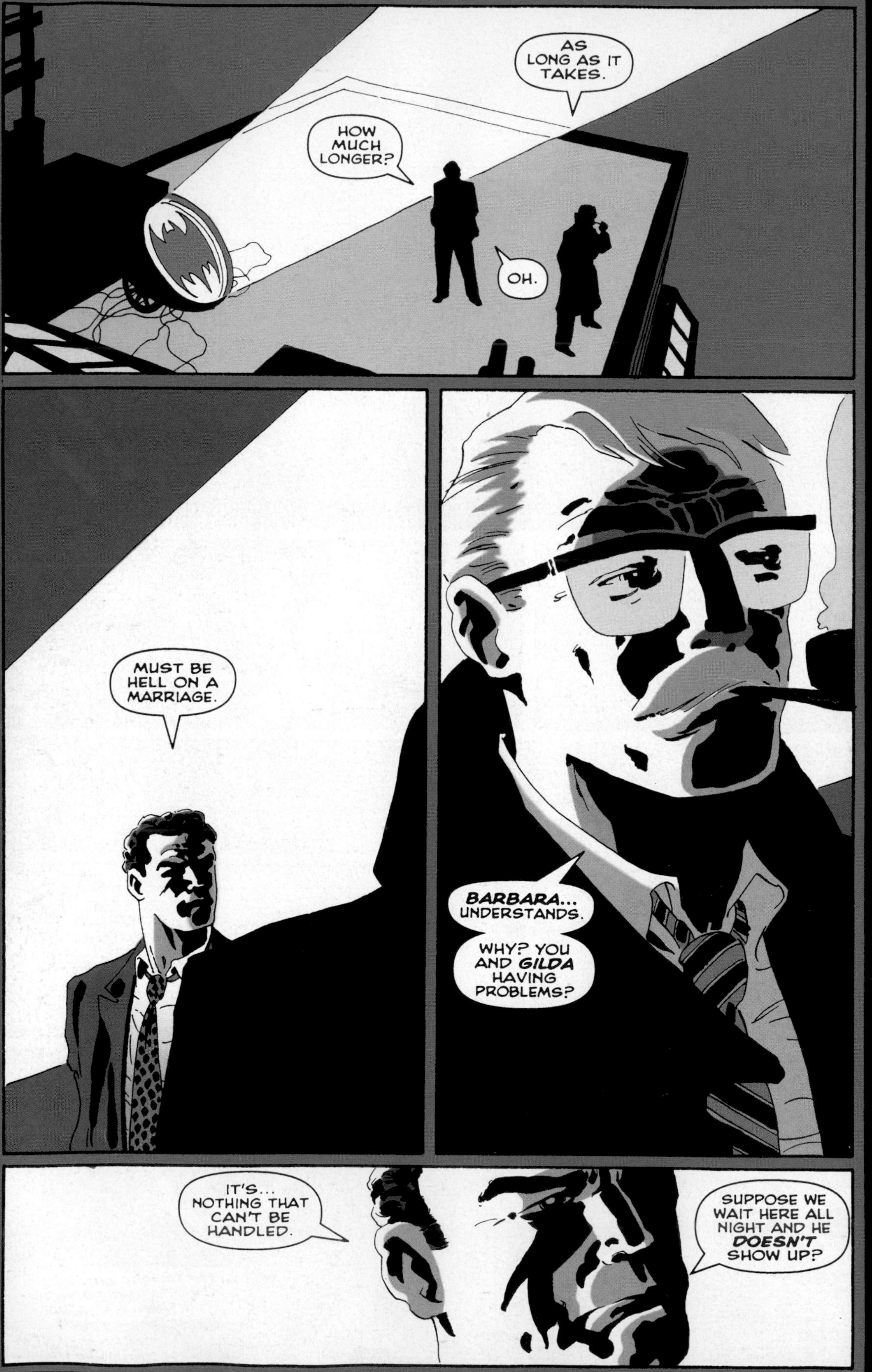
HOW MUCH LONGER?
AS LONG AS IT TAKES.
OH.
MUST BE HELL ON A MARRIAGE.
BARBARA... UNDERSTANDS.
WHY? YOU AND GILDA HAVING PROBLEMS?
IT'S... NOTHING THAT CAN'T BE HANDLED.
SUPPOSE WE WAIT HERE ALL NIGHT AND HE DOESN'T SHOW UP?

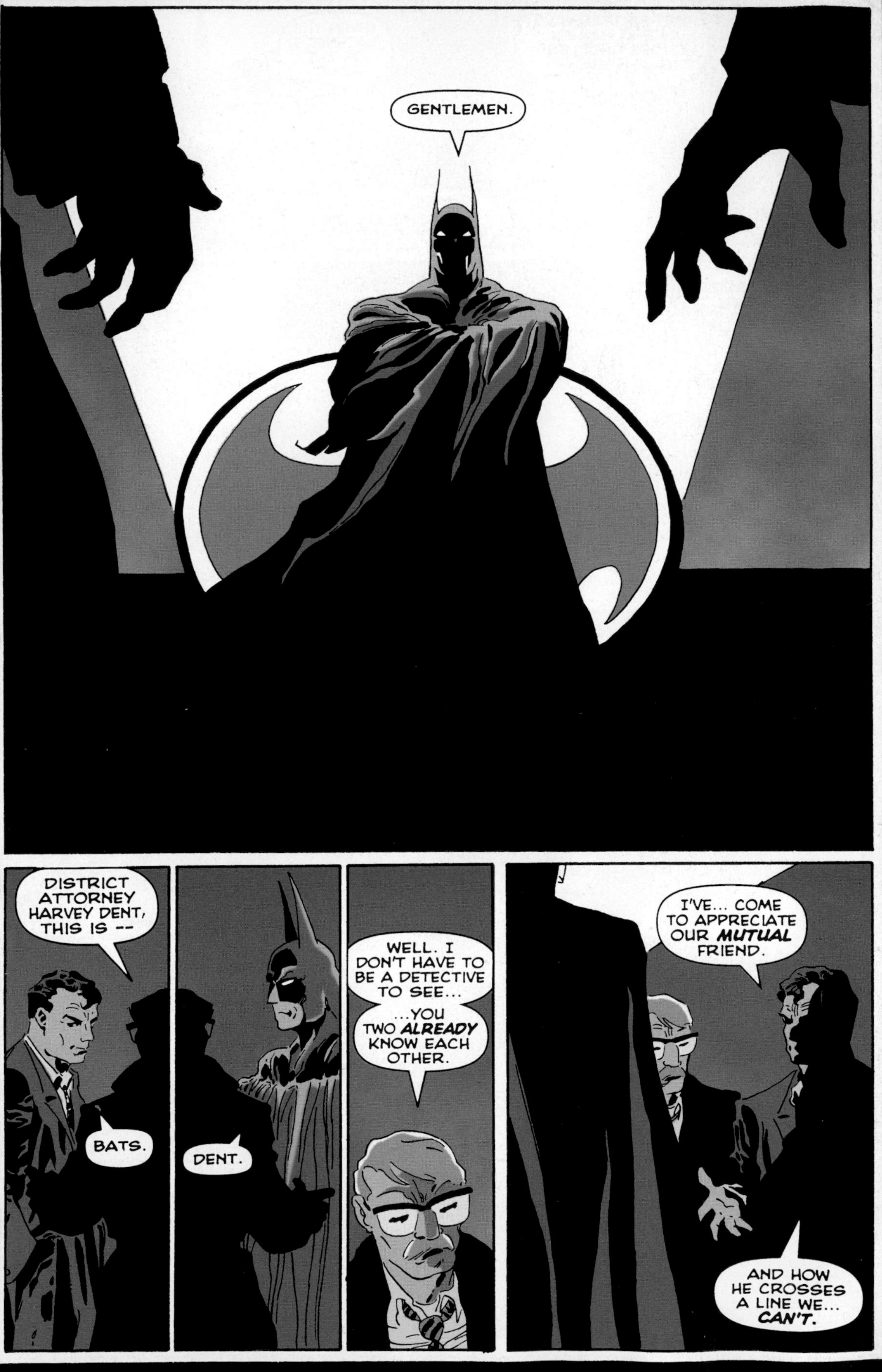
GENTLEMEN.
DISTRICT ATTORNEY HARVEY DENT, THIS IS --
BATS.
DENT.
WELL. I DON'T HAVE TO BE A DETECTIVE TO SEE...
...YOU TWO ALREADY KNOW EACH OTHER.
I'VE... COME TO APPRECIATE OUR MUTUAL FRIEND.
AND HOW HE CROSSES A LINE WE... CAN'T.

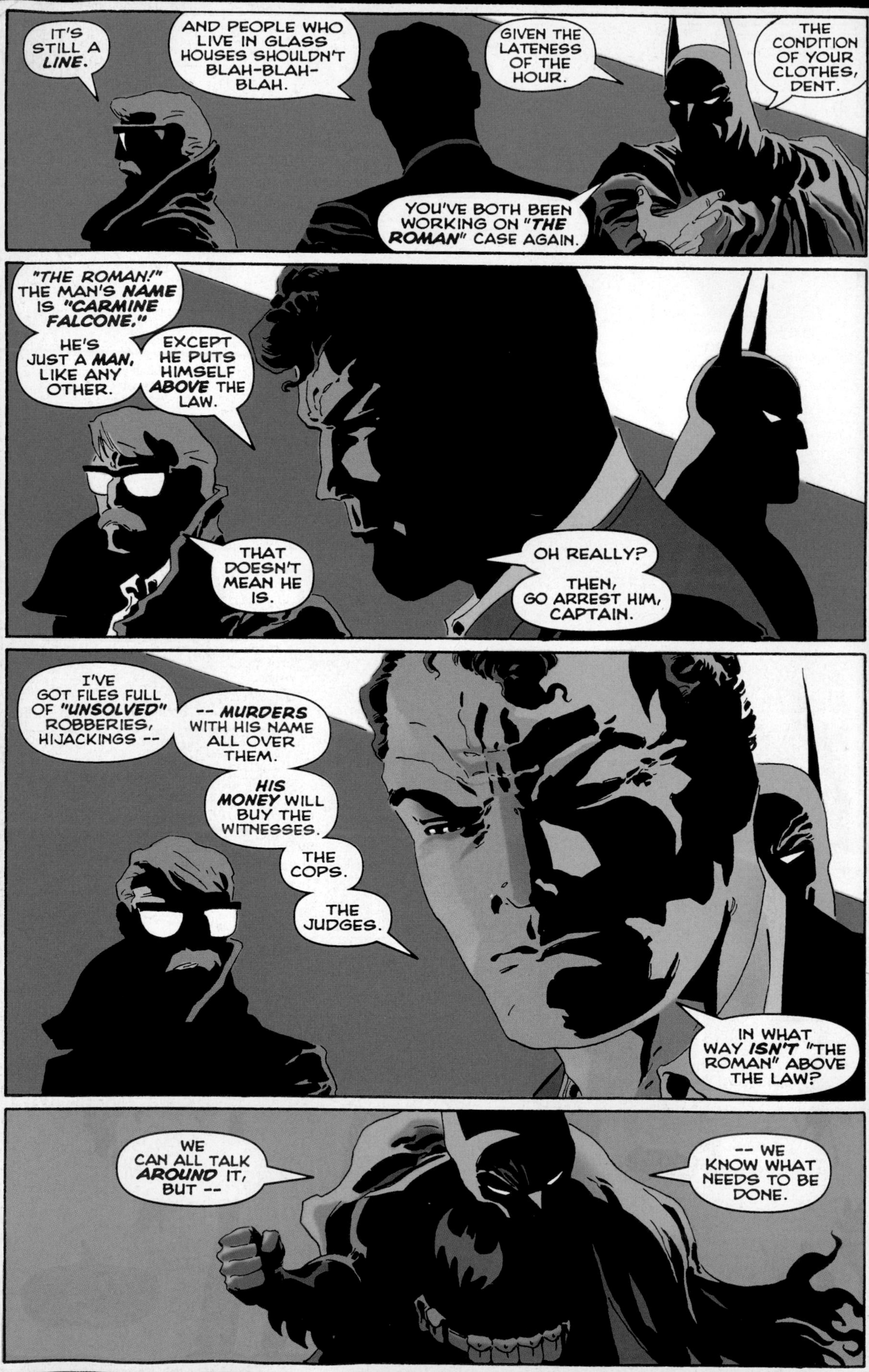
IT'S STILL A LINE.
AND PEOPLE WHO LIVE IN GLASS HOUSES SHOULDN'T BLAH-BLAH-BLAH.
GIVEN THE LATENESS OF THE HOUR.
THE CONDITION OF YOUR CLOTHES, DENT.
YOU'VE BOTH BEEN WORKING ON "THE ROMAN" CASE AGAIN.
"THE ROMAN!" THE MAN'S NAME IS "CARMINE FALCONE."
HE'S JUST A MAN, LIKE ANY OTHER.
EXCEPT HE PUTS HIMSELF ABOVE THE LAW.
THAT DOESN'T MEAN HE IS.
OH REALLY?
THEN, GO ARREST HIM, CAPTAIN.
I'VE GOT FILES FULL OF "UNSOLVED" ROBBERIES, HIJACKINGS --
-- MURDERS WITH HIS NAME ALL OVER THEM.
HIS MONEY WILL BUY THE WITNESSES.
THE COPS.
THE JUDGES.
IN WHAT WAY ISN'T "THE ROMAN" ABOVE THE LAW?
WE CAN ALL TALK AROUND IT, BUT --
-- WE KNOW WHAT NEEDS TO BE DONE.

I WANT TO BE *CLEAR* ON THIS. IN OUR...ZEAL... TO BRING FALCONE TO JUSTICE.

I'LL LET YOU *BEND* THE RULES, BUT WE CANNOT *BREAK* THEM. OTHERWISE, HOW ARE WE DIFFERENT FROM *HIM?*

OF COURSE.

I made a promise on the grave of my slain parents.

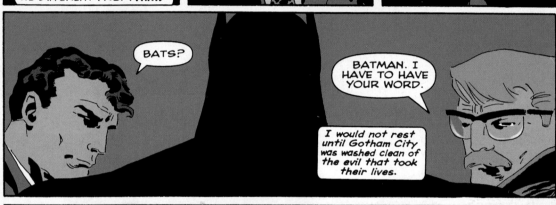

BATS?

BATMAN. I HAVE TO HAVE YOUR WORD.

I would not rest until Gotham City was washed clean of the evil that took their lives.

There could be no compromises.

And yet...

AGREED.

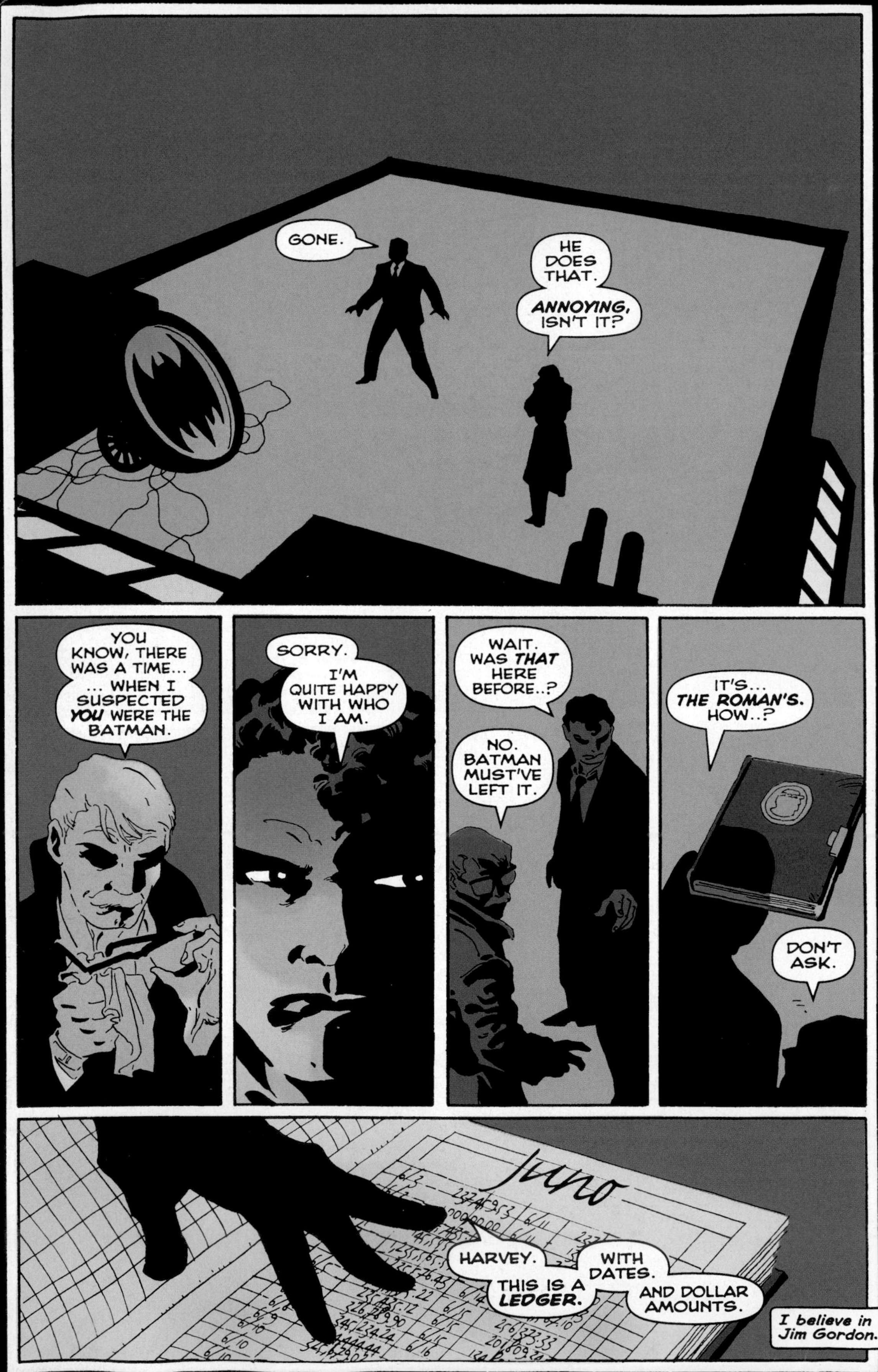
GONE.
HE DOES THAT.
ANNOYING, ISN'T IT?
YOU KNOW, THERE WAS A TIME...
... WHEN I SUSPECTED YOU WERE THE BATMAN.
SORRY.
I'M QUITE HAPPY WITH WHO I AM.
WAIT. WAS THAT HERE BEFORE..?
NO. BATMAN MUST'VE LEFT IT.
IT'S... THE ROMAN'S. HOW..?
DON'T ASK.
Juno
HARVEY.
THIS IS A LEDGER.
WITH DATES.
AND DOLLAR AMOUNTS.
I believe in Jim Gordon.

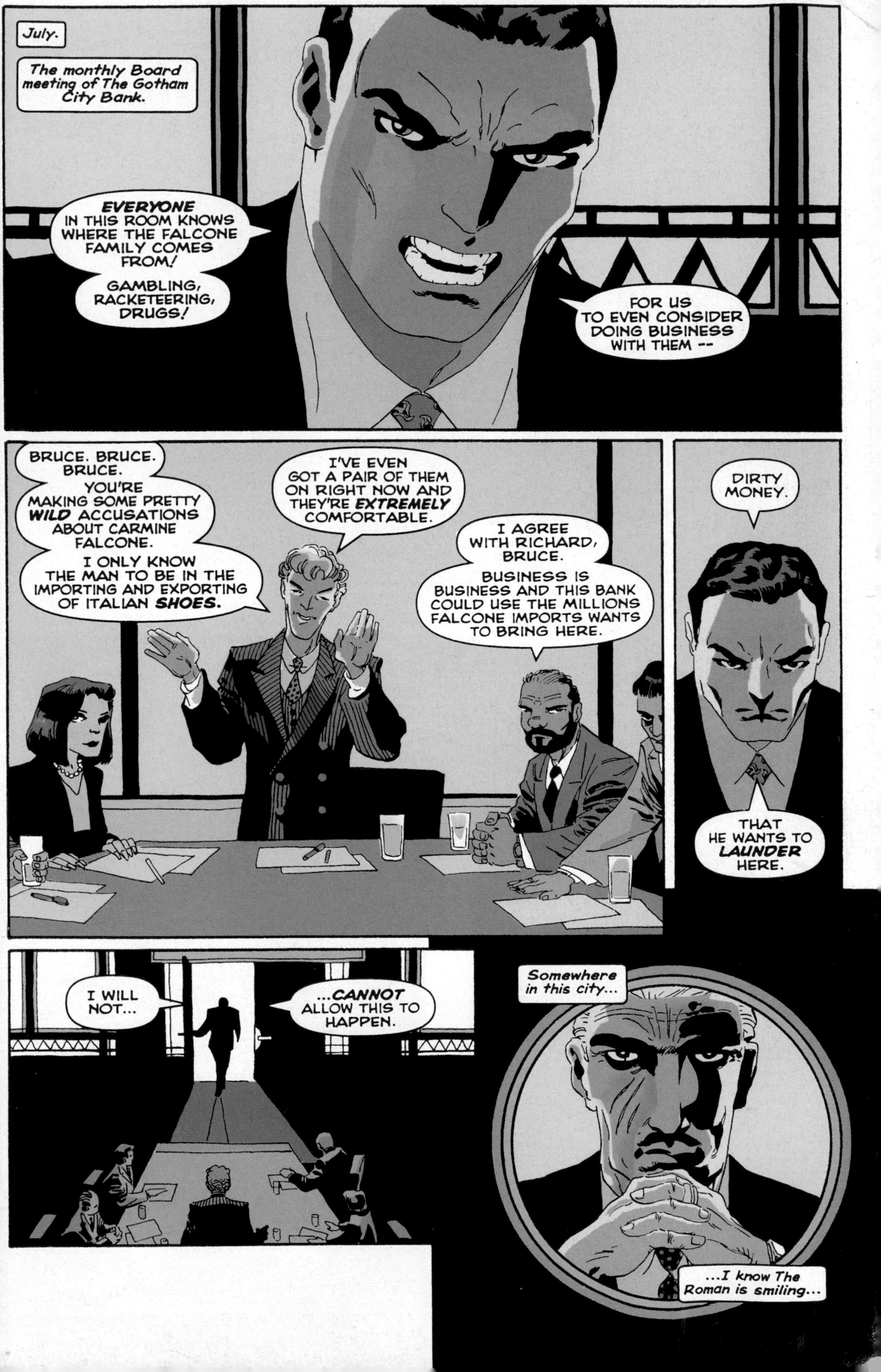
July.
The monthly Board meeting of The Gotham City Bank.
EVERYONE IN THIS ROOM KNOWS WHERE THE FALCONE FAMILY COMES FROM!
GAMBLING, RACKETEERING, DRUGS!
FOR US TO EVEN CONSIDER DOING BUSINESS WITH THEM --
BRUCE. BRUCE. BRUCE.
YOU'RE MAKING SOME PRETTY WILD ACCUSATIONS ABOUT CARMINE FALCONE.
I ONLY KNOW THE MAN TO BE IN THE IMPORTING AND EXPORTING OF ITALIAN SHOES.
I'VE EVEN GOT A PAIR OF THEM ON RIGHT NOW AND THEY'RE EXTREMELY COMFORTABLE.
I AGREE WITH RICHARD, BRUCE.
BUSINESS IS BUSINESS AND THIS BANK COULD USE THE MILLIONS FALCONE IMPORTS WANTS TO BRING HERE.
DIRTY MONEY.
THAT HE WANTS TO LAUNDER HERE.
I WILL NOT...
...CANNOT ALLOW THIS TO HAPPEN.
Somewhere in this city...
...I know The Roman is smiling...

Richard Daniel's penthouse.

Far more luxurious than one could afford on a BANK PRESIDENT'S salary.

DARLING, HURRY ALONG! THE RESERVATION IS IN HALF AN HOUR.

RICHARD DANIEL.

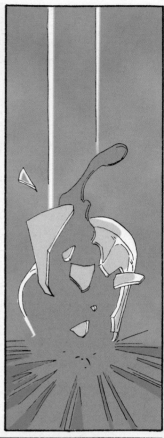

THE FALCONE MONEY.

KEEP IT OUT OF THE BANK.

GOTHAM GAZE
BANK CHIEF
DANIEL RESIGNS
BRUCE WAYNE TO HEAD

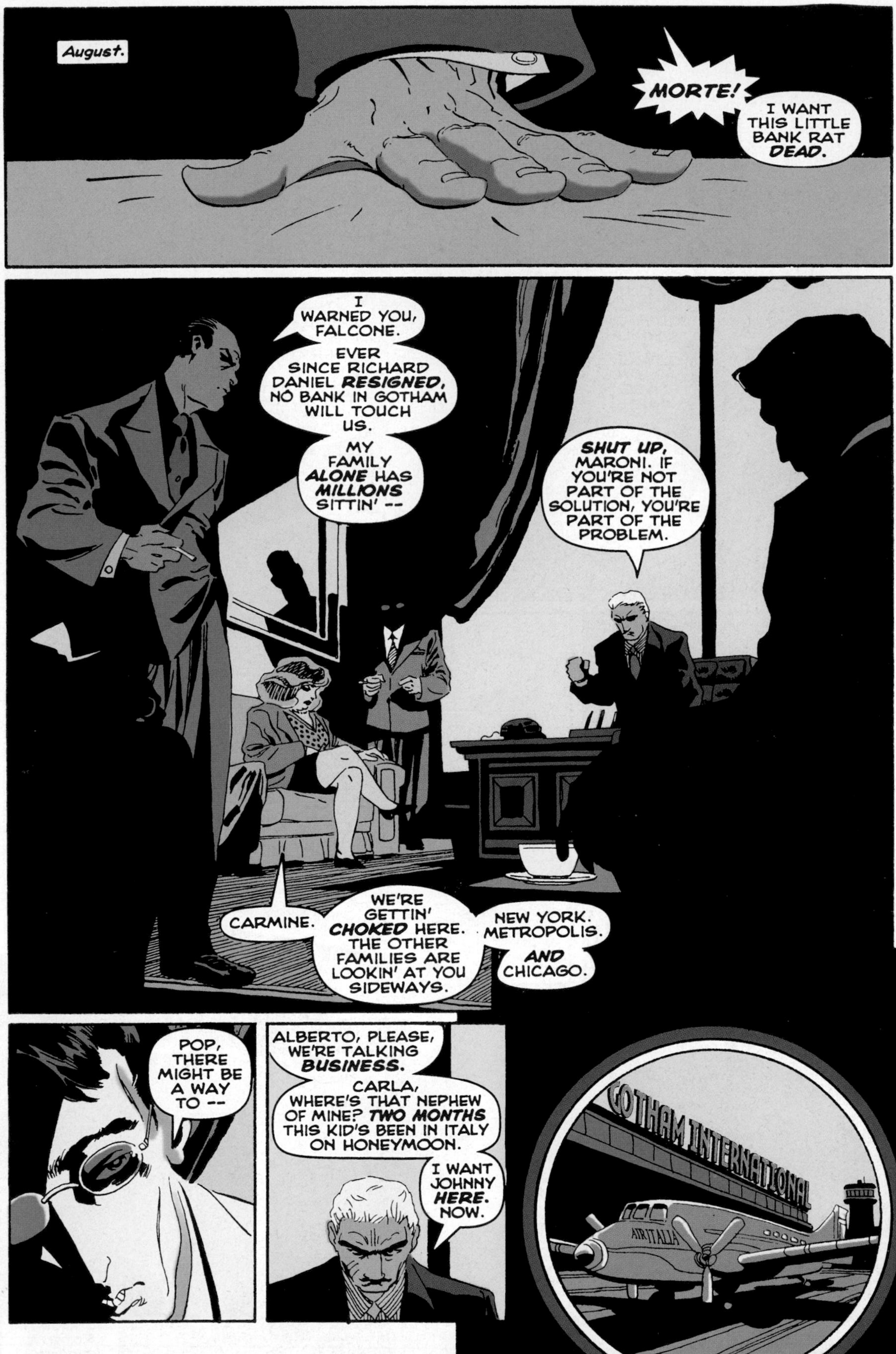
August.
MORTE!
I WANT THIS LITTLE BANK RAT DEAD.
I WARNED YOU, FALCONE.
EVER SINCE RICHARD DANIEL RESIGNED, NO BANK IN GOTHAM WILL TOUCH US.
MY FAMILY ALONE HAS MILLIONS SITTIN' --
SHUT UP, MARONI. IF YOU'RE NOT PART OF THE SOLUTION, YOU'RE PART OF THE PROBLEM.
CARMINE.
WE'RE GETTIN' CHOKED HERE. THE OTHER FAMILIES ARE LOOKIN' AT YOU SIDEWAYS.
NEW YORK. METROPOLIS.
AND CHICAGO.
POP, THERE MIGHT BE A WAY TO --
ALBERTO, PLEASE, WE'RE TALKING BUSINESS.
CARLA, WHERE'S THAT NEPHEW OF MINE? TWO MONTHS THIS KID'S BEEN IN ITALY ON HONEYMOON.
I WANT JOHNNY HERE. NOW.
GOTHAM INTERNATIONAL
AIR ITALIA

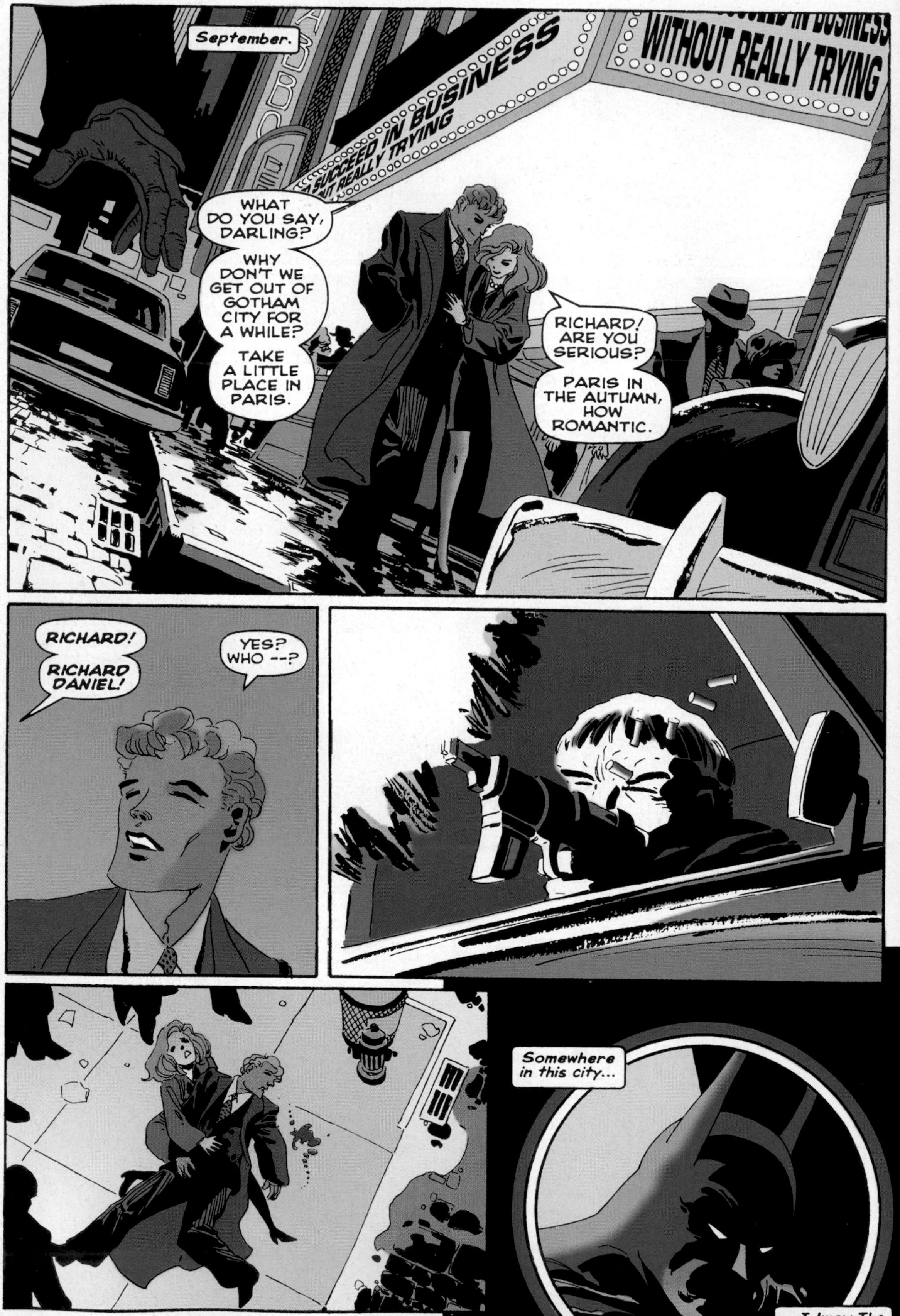
September.
HOW TO SUCCEED IN BUSINESS WITHOUT REALLY TRYING
WITHOUT REALLY TRYING
WHAT DO YOU SAY, DARLING?
WHY DON'T WE GET OUT OF GOTHAM CITY FOR A WHILE?
TAKE A LITTLE PLACE IN PARIS.
RICHARD! ARE YOU SERIOUS?
PARIS IN THE AUTUMN, HOW ROMANTIC.
RICHARD! RICHARD DANIEL!
YES? WHO --?
Somewhere in this city...
...I know The Roman is laughing...

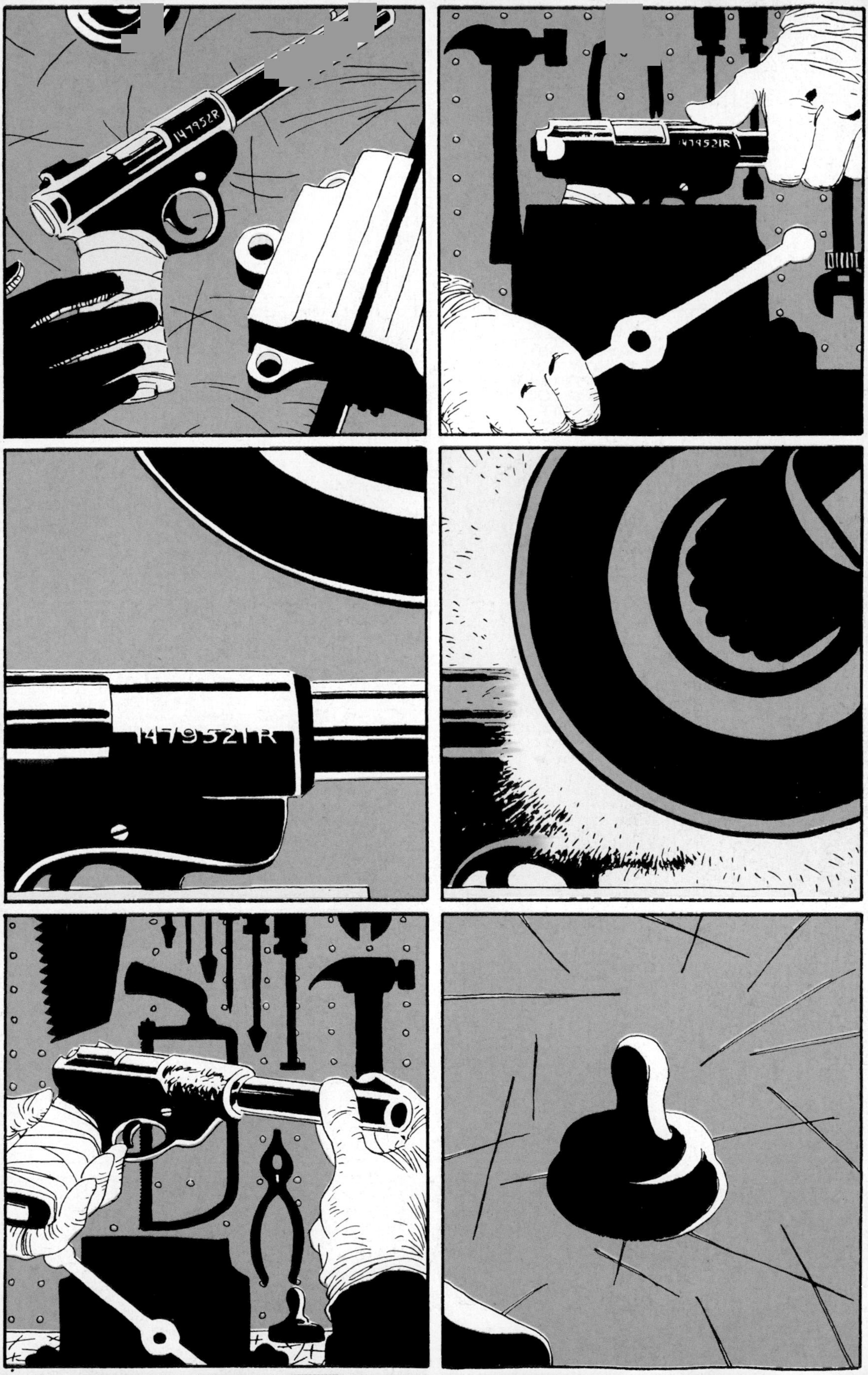
147952R
1479521R
1479521R

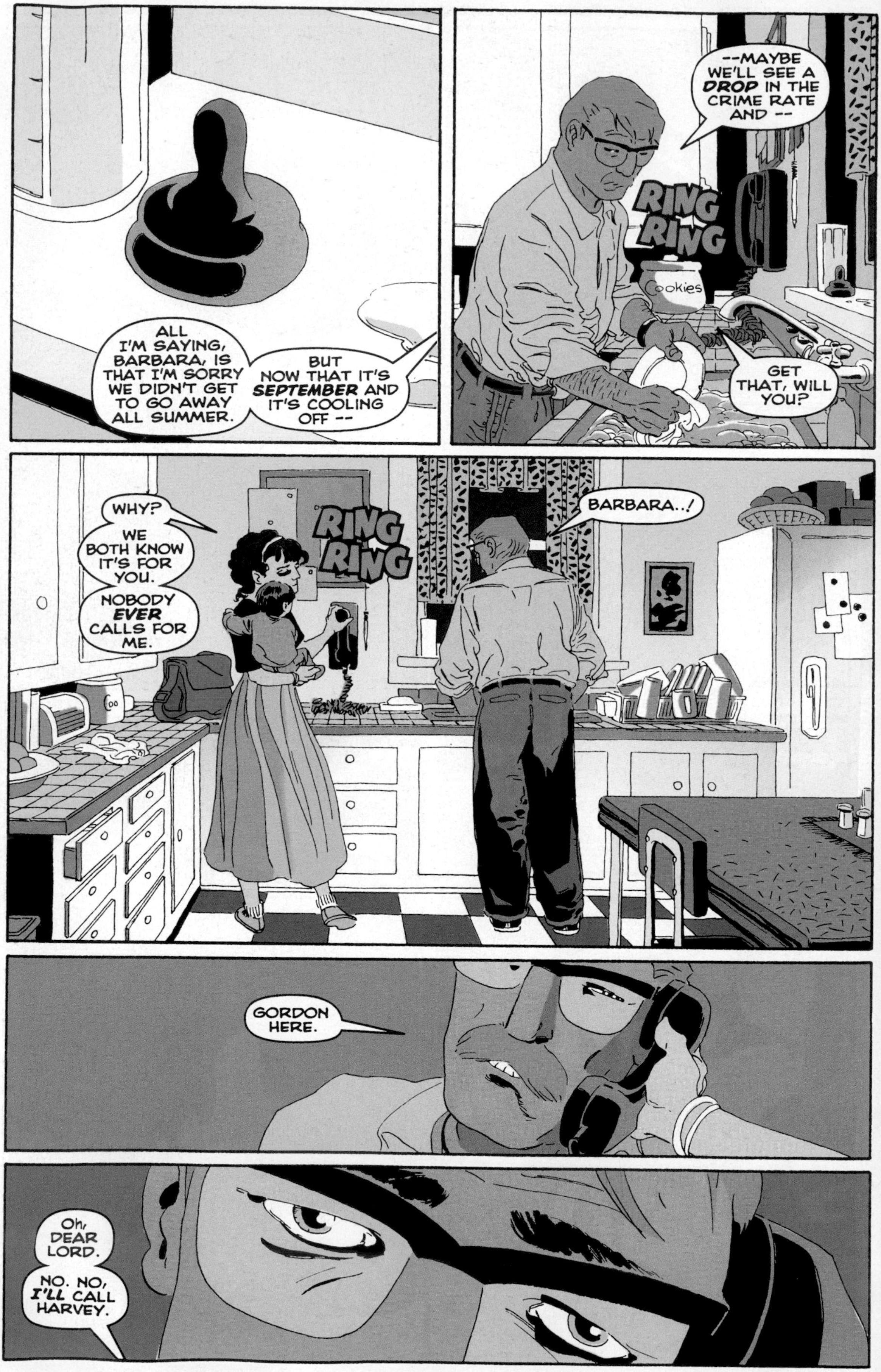
ALL I'M SAYING, BARBARA, IS THAT I'M SORRY WE DIDN'T GET TO GO AWAY ALL SUMMER.
BUT NOW THAT IT'S SEPTEMBER AND IT'S COOLING OFF --
--MAYBE WE'LL SEE A DROP IN THE CRIME RATE AND --
RING RING
Cookies
GET THAT, WILL YOU?
RING RING
WHY?
WE BOTH KNOW IT'S FOR YOU.
NOBODY EVER CALLS FOR ME.
BARBARA..!
GORDON HERE.
Oh, DEAR LORD.
NO. NO, I'LL CALL HARVEY.

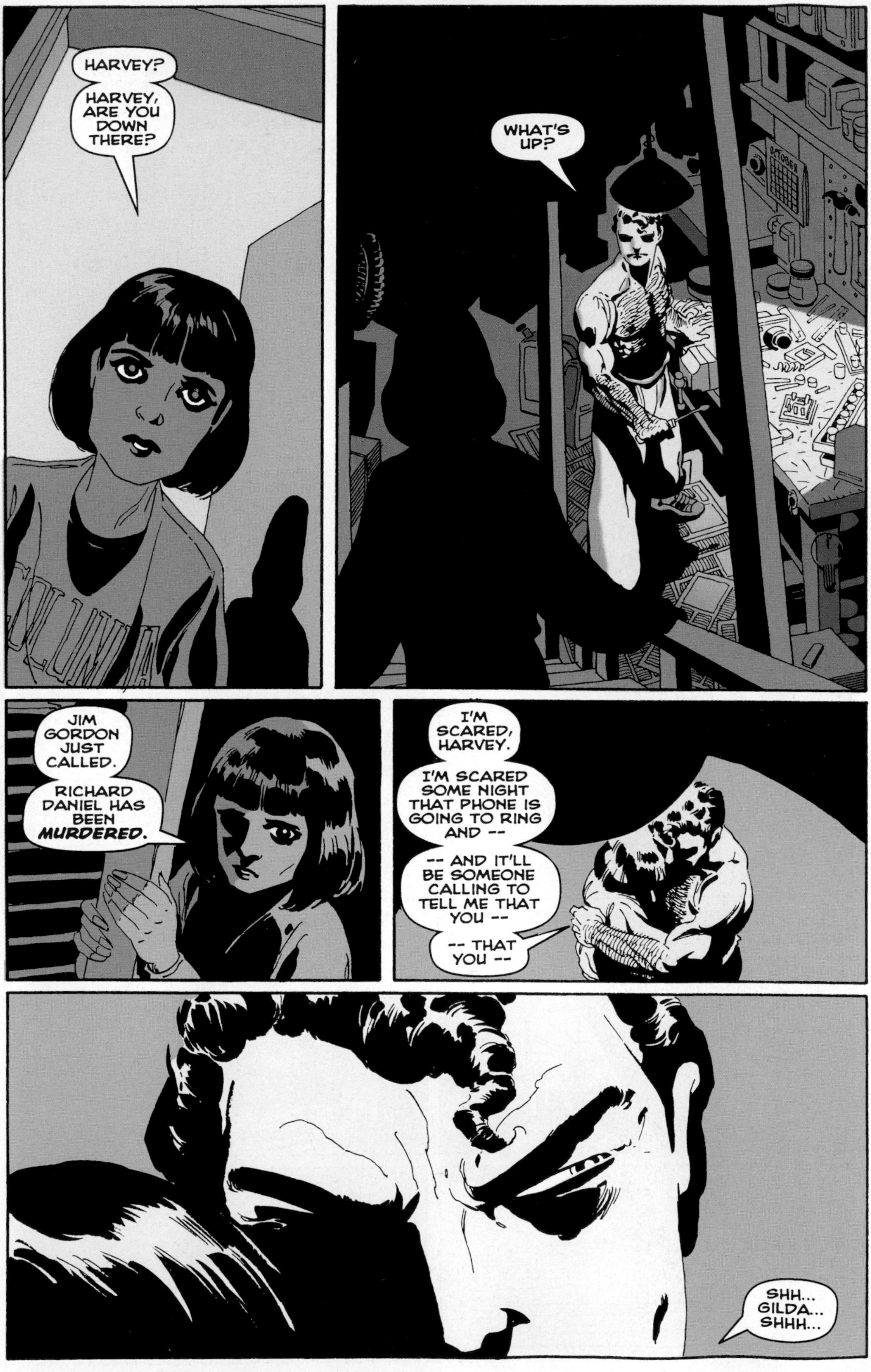
HARVEY?
HARVEY, ARE YOU DOWN THERE?
WHAT'S UP?
JIM GORDON JUST CALLED.
RICHARD DANIEL HAS BEEN *MURDERED*.
I'M SCARED, HARVEY.
I'M SCARED SOME NIGHT THAT PHONE IS GOING TO RING AND --
-- AND IT'LL BE SOMEONE CALLING TO TELL ME THAT YOU --
-- THAT YOU --
SHH... GILDA... SHHH...

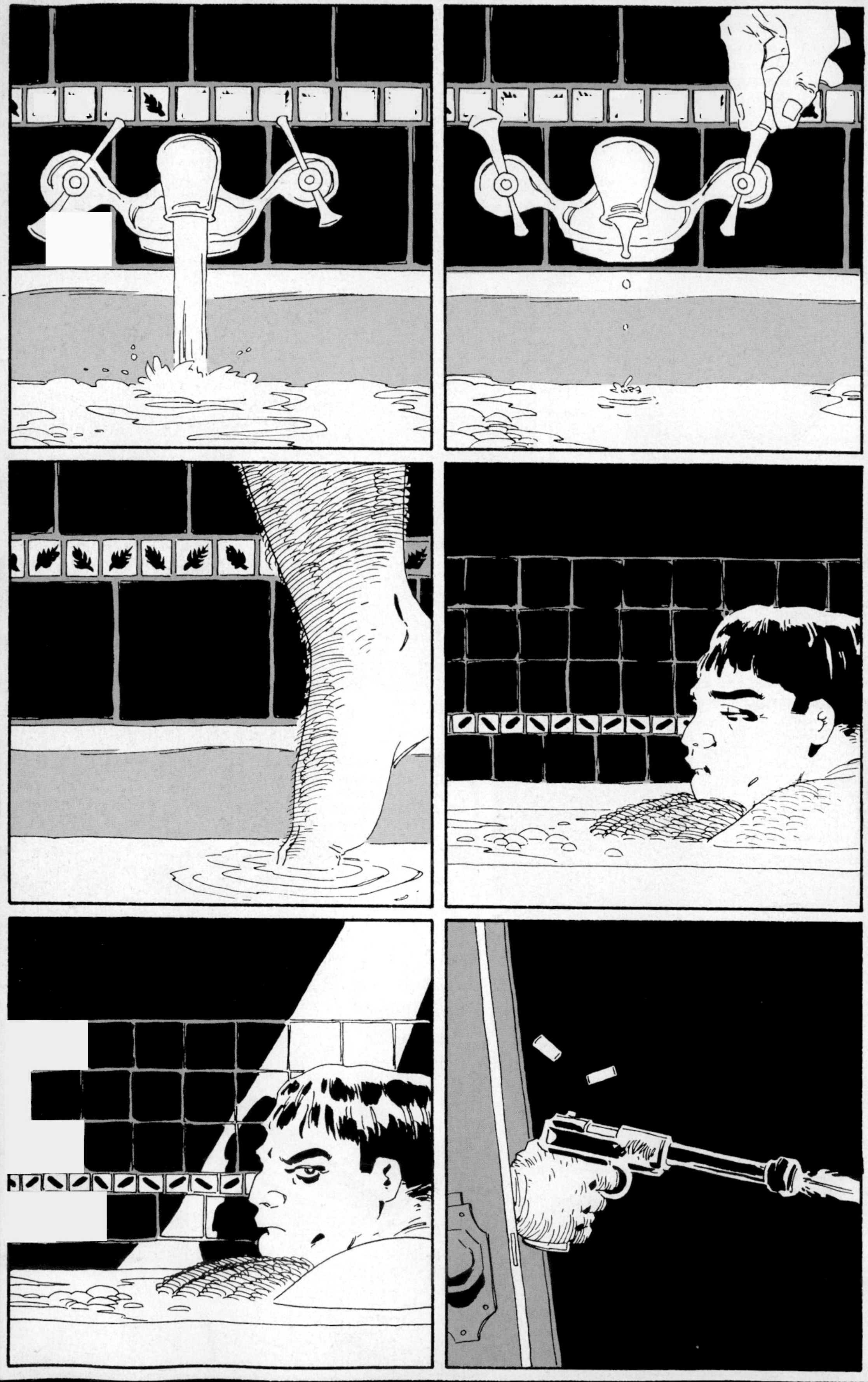

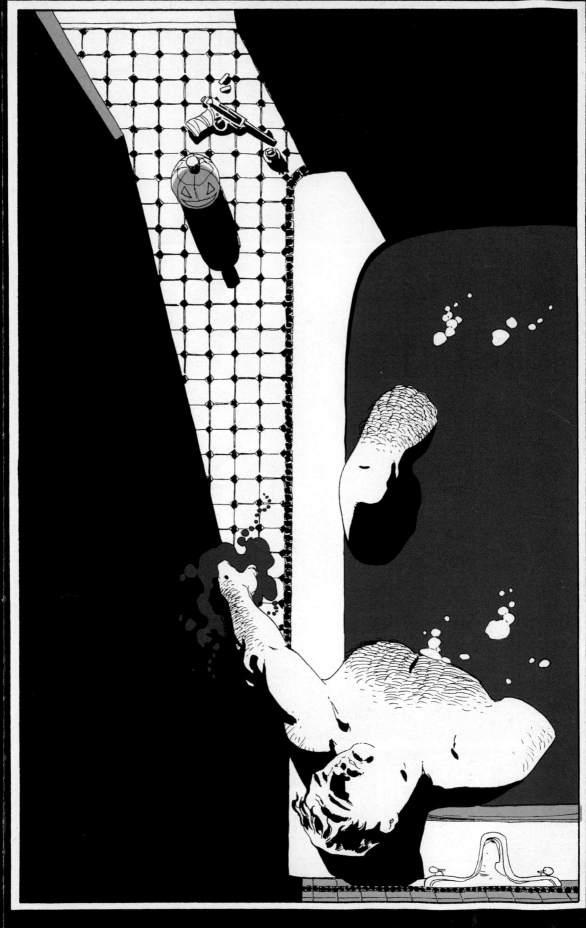

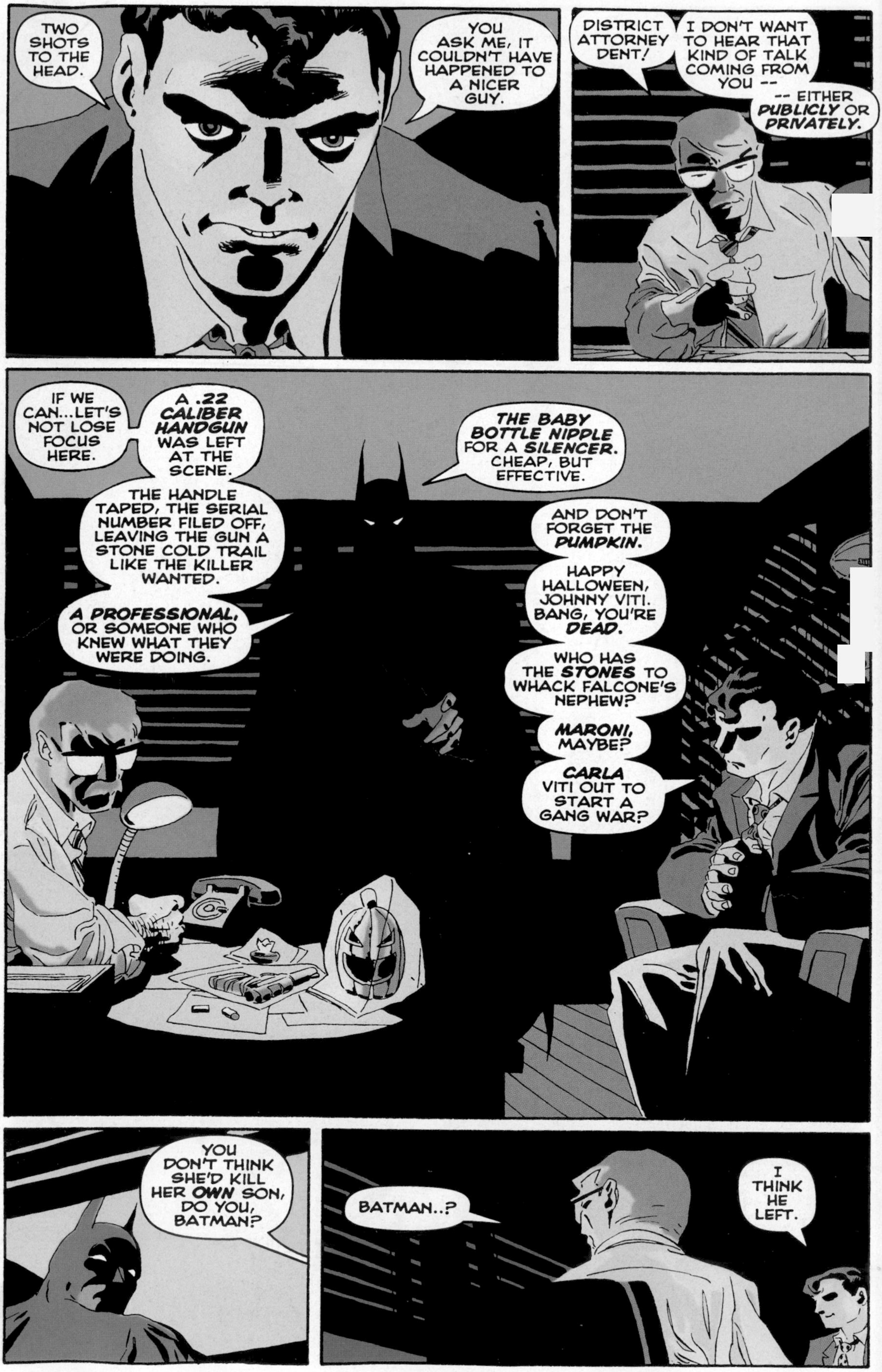
TWO SHOTS TO THE HEAD.
YOU ASK ME, IT COULDN'T HAVE HAPPENED TO A NICER GUY.
DISTRICT ATTORNEY DENT!
I DON'T WANT TO HEAR THAT KIND OF TALK COMING FROM YOU --
-- EITHER PUBLICLY OR PRIVATELY.
IF WE CAN...LET'S NOT LOSE FOCUS HERE.
A .22 CALIBER HANDGUN WAS LEFT AT THE SCENE.
THE HANDLE TAPED, THE SERIAL NUMBER FILED OFF, LEAVING THE GUN A STONE COLD TRAIL LIKE THE KILLER WANTED.
A PROFESSIONAL, OR SOMEONE WHO KNEW WHAT THEY WERE DOING.
THE BABY BOTTLE NIPPLE FOR A SILENCER. CHEAP, BUT EFFECTIVE.
AND DON'T FORGET THE PUMPKIN.
HAPPY HALLOWEEN, JOHNNY VITI. BANG, YOU'RE DEAD.
WHO HAS THE STONES TO WHACK FALCONE'S NEPHEW?
MARONI, MAYBE?
CARLA VITI OUT TO START A GANG WAR?
YOU DON'T THINK SHE'D KILL HER OWN SON, DO YOU, BATMAN?
BATMAN..?
I THINK HE LEFT.

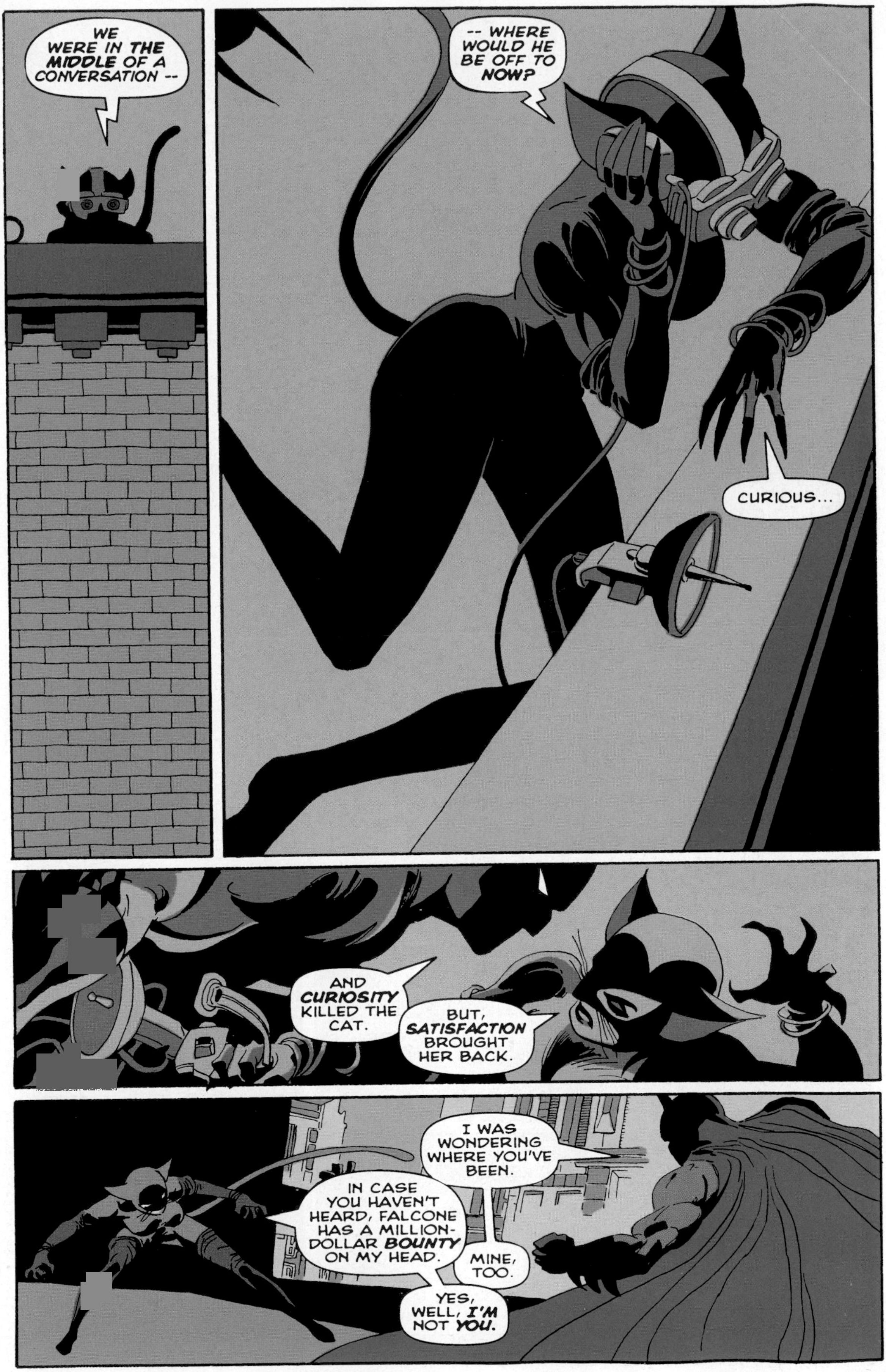
WE WERE IN THE MIDDLE OF A CONVERSATION --
-- WHERE WOULD HE BE OFF TO NOW?
CURIOUS...
AND CURIOSITY KILLED THE CAT.
BUT, SATISFACTION BROUGHT HER BACK.
I WAS WONDERING WHERE YOU'VE BEEN.
IN CASE YOU HAVEN'T HEARD, FALCONE HAS A MILLION-DOLLAR BOUNTY ON MY HEAD.
MINE, TOO.
YES, WELL, I'M NOT YOU.

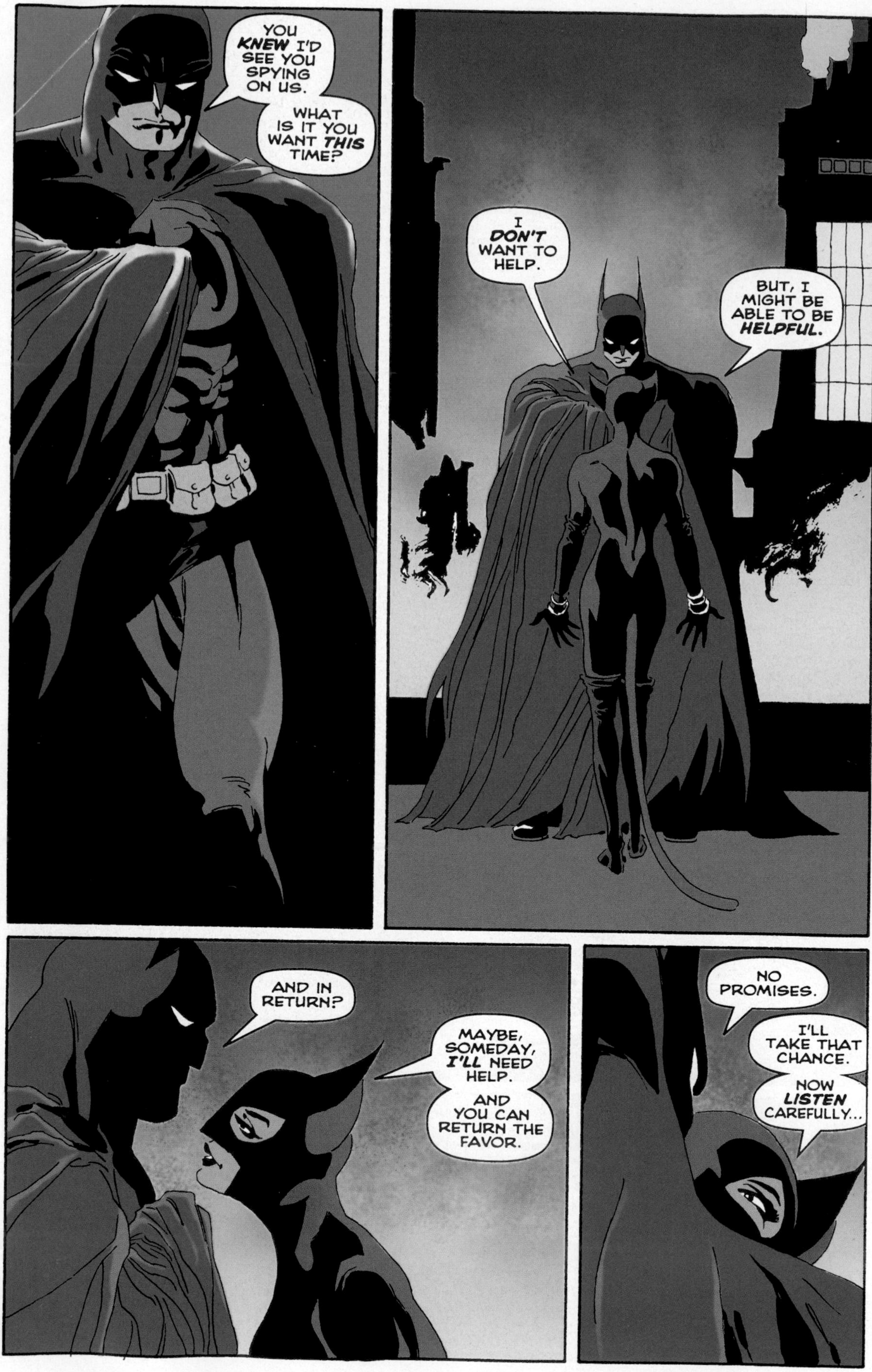
YOU KNEW I'D SEE YOU SPYING ON US.
WHAT IS IT YOU WANT THIS TIME?
I DON'T WANT TO HELP.
BUT, I MIGHT BE ABLE TO BE HELPFUL.
AND IN RETURN?
MAYBE, SOMEDAY, I'LL NEED HELP.
AND YOU CAN RETURN THE FAVOR.
NO PROMISES.
I'LL TAKE THAT CHANCE.
NOW LISTEN CAREFULLY...

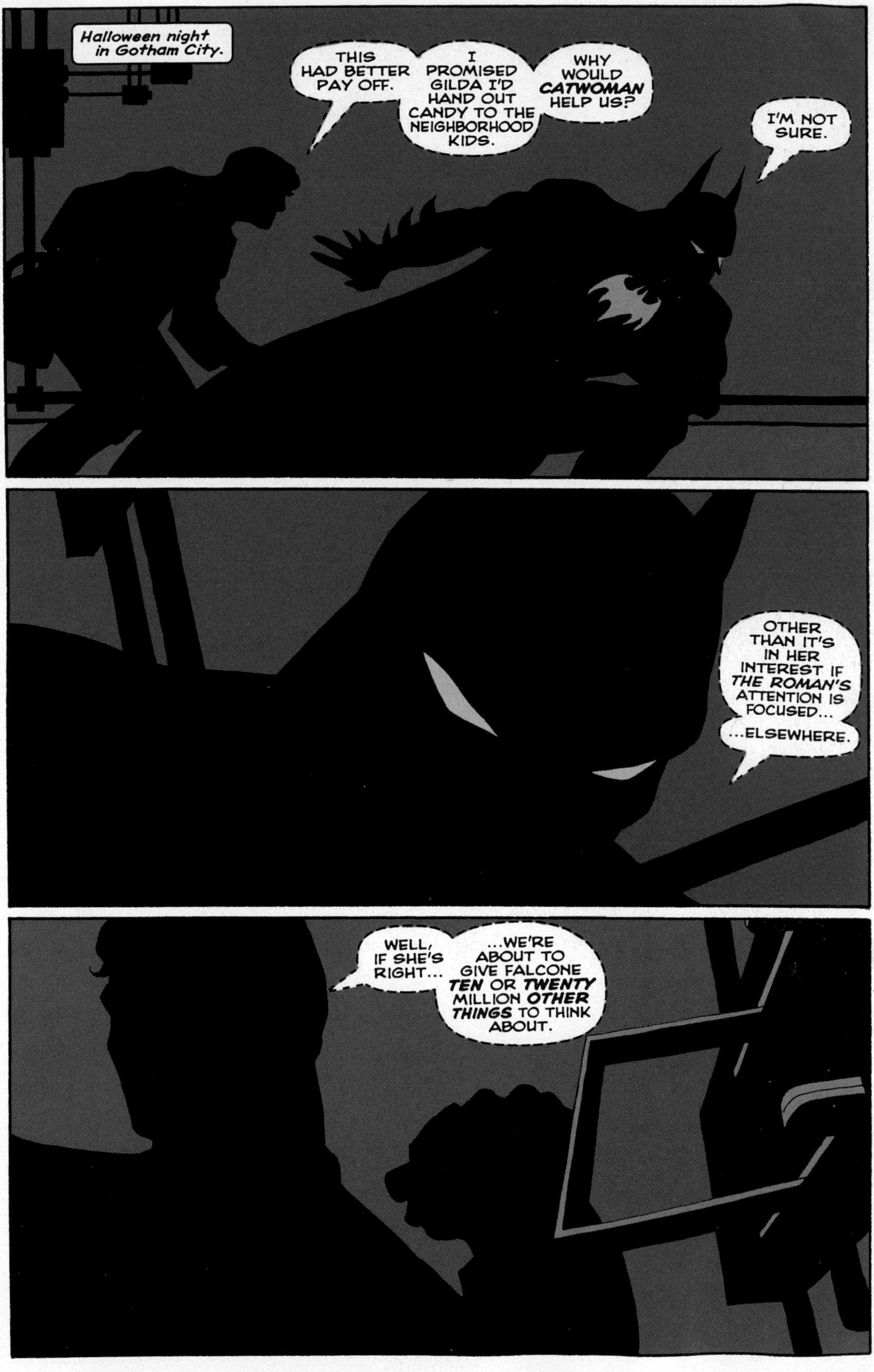
Halloween night in Gotham City.
THIS HAD BETTER PAY OFF.
I PROMISED GILDA I'D HAND OUT CANDY TO THE NEIGHBORHOOD KIDS.
WHY WOULD CATWOMAN HELP US?
I'M NOT SURE.
OTHER THAN IT'S IN HER INTEREST IF THE ROMAN'S ATTENTION IS FOCUSED...
...ELSEWHERE.
WELL, IF SHE'S RIGHT...
...WE'RE ABOUT TO GIVE FALCONE TEN OR TWENTY MILLION OTHER THINGS TO THINK ABOUT.

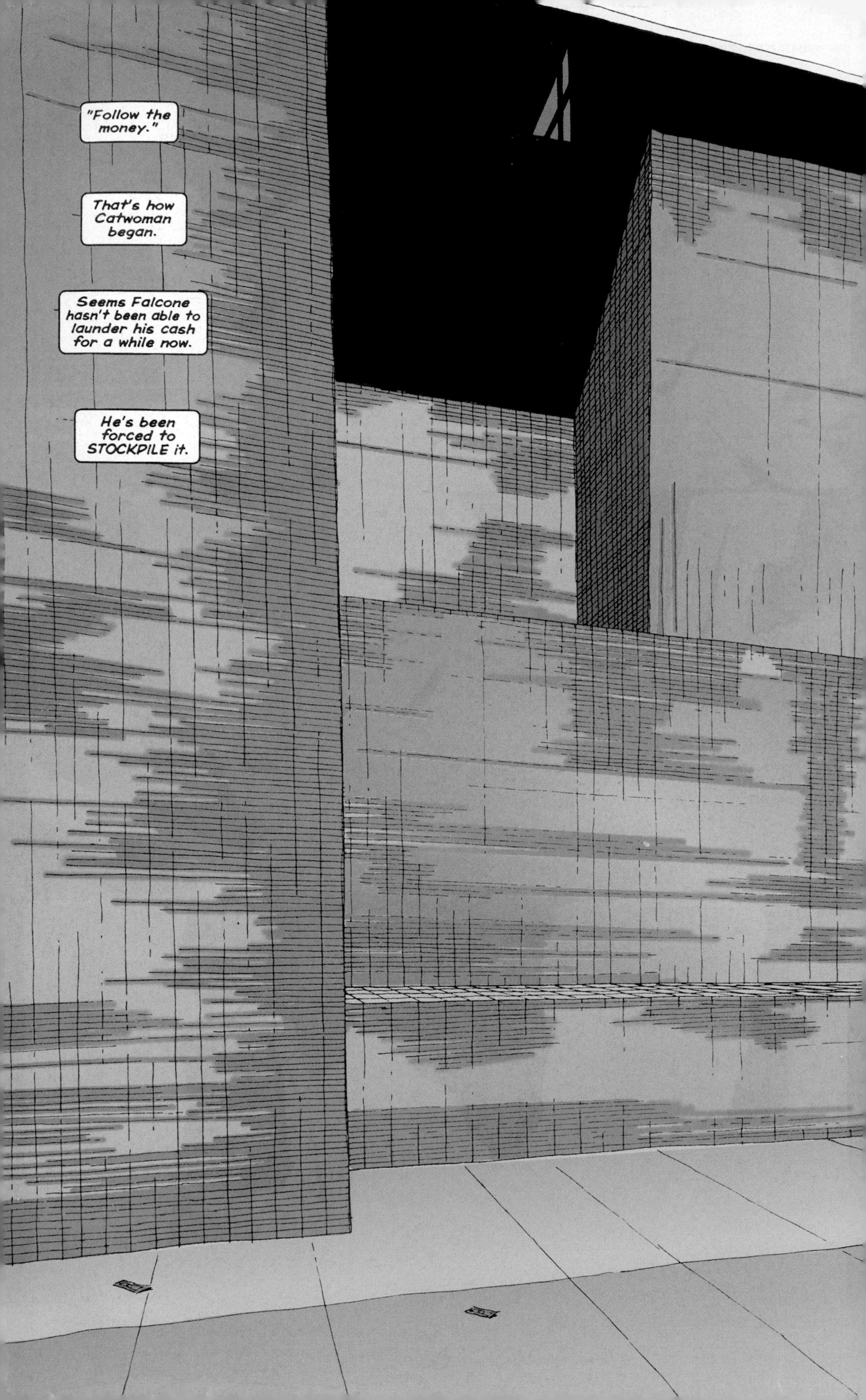
"Follow the money."
That's how Catwoman began.
Seems Falcone hasn't been able to launder his cash for a while now.
He's been forced to STOCKPILE it.

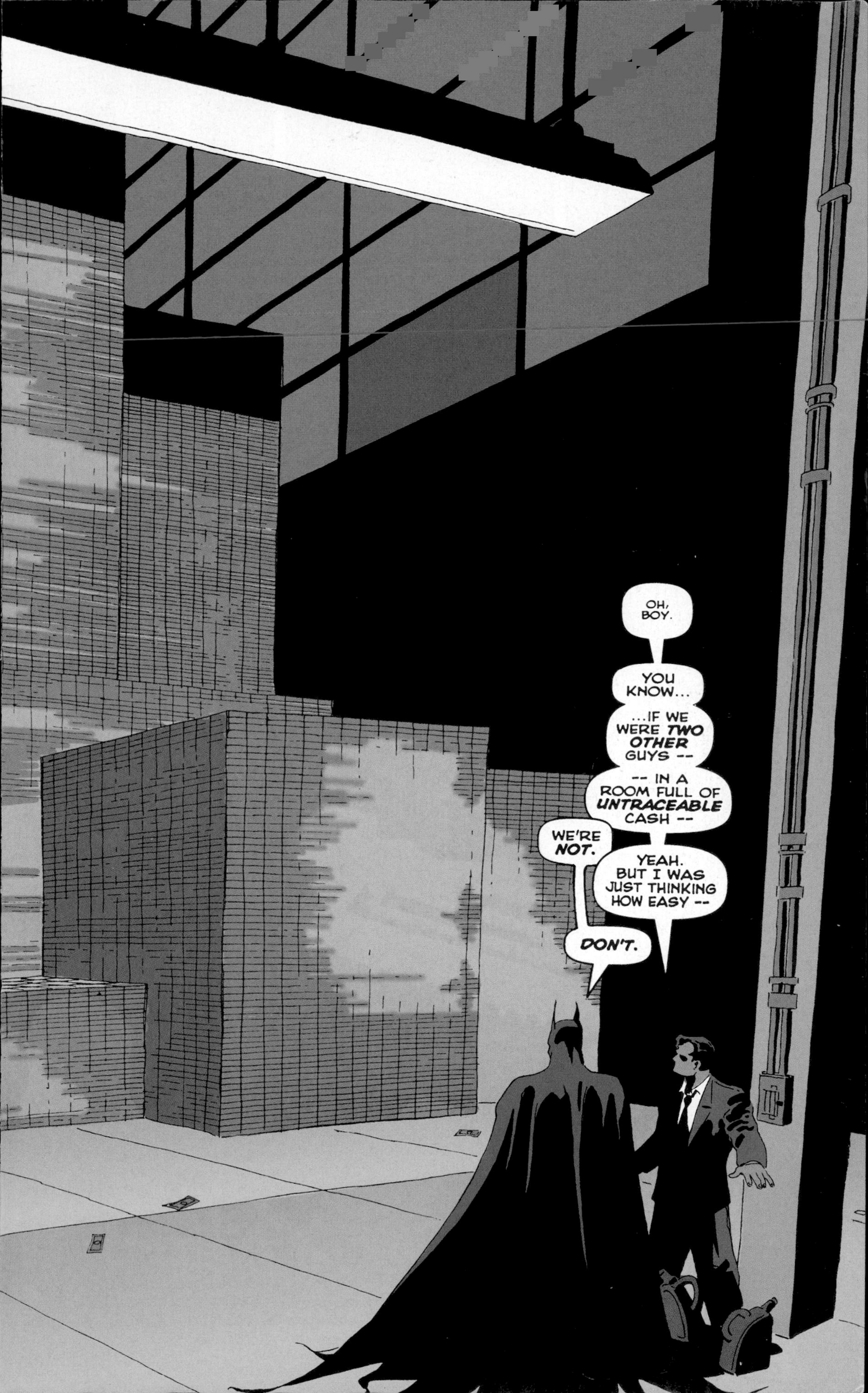
OH, BOY.
YOU KNOW...
...IF WE WERE TWO OTHER GUYS --
-- IN A ROOM FULL OF UNTRACEABLE CASH --
WE'RE NOT.
YEAH. BUT I WAS JUST THINKING HOW EASY --
DON'T.

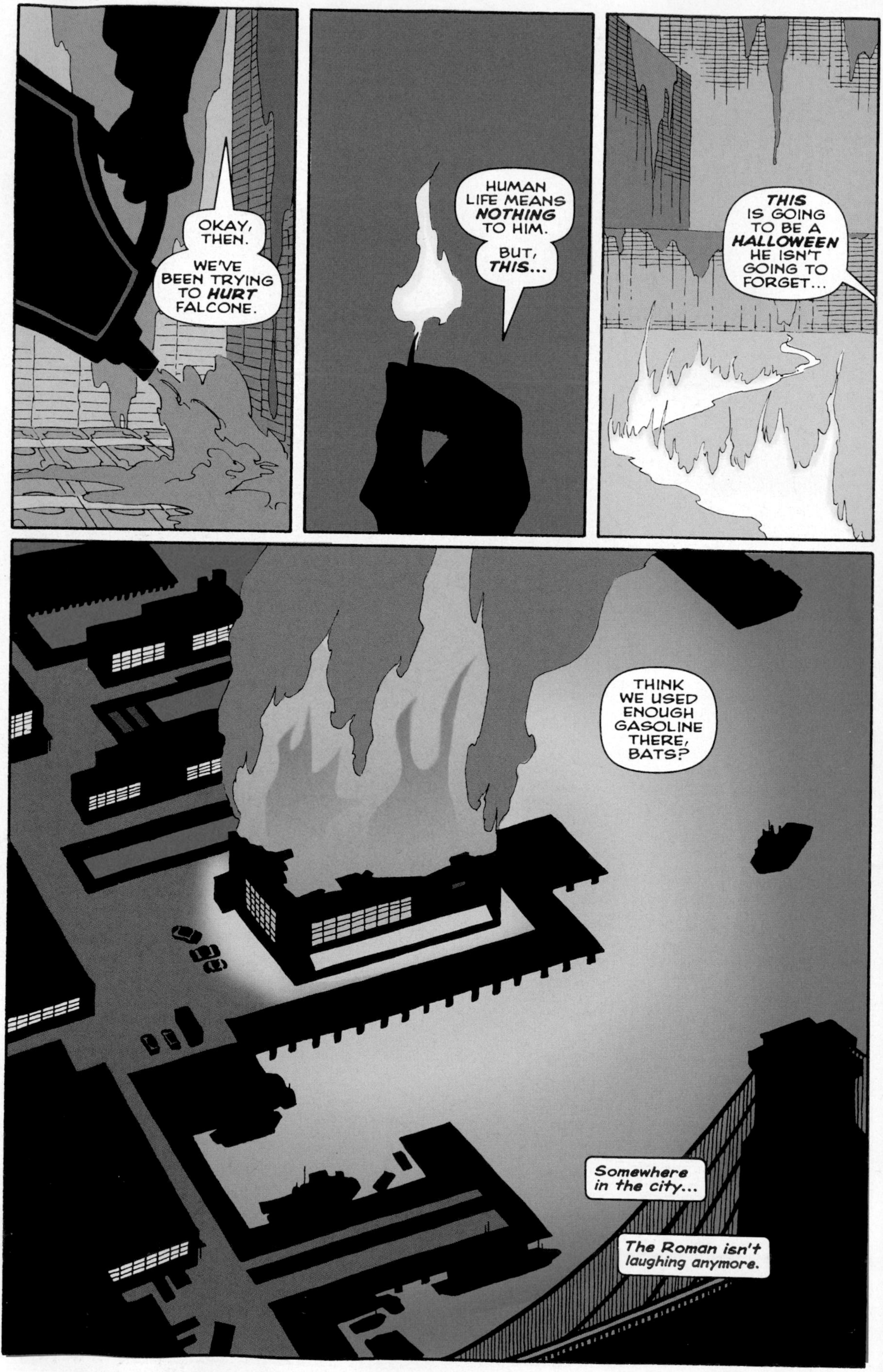
OKAY, THEN.
WE'VE BEEN TRYING TO HURT FALCONE.
HUMAN LIFE MEANS NOTHING TO HIM.
BUT, THIS...
THIS IS GOING TO BE A HALLOWEEN HE ISN'T GOING TO FORGET...
THINK WE USED ENOUGH GASOLINE THERE, BATS?
Somewhere in the city...
The Roman isn't laughing anymore.

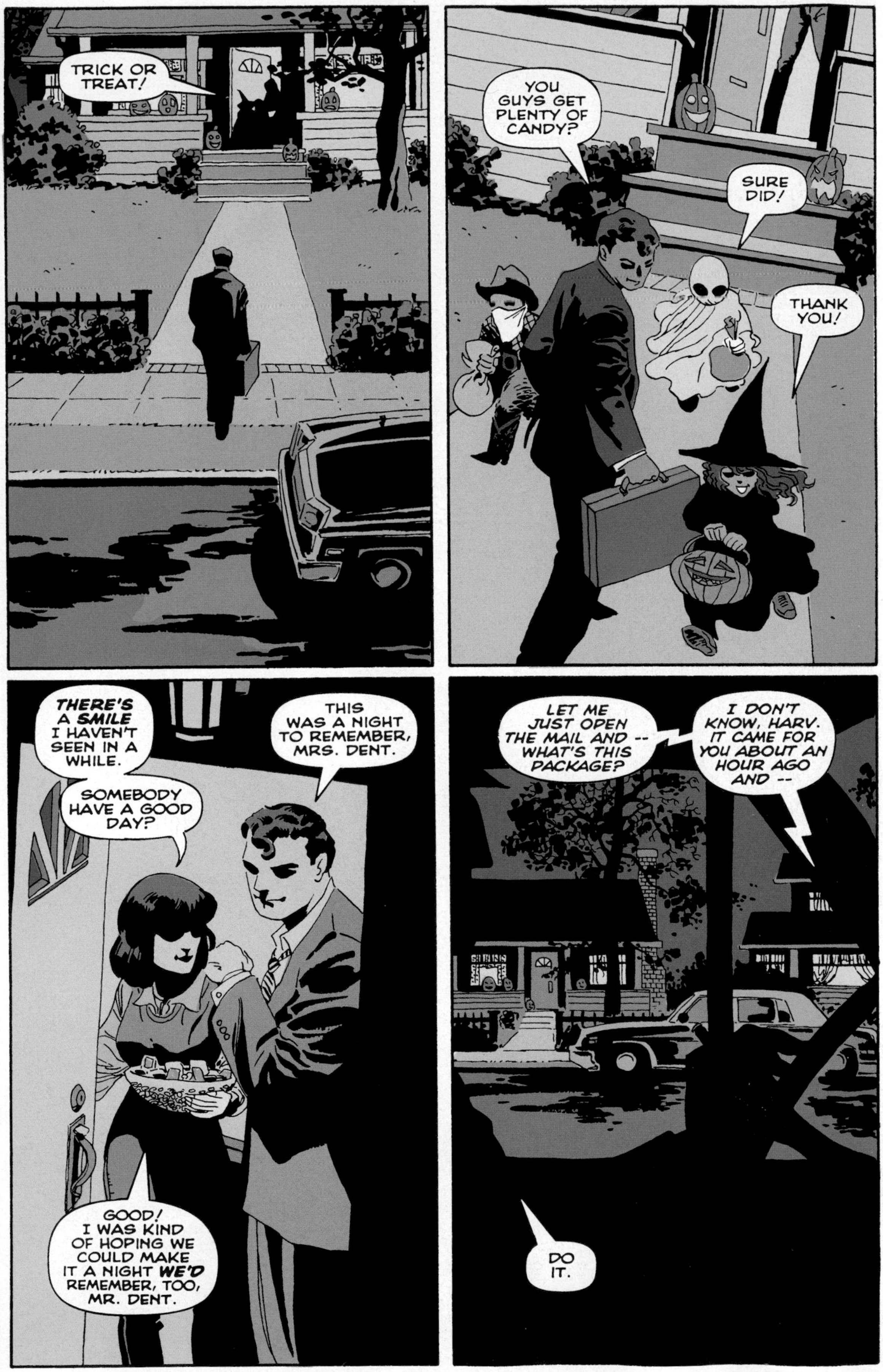
TRICK OR TREAT!
YOU GUYS GET PLENTY OF CANDY?
SURE DID!
THANK YOU!
THERE'S A SMILE I HAVEN'T SEEN IN A WHILE.
SOMEBODY HAVE A GOOD DAY?
THIS WAS A NIGHT TO REMEMBER, MRS. DENT.
GOOD! I WAS KIND OF HOPING WE COULD MAKE IT A NIGHT WE'D REMEMBER, TOO, MR. DENT.
LET ME JUST OPEN THE MAIL AND -- WHAT'S THIS PACKAGE?
I DON'T KNOW, HARV. IT CAME FOR YOU ABOUT AN HOUR AGO AND --
DO IT.

CHAPTER TWO
THANKSGIVING

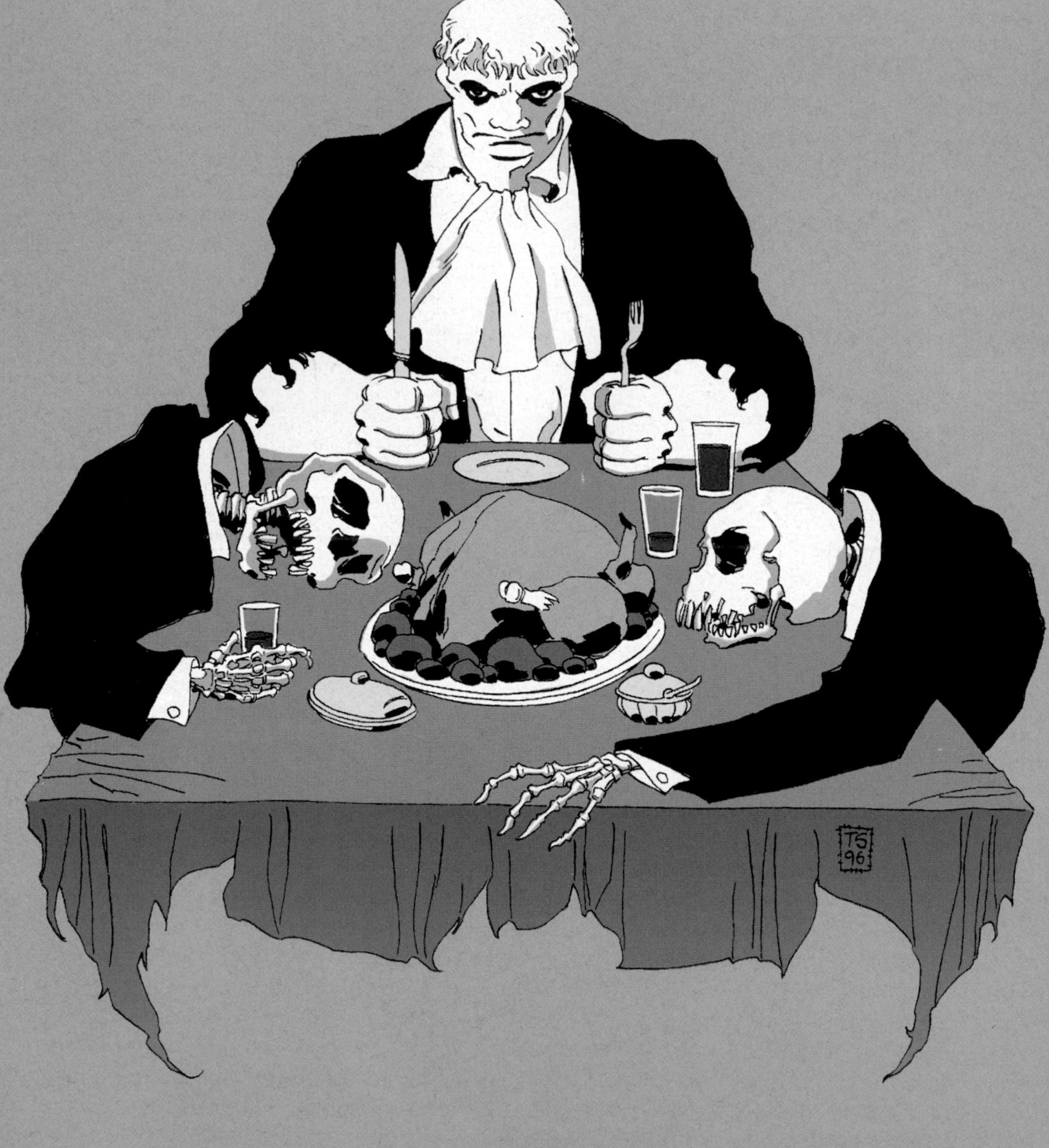
TS 96

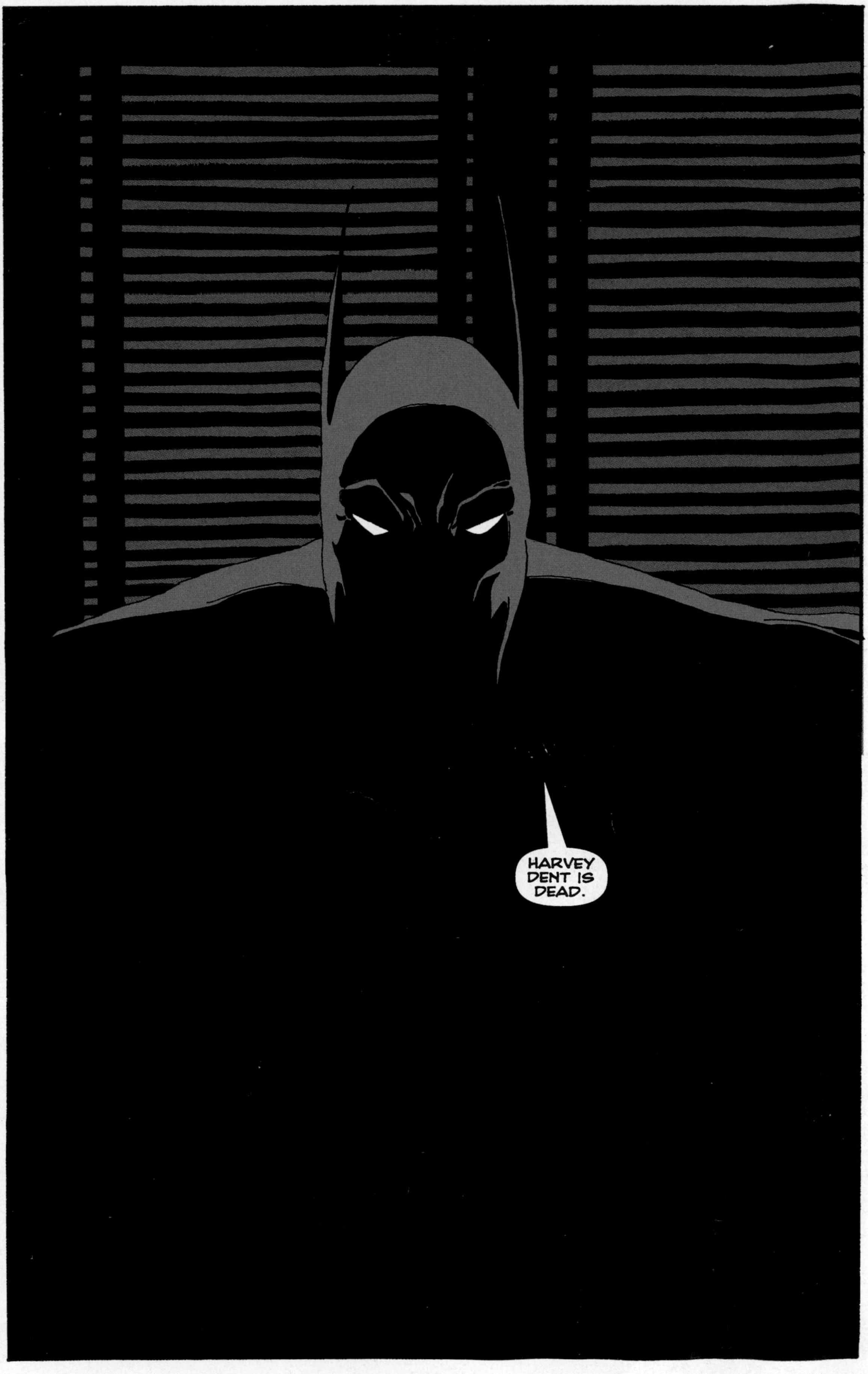
HARVEY DENT IS DEAD.

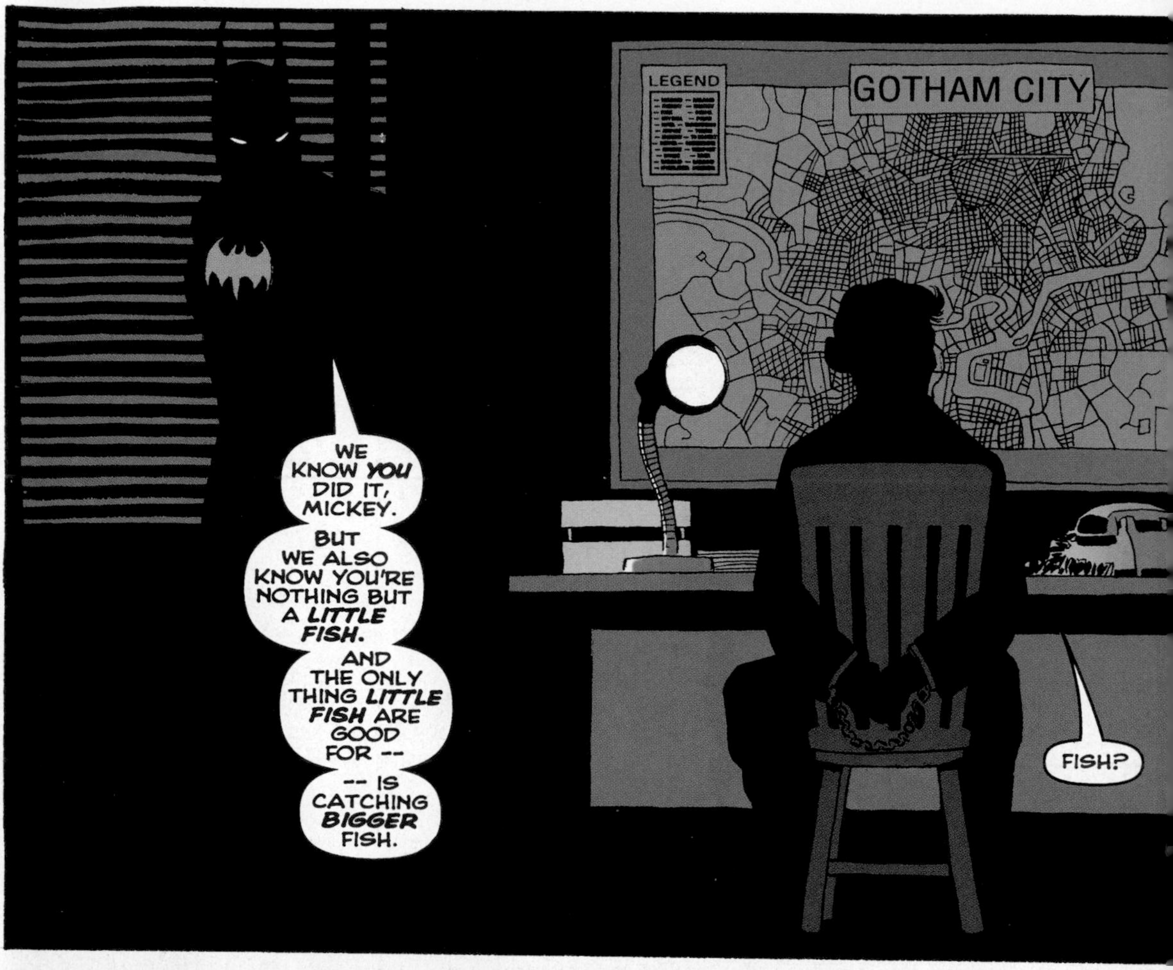
GOTHAM CITY
LEGEND
WE KNOW YOU DID IT, MICKEY.
BUT WE ALSO KNOW YOU'RE NOTHING BUT A LITTLE FISH.
AND THE ONLY THING LITTLE FISH ARE GOOD FOR --
-- IS CATCHING BIGGER FISH.
FISH?

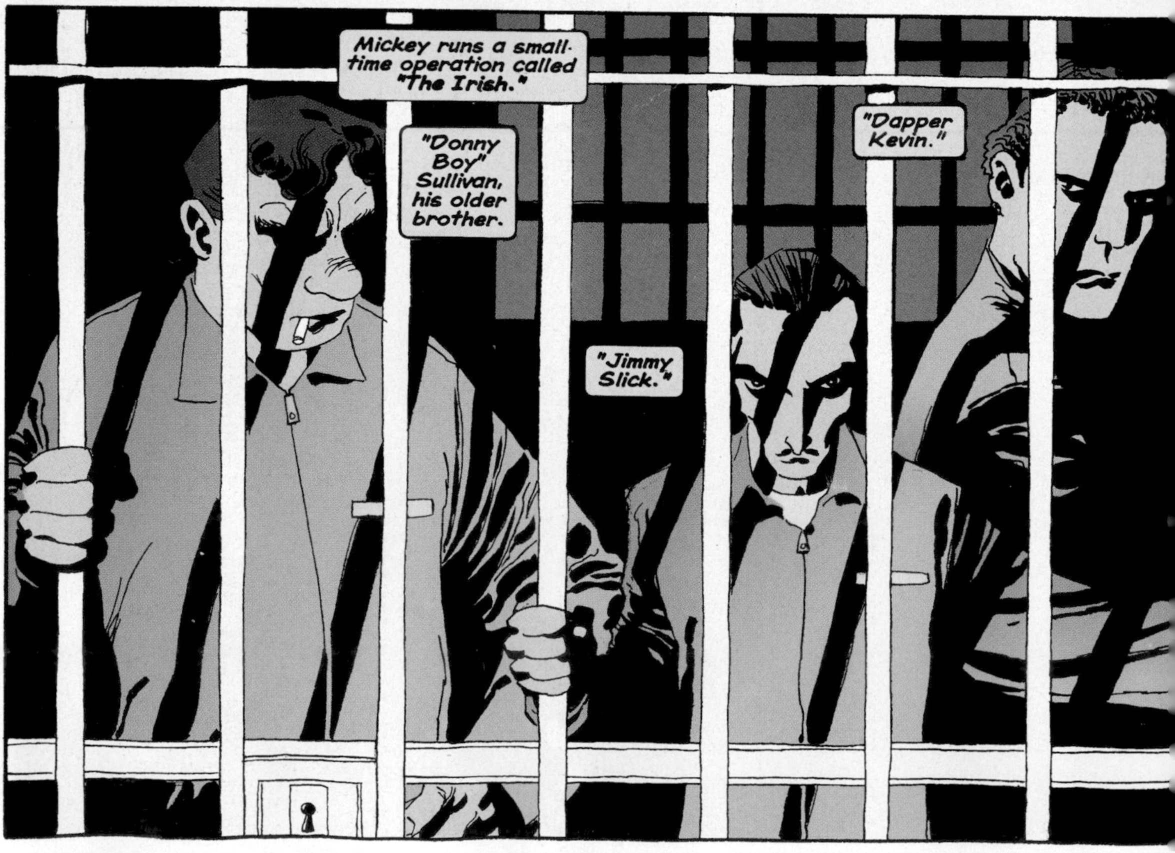
Mickey runs a small-time operation called "The Irish."
"Donny Boy" Sullivan, his older brother.
"Dapper Kevin."
"Jimmy Slick."

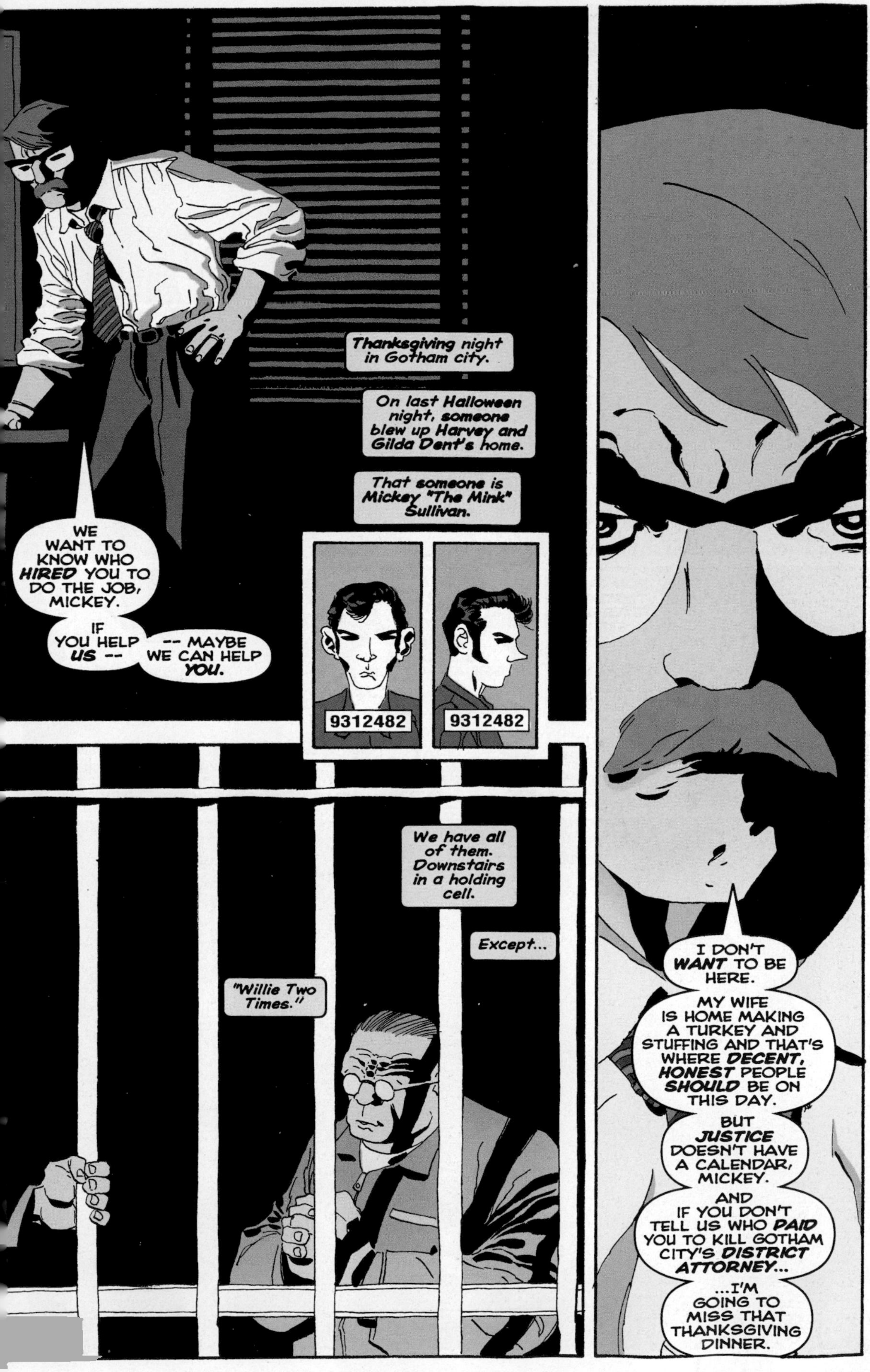
Thanksgiving night in Gotham city.
On last Halloween night, someone blew up Harvey and Gilda Dent's home.
That someone is Mickey "The Mink" Sullivan.
9312482
9312482
WE WANT TO KNOW WHO HIRED YOU TO DO THE JOB, MICKEY.
IF YOU HELP US --
-- MAYBE WE CAN HELP YOU.
We have all of them. Downstairs in a holding cell.
Except...
"Willie Two Times."
I DON'T WANT TO BE HERE.
MY WIFE IS HOME MAKING A TURKEY AND STUFFING AND THAT'S WHERE DECENT, HONEST PEOPLE SHOULD BE ON THIS DAY.
BUT JUSTICE DOESN'T HAVE A CALENDAR, MICKEY.
AND IF YOU DON'T TELL US WHO PAID YOU TO KILL GOTHAM CITY'S DISTRICT ATTORNEY...
...I'M GOING TO MISS THAT THANKSGIVING DINNER.

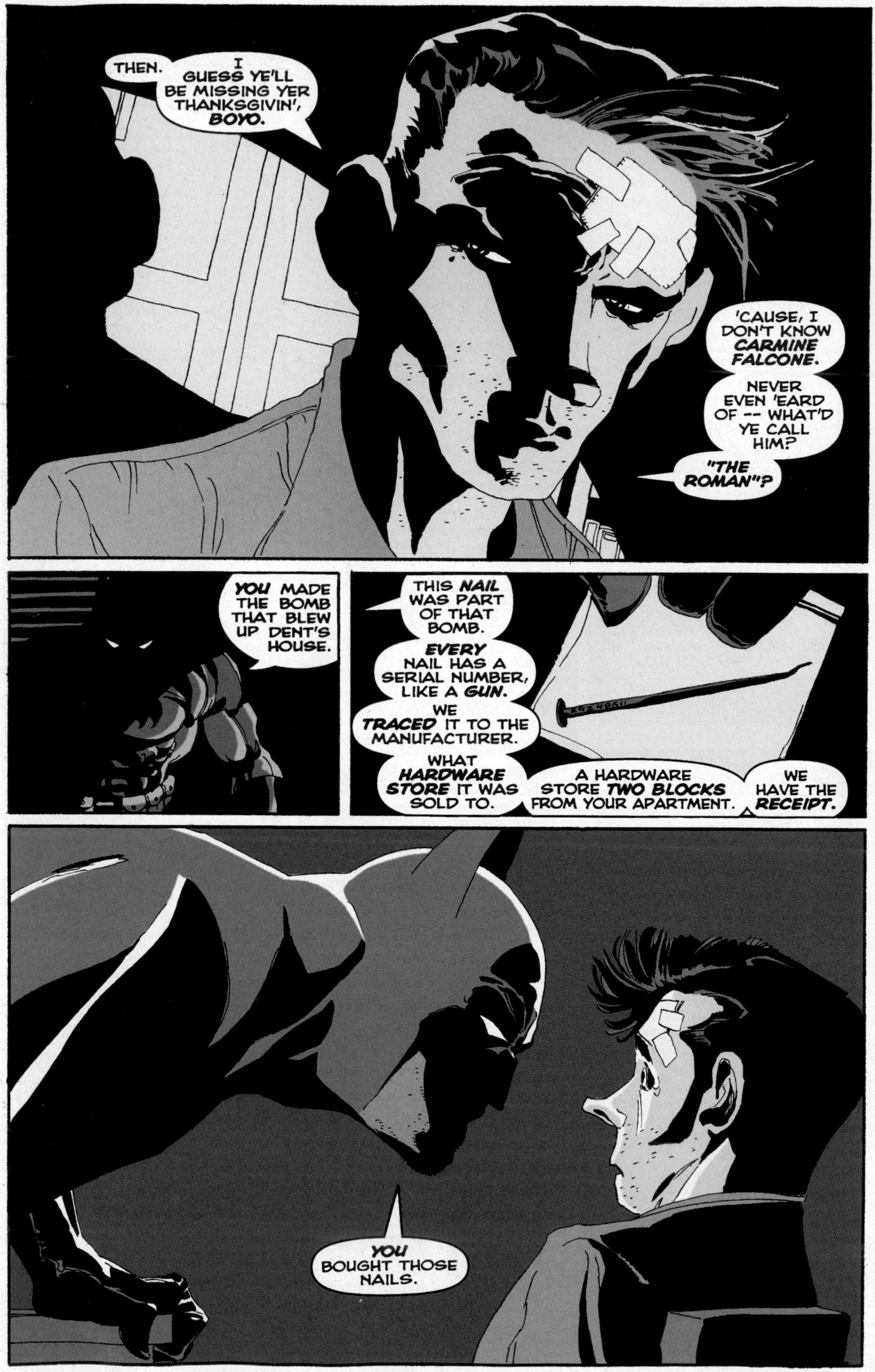
THEN.
I GUESS YE'LL BE MISSING YER THANKSGIVIN', BOYO.
'CAUSE, I DON'T KNOW CARMINE FALCONE.
NEVER EVEN 'EARD OF -- WHAT'D YE CALL HIM?
"THE ROMAN"?
YOU MADE THE BOMB THAT BLEW UP DENT'S HOUSE.
THIS NAIL WAS PART OF THAT BOMB.
EVERY NAIL HAS A SERIAL NUMBER, LIKE A GUN.
WE TRACED IT TO THE MANUFACTURER.
WHAT HARDWARE STORE IT WAS SOLD TO.
A HARDWARE STORE TWO BLOCKS FROM YOUR APARTMENT.
WE HAVE THE RECEIPT.
YOU BOUGHT THOSE NAILS.

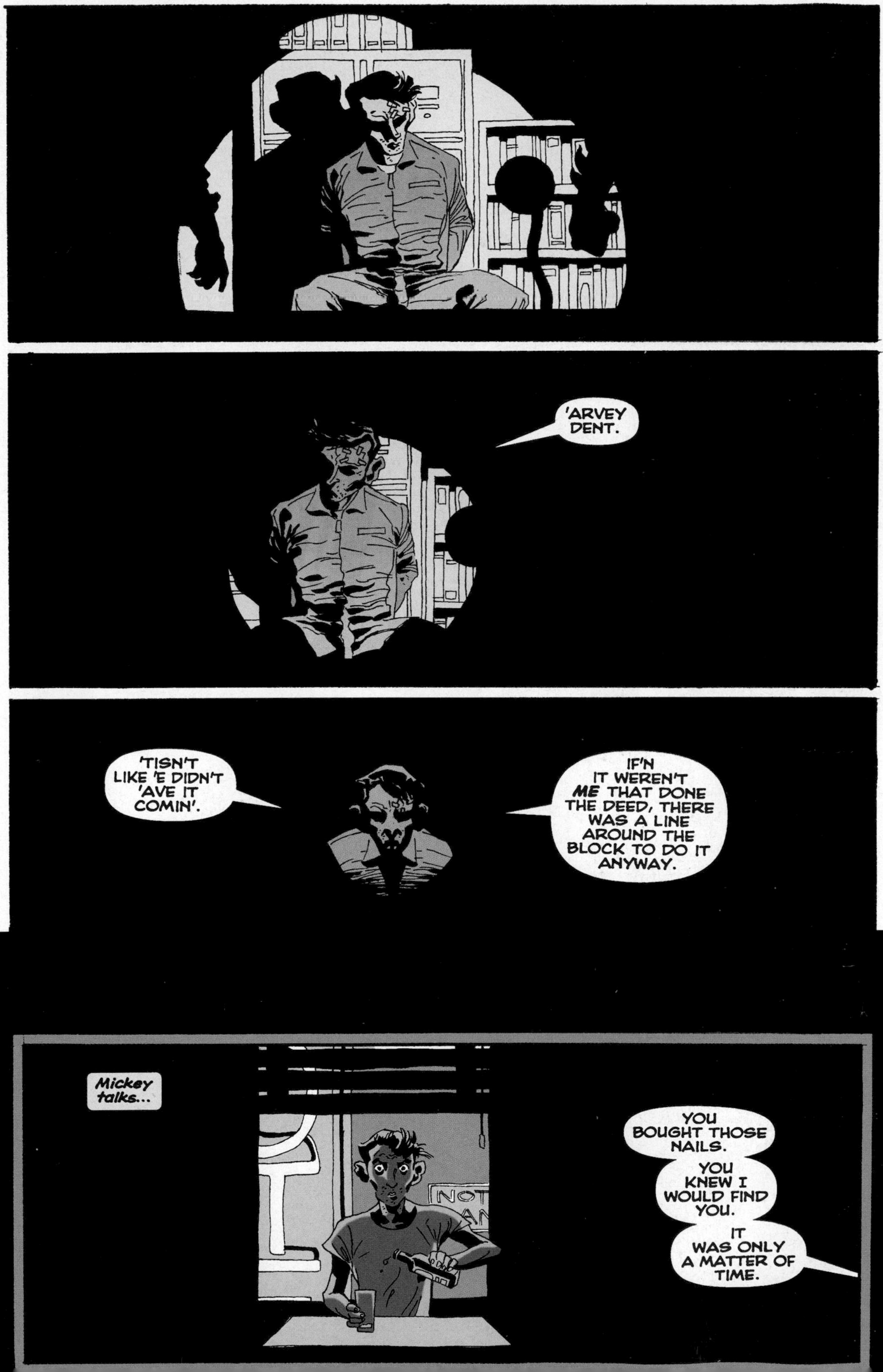
'ARVEY DENT.
'TISN'T LIKE 'E DIDN'T 'AVE IT COMIN'.
IF'N IT WEREN'T *ME* THAT DONE THE DEED, THERE WAS A LINE AROUND THE BLOCK TO DO IT ANYWAY.
Mickey talks...
YOU BOUGHT THOSE NAILS.
YOU KNEW I WOULD FIND YOU.
IT WAS ONLY A MATTER OF TIME.
NOT
AN

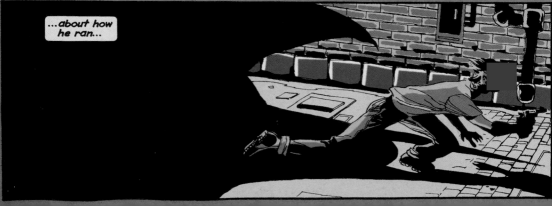

...about how
he ran...

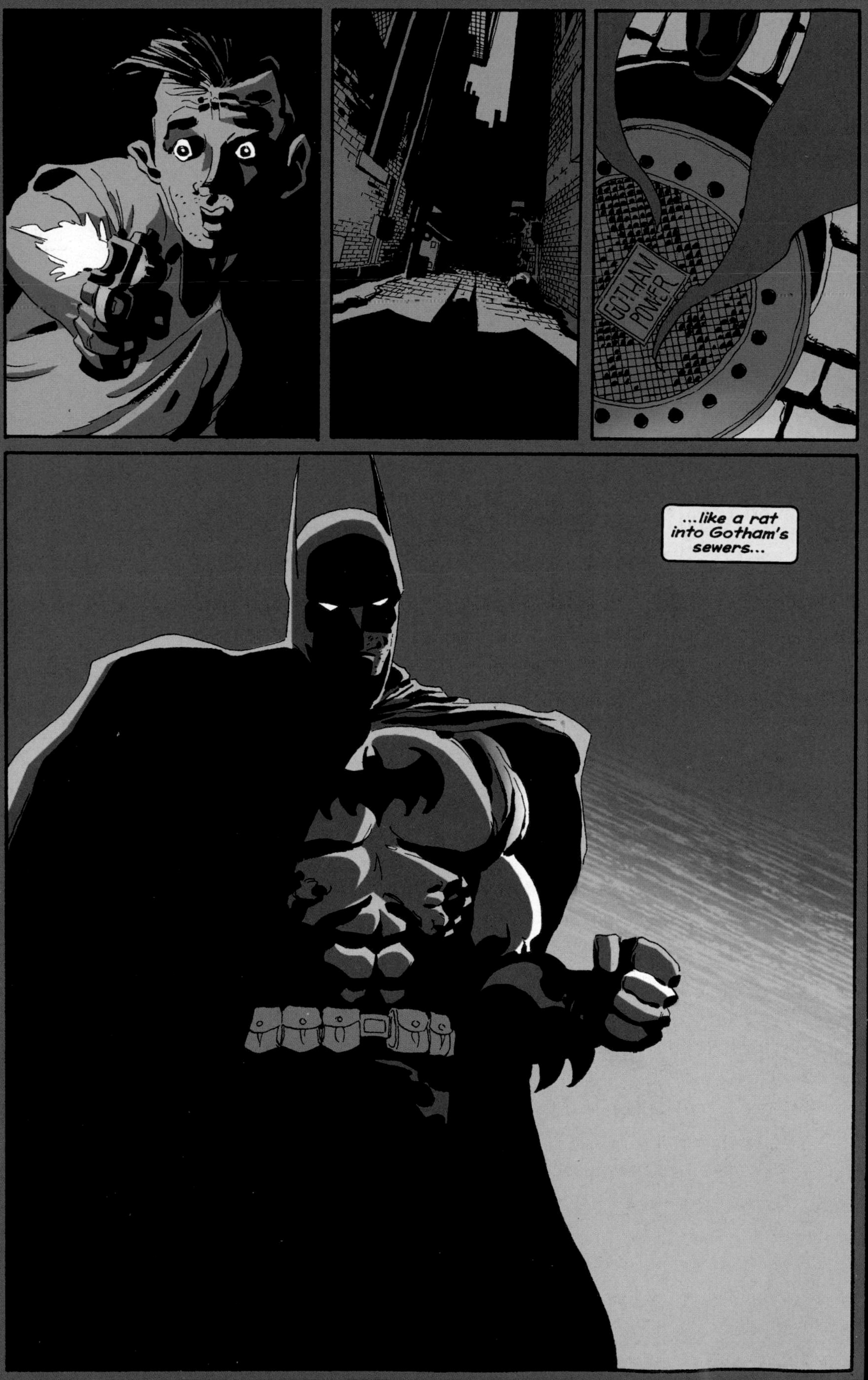
GOTHAM POWER
...like a rat into Gotham's sewers...

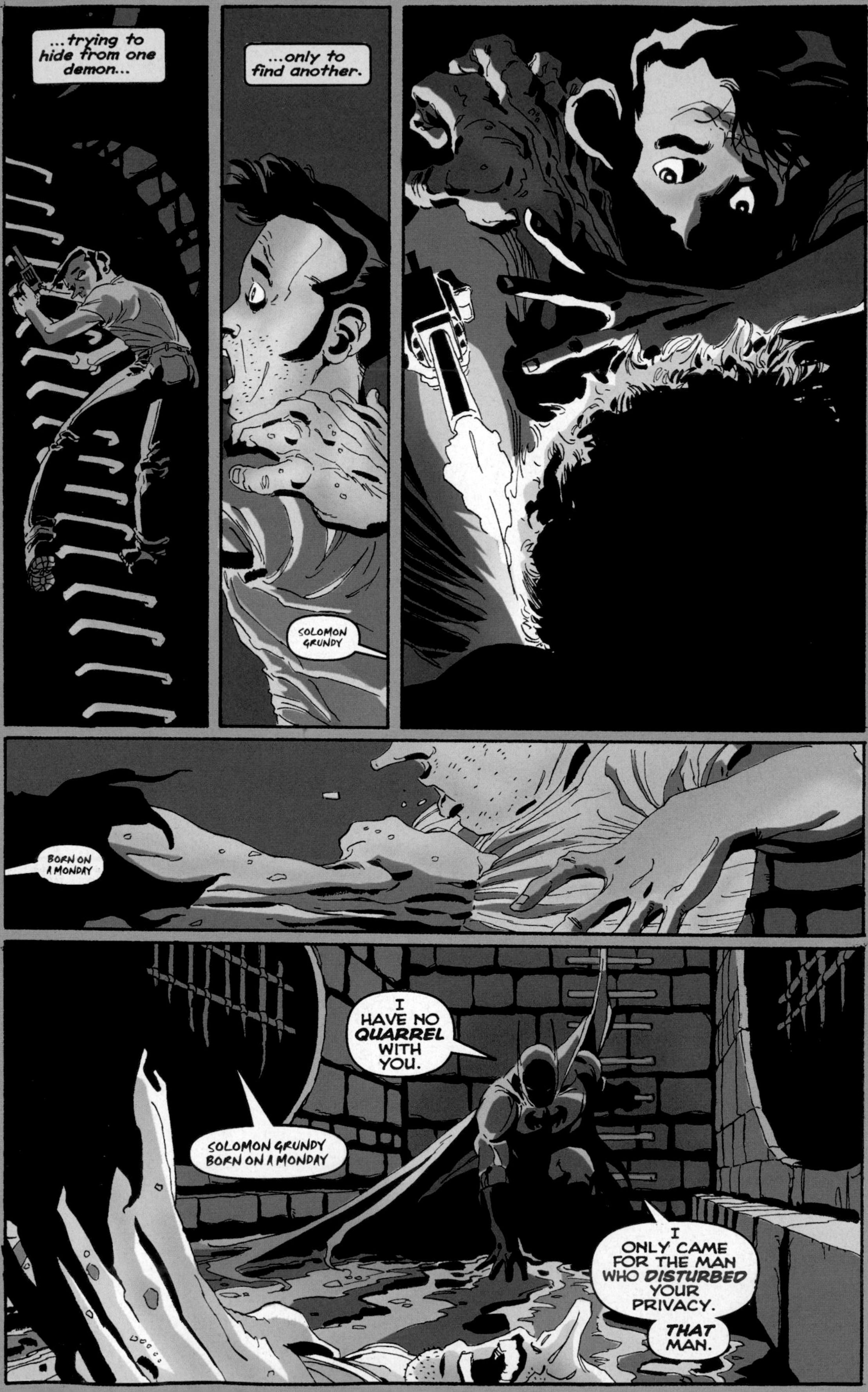

...trying to hide from one demon...
...only to find another.
SOLOMON GRUNDY
BORN ON A MONDAY
I HAVE NO QUARREL WITH YOU.
SOLOMON GRUNDY BORN ON A MONDAY
I ONLY CAME FOR THE MAN WHO DISTURBED YOUR PRIVACY.
THAT MAN.

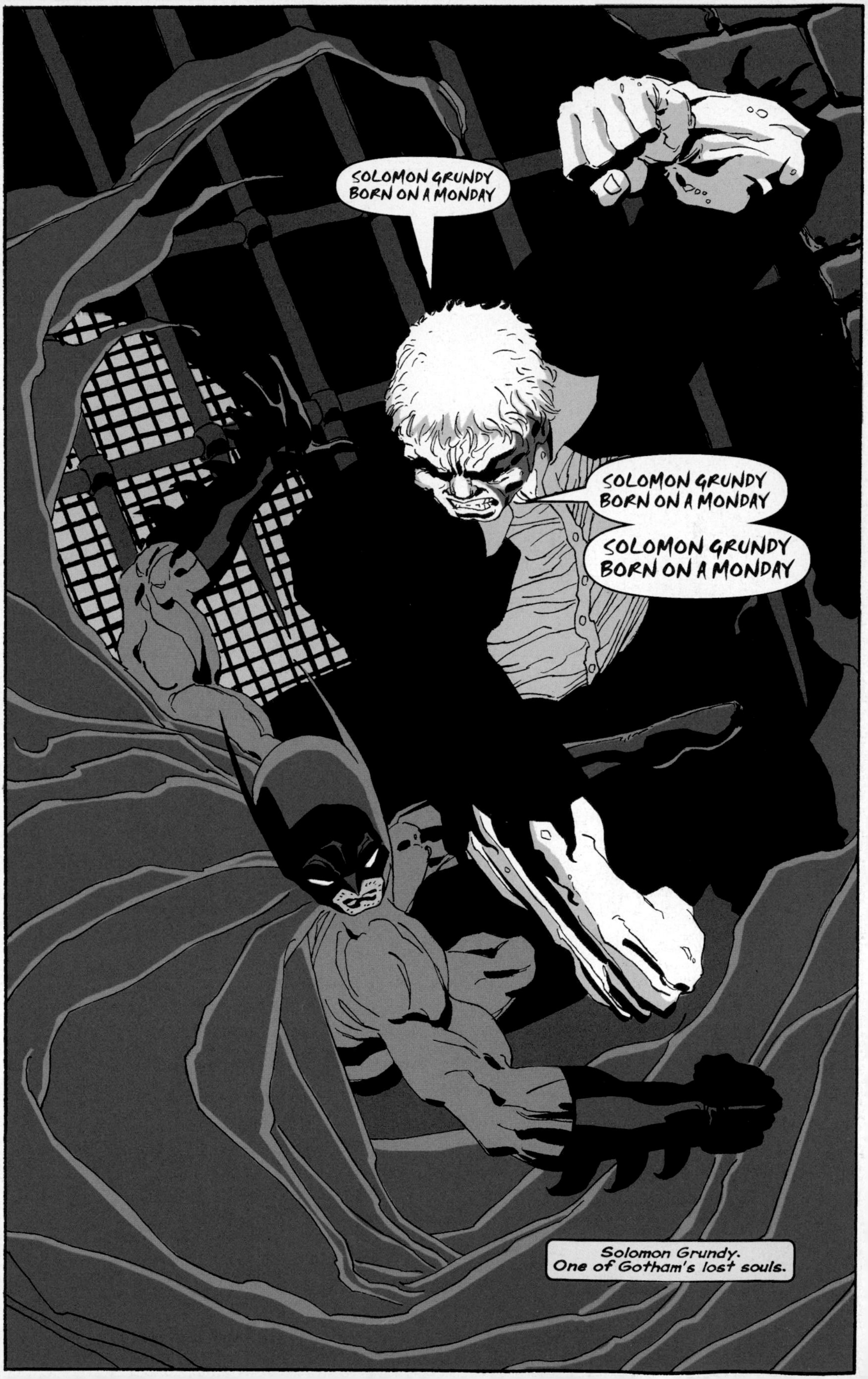
SOLOMON GRUNDY BORN ON A MONDAY
SOLOMON GRUNDY BORN ON A MONDAY
SOLOMON GRUNDY BORN ON A MONDAY
Solomon Grundy. One of Gotham's lost souls.

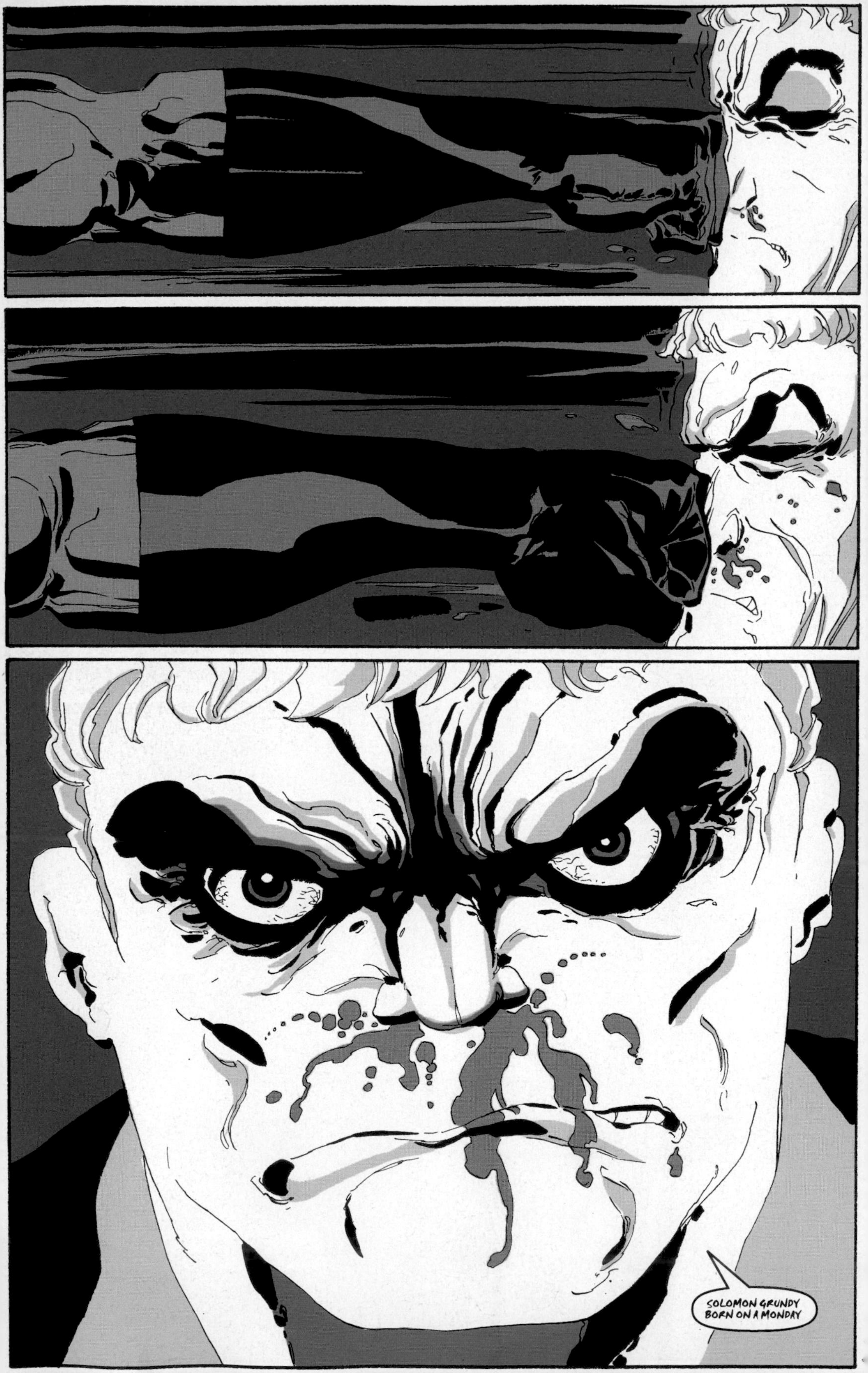
SOLOMON GRUNDY
BORN ON A MONDAY

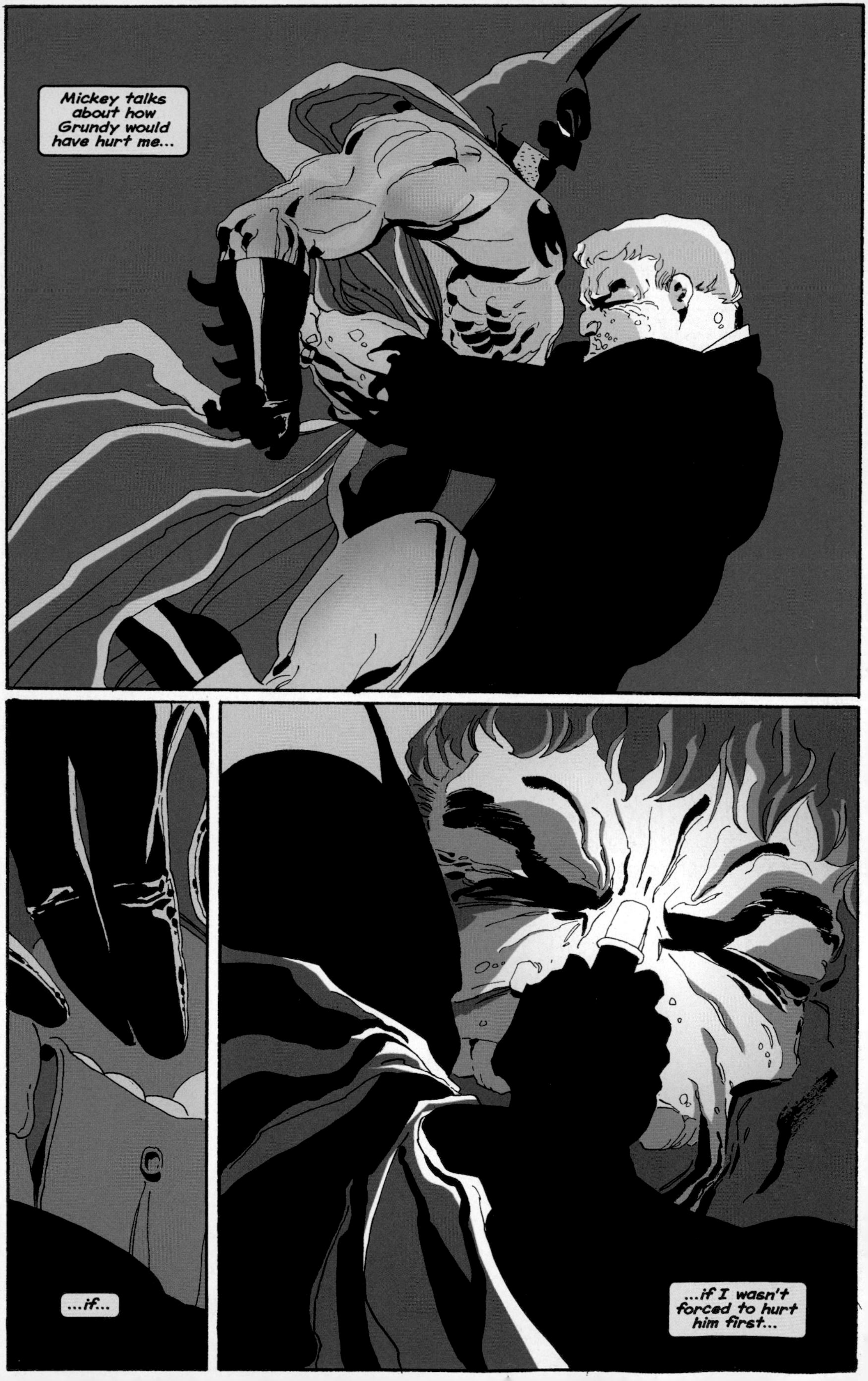
Mickey talks about how Grundy would have hurt me...
...if...
...if I wasn't forced to hurt him first...

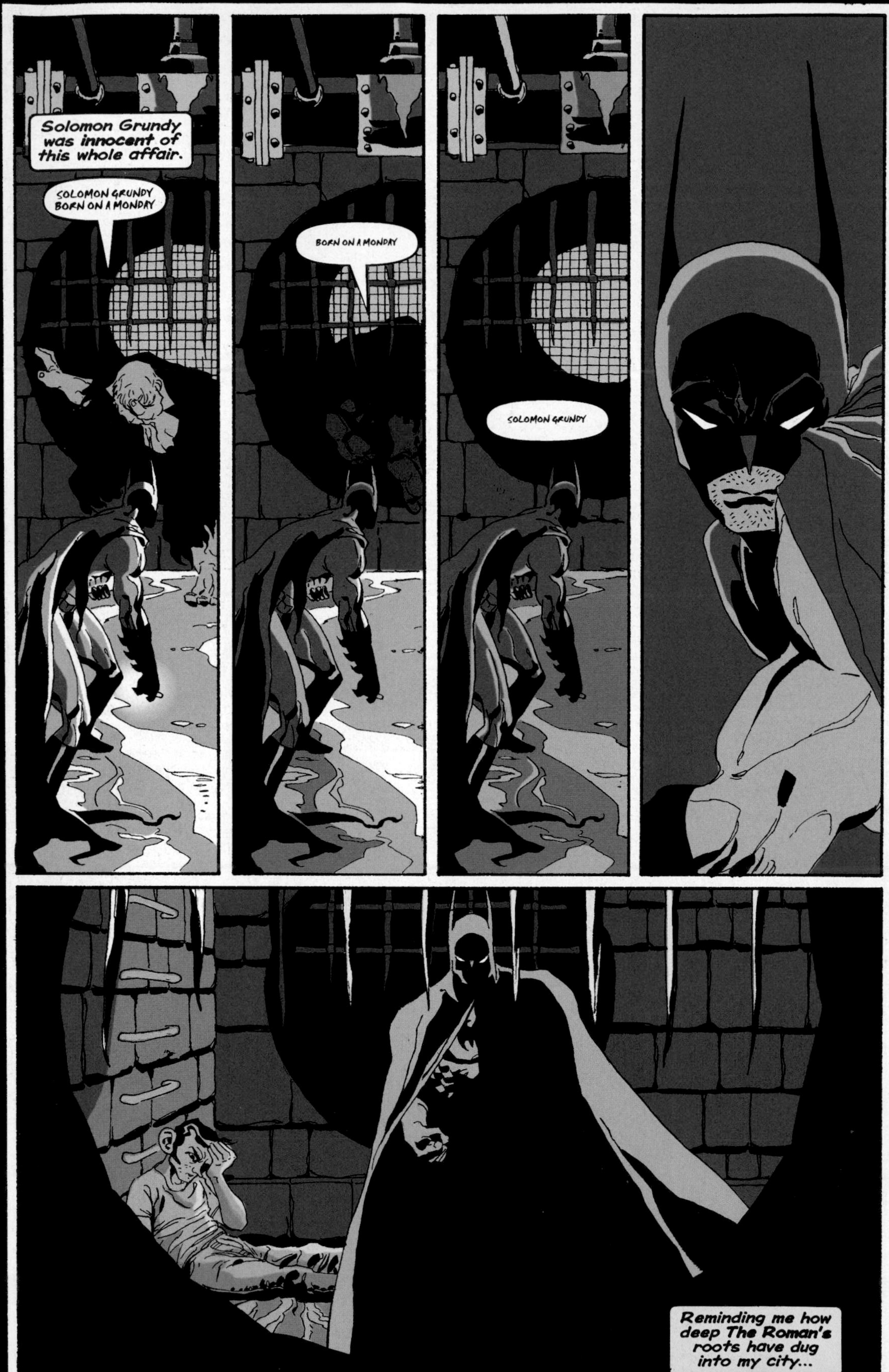
Solomon Grundy was innocent of this whole affair.
SOLOMON GRUNDY BORN ON A MONDAY
BORN ON A MONDAY
SOLOMON GRUNDY
Reminding me how deep The Roman's roots have dug into my city...

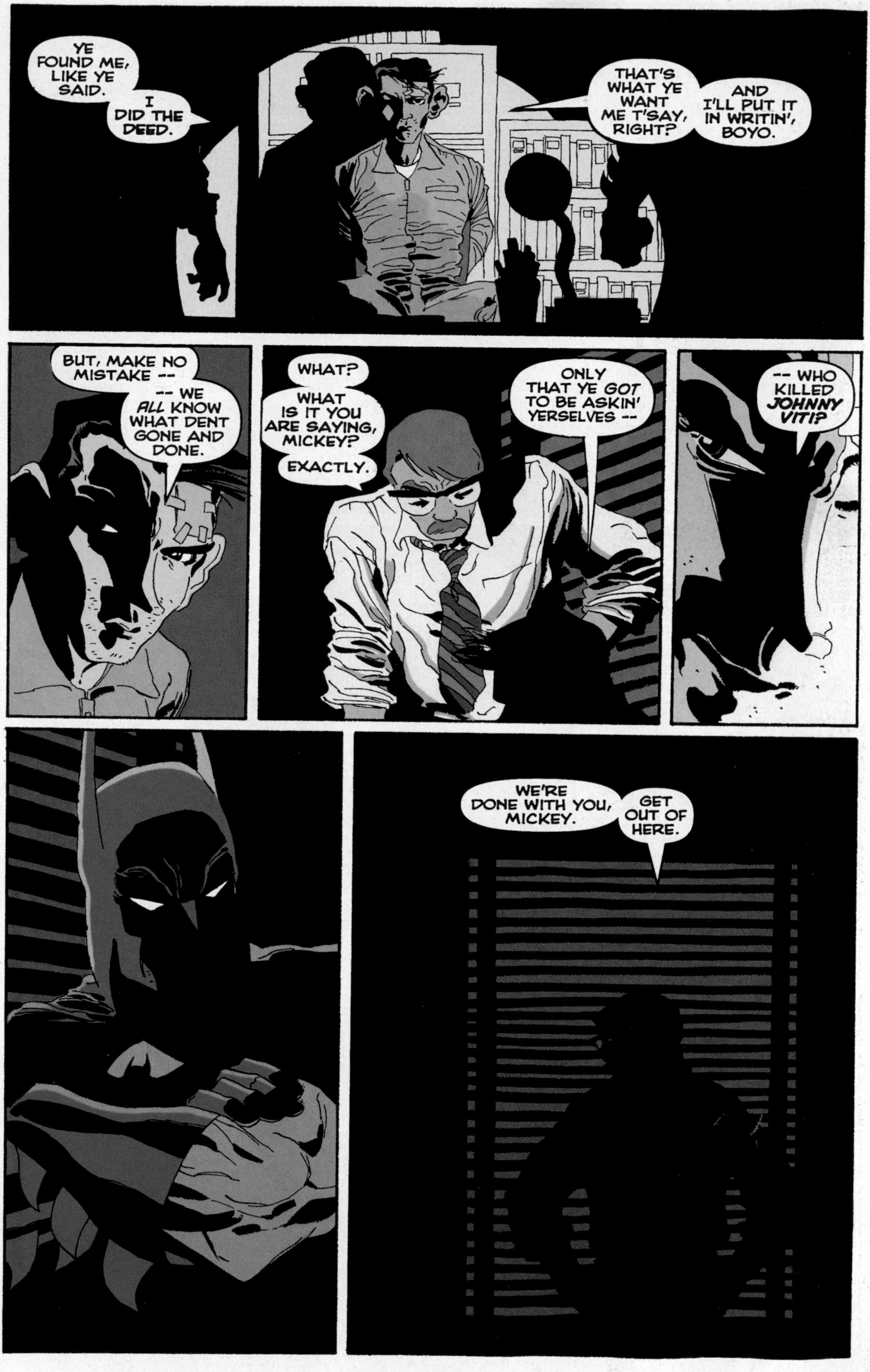
YE FOUND ME, LIKE YE SAID.
I DID THE DEED.
THAT'S WHAT YE WANT ME T'SAY, RIGHT?
AND I'LL PUT IT IN WRITIN', BOYO.
BUT, MAKE NO MISTAKE --
-- WE ALL KNOW WHAT DENT GONE AND DONE.
WHAT?
WHAT IS IT YOU ARE SAYING, MICKEY?
EXACTLY.
ONLY THAT YE GOT TO BE ASKIN' YERSELVES --
-- WHO KILLED JOHNNY VITI?
WE'RE DONE WITH YOU, MICKEY.
GET OUT OF HERE.

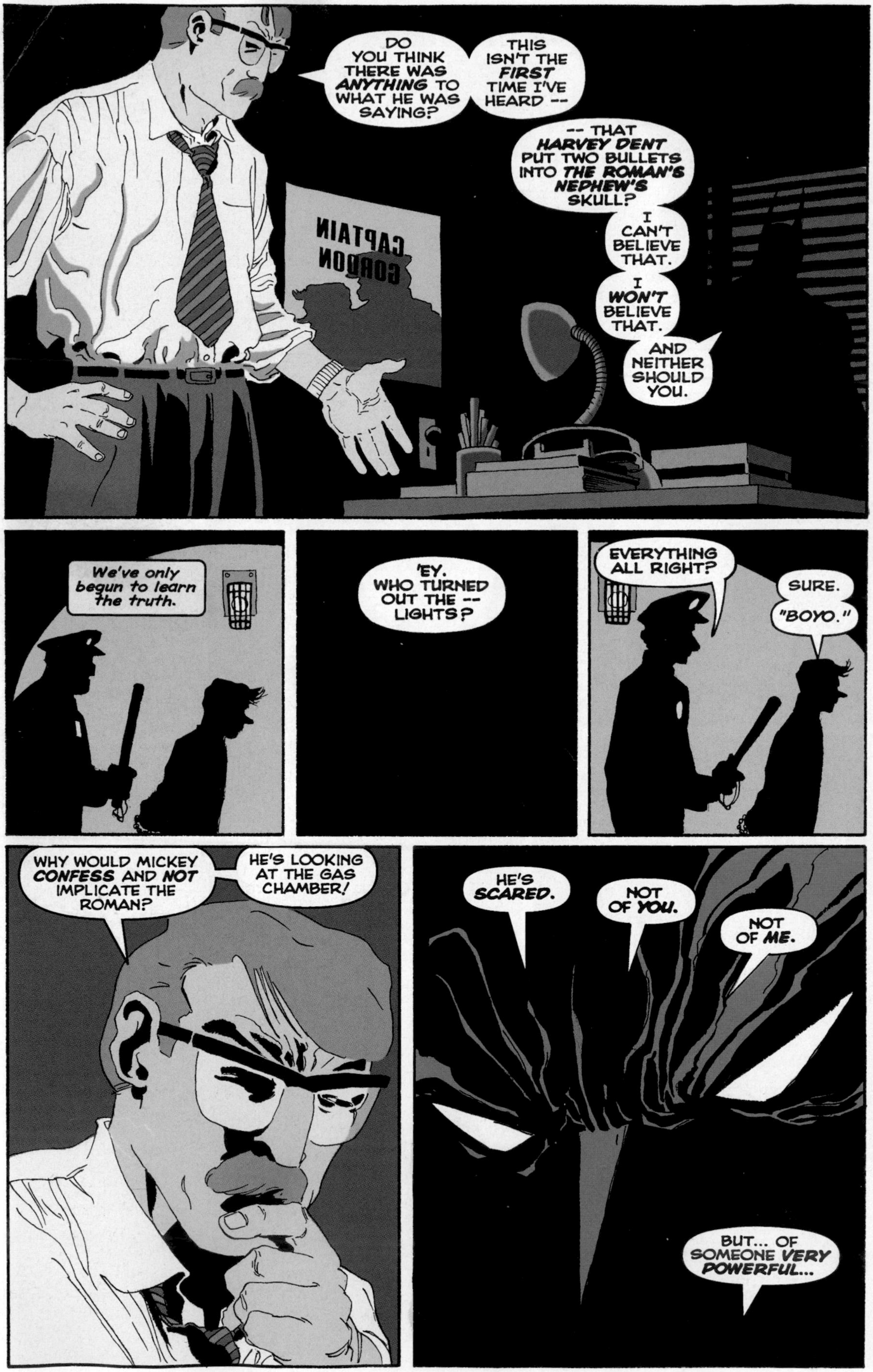

DO YOU THINK THERE WAS ANYTHING TO WHAT HE WAS SAYING?
THIS ISN'T THE FIRST TIME I'VE HEARD --
-- THAT HARVEY DENT PUT TWO BULLETS INTO THE ROMAN'S NEPHEW'S SKULL?
I CAN'T BELIEVE THAT.
I WON'T BELIEVE THAT.
AND NEITHER SHOULD YOU.
CAPTAIN GORDON
We've only begun to learn the truth.
'EY. WHO TURNED OUT THE -- LIGHTS?
EVERYTHING ALL RIGHT?
SURE.
"BOYO."
WHY WOULD MICKEY CONFESS AND NOT IMPLICATE THE ROMAN?
HE'S LOOKING AT THE GAS CHAMBER!
HE'S SCARED.
NOT OF YOU.
NOT OF ME.
BUT... OF SOMEONE VERY POWERFUL...

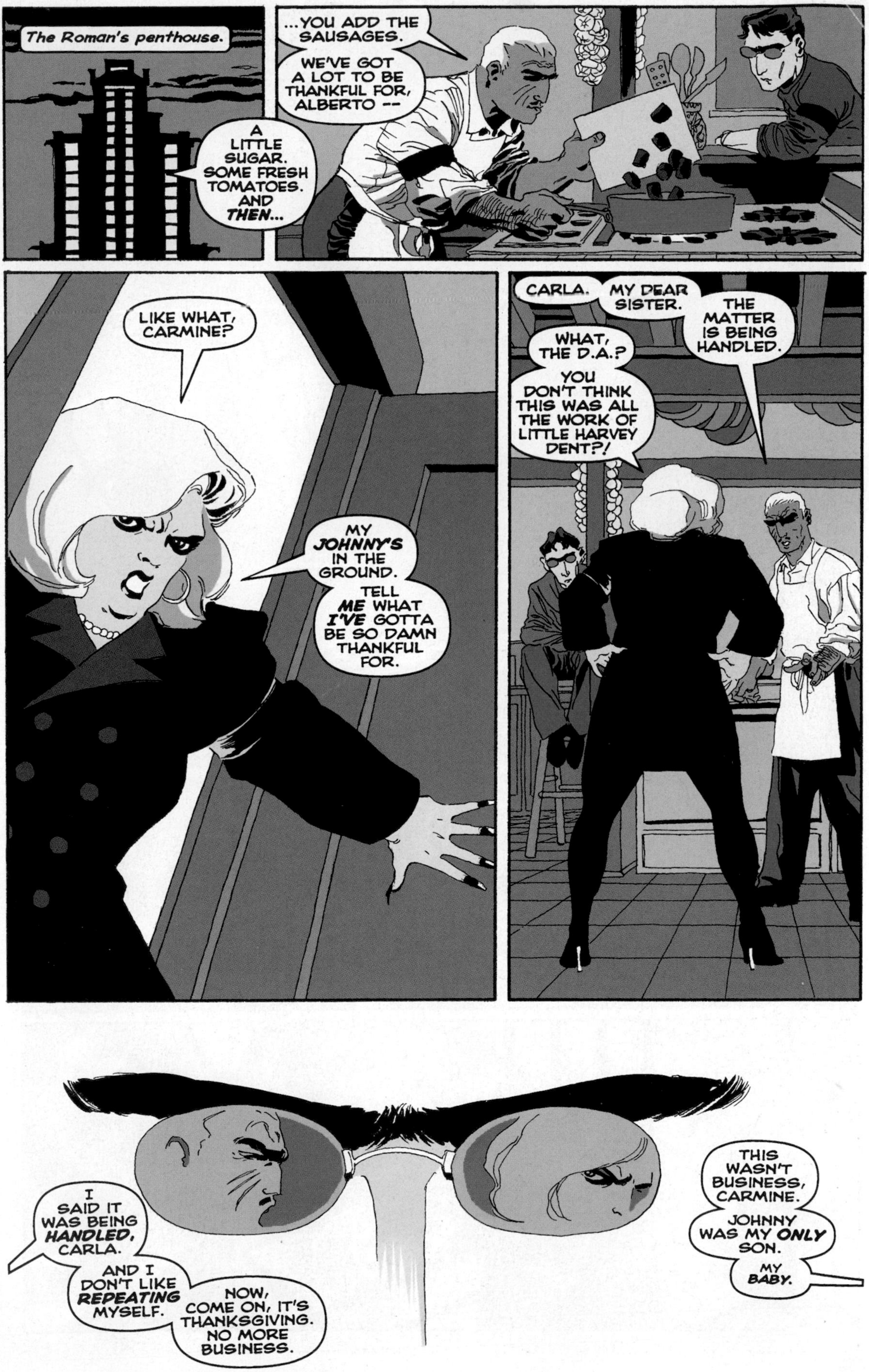
The Roman's penthouse.
A LITTLE SUGAR. SOME FRESH TOMATOES. AND THEN...
...YOU ADD THE SAUSAGES.
WE'VE GOT A LOT TO BE THANKFUL FOR, ALBERTO --
LIKE WHAT, CARMINE?
MY JOHNNY'S IN THE GROUND.
TELL ME WHAT I'VE GOTTA BE SO DAMN THANKFUL FOR.
CARLA.
MY DEAR SISTER.
THE MATTER IS BEING HANDLED.
WHAT, THE D.A.?
YOU DON'T THINK THIS WAS ALL THE WORK OF LITTLE HARVEY DENT?!
THIS WASN'T BUSINESS, CARMINE.
JOHNNY WAS MY ONLY SON.
MY BABY.
I SAID IT WAS BEING HANDLED, CARLA.
AND I DON'T LIKE REPEATING MYSELF.
NOW, COME ON, IT'S THANKSGIVING. NO MORE BUSINESS.

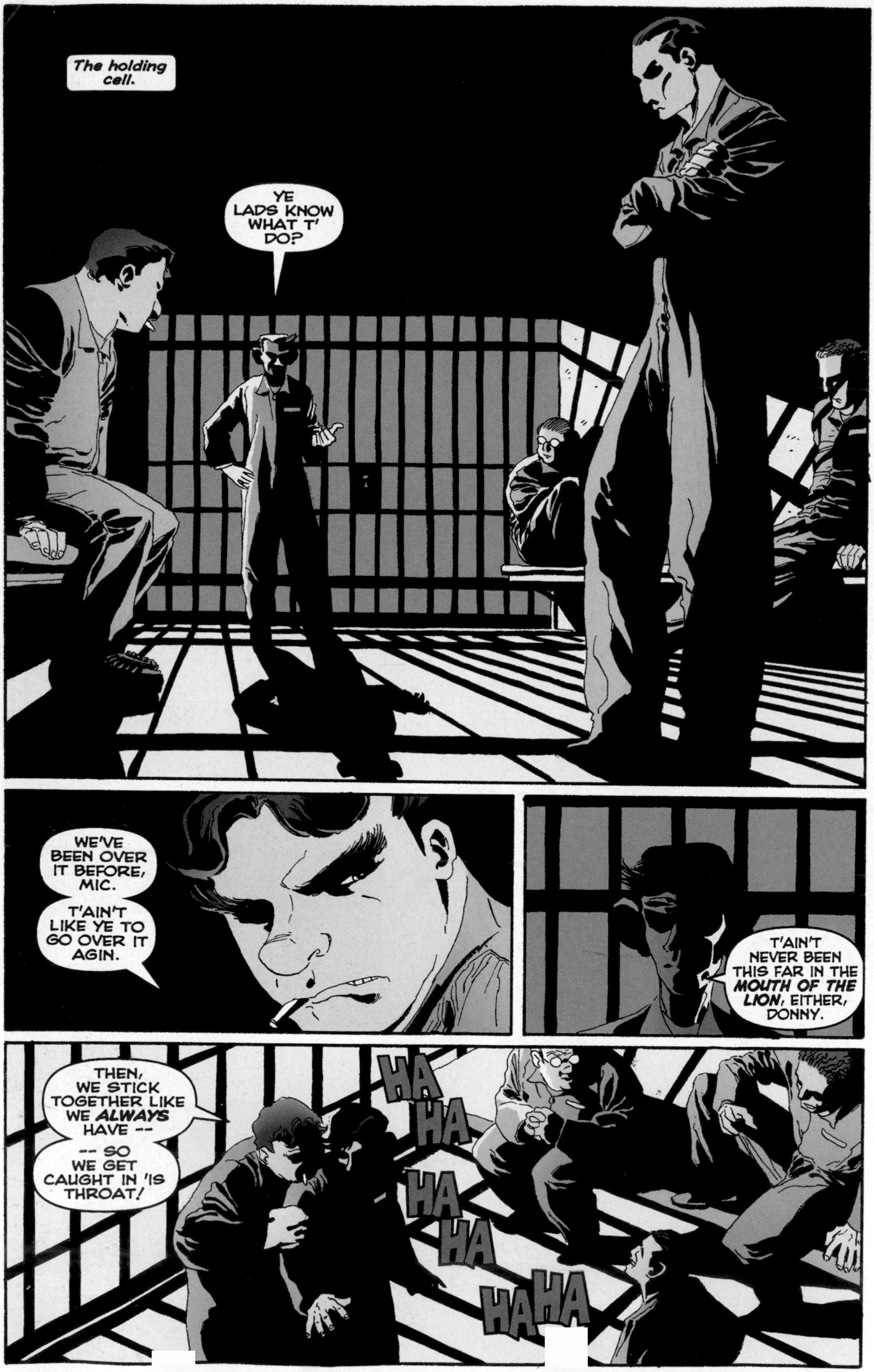
The holding cell.
YE LADS KNOW WHAT T' DO?
WE'VE BEEN OVER IT BEFORE, MIC.
T'AIN'T LIKE YE TO GO OVER IT AGIN.
T'AIN'T NEVER BEEN THIS FAR IN THE MOUTH OF THE LION, EITHER, DONNY.
THEN, WE STICK TOGETHER LIKE WE ALWAYS HAVE --
-- SO WE GET CAUGHT IN 'IS THROAT!
HA HA HA HA HAHA

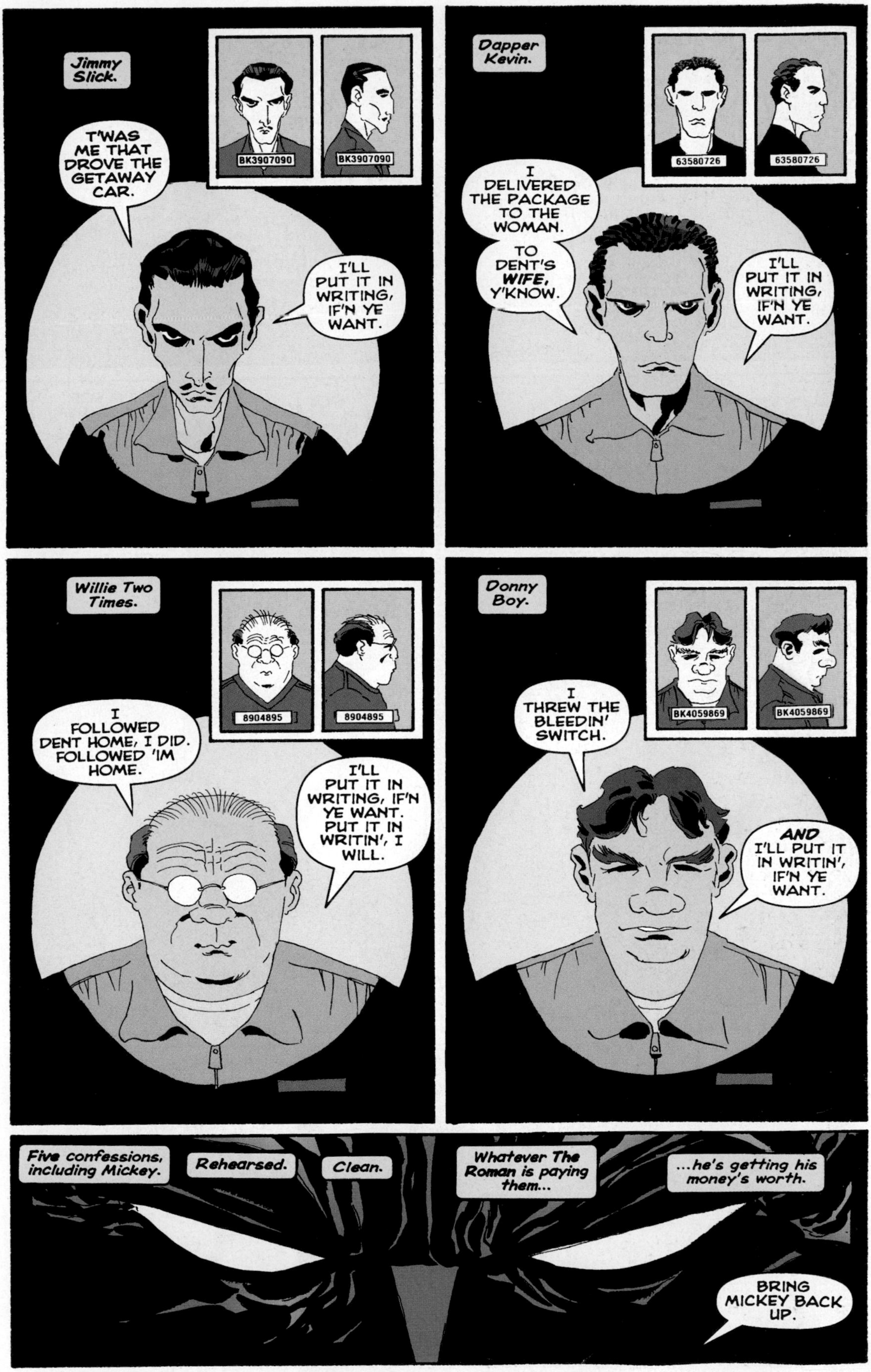
Jimmy Slick.
BK3907090
BK3907090
T'WAS ME THAT DROVE THE GETAWAY CAR.
I'LL PUT IT IN WRITING, IF'N YE WANT.
Dapper Kevin.
63580726
63580726
I DELIVERED THE PACKAGE TO THE WOMAN.
TO DENT'S *WIFE,* Y'KNOW.
I'LL PUT IT IN WRITING, IF'N YE WANT.
Willie Two Times.
8904895
8904895
I FOLLOWED DENT HOME, I DID. FOLLOWED 'IM HOME.
I'LL PUT IT IN WRITING, IF'N YE WANT. PUT IT IN WRITIN', I WILL.
Donny Boy.
BK4059869
BK4059869
I THREW THE BLEEDIN' SWITCH.
AND I'LL PUT IT IN WRITIN', IF'N YE WANT.
Five confessions, including Mickey.
Rehearsed.
Clean.
Whatever The Roman is paying them...
...he's getting his money's worth.
BRING MICKEY BACK UP.

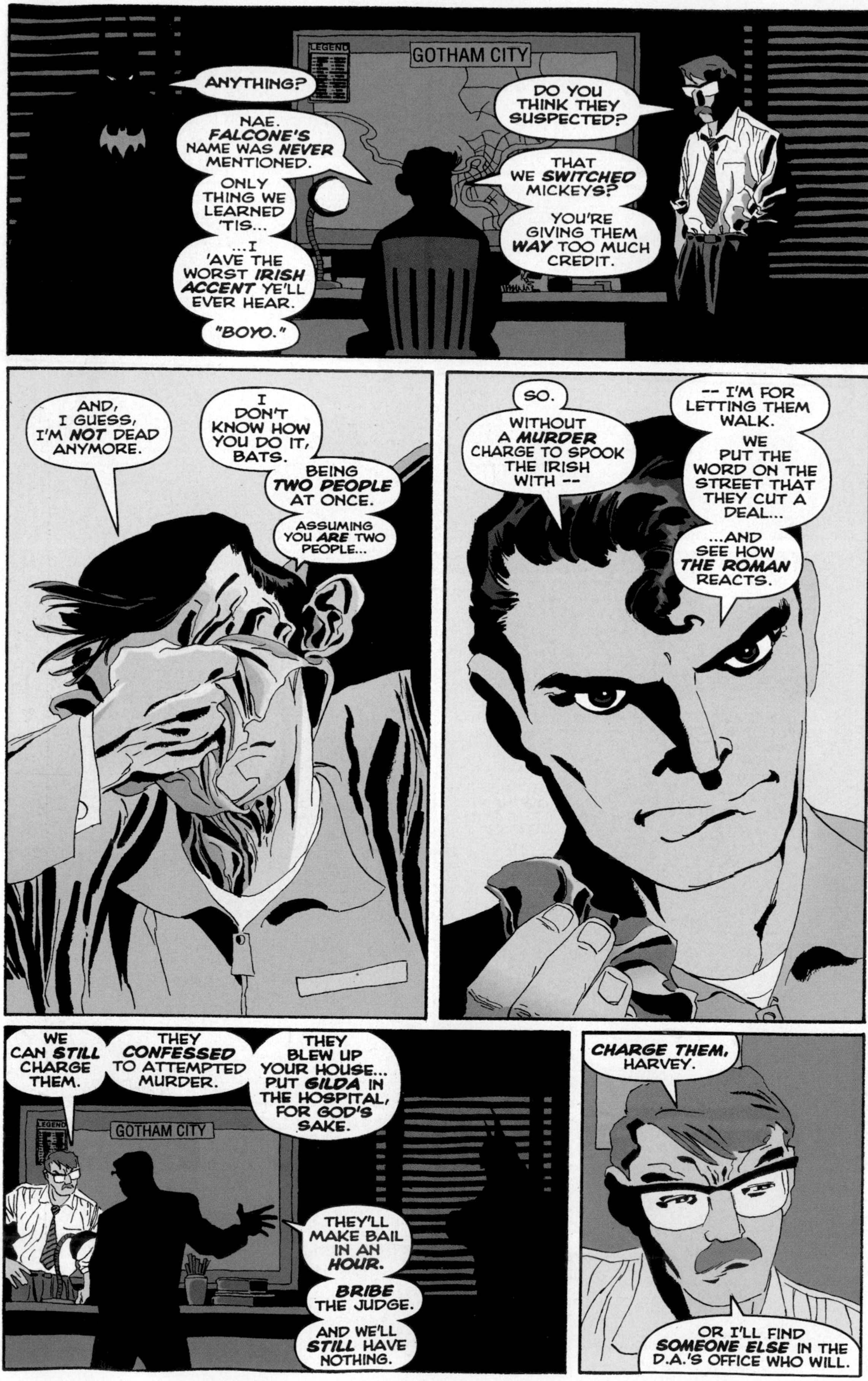
GOTHAM CITY
LEGEND
ANYTHING?
NAE. FALCONE'S NAME WAS NEVER MENTIONED.
ONLY THING WE LEARNED 'TIS...
...I 'AVE THE WORST IRISH ACCENT YE'LL EVER HEAR.
"BOYO."
DO YOU THINK THEY SUSPECTED?
THAT WE SWITCHED MICKEYS?
YOU'RE GIVING THEM WAY TOO MUCH CREDIT.
AND, I GUESS, I'M NOT DEAD ANYMORE.
I DON'T KNOW HOW YOU DO IT, BATS.
BEING TWO PEOPLE AT ONCE.
ASSUMING YOU ARE TWO PEOPLE...
SO.
WITHOUT A MURDER CHARGE TO SPOOK THE IRISH WITH --
-- I'M FOR LETTING THEM WALK.
WE PUT THE WORD ON THE STREET THAT THEY CUT A DEAL...
...AND SEE HOW THE ROMAN REACTS.
WE CAN STILL CHARGE THEM.
THEY CONFESSED TO ATTEMPTED MURDER.
THEY BLEW UP YOUR HOUSE... PUT GILDA IN THE HOSPITAL, FOR GOD'S SAKE.
LEGEND
GOTHAM CITY
THEY'LL MAKE BAIL IN AN HOUR.
BRIBE THE JUDGE.
AND WE'LL STILL HAVE NOTHING.
CHARGE THEM, HARVEY.
OR I'LL FIND SOMEONE ELSE IN THE D.A.'S OFFICE WHO WILL.

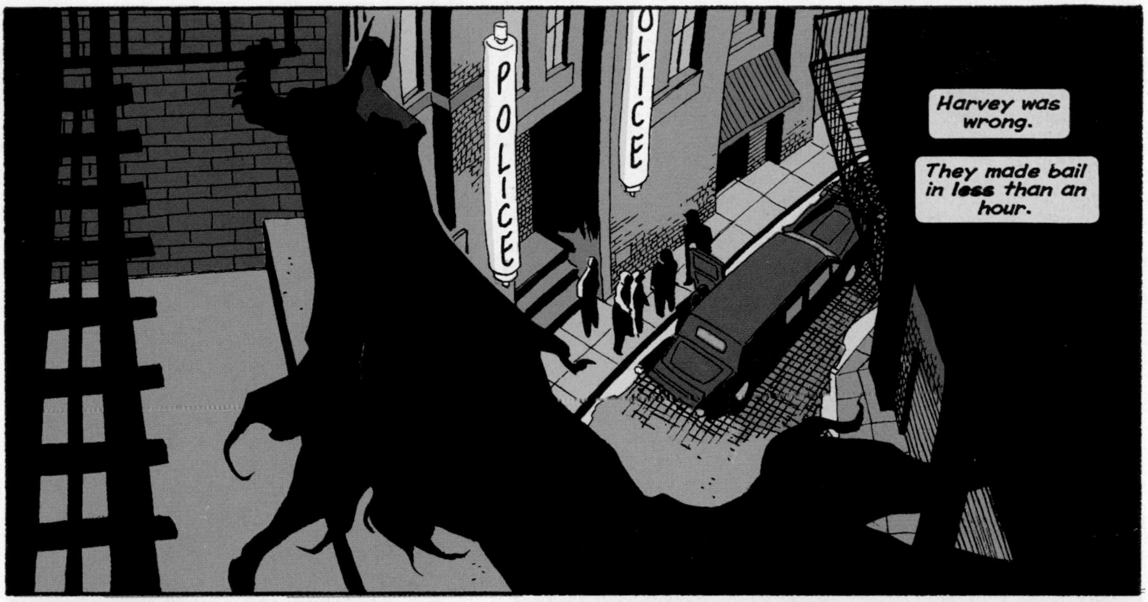
POLICE
POLICE
Harvey was wrong.
They made bail in less than an hour.

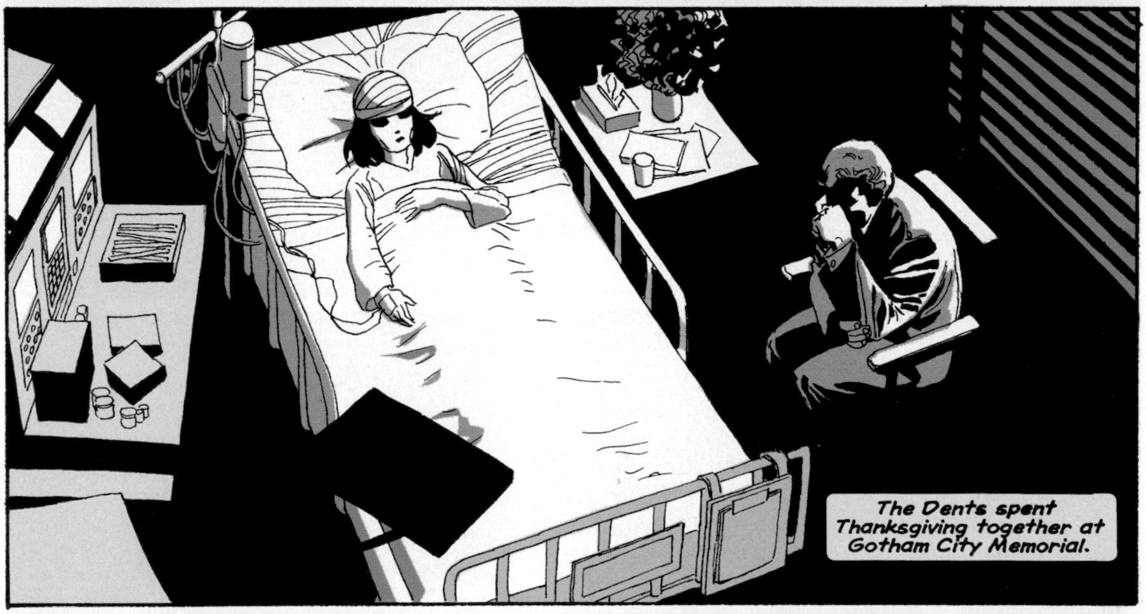
The Dents spent Thanksgiving together at Gotham City Memorial.

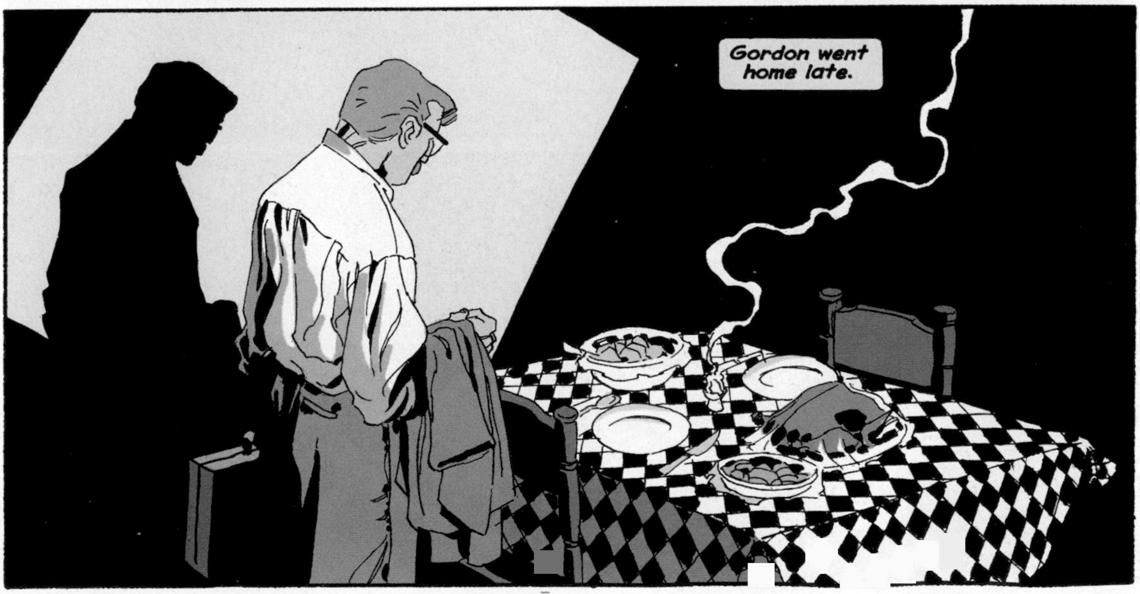
Gordon went home late.

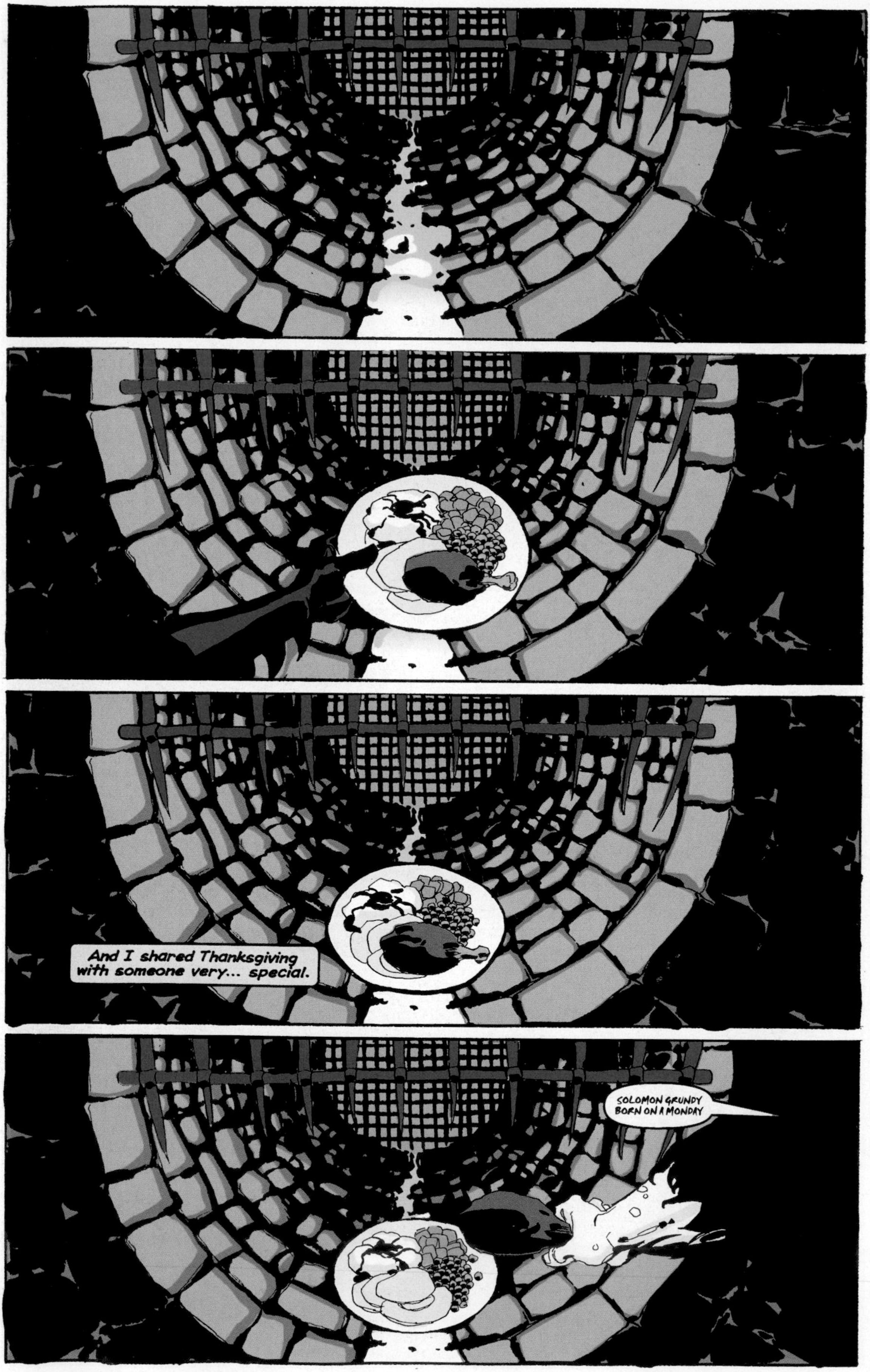
And I shared Thanksgiving with someone very... special.
SOLOMON GRUNDY BORN ON A MONDAY

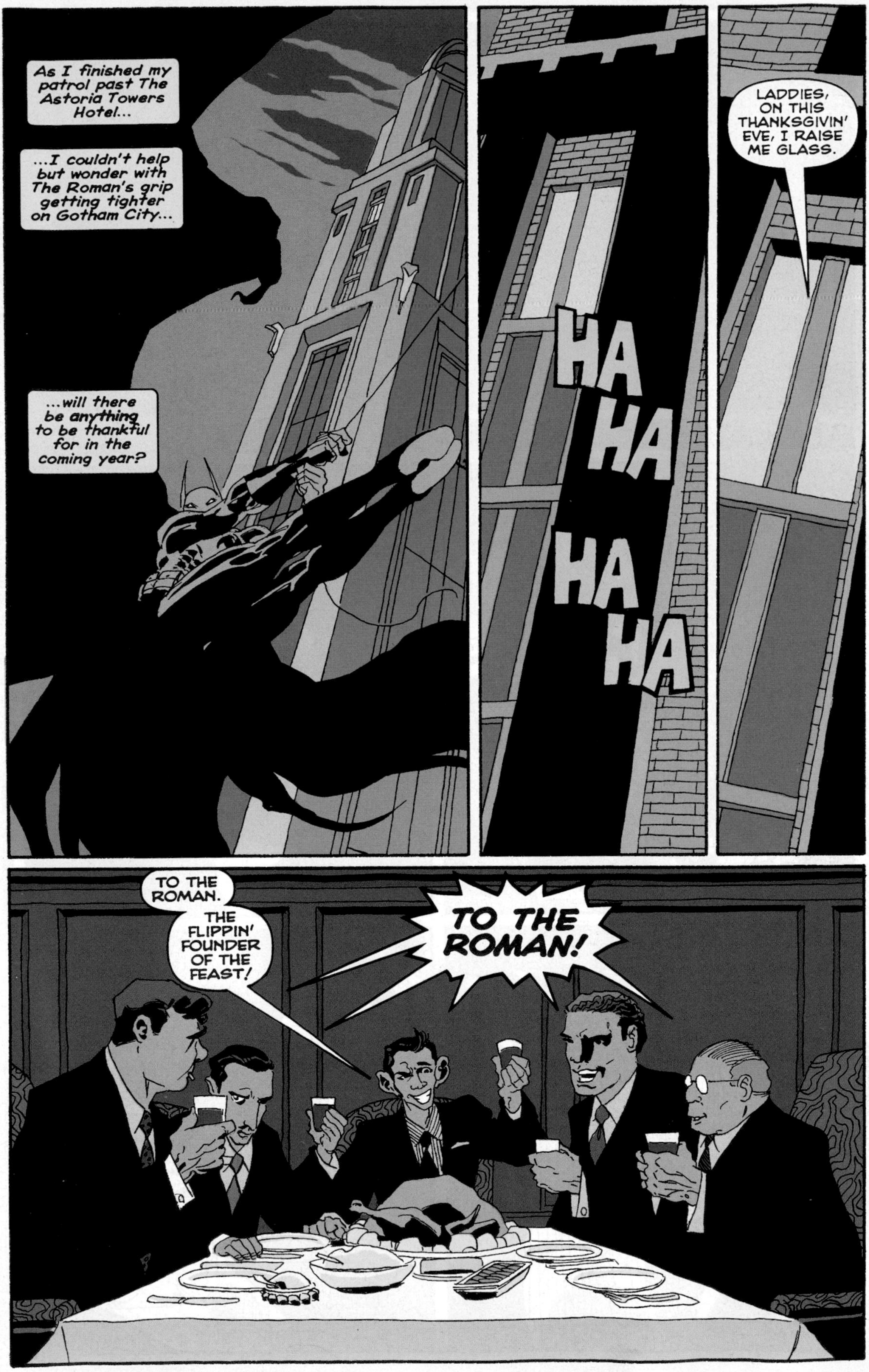
As I finished my patrol past The Astoria Towers Hotel...
...I couldn't help but wonder with The Roman's grip getting tighter on Gotham City...
...will there be anything to be thankful for in the coming year?
HA HA HA HA
LADDIES, ON THIS THANKSGIVIN' EVE, I RAISE ME GLASS.
TO THE ROMAN.
THE FLIPPIN' FOUNDER OF THE FEAST!
TO THE ROMAN!

CHAPTER THREE
CHRISTMAS

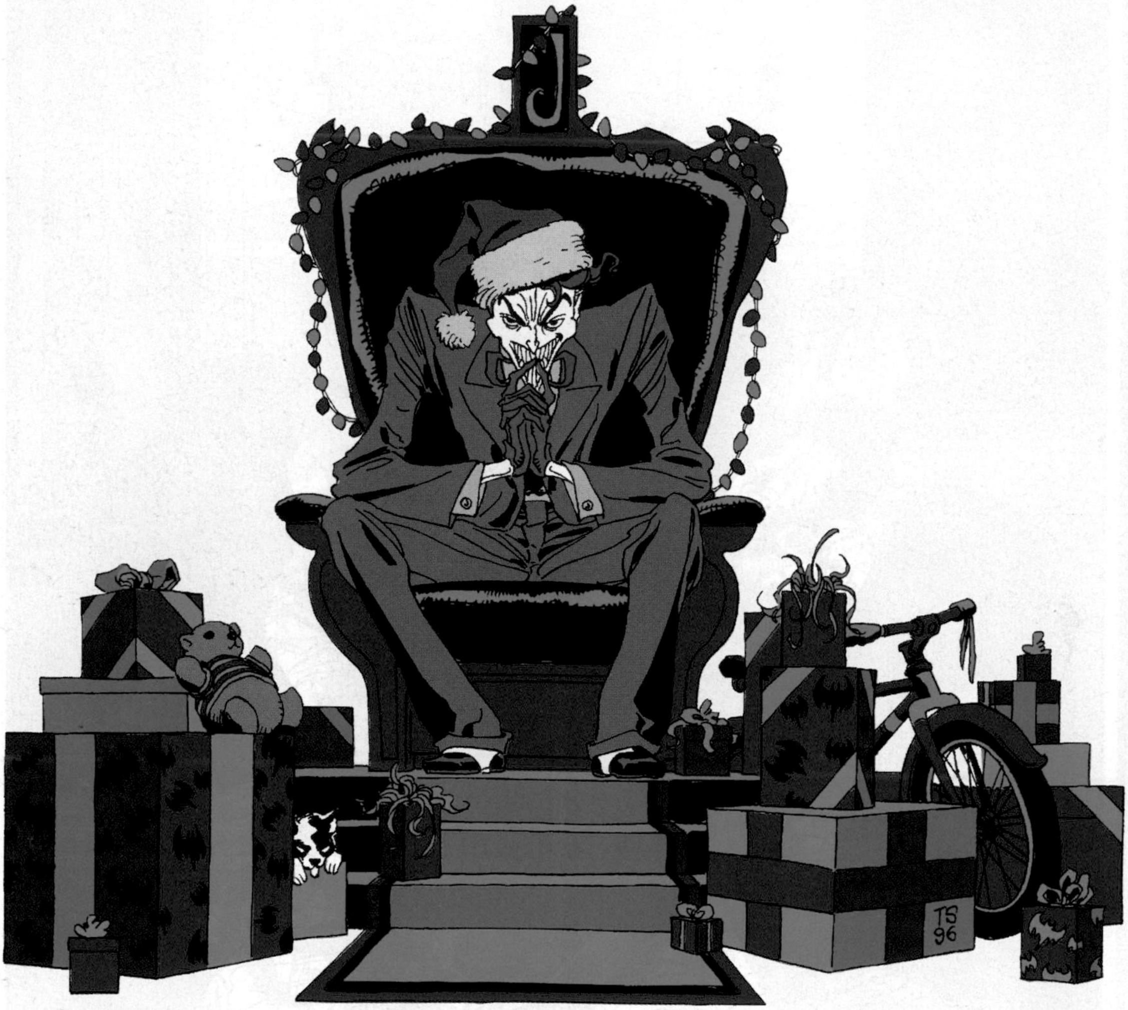

TS
96

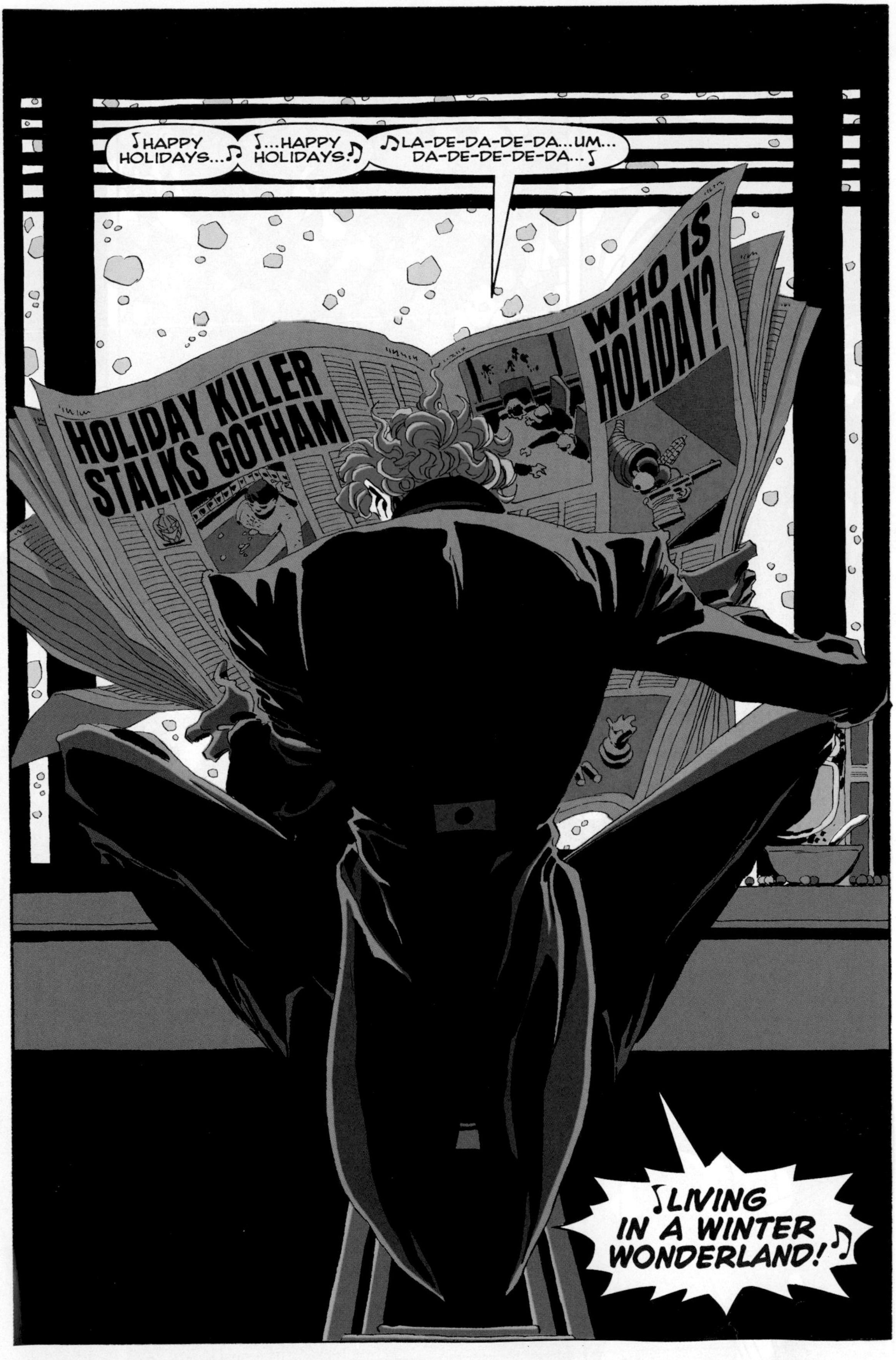

♪HAPPY HOLIDAYS...♪
♪...HAPPY HOLIDAYS♪
♪LA-DE-DA-DE-DA...UM... DA-DE-DE-DE-DA...♪
HOLIDAY KILLER STALKS GOTHAM
WHO IS HOLIDAY?
♪LIVING IN A WINTER WONDERLAND!♪

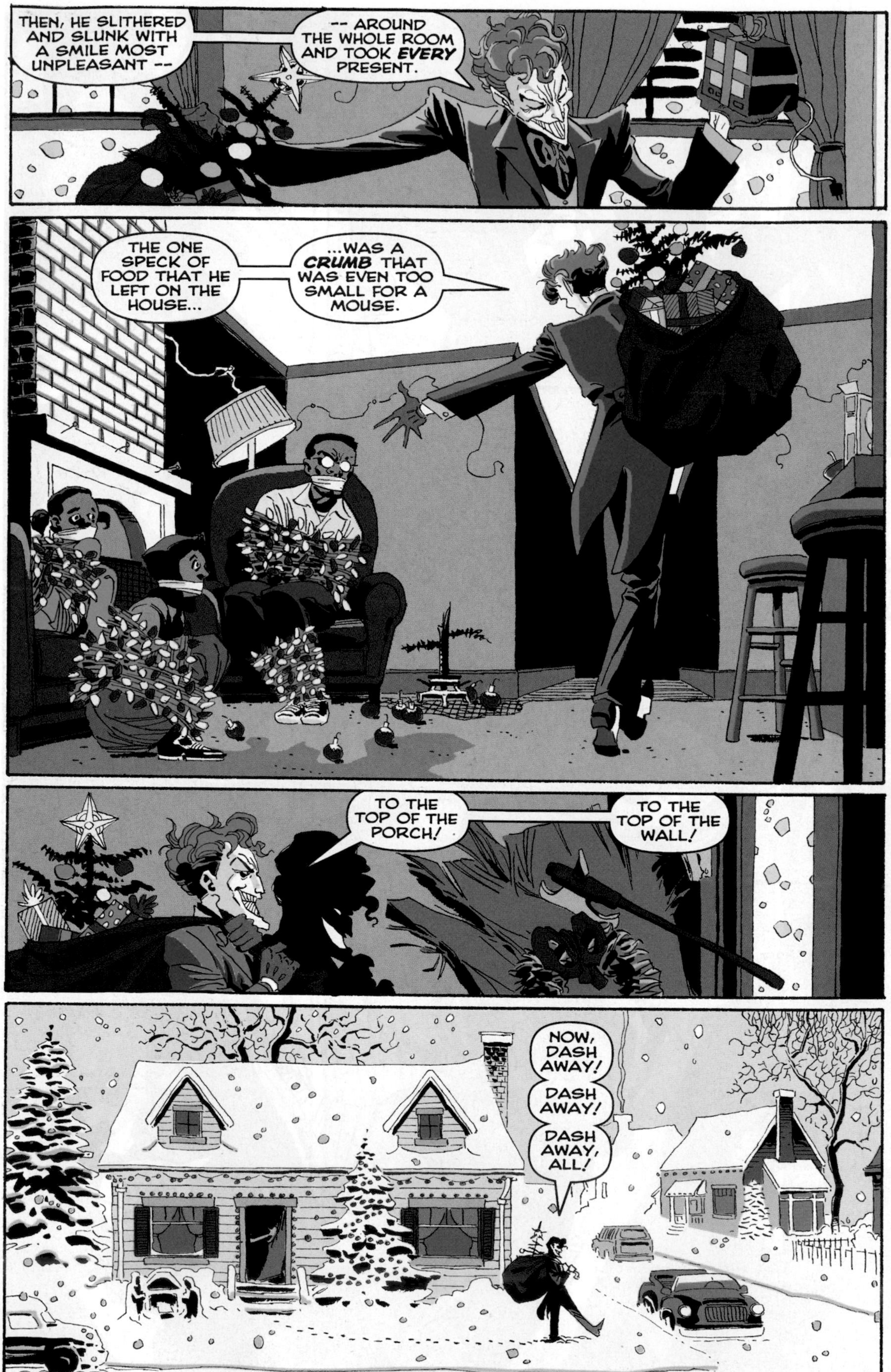
THEN, HE SLITHERED AND SLUNK WITH A SMILE MOST UNPLEASANT --
-- AROUND THE WHOLE ROOM AND TOOK EVERY PRESENT.
THE ONE SPECK OF FOOD THAT HE LEFT ON THE HOUSE...
...WAS A CRUMB THAT WAS EVEN TOO SMALL FOR A MOUSE.
TO THE TOP OF THE PORCH!
TO THE TOP OF THE WALL!
NOW, DASH AWAY!
DASH AWAY!
DASH AWAY, ALL!

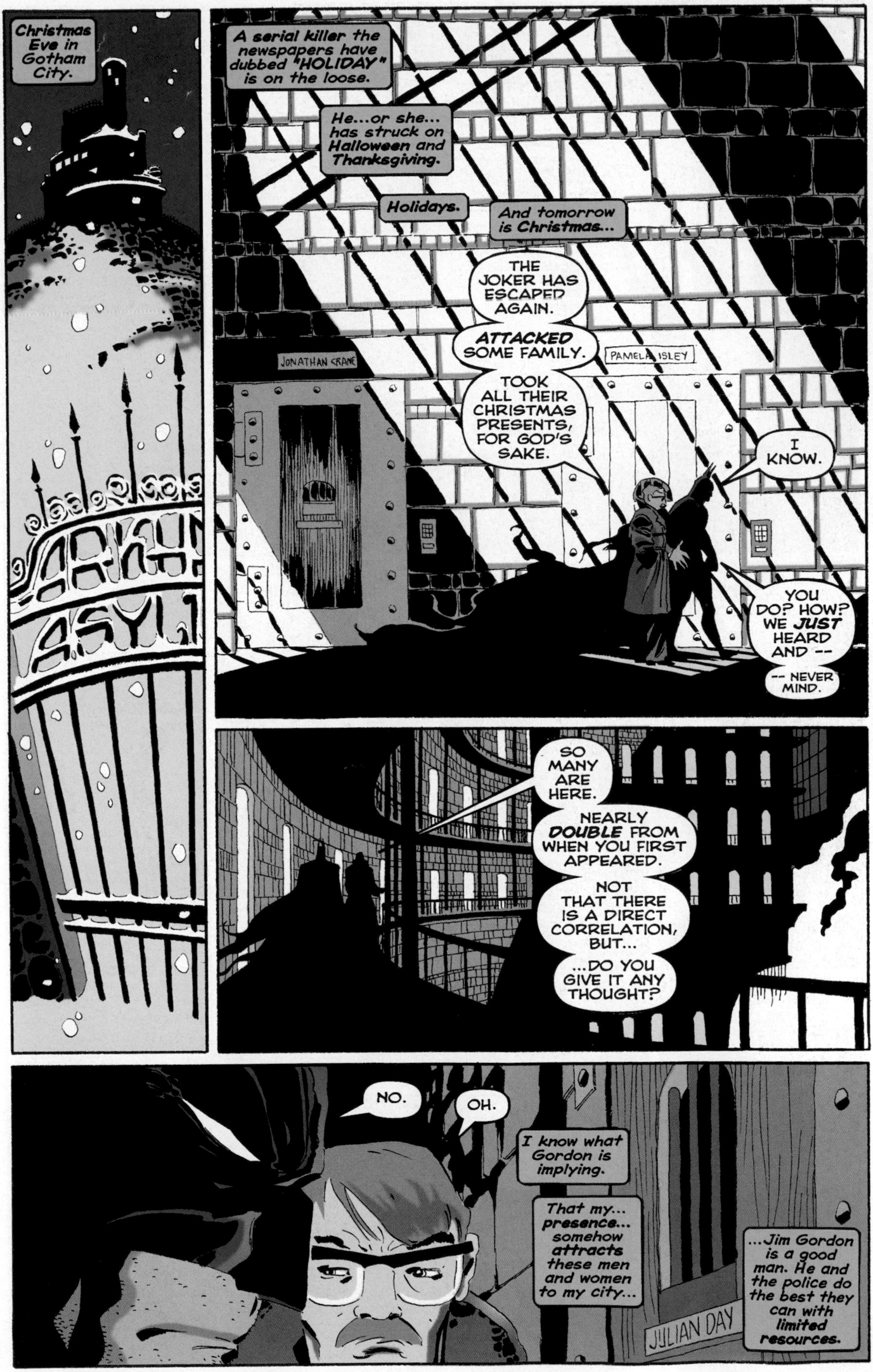
Christmas Eve in Gotham City.
ARKHAM ASYLUM
A serial killer the newspapers have dubbed "HOLIDAY" is on the loose.
He...or she... has struck on Halloween and Thanksgiving.
Holidays.
And tomorrow is Christmas...
JONATHAN CRANE
PAMELA ISLEY
THE JOKER HAS ESCAPED AGAIN.
ATTACKED SOME FAMILY.
TOOK ALL THEIR CHRISTMAS PRESENTS, FOR GOD'S SAKE.
I KNOW.
YOU DO? HOW? WE JUST HEARD AND --
-- NEVER MIND.
SO MANY ARE HERE.
NEARLY DOUBLE FROM WHEN YOU FIRST APPEARED.
NOT THAT THERE IS A DIRECT CORRELATION, BUT...
...DO YOU GIVE IT ANY THOUGHT?
NO.
OH.
I know what Gordon is implying.
That my... presence... somehow attracts these men and women to my city...
JULIAN DAY
...Jim Gordon is a good man. He and the police do the best they can with limited resources.

But, Gotham City needs Batman to protect her.

From criminals such as Julian Day.

The Calendar Man.

STAND AWAY FROM GLASS

THIRTY DAYS HATH SEPTEMBER, APRIL, JUNE, AND --

I'VE SPOKEN TO THE DISTRICT ATTORNEY'S OFFICE, JULIAN --

-- AND THEY ARE WILLING TO COMMUTE YOUR SENTENCE TO "TIME SERVED," IF YOU'LL HELP US WITH THESE MURDERS.

OUR FEELING IS WITH YOUR INTEREST IN COMMITTING CRIME TO COINCIDE WITH THE CALENDAR --

-- YOU MIGHT HAVE SOME INSIGHT?

DEC 24

TOMORROW IS THE BIG DAY.

SHE'LL BE KILLING AGAIN.

WHAT MAKES YOU THINK IT'S A WOMAN?

BECAUSE HE LIKES IT. THE ATTENTION.

NO ONE KNOWS WHO SHE IS AND ALREADY HE HAS MADE A NAME FOR HIMSELF.

OR HERSELF.

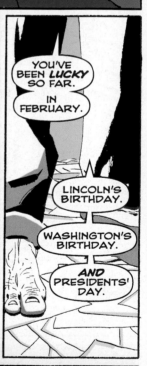

YOU'VE BEEN LUCKY SO FAR. IN FEBRUARY.

LINCOLN'S BIRTHDAY.

WASHINGTON'S BIRTHDAY.

AND PRESIDENTS' DAY.

FEBRUARY.

SURELY WE'LL HAVE CAUGHT THE KILLER BY THEN.

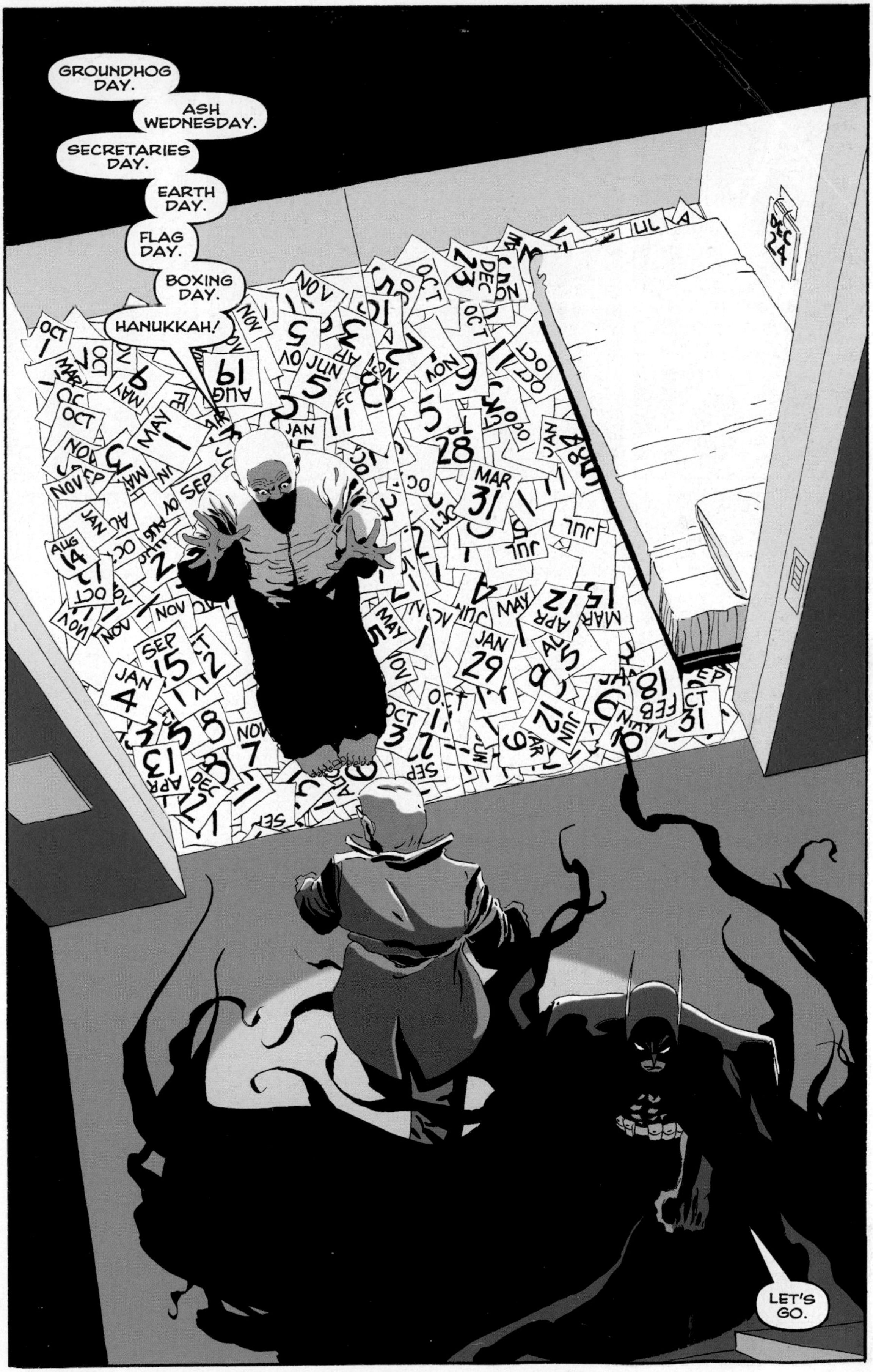
GROUNDHOG DAY.
ASH WEDNESDAY.
SECRETARIES DAY.
EARTH DAY.
FLAG DAY.
BOXING DAY.
HANUKKAH!
LET'S GO.

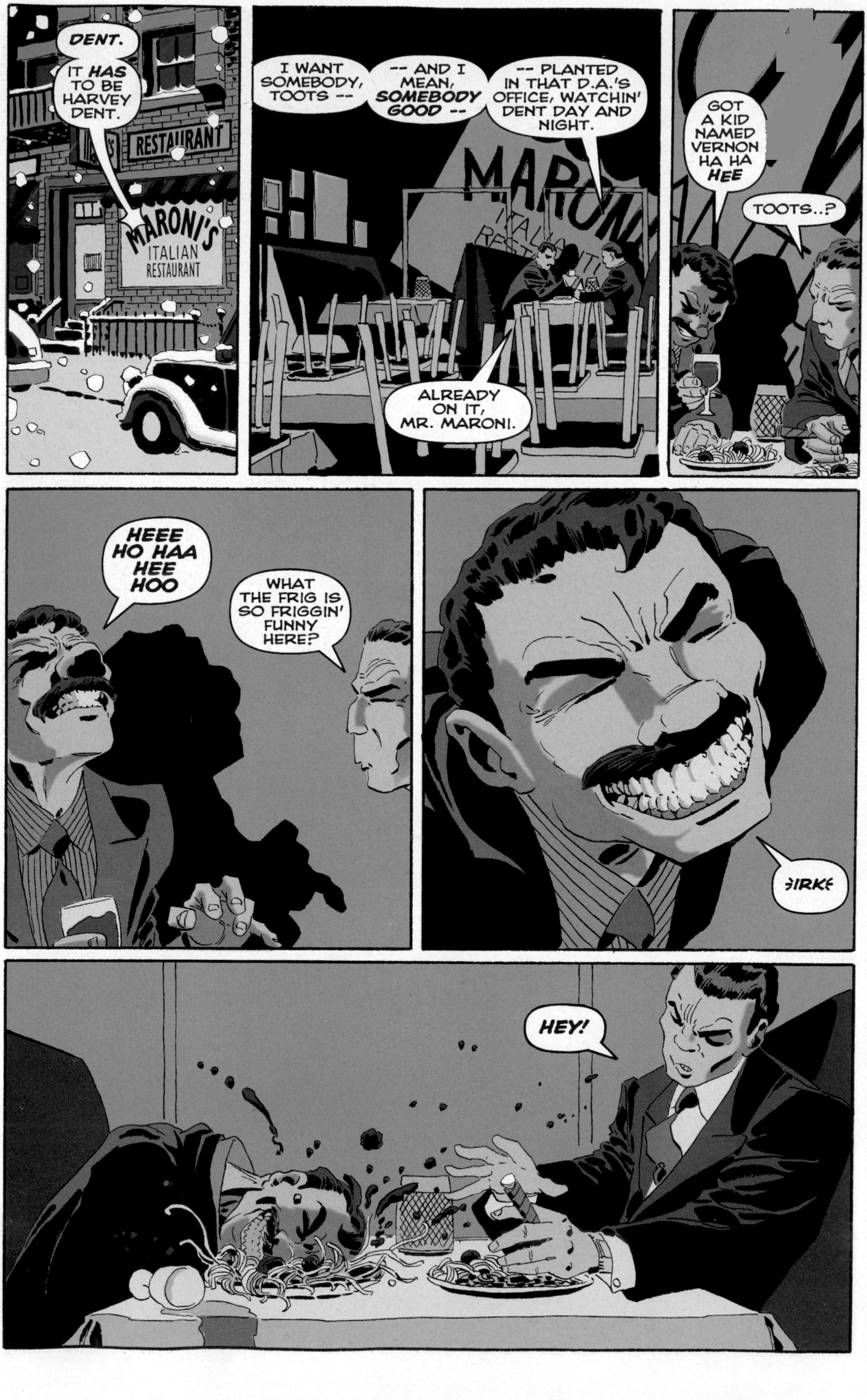
DENT.
IT HAS TO BE HARVEY DENT.
RESTAURANT
MARONI'S ITALIAN RESTAURANT
I WANT SOMEBODY, TOOTS --
-- AND I MEAN, SOMEBODY GOOD --
-- PLANTED IN THAT D.A.'S OFFICE, WATCHIN' DENT DAY AND NIGHT.
ALREADY ON IT, MR. MARONI.
GOT A KID NAMED VERNON HA HA HEE
TOOTS..?
HEEE HO HAA HEE HOO
WHAT THE FRIG IS SO FRIGGIN' FUNNY HERE?
HEY!

CARE FOR SOME MORE WINE, MR. MARONI?

A CLOWN.

NO *CLOWN* COMES INTO *MY* PLACE AND --

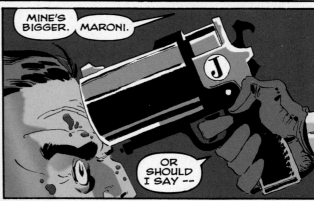

MINE'S BIGGER. MARONI.

OR SHOULD I SAY --

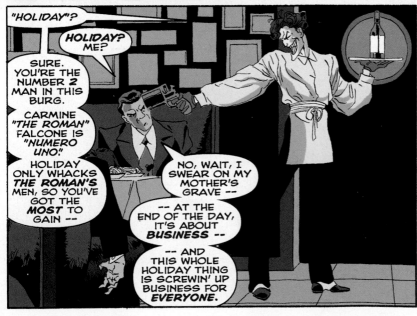

"HOLIDAY"?

HOLIDAY? ME?

SURE. YOU'RE THE NUMBER *2* MAN IN THIS BURG. CARMINE "THE ROMAN" FALCONE IS "NUMERO UNO." HOLIDAY ONLY WHACKS *THE ROMAN'S* MEN, SO YOU'VE GOT THE *MOST* TO GAIN --

NO, WAIT, I SWEAR ON MY MOTHER'S GRAVE --

-- AT THE END OF THE DAY, IT'S ABOUT *BUSINESS* --

-- AND THIS WHOLE HOLIDAY THING IS SCREWIN' UP BUSINESS FOR *EVERYONE.*

THEN... *WHO* IS HOLIDAY?

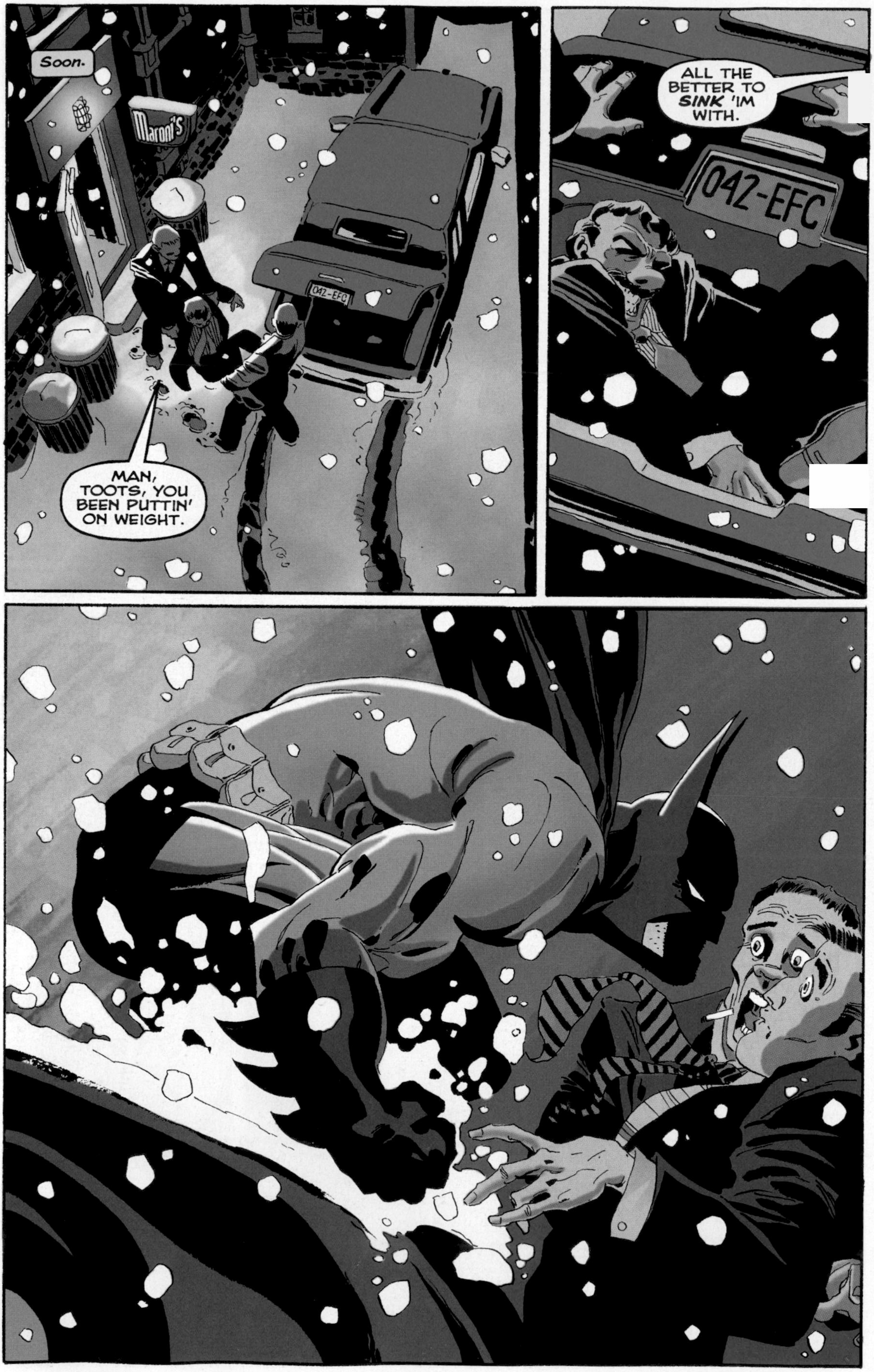
Soon.
Maroni's
042-EFC
MAN, TOOTS, YOU BEEN PUTTIN' ON WEIGHT.
ALL THE BETTER TO SINK 'IM WITH.
042-EFC

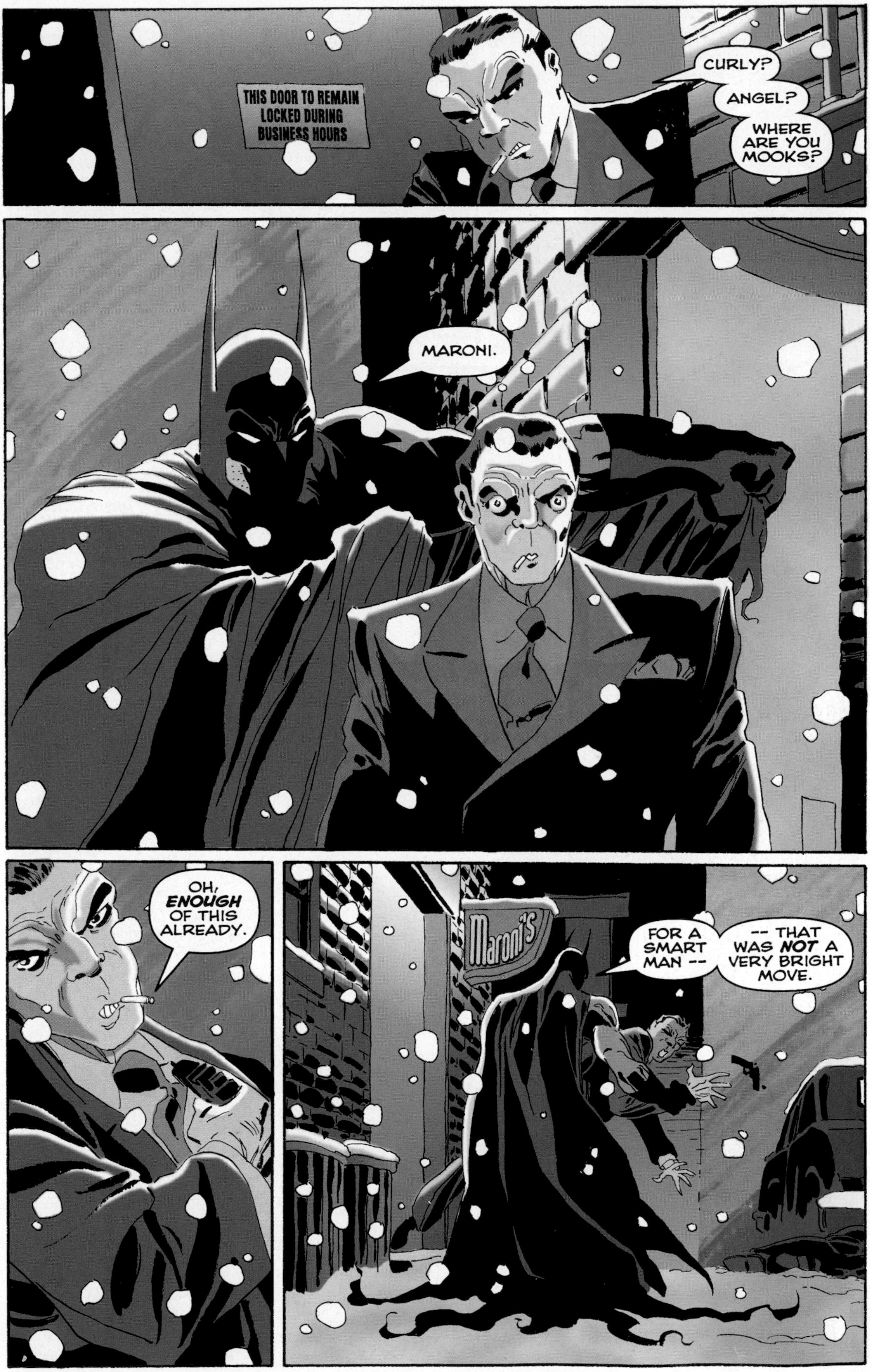
THIS DOOR TO REMAIN LOCKED DURING BUSINESS HOURS
CURLY?
ANGEL?
WHERE ARE YOU MOOKS?
MARONI.
OH, ***ENOUGH*** OF THIS ALREADY.
Maroni's
FOR A SMART MAN --
-- THAT WAS ***NOT*** A VERY BRIGHT MOVE.

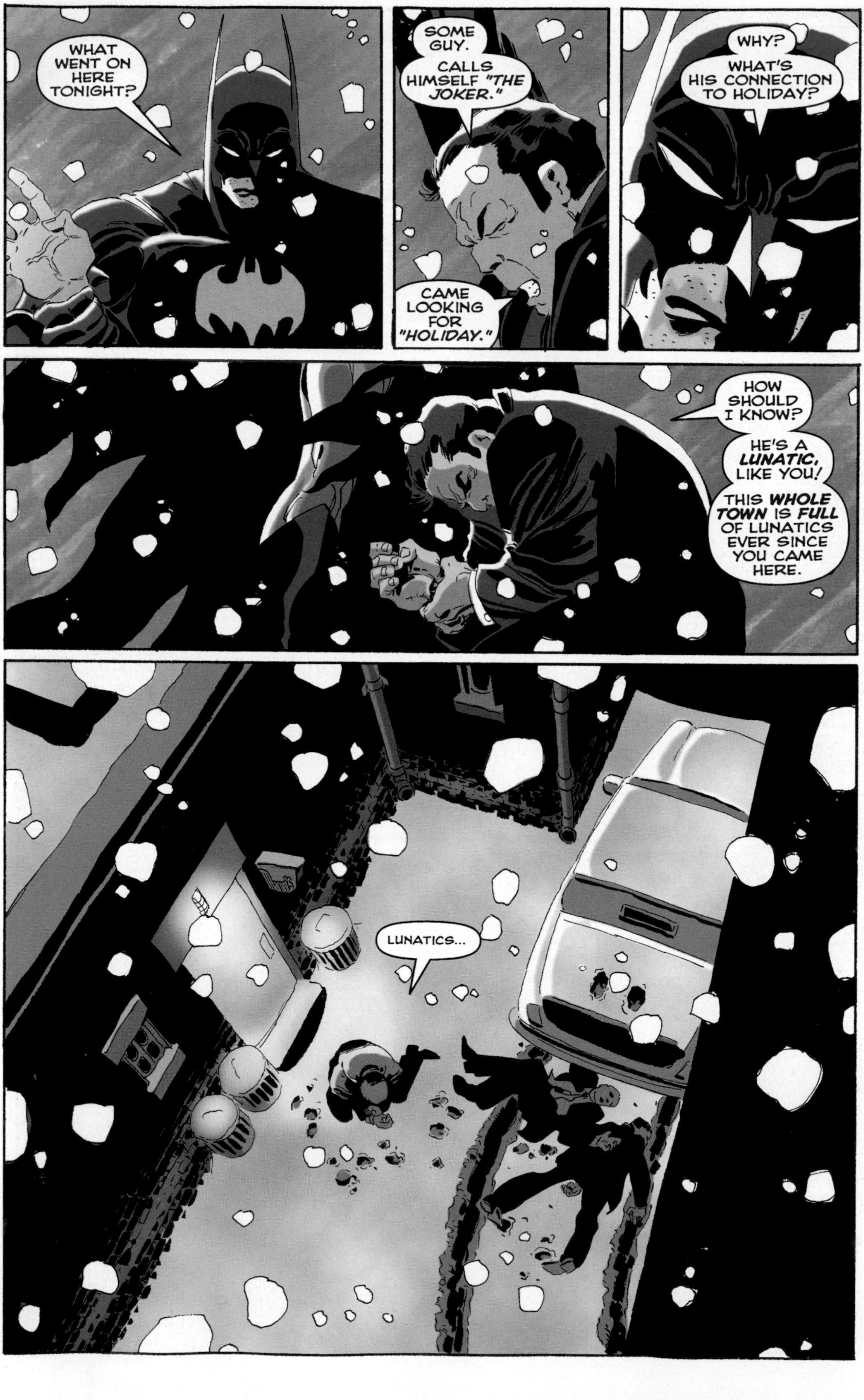
WHAT WENT ON HERE TONIGHT?
SOME GUY.
CALLS HIMSELF "THE JOKER."
CAME LOOKING FOR "HOLIDAY."
WHY?
WHAT'S HIS CONNECTION TO HOLIDAY?
HOW SHOULD I KNOW?
HE'S A LUNATIC, LIKE YOU!
THIS WHOLE TOWN IS FULL OF LUNATICS EVER SINCE YOU CAME HERE.
LUNATICS...

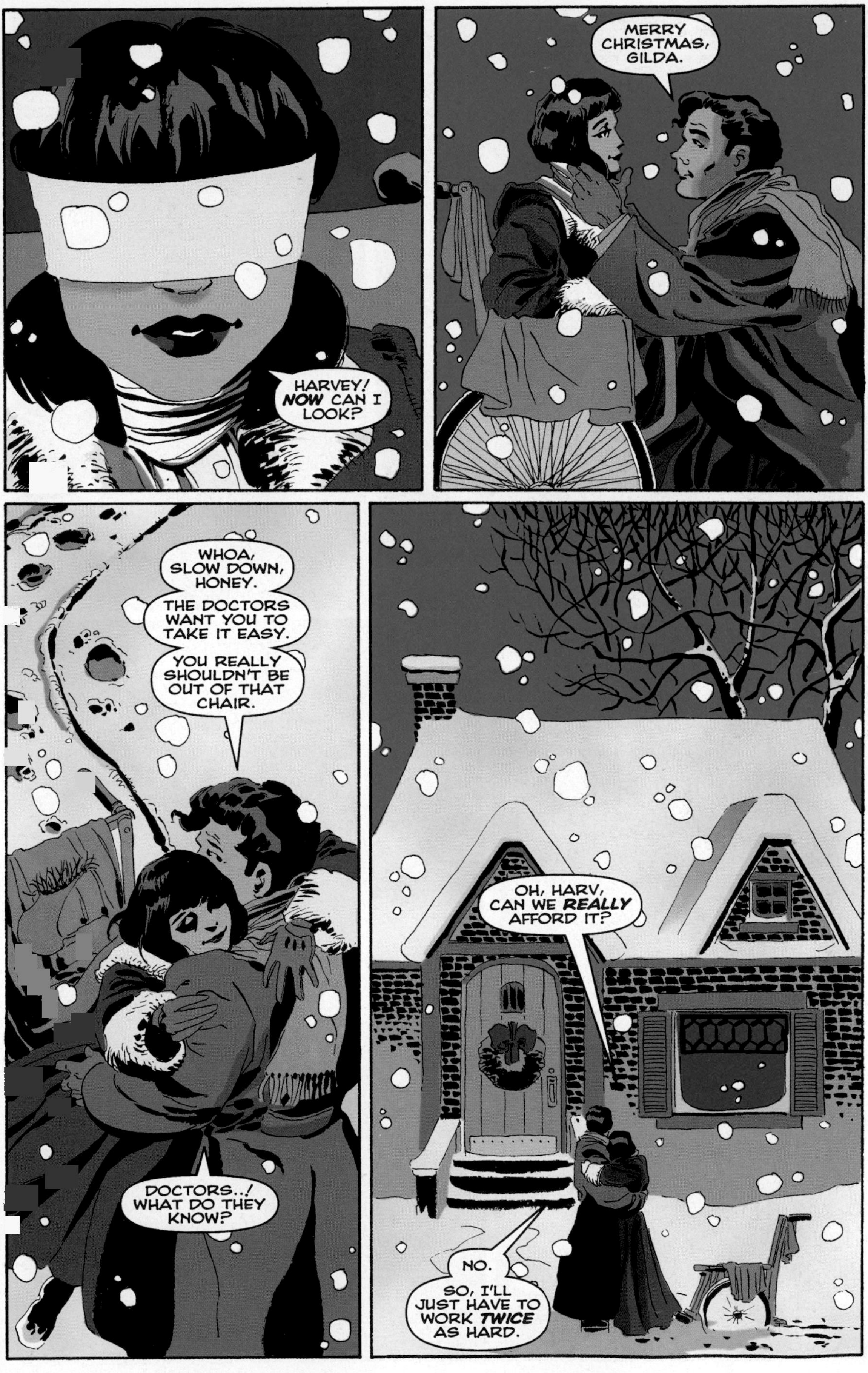
HARVEY! *NOW* CAN I LOOK?
MERRY CHRISTMAS, GILDA.
WHOA, SLOW DOWN, HONEY.
THE DOCTORS WANT YOU TO TAKE IT EASY.
YOU REALLY SHOULDN'T BE OUT OF THAT CHAIR.
DOCTORS..! WHAT DO THEY KNOW?
OH, HARV, CAN WE *REALLY* AFFORD IT?
NO.
SO, I'LL JUST HAVE TO WORK *TWICE* AS HARD.

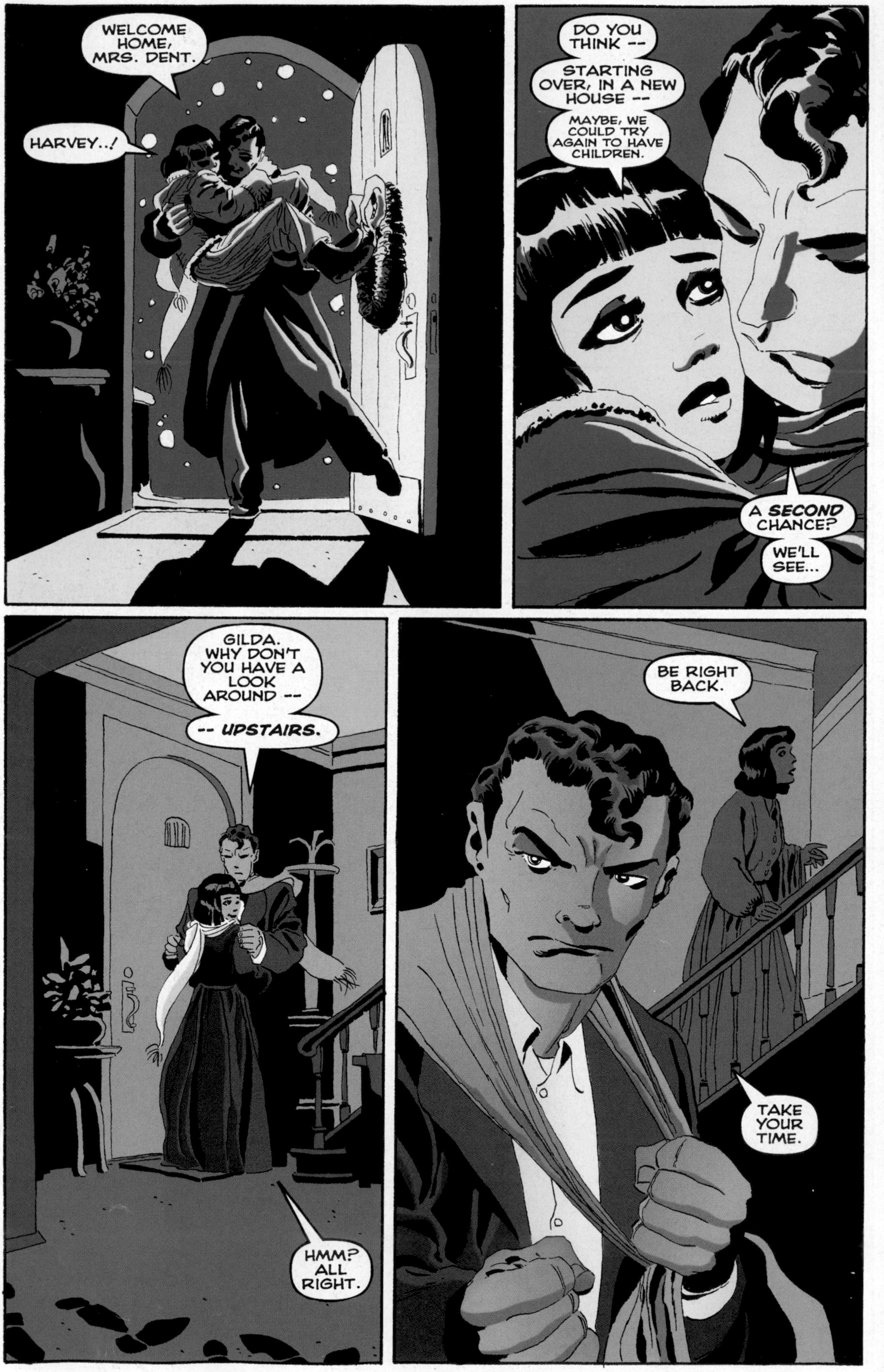
WELCOME HOME, MRS. DENT.
HARVEY..!
DO YOU THINK --
STARTING OVER, IN A NEW HOUSE --
MAYBE, WE COULD TRY AGAIN TO HAVE CHILDREN.
A SECOND CHANCE?
WE'LL SEE...
GILDA. WHY DON'T YOU HAVE A LOOK AROUND --
-- UPSTAIRS.
HMM? ALL RIGHT.
BE RIGHT BACK.
TAKE YOUR TIME.

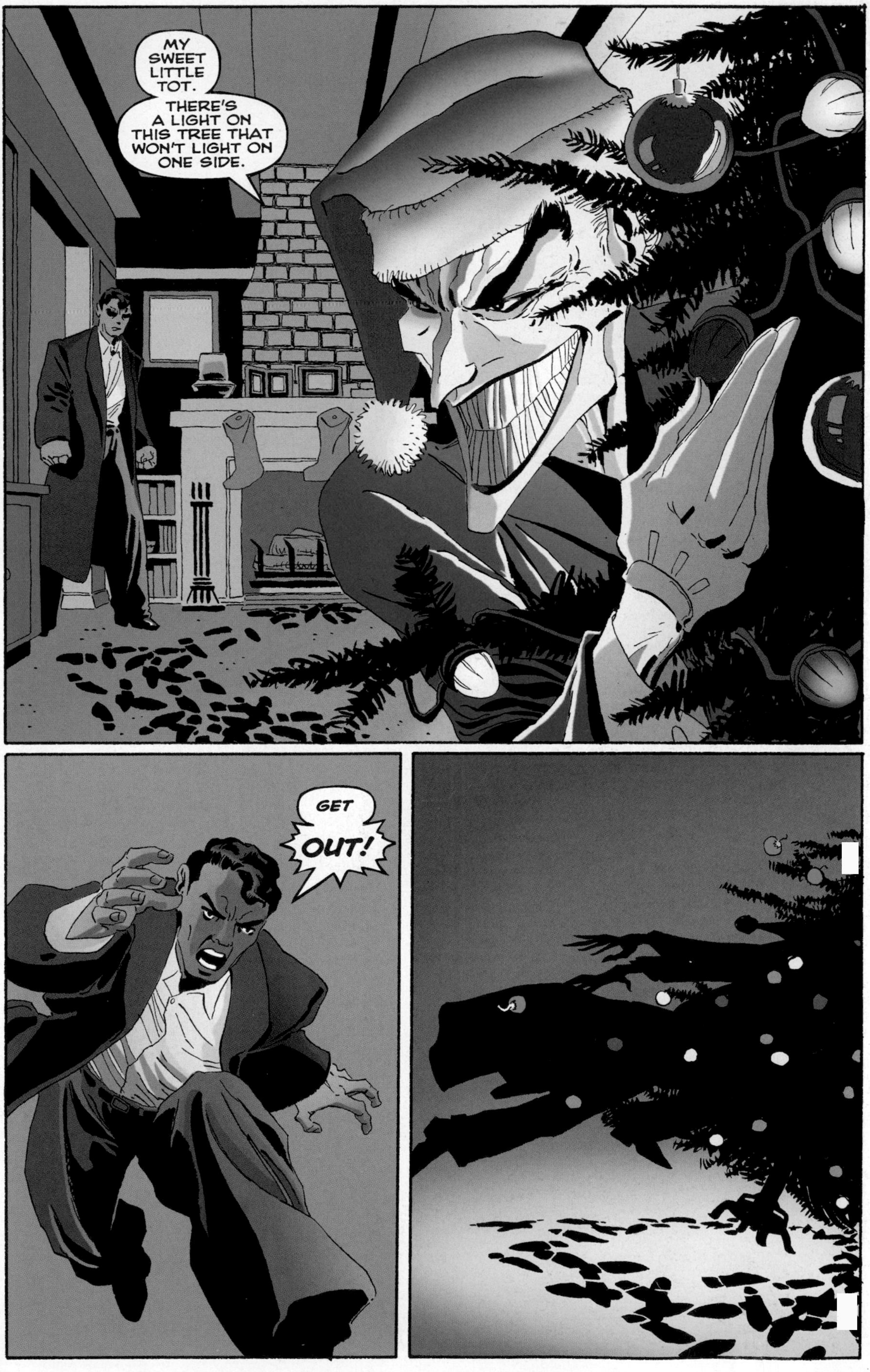
MY SWEET LITTLE TOT.
THERE'S A LIGHT ON THIS TREE THAT WON'T LIGHT ON ONE SIDE.
GET OUT!

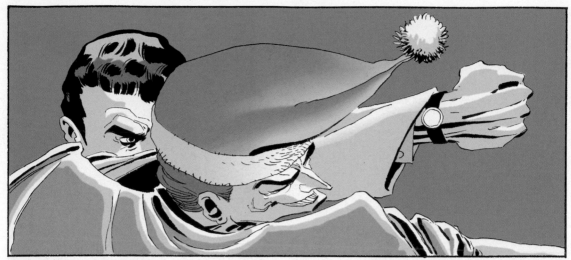

YOU'RE GOOD, DENT.

BUT, YOU'RE NO BATMAN.

THE QUESTION IS...

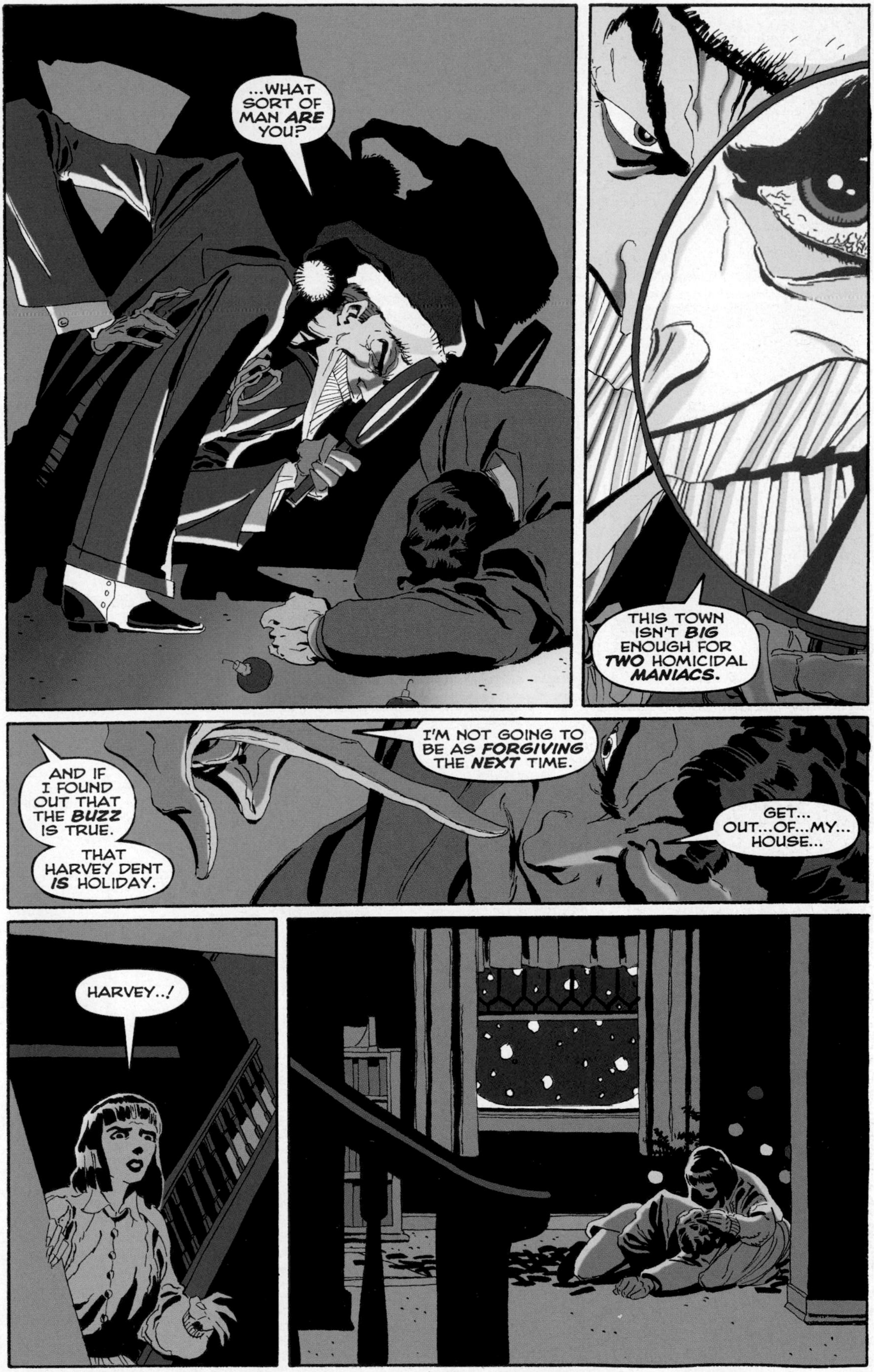
...WHAT SORT OF MAN ARE YOU?
THIS TOWN ISN'T BIG ENOUGH FOR TWO HOMICIDAL MANIACS.
AND IF I FOUND OUT THAT THE BUZZ IS TRUE.
THAT HARVEY DENT IS HOLIDAY.
I'M NOT GOING TO BE AS FORGIVING THE NEXT TIME.
GET... OUT...OF...MY... HOUSE...
HARVEY..!

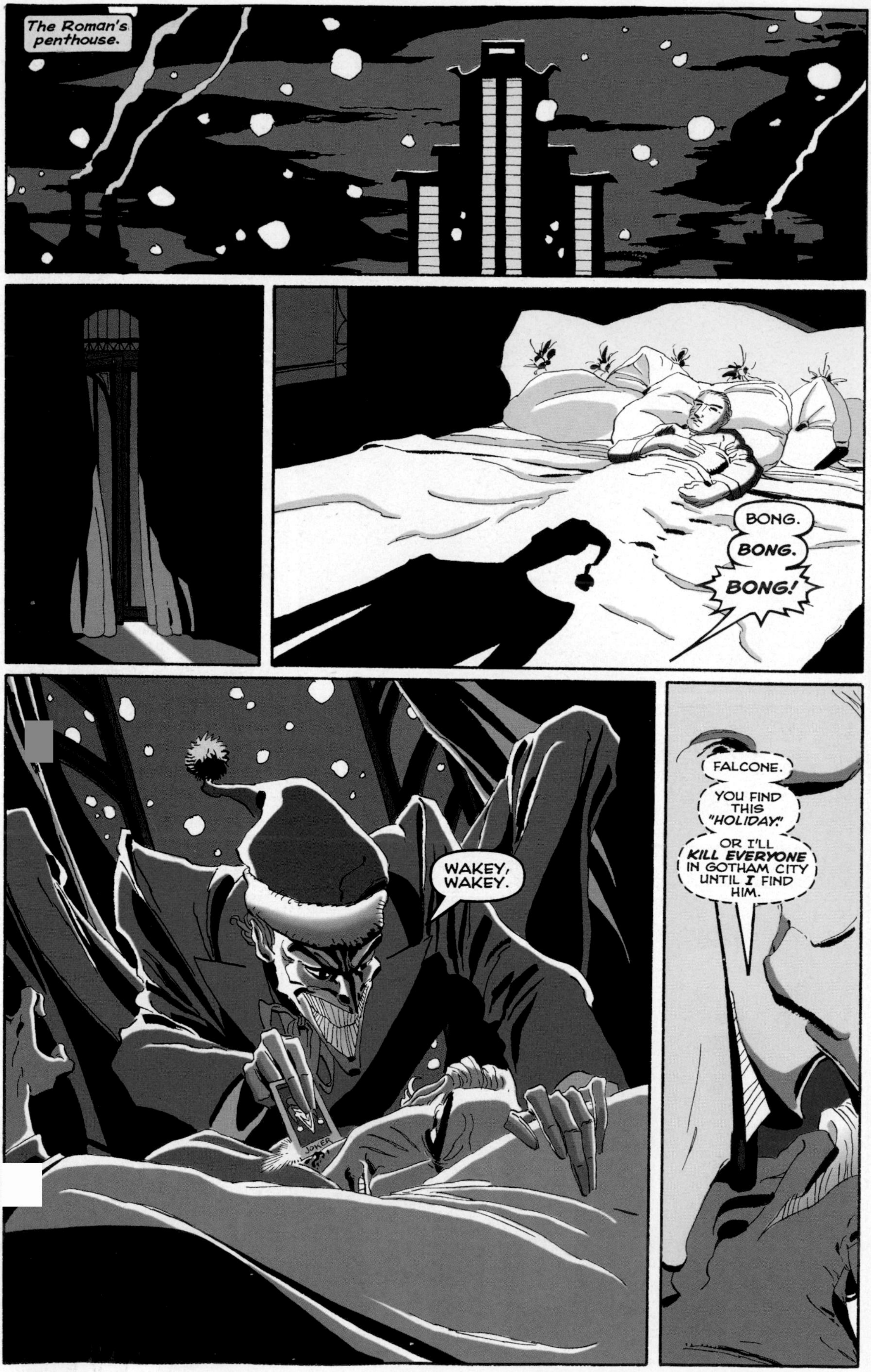
The Roman's penthouse.
BONG.
BONG.
BONG!
WAKEY, WAKEY.
JOKER
FALCONE.
YOU FIND THIS "HOLIDAY."
OR I'LL KILL EVERYONE IN GOTHAM CITY UNTIL I FIND HIM.

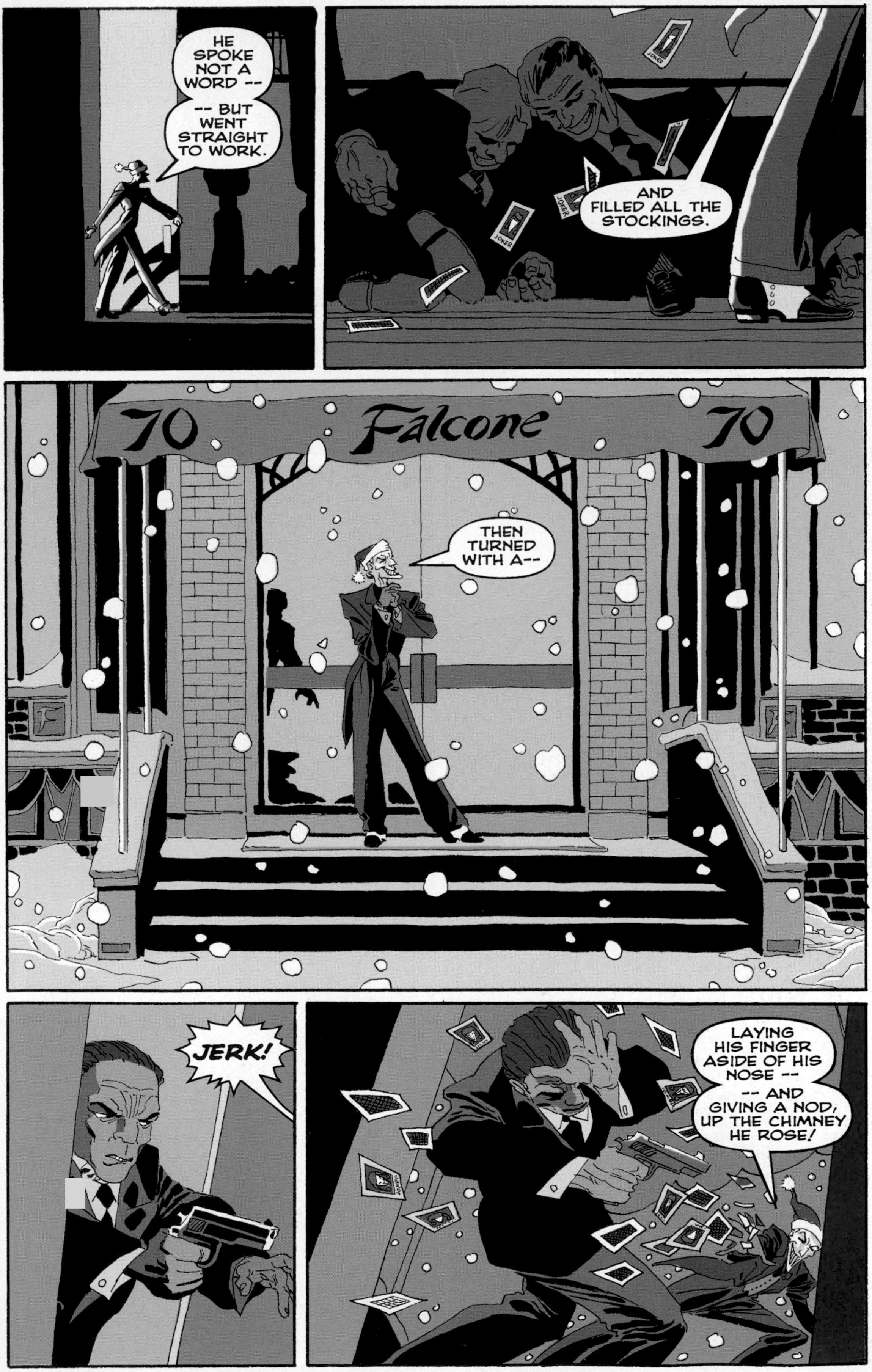
HE SPOKE NOT A WORD --
-- BUT WENT STRAIGHT TO WORK.
AND FILLED ALL THE STOCKINGS.
70
Falcone
70
THEN TURNED WITH A--
JERK!
LAYING HIS FINGER ASIDE OF HIS NOSE --
-- AND GIVING A NOD, UP THE CHIMNEY HE ROSE!

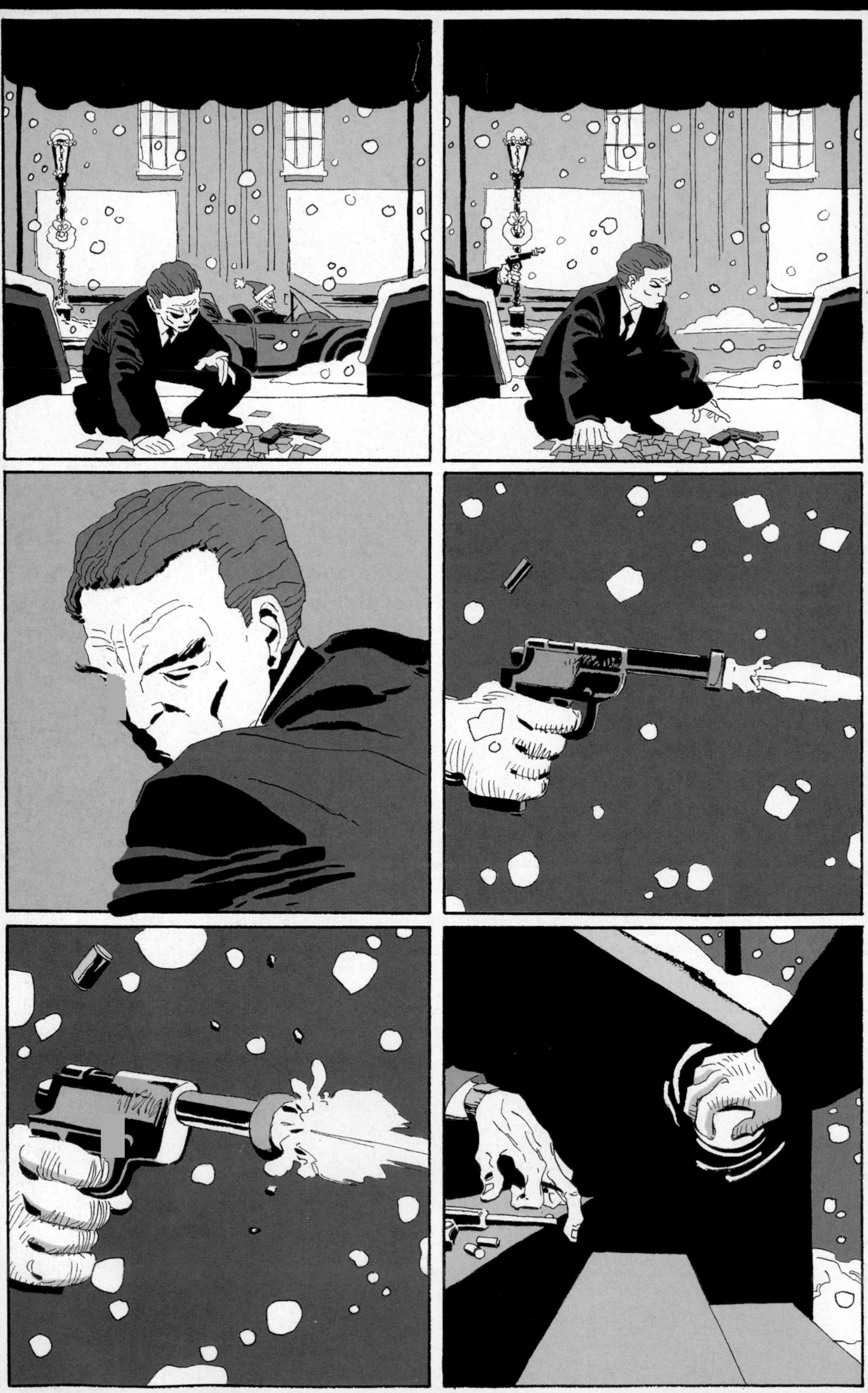

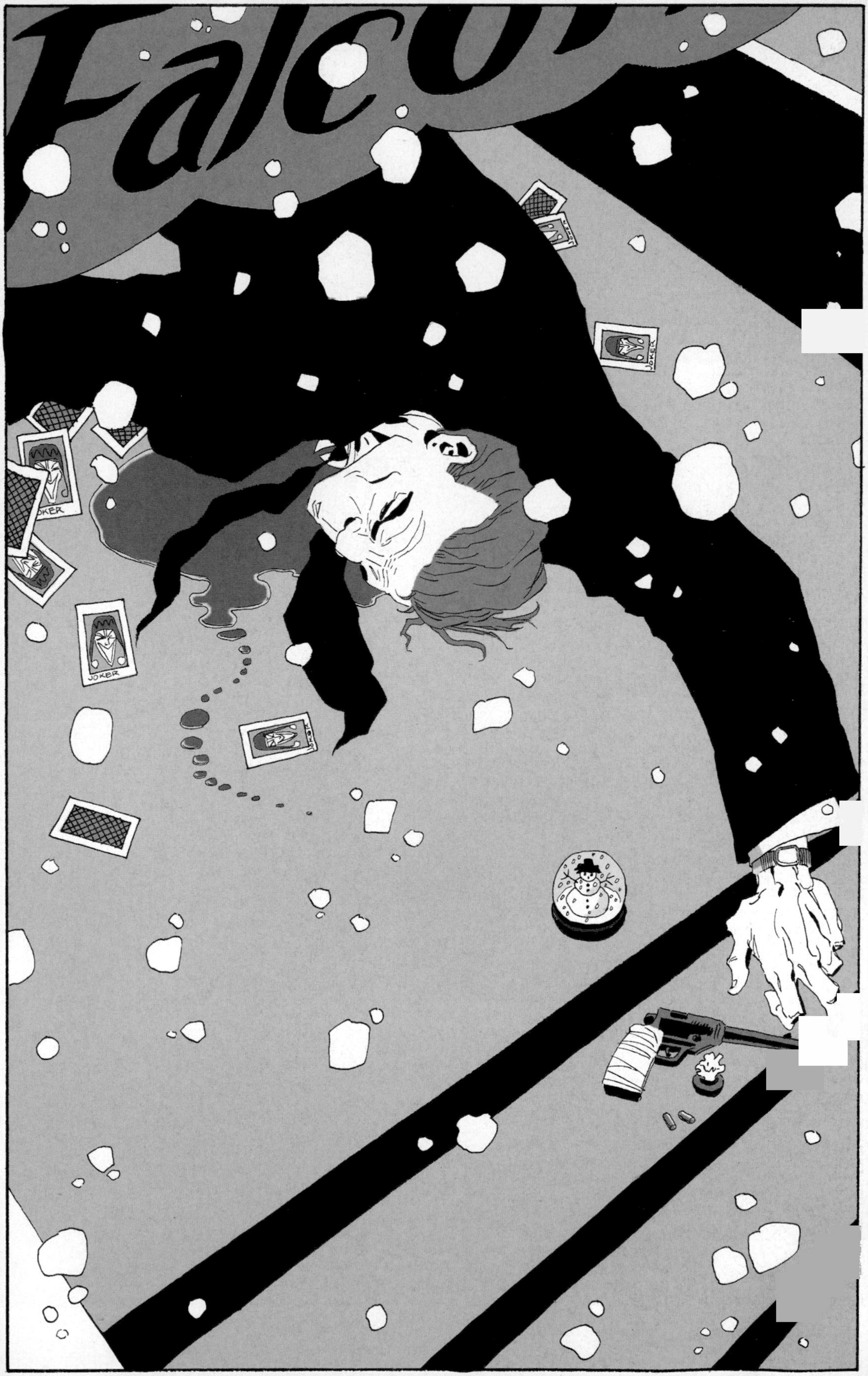
Falco
JOKER

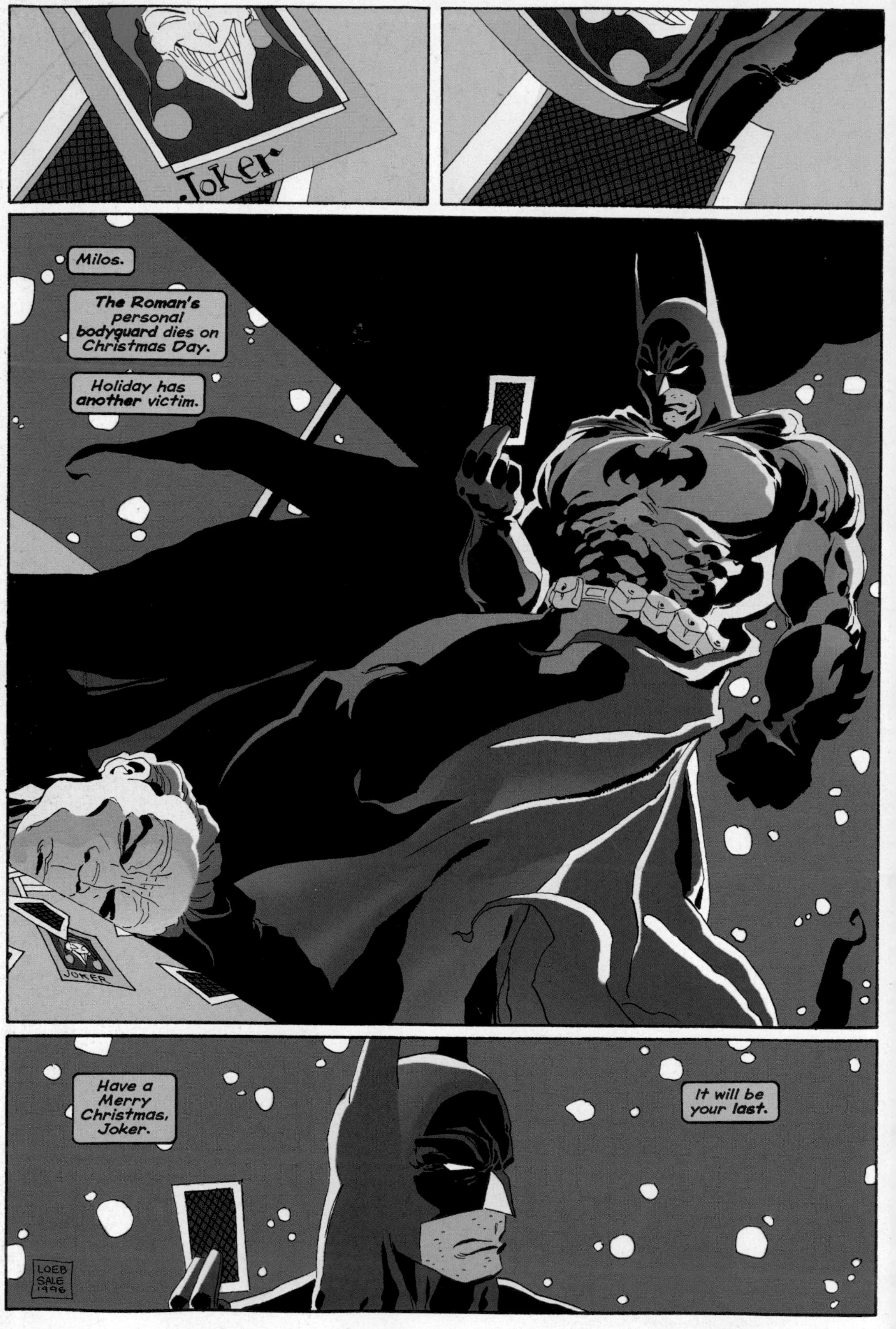
Joker
Milos.
The Roman's personal bodyguard dies on Christmas Day.
Holiday has another victim.
JOKER
Have a Merry Christmas, Joker.
It will be your last.
LOEB SALE 1996

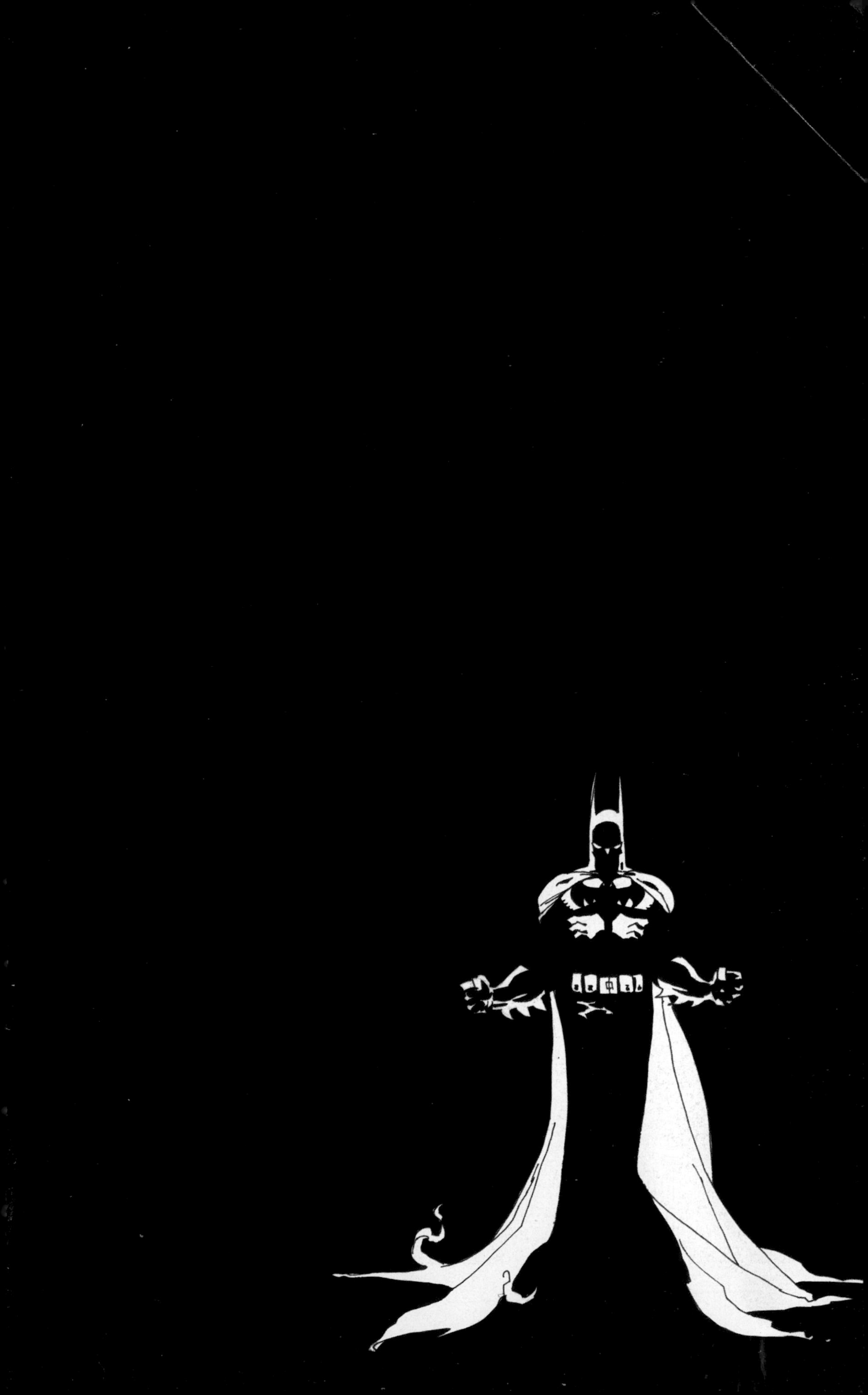

CHAPTER FOUR
NEW YEAR'S EVE

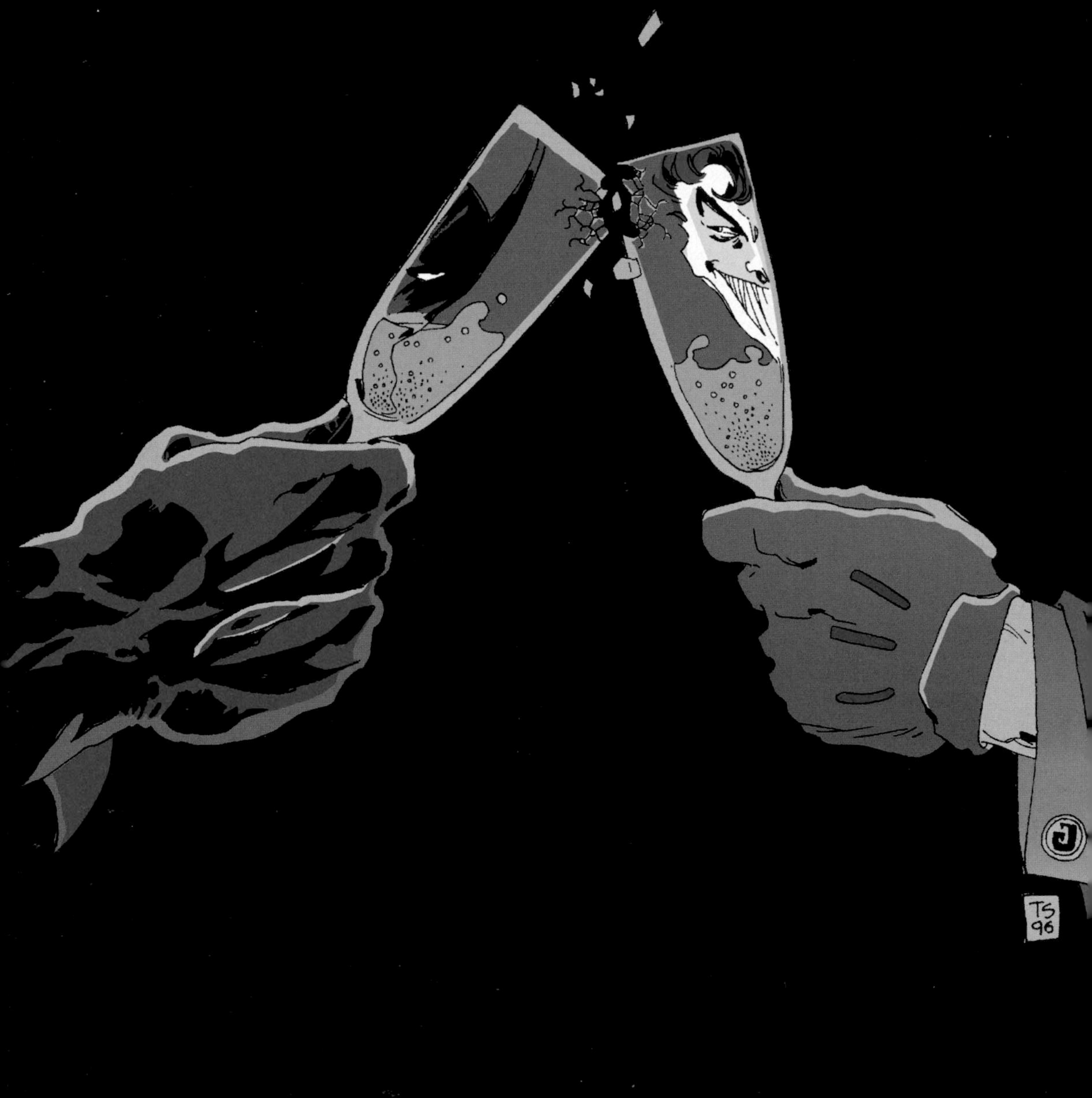
TS
96

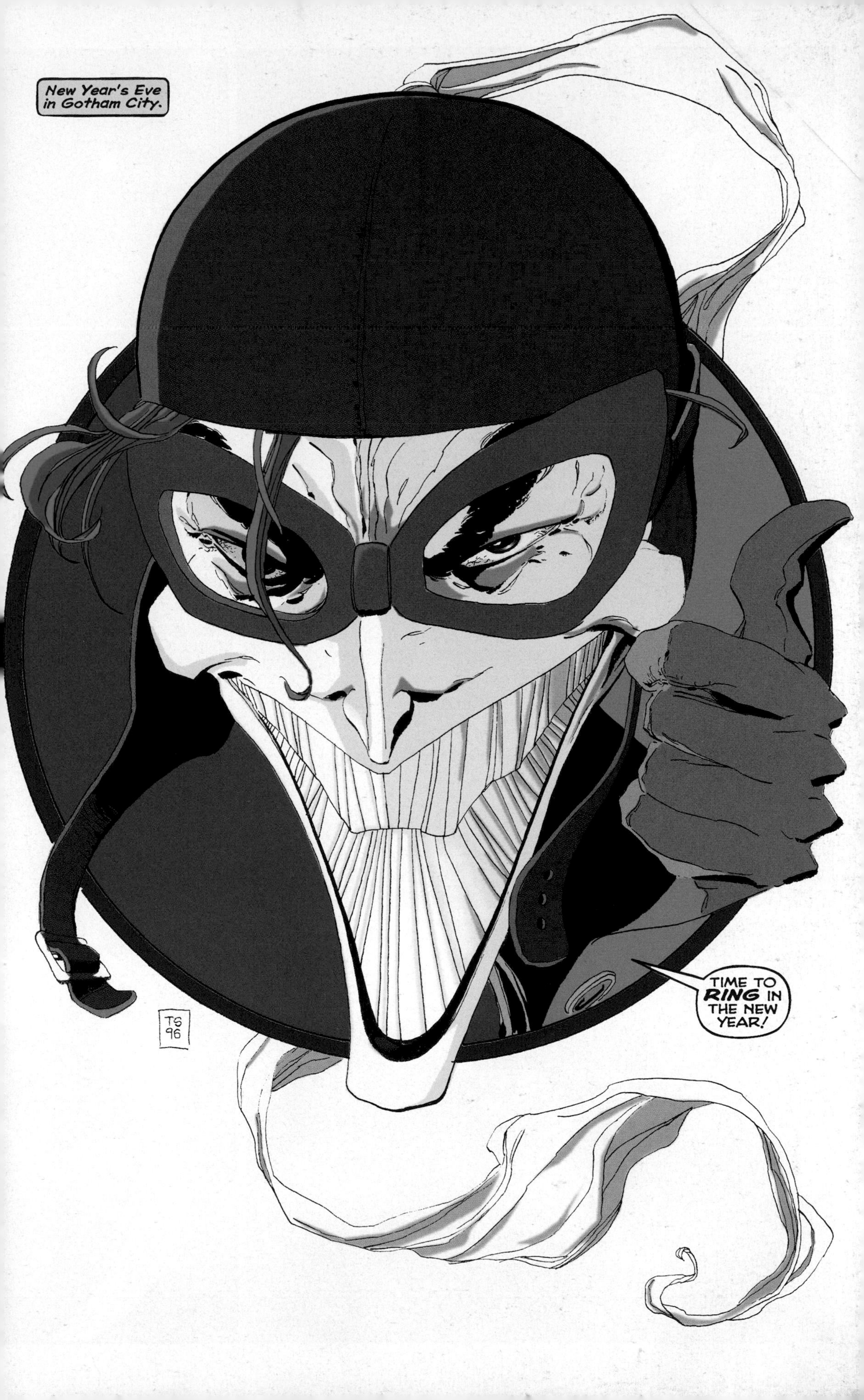
New Year's Eve in Gotham City.
TIME TO RING IN THE NEW YEAR!
TS 96

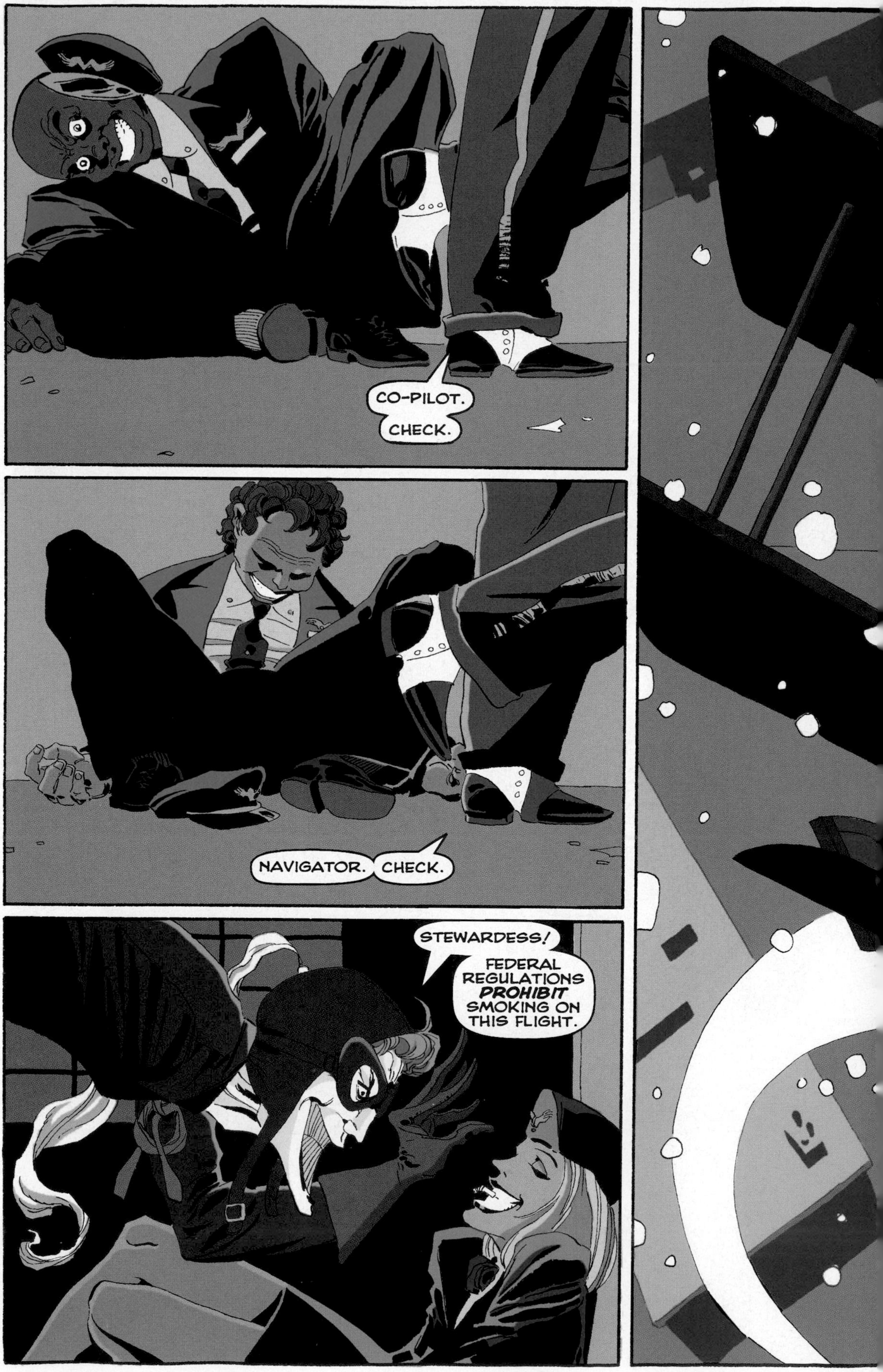
CO-PILOT.
CHECK.
NAVIGATOR.
CHECK.
STEWARDESS!
FEDERAL REGULATIONS PROHIBIT SMOKING ON THIS FLIGHT.

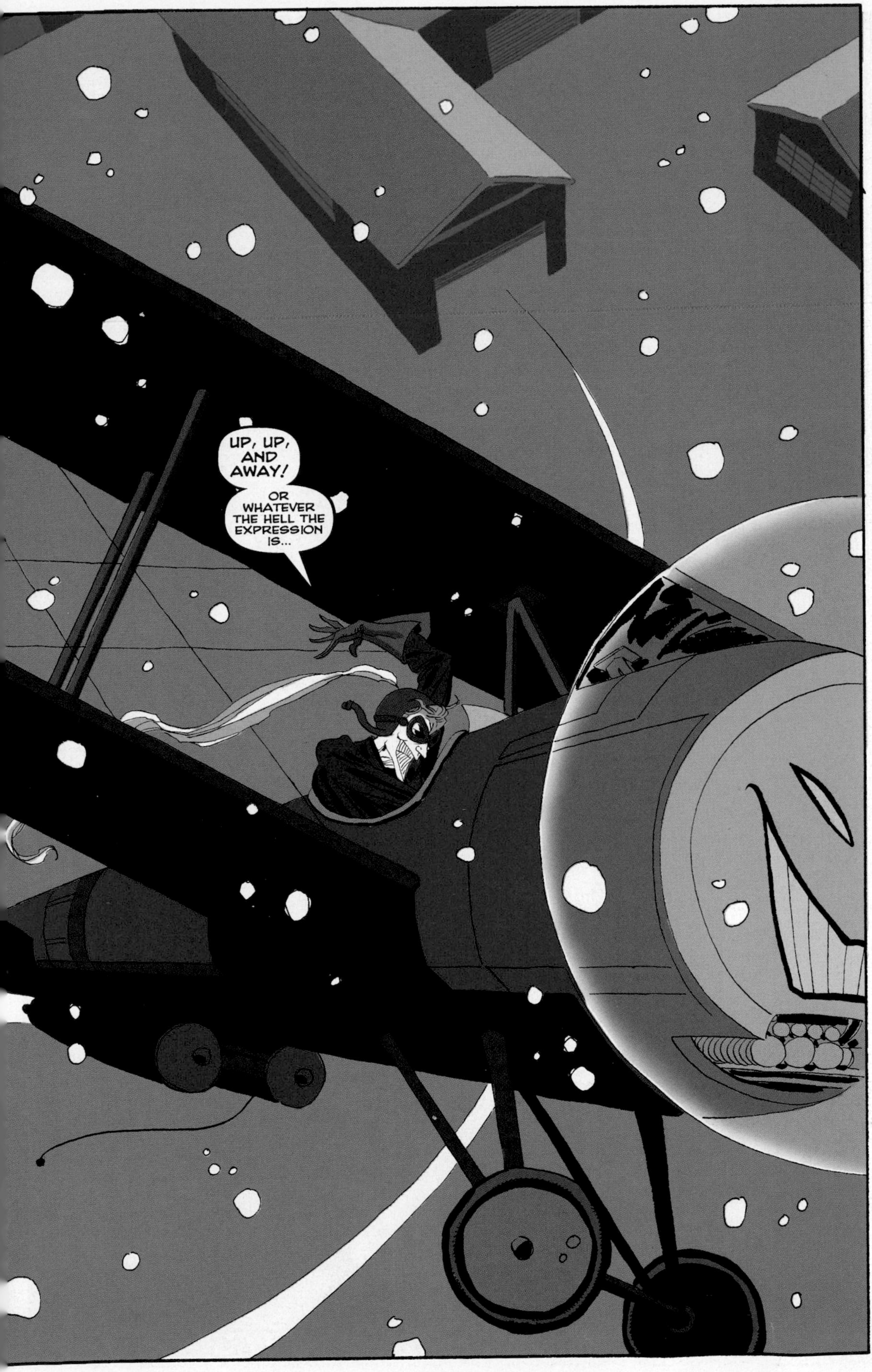
UP, UP, AND AWAY!
OR WHATEVER THE HELL THE EXPRESSION IS...

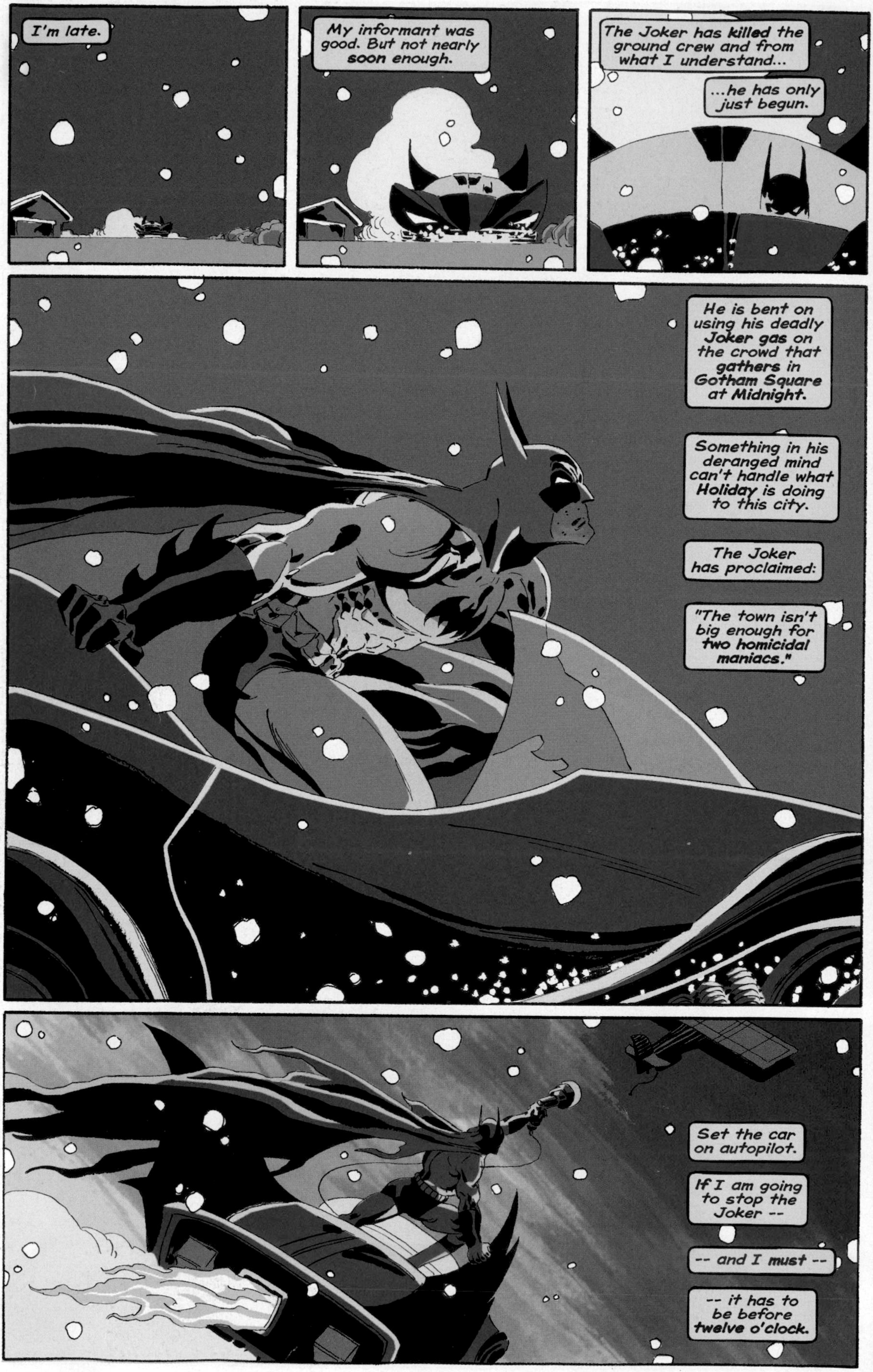
I'm late.
My informant was good. But not nearly soon enough.
The Joker has killed the ground crew and from what I understand...
...he has only just begun.
He is bent on using his deadly Joker gas on the crowd that gathers in Gotham Square at Midnight.
Something in his deranged mind can't handle what Holiday is doing to this city.
The Joker has proclaimed:
"The town isn't big enough for two homicidal maniacs."
Set the car on autopilot.
If I am going to stop the Joker --
-- and I must --
-- it has to be before twelve o'clock.

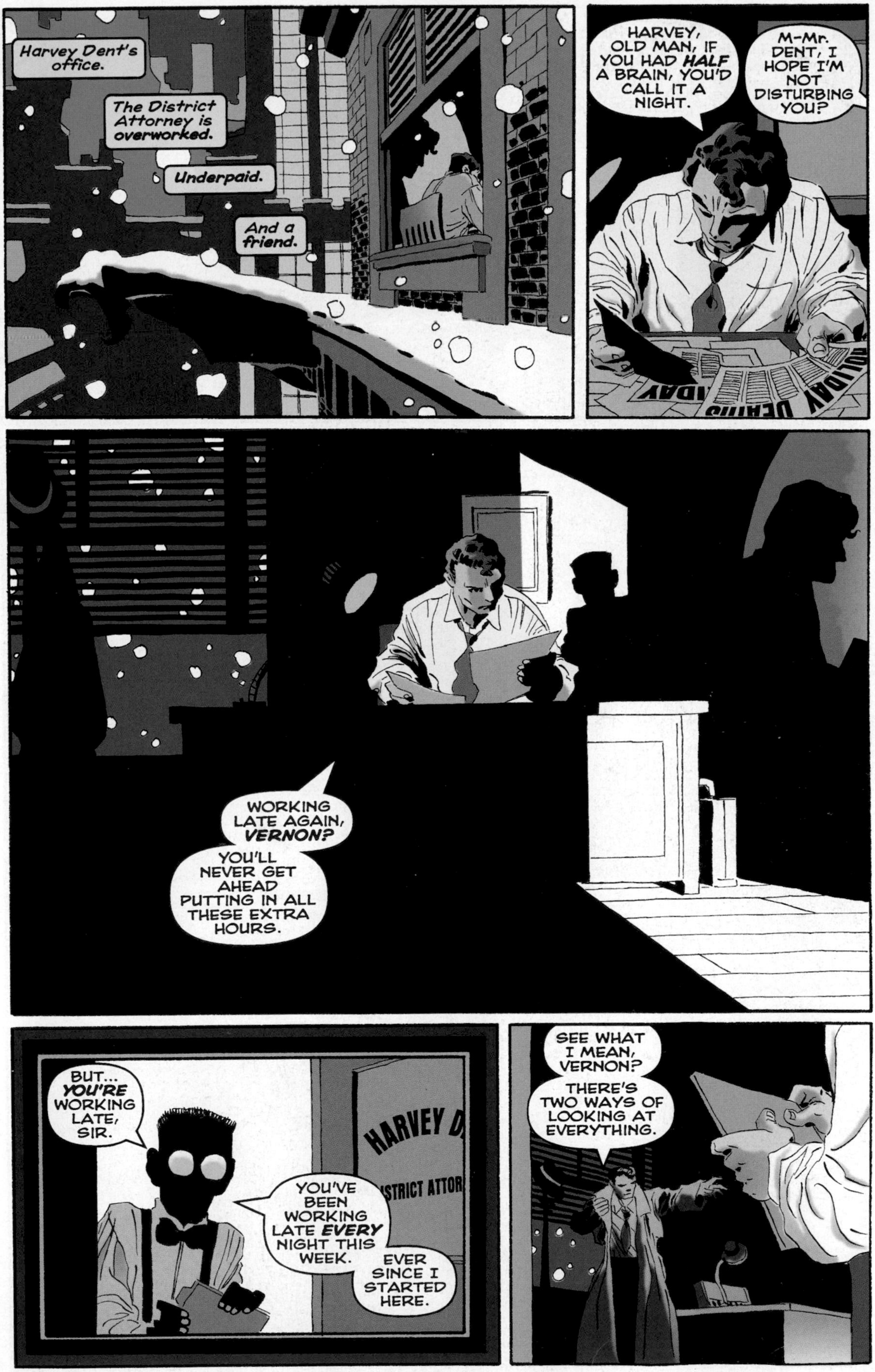
Harvey Dent's office.
The District Attorney is overworked.
Underpaid.
And a friend.
HARVEY, OLD MAN, IF YOU HAD HALF A BRAIN, YOU'D CALL IT A NIGHT.
M-Mr. DENT, I HOPE I'M NOT DISTURBING YOU?
HOLIDAY DEATHS
WORKING LATE AGAIN, VERNON?
YOU'LL NEVER GET AHEAD PUTTING IN ALL THESE EXTRA HOURS.
BUT... YOU'RE WORKING LATE, SIR.
HARVEY D
STRICT ATTOR
YOU'VE BEEN WORKING LATE EVERY NIGHT THIS WEEK.
EVER SINCE I STARTED HERE.
SEE WHAT I MEAN, VERNON?
THERE'S TWO WAYS OF LOOKING AT EVERYTHING.

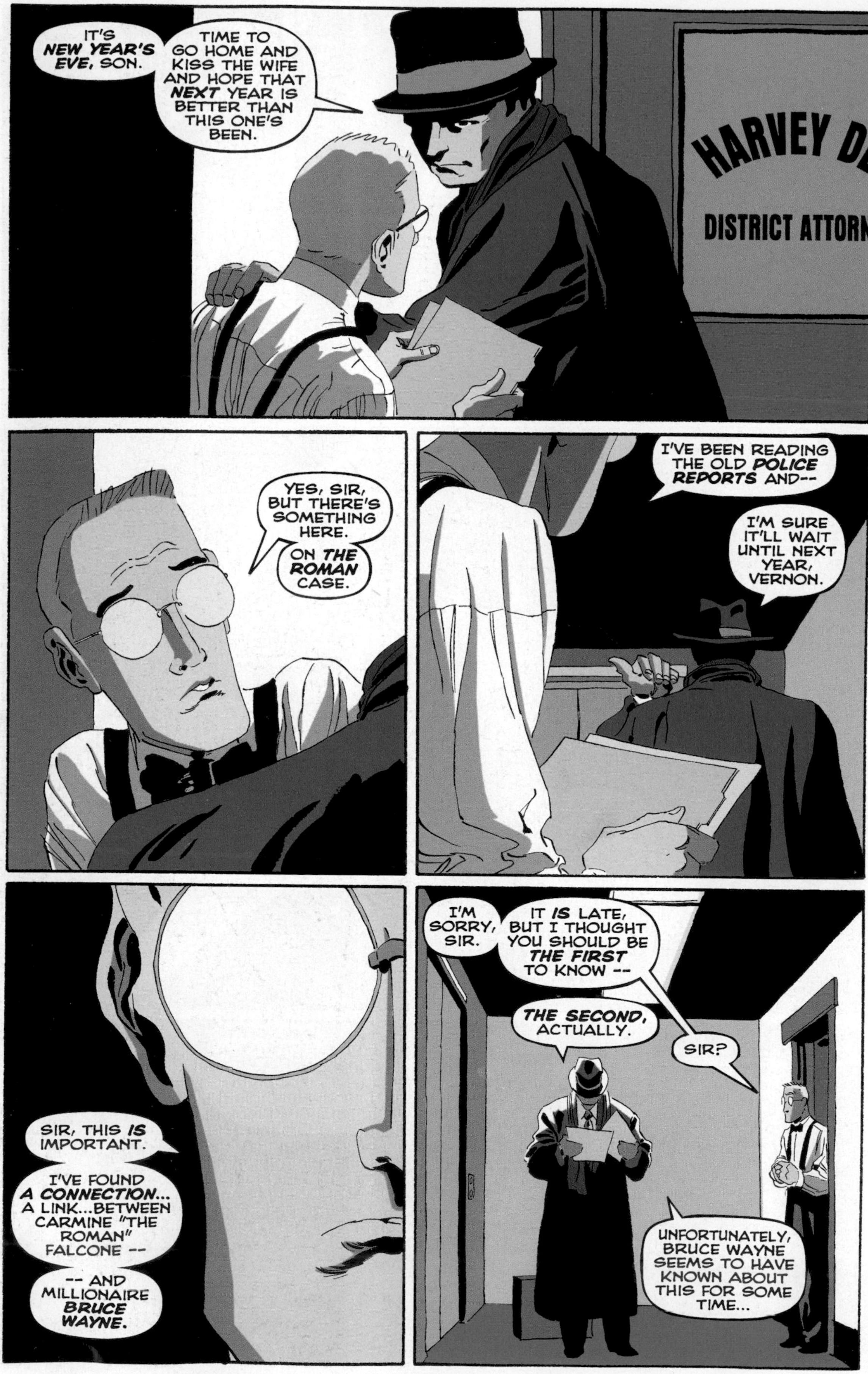

IT'S NEW YEAR'S EVE, SON.
TIME TO GO HOME AND KISS THE WIFE AND HOPE THAT NEXT YEAR IS BETTER THAN THIS ONE'S BEEN.
HARVEY DE
DISTRICT ATTORN
YES, SIR, BUT THERE'S SOMETHING HERE.
ON THE ROMAN CASE.
I'VE BEEN READING THE OLD POLICE REPORTS AND--
I'M SURE IT'LL WAIT UNTIL NEXT YEAR, VERNON.
SIR, THIS IS IMPORTANT.
I'VE FOUND A CONNECTION... A LINK...BETWEEN CARMINE "THE ROMAN" FALCONE --
-- AND MILLIONAIRE BRUCE WAYNE.
I'M SORRY, SIR.
IT IS LATE, BUT I THOUGHT YOU SHOULD BE THE FIRST TO KNOW --
THE SECOND, ACTUALLY.
SIR?
UNFORTUNATELY, BRUCE WAYNE SEEMS TO HAVE KNOWN ABOUT THIS FOR SOME TIME...

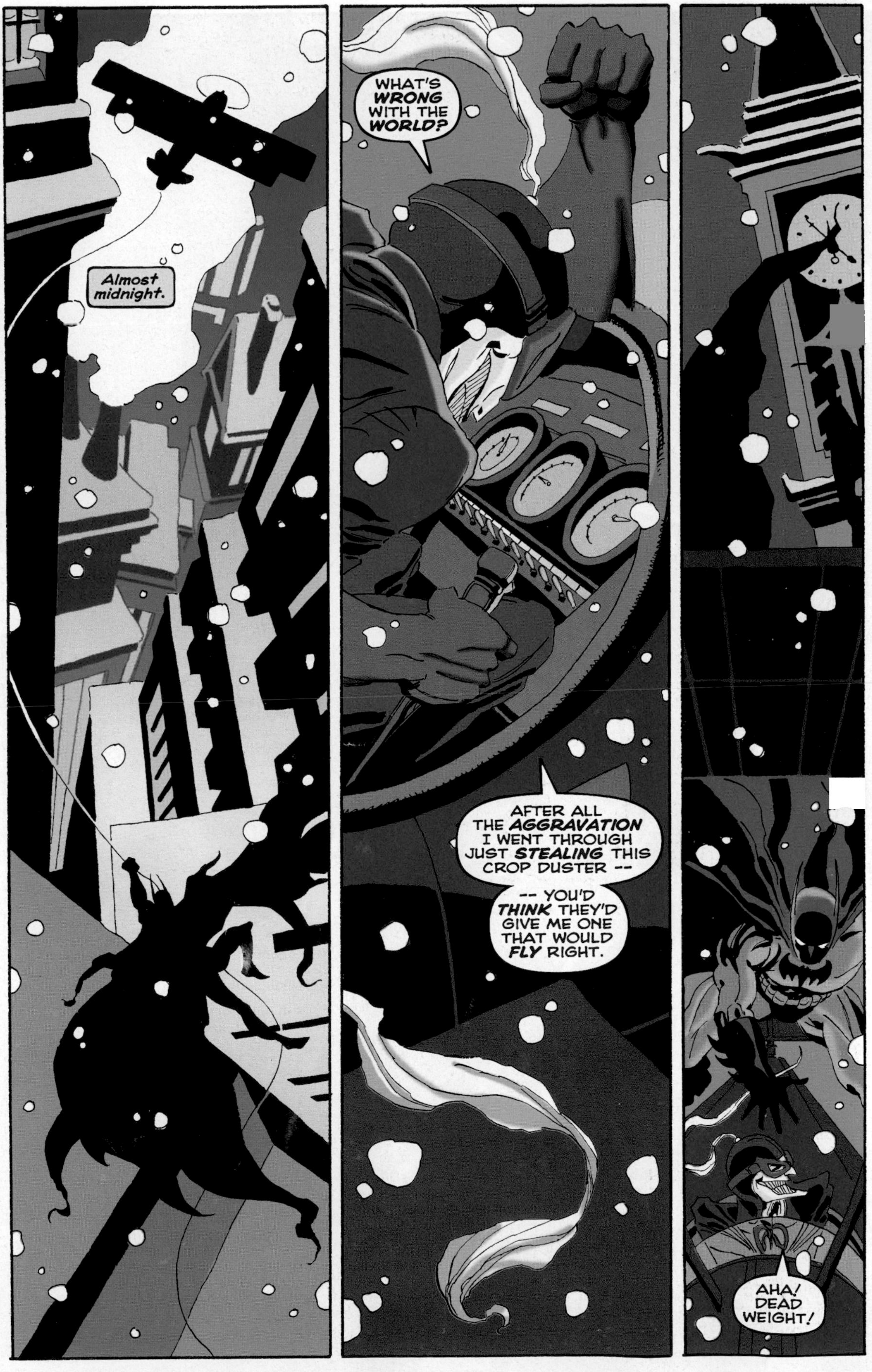
Almost midnight.
WHAT'S WRONG WITH THE WORLD?
AFTER ALL THE AGGRAVATION I WENT THROUGH JUST STEALING THIS CROP DUSTER --
-- YOU'D THINK THEY'D GIVE ME ONE THAT WOULD FLY RIGHT.
AHA! DEAD WEIGHT!

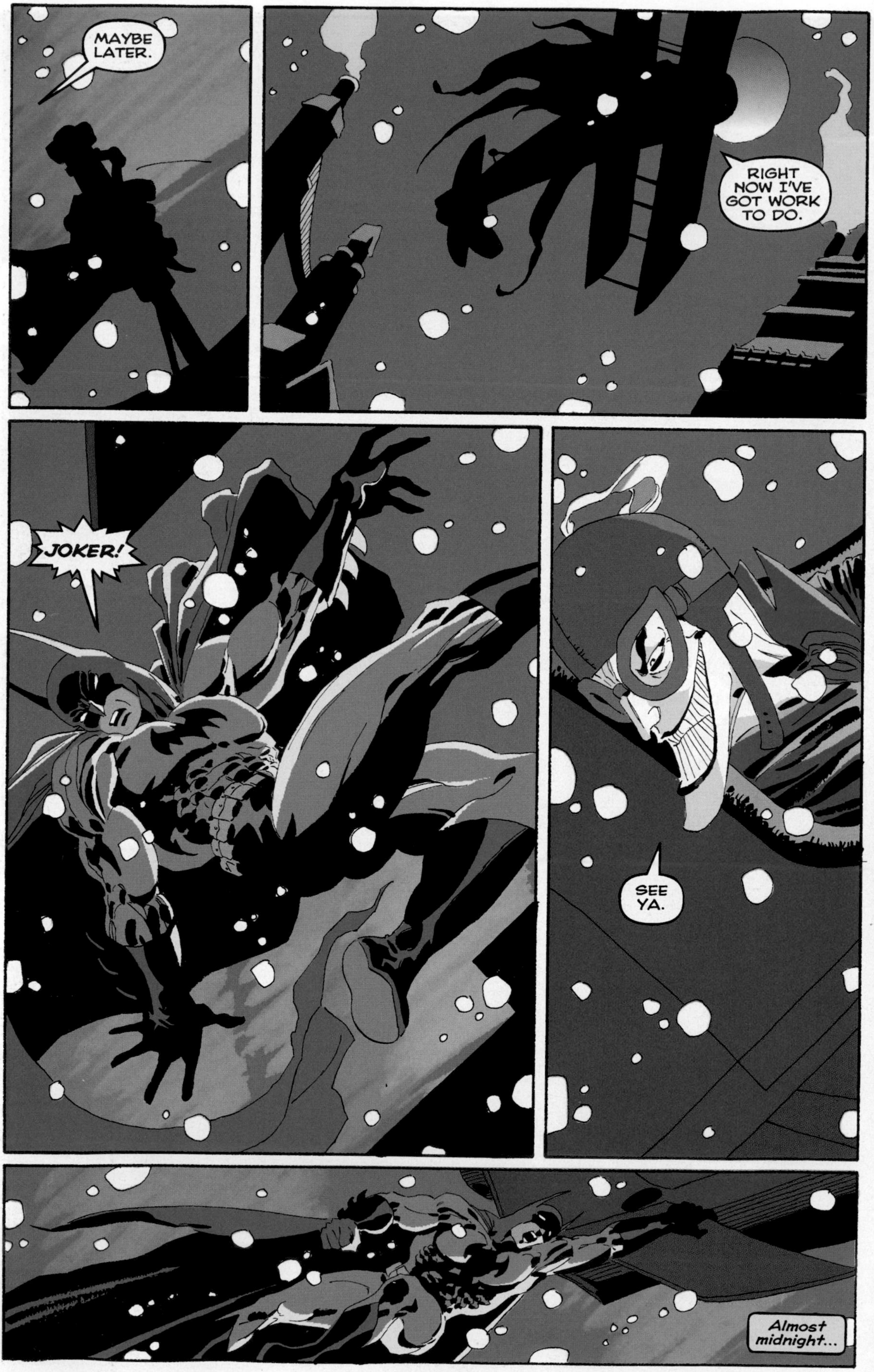
MAYBE LATER.
RIGHT NOW I'VE GOT WORK TO DO.
JOKER!
SEE YA.
Almost midnight...

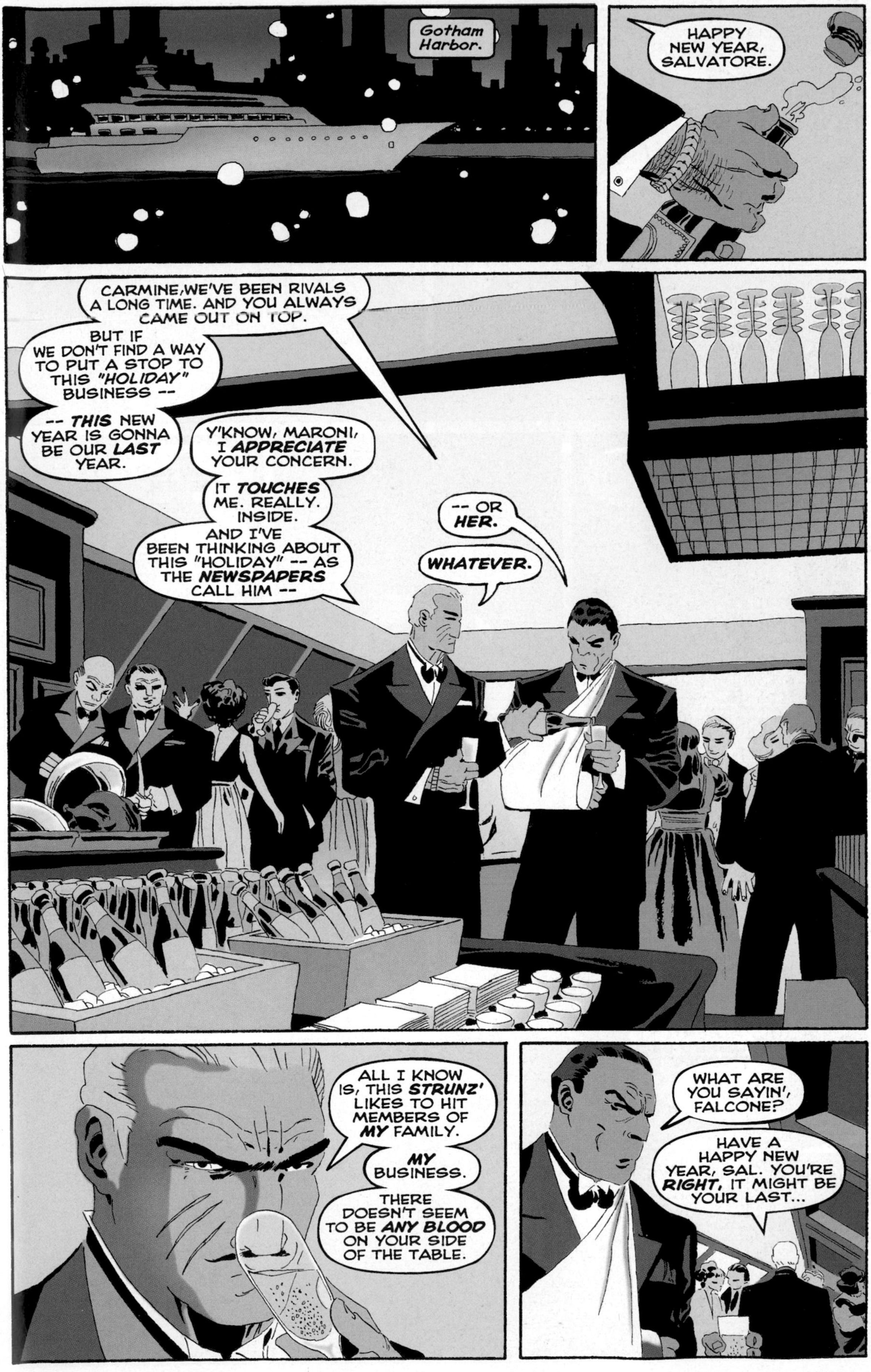
Gotham Harbor.
HAPPY NEW YEAR, SALVATORE.
CARMINE, WE'VE BEEN RIVALS A LONG TIME. AND YOU ALWAYS CAME OUT ON TOP.
BUT IF WE DON'T FIND A WAY TO PUT A STOP TO THIS "HOLIDAY" BUSINESS --
-- THIS NEW YEAR IS GONNA BE OUR LAST YEAR.
Y'KNOW, MARONI, I APPRECIATE YOUR CONCERN.
IT TOUCHES ME. REALLY. INSIDE.
AND I'VE BEEN THINKING ABOUT THIS "HOLIDAY" -- AS THE NEWSPAPERS CALL HIM --
-- OR HER.
WHATEVER.
ALL I KNOW IS, THIS STRUNZ' LIKES TO HIT MEMBERS OF MY FAMILY.
MY BUSINESS.
THERE DOESN'T SEEM TO BE ANY BLOOD ON YOUR SIDE OF THE TABLE.
WHAT ARE YOU SAYIN', FALCONE?
HAVE A HAPPY NEW YEAR, SAL. YOU'RE RIGHT, IT MIGHT BE YOUR LAST...

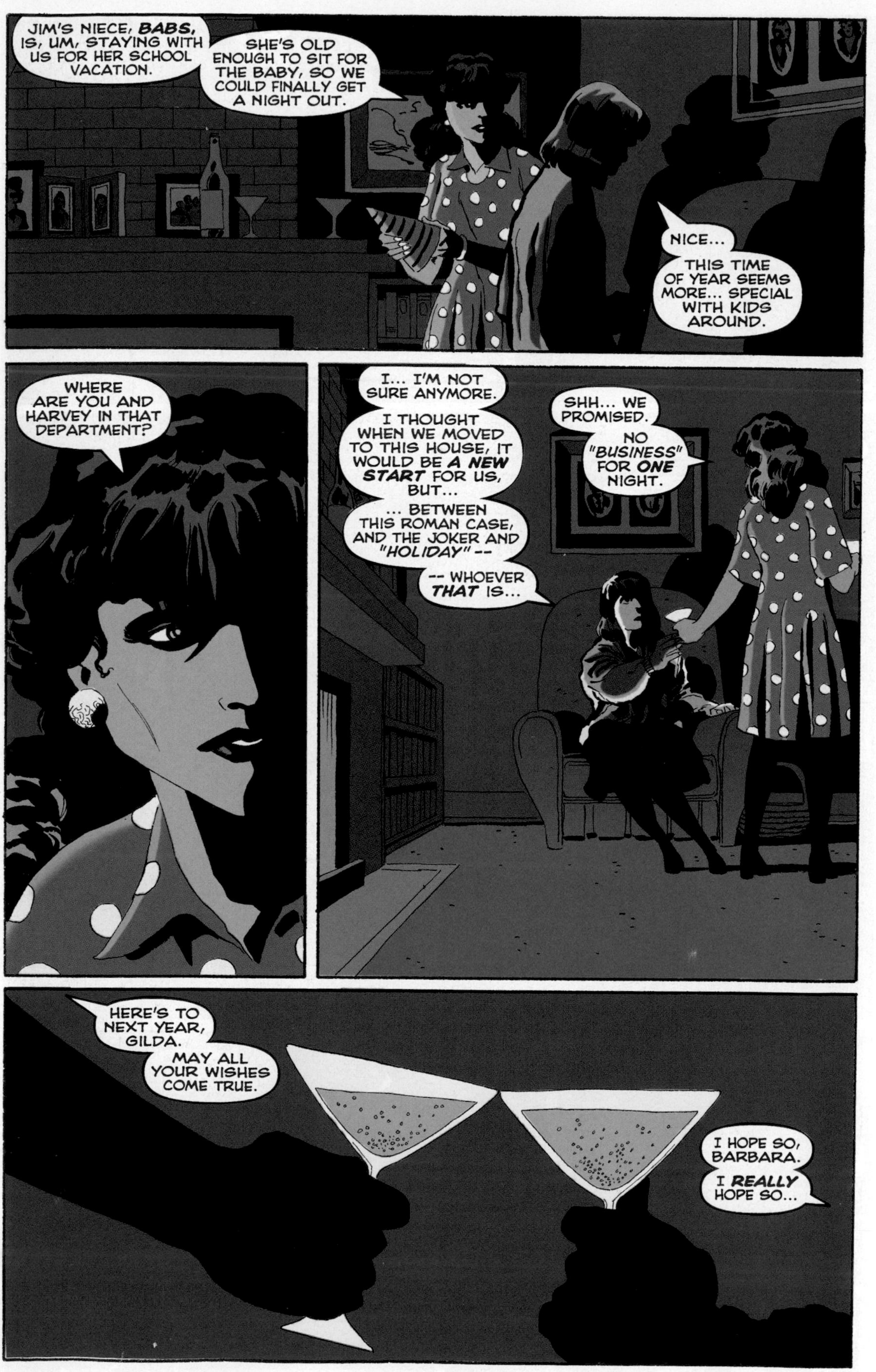

JIM'S NIECE, BABS, IS, UM, STAYING WITH US FOR HER SCHOOL VACATION.
SHE'S OLD ENOUGH TO SIT FOR THE BABY, SO WE COULD FINALLY GET A NIGHT OUT.
NICE...
THIS TIME OF YEAR SEEMS MORE... SPECIAL WITH KIDS AROUND.
WHERE ARE YOU AND HARVEY IN THAT DEPARTMENT?
I... I'M NOT SURE ANYMORE.
I THOUGHT WHEN WE MOVED TO THIS HOUSE, IT WOULD BE A NEW START FOR US, BUT...
... BETWEEN THIS ROMAN CASE, AND THE JOKER AND "HOLIDAY" --
-- WHOEVER THAT IS...
SHH... WE PROMISED.
NO "BUSINESS" FOR ONE NIGHT.
HERE'S TO NEXT YEAR, GILDA.
MAY ALL YOUR WISHES COME TRUE.
I HOPE SO, BARBARA.
I REALLY HOPE SO...

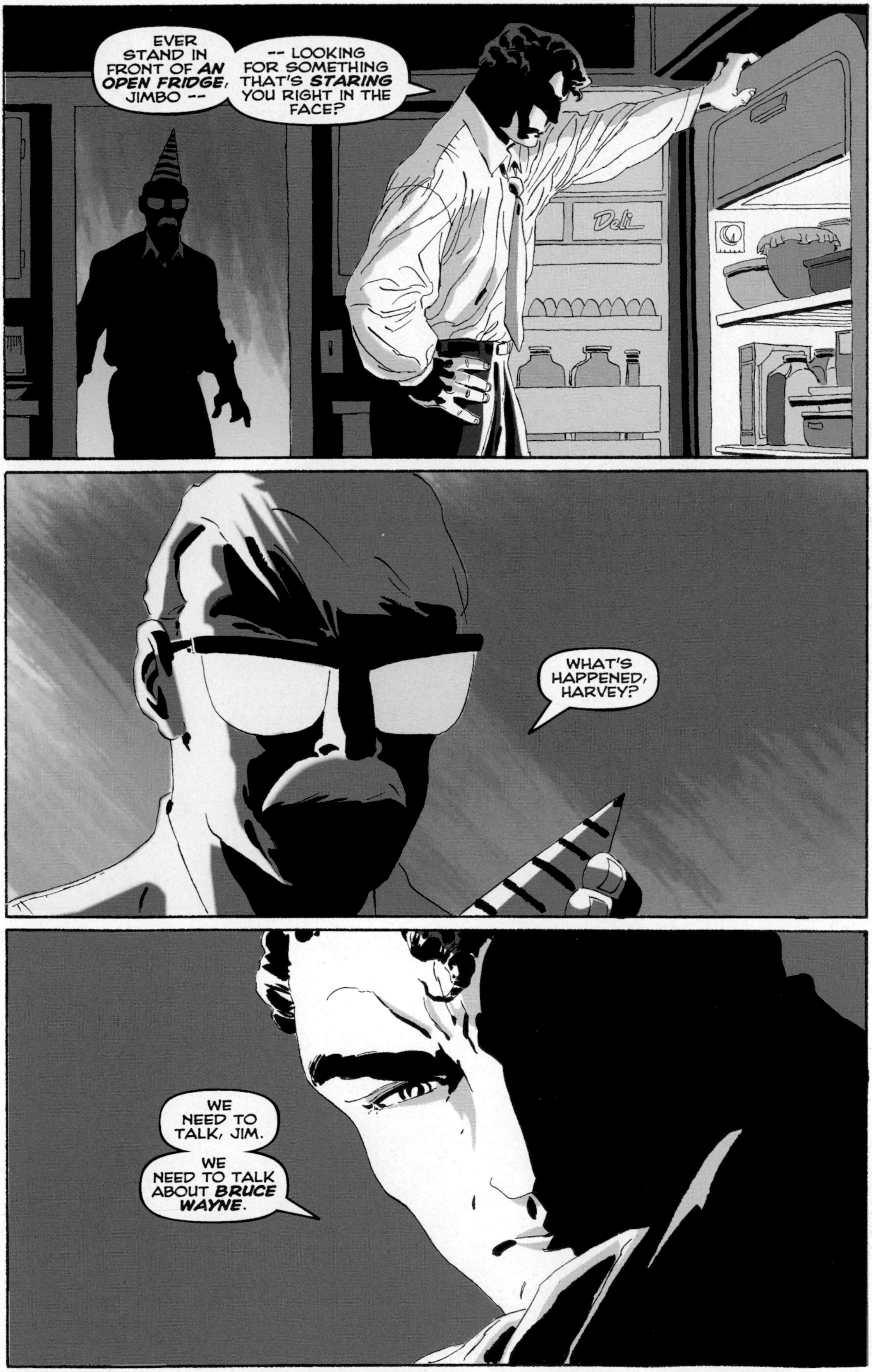
EVER STAND IN FRONT OF AN OPEN FRIDGE, JIMBO --
-- LOOKING FOR SOMETHING THAT'S STARING YOU RIGHT IN THE FACE?
WHAT'S HAPPENED, HARVEY?
WE NEED TO TALK, JIM.
WE NEED TO TALK ABOUT BRUCE WAYNE.

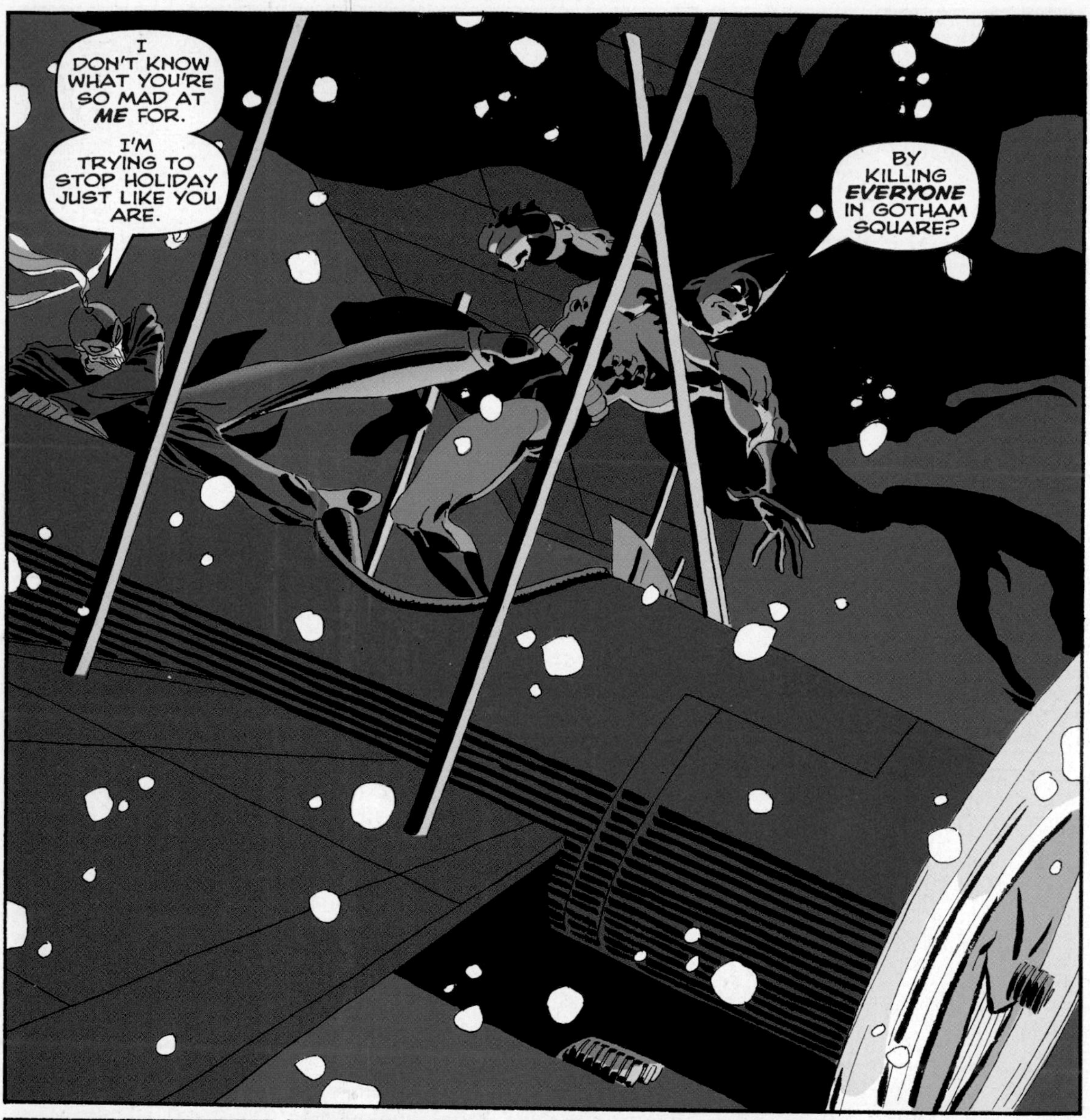
I DON'T KNOW WHAT YOU'RE SO MAD AT *ME* FOR.
I'M TRYING TO STOP HOLIDAY JUST LIKE YOU ARE.
BY KILLING *EVERYONE* IN GOTHAM SQUARE?

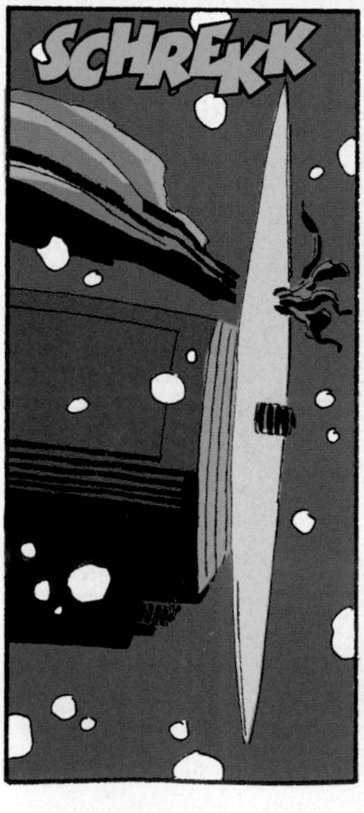
SCHREKK

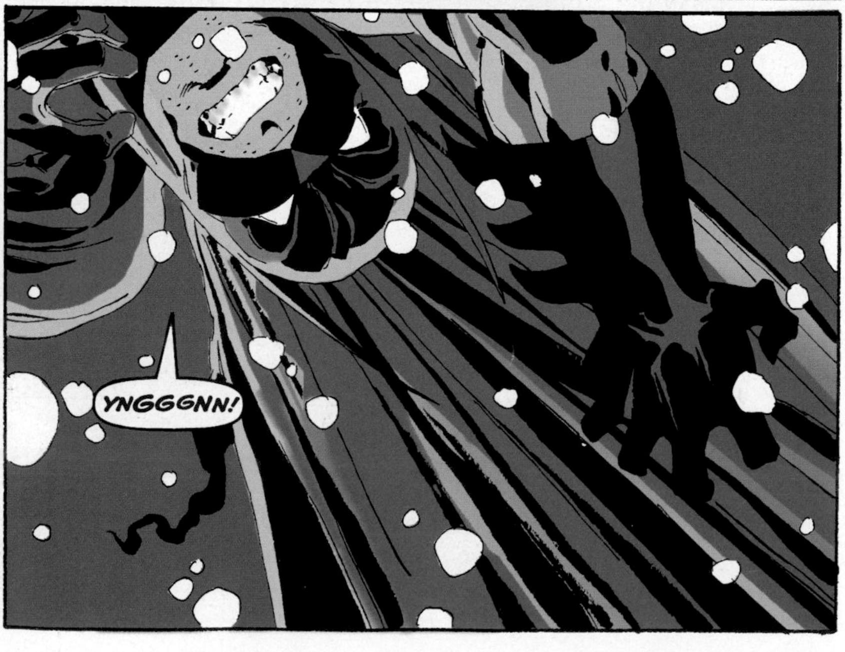
YNGGGNN!

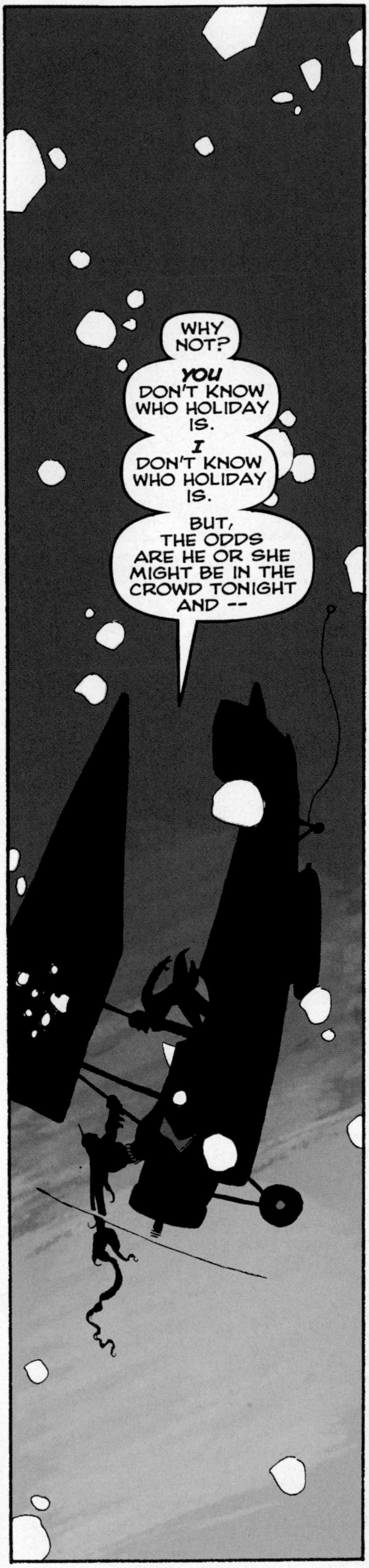
WHY NOT?
YOU DON'T KNOW WHO HOLIDAY IS.
I DON'T KNOW WHO HOLIDAY IS.
BUT, THE ODDS ARE HE OR SHE MIGHT BE IN THE CROWD TONIGHT AND --

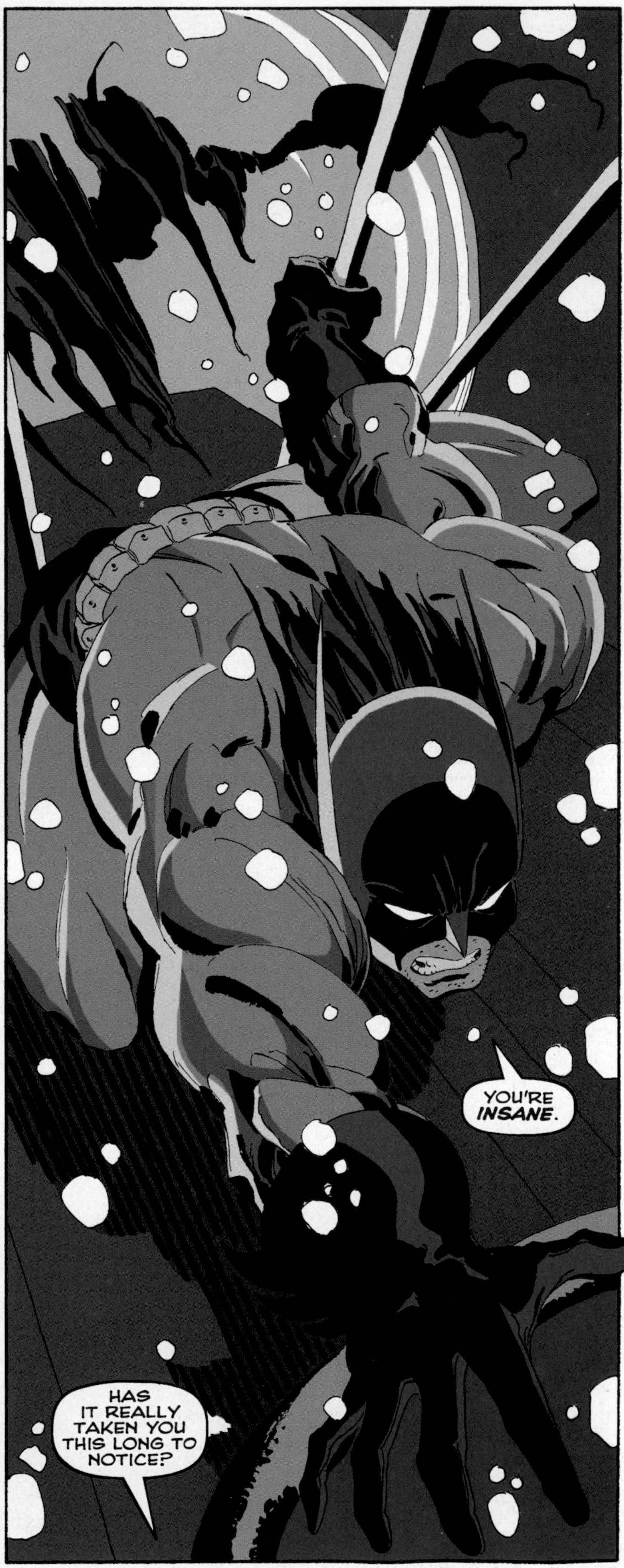
YOU'RE INSANE.
HAS IT REALLY TAKEN YOU THIS LONG TO NOTICE?

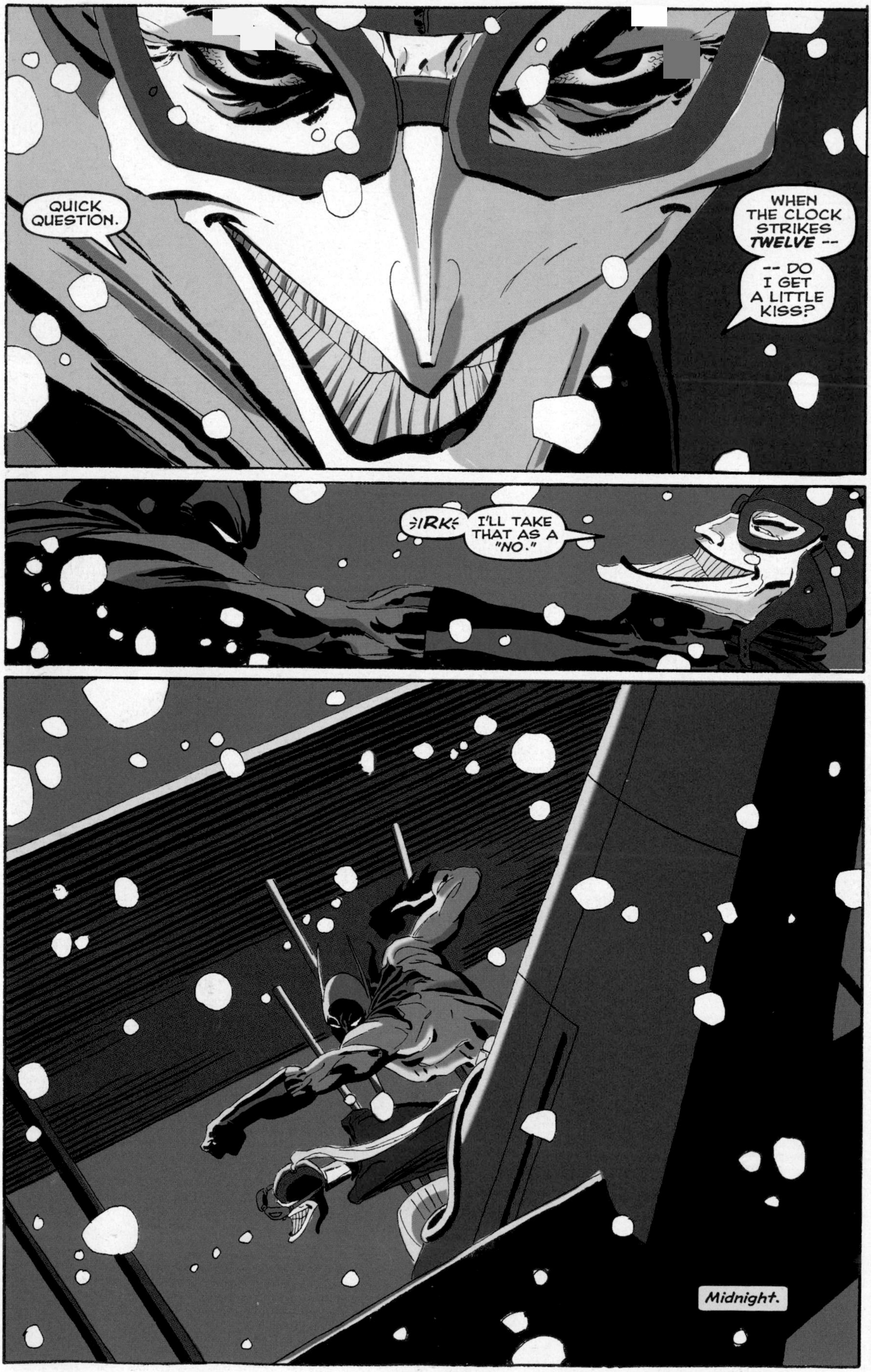
QUICK QUESTION.
WHEN THE CLOCK STRIKES *TWELVE* --
-- DO I GET A LITTLE KISS?
IRK
I'LL TAKE THAT AS A "*NO*."
Midnight.

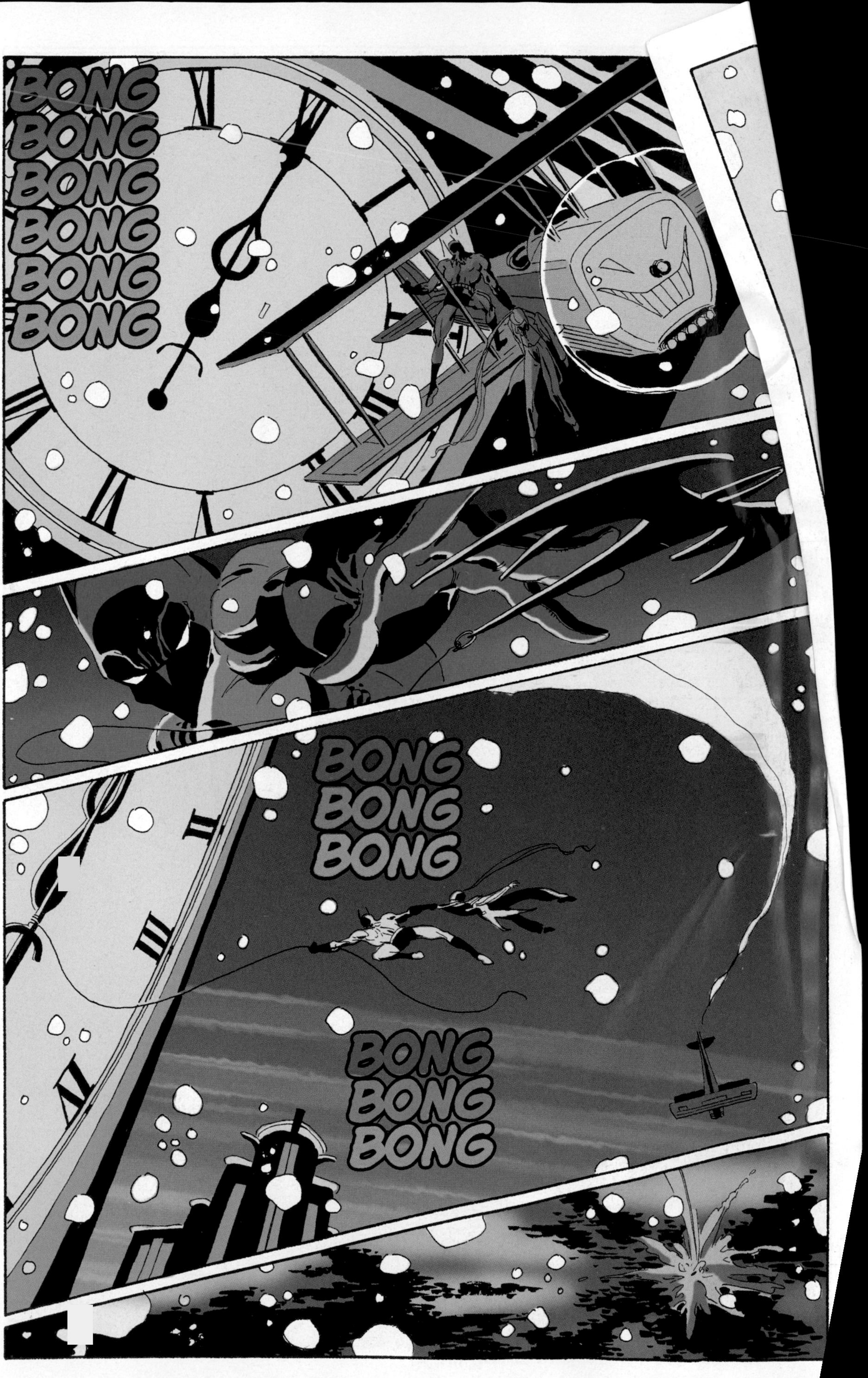
BONG
BONG
BONG
BONG
BONG
BONG
BONG
BONG
BONG
BONG
BONG
BONG

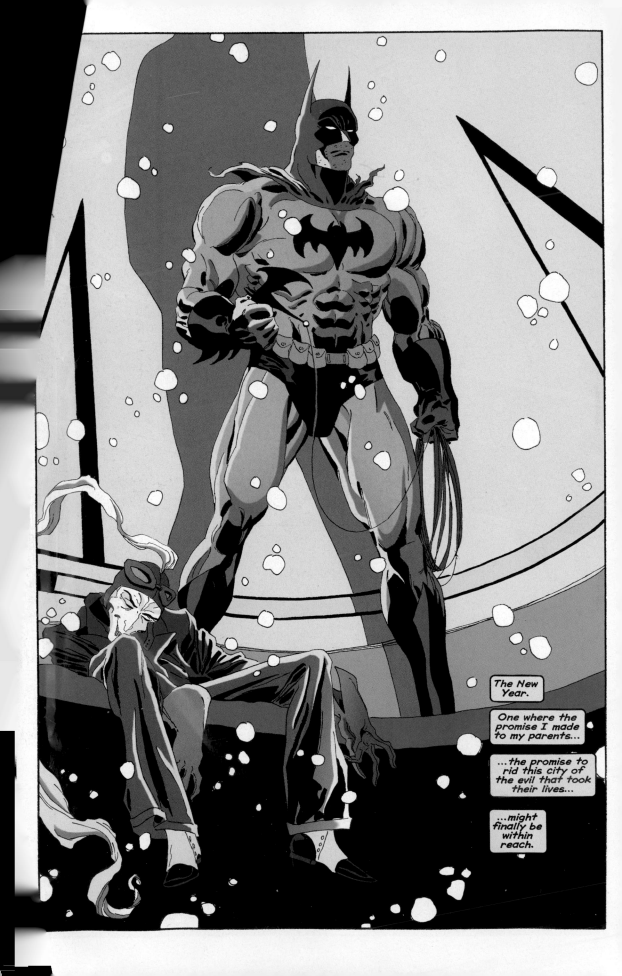

The New Year.

One where the promise I made to my parents...

...the promise to rid this city of the evil that took their lives...

...might finally be within reach.

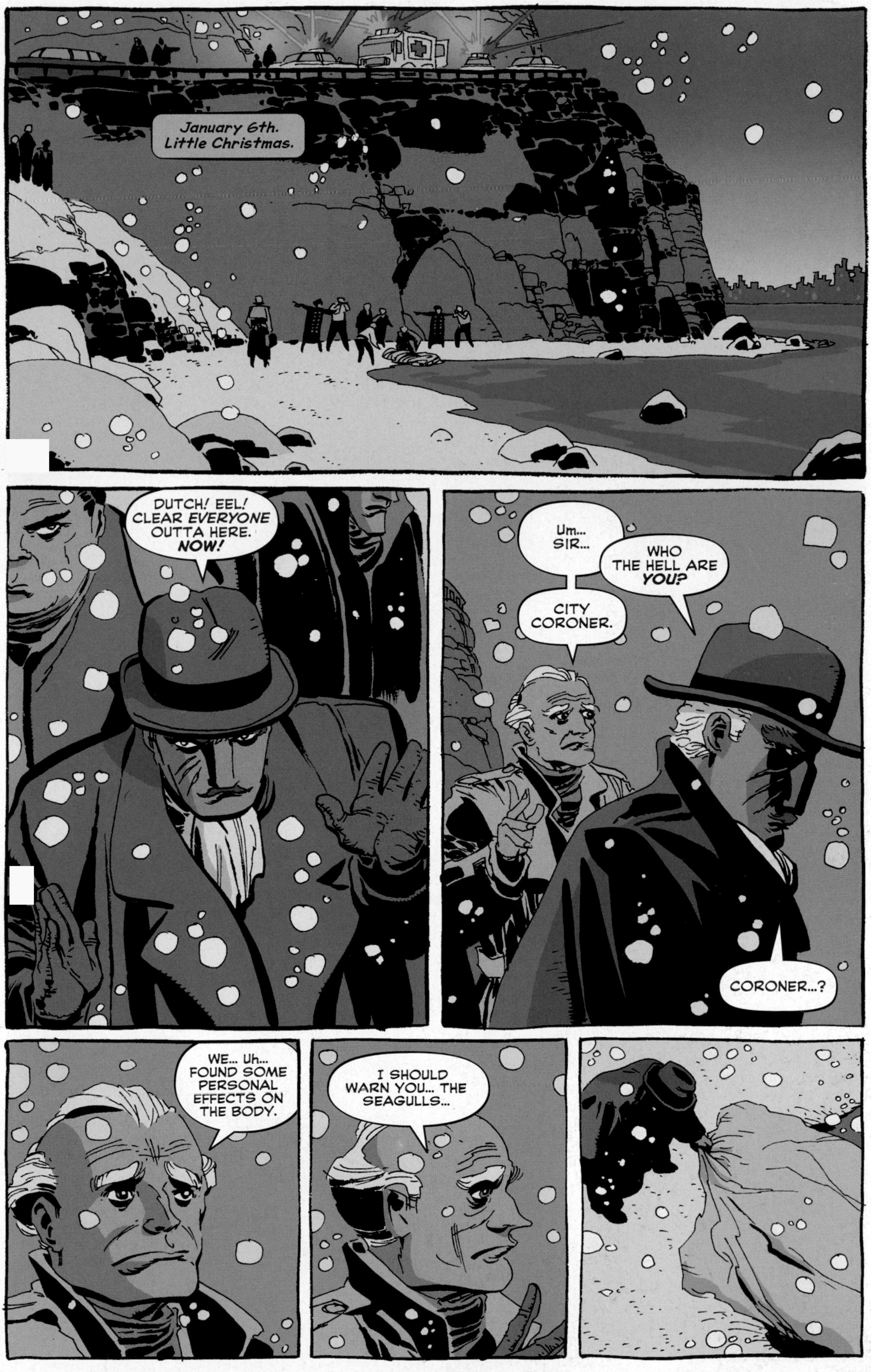
January 6th. Little Christmas.
DUTCH! EEL! CLEAR EVERYONE OUTTA HERE. NOW!
Um... SIR...
CITY CORONER.
WHO THE HELL ARE YOU?
CORONER...?
WE... Uh... FOUND SOME PERSONAL EFFECTS ON THE BODY.
I SHOULD WARN YOU... THE SEAGULLS...

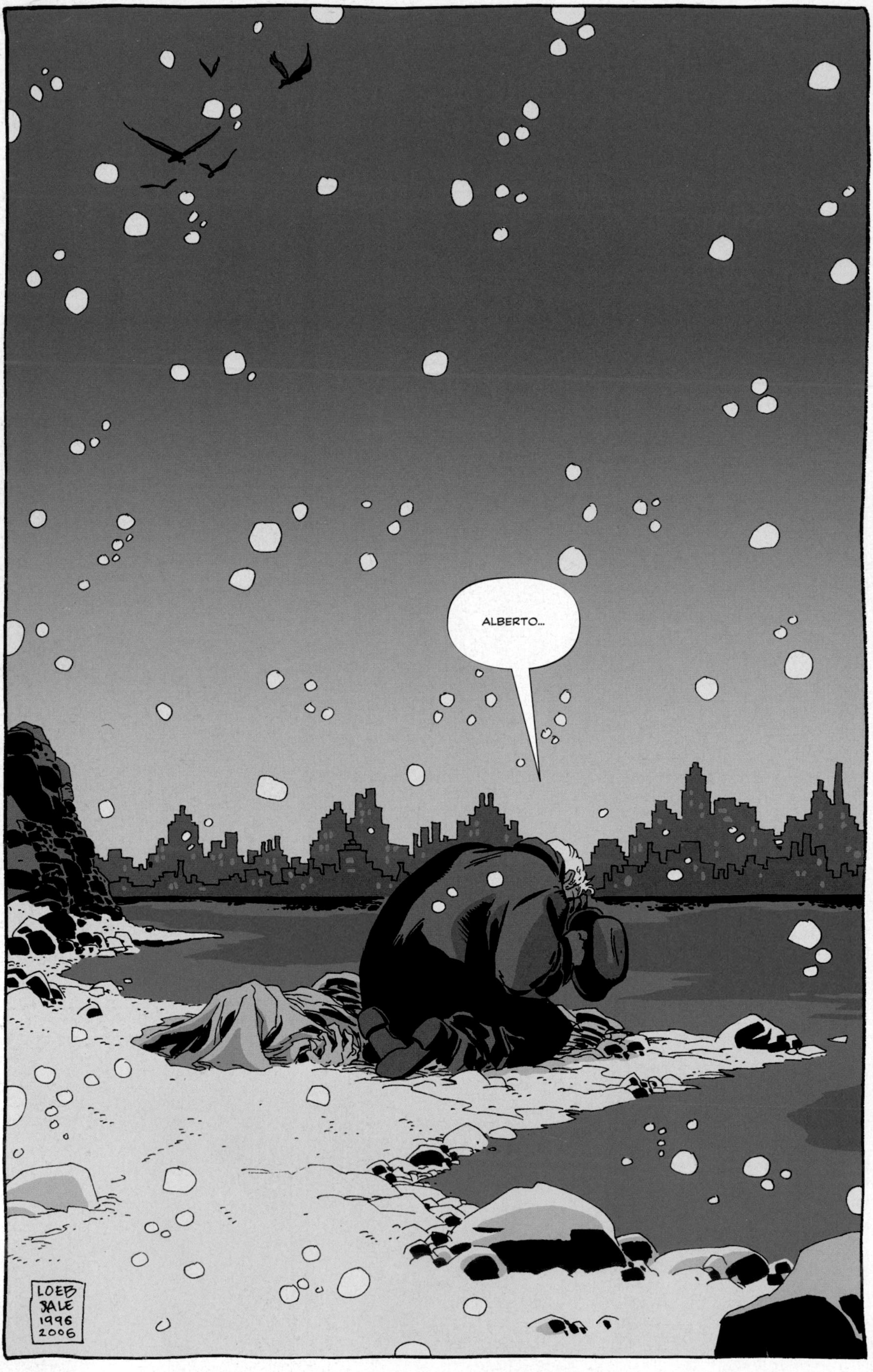
ALBERTO...
LOEB
SALE
1996
2006

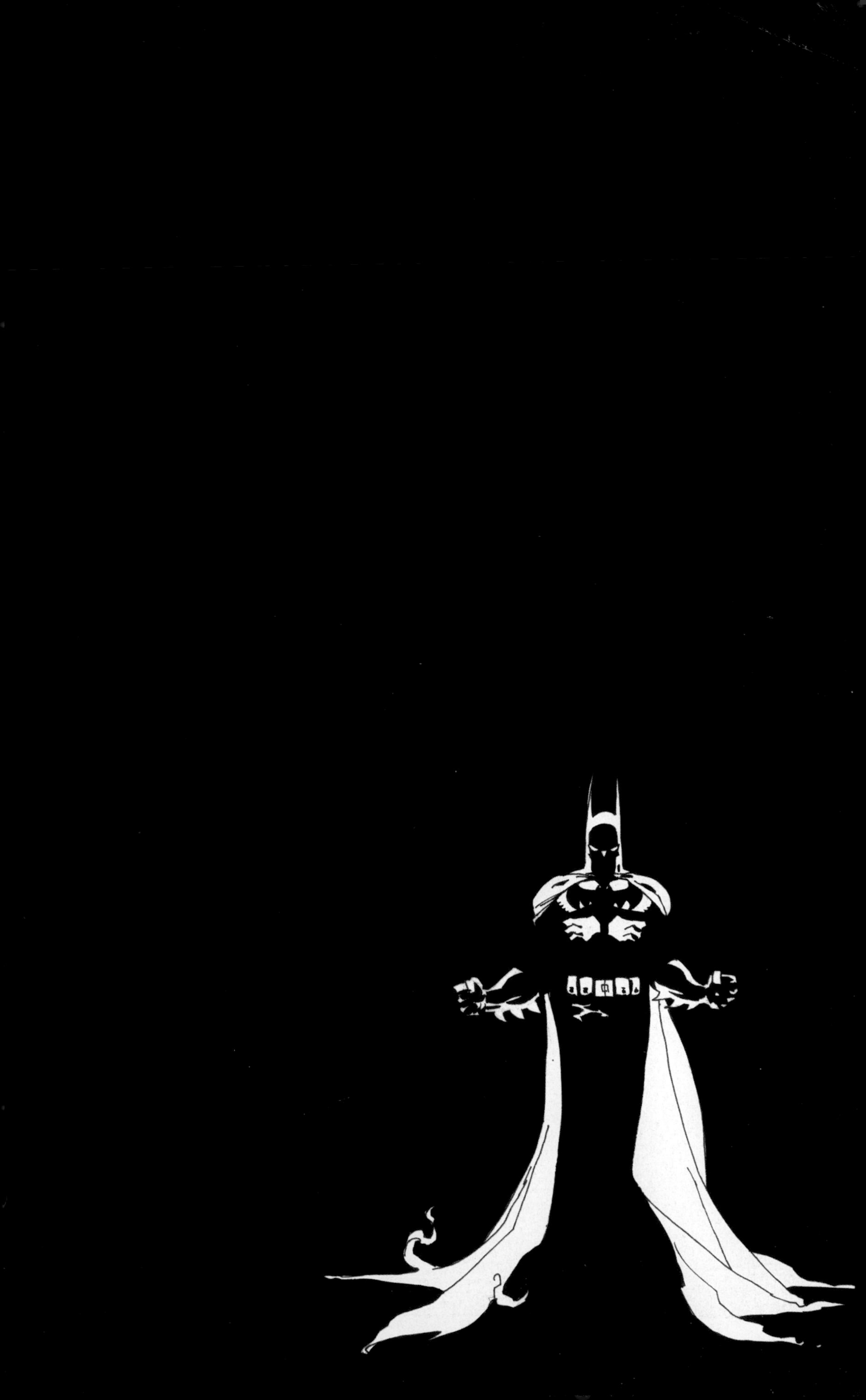

CHAPTER FIVE

VALENTINE'S DAY

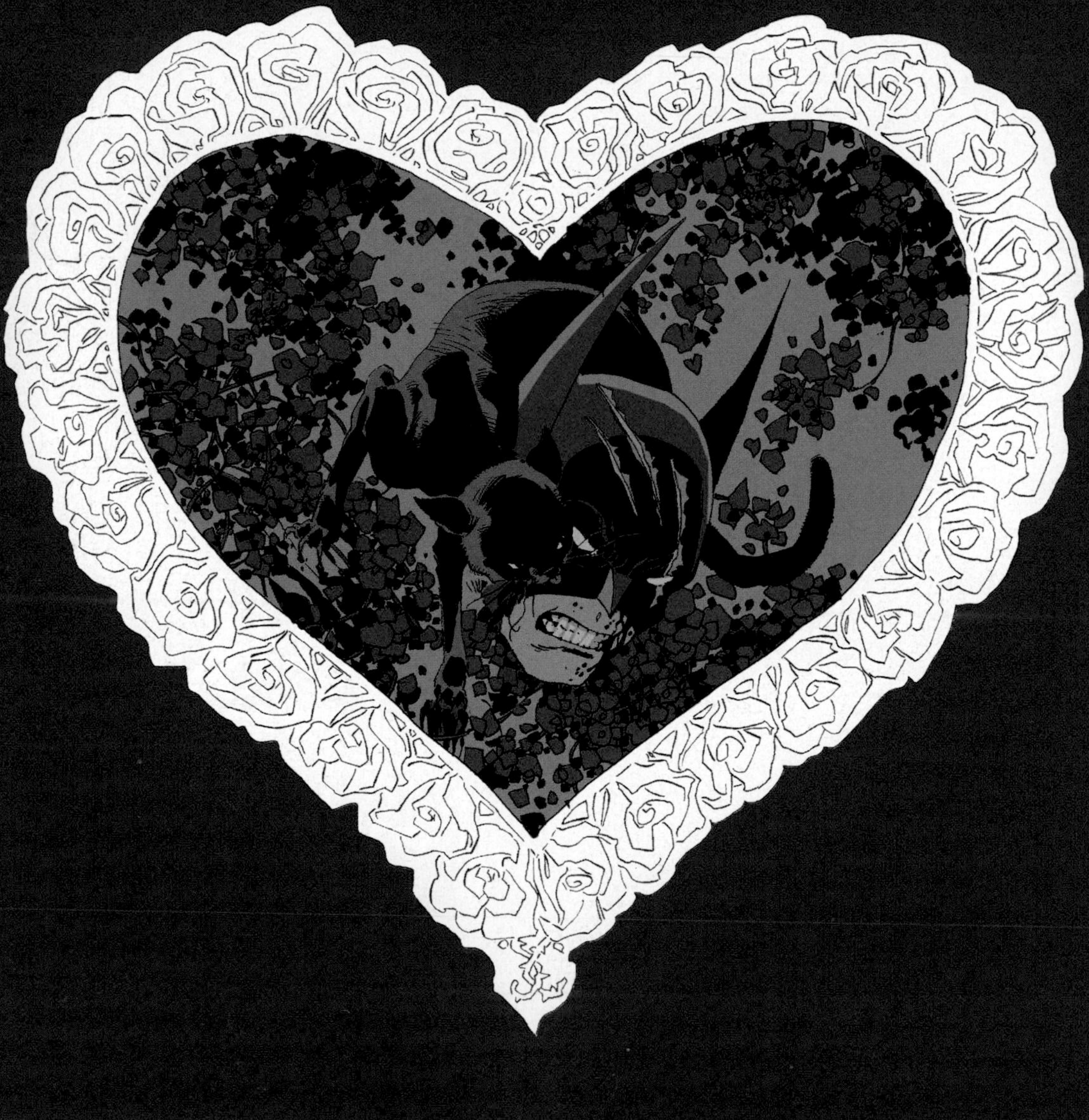

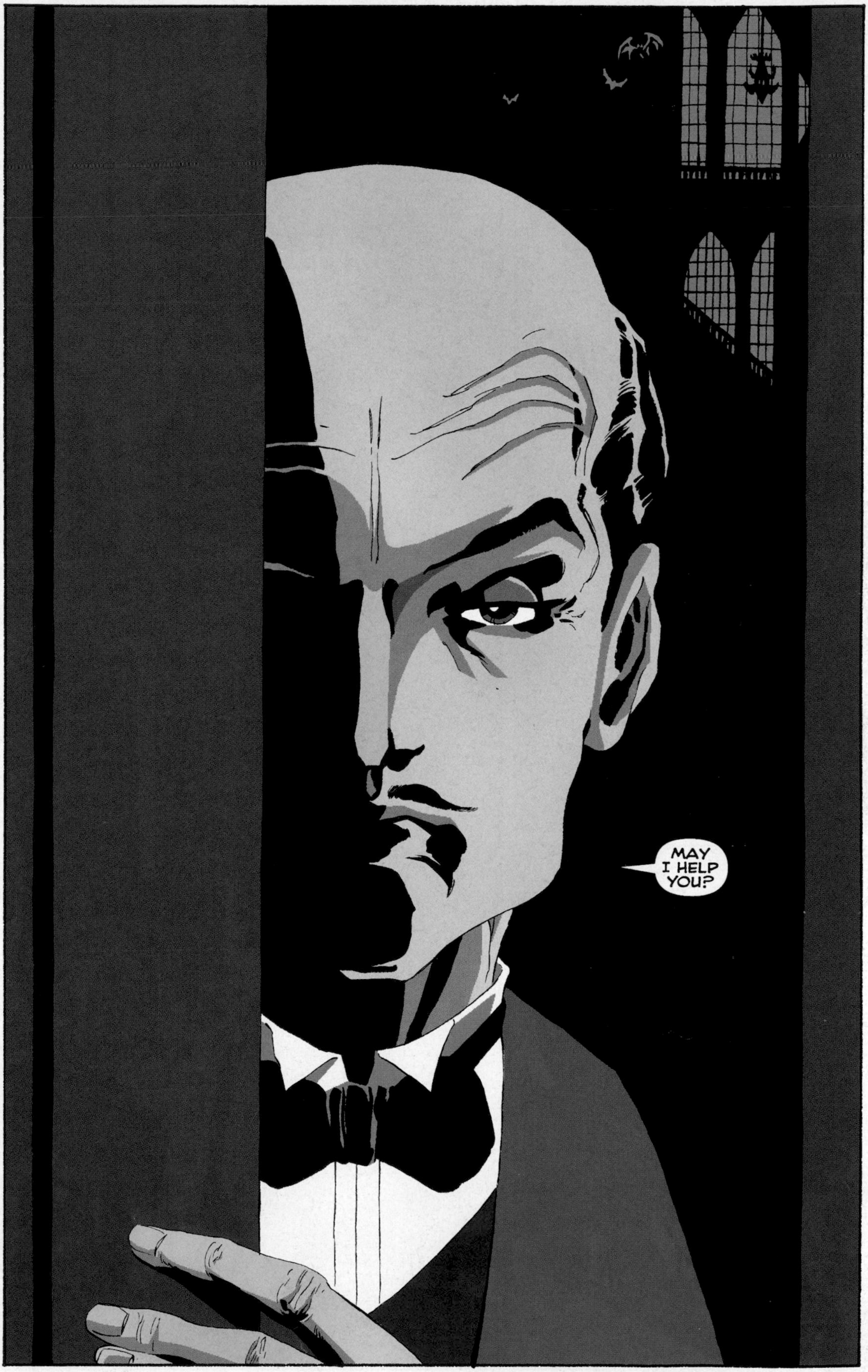
MAY I HELP YOU?

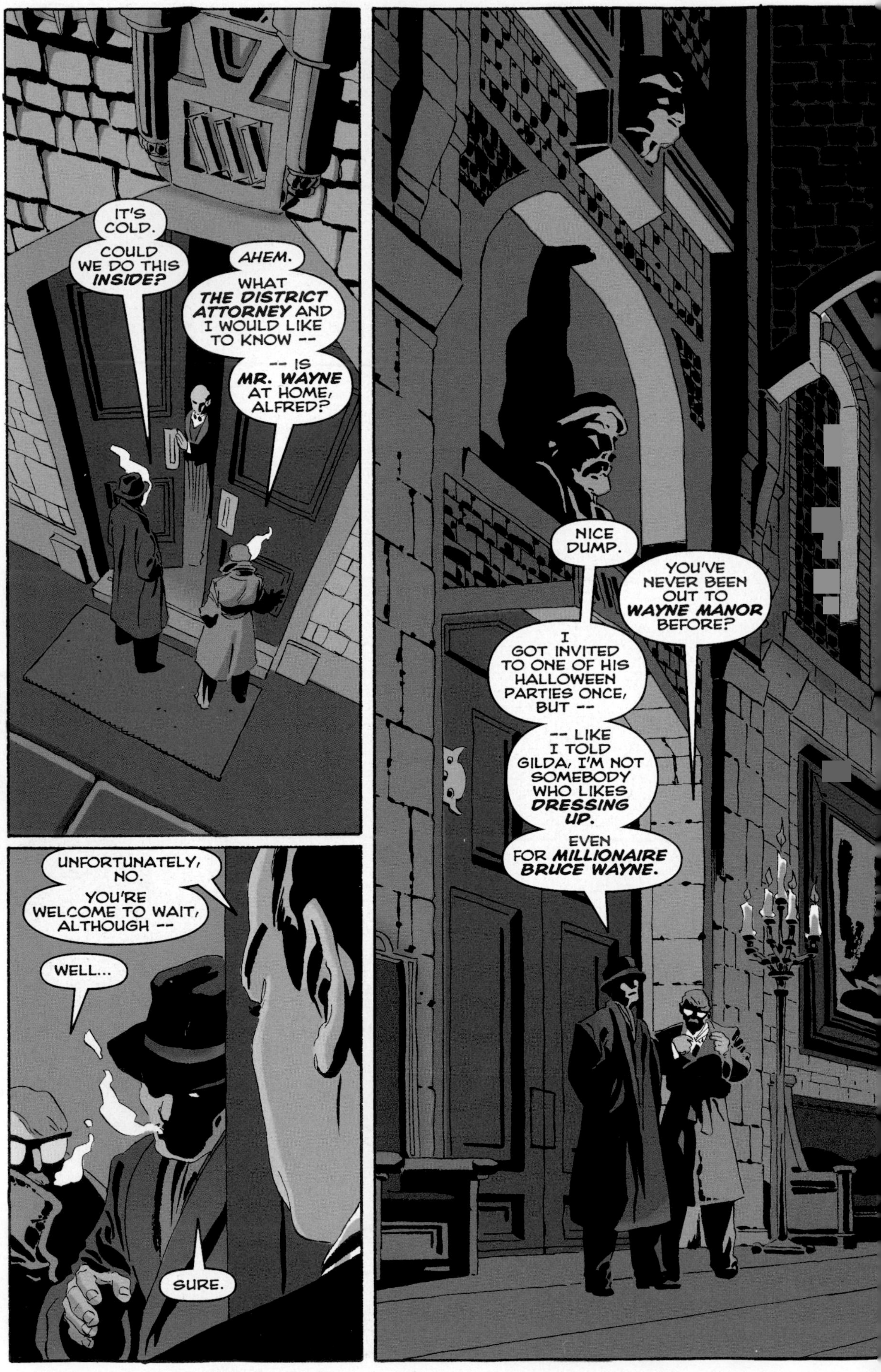
IT'S COLD.
COULD WE DO THIS INSIDE?
AHEM.
WHAT THE DISTRICT ATTORNEY AND I WOULD LIKE TO KNOW --
-- IS MR. WAYNE AT HOME, ALFRED?
UNFORTUNATELY, NO.
YOU'RE WELCOME TO WAIT, ALTHOUGH --
WELL...
SURE.
NICE DUMP.
YOU'VE NEVER BEEN OUT TO WAYNE MANOR BEFORE?
I GOT INVITED TO ONE OF HIS HALLOWEEN PARTIES ONCE, BUT --
-- LIKE I TOLD GILDA, I'M NOT SOMEBODY WHO LIKES DRESSING UP.
EVEN FOR MILLIONAIRE BRUCE WAYNE.

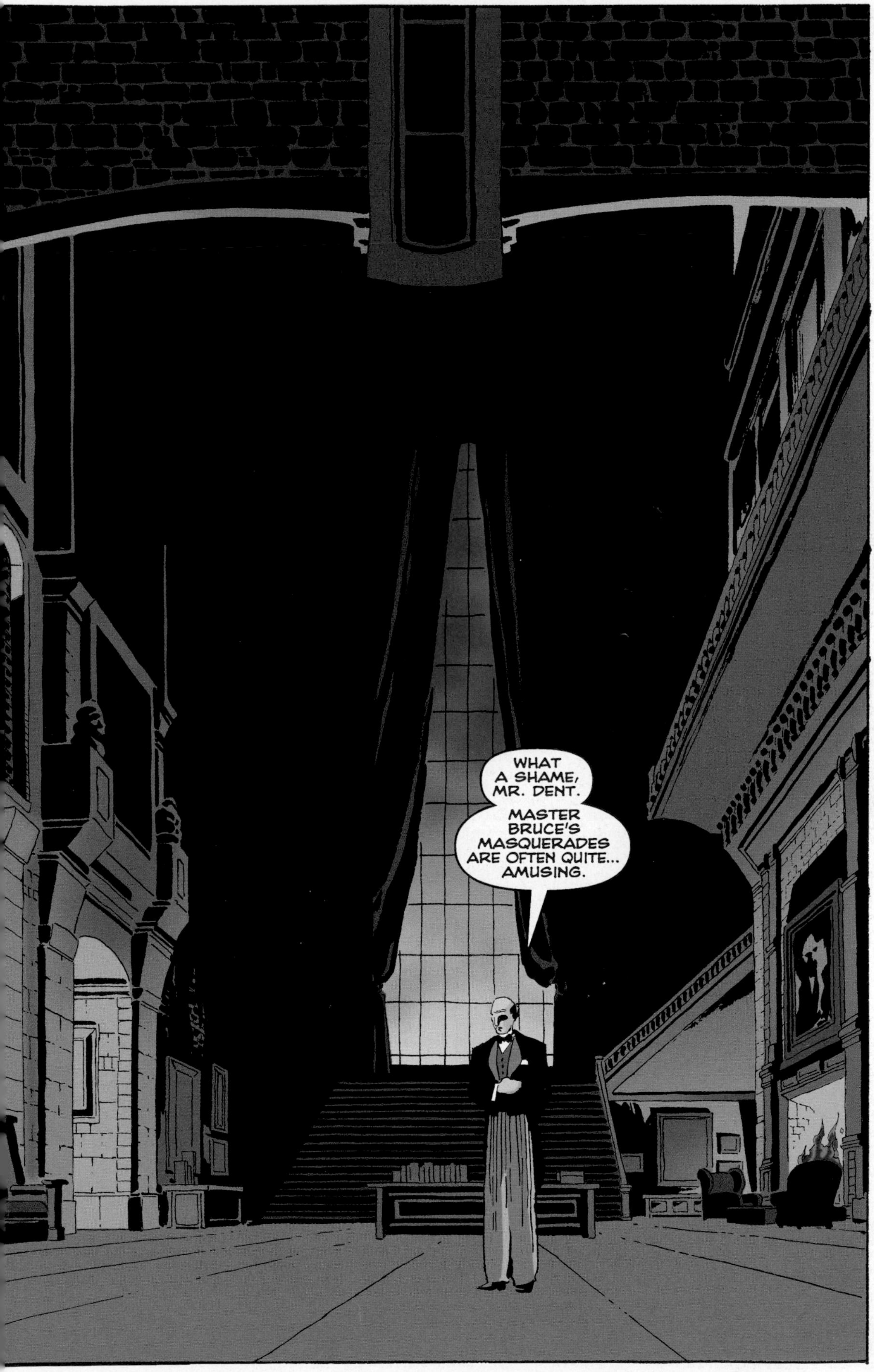
WHAT A SHAME, MR. DENT.
MASTER BRUCE'S MASQUERADES ARE OFTEN QUITE... AMUSING.

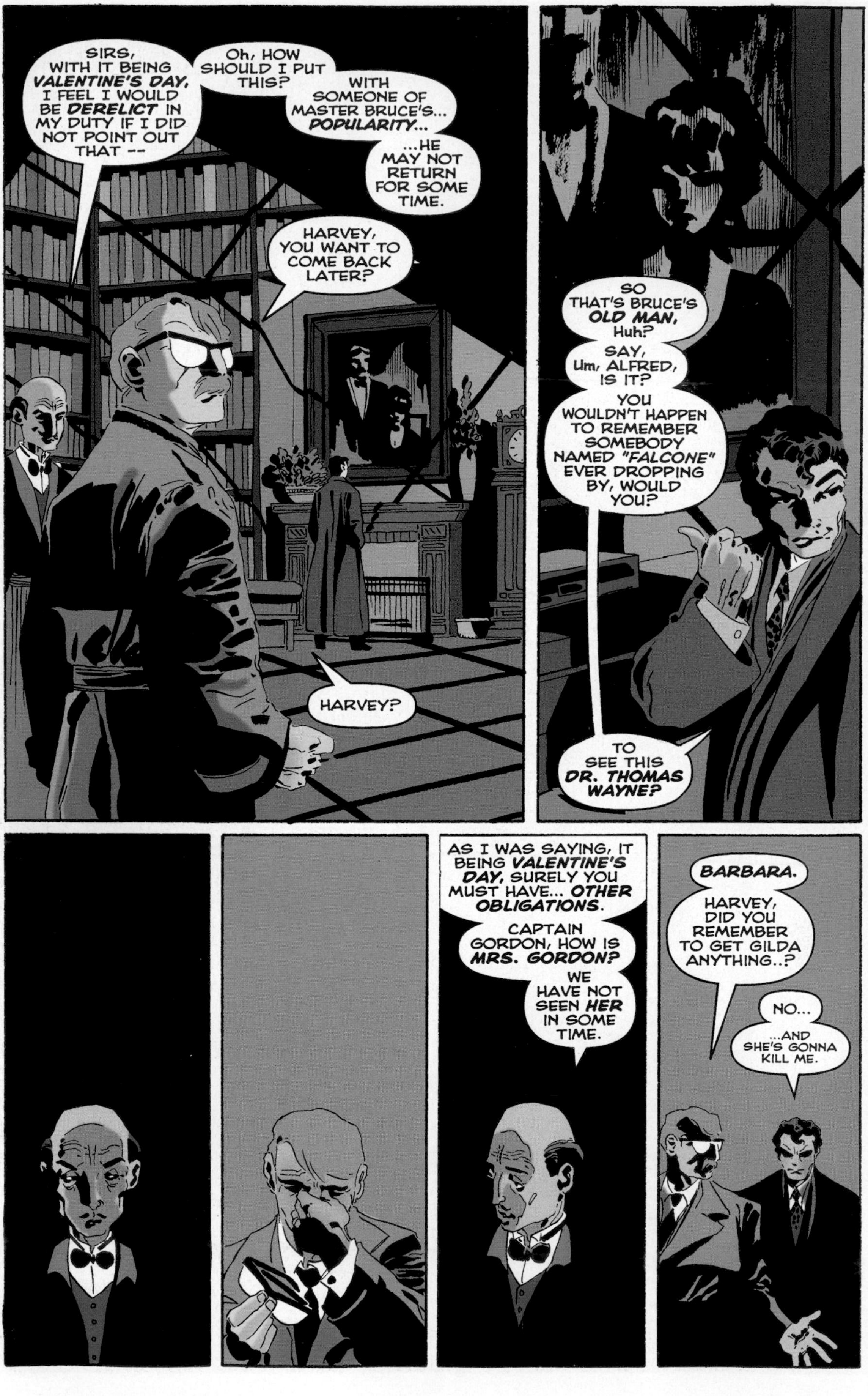
SIRS, WITH IT BEING VALENTINE'S DAY, I FEEL I WOULD BE DERELICT IN MY DUTY IF I DID NOT POINT OUT THAT --
Oh, HOW SHOULD I PUT THIS?
WITH SOMEONE OF MASTER BRUCE'S... POPULARITY...
...HE MAY NOT RETURN FOR SOME TIME.
HARVEY, YOU WANT TO COME BACK LATER?
HARVEY?
SO THAT'S BRUCE'S OLD MAN, Huh?
SAY, Um, ALFRED, IS IT?
YOU WOULDN'T HAPPEN TO REMEMBER SOMEBODY NAMED "FALCONE" EVER DROPPING BY, WOULD YOU?
TO SEE THIS DR. THOMAS WAYNE?
AS I WAS SAYING, IT BEING VALENTINE'S DAY, SURELY YOU MUST HAVE... OTHER OBLIGATIONS.
CAPTAIN GORDON, HOW IS MRS. GORDON?
WE HAVE NOT SEEN HER IN SOME TIME.
BARBARA.
HARVEY, DID YOU REMEMBER TO GET GILDA ANYTHING..?
NO...
...AND SHE'S GONNA KILL ME.

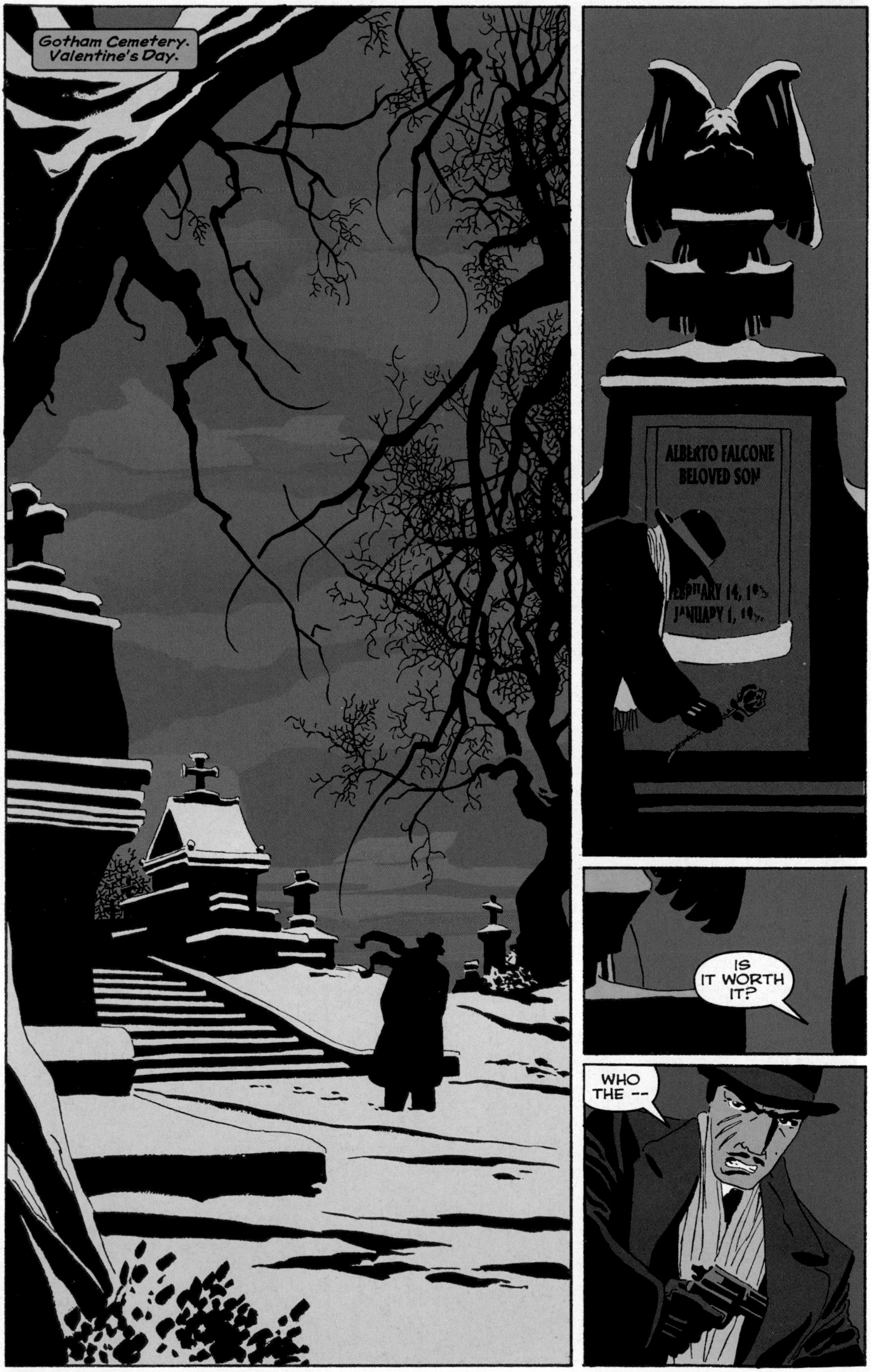
Gotham Cemetery. Valentine's Day.
ALBERTO FALCONE
BELOVED SON
IS IT WORTH IT?
WHO THE --

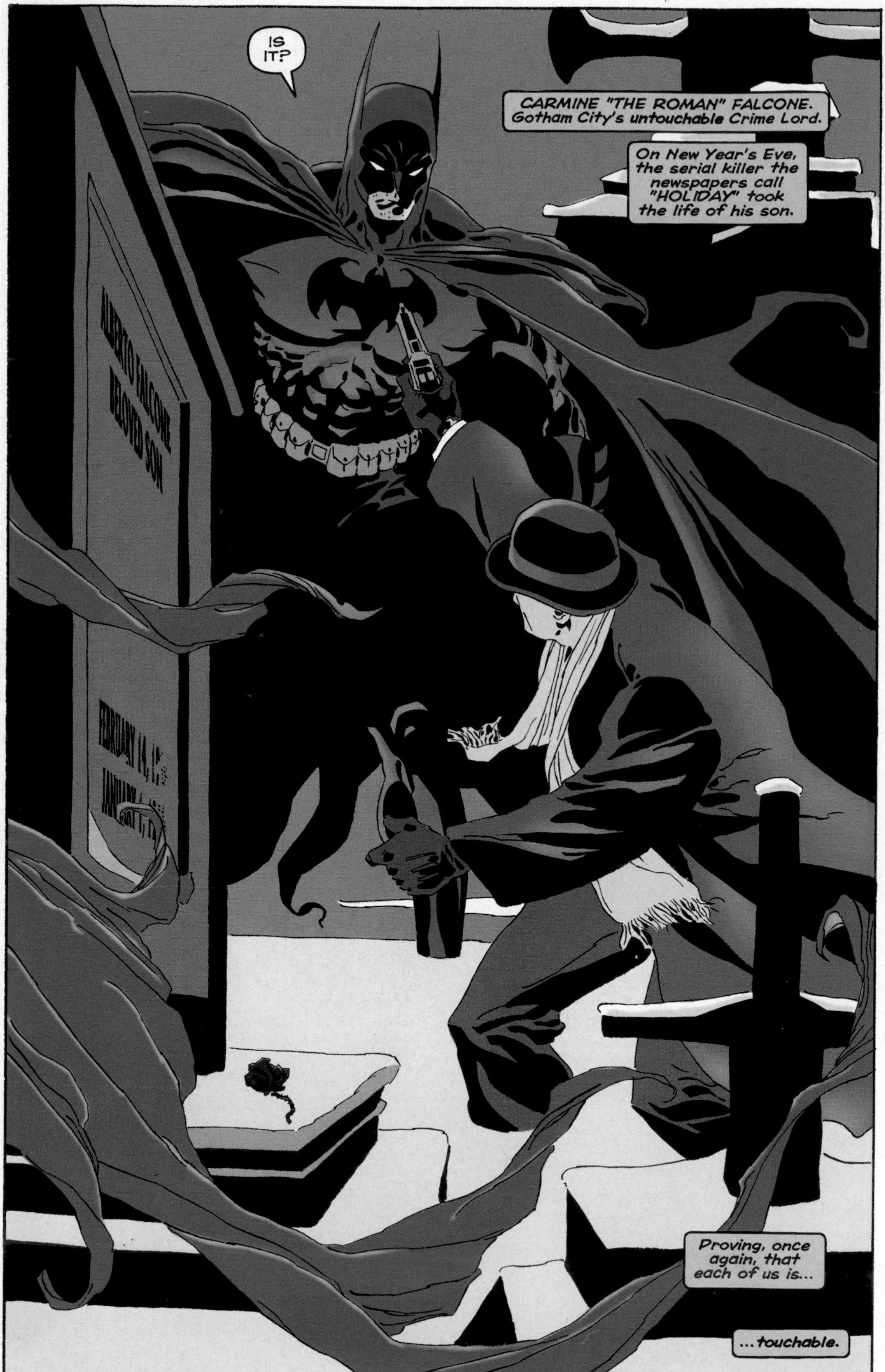
IS IT?
CARMINE "THE ROMAN" FALCONE. Gotham City's untouchable Crime Lord.
On New Year's Eve, the serial killer the newspapers call "HOLIDAY" took the life of his son.
ALBERTO FALCONE
BELOVED SON
Proving, once again, that each of us is...
...touchable.

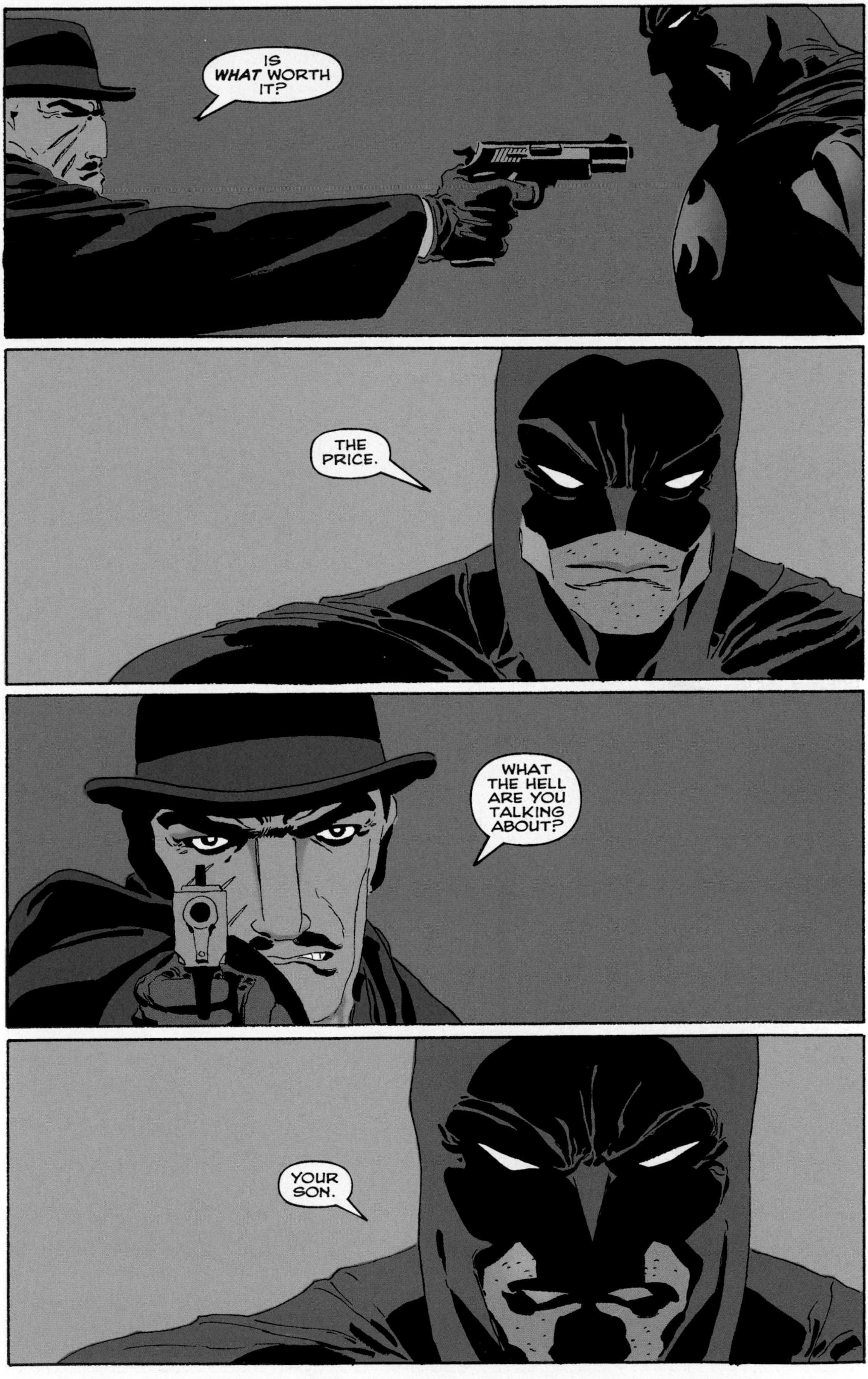
IS *WHAT* WORTH IT?
THE PRICE.
WHAT THE HELL ARE YOU TALKING ABOUT?
YOUR SON.

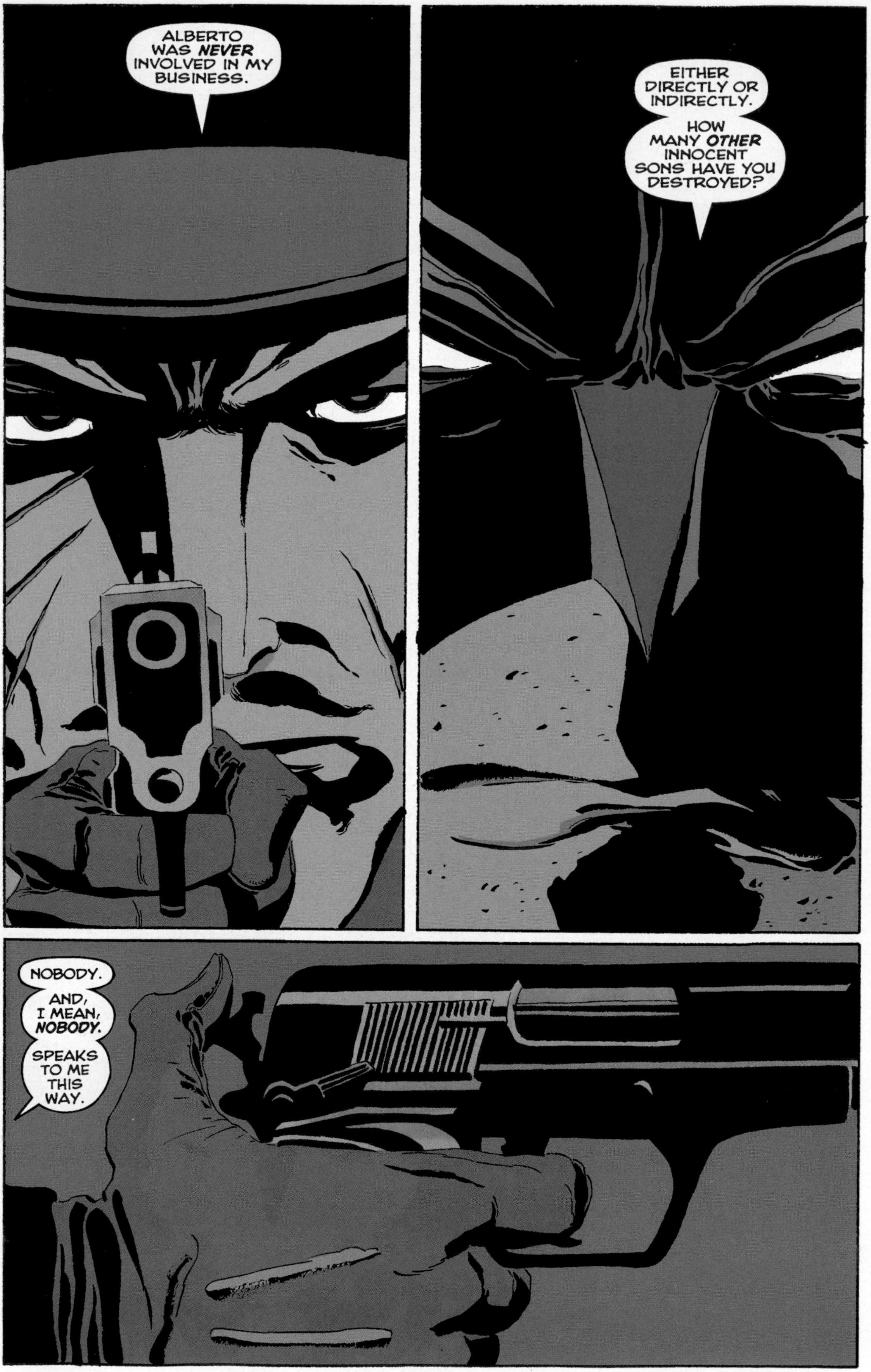

ALBERTO WAS NEVER INVOLVED IN MY BUSINESS.
EITHER DIRECTLY OR INDIRECTLY.
HOW MANY OTHER INNOCENT SONS HAVE YOU DESTROYED?
NOBODY.
AND, I MEAN, NOBODY.
SPEAKS TO ME THIS WAY.

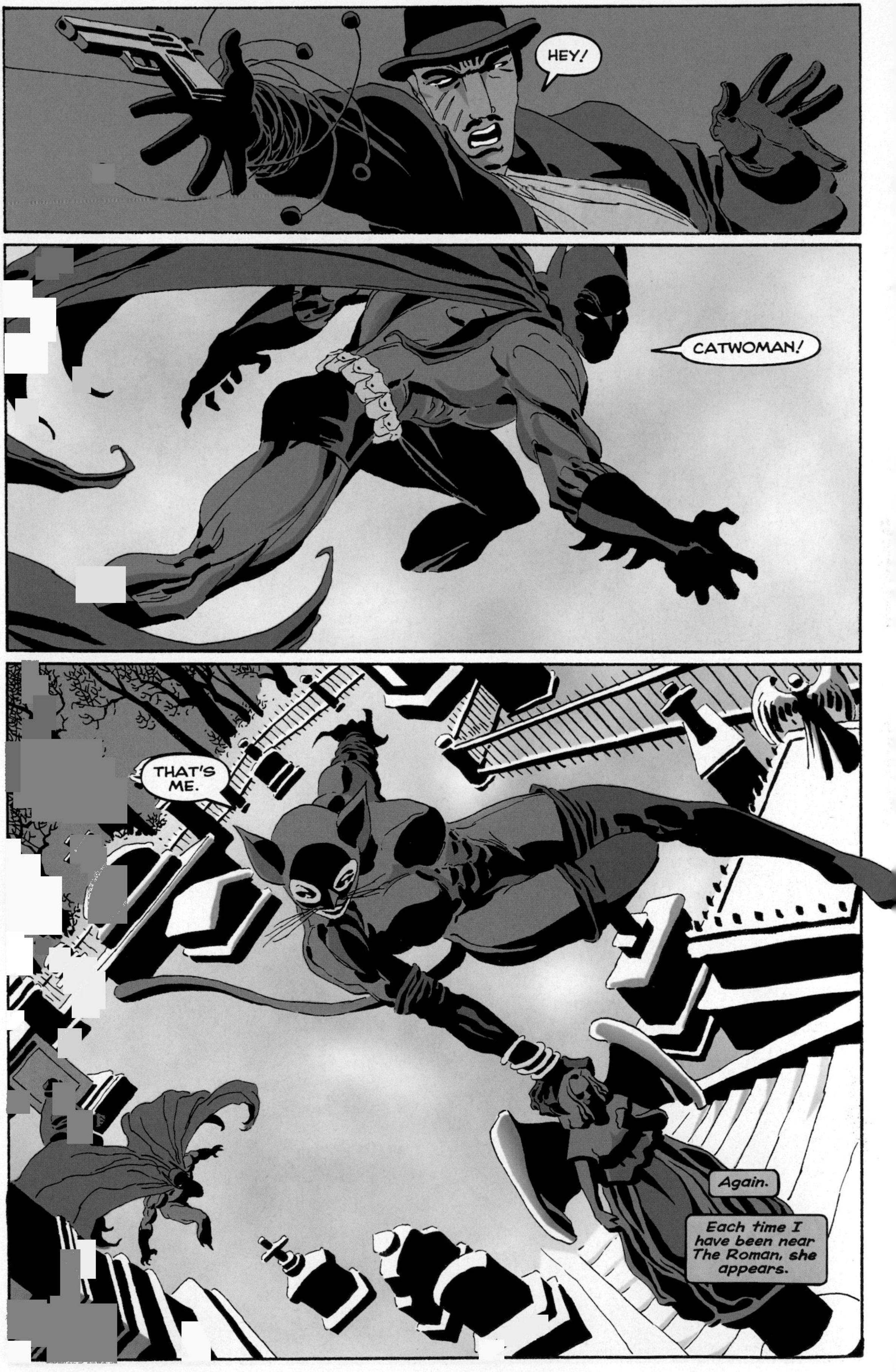
HEY!
CATWOMAN!
THAT'S ME.
Again.
Each time I have been near The Roman, she appears.

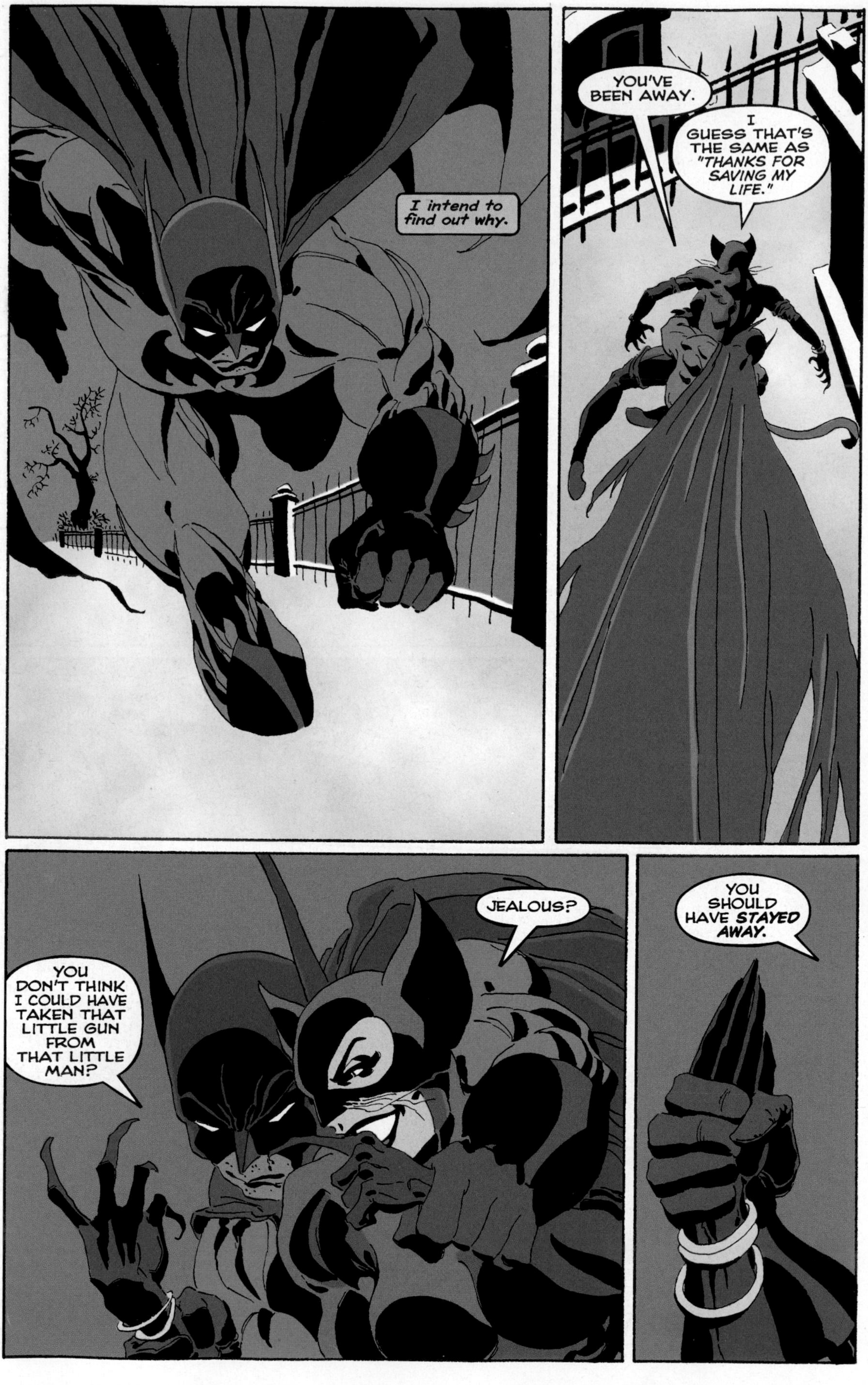
I intend to find out why.
YOU'VE BEEN AWAY.
I GUESS THAT'S THE SAME AS "THANKS FOR SAVING MY LIFE."
JEALOUS?
YOU DON'T THINK I COULD HAVE TAKEN THAT LITTLE GUN FROM THAT LITTLE MAN?
YOU SHOULD HAVE STAYED AWAY.

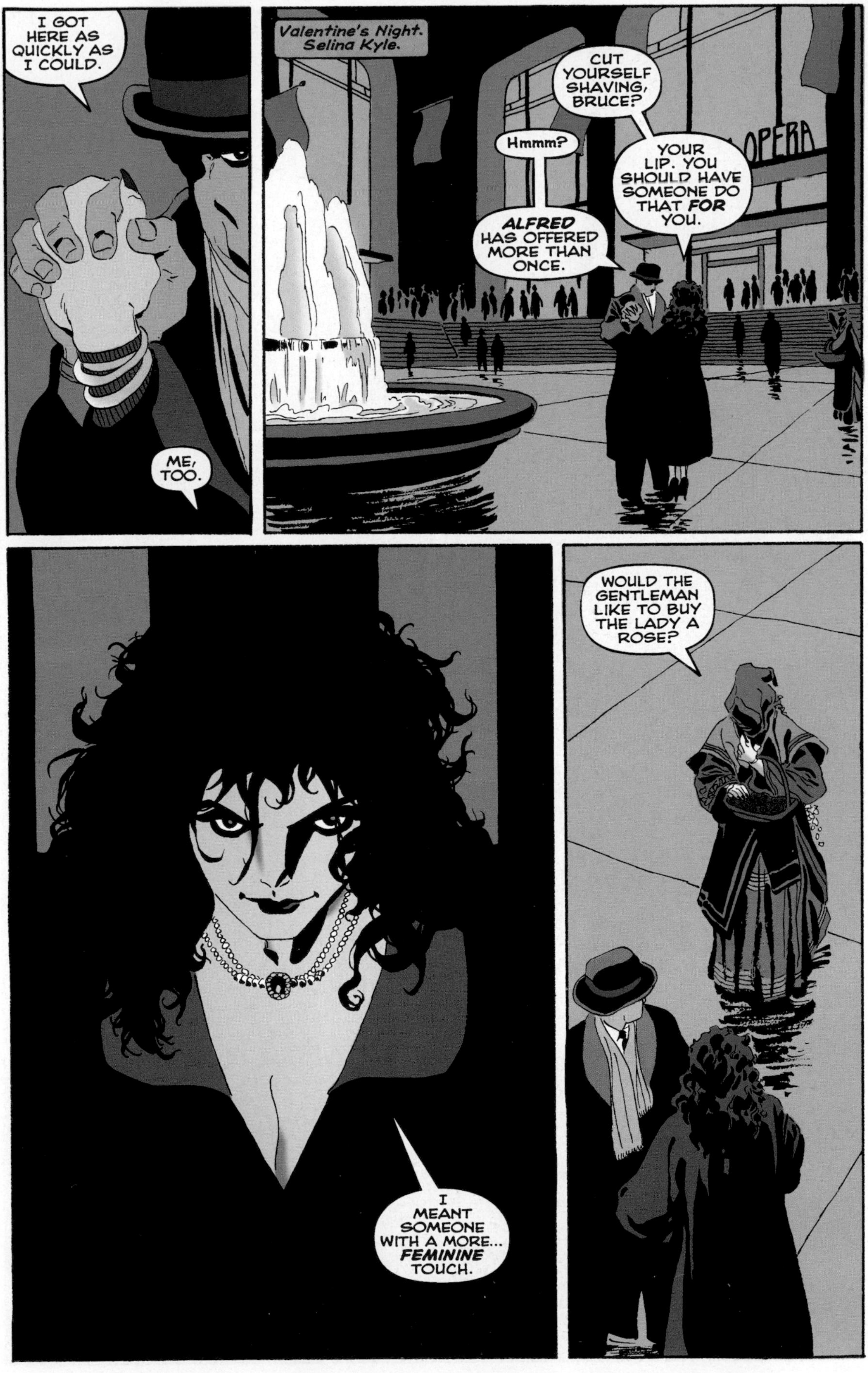
I GOT HERE AS QUICKLY AS I COULD.
ME, TOO.
Valentine's Night. Selina Kyle.
CUT YOURSELF SHAVING, BRUCE?
Hmmm?
YOUR LIP. YOU SHOULD HAVE SOMEONE DO THAT FOR YOU.
ALFRED HAS OFFERED MORE THAN ONCE.
OPERA
I MEANT SOMEONE WITH A MORE... FEMININE TOUCH.
WOULD THE GENTLEMAN LIKE TO BUY THE LADY A ROSE?

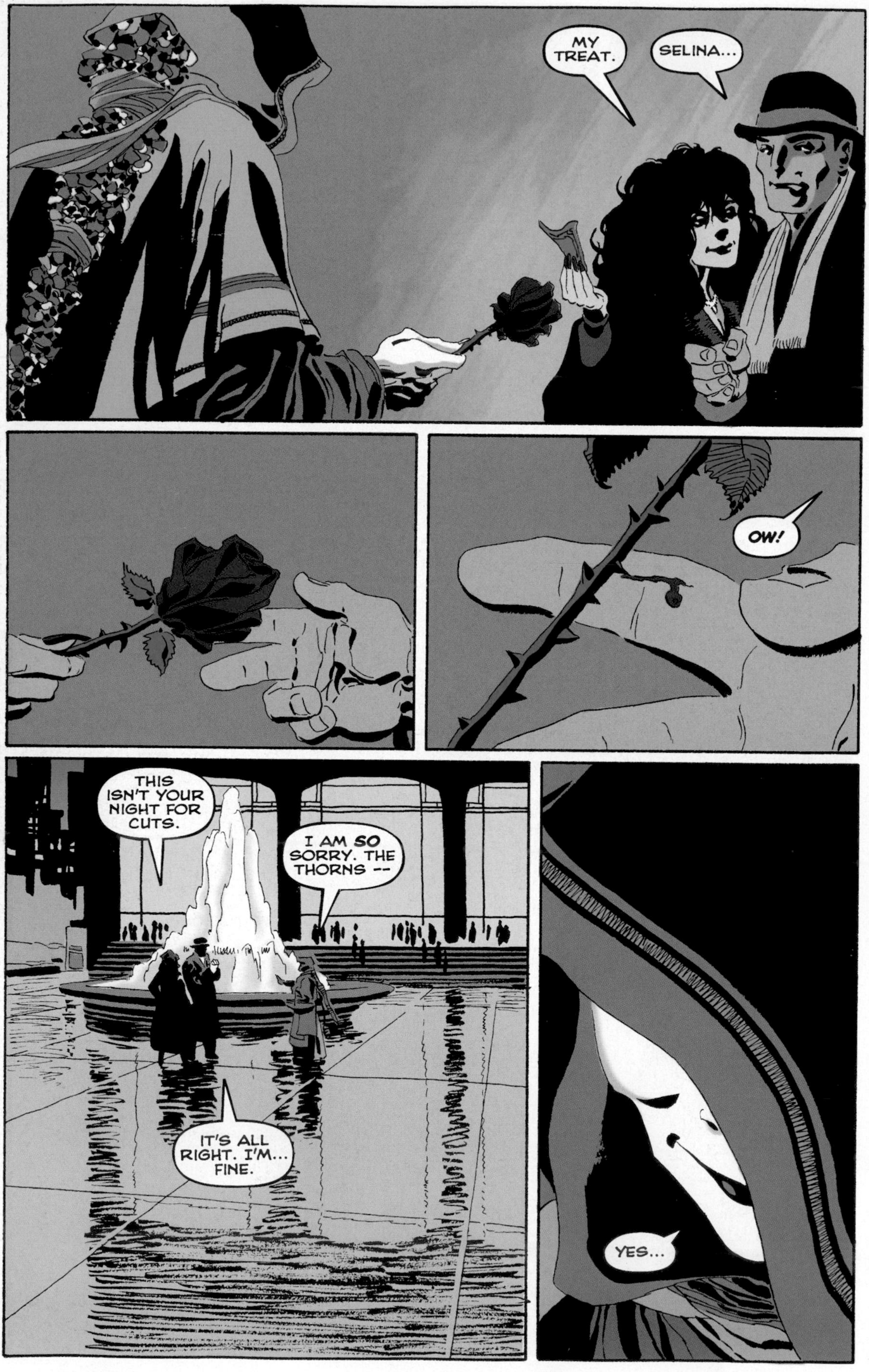
MY TREAT.
SELINA...
OW!
THIS ISN'T YOUR NIGHT FOR CUTS.
I AM SO SORRY. THE THORNS --
IT'S ALL RIGHT. I'M... FINE.
YES...

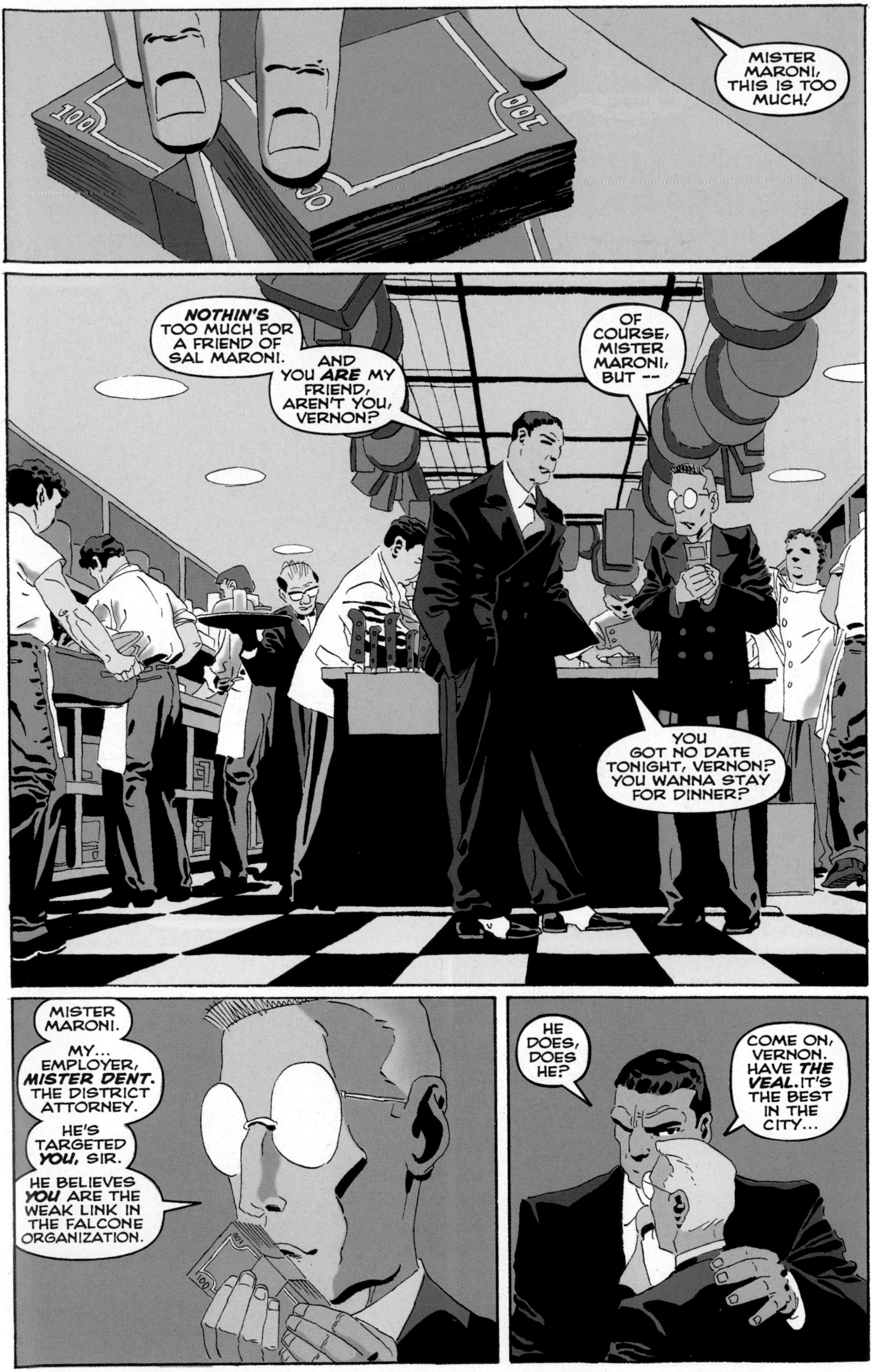
MISTER MARONI, THIS IS TOO MUCH!
NOTHIN'S TOO MUCH FOR A FRIEND OF SAL MARONI.
AND YOU ARE MY FRIEND, AREN'T YOU, VERNON?
OF COURSE, MISTER MARONI, BUT --
YOU GOT NO DATE TONIGHT, VERNON? YOU WANNA STAY FOR DINNER?
MISTER MARONI.
MY... EMPLOYER, MISTER DENT. THE DISTRICT ATTORNEY.
HE'S TARGETED YOU, SIR.
HE BELIEVES YOU ARE THE WEAK LINK IN THE FALCONE ORGANIZATION.
HE DOES, DOES HE?
COME ON, VERNON. HAVE THE VEAL. IT'S THE BEST IN THE CITY...

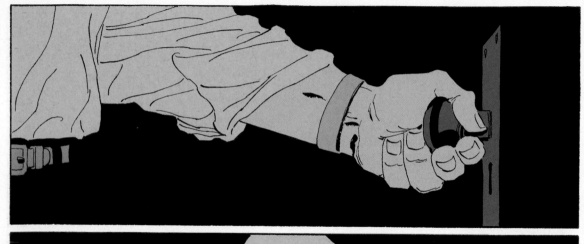

I WAS *WONDERING* WHEN YOU'D GET HOME.

BARBARA... I...I KNOW I'VE ALREADY TOLD YOU TOO MANY TIMES, BUT --

I *AM* SORRY...

Shhh... IT CAN *NEVER* BE TOO MANY TIMES...

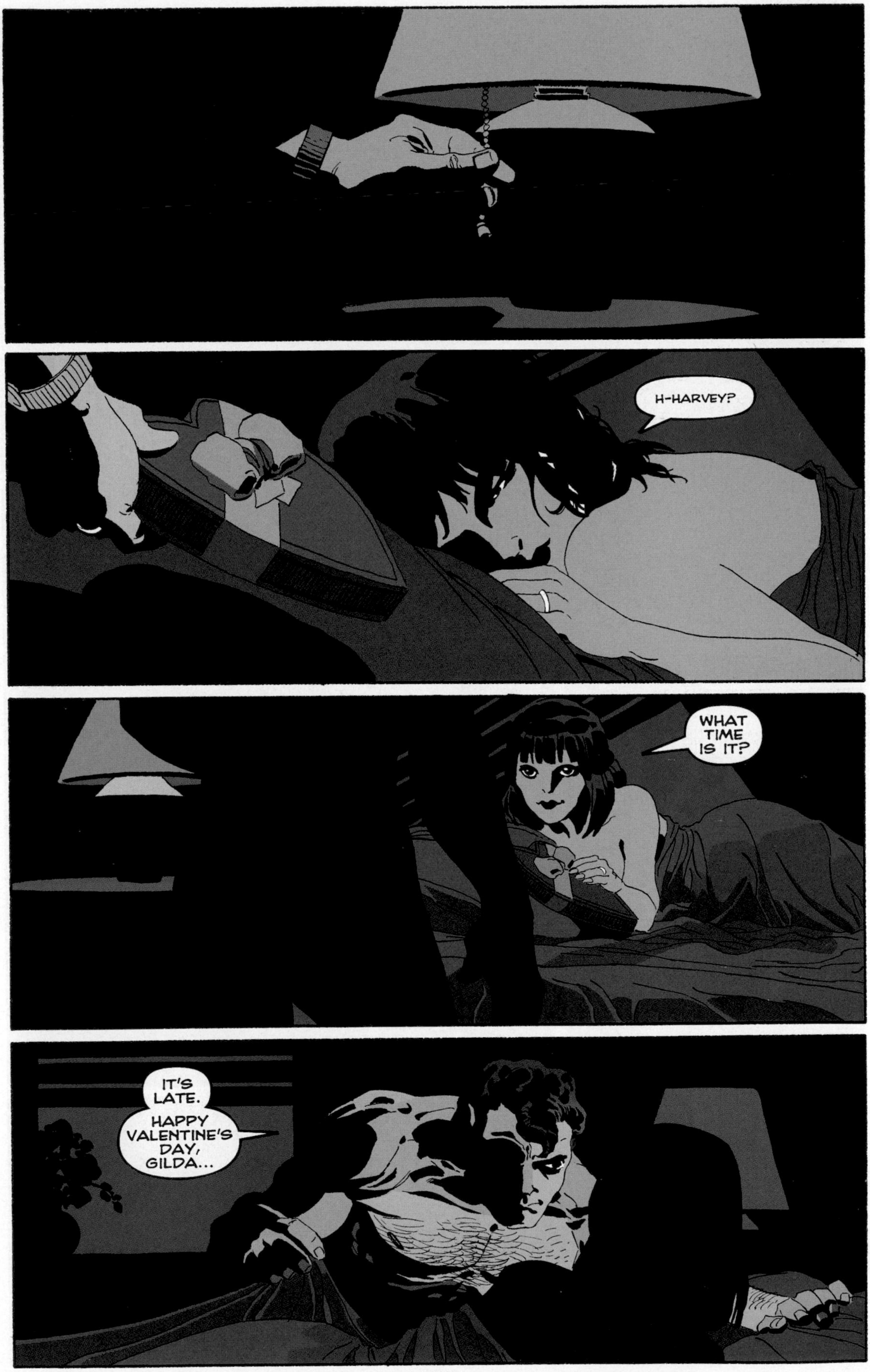
H-HARVEY?
WHAT TIME IS IT?
IT'S LATE.
HAPPY VALENTINE'S DAY, GILDA...

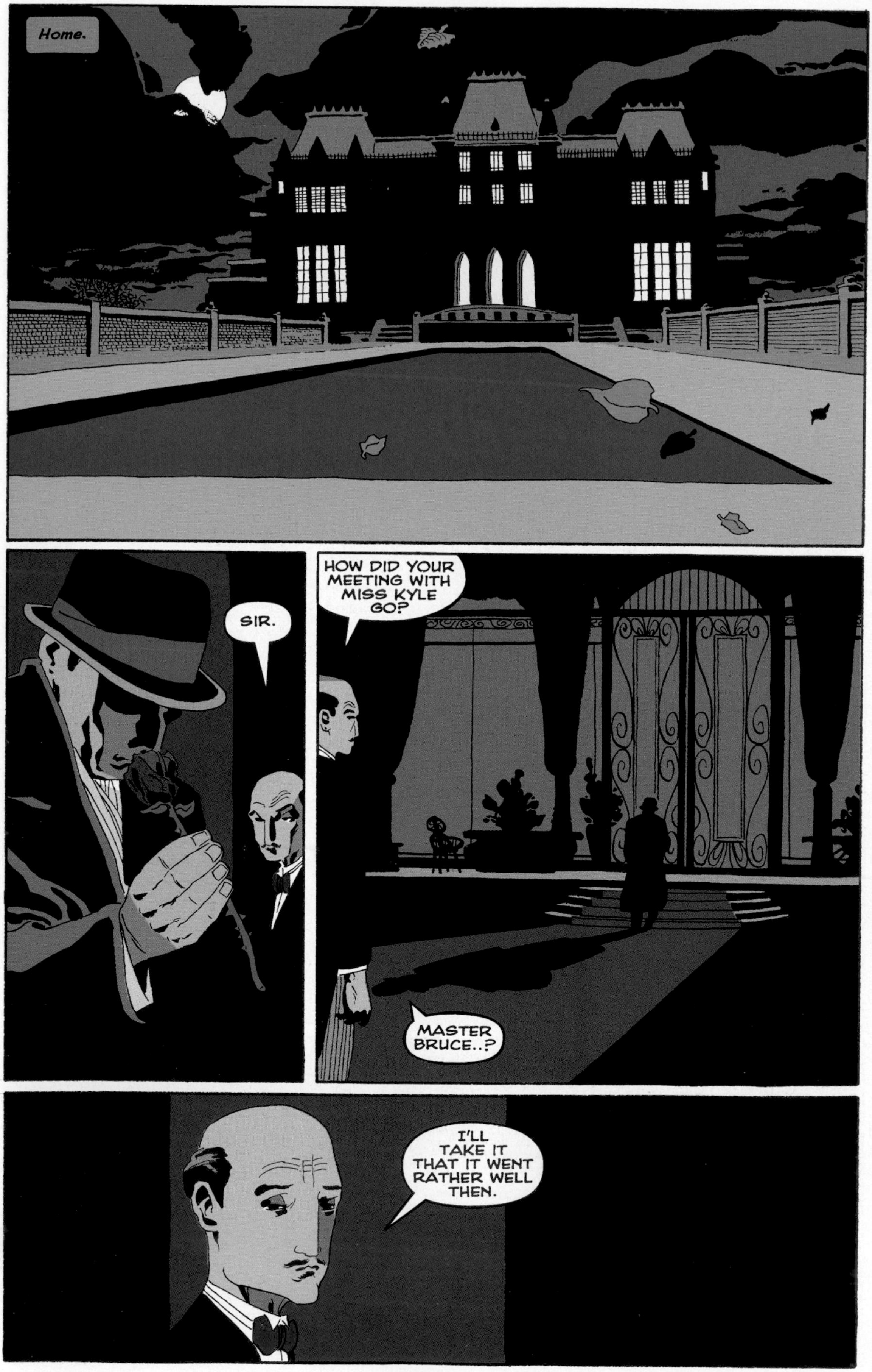
Home.
SIR.
HOW DID YOUR MEETING WITH MISS KYLE GO?
MASTER BRUCE..?
I'LL TAKE IT THAT IT WENT RATHER WELL THEN.

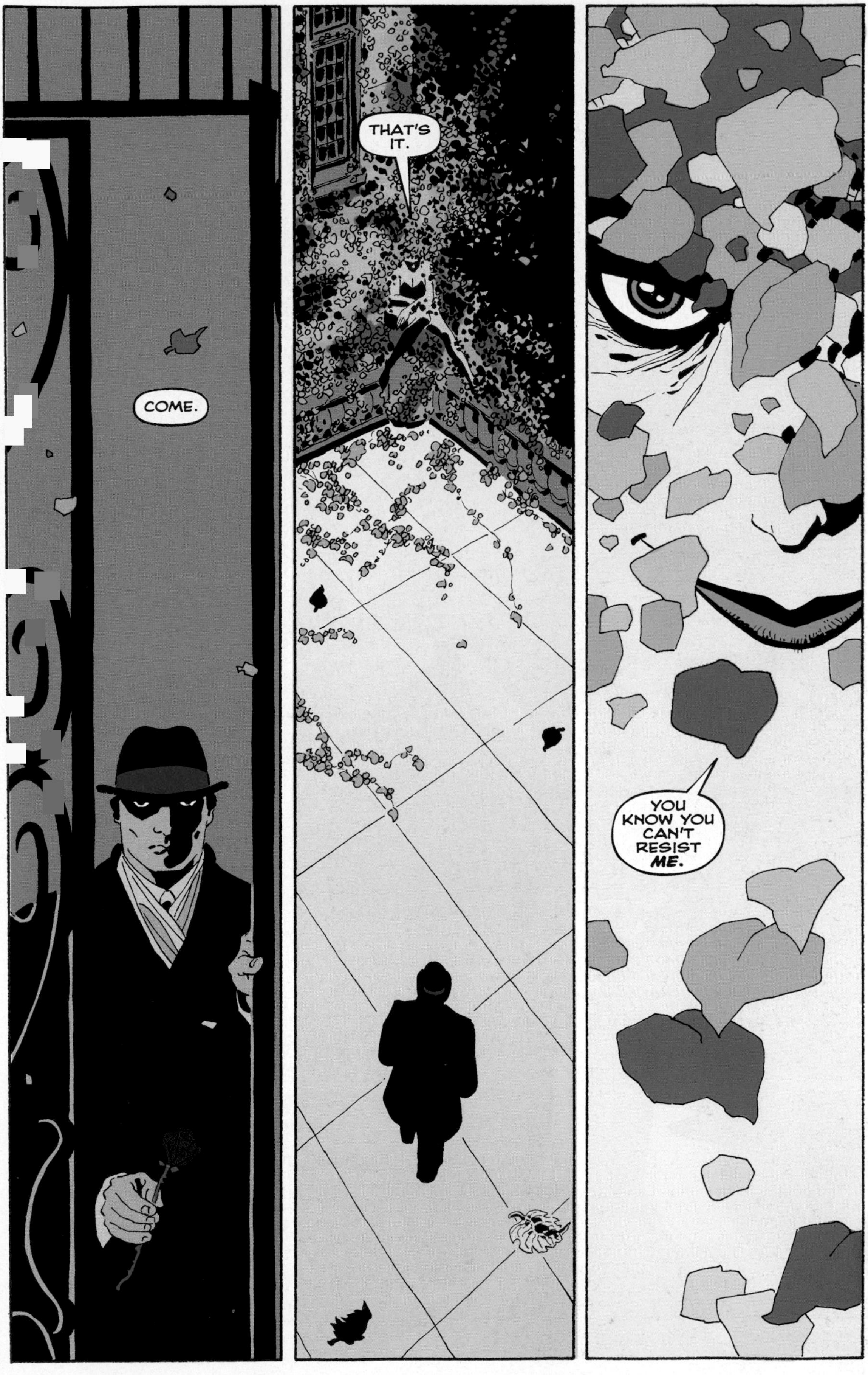
COME.
THAT'S IT.
YOU KNOW YOU CAN'T RESIST *ME.*

CHAPTER SIX
ST. PATRICK'S DAY

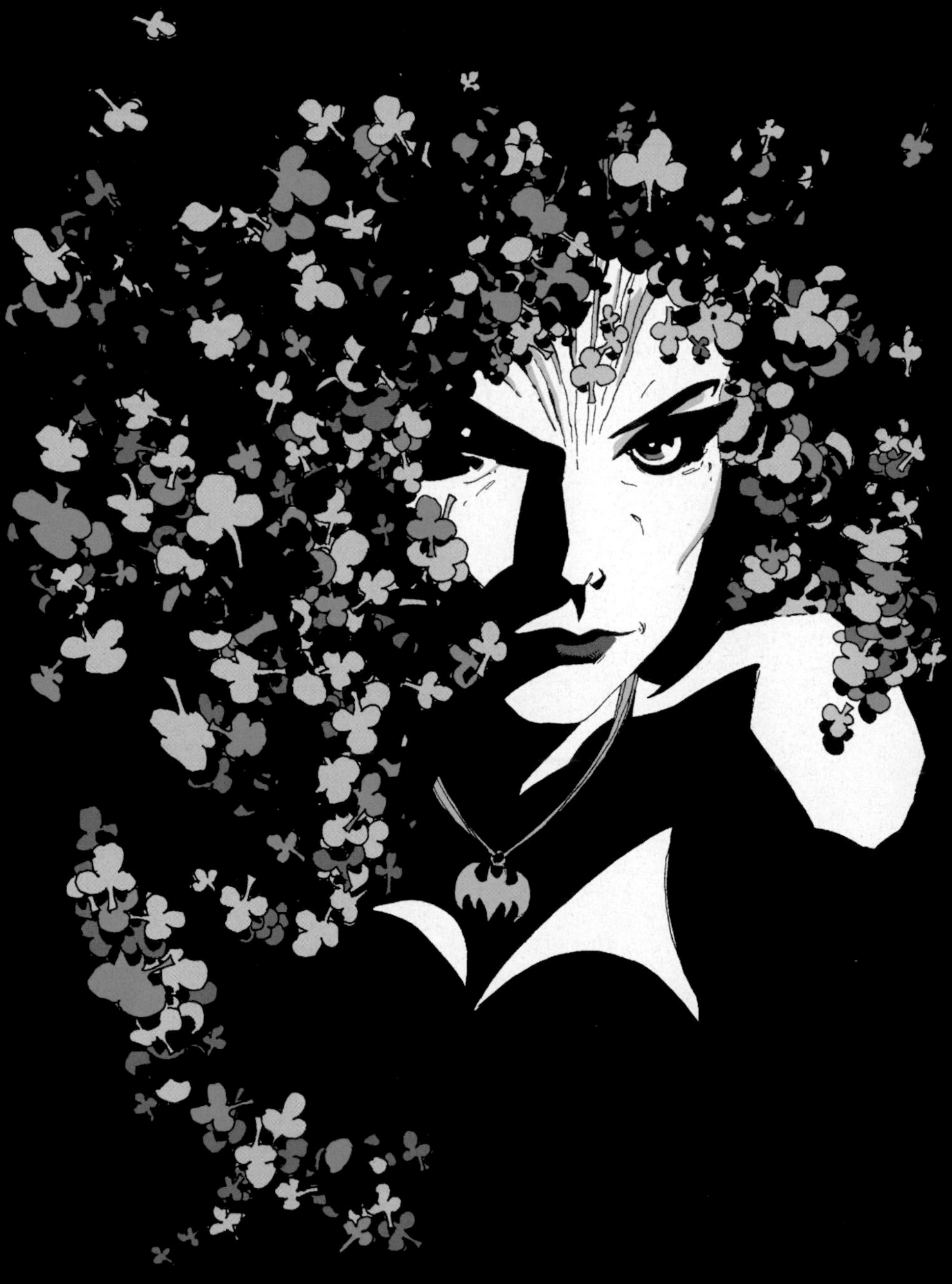

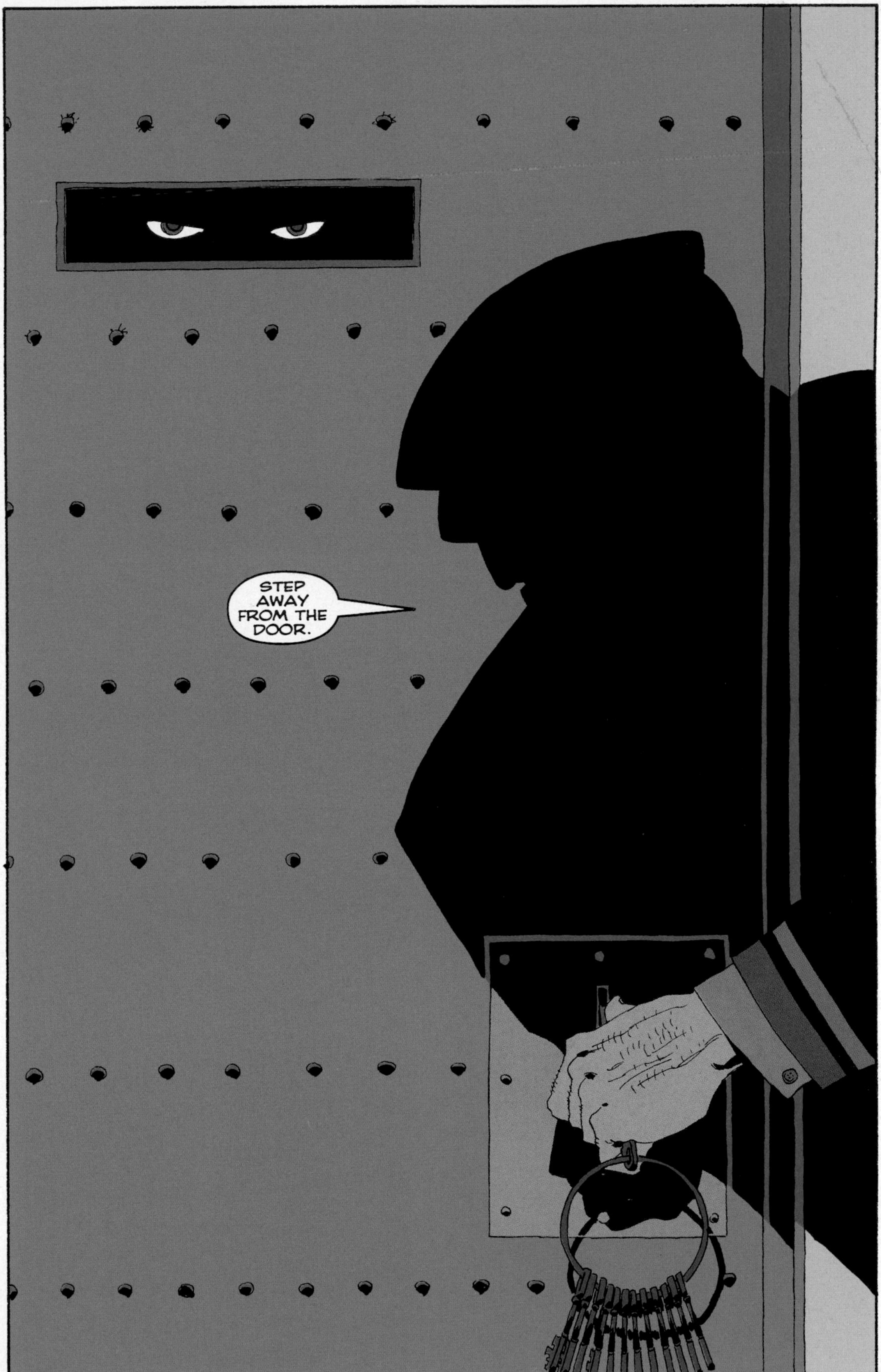
STEP AWAY FROM THE DOOR.

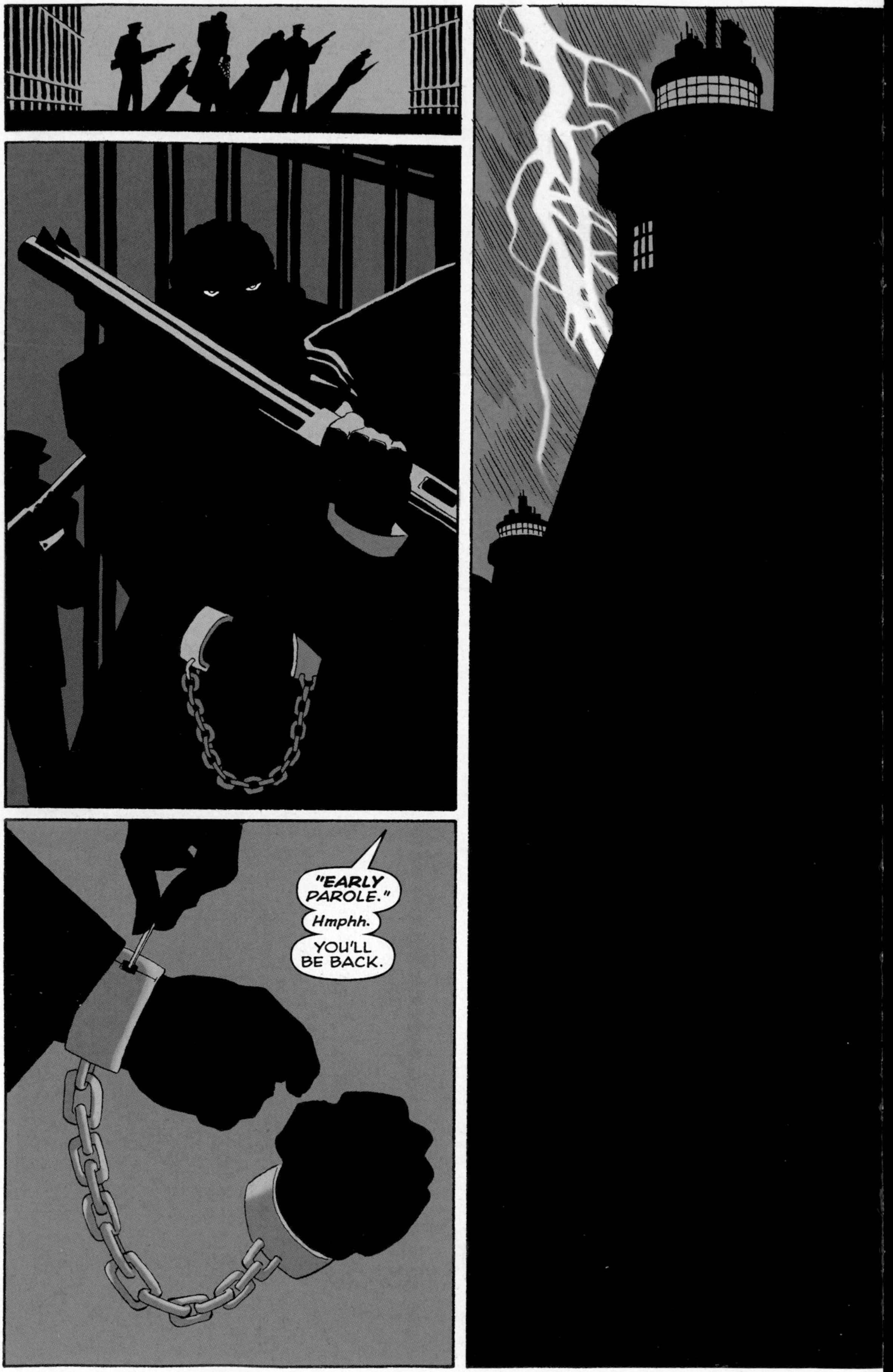
"EARLY PAROLE."
Hmphh.
YOU'LL BE BACK.

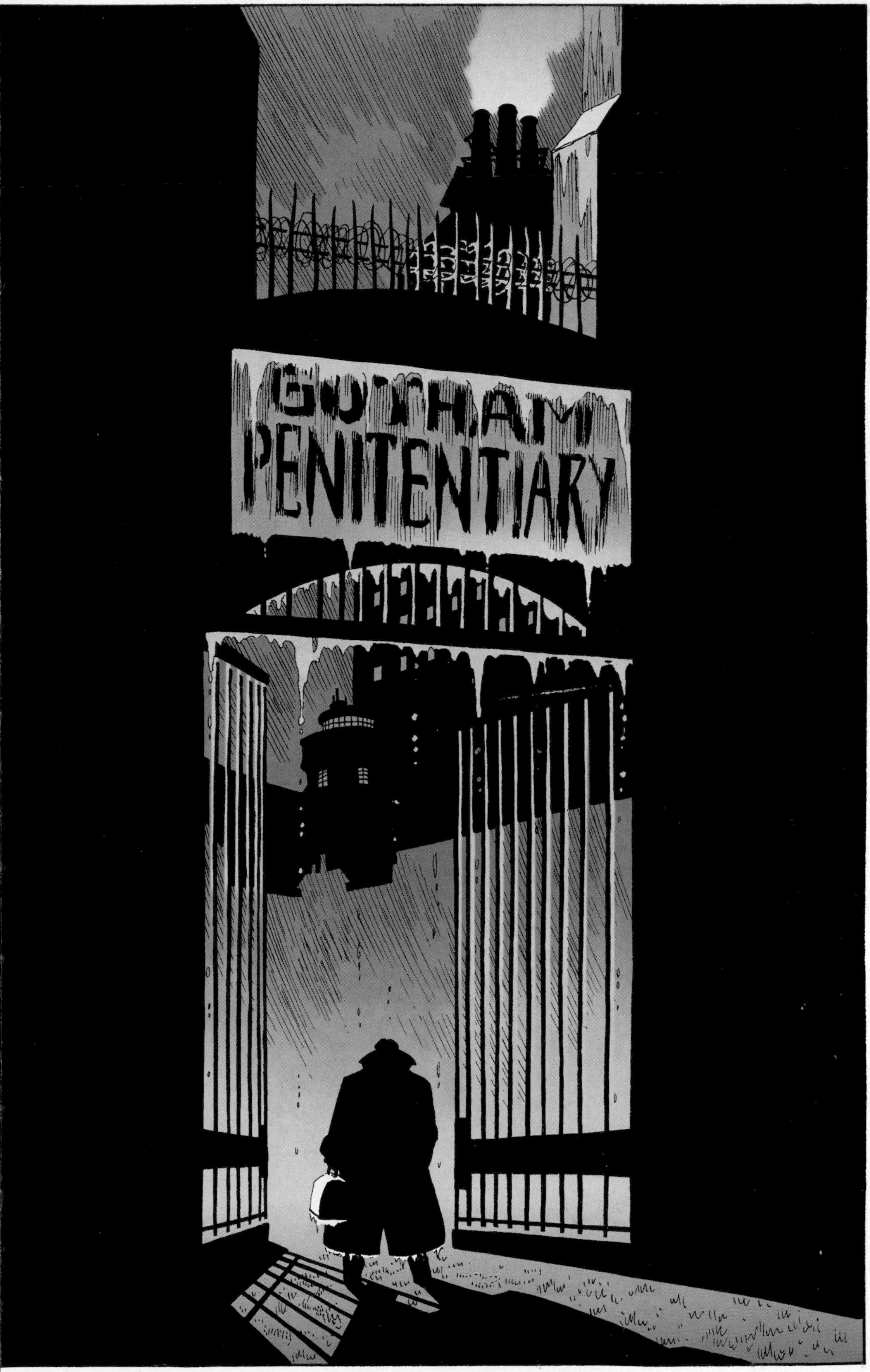
GOTHAM PENITENTIARY

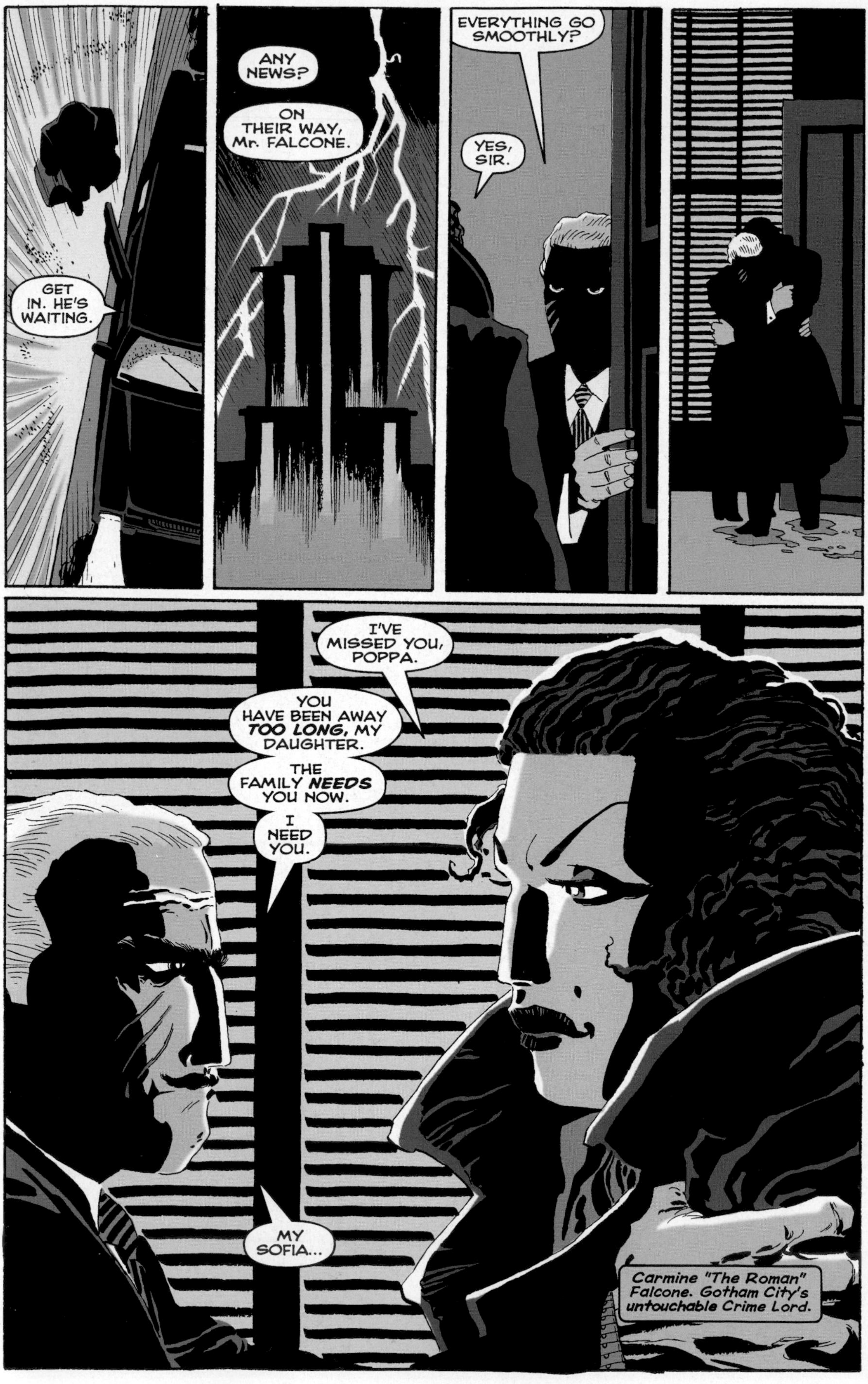
GET IN. HE'S WAITING.
ANY NEWS?
ON THEIR WAY, Mr. FALCONE.
EVERYTHING GO SMOOTHLY?
YES, SIR.
I'VE MISSED YOU, POPPA.
YOU HAVE BEEN AWAY TOO LONG, MY DAUGHTER.
THE FAMILY NEEDS YOU NOW.
I NEED YOU.
MY SOFIA...
Carmine "The Roman" Falcone. Gotham City's untouchable Crime Lord.

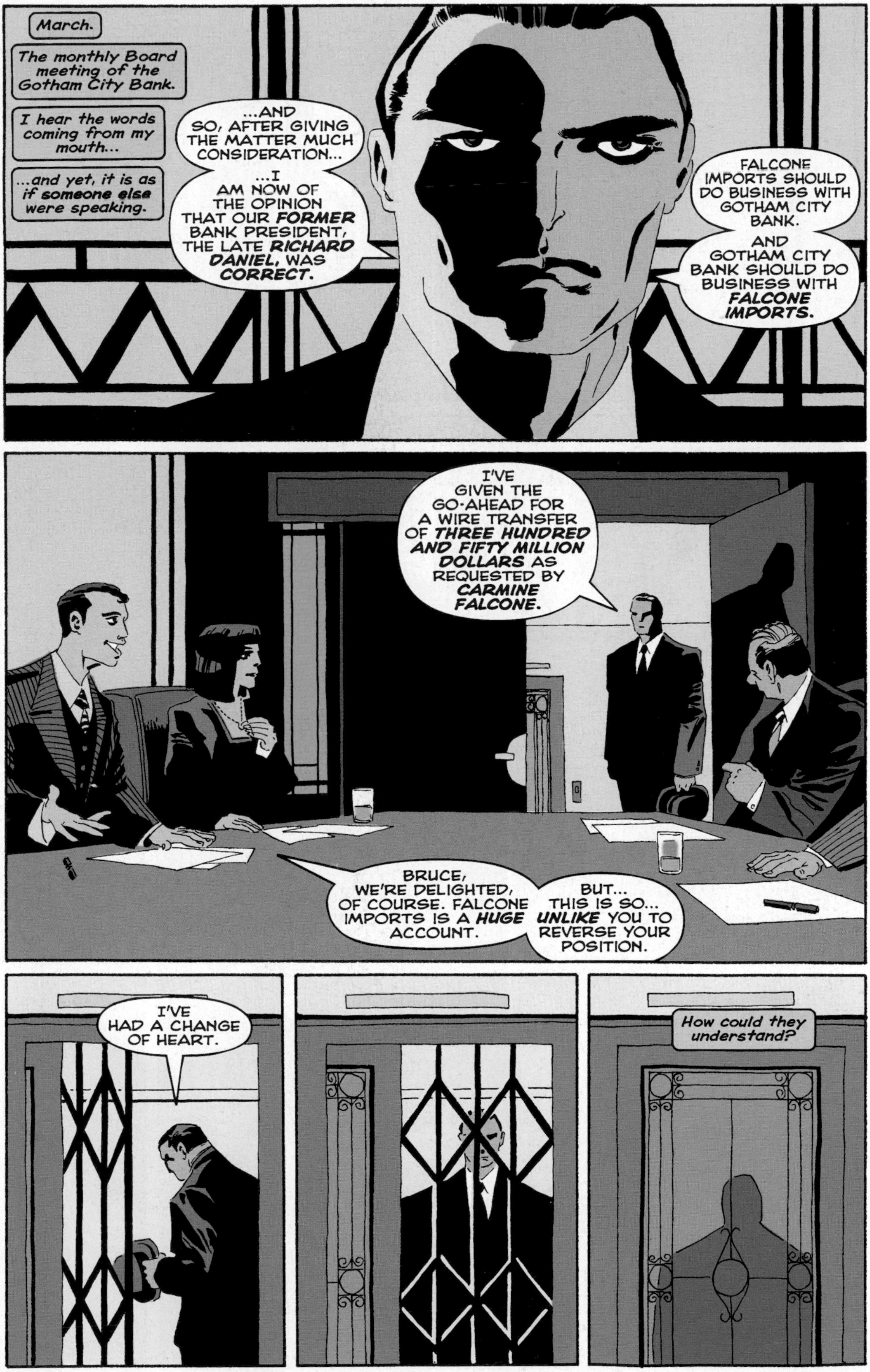
March.
The monthly Board meeting of the Gotham City Bank.
I hear the words coming from my mouth...
...and yet, it is as if someone else were speaking.
...AND SO, AFTER GIVING THE MATTER MUCH CONSIDERATION...
...I AM NOW OF THE OPINION THAT OUR FORMER BANK PRESIDENT, THE LATE RICHARD DANIEL, WAS CORRECT.
FALCONE IMPORTS SHOULD DO BUSINESS WITH GOTHAM CITY BANK.
AND GOTHAM CITY BANK SHOULD DO BUSINESS WITH FALCONE IMPORTS.
I'VE GIVEN THE GO-AHEAD FOR A WIRE TRANSFER OF THREE HUNDRED AND FIFTY MILLION DOLLARS AS REQUESTED BY CARMINE FALCONE.
BRUCE, WE'RE DELIGHTED, OF COURSE. FALCONE IMPORTS IS A HUGE ACCOUNT.
BUT... THIS IS SO... UNLIKE YOU TO REVERSE YOUR POSITION.
I'VE HAD A CHANGE OF HEART.
How could they understand?

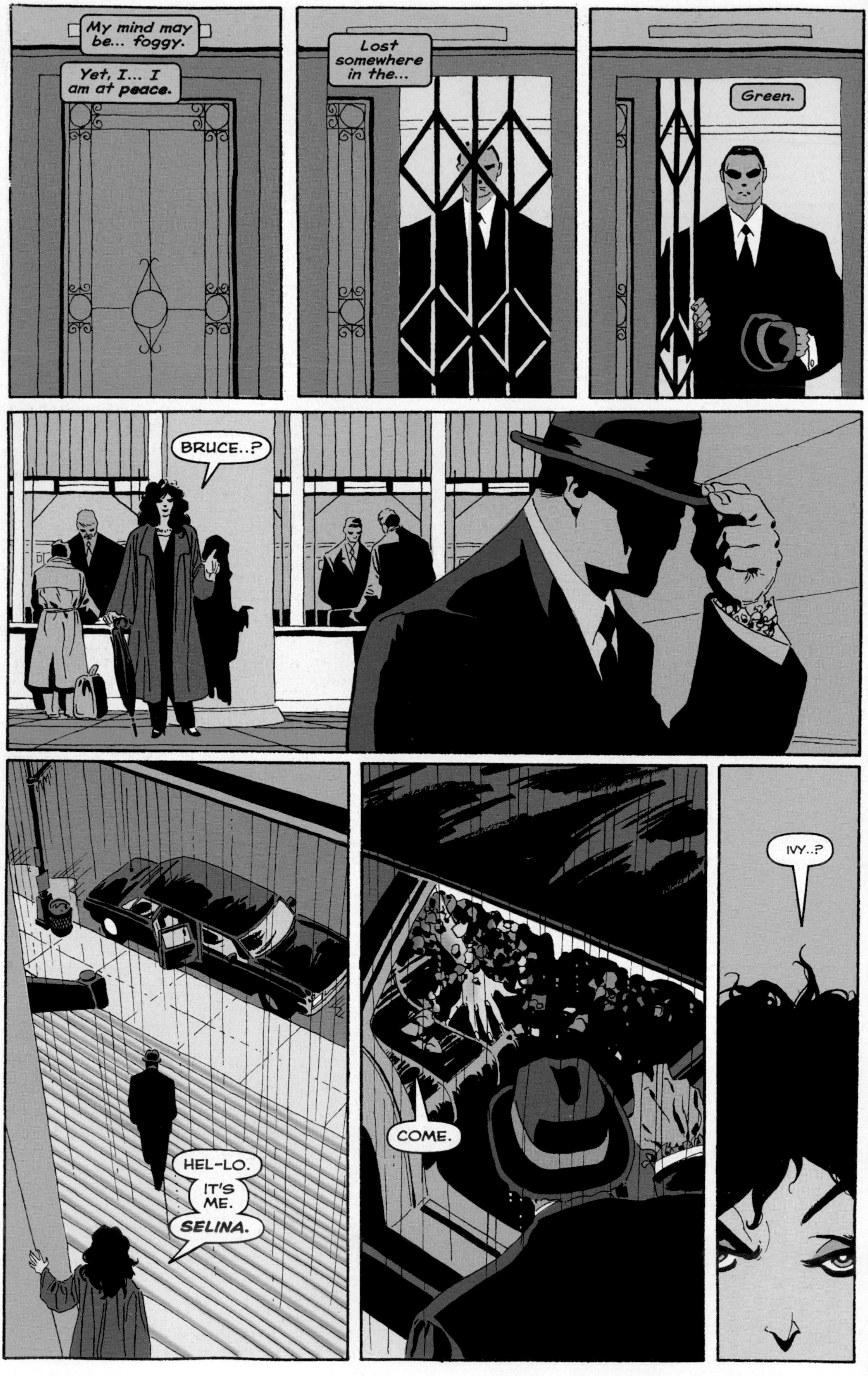
My mind may be... foggy.
Yet, I... I am at peace.
Lost somewhere in the...
Green.
BRUCE..?
HEL-LO.
IT'S ME.
SELINA.
COME.
IVY..?

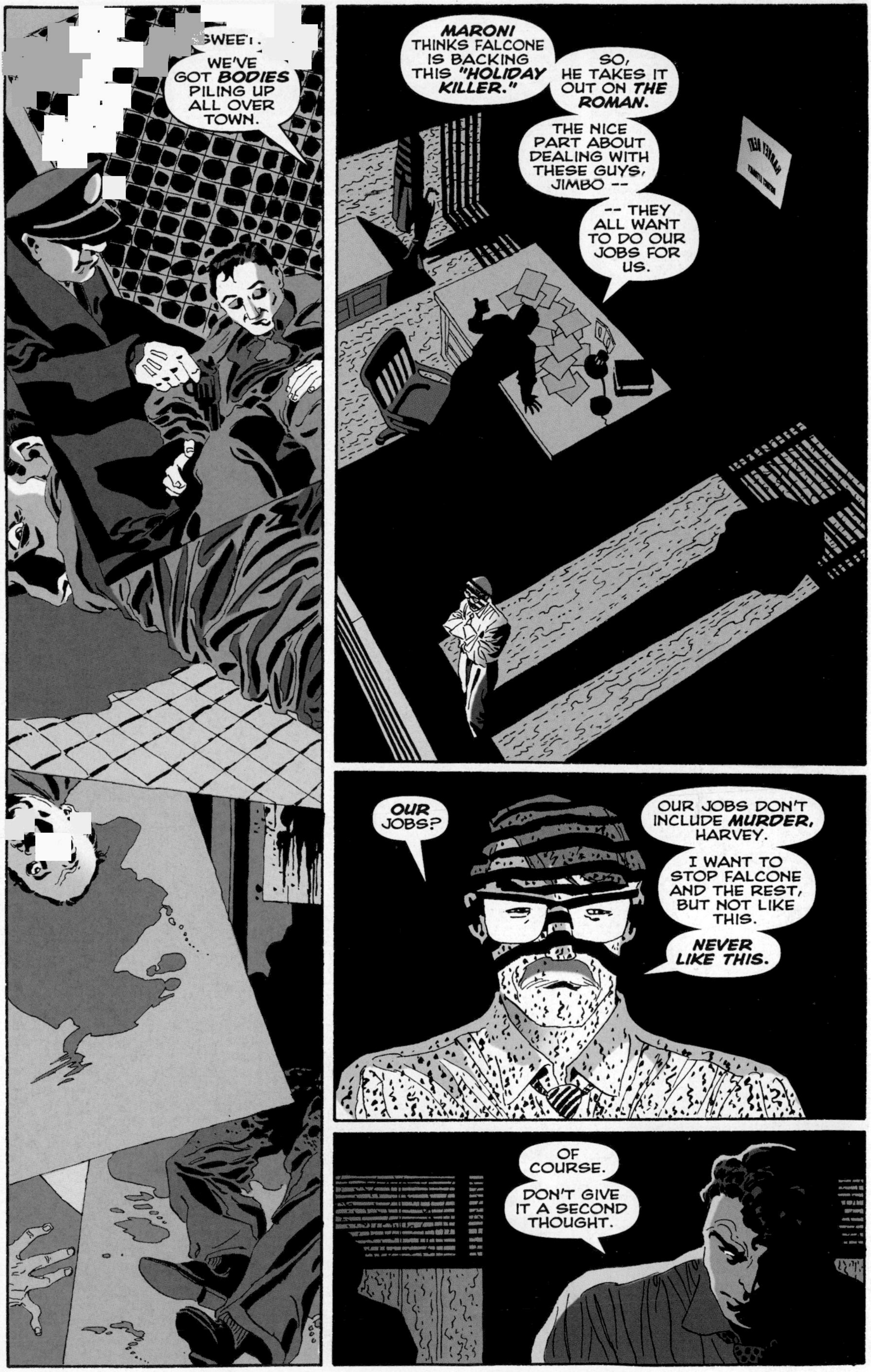
SWEET.
WE'VE GOT BODIES PILING UP ALL OVER TOWN.
MARONI THINKS FALCONE IS BACKING THIS "HOLIDAY KILLER."
SO, HE TAKES IT OUT ON THE ROMAN.
THE NICE PART ABOUT DEALING WITH THESE GUYS, JIMBO --
-- THEY ALL WANT TO DO OUR JOBS FOR US.
OUR JOBS?
OUR JOBS DON'T INCLUDE MURDER, HARVEY.
I WANT TO STOP FALCONE AND THE REST, BUT NOT LIKE THIS.
NEVER LIKE THIS.
OF COURSE.
DON'T GIVE IT A SECOND THOUGHT.

GREEN.

Huh?

WHEN I WAS A CHILD, GROWING UP IN *CHICAGO*, WE LOOKED FORWARD TO SAINT PATRICK'S DAY.

THEY WOULD *CLOSE THE SCHOOLS* SO WE COULD GO DOWNTOWN AND SEE THE PARADE.

THE CITY WOULD TURN THE RIVER *GREEN* AND WE ALL THOUGHT IT WAS THE WORK OF *LEPRECHAUNS.*

WHAT DO YOU WANT TO DO ABOUT *BRUCE WAYNE?*

WITH WHAT WE *SUSPECT* ABOUT HIS *CONNECTION* TO THE ROMAN, WE COULD HURT THEM.

SAINT PATRICK'S DAY.

WE ALL THINK OF GREEN.

NOW. IT'S RED.

BLOOD RED.

SAINT PATRICK'S DAY IS COMING AND WE'RE NO CLOSER TO FINDING OUT WHO THIS *MADMAN* IS.

"HOLIDAY."

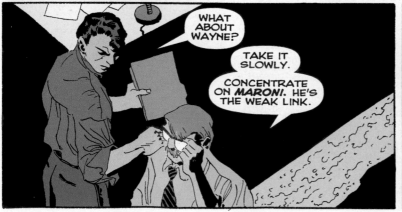

WHAT ABOUT WAYNE?

TAKE IT SLOWLY.

CONCENTRATE ON *MARONI.* HE'S THE WEAK LINK.

MARONI *AND* WAYNE.

TWO FOR ONE.

I LIKE IT...

HARVE DEN

DISTRICT ATTORN

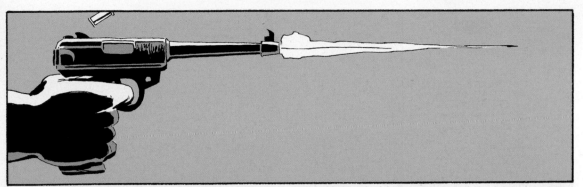

MORTE!

Carla Viti.
The Roman's
sister.

The Viti family
rules Chicago.
With designs on
Gotham City.

I RANG THE BELL.

YOU DIDN'T ANSWER.

I'M NOT INTERRUPTING *ANYTHING*, AM I --

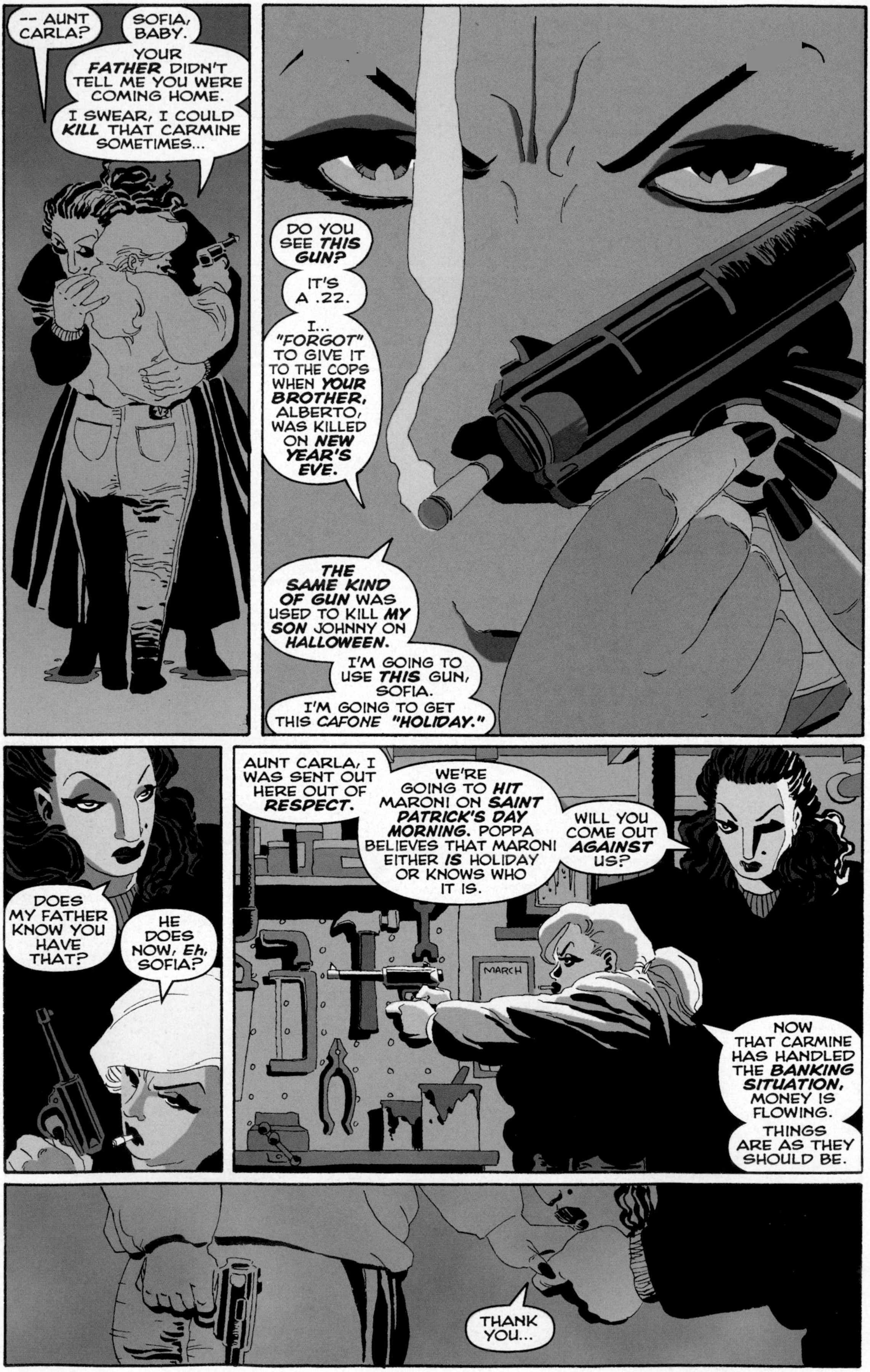

-- AUNT CARLA?
SOFIA, BABY.
YOUR FATHER DIDN'T TELL ME YOU WERE COMING HOME.
I SWEAR, I COULD KILL THAT CARMINE SOMETIMES...
DO YOU SEE THIS GUN?
IT'S A .22.
I... "FORGOT" TO GIVE IT TO THE COPS WHEN YOUR BROTHER, ALBERTO, WAS KILLED ON NEW YEAR'S EVE.
THE SAME KIND OF GUN WAS USED TO KILL MY SON JOHNNY ON HALLOWEEN.
I'M GOING TO USE THIS GUN, SOFIA.
I'M GOING TO GET THIS CAFONE "HOLIDAY."
DOES MY FATHER KNOW YOU HAVE THAT?
HE DOES NOW, Eh, SOFIA?
AUNT CARLA, I WAS SENT OUT HERE OUT OF RESPECT.
WE'RE GOING TO HIT MARONI ON SAINT PATRICK'S DAY MORNING. POPPA BELIEVES THAT MARONI EITHER IS HOLIDAY OR KNOWS WHO IT IS.
WILL YOU COME OUT AGAINST US?
MARCH
NOW THAT CARMINE HAS HANDLED THE BANKING SITUATION, MONEY IS FLOWING.
THINGS ARE AS THEY SHOULD BE.
THANK YOU...

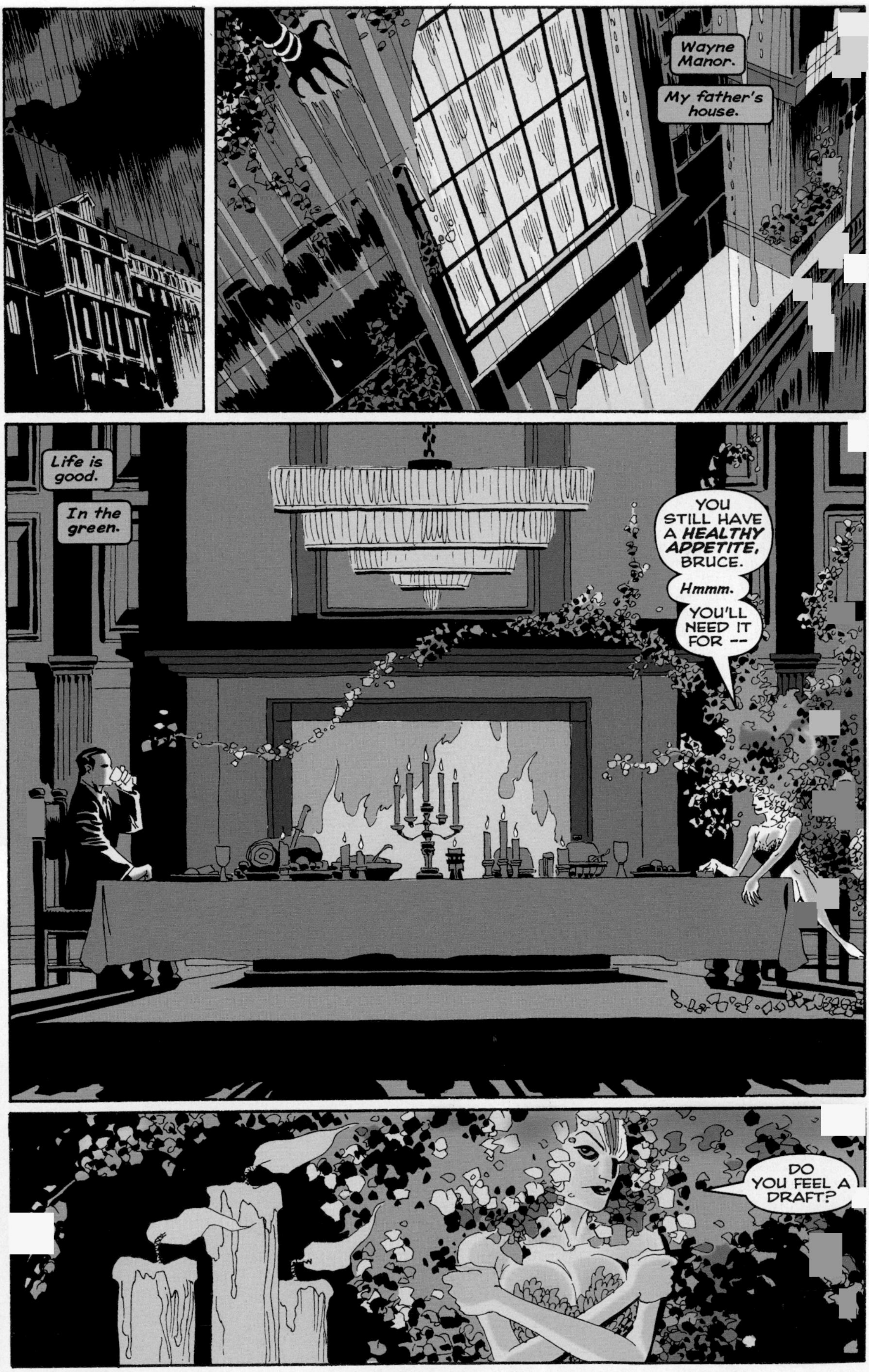
Wayne Manor.
My father's house.
Life is good.
In the green.
YOU STILL HAVE A HEALTHY APPETITE, BRUCE.
Hmmm.
YOU'LL NEED IT FOR --
DO YOU FEEL A DRAFT?

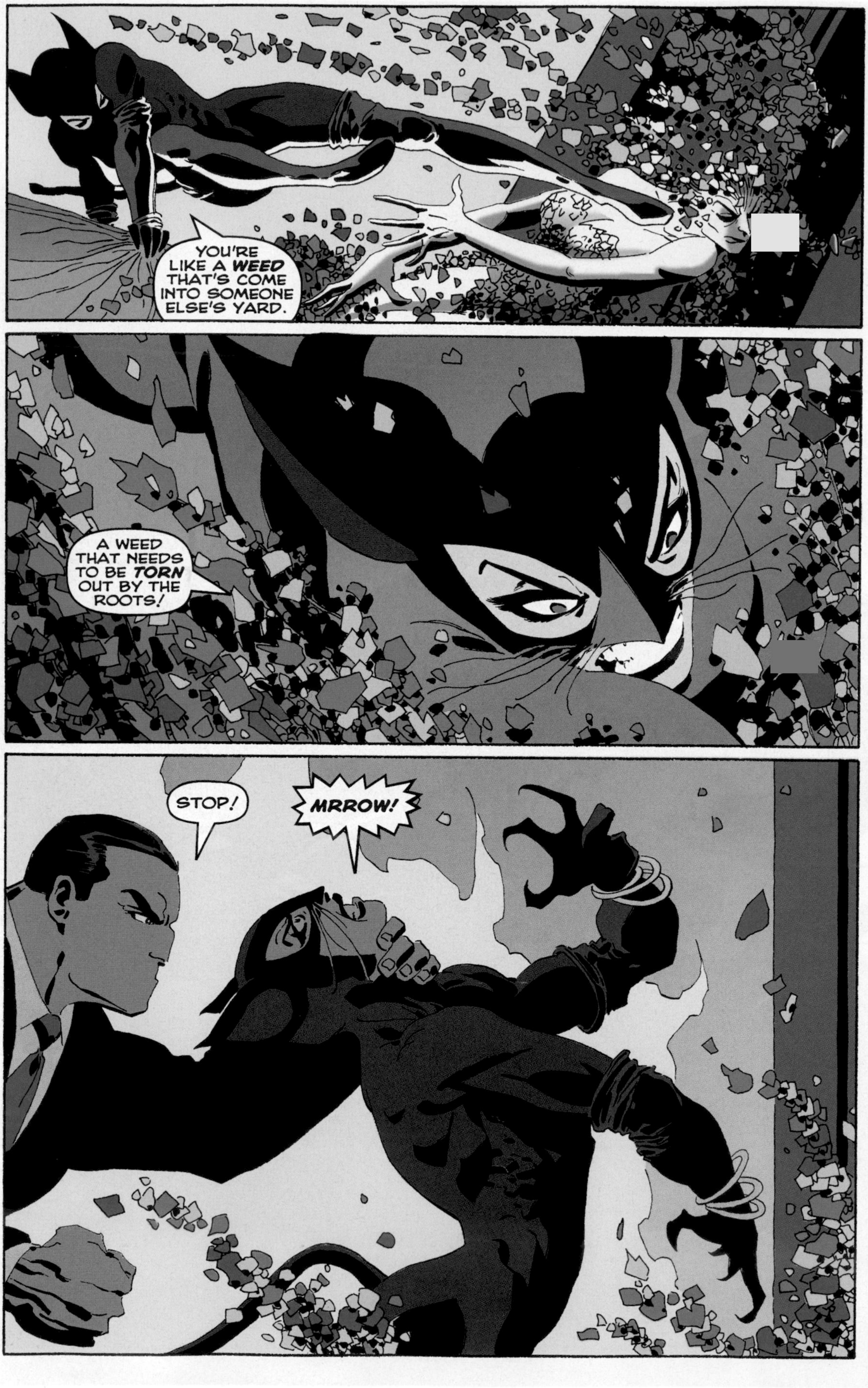
YOU'RE LIKE A WEED THAT'S COME INTO SOMEONE ELSE'S YARD.
A WEED THAT NEEDS TO BE TORN OUT BY THE ROOTS!
STOP!
MRROW!

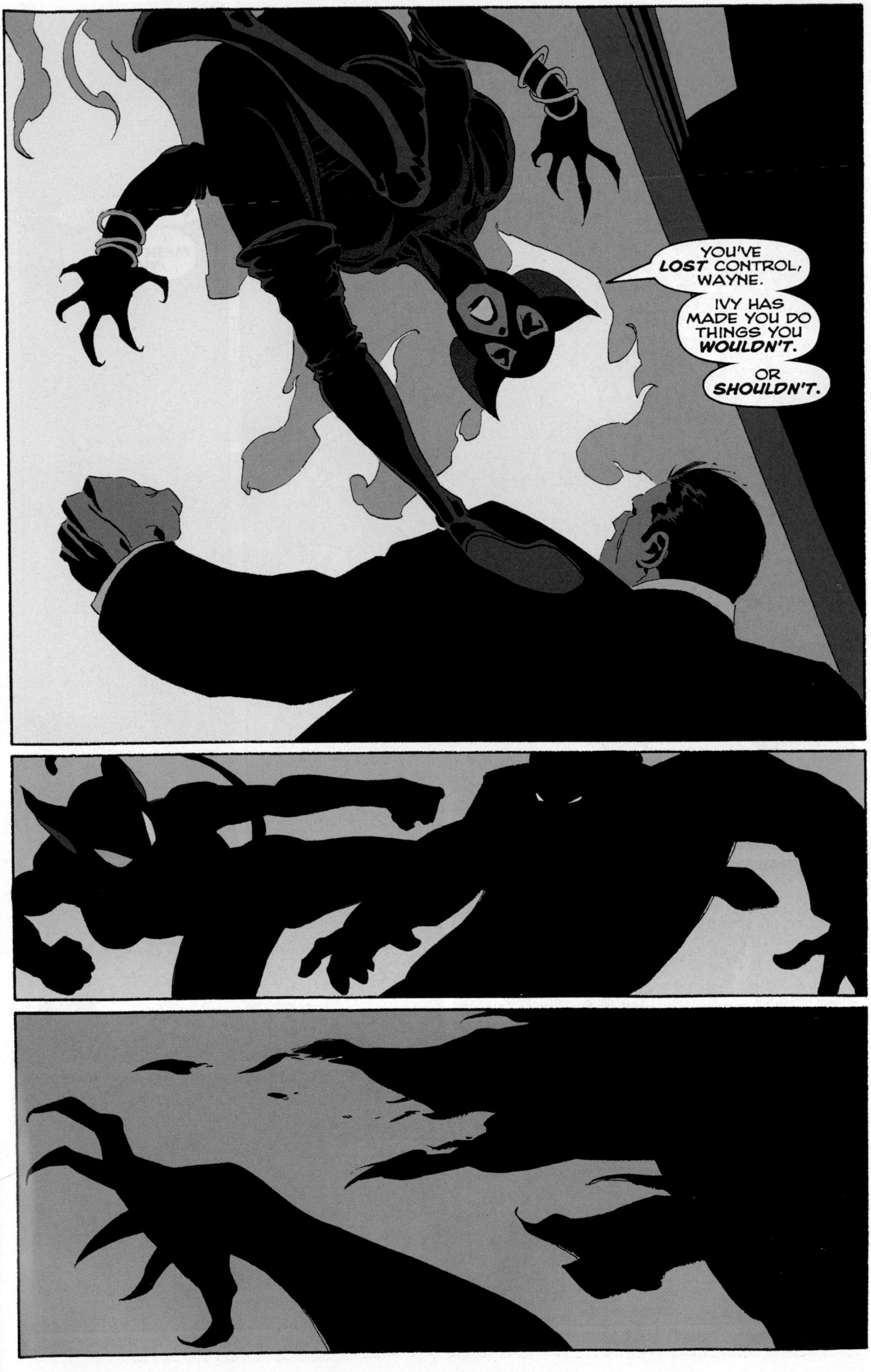
YOU'VE LOST CONTROL, WAYNE.
IVY HAS MADE YOU DO THINGS YOU WOULDN'T.
OR SHOULDN'T.

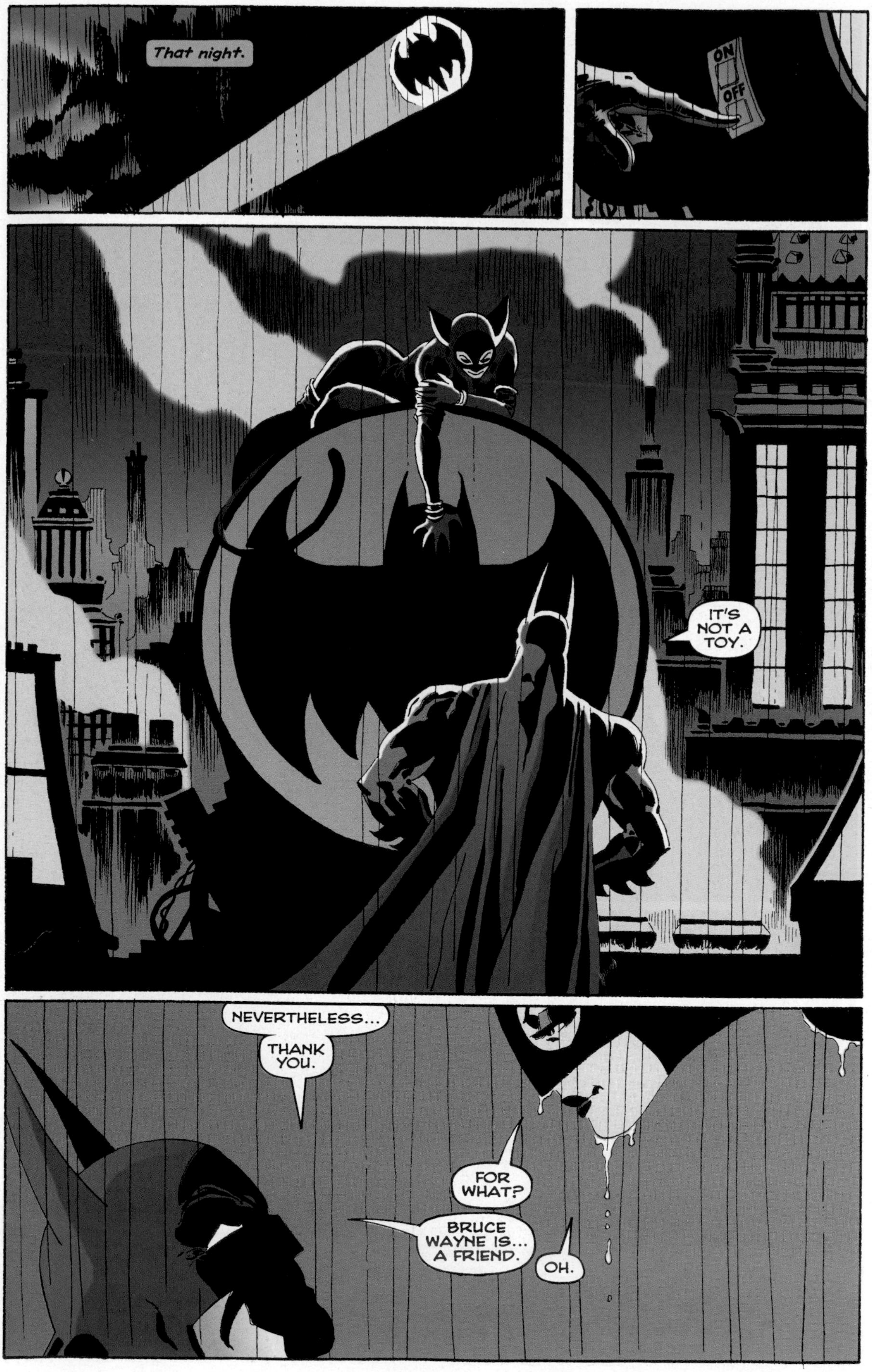
That night.
ON
OFF
IT'S NOT A TOY.
NEVERTHELESS...
THANK YOU.
FOR WHAT?
BRUCE WAYNE IS... A FRIEND.
OH.

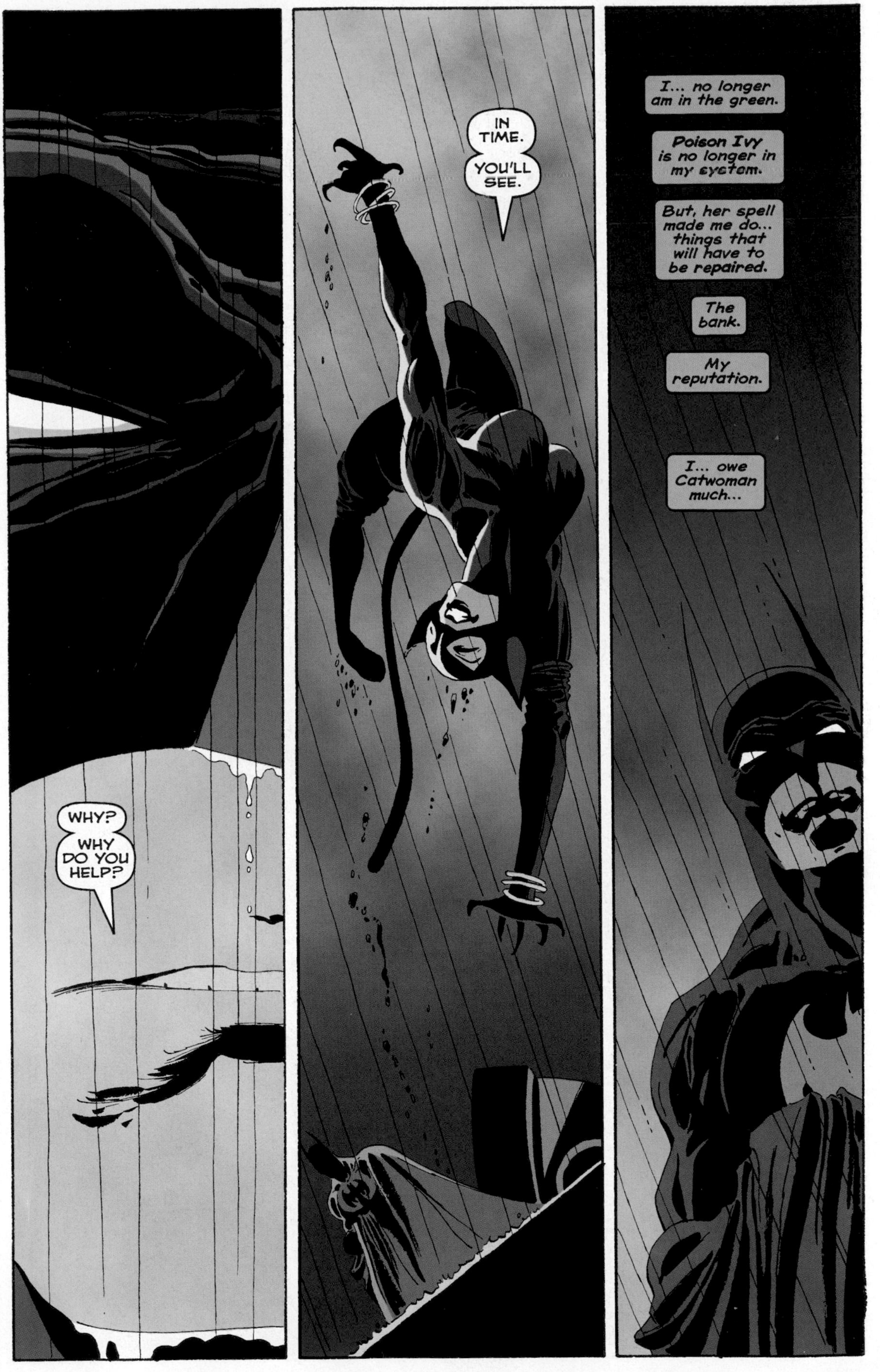
WHY? WHY DO YOU HELP?
IN TIME.
YOU'LL SEE.
I... no longer am in the green.
Poison Ivy is no longer in my system.
But, her spell made me do... things that will have to be repaired.
The bank.
My reputation.
I... owe Catwoman much...

CHAPTER SEVEN

APRIL FOOL'S DAY

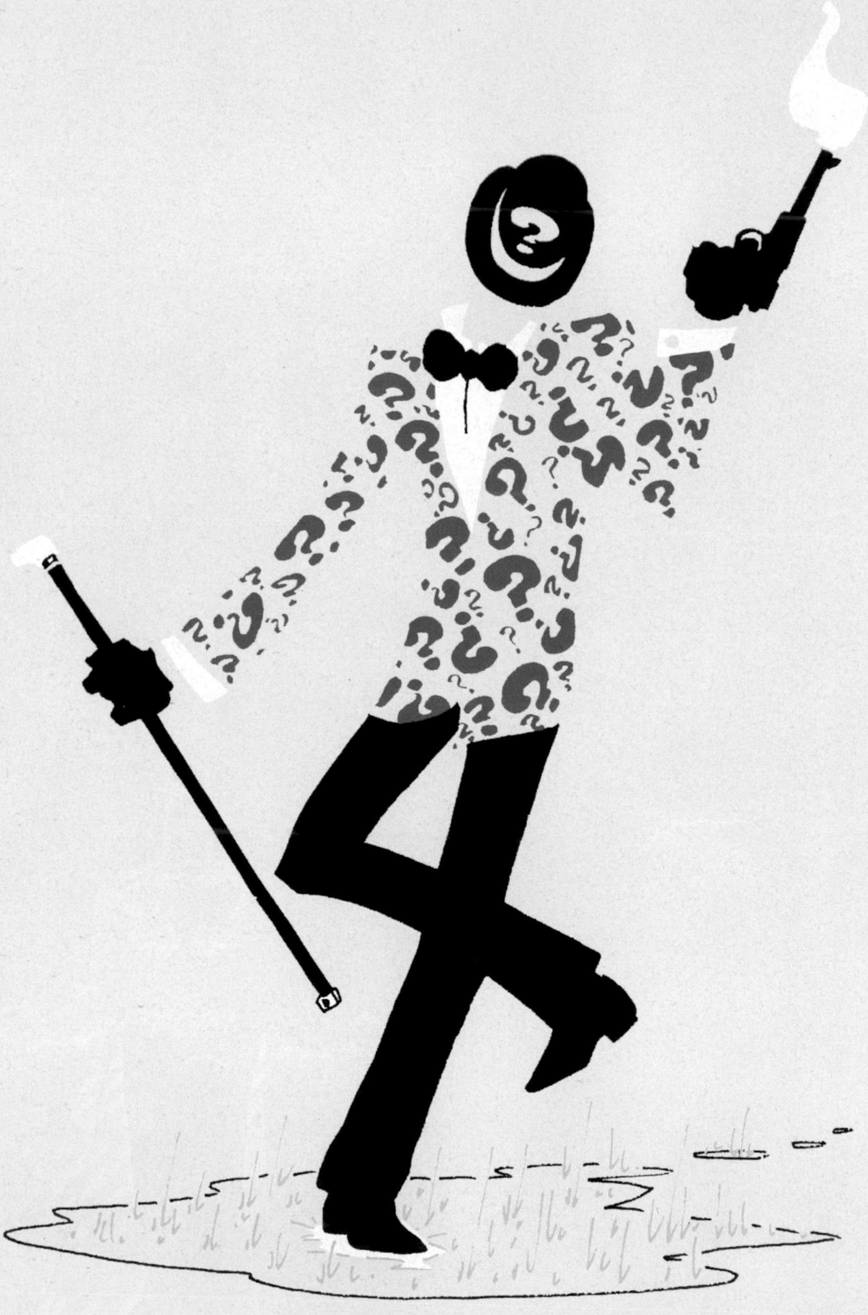

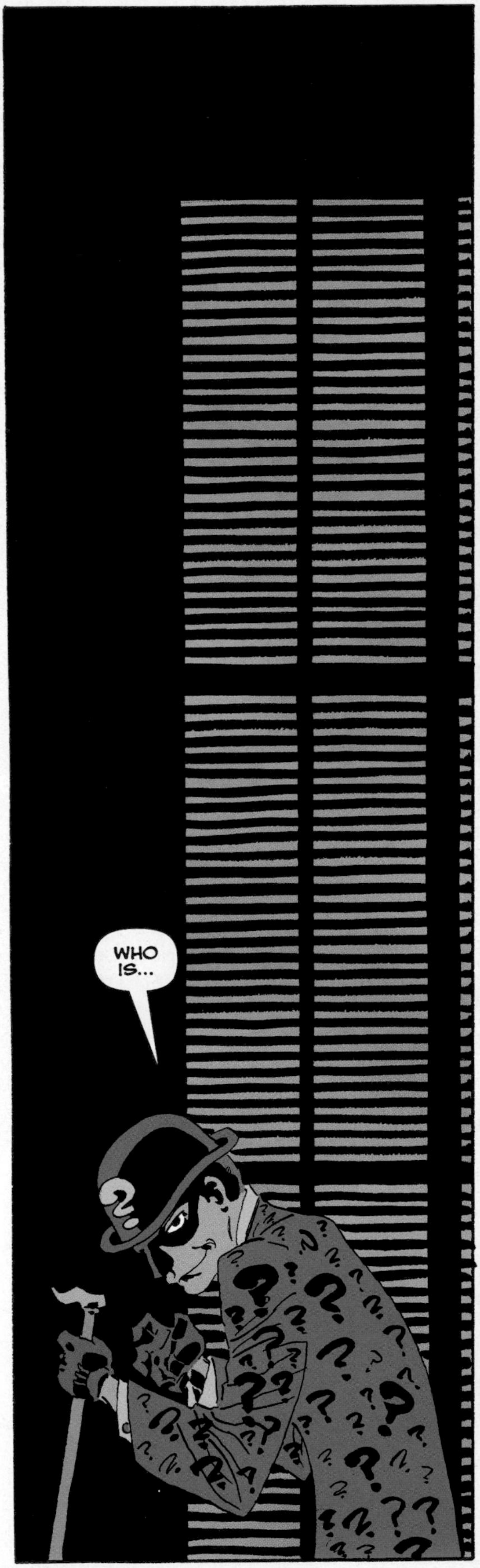
WHO IS...

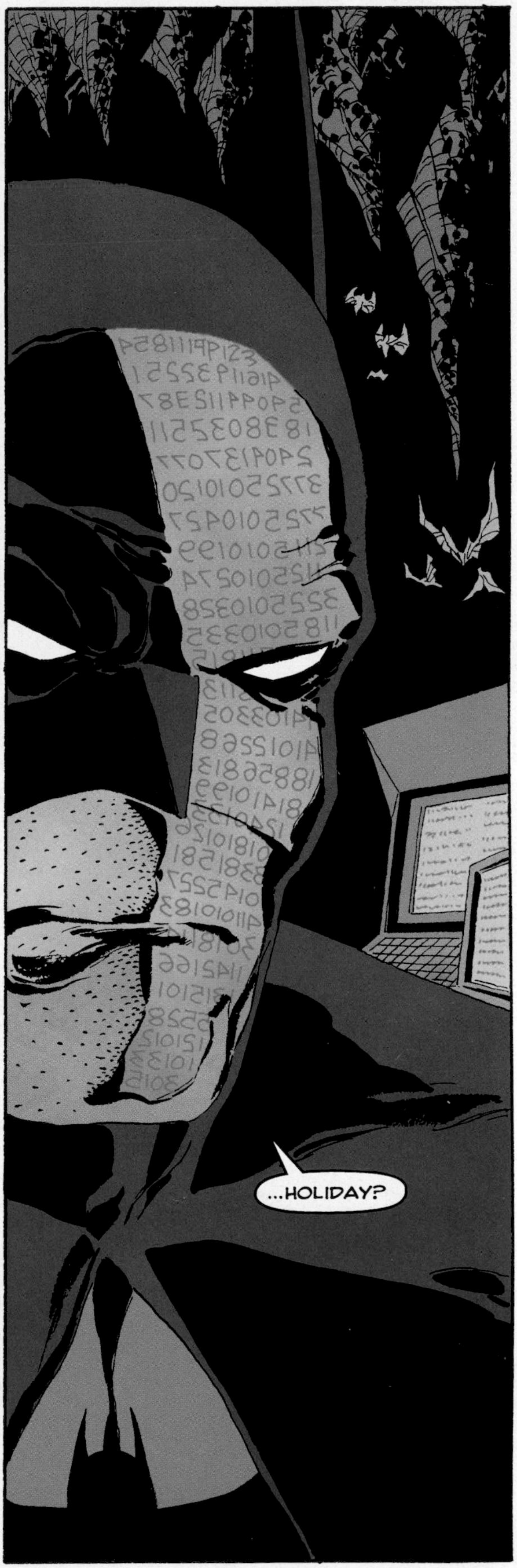
...HOLIDAY?

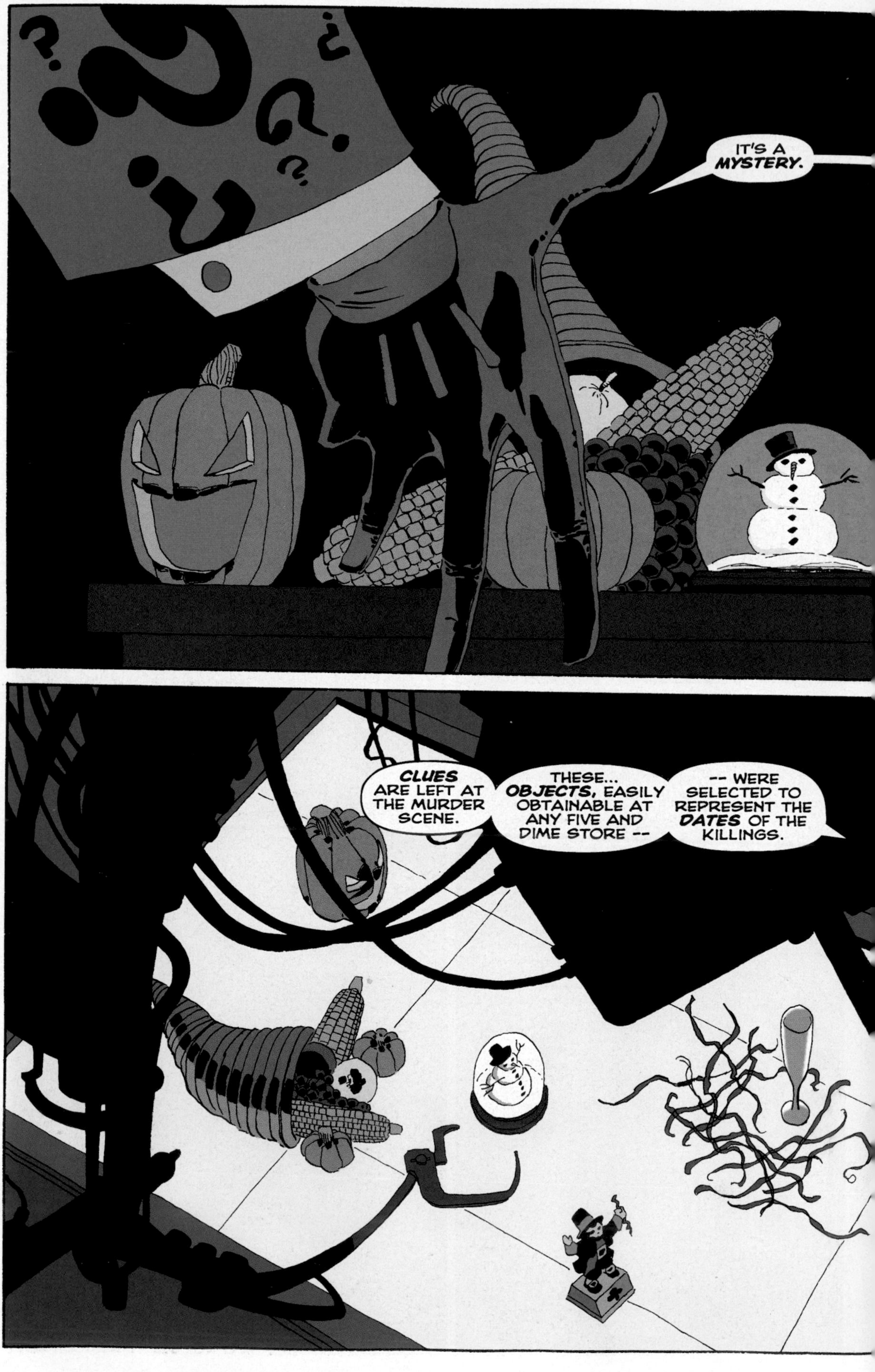
IT'S A MYSTERY.
CLUES ARE LEFT AT THE MURDER SCENE.
THESE... OBJECTS, EASILY OBTAINABLE AT ANY FIVE AND DIME STORE --
-- WERE SELECTED TO REPRESENT THE DATES OF THE KILLINGS.

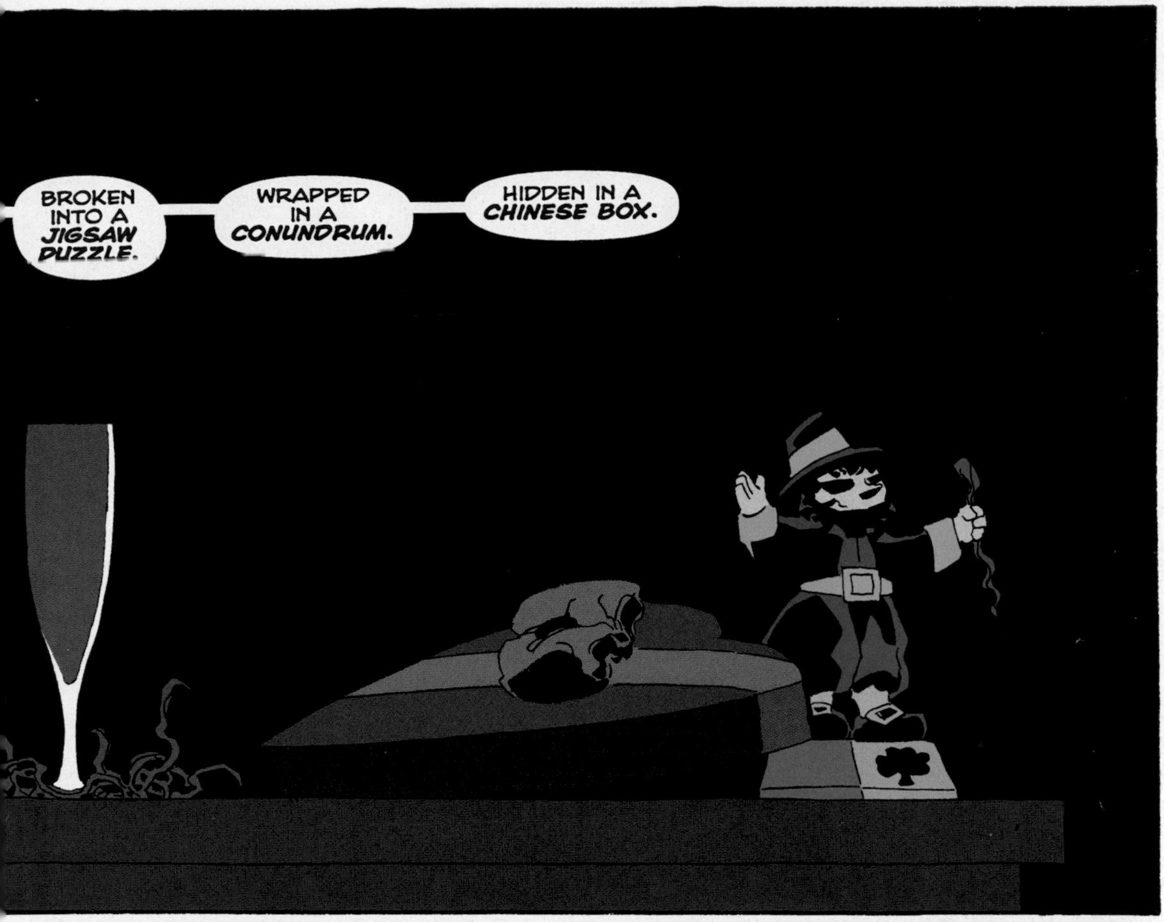
BROKEN INTO A JIGSAW PUZZLE.
WRAPPED IN A CONUNDRUM.
HIDDEN IN A CHINESE BOX.

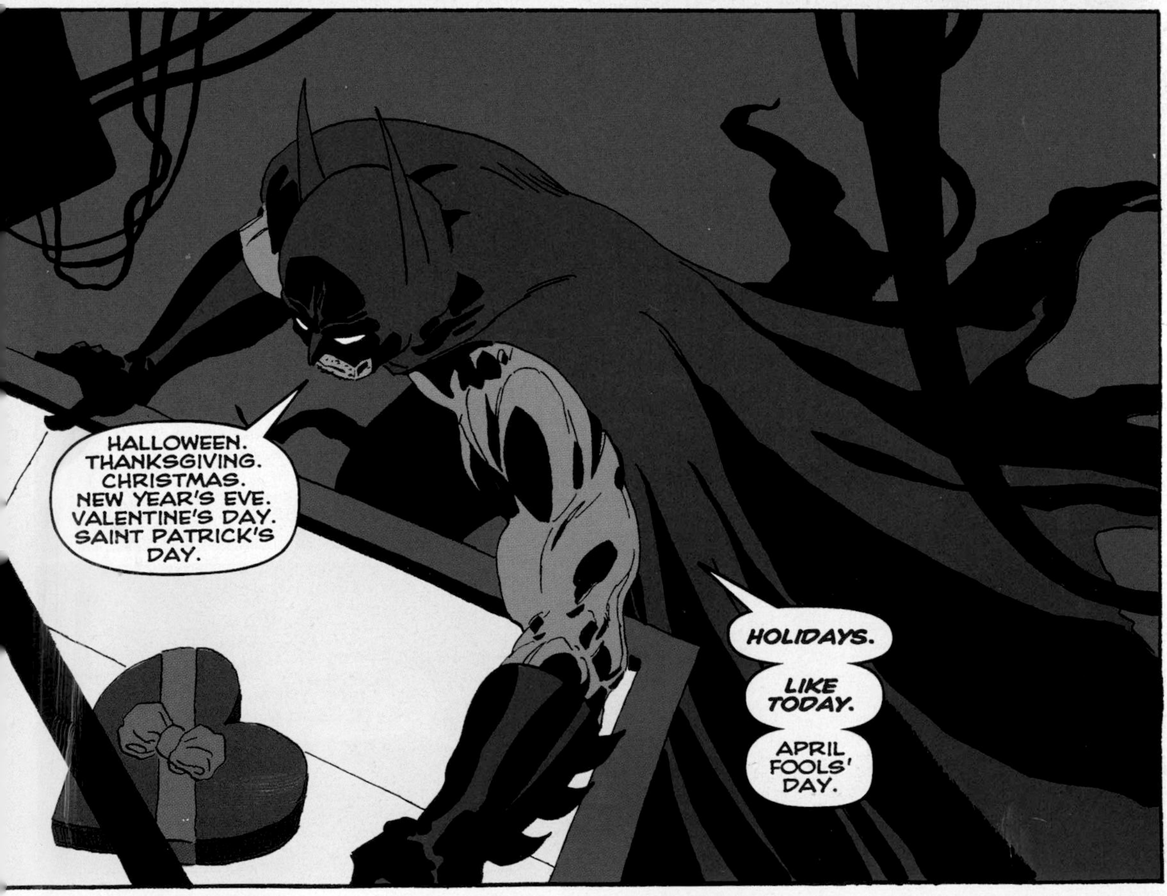
HALLOWEEN. THANKSGIVING. CHRISTMAS. NEW YEAR'S EVE. VALENTINE'S DAY. SAINT PATRICK'S DAY.
HOLIDAYS.
LIKE TODAY.
APRIL FOOLS' DAY.

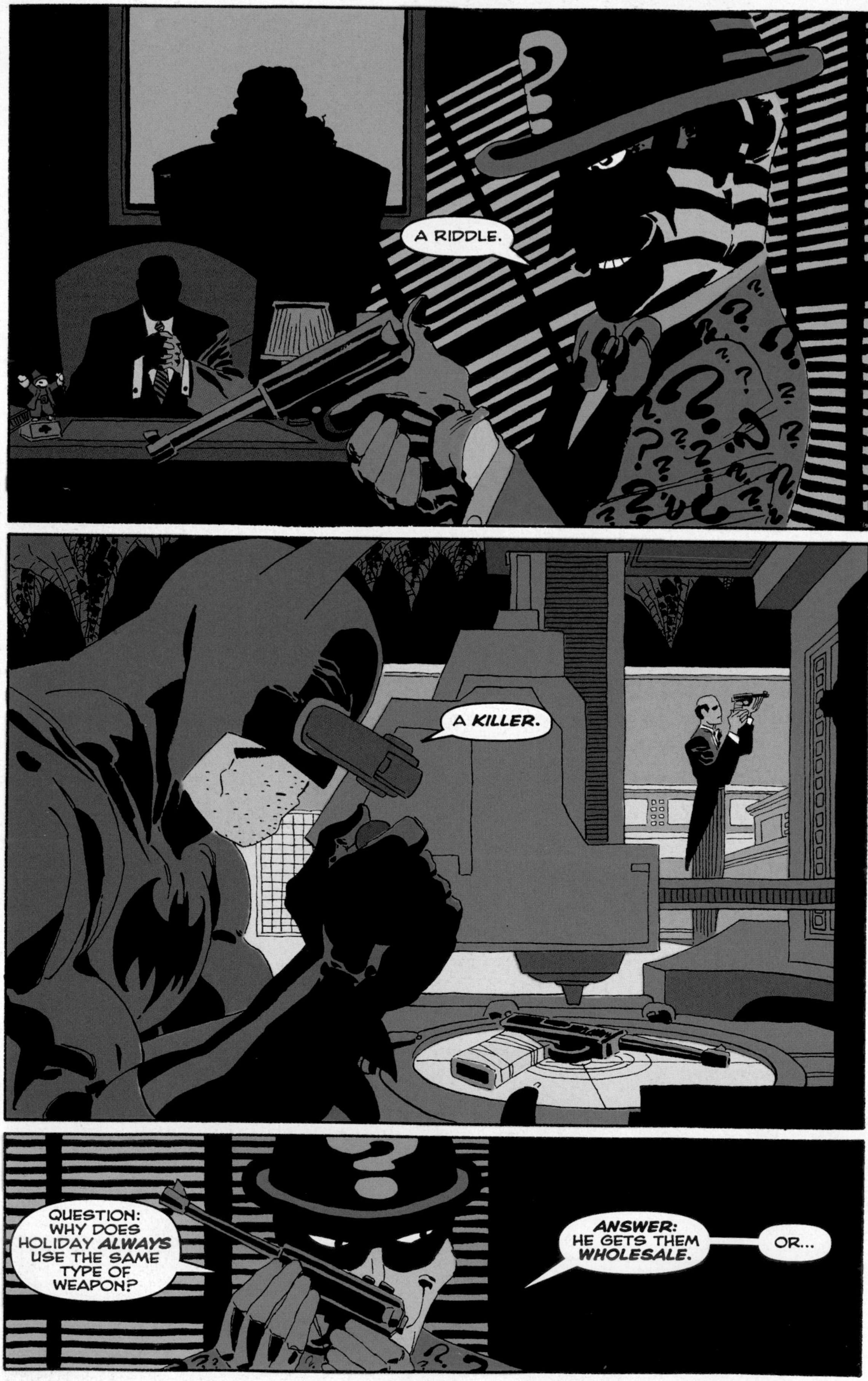
A RIDDLE.
A KILLER.
QUESTION: WHY DOES HOLIDAY ALWAYS USE THE SAME TYPE OF WEAPON?
ANSWER: HE GETS THEM WHOLESALE.
OR...

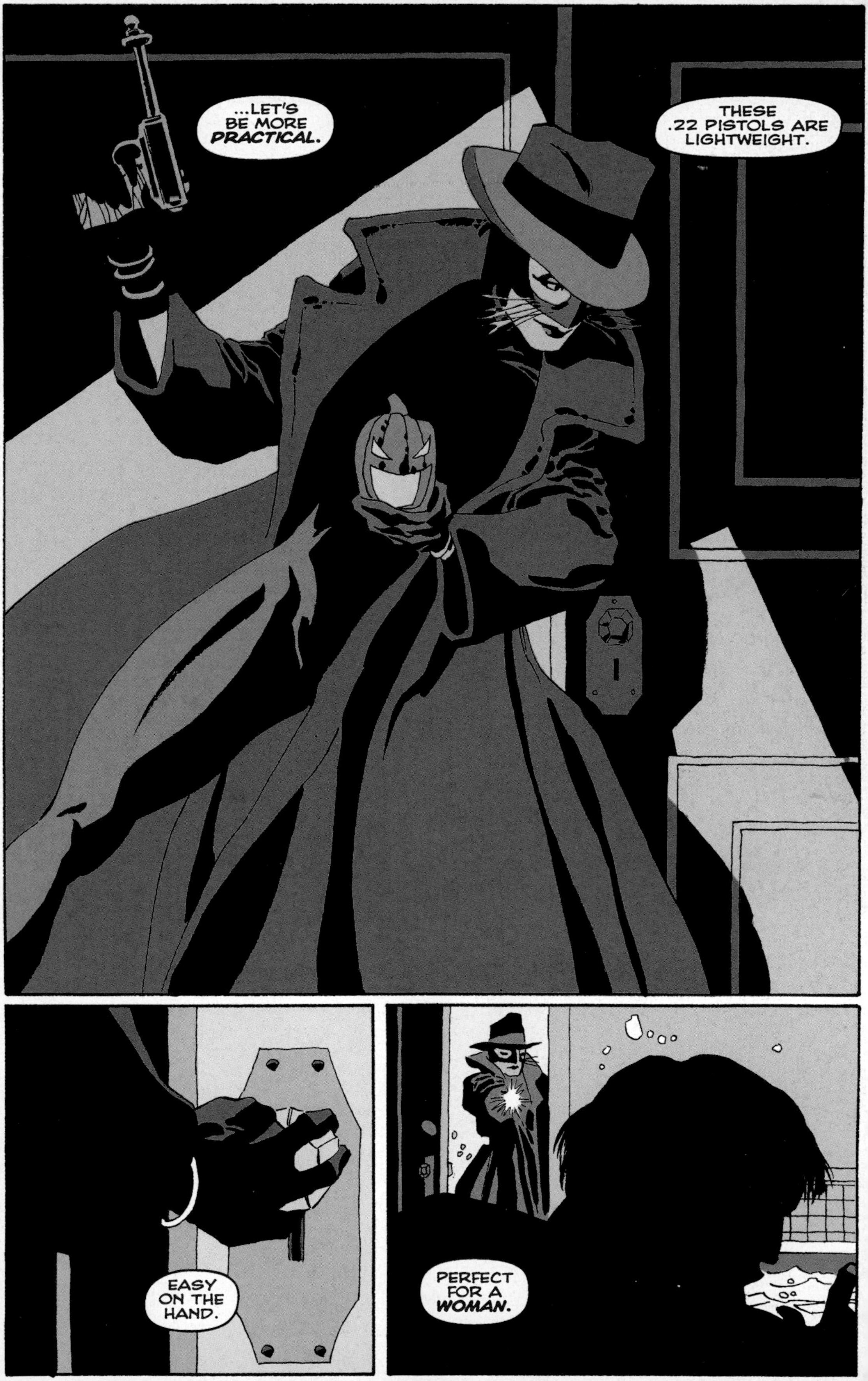
...LET'S BE MORE PRACTICAL.
THESE .22 PISTOLS ARE LIGHTWEIGHT.
EASY ON THE HAND.
PERFECT FOR A WOMAN.

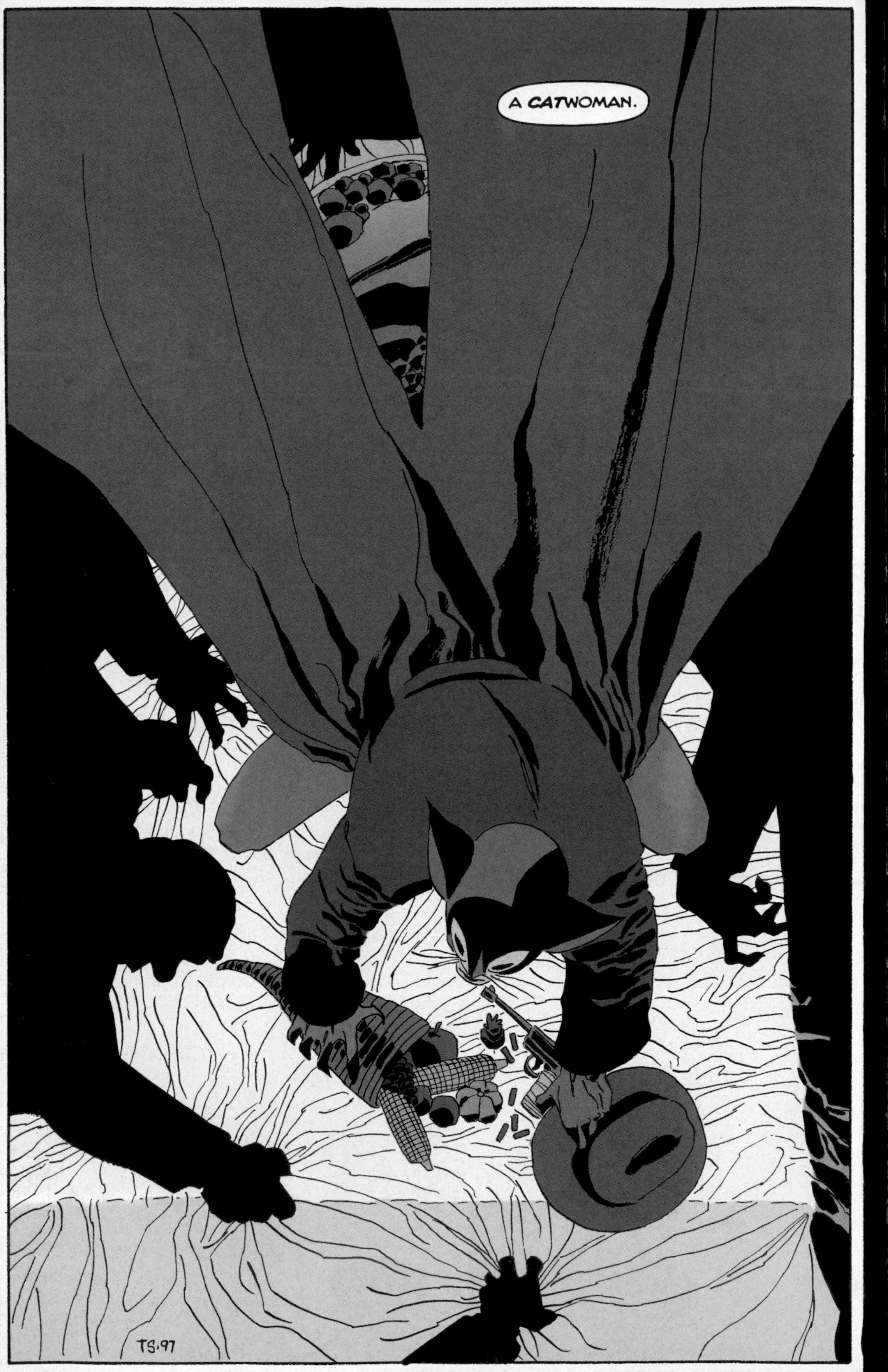
A CATWOMAN.
TS·97

WITH THE BREAK-IN LAST JUNE, SHE HAD ACCESS TO *MR. FALCONE'S SAFE.*

AND THEREFORE, THE *NAMES* OF EVERYONE IN *"THE ROMAN"* EMPIRE.

ADD TO THAT, THE *MILLION DOLLAR BOUNTY* MR. FALCONE SUBSEQUENTLY PUT ON HER HEAD.

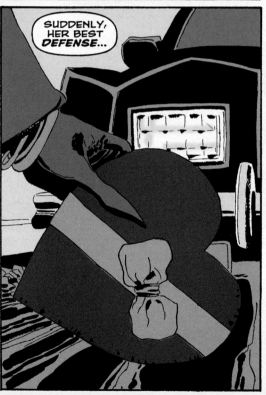

SUDDENLY, HER BEST *DEFENSE...*

...IS A GOOD *OFFENSE...*

MARONI.

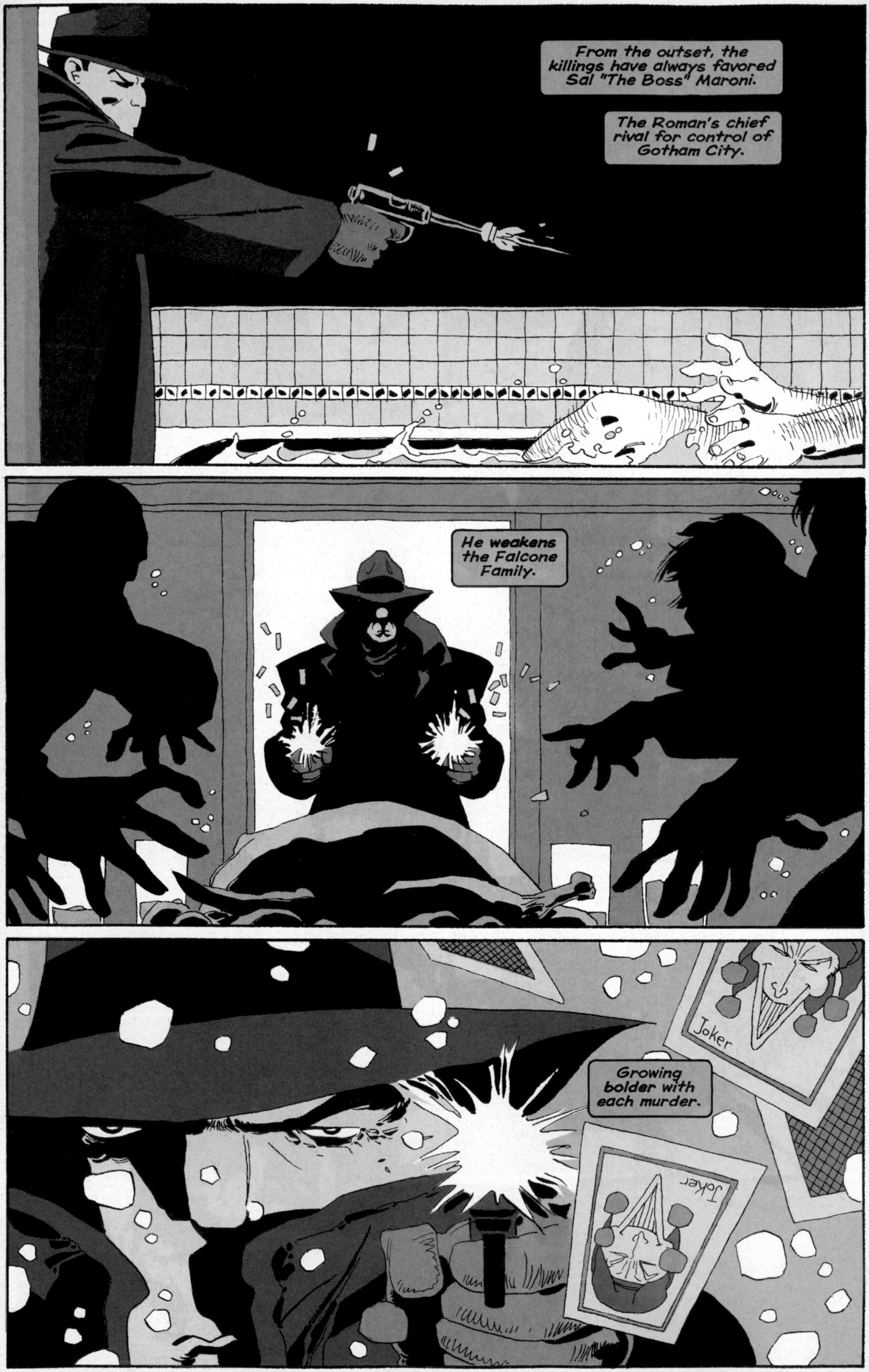
From the outset, the killings have always favored Sal "The Boss" Maroni.
The Roman's chief rival for control of Gotham City.
He weakens the Falcone Family.
Joker
Growing bolder with each murder.
Joker

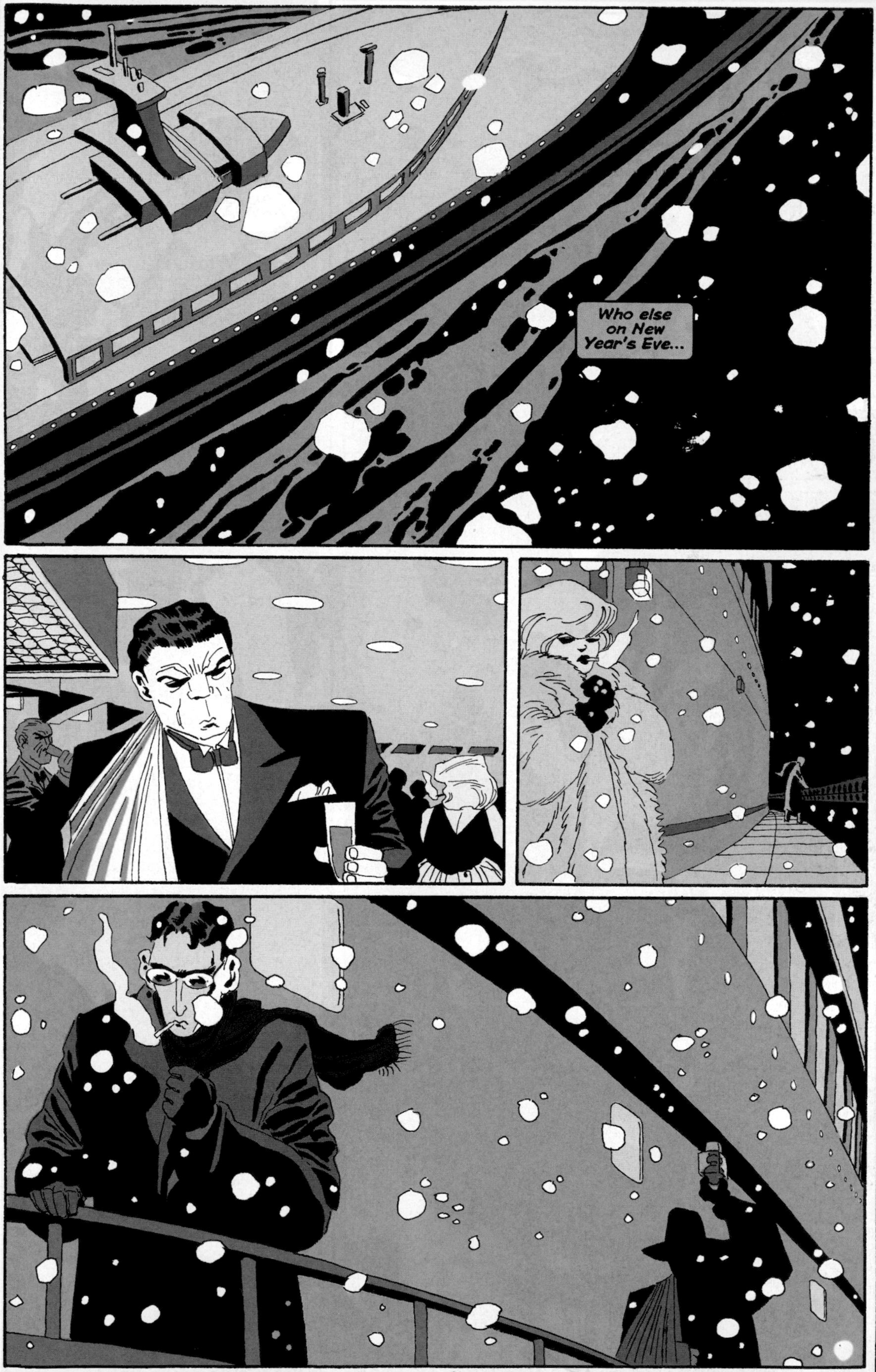
Who else on New Year's Eve...

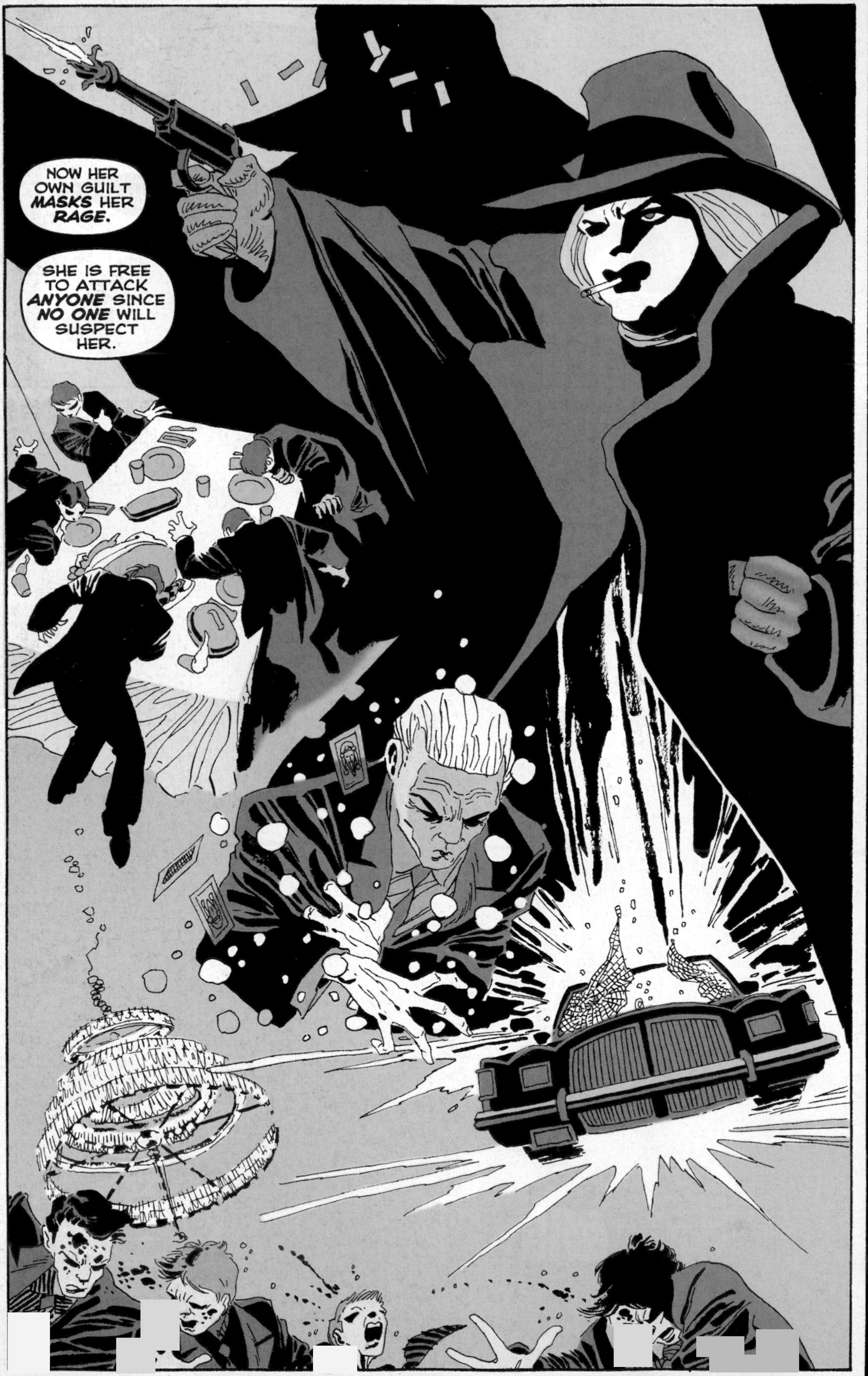
NOW HER OWN GUILT MASKS HER RAGE.
SHE IS FREE TO ATTACK ANYONE SINCE NO ONE WILL SUSPECT HER.

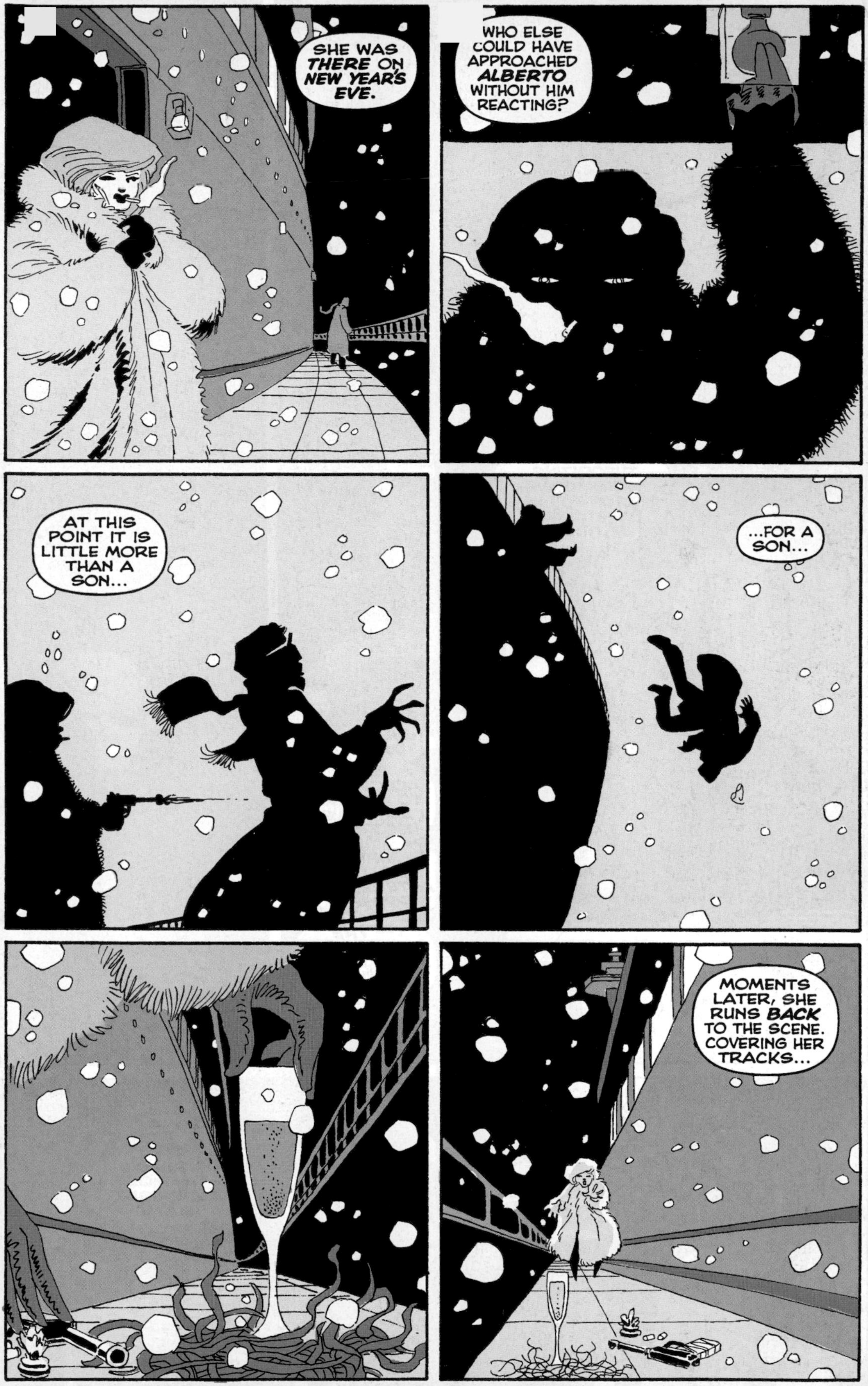
SHE WAS *THERE* ON *NEW YEAR'S EVE.*
WHO ELSE COULD HAVE APPROACHED *ALBERTO* WITHOUT HIM REACTING?
AT THIS POINT IT IS LITTLE MORE THAN A SON...
...FOR A SON...
MOMENTS LATER, SHE RUNS *BACK* TO THE SCENE. COVERING HER TRACKS...

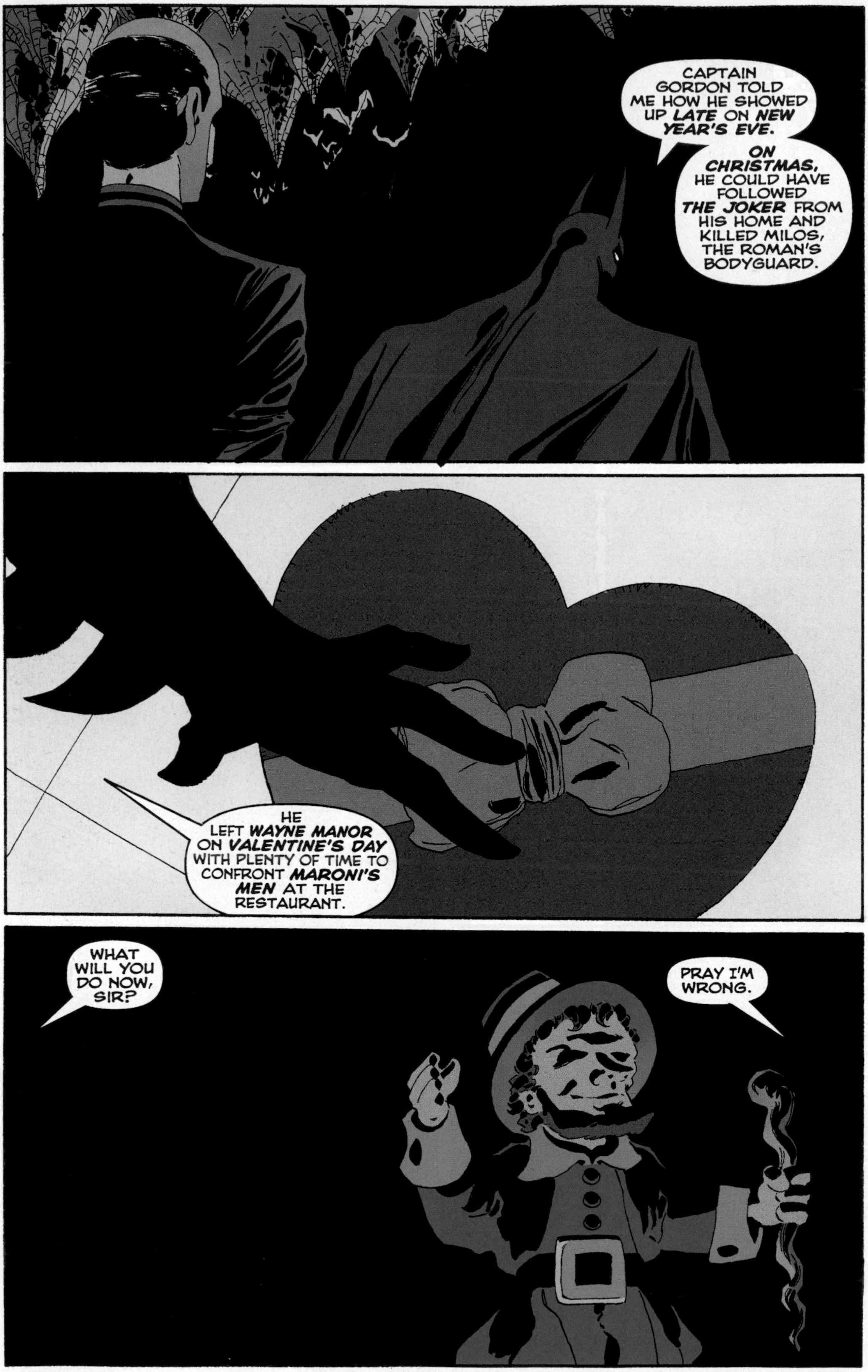
CAPTAIN GORDON TOLD ME HOW HE SHOWED UP LATE ON NEW YEAR'S EVE.
ON CHRISTMAS, HE COULD HAVE FOLLOWED THE JOKER FROM HIS HOME AND KILLED MILOS, THE ROMAN'S BODYGUARD.
HE LEFT WAYNE MANOR ON VALENTINE'S DAY WITH PLENTY OF TIME TO CONFRONT MARONI'S MEN AT THE RESTAURANT.
WHAT WILL YOU DO NOW, SIR?
PRAY I'M WRONG.

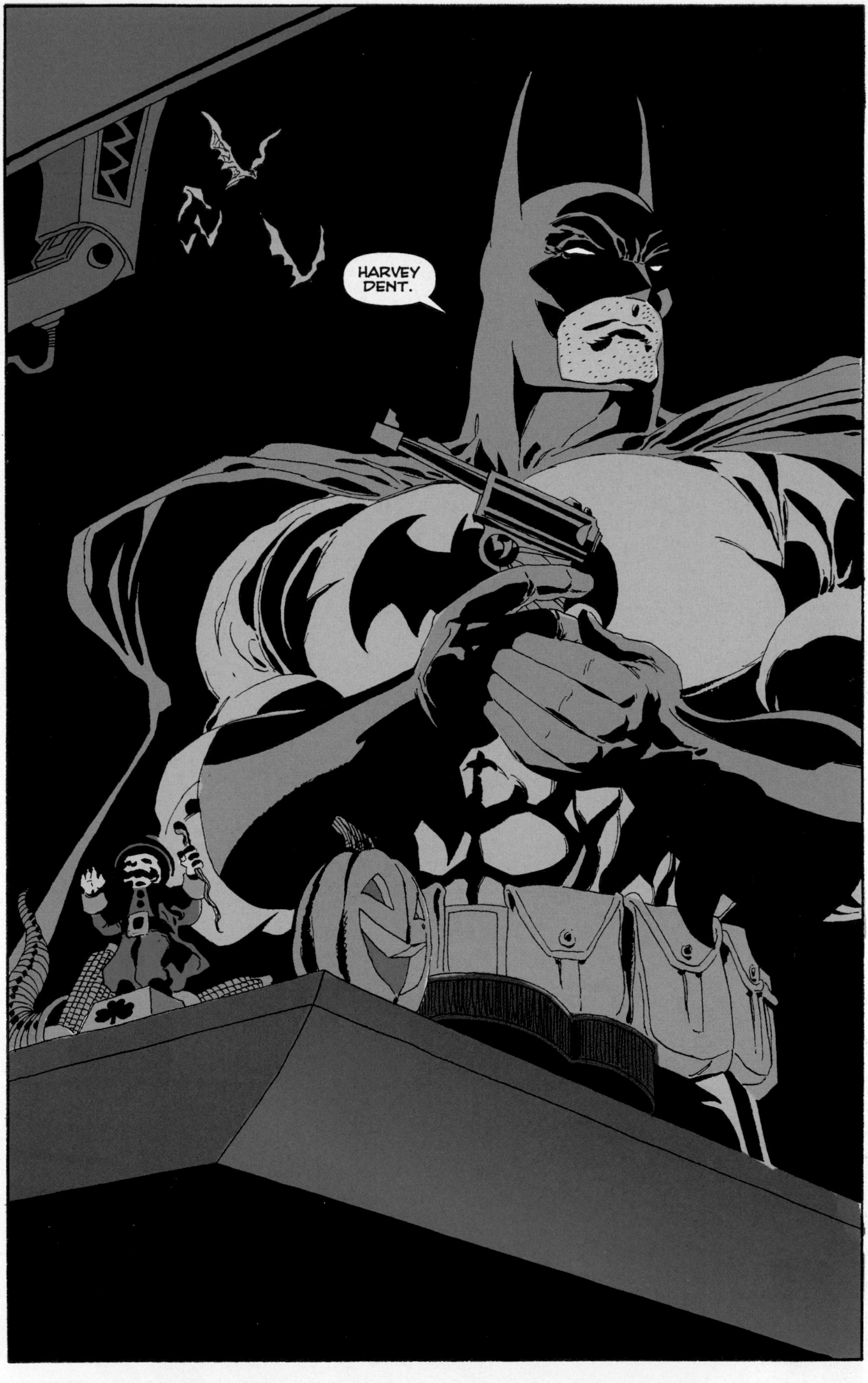
HARVEY DENT.

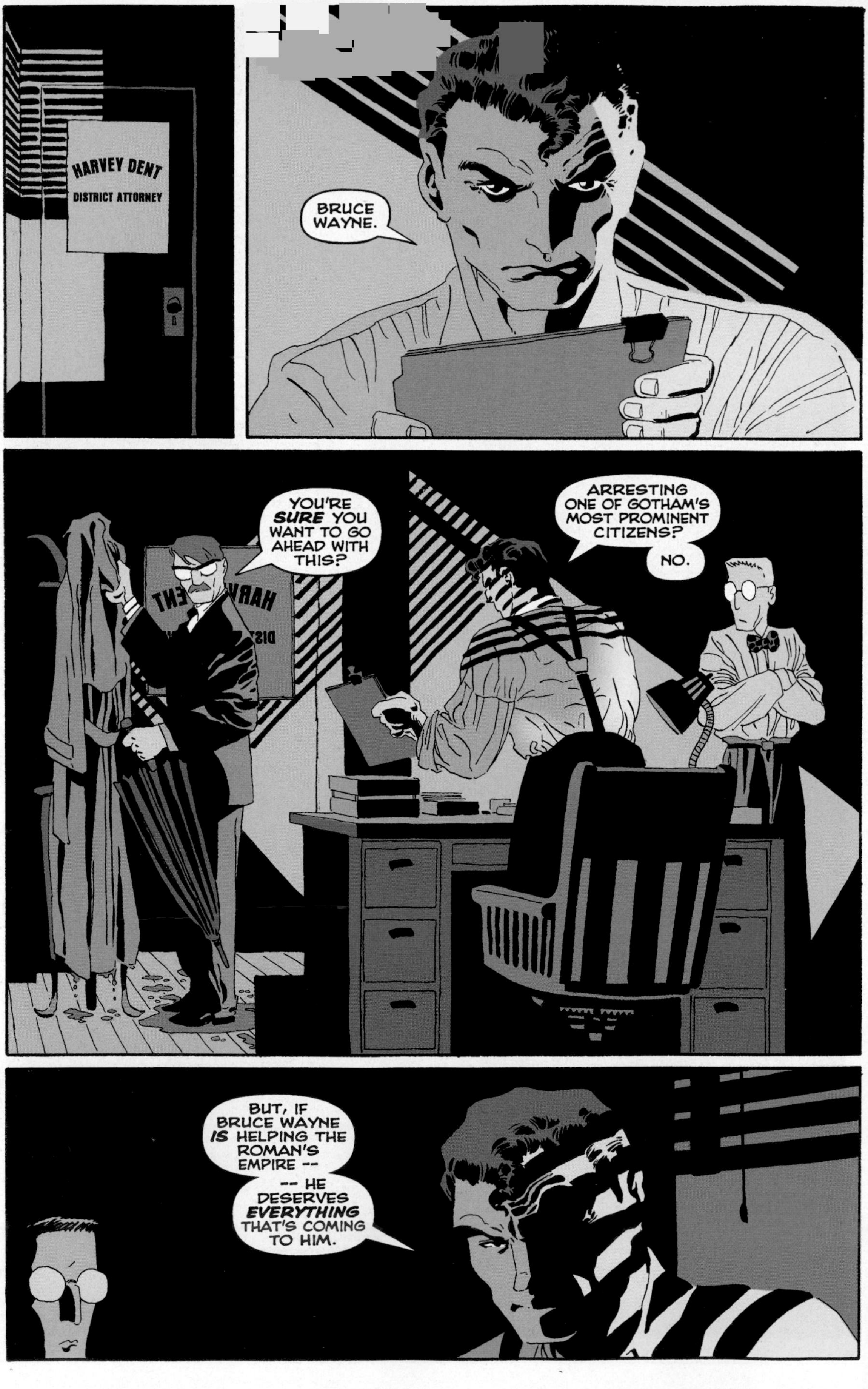
HARVEY DENT
DISTRICT ATTORNEY
BRUCE WAYNE.
YOU'RE *SURE* YOU WANT TO GO AHEAD WITH THIS?
ARRESTING ONE OF GOTHAM'S MOST PROMINENT CITIZENS?
NO.
BUT, IF BRUCE WAYNE *IS* HELPING THE ROMAN'S EMPIRE --
-- HE DESERVES *EVERYTHING* THAT'S COMING TO HIM.

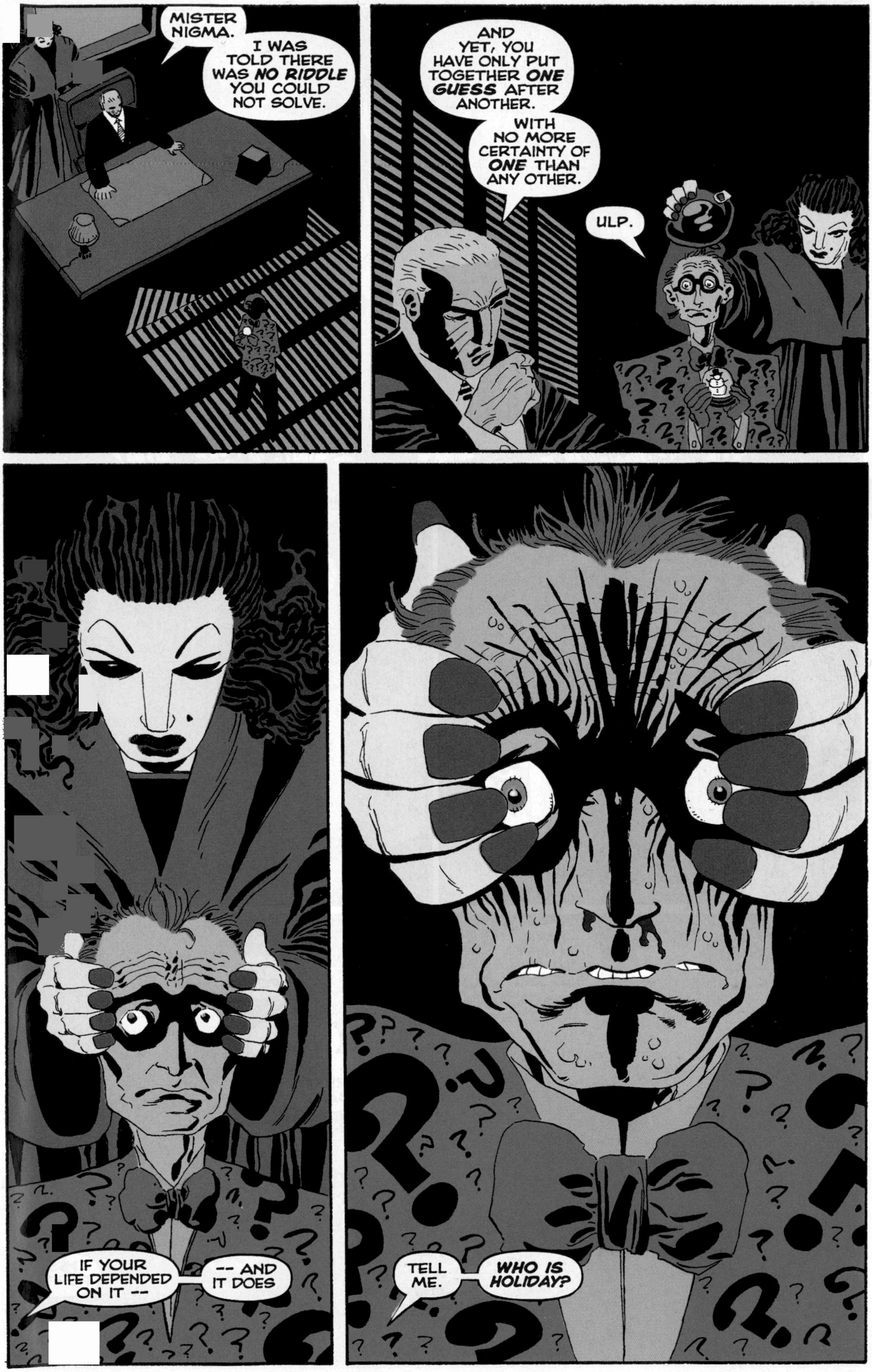
MISTER NIGMA.
I WAS TOLD THERE WAS NO RIDDLE YOU COULD NOT SOLVE.
AND YET, YOU HAVE ONLY PUT TOGETHER ONE GUESS AFTER ANOTHER.
WITH NO MORE CERTAINTY OF ONE THAN ANY OTHER.
ULP.
IF YOUR LIFE DEPENDED ON IT --
-- AND IT DOES
TELL ME.
WHO IS HOLIDAY?

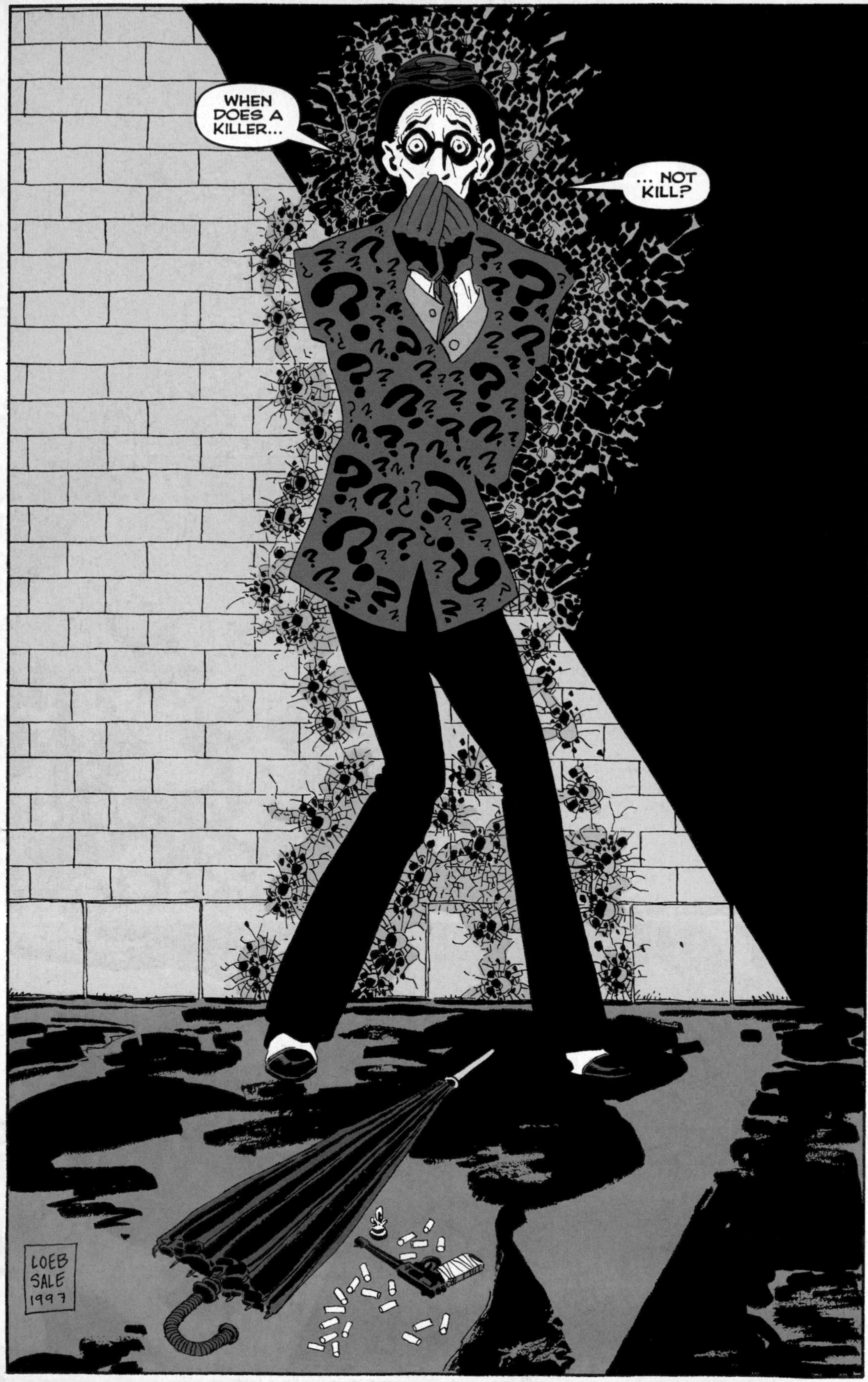
WHEN DOES A KILLER...
... NOT KILL?
LOEB SALE 1997

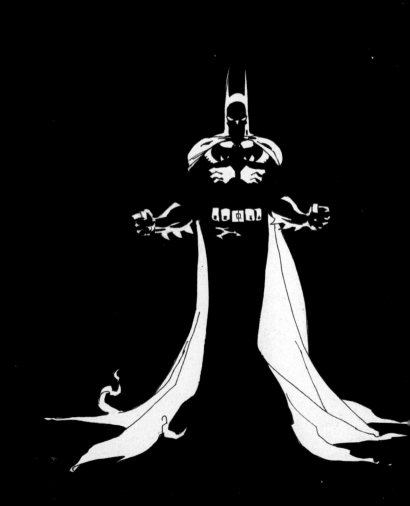

CHAPTER EIGHT

MOTHER'S DAY

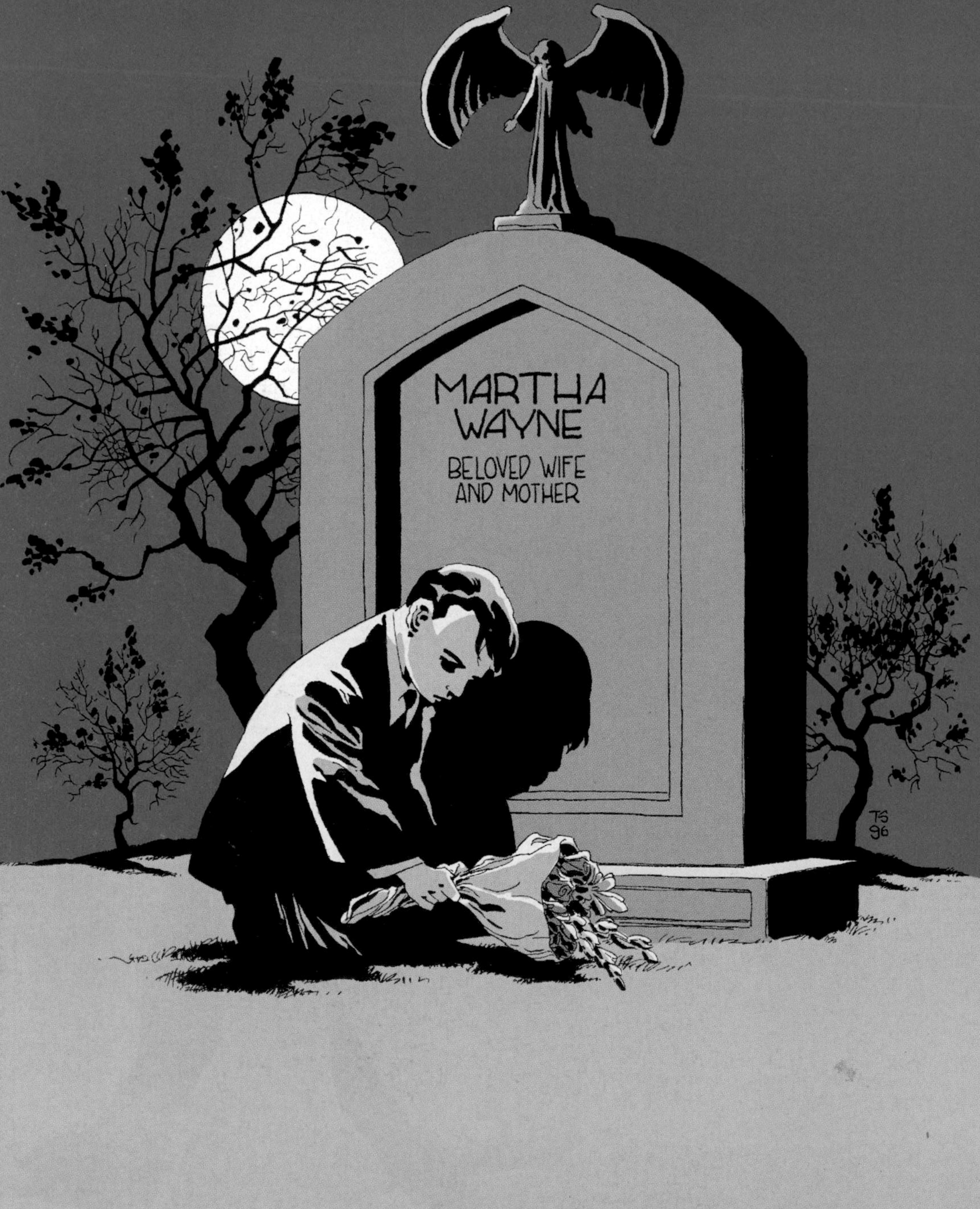

MARTHA WAYNE
BELOVED WIFE AND MOTHER
TS 96

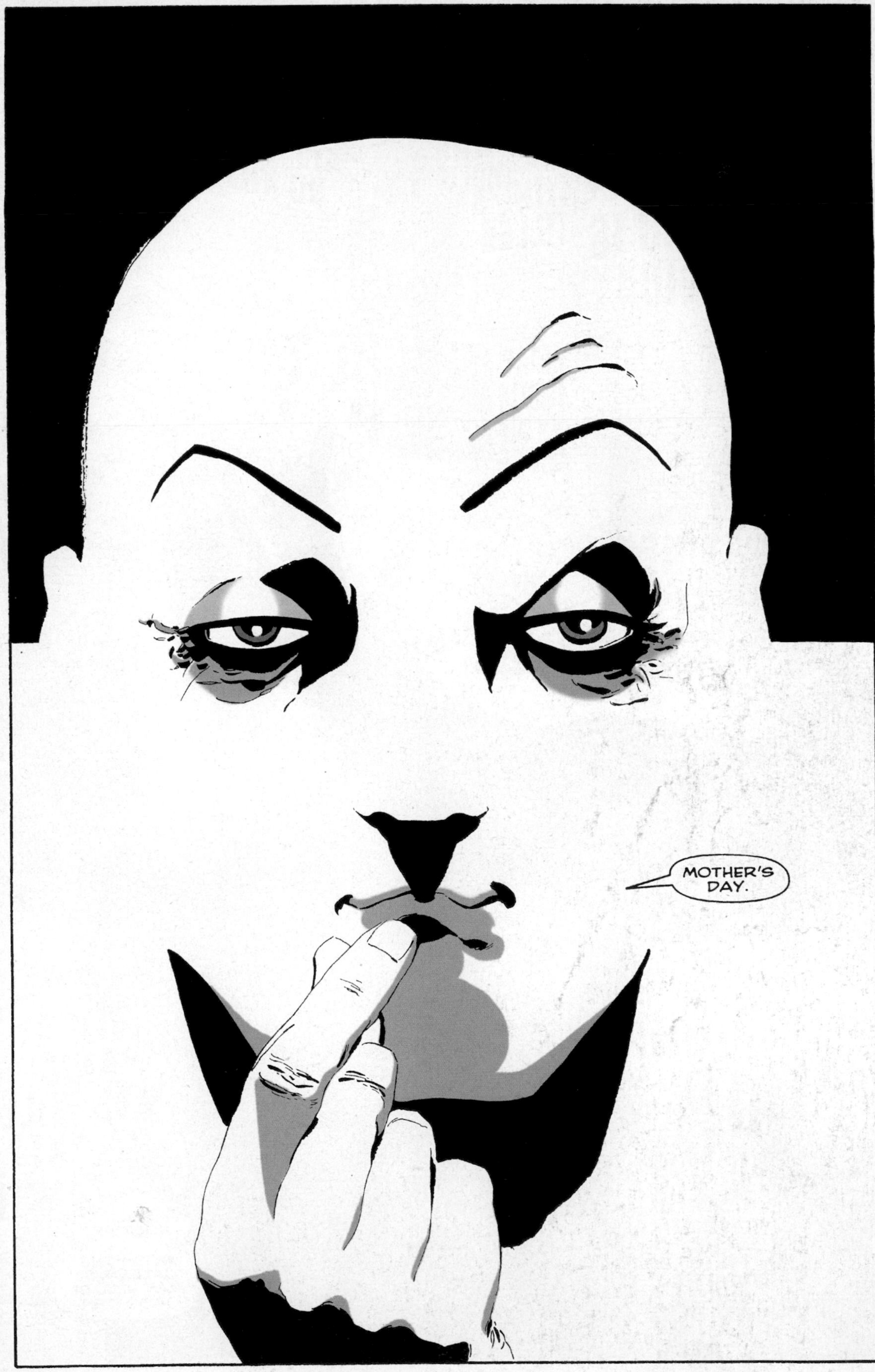
MOTHER'S DAY.

IT'S *MAY.*
YOU *SAID* YOU WOULD HAVE CAUGHT HER BY *FEBRUARY.*
HE'S MAKING QUITE A NAME FOR *HER*SELF.
"HOLIDAY."
SOON *THE CALENDAR MAN* WILL BE FORGOTTEN...
WHO IS HOLIDAY?

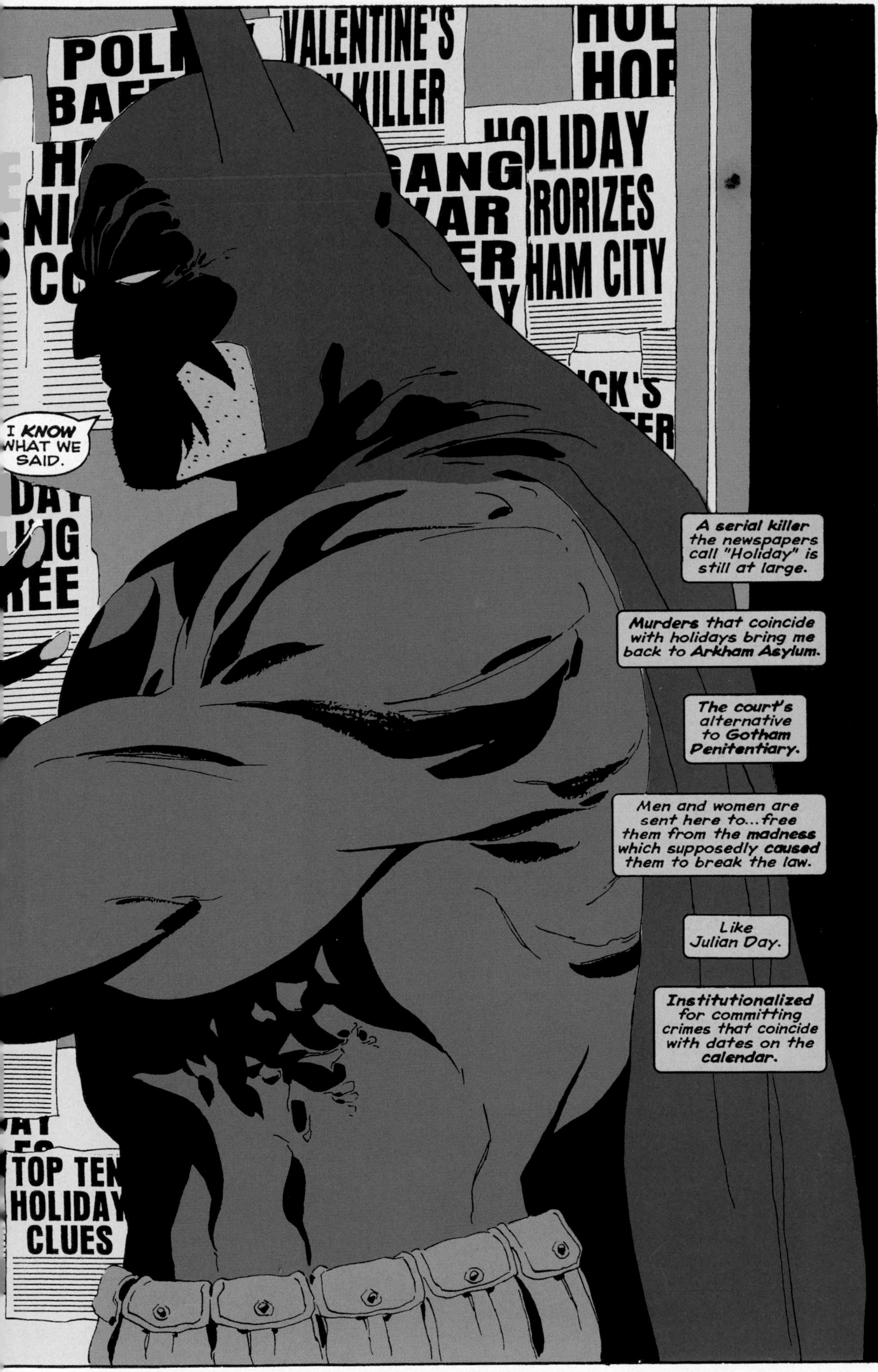
VALENTINE'S
KILLER
HOLIDAY
TOP TEN HOLIDAY CLUES
I *KNOW* WHAT WE SAID.
A serial killer the newspapers call "Holiday" is still at large.
Murders that coincide with holidays bring me back to Arkham Asylum.
The court's alternative to Gotham Penitentiary.
Men and women are sent here to...free them from the madness which supposedly caused them to break the law.
Like Julian Day.
Institutionalized for committing crimes that coincide with dates on the calendar.

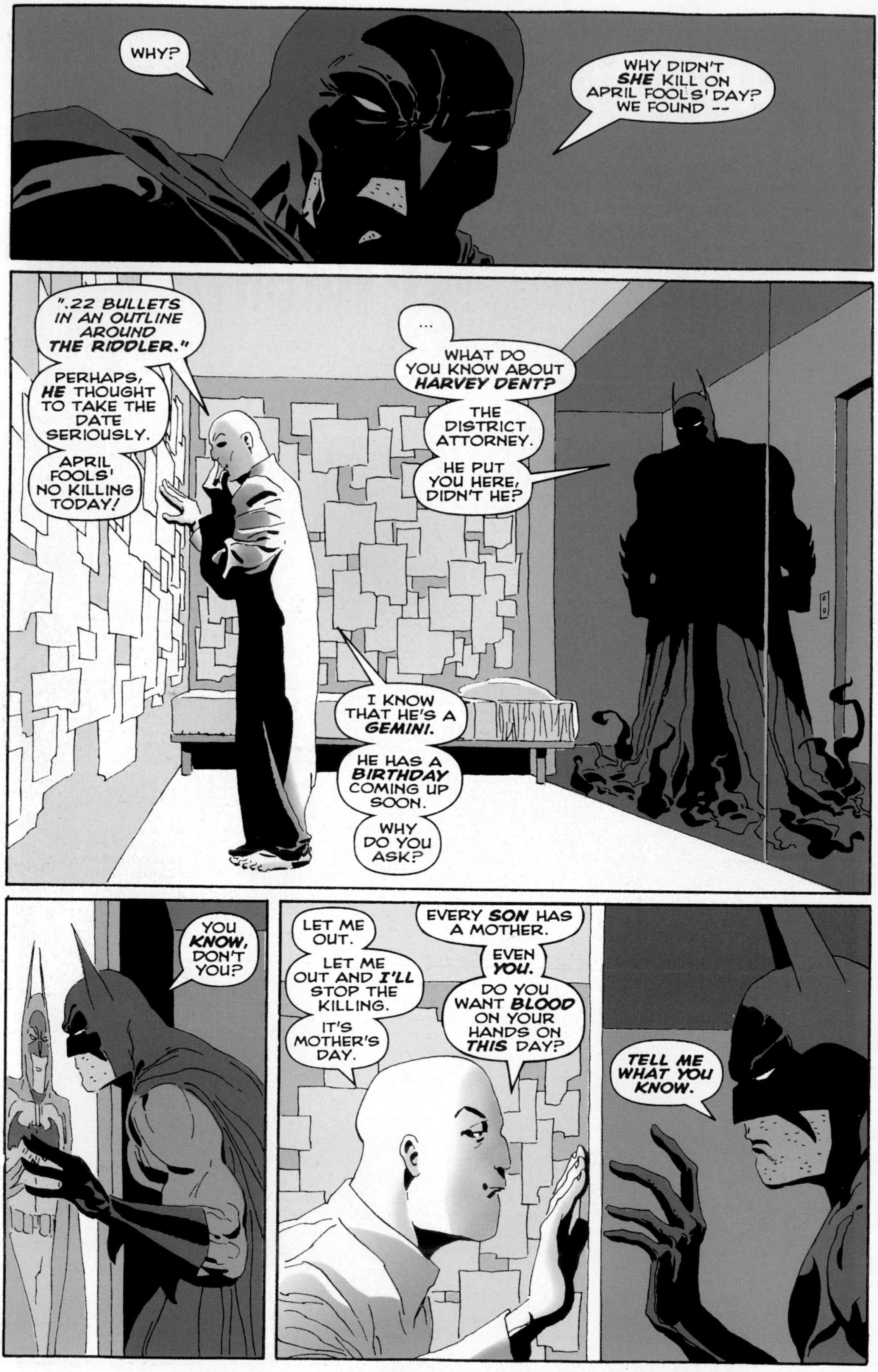
WHY?
WHY DIDN'T SHE KILL ON APRIL FOOLS' DAY? WE FOUND --
".22 BULLETS IN AN OUTLINE AROUND THE RIDDLER."
PERHAPS, HE THOUGHT TO TAKE THE DATE SERIOUSLY.
APRIL FOOLS' NO KILLING TODAY!
...
WHAT DO YOU KNOW ABOUT HARVEY DENT?
THE DISTRICT ATTORNEY.
HE PUT YOU HERE, DIDN'T HE?
I KNOW THAT HE'S A GEMINI.
HE HAS A BIRTHDAY COMING UP SOON.
WHY DO YOU ASK?
YOU KNOW, DON'T YOU?
LET ME OUT.
LET ME OUT AND I'LL STOP THE KILLING.
IT'S MOTHER'S DAY.
EVERY SON HAS A MOTHER.
EVEN YOU.
DO YOU WANT BLOOD ON YOUR HANDS ON THIS DAY?
TELL ME WHAT YOU KNOW.

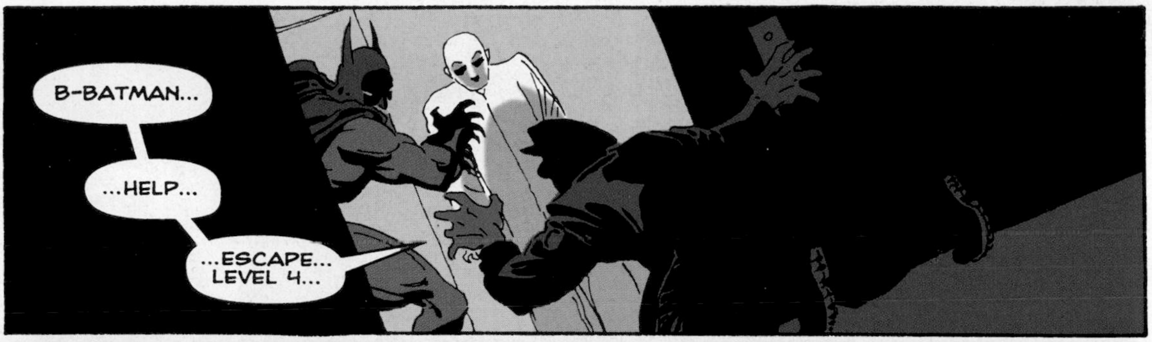
B-BATMAN...
...HELP...
...ESCAPE... LEVEL 4...

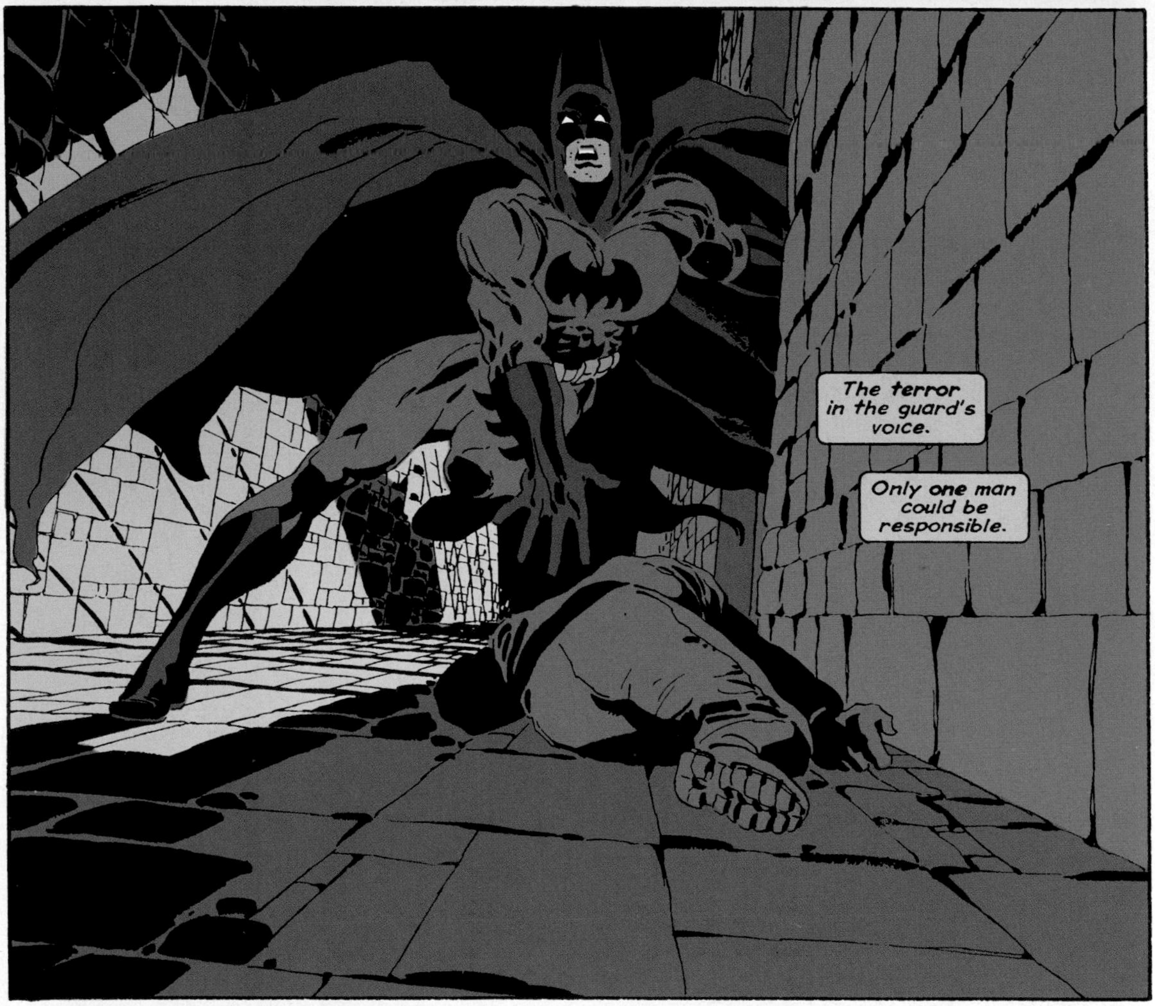
The terror in the guard's voice.
Only one man could be responsible.

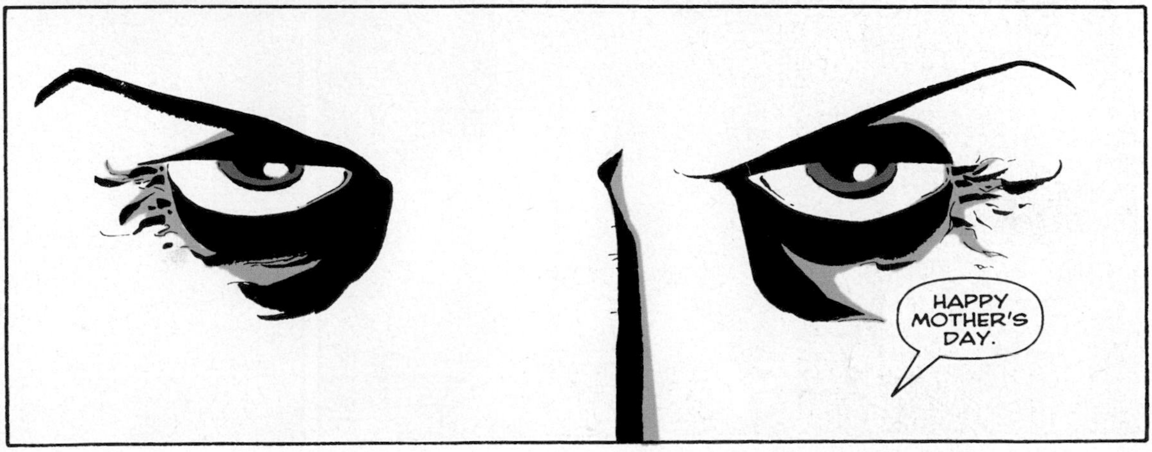
HAPPY MOTHER'S DAY.

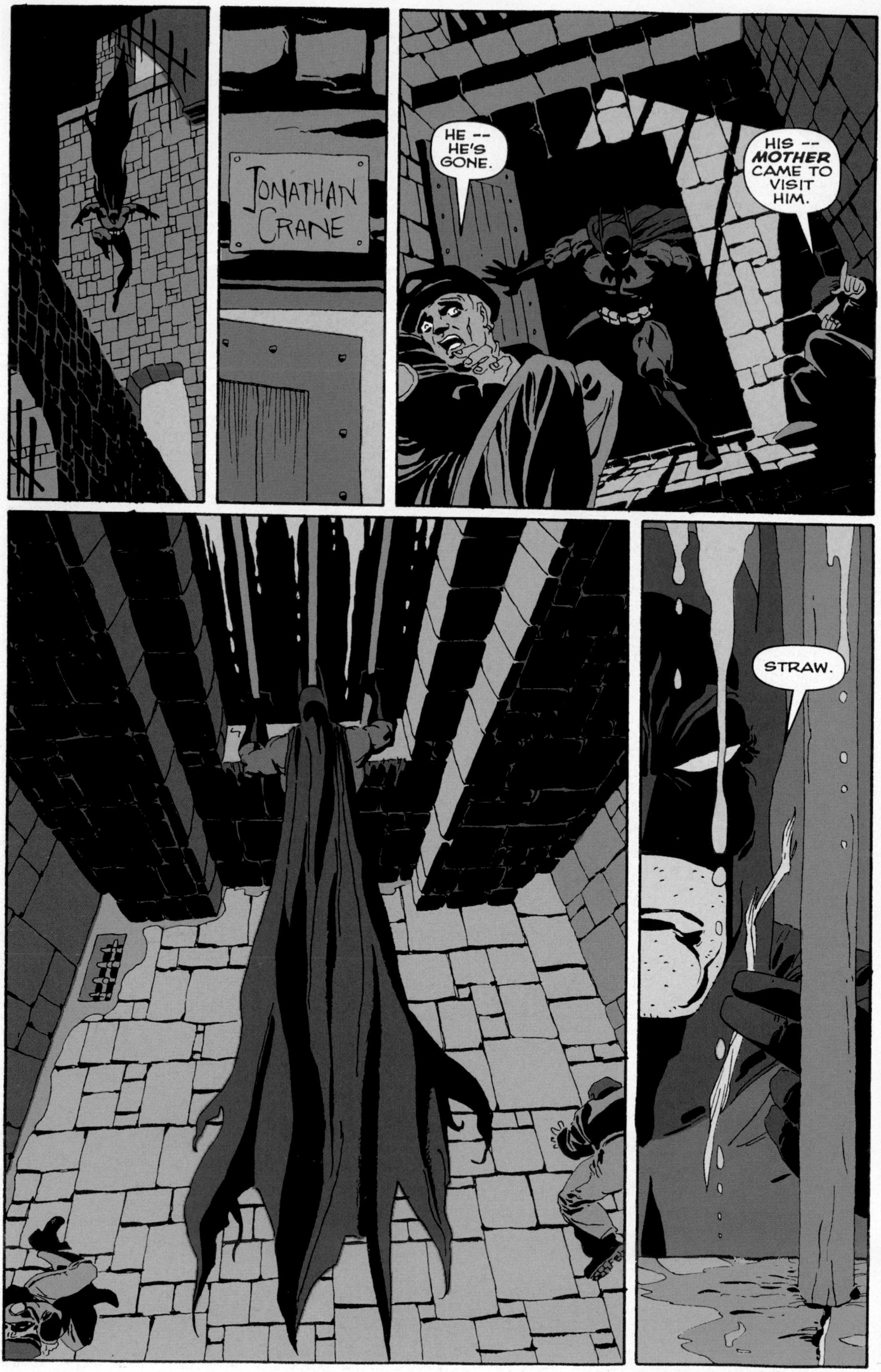

JONATHAN CRANE
HE -- HE'S GONE.
HIS -- MOTHER CAME TO VISIT HIM.
STRAW.

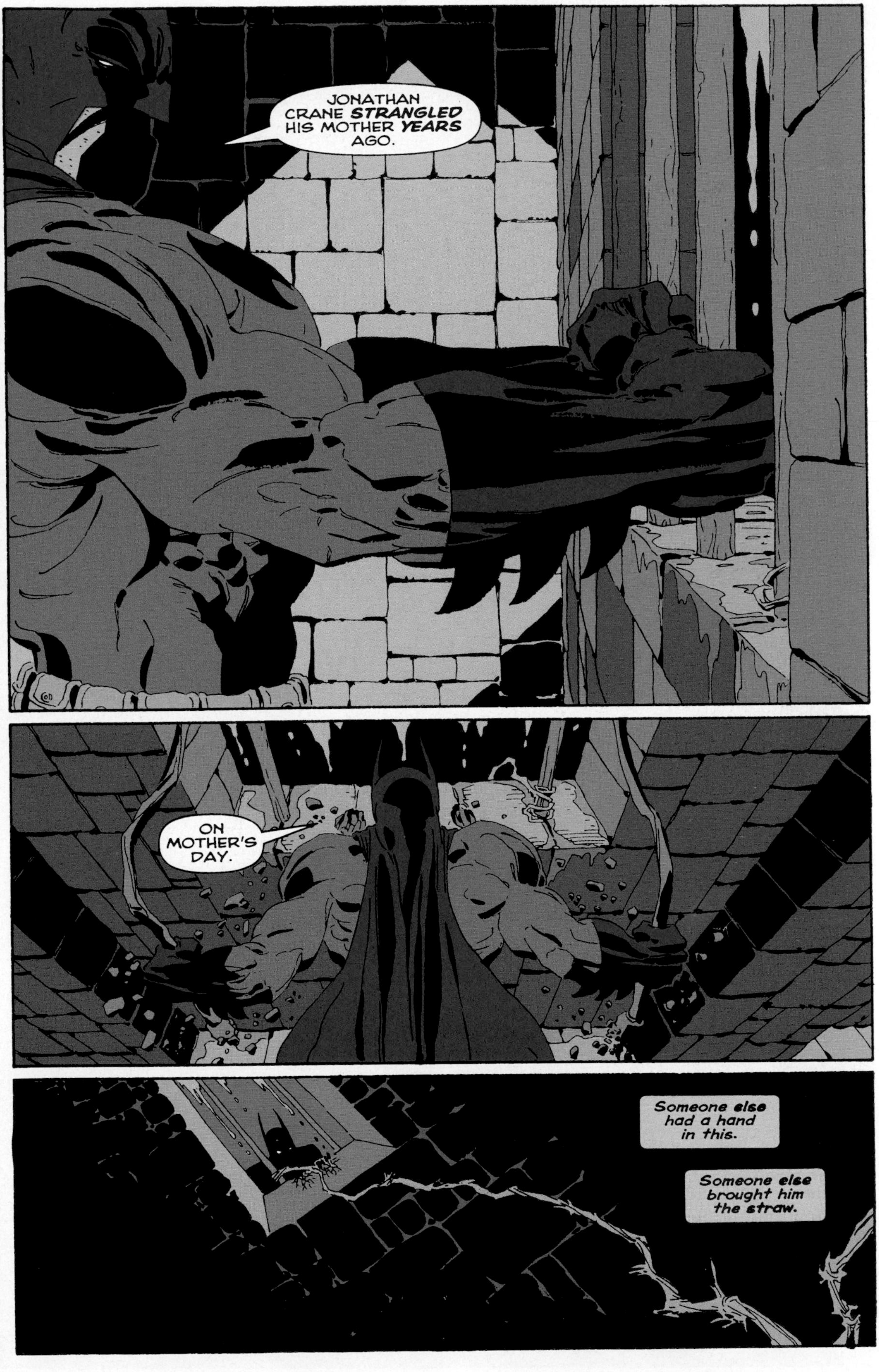
JONATHAN CRANE STRANGLED HIS MOTHER YEARS AGO.
ON MOTHER'S DAY.
Someone else had a hand in this.
Someone else brought him the straw.

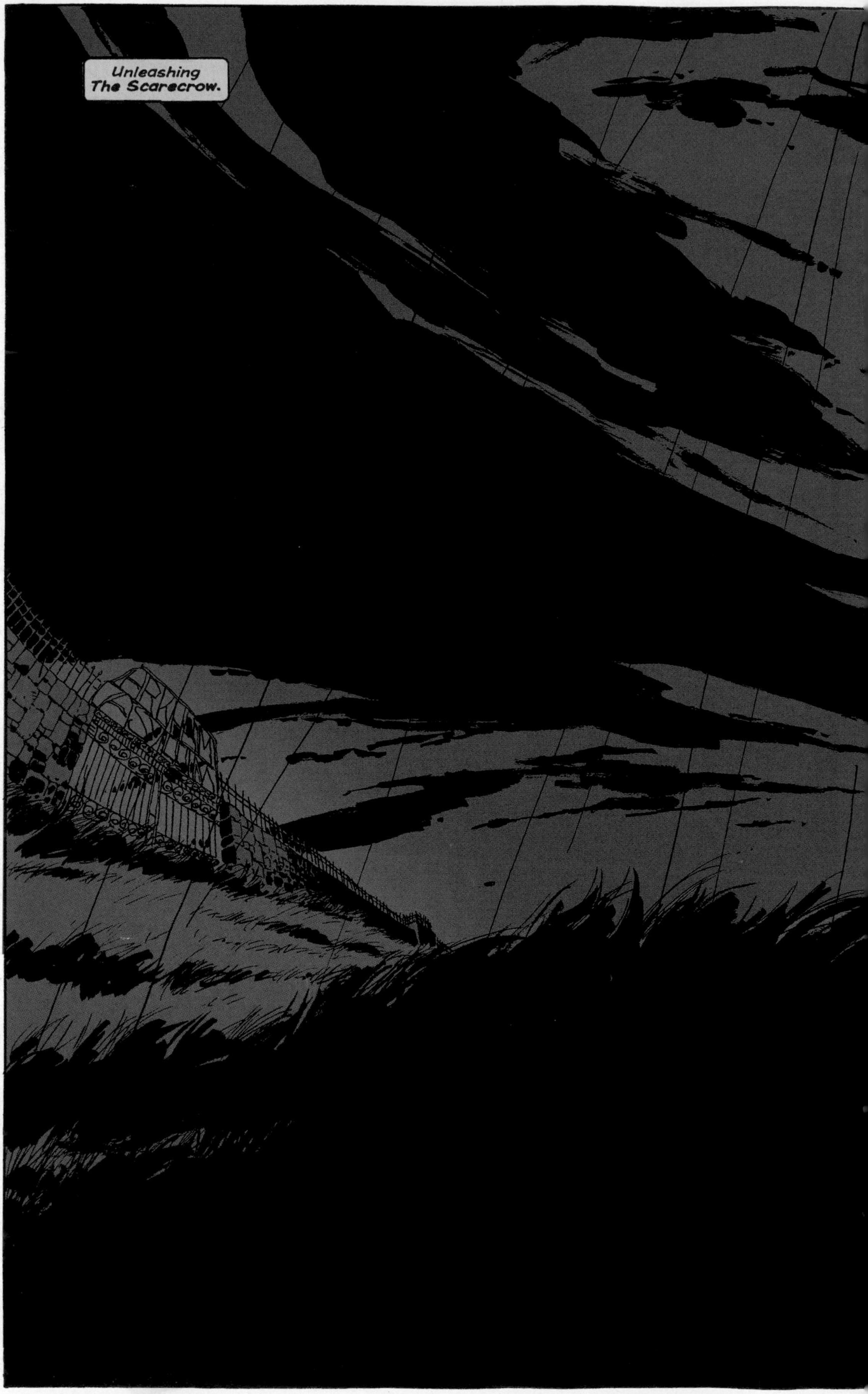
Unleashing The Scarecrow.

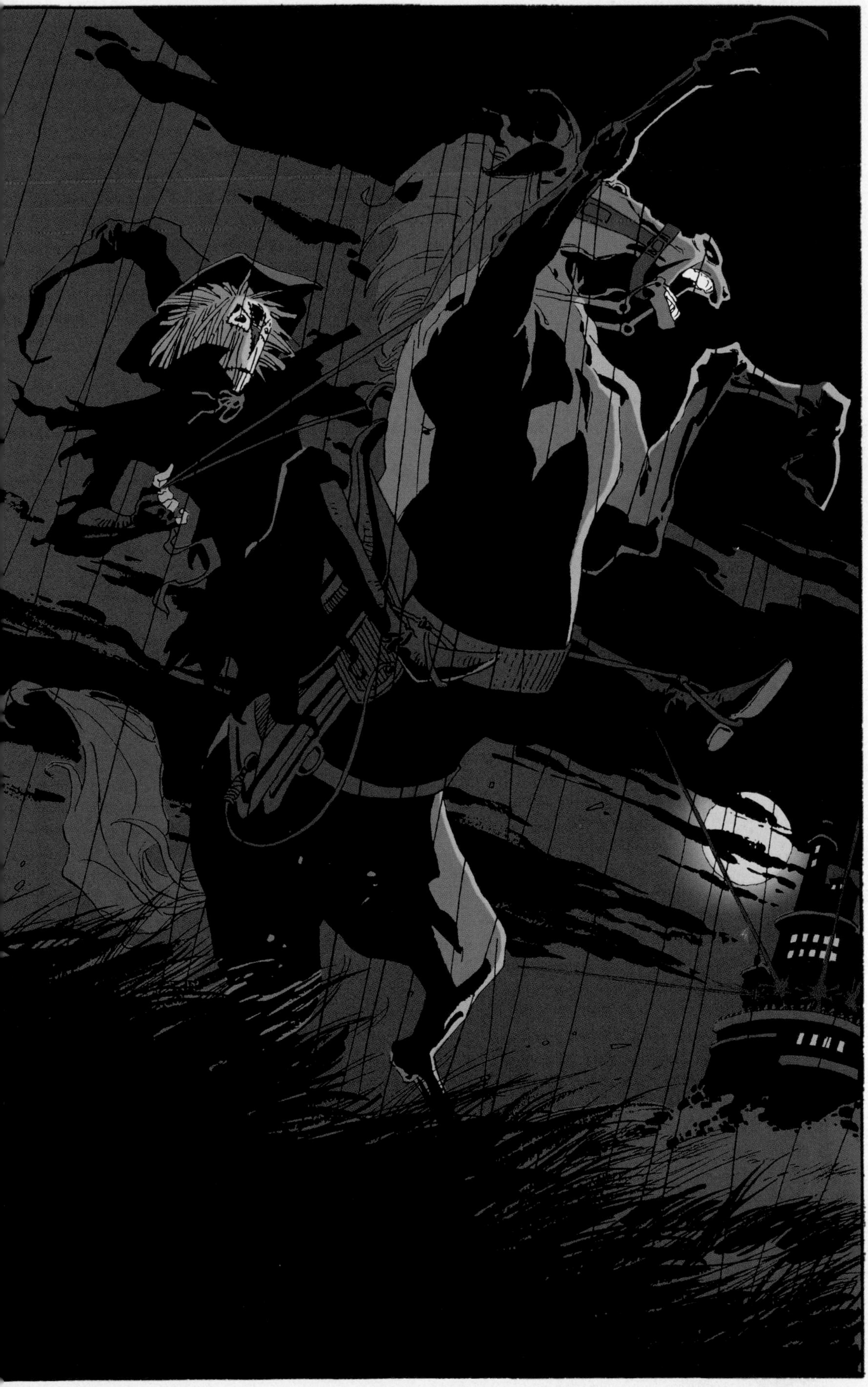

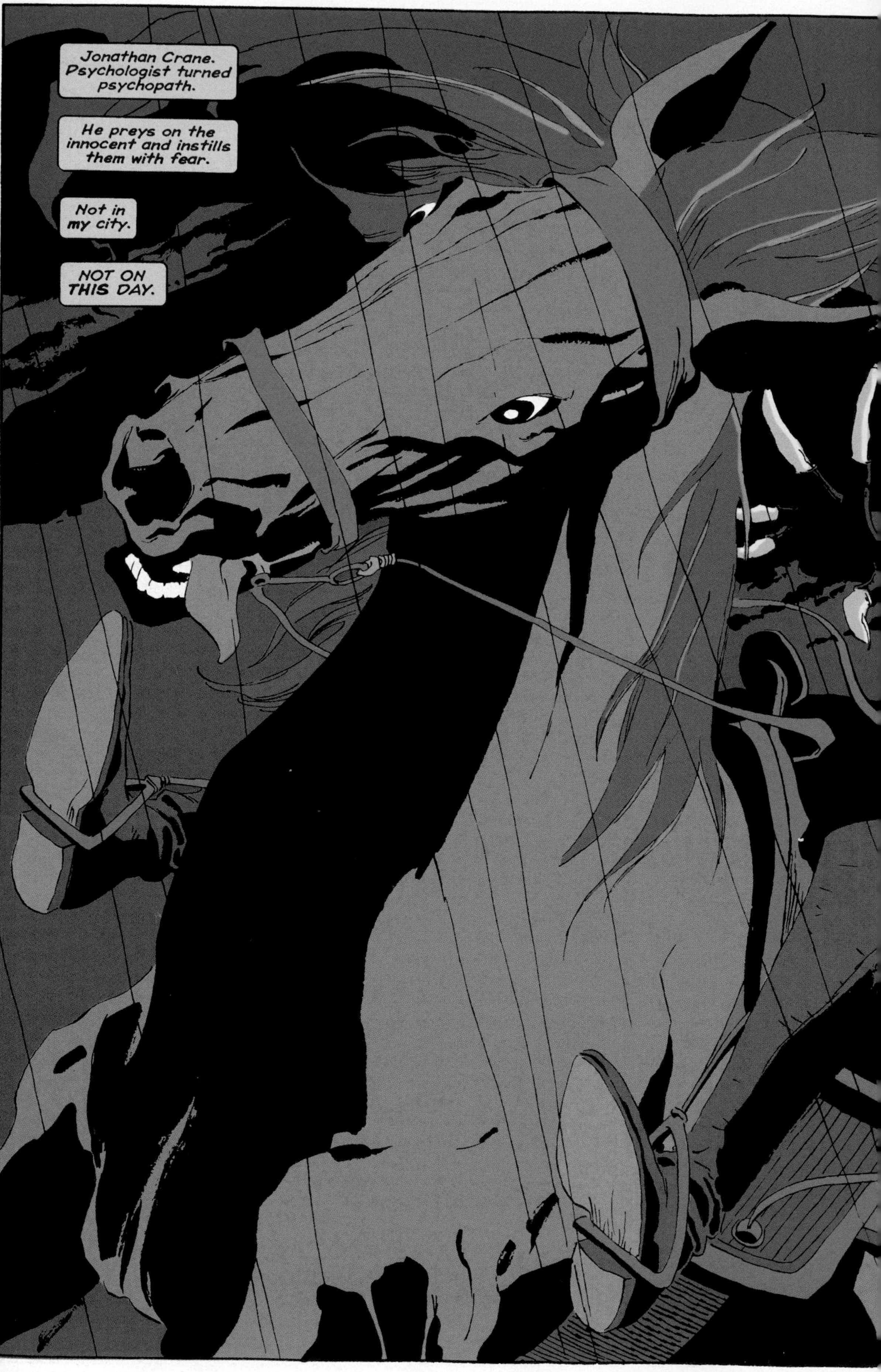
Jonathan Crane. Psychologist turned psychopath.
He preys on the innocent and instills them with fear.
Not in my city.
NOT ON THIS DAY.

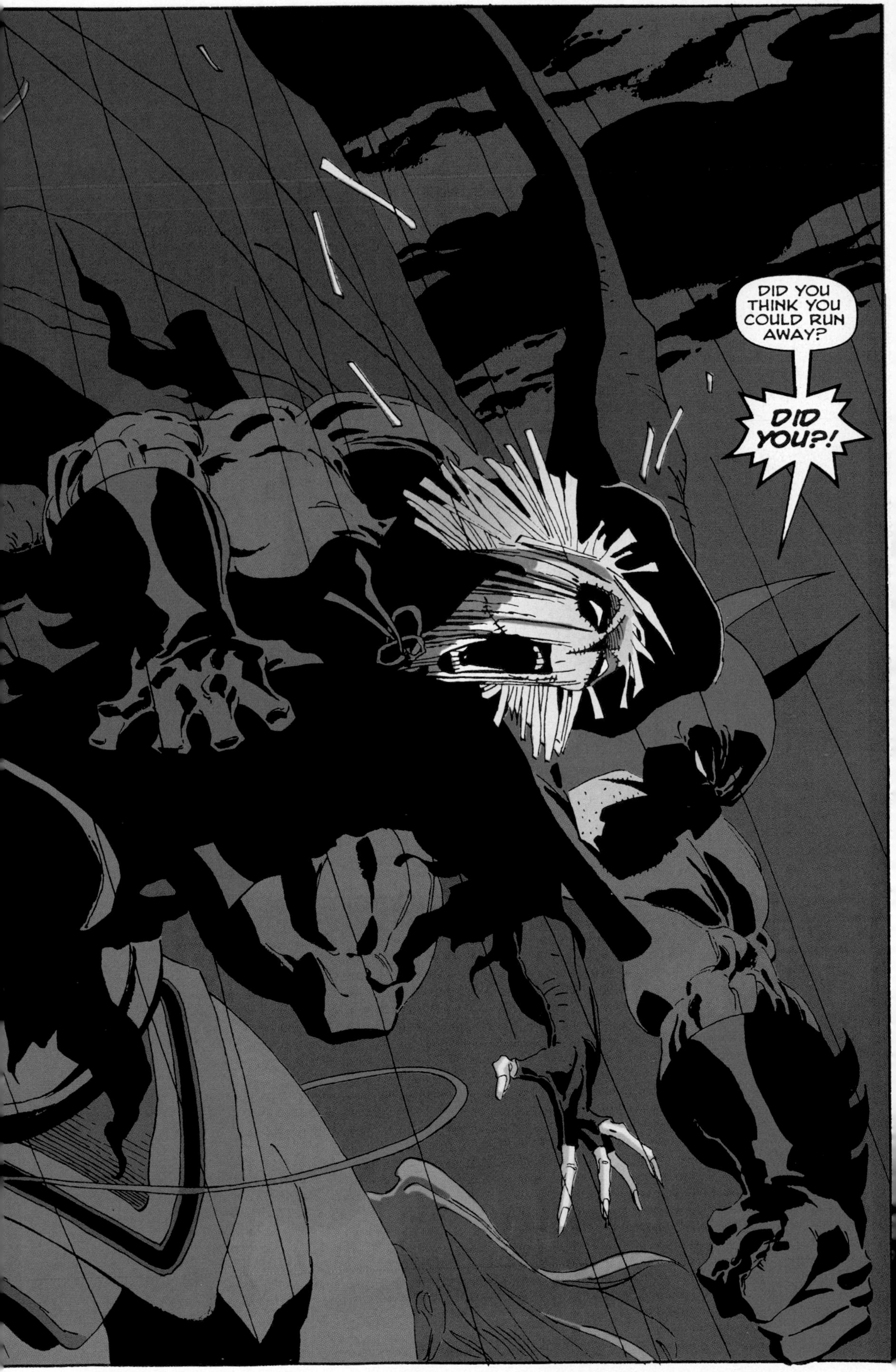
DID YOU THINK YOU COULD RUN AWAY?
DID YOU?!

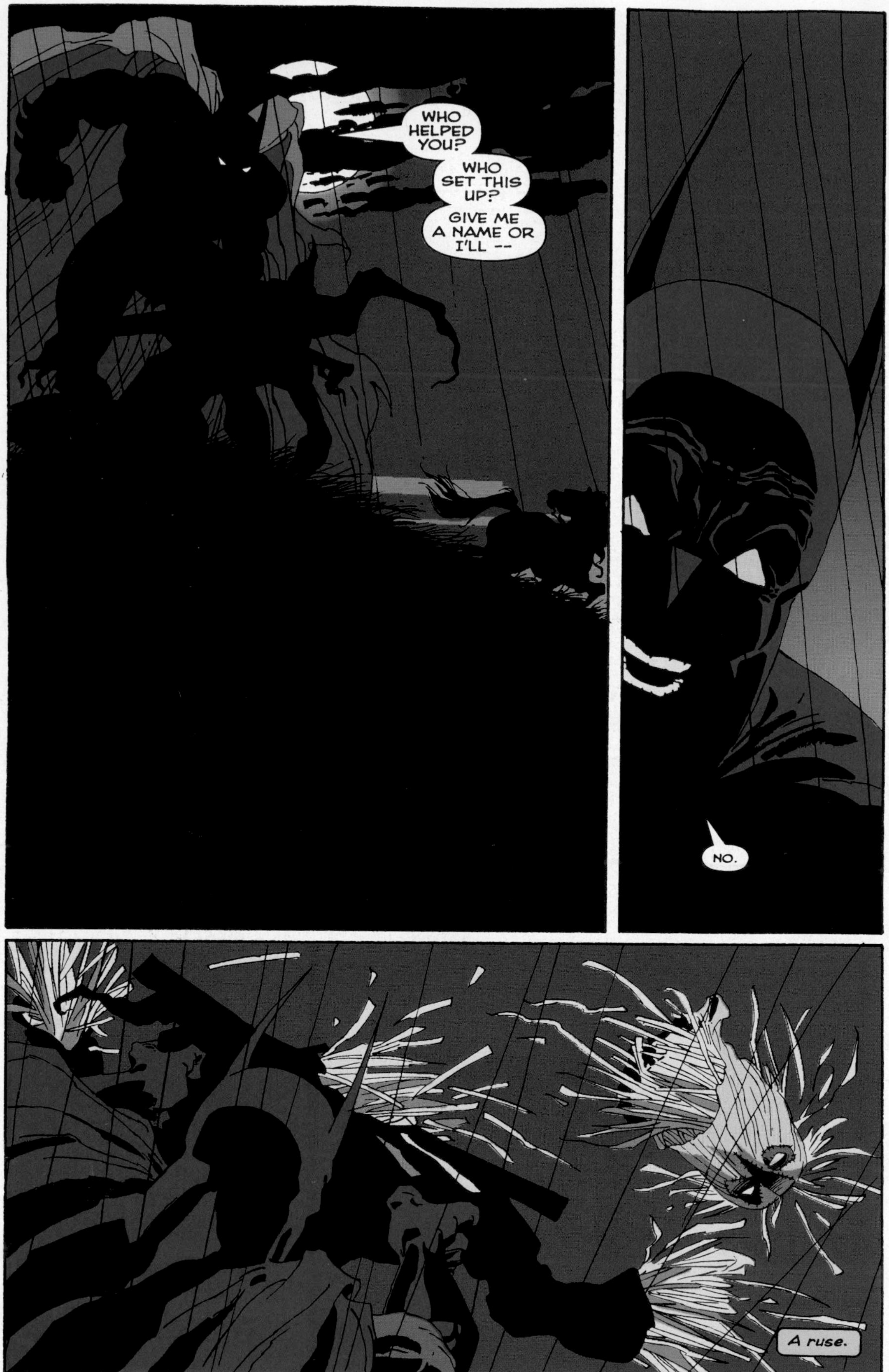
WHO HELPED YOU?
WHO SET THIS UP?
GIVE ME A NAME OR I'LL --
NO.
A ruse.

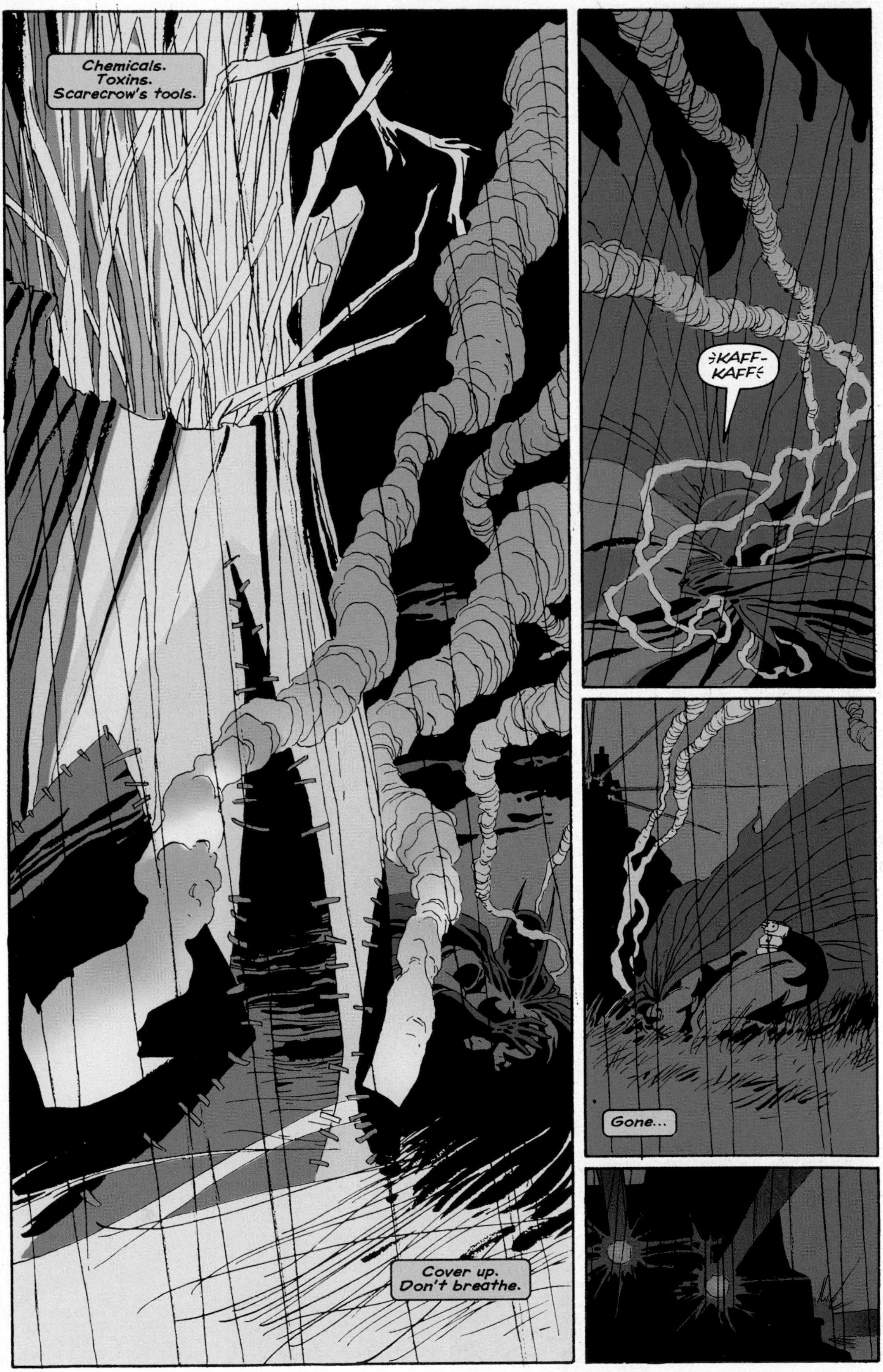
Chemicals.
Toxins.
Scarecrow's tools.
Cover up.
Don't breathe.
KAFF-
KAFF
Gone...

Wayne Manor. My father's house.

AT THE RISK OF SOUNDING **REDUNDANT**, CAPTAIN GORDON...

...MISTER WAYNE IS **NOT** AT HOME.

MISTER PENNYWORTH.

YOU **MUST** KNOW I DON'T **WANT** TO BE HERE.

CERTAINLY NOT UNDER **THESE** CIRCUMSTANCES.

IS IT NOT POSSIBLE THAT THIS IS SOME SORT OF TERRIBLE MISTAKE?

MISTER WAYNE HAS **NO** CONNECTION TO THIS "**FALCONE**" PERSON.

THEN, **ONLY BY COOPERATING** CAN WE CLEAR THE WHOLE THING UP.

ALFRED.

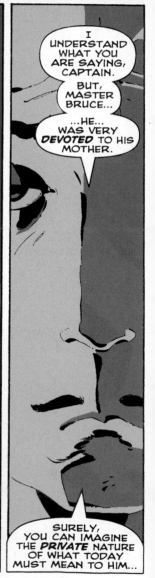

I UNDERSTAND WHAT YOU ARE SAYING, CAPTAIN.

BUT, MASTER BRUCE...

...HE... WAS VERY **DEVOTED** TO HIS MOTHER.

SURELY, YOU CAN IMAGINE THE **PRIVATE** NATURE OF WHAT TODAY MUST MEAN TO HIM...

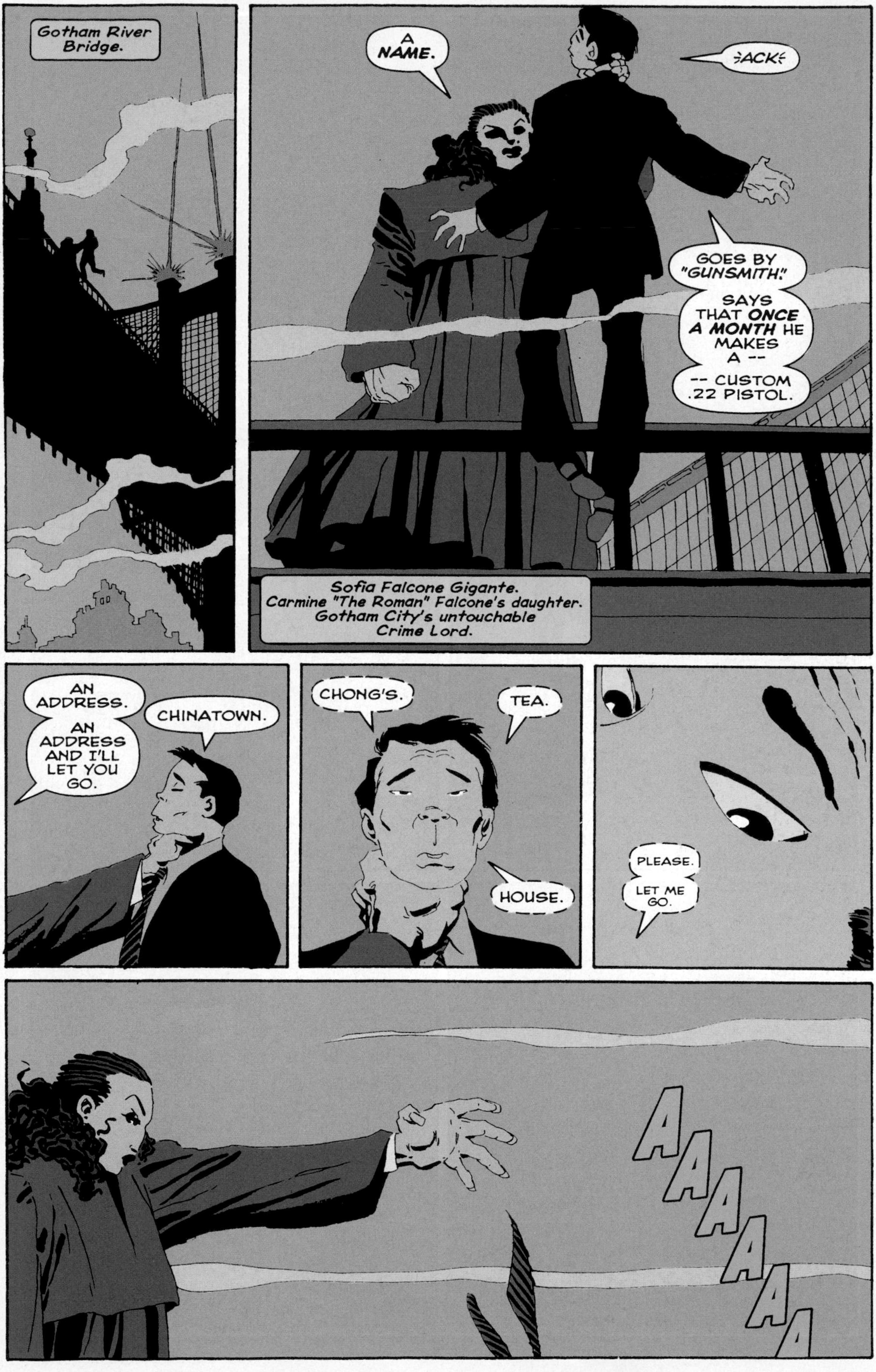
Gotham River Bridge.
A NAME.
ACK
GOES BY "GUNSMITH."
SAYS THAT ONCE A MONTH HE MAKES A --
-- CUSTOM .22 PISTOL.
Sofia Falcone Gigante. Carmine "The Roman" Falcone's daughter. Gotham City's untouchable Crime Lord.
AN ADDRESS.
AN ADDRESS AND I'LL LET YOU GO.
CHINATOWN.
CHONG'S.
TEA.
HOUSE.
PLEASE.
LET ME GO.
AAAAAAAA

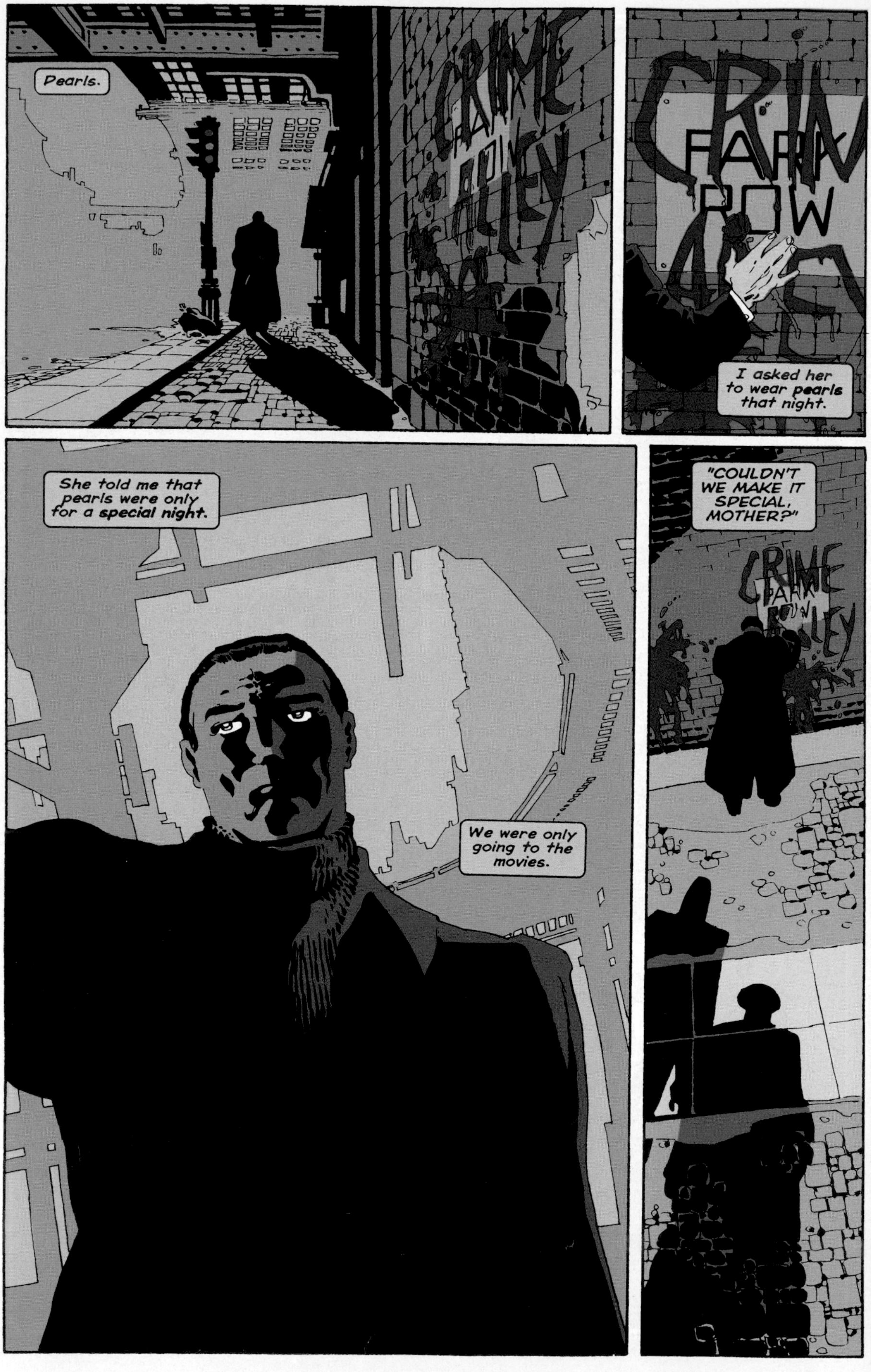
Pearls.
CRIME
ALLEY
PARK
ROW
I asked her to wear pearls that night.
She told me that pearls were only for a special night.
We were only going to the movies.
"COULDN'T WE MAKE IT SPECIAL, MOTHER?"

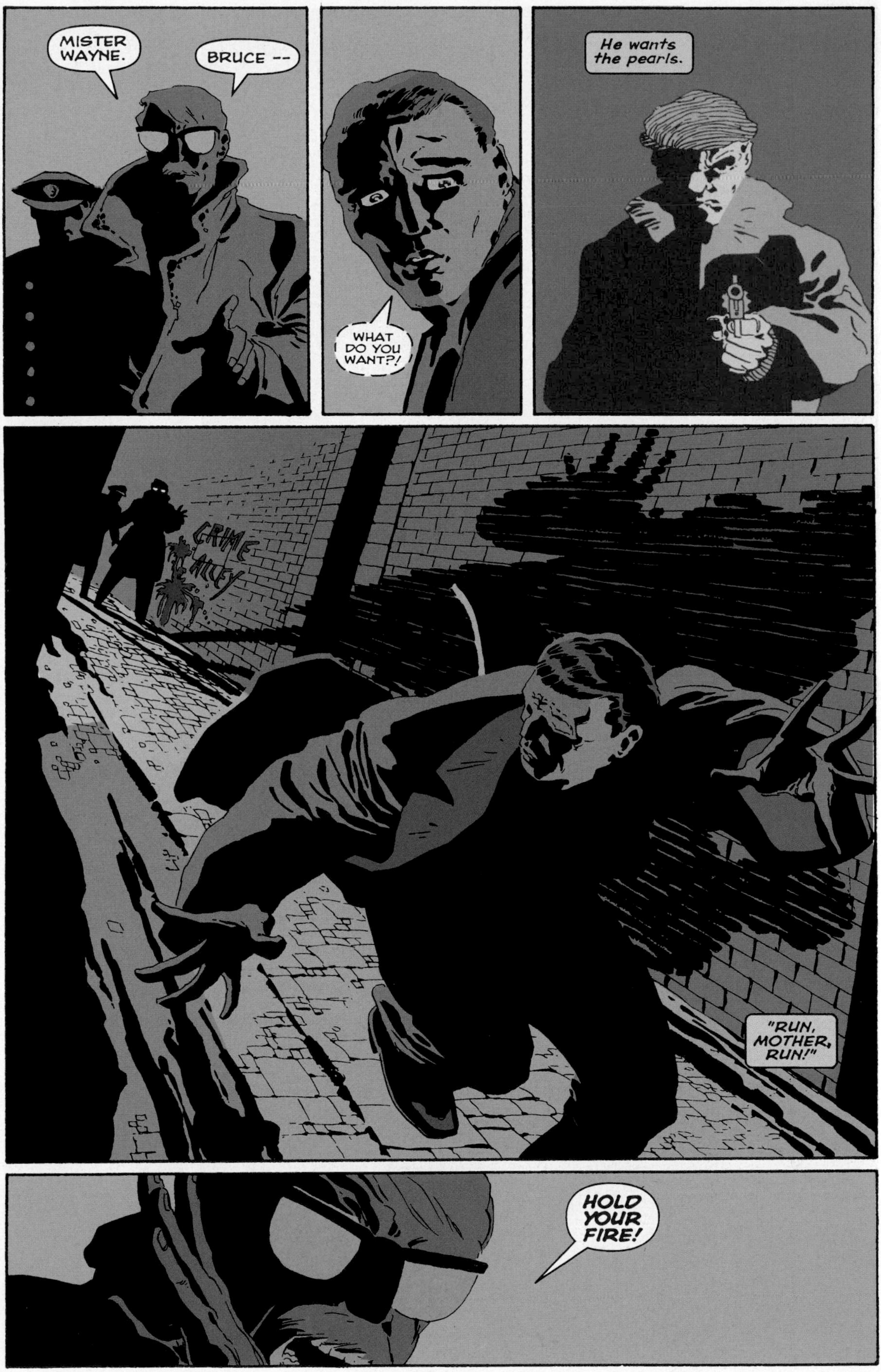
MISTER WAYNE.
BRUCE --
WHAT DO YOU WANT?!
He wants the pearls.
CRIME ALLEY
"RUN, MOTHER, RUN!"
HOLD YOUR FIRE!

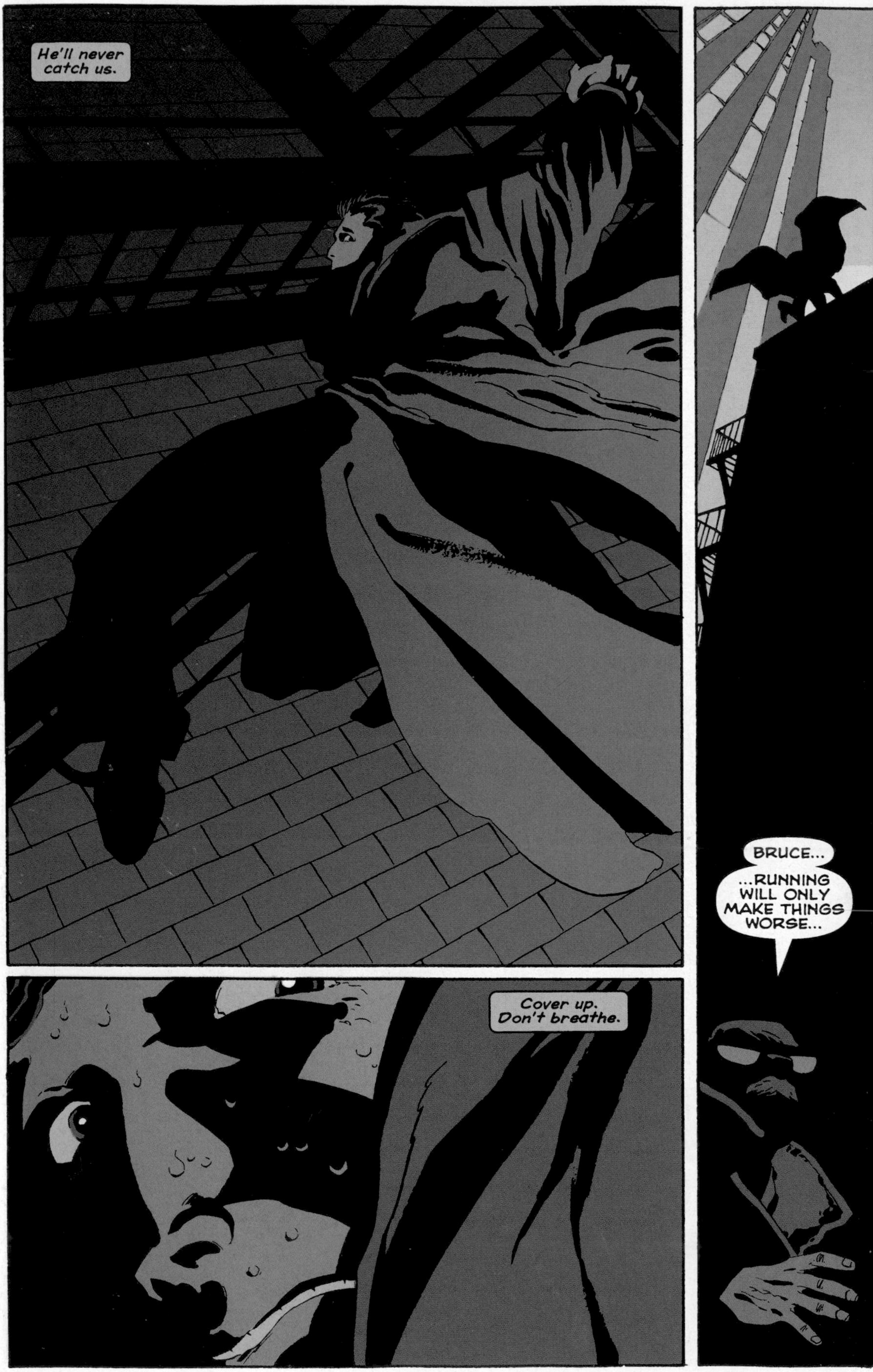
He'll never catch us.
BRUCE...
...RUNNING WILL ONLY MAKE THINGS WORSE...
Cover up. Don't breathe.

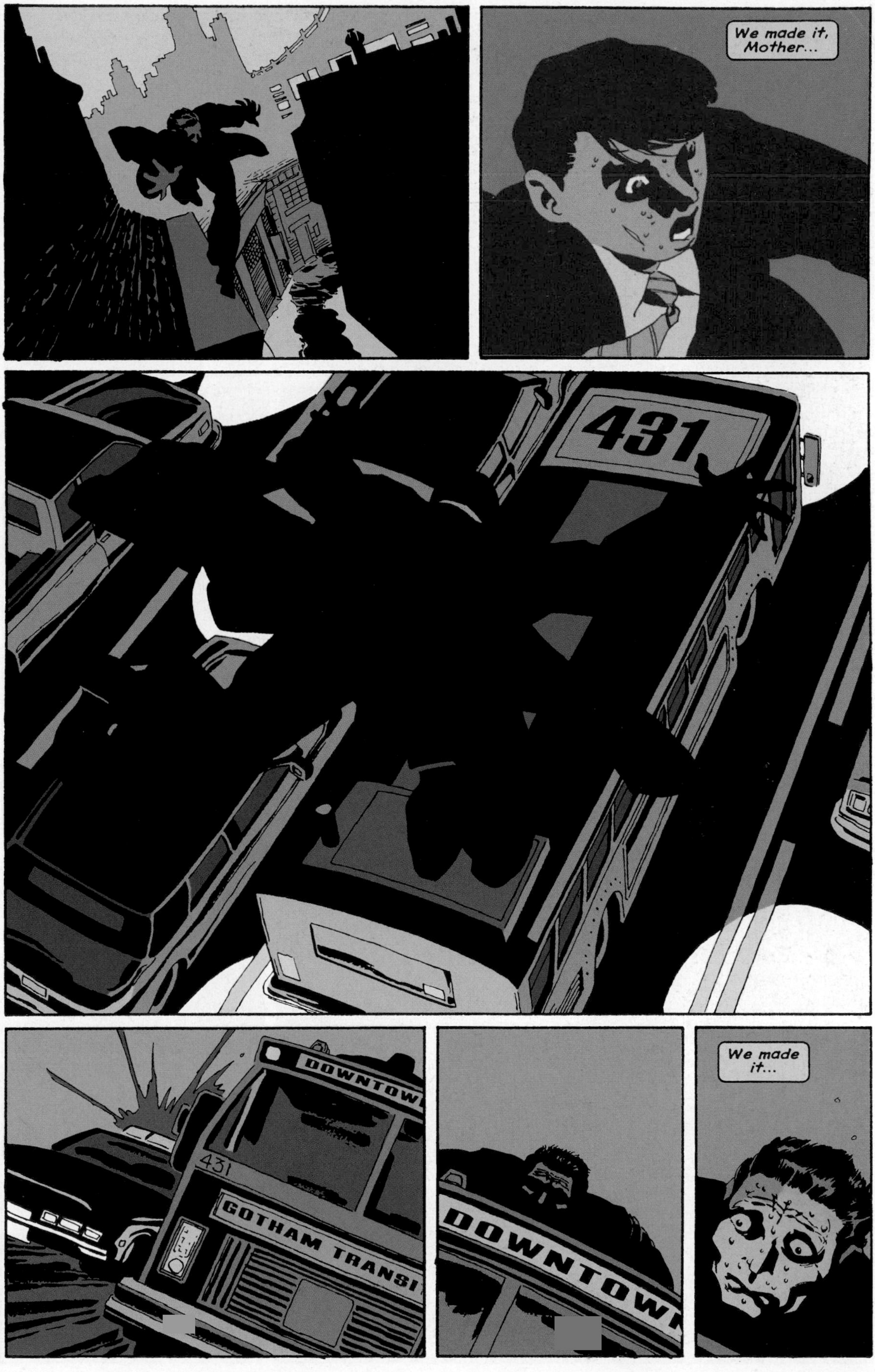
We made it, Mother...
431
DOWNTOWN
431
GOTHAM TRANSI
DOWNTOWN
We made it...

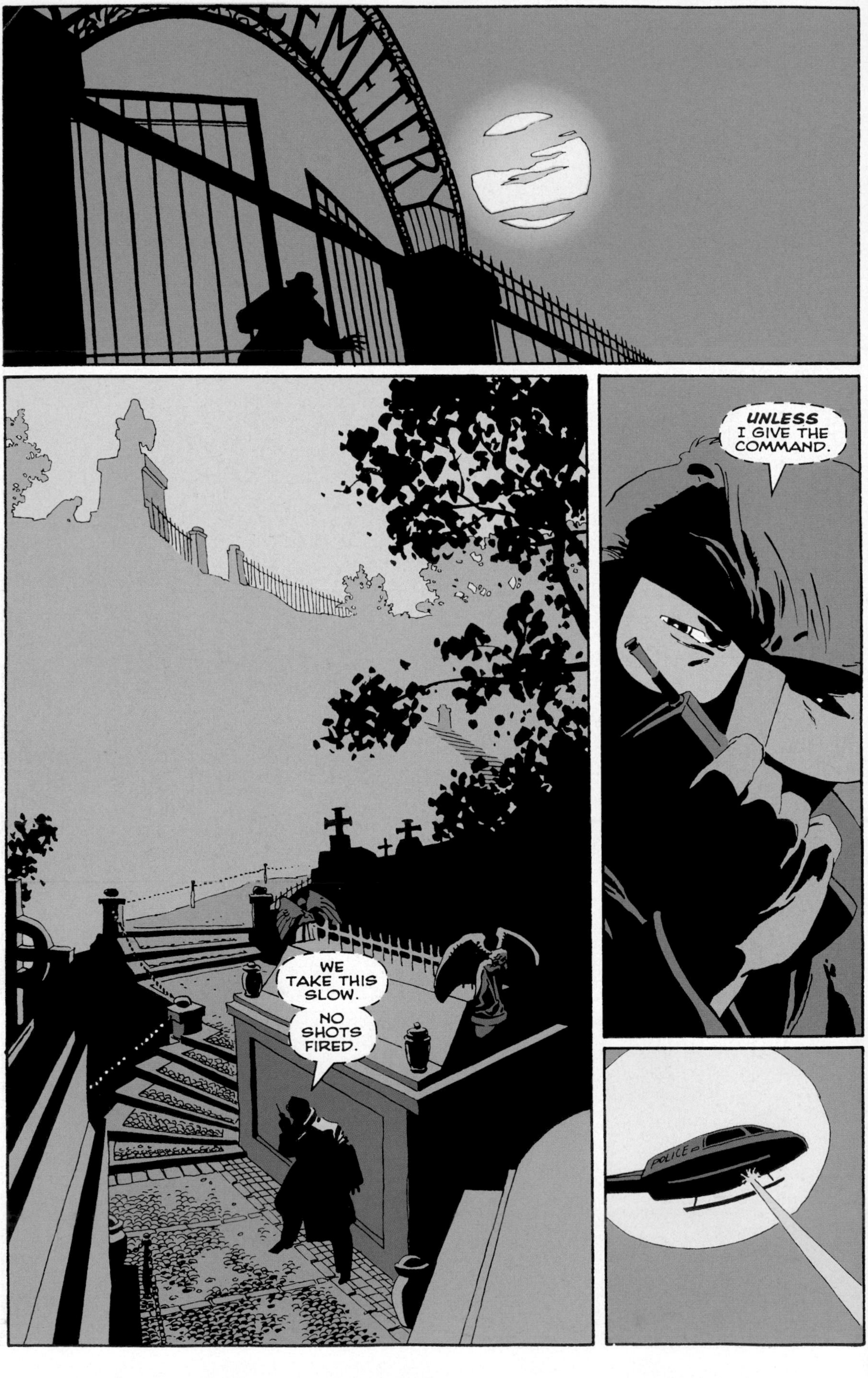
CEMETERY
WE TAKE THIS SLOW.
NO SHOTS FIRED.
UNLESS I GIVE THE COMMAND.
POLICE

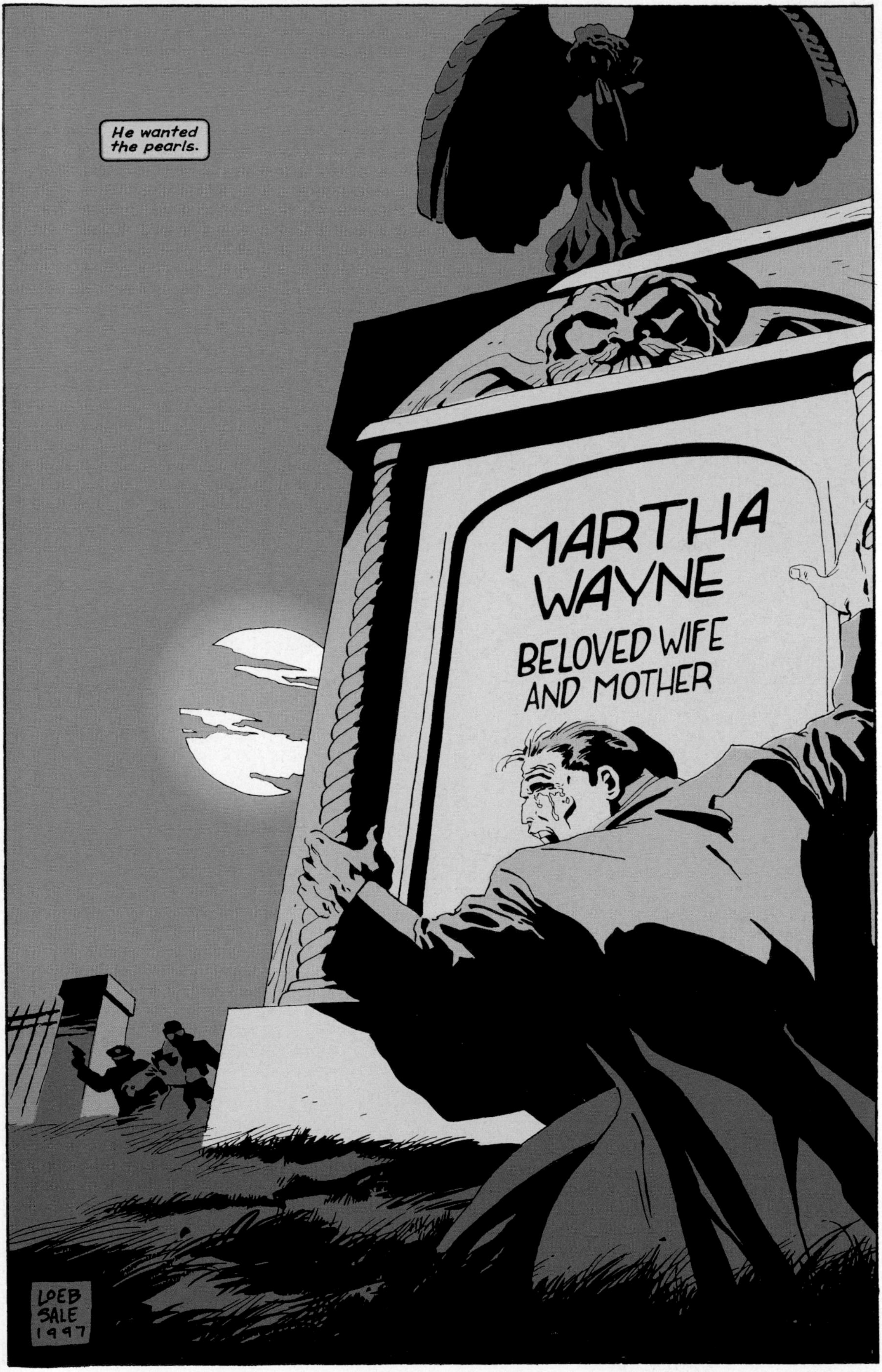
He wanted the pearls.
MARTHA WAYNE
BELOVED WIFE AND MOTHER
LOEB SALE 1997

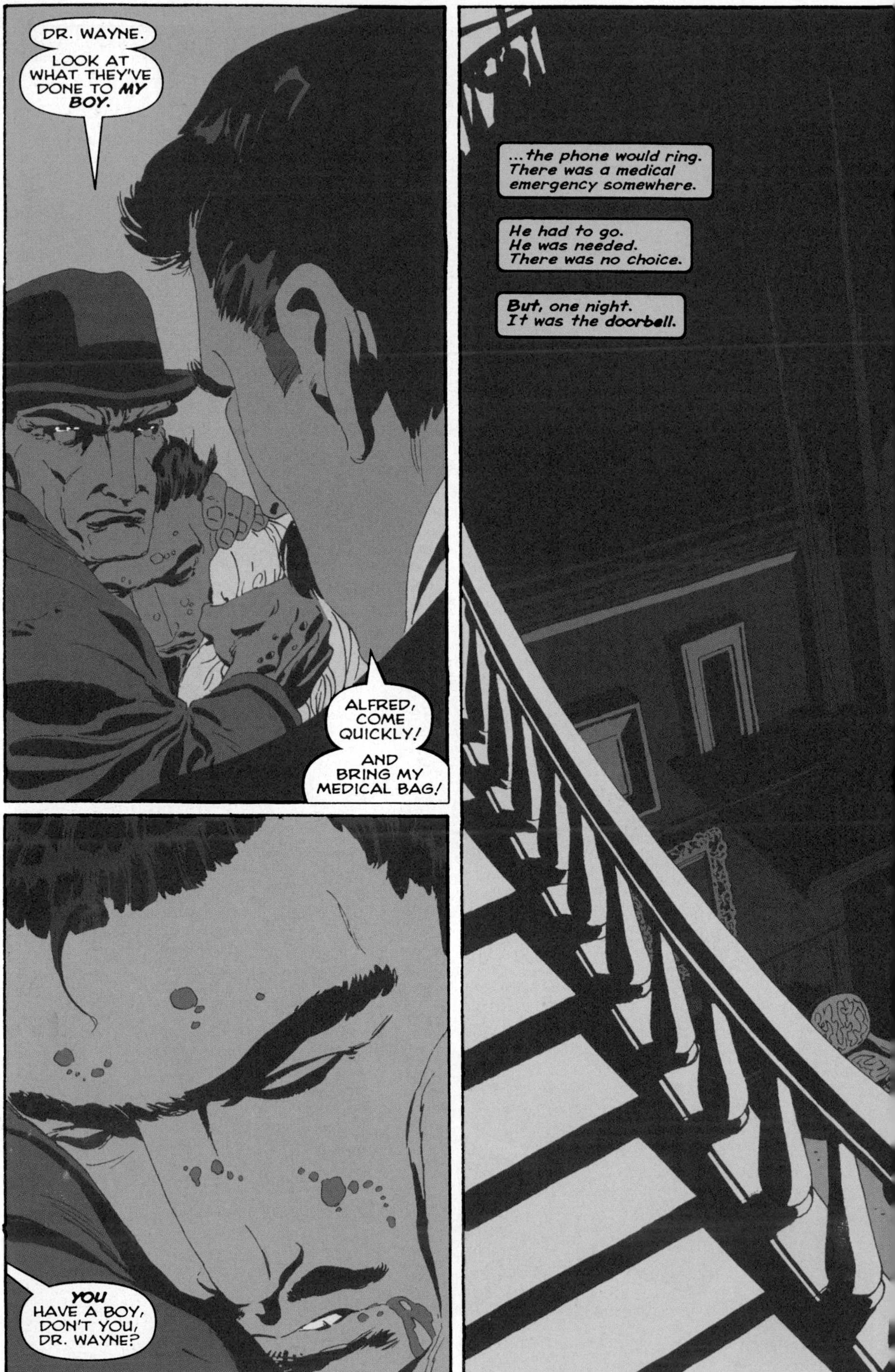

DR. WAYNE.
LOOK AT WHAT THEY'VE DONE TO *MY BOY.*
ALFRED, COME QUICKLY!
AND BRING MY MEDICAL BAG!
YOU HAVE A BOY, DON'T YOU, DR. WAYNE?
...the phone would ring. There was a medical emergency somewhere.
He had to go. He was needed. There was no choice.
But, one night. It was the *doorbell.*

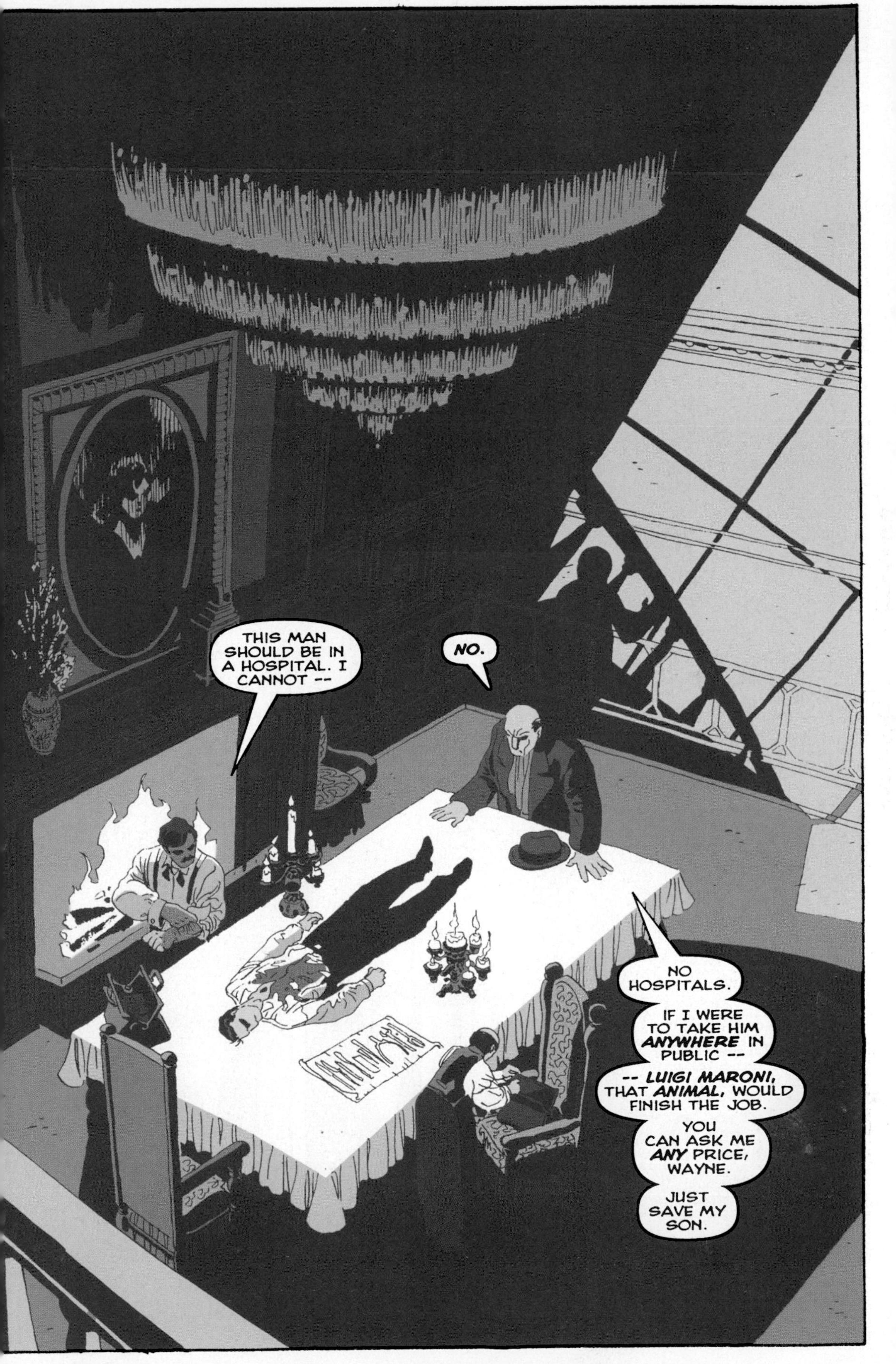
THIS MAN SHOULD BE IN A HOSPITAL. I CANNOT --
NO.
NO HOSPITALS.
IF I WERE TO TAKE HIM ANYWHERE IN PUBLIC --
-- LUIGI MARONI, THAT ANIMAL, WOULD FINISH THE JOB.
YOU CAN ASK ME ANY PRICE, WAYNE.
JUST SAVE MY SON.

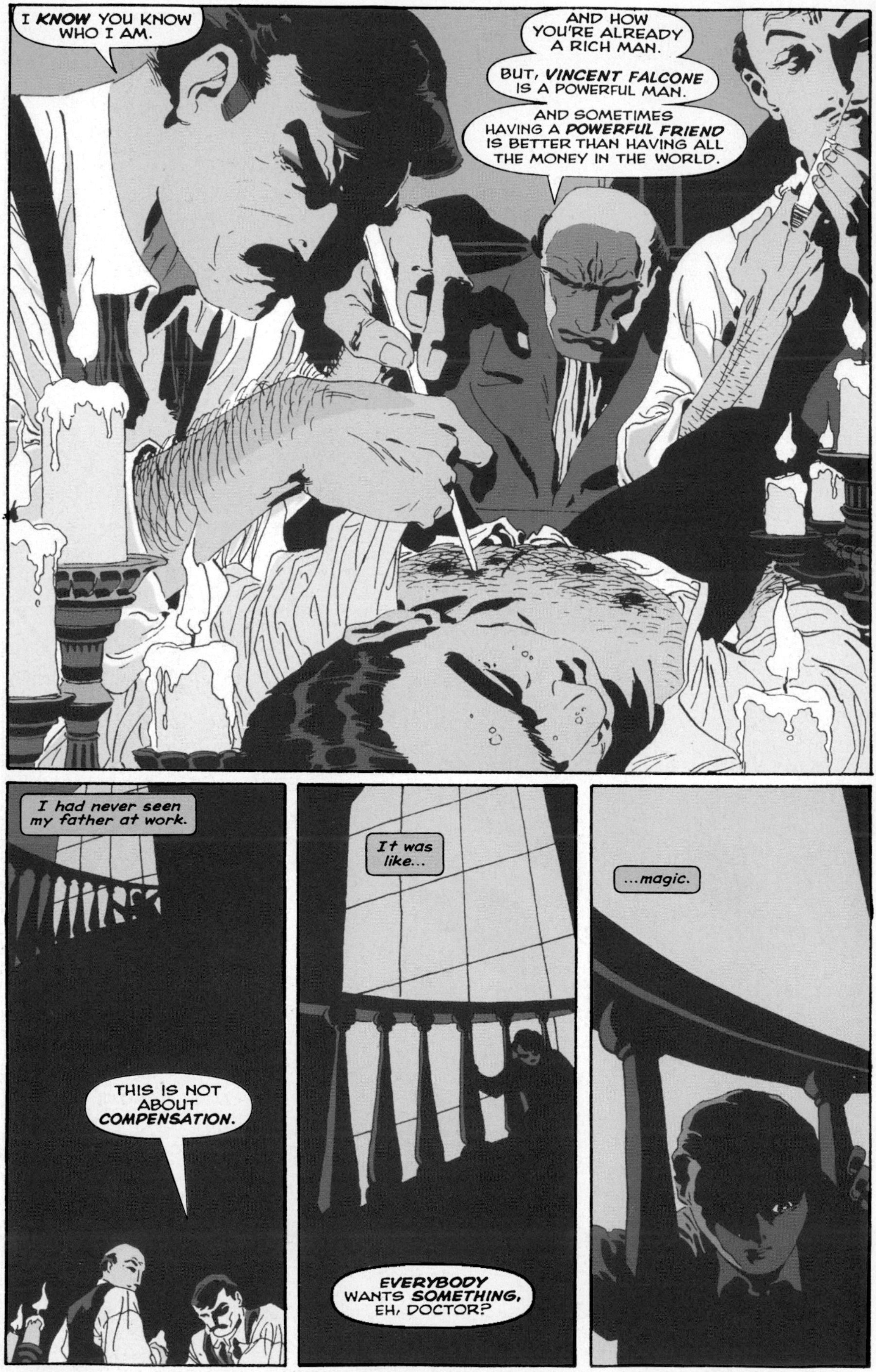

I KNOW YOU KNOW WHO I AM.
AND HOW YOU'RE ALREADY A RICH MAN.
BUT, VINCENT FALCONE IS A POWERFUL MAN.
AND SOMETIMES HAVING A POWERFUL FRIEND IS BETTER THAN HAVING ALL THE MONEY IN THE WORLD.
I had never seen my father at work.
THIS IS NOT ABOUT COMPENSATION.
It was like...
EVERYBODY WANTS SOMETHING, EH, DOCTOR?
...magic.

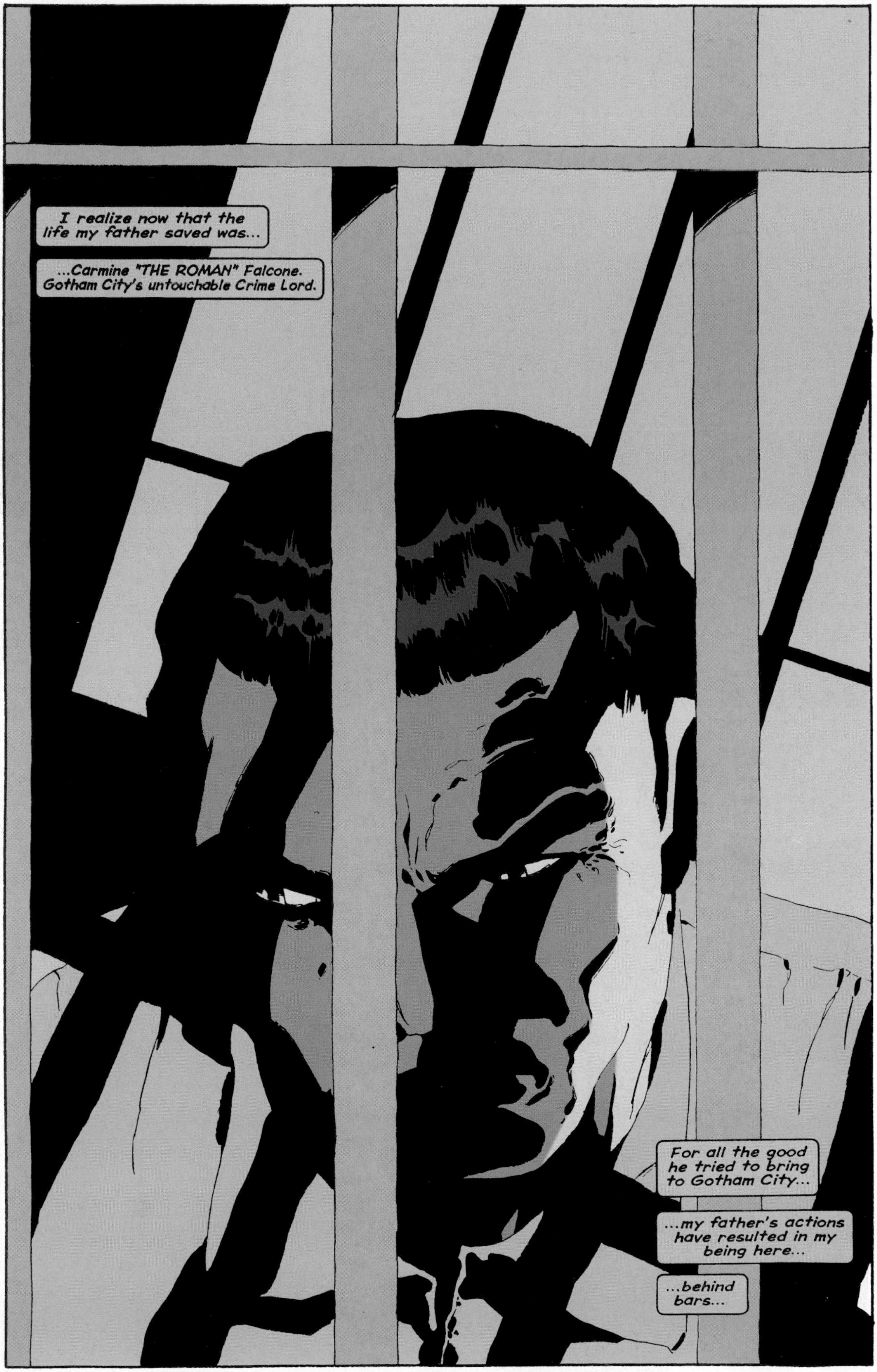
I realize now that the life my father saved was...
...Carmine "THE ROMAN" Falcone. Gotham City's untouchable Crime Lord.
For all the good he tried to bring to Gotham City...
...my father's actions have resulted in my being here...
...behind bars...

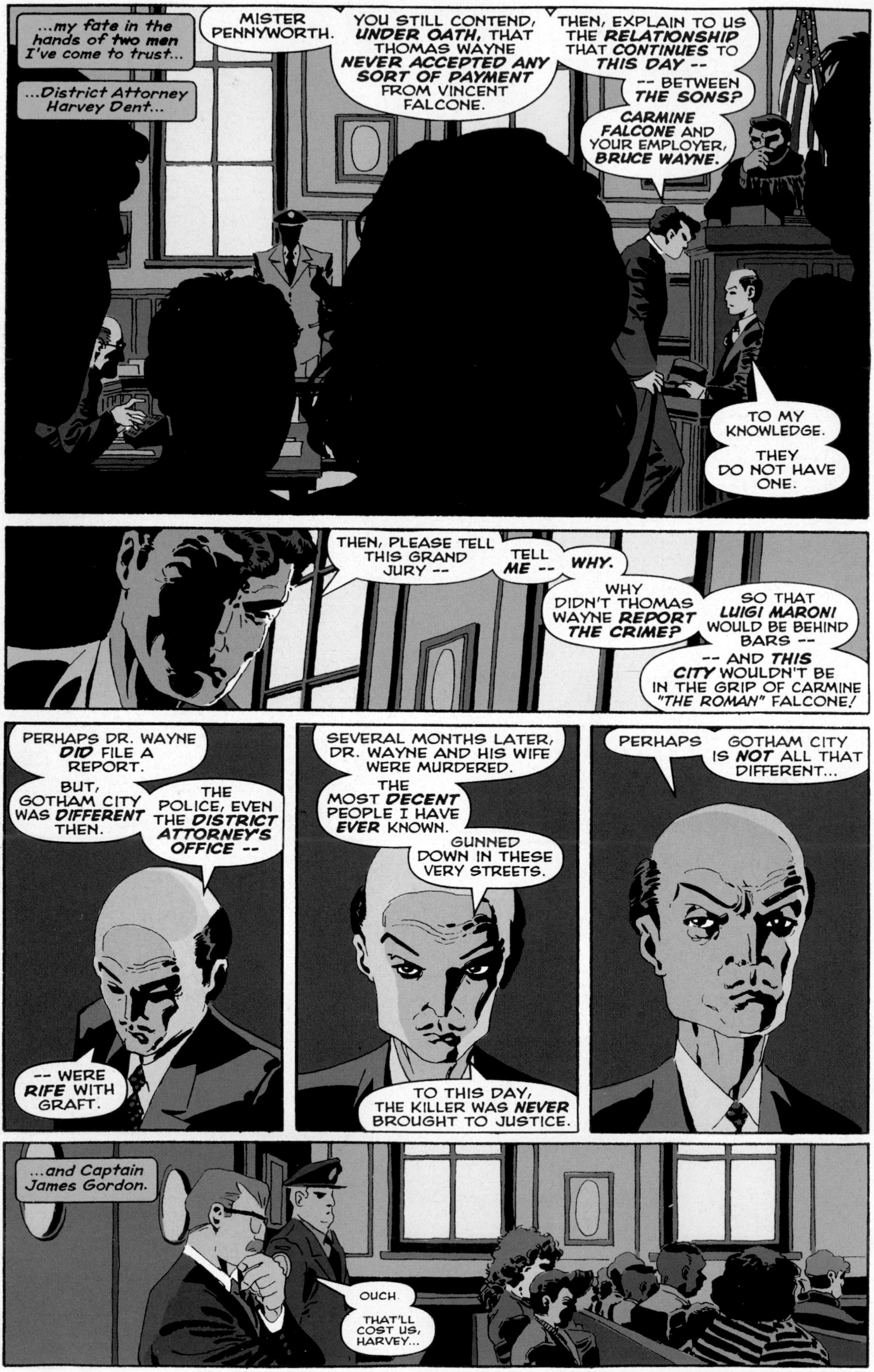
...my fate in the hands of two men I've come to trust...
...District Attorney Harvey Dent...
MISTER PENNYWORTH.
YOU STILL CONTEND, UNDER OATH, THAT THOMAS WAYNE NEVER ACCEPTED ANY SORT OF PAYMENT FROM VINCENT FALCONE.
THEN, EXPLAIN TO US THE RELATIONSHIP THAT CONTINUES TO THIS DAY --
-- BETWEEN THE SONS?
CARMINE FALCONE AND YOUR EMPLOYER, BRUCE WAYNE.
TO MY KNOWLEDGE.
THEY DO NOT HAVE ONE.
THEN, PLEASE TELL THIS GRAND JURY --
TELL ME --
WHY.
WHY DIDN'T THOMAS WAYNE REPORT THE CRIME?
SO THAT LUIGI MARONI WOULD BE BEHIND BARS --
-- AND THIS CITY WOULDN'T BE IN THE GRIP OF CARMINE "THE ROMAN" FALCONE!
PERHAPS DR. WAYNE DID FILE A REPORT.
BUT, GOTHAM CITY WAS DIFFERENT THEN.
THE POLICE, EVEN THE DISTRICT ATTORNEY'S OFFICE --
-- WERE RIFE WITH GRAFT.
SEVERAL MONTHS LATER, DR. WAYNE AND HIS WIFE WERE MURDERED.
THE MOST DECENT PEOPLE I HAVE EVER KNOWN.
GUNNED DOWN IN THESE VERY STREETS.
TO THIS DAY, THE KILLER WAS NEVER BROUGHT TO JUSTICE.
PERHAPS
GOTHAM CITY IS NOT ALL THAT DIFFERENT...
...and Captain James Gordon.
OUCH.
THAT'LL COST US, HARVEY...

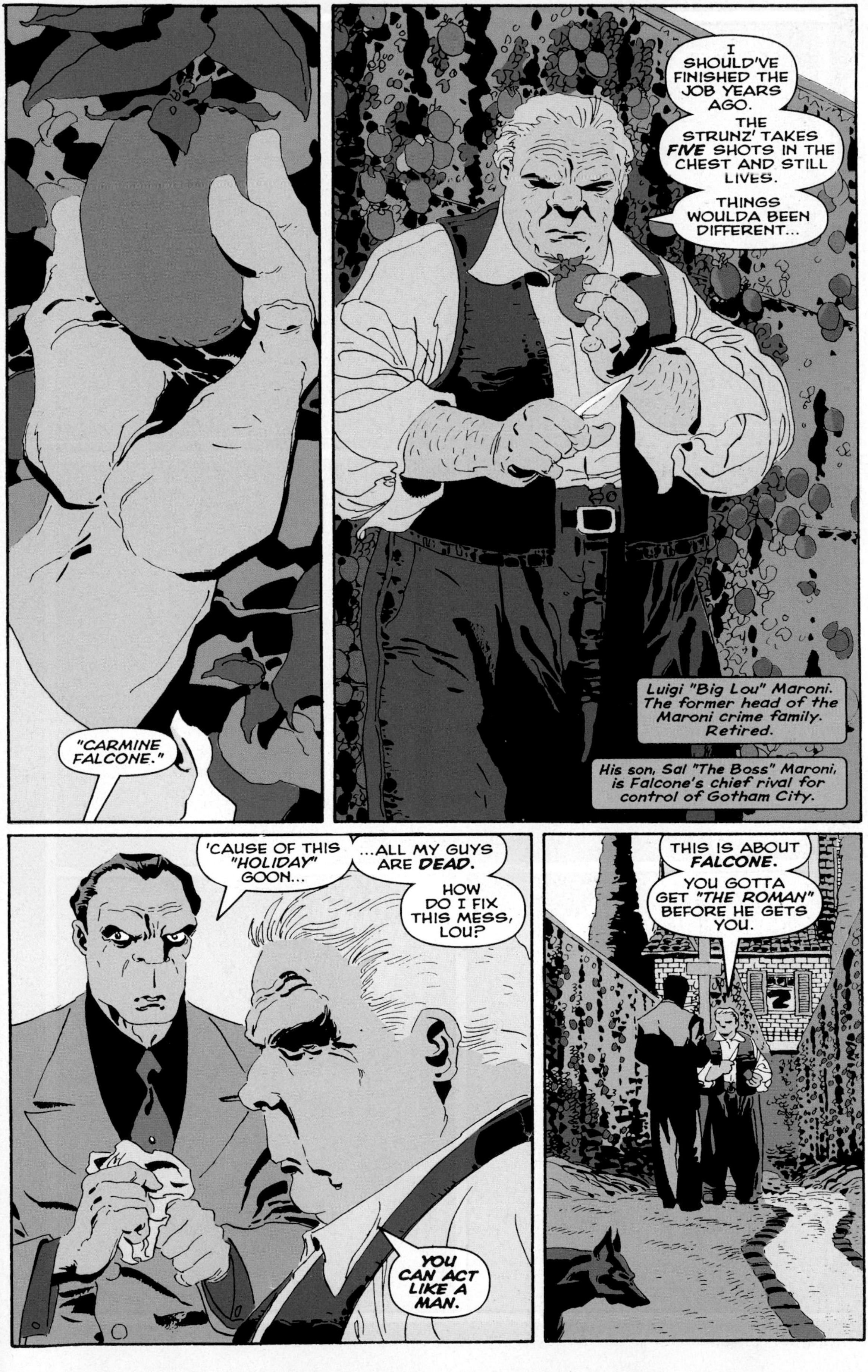
"CARMINE FALCONE."
I SHOULD'VE FINISHED THE JOB YEARS AGO.
THE STRUNZ' TAKES FIVE SHOTS IN THE CHEST AND STILL LIVES.
THINGS WOULDA BEEN DIFFERENT...
Luigi "Big Lou" Maroni. The former head of the Maroni crime family. Retired.
His son, Sal "The Boss" Maroni, is Falcone's chief rival for control of Gotham City.
'CAUSE OF THIS "HOLIDAY" GOON...
...ALL MY GUYS ARE DEAD.
HOW DO I FIX THIS MESS, LOU?
YOU CAN ACT LIKE A MAN.
THIS IS ABOUT FALCONE.
YOU GOTTA GET "THE ROMAN" BEFORE HE GETS YOU.

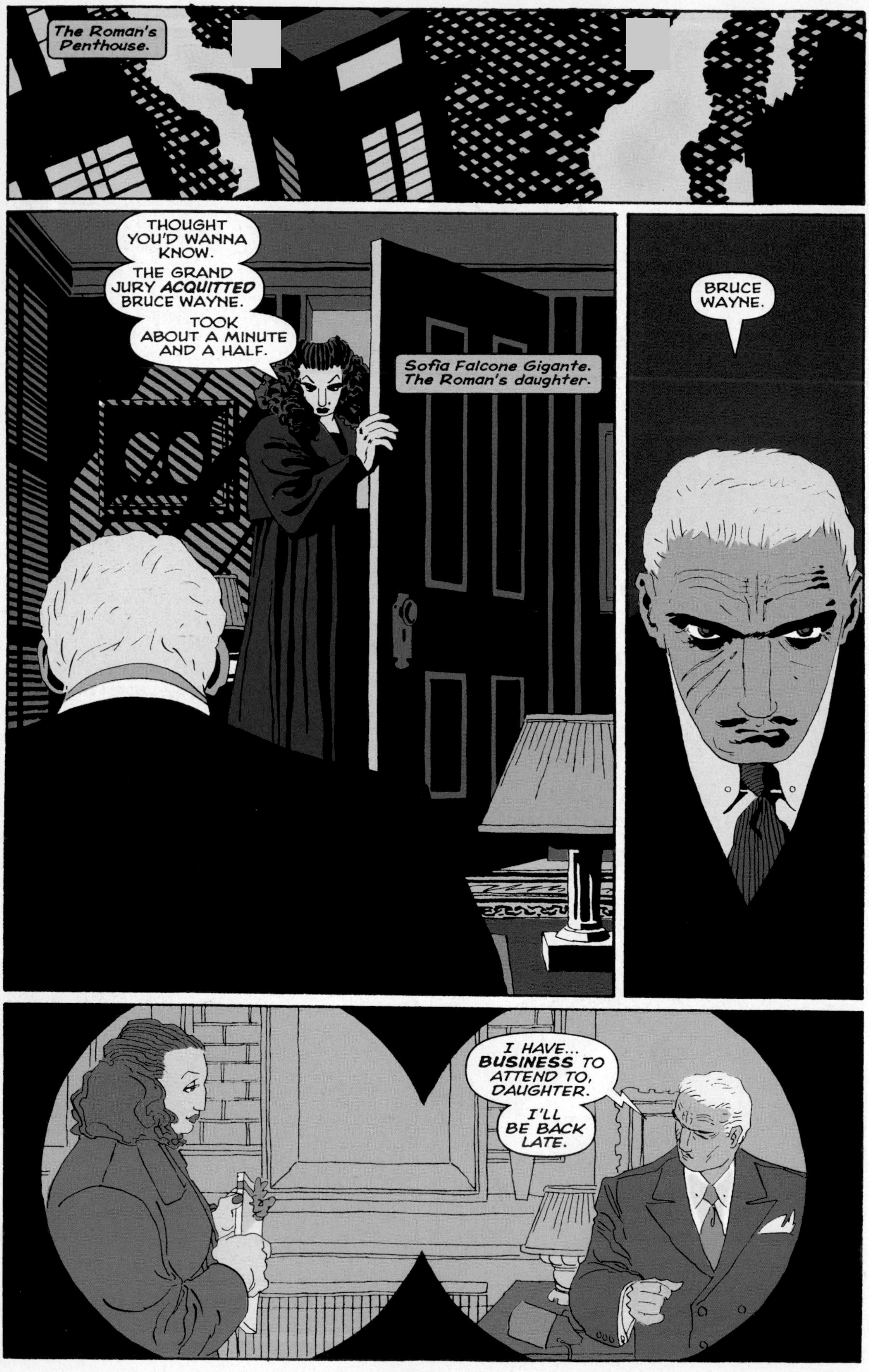
The Roman's Penthouse.
THOUGHT YOU'D WANNA KNOW.
THE GRAND JURY ACQUITTED BRUCE WAYNE.
TOOK ABOUT A MINUTE AND A HALF.
Sofia Falcone Gigante. The Roman's daughter.
BRUCE WAYNE.
I HAVE... BUSINESS TO ATTEND TO, DAUGHTER.
I'LL BE BACK LATE.

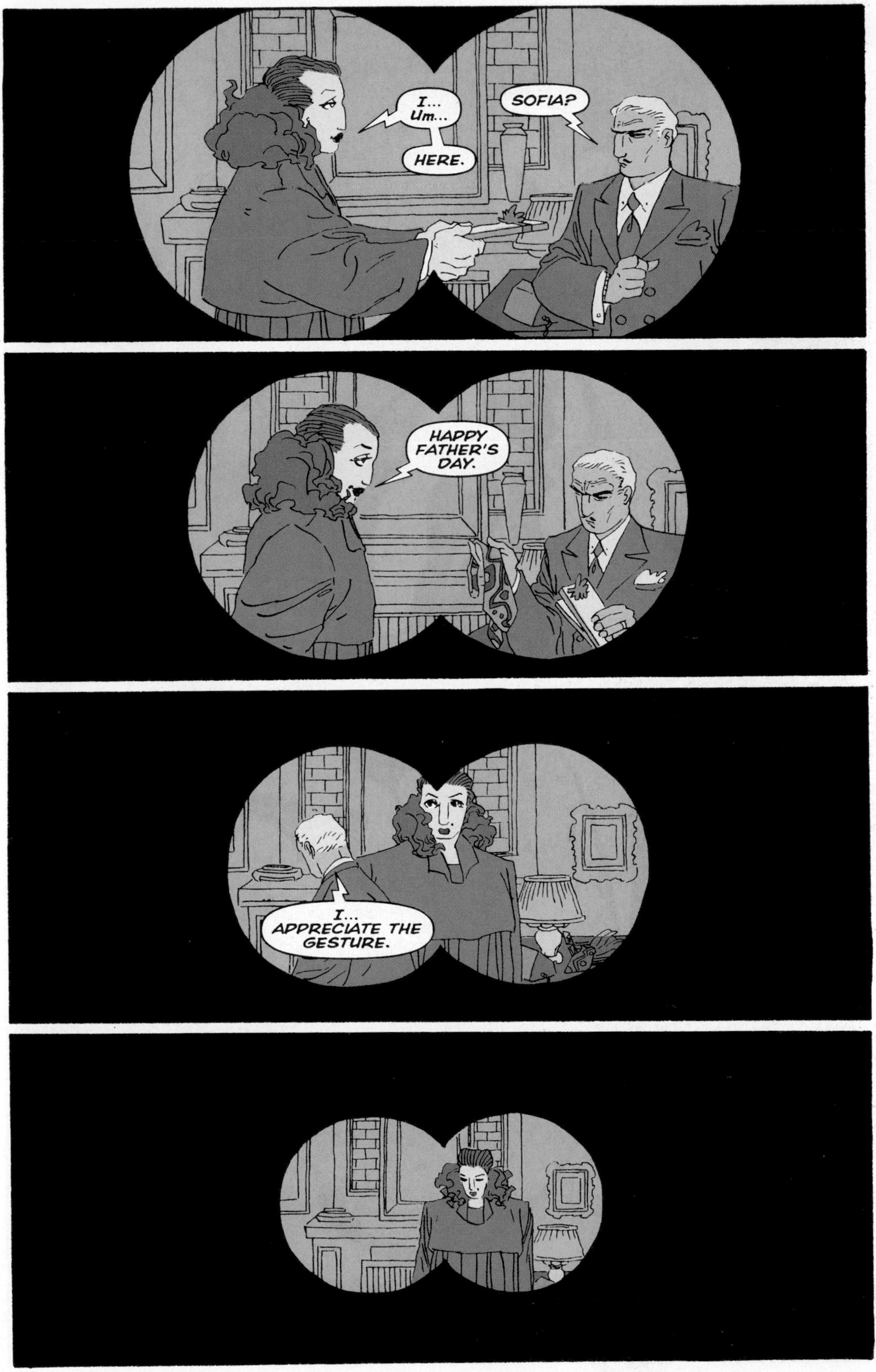
SOFIA?
I... Um...
HERE.
HAPPY FATHER'S DAY.
I... APPRECIATE THE GESTURE.

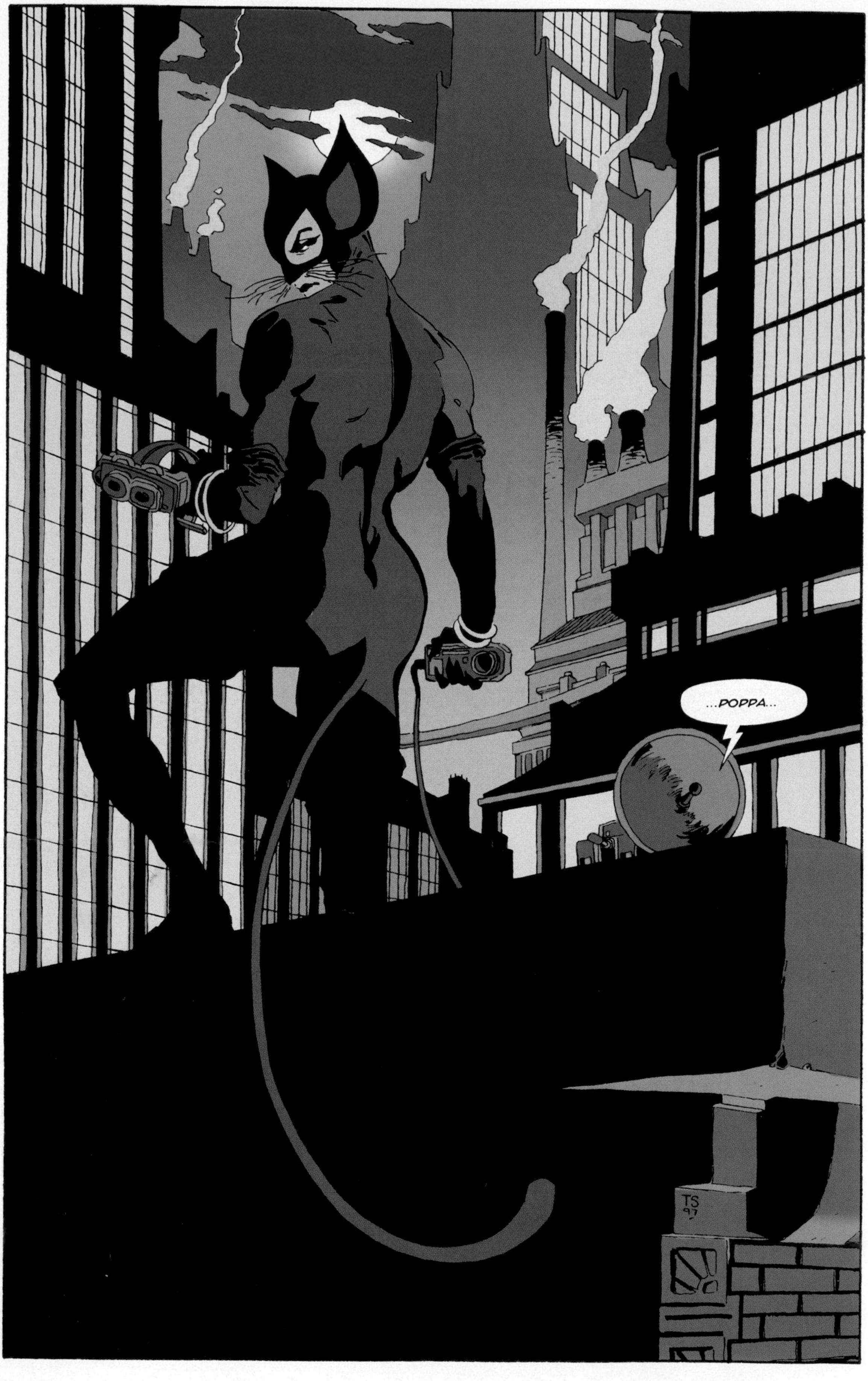
...POPPA...
TS 97

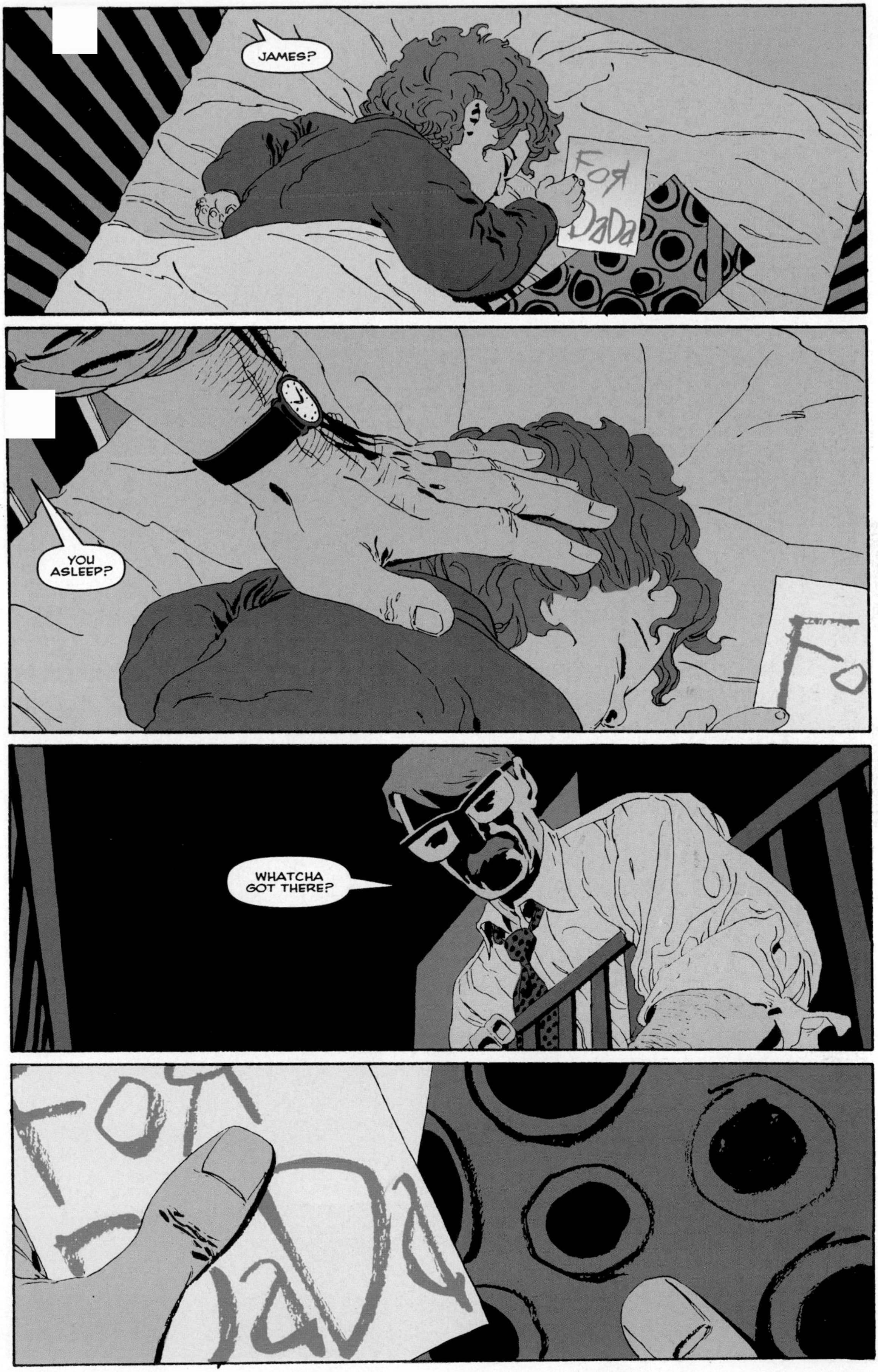
JAMES?
FOR DADA
YOU ASLEEP?
WHATCHA GOT THERE?

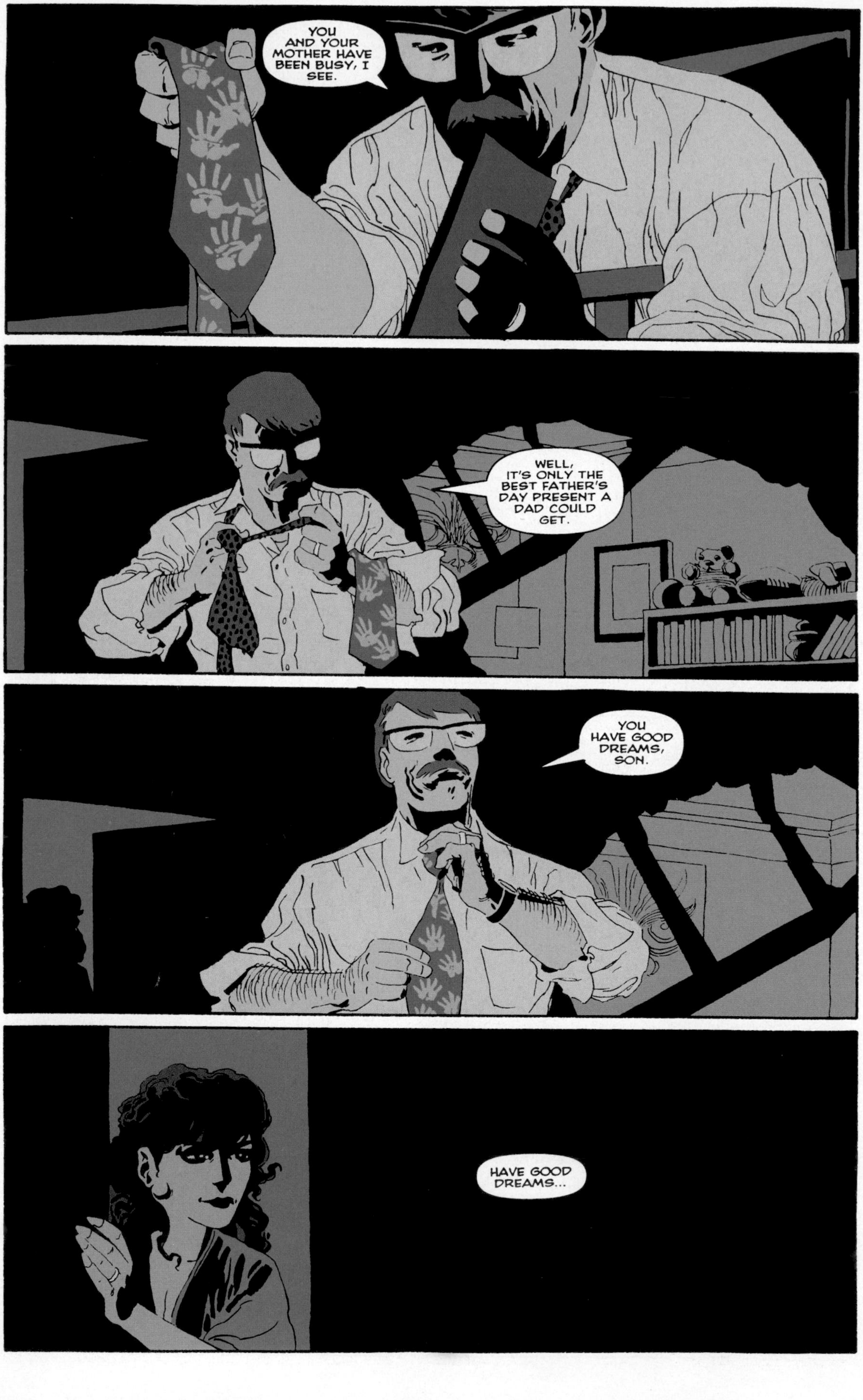
YOU AND YOUR MOTHER HAVE BEEN BUSY, I SEE.
WELL, IT'S ONLY THE BEST FATHER'S DAY PRESENT A DAD COULD GET.
YOU HAVE GOOD DREAMS, SON.
HAVE GOOD DREAMS...

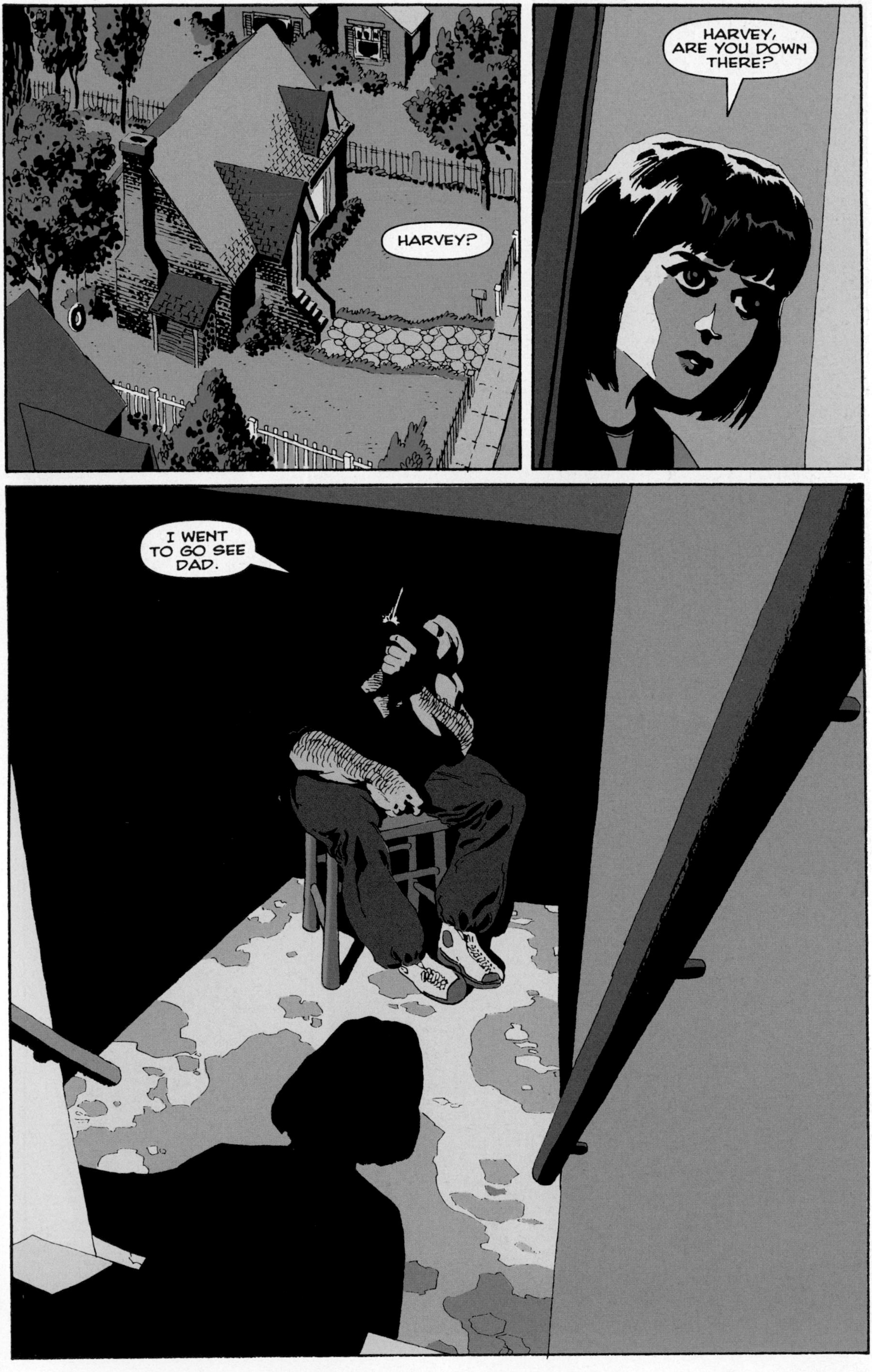
HARVEY?
HARVEY, ARE YOU DOWN THERE?
I WENT TO GO SEE DAD.

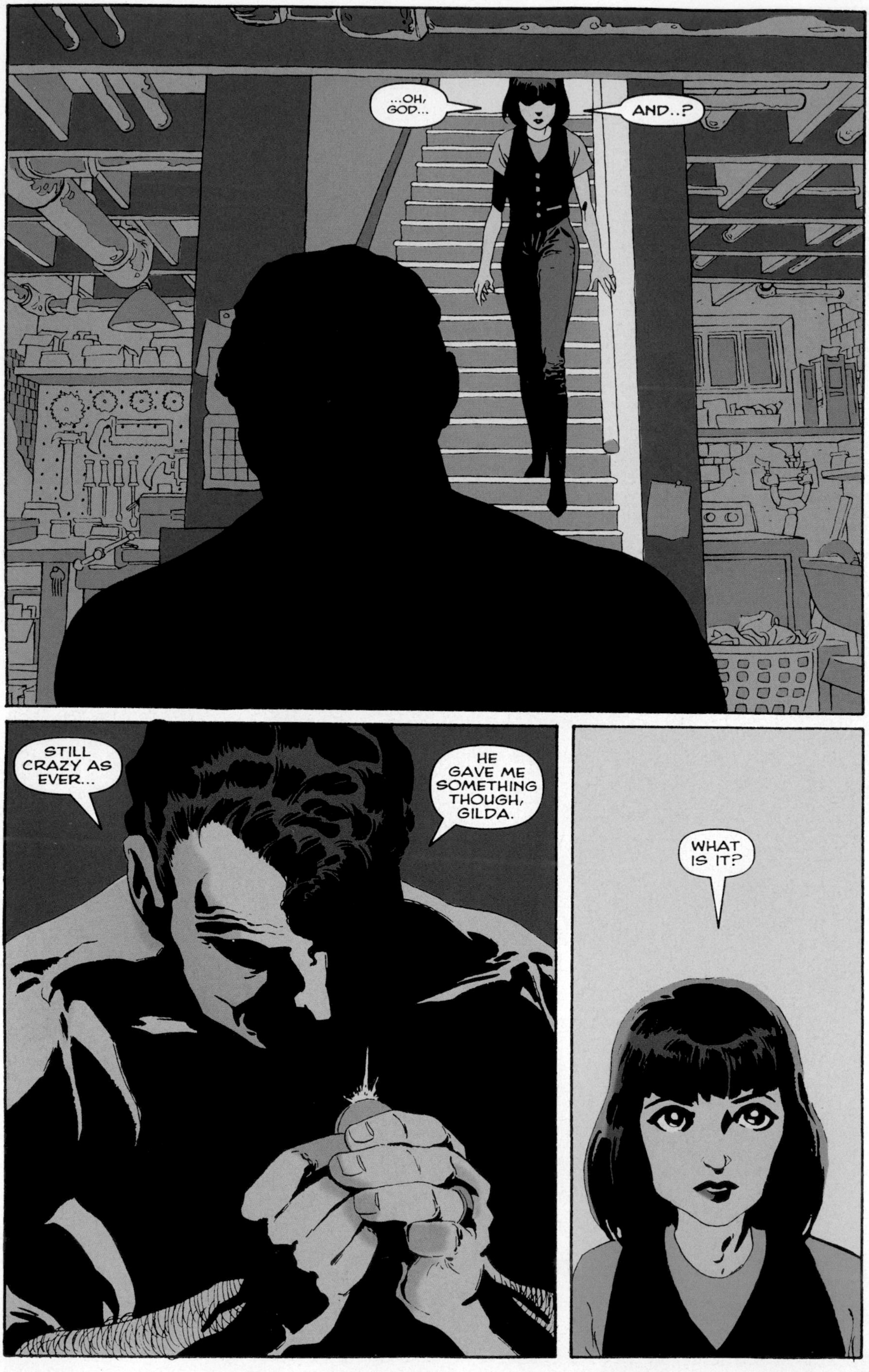
...OH, GOD...
AND..?
STILL CRAZY AS EVER...
HE GAVE ME SOMETHING THOUGH, GILDA.
WHAT IS IT?

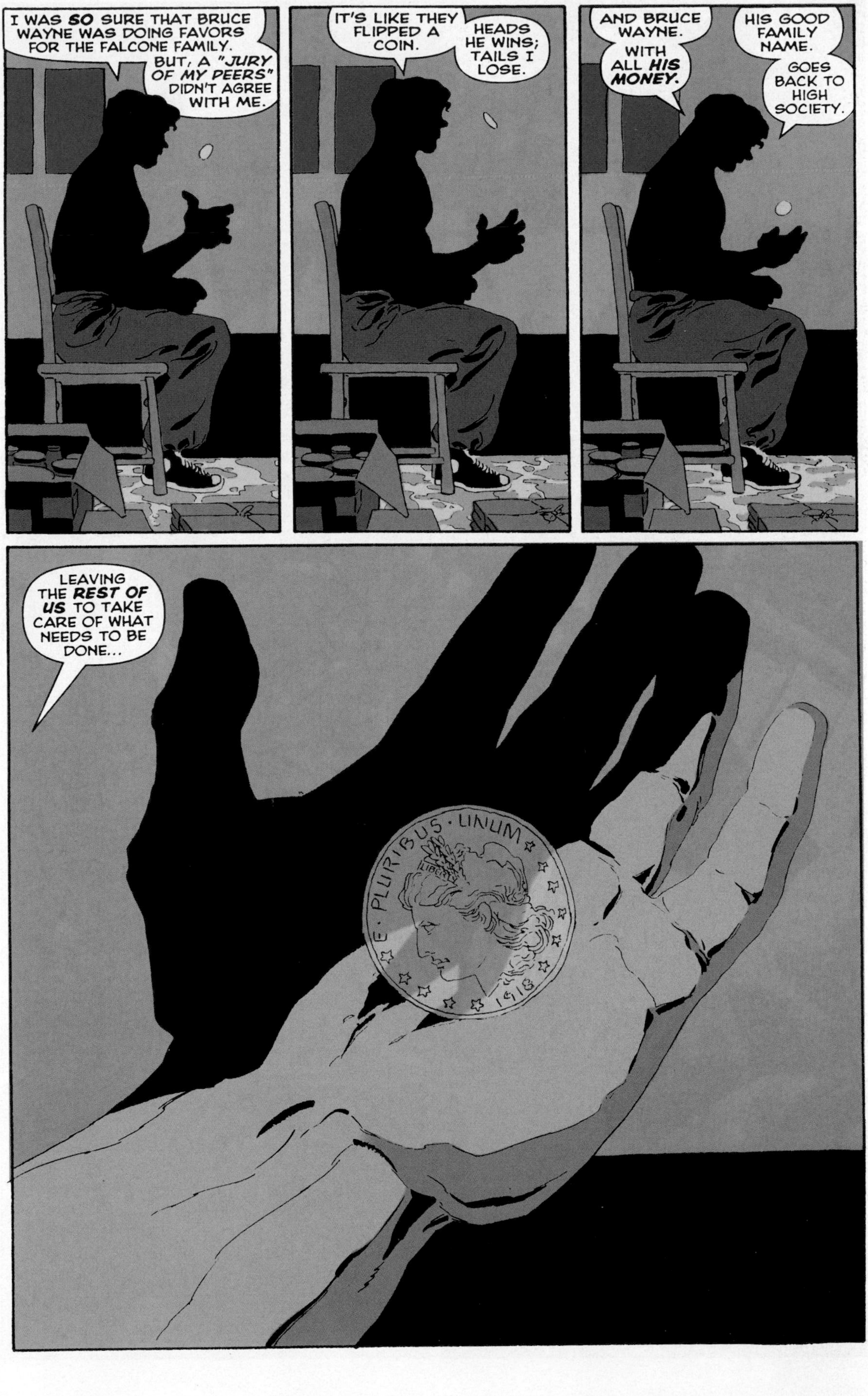
I WAS SO SURE THAT BRUCE WAYNE WAS DOING FAVORS FOR THE FALCONE FAMILY.
BUT, A "JURY OF MY PEERS" DIDN'T AGREE WITH ME.
IT'S LIKE THEY FLIPPED A COIN.
HEADS HE WINS; TAILS I LOSE.
AND BRUCE WAYNE.
WITH ALL HIS MONEY.
HIS GOOD FAMILY NAME.
GOES BACK TO HIGH SOCIETY.
LEAVING THE REST OF US TO TAKE CARE OF WHAT NEEDS TO BE DONE...
E · PLURIBUS · UNUM
LIBERTY
1918

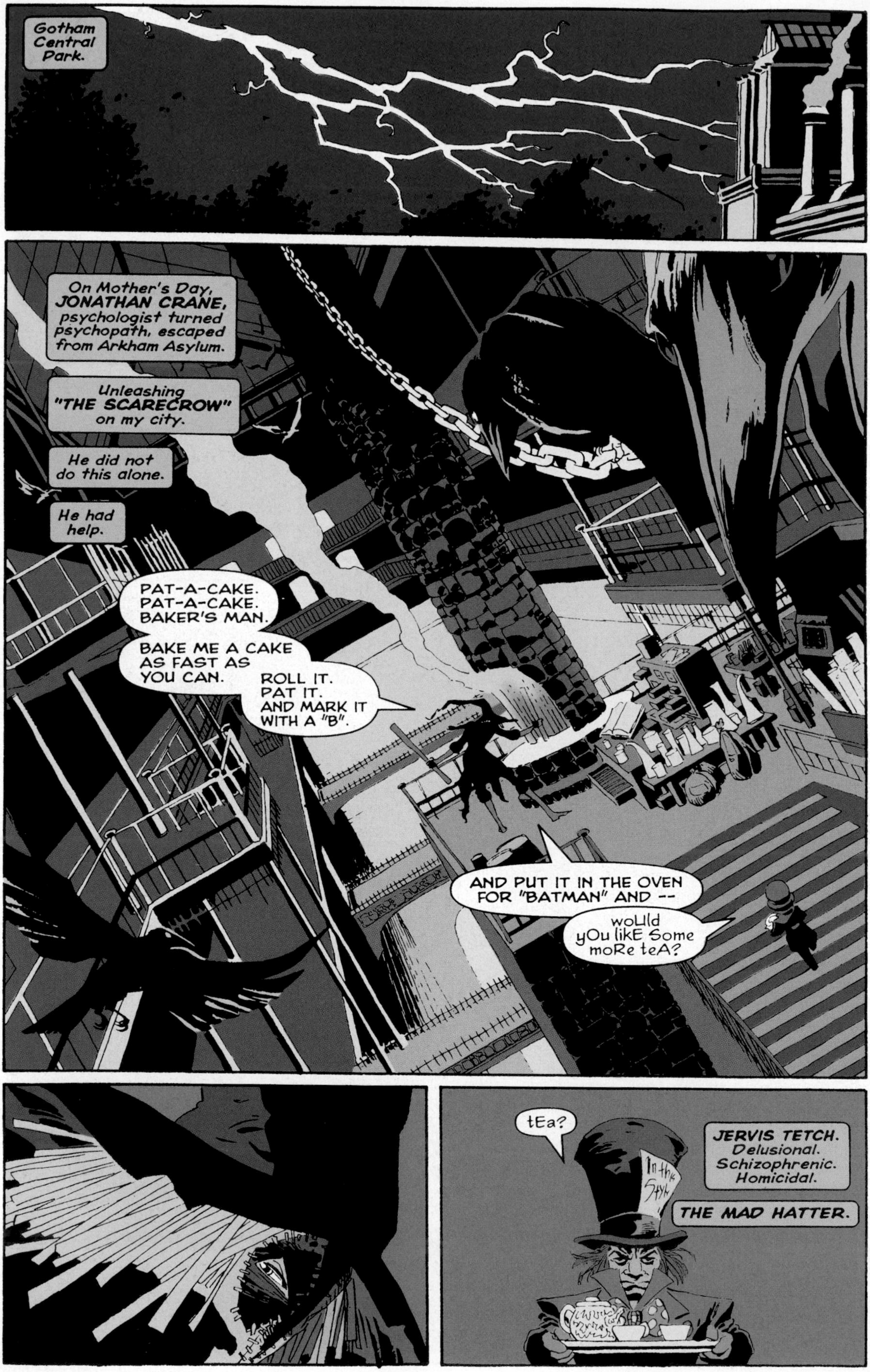
Gotham Central Park.
On Mother's Day, JONATHAN CRANE, psychologist turned psychopath, escaped from Arkham Asylum.
Unleashing "THE SCARECROW" on my city.
He did not do this alone.
He had help.
PAT-A-CAKE. PAT-A-CAKE. BAKER'S MAN.
BAKE ME A CAKE AS FAST AS YOU CAN.
ROLL IT. PAT IT. AND MARK IT WITH A "B".
AND PUT IT IN THE OVEN FOR "BATMAN" AND --
woUld yOu likE Some moRe teA?
tEa?
JERVIS TETCH. Delusional. Schizophrenic. Homicidal.
THE MAD HATTER.

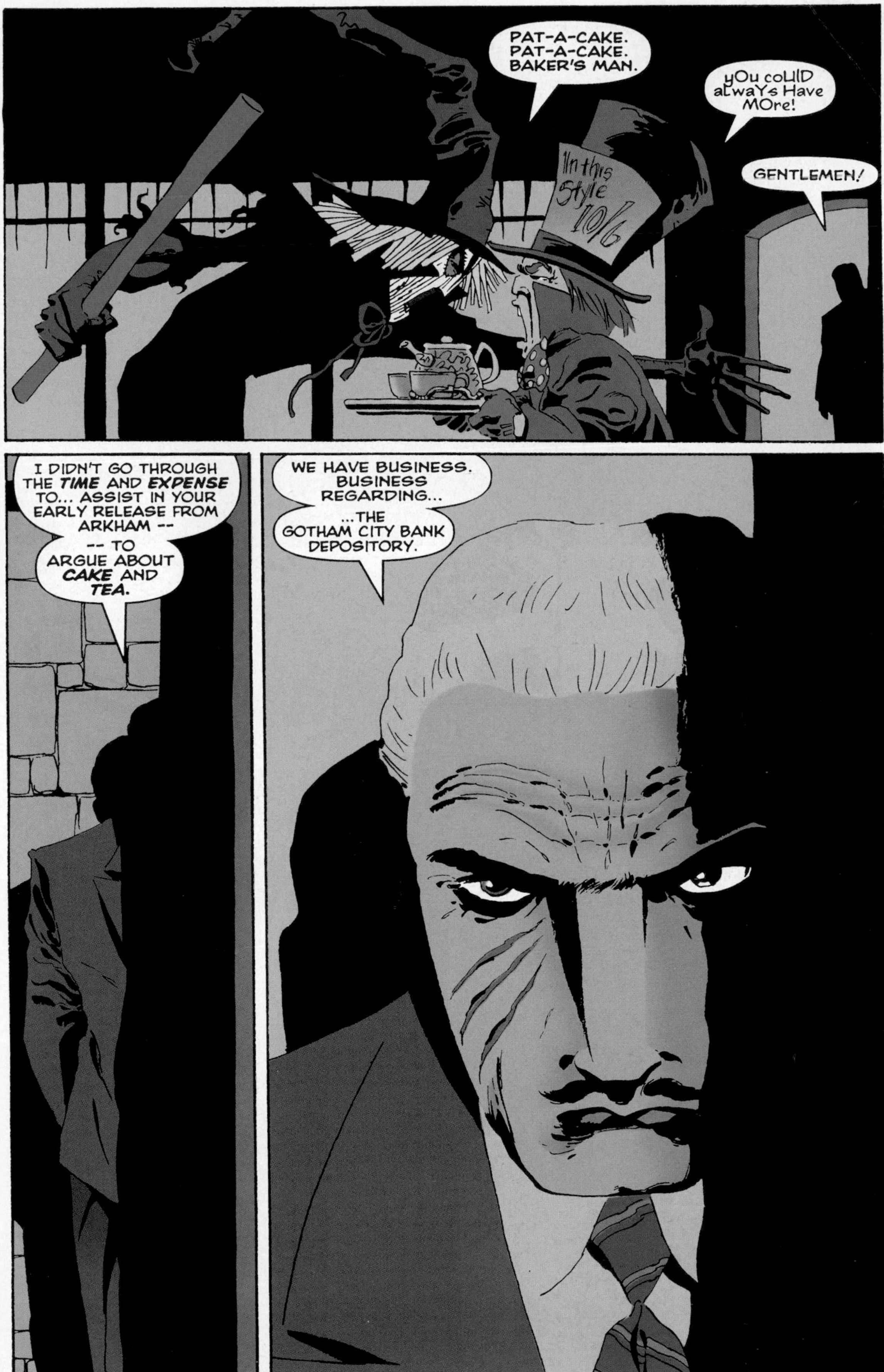
PAT-A-CAKE. PAT-A-CAKE. BAKER'S MAN.
In this Style 10/6
yOu coUlD aLwaYs Have MOre!
GENTLEMEN!
I DIDN'T GO THROUGH THE *TIME* AND *EXPENSE* TO... ASSIST IN YOUR EARLY RELEASE FROM ARKHAM --
-- TO ARGUE ABOUT *CAKE* AND *TEA*.
WE HAVE BUSINESS. BUSINESS REGARDING...
...THE GOTHAM CITY BANK DEPOSITORY.

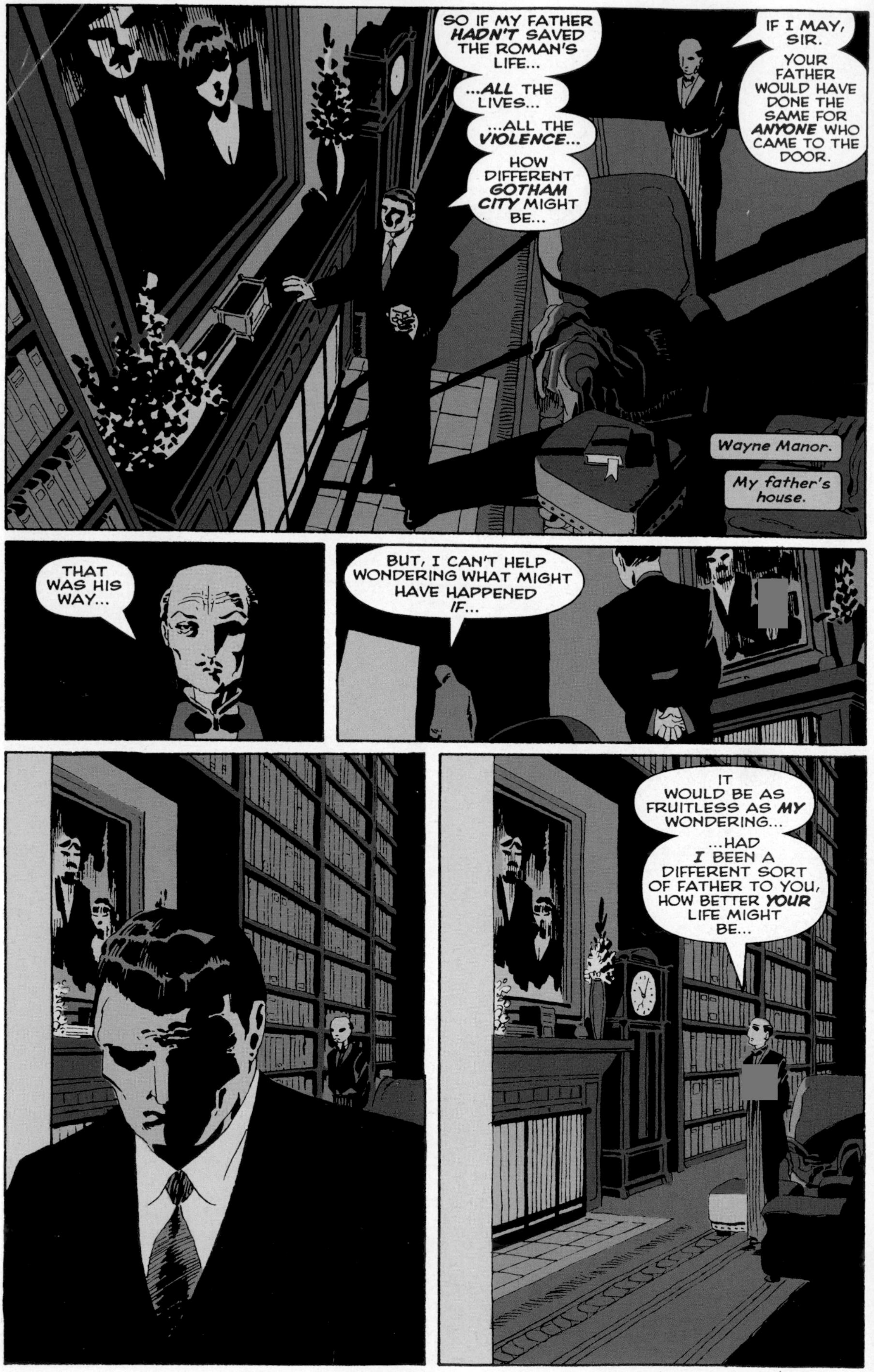
SO IF MY FATHER HADN'T SAVED THE ROMAN'S LIFE...
...ALL THE LIVES...
...ALL THE VIOLENCE...
HOW DIFFERENT GOTHAM CITY MIGHT BE...
IF I MAY, SIR.
YOUR FATHER WOULD HAVE DONE THE SAME FOR ANYONE WHO CAME TO THE DOOR.
Wayne Manor.
My father's house.
THAT WAS HIS WAY...
BUT, I CAN'T HELP WONDERING WHAT MIGHT HAVE HAPPENED IF...
IT WOULD BE AS FRUITLESS AS MY WONDERING...
...HAD I BEEN A DIFFERENT SORT OF FATHER TO YOU, HOW BETTER YOUR LIFE MIGHT BE...

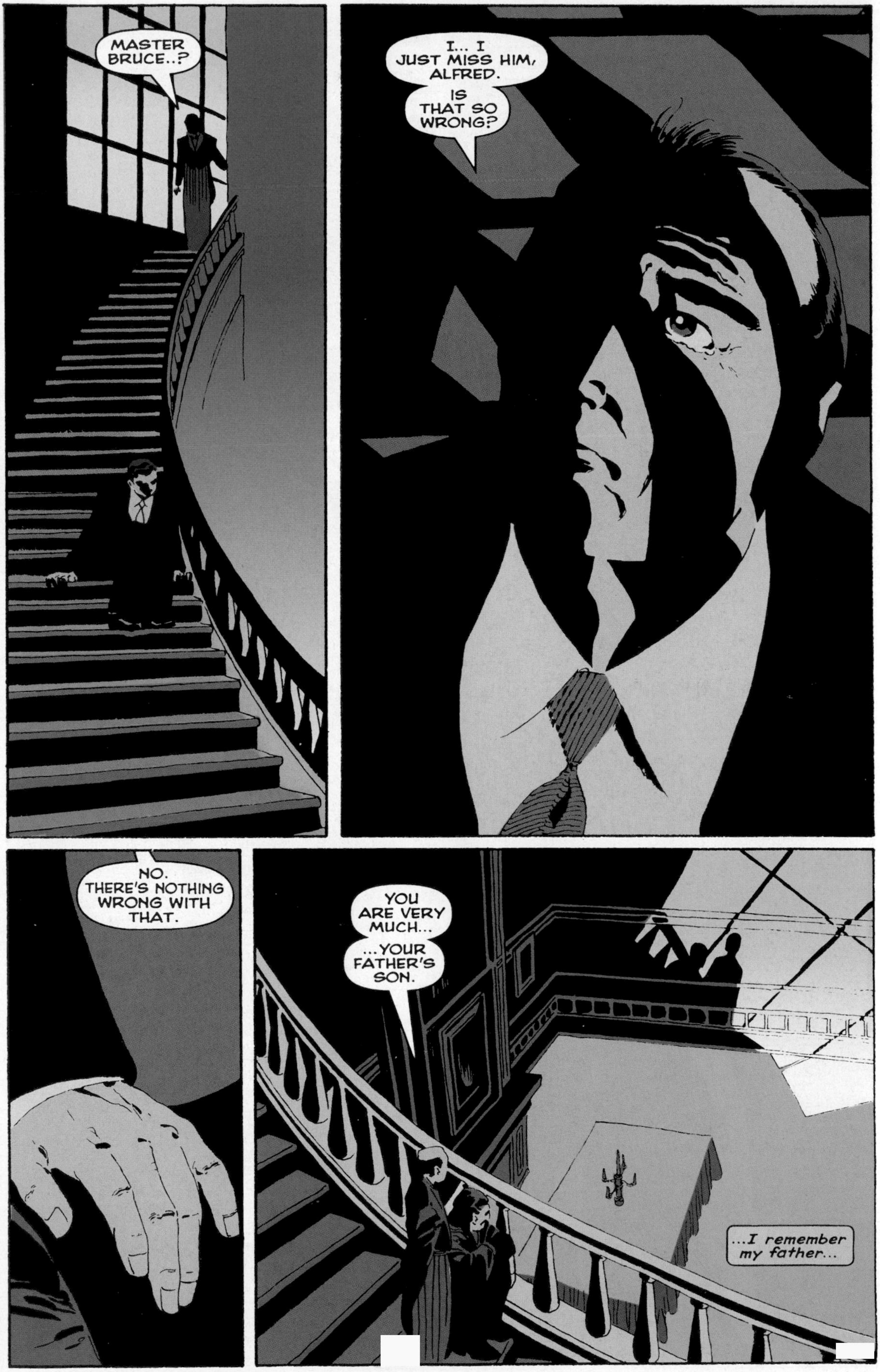
MASTER BRUCE..?
I... I JUST MISS HIM, ALFRED.
IS THAT SO WRONG?
NO. THERE'S NOTHING WRONG WITH THAT.
YOU ARE VERY MUCH...
...YOUR FATHER'S SON.
...I remember my father...

CHAPTER TEN

INDEPENDENCE DAY

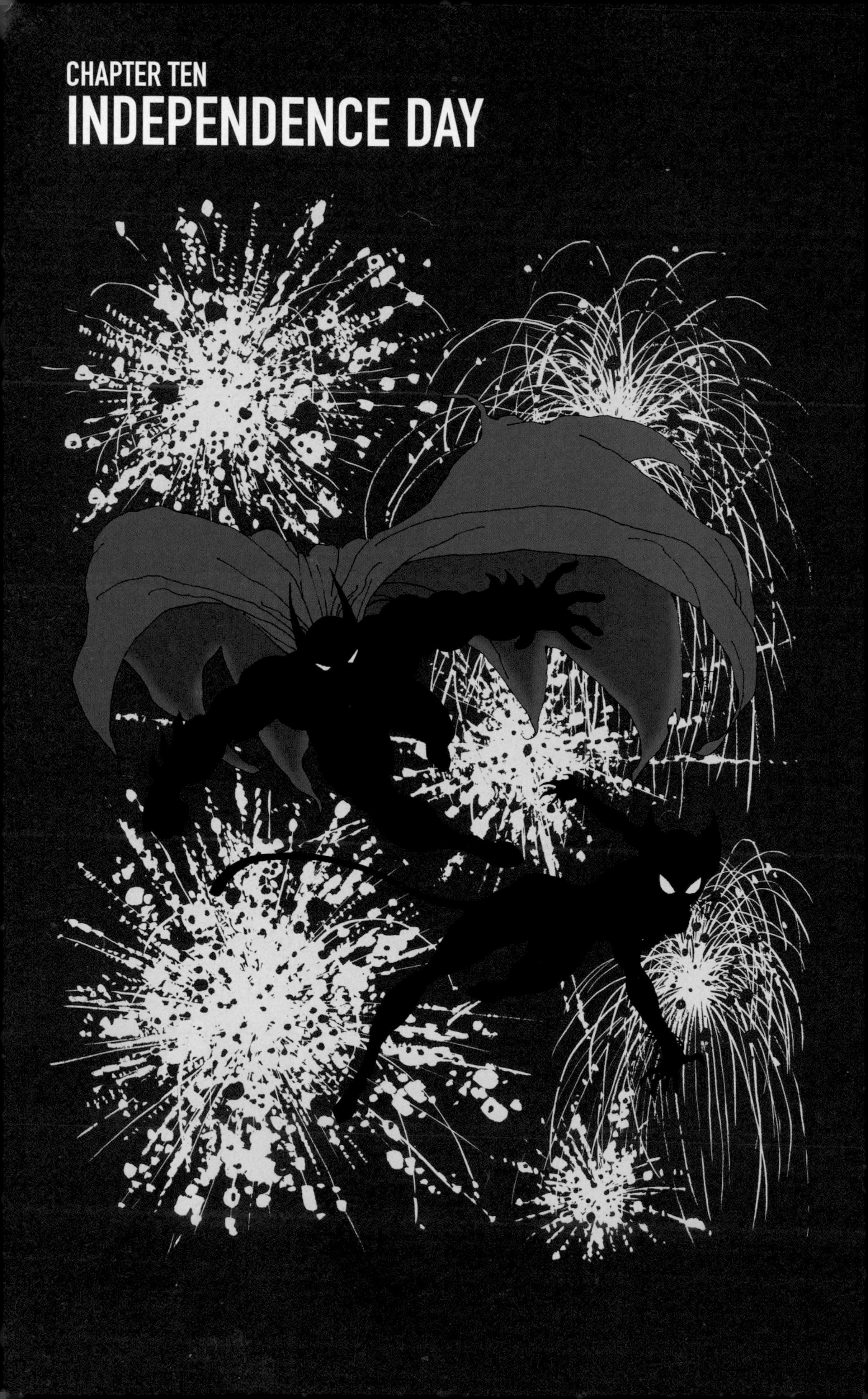

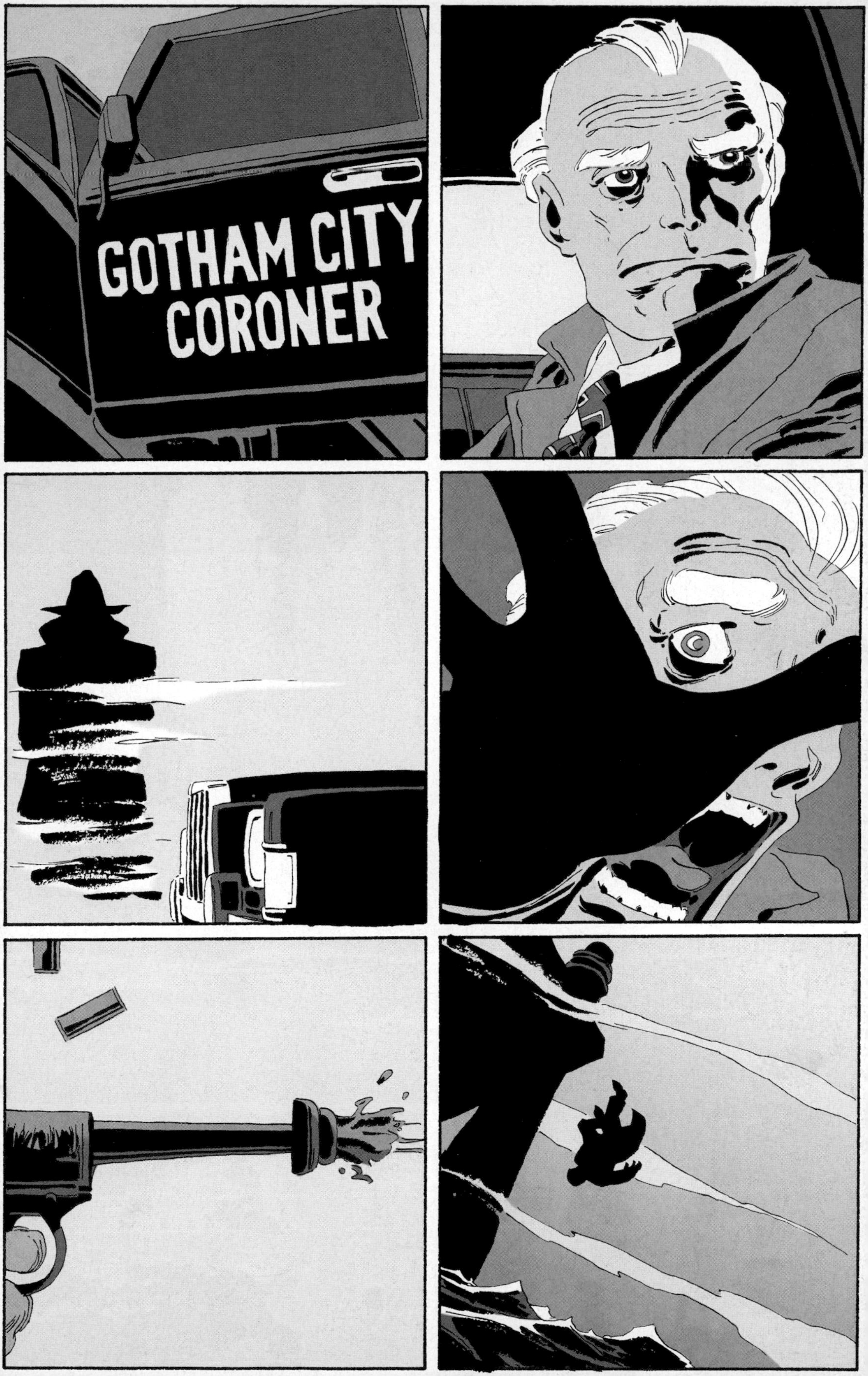
GOTHAM CITY
CORONER

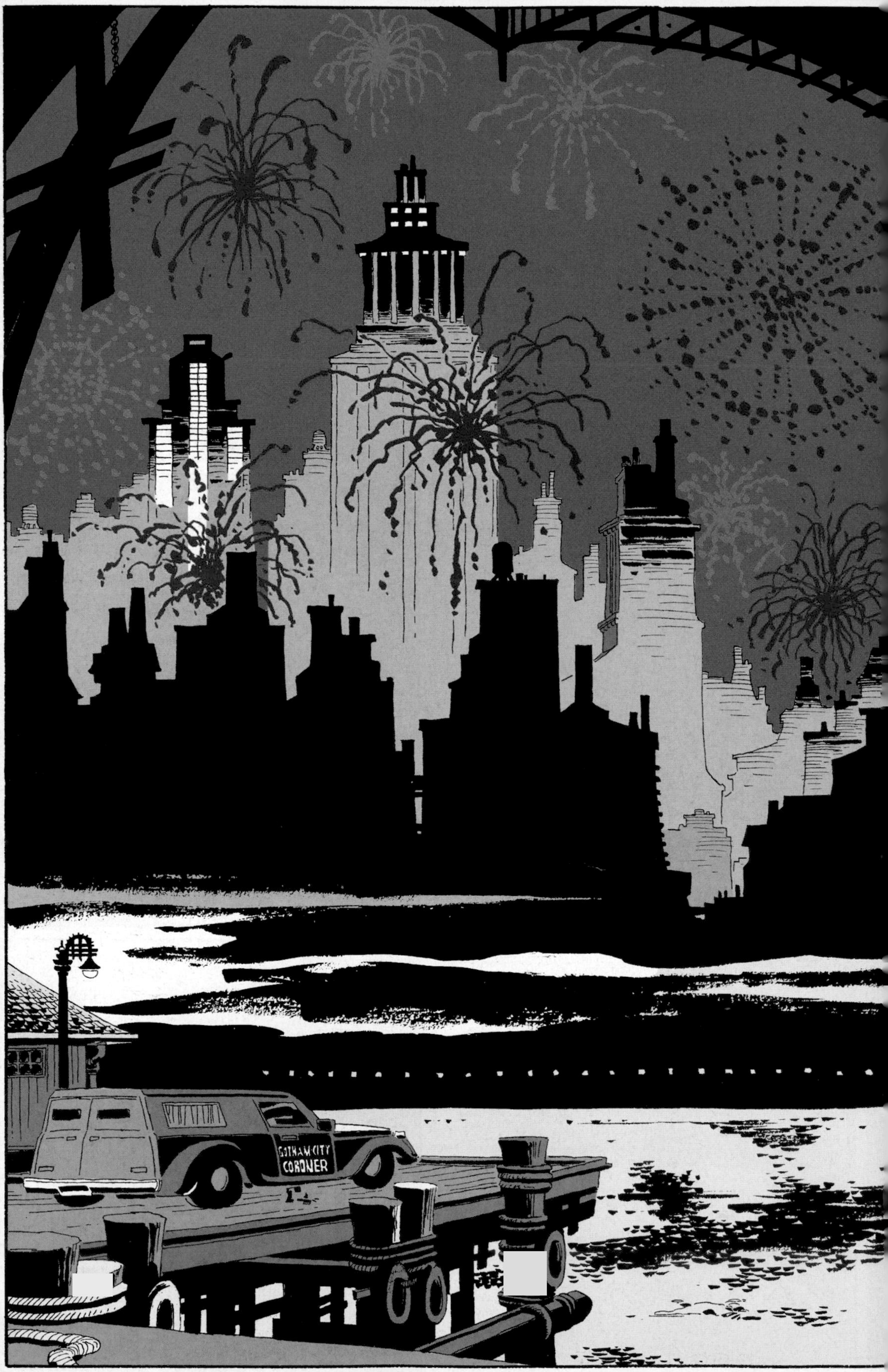
GOTHAM CITY
CORONER

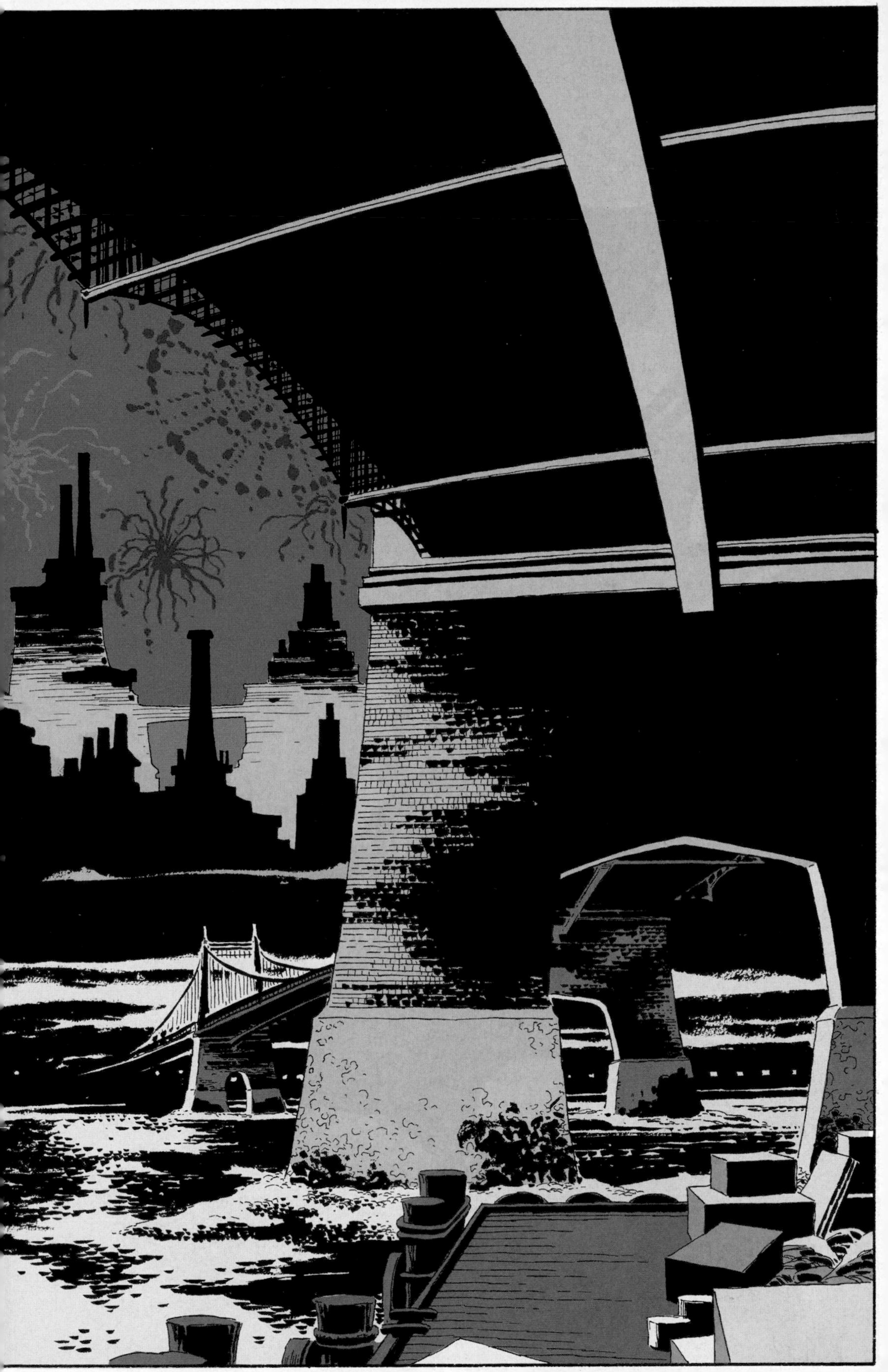

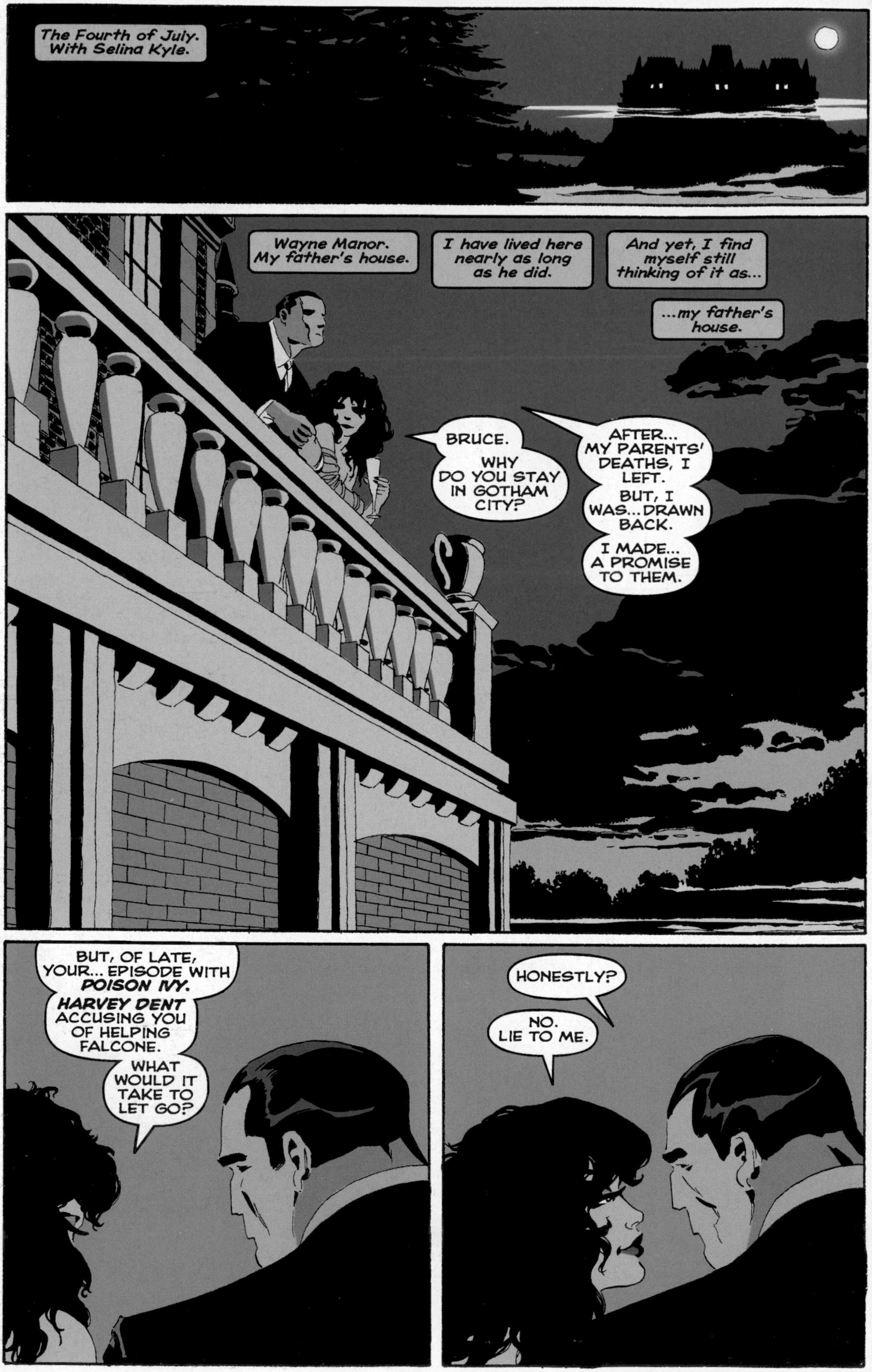
The Fourth of July. With Selina Kyle.
Wayne Manor. My father's house.
I have lived here nearly as long as he did.
And yet, I find myself still thinking of it as...
...my father's house.
BRUCE.
WHY DO YOU STAY IN GOTHAM CITY?
AFTER... MY PARENTS' DEATHS, I LEFT.
BUT, I WAS... DRAWN BACK.
I MADE... A PROMISE TO THEM.
BUT, OF LATE, YOUR... EPISODE WITH **POISON IVY.**
HARVEY DENT ACCUSING YOU OF HELPING FALCONE.
WHAT WOULD IT TAKE TO LET GO?
HONESTLY?
NO. LIE TO ME.

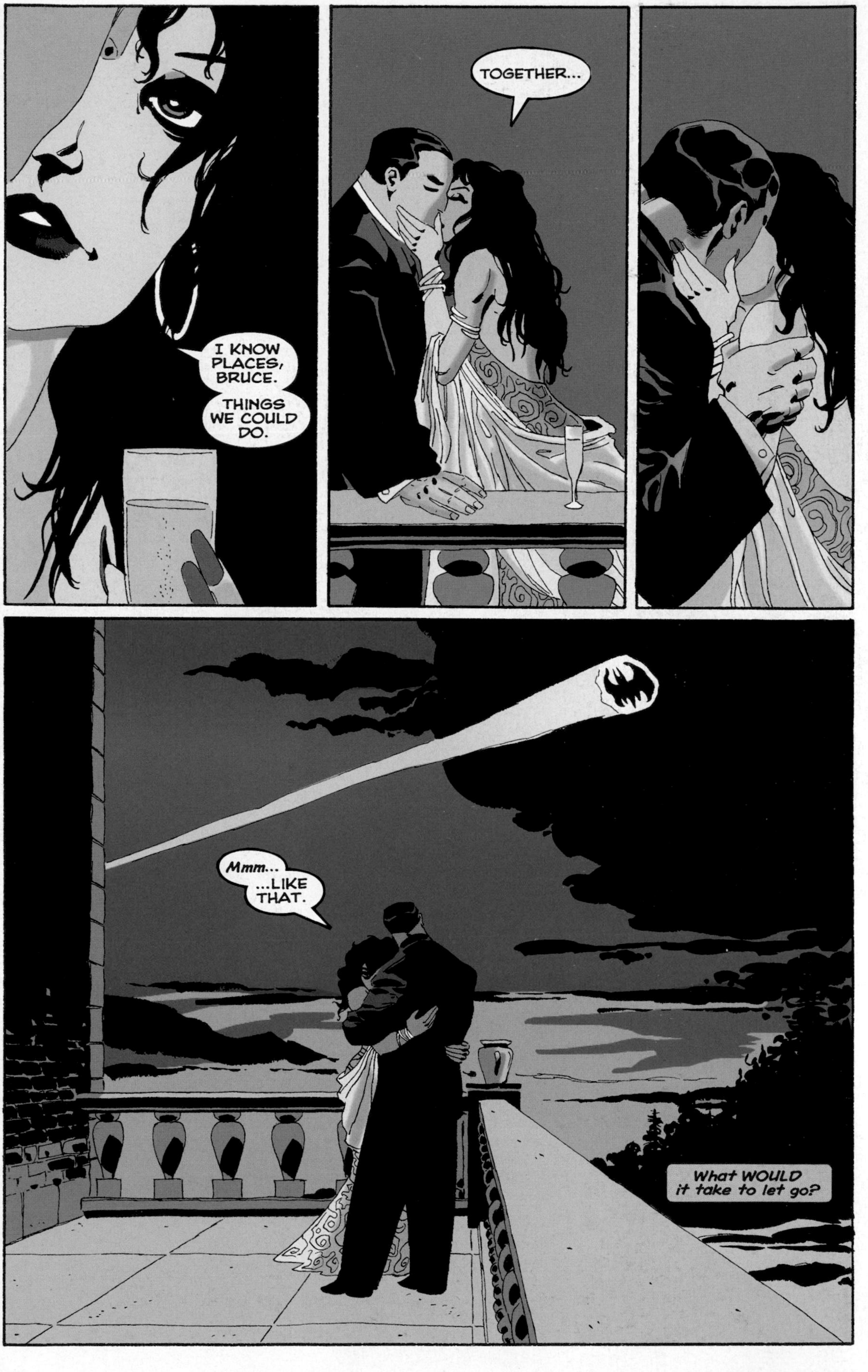
I KNOW PLACES, BRUCE.
THINGS WE COULD DO.
TOGETHER...
Mmm... ...LIKE THAT.
What WOULD it take to let go?

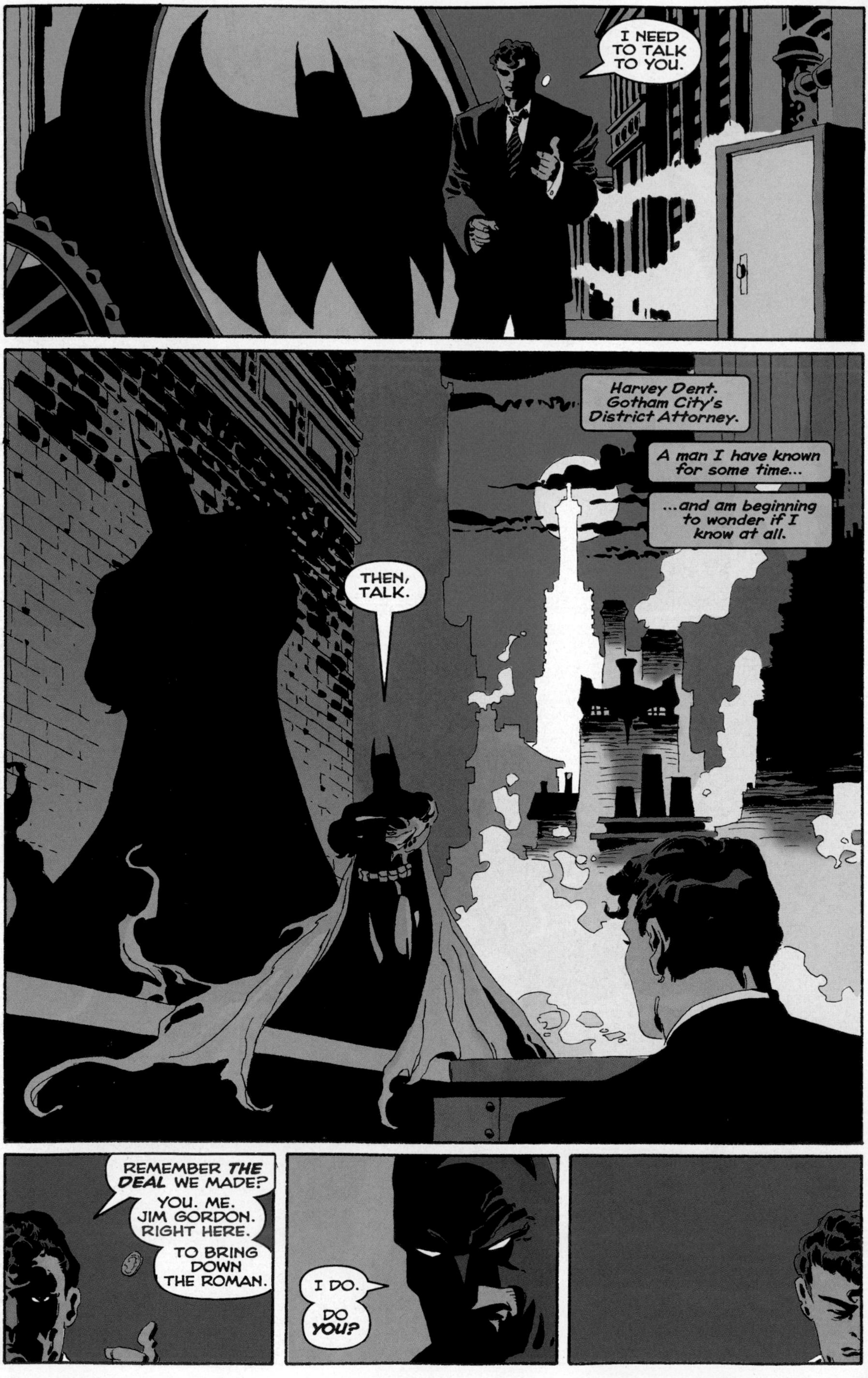

I NEED TO TALK TO YOU.
Harvey Dent. Gotham City's District Attorney.
A man I have known for some time...
...and am beginning to wonder if I know at all.
THEN, TALK.
REMEMBER THE DEAL WE MADE?
YOU. ME. JIM GORDON. RIGHT HERE.
TO BRING DOWN THE ROMAN.
I DO.
DO YOU?

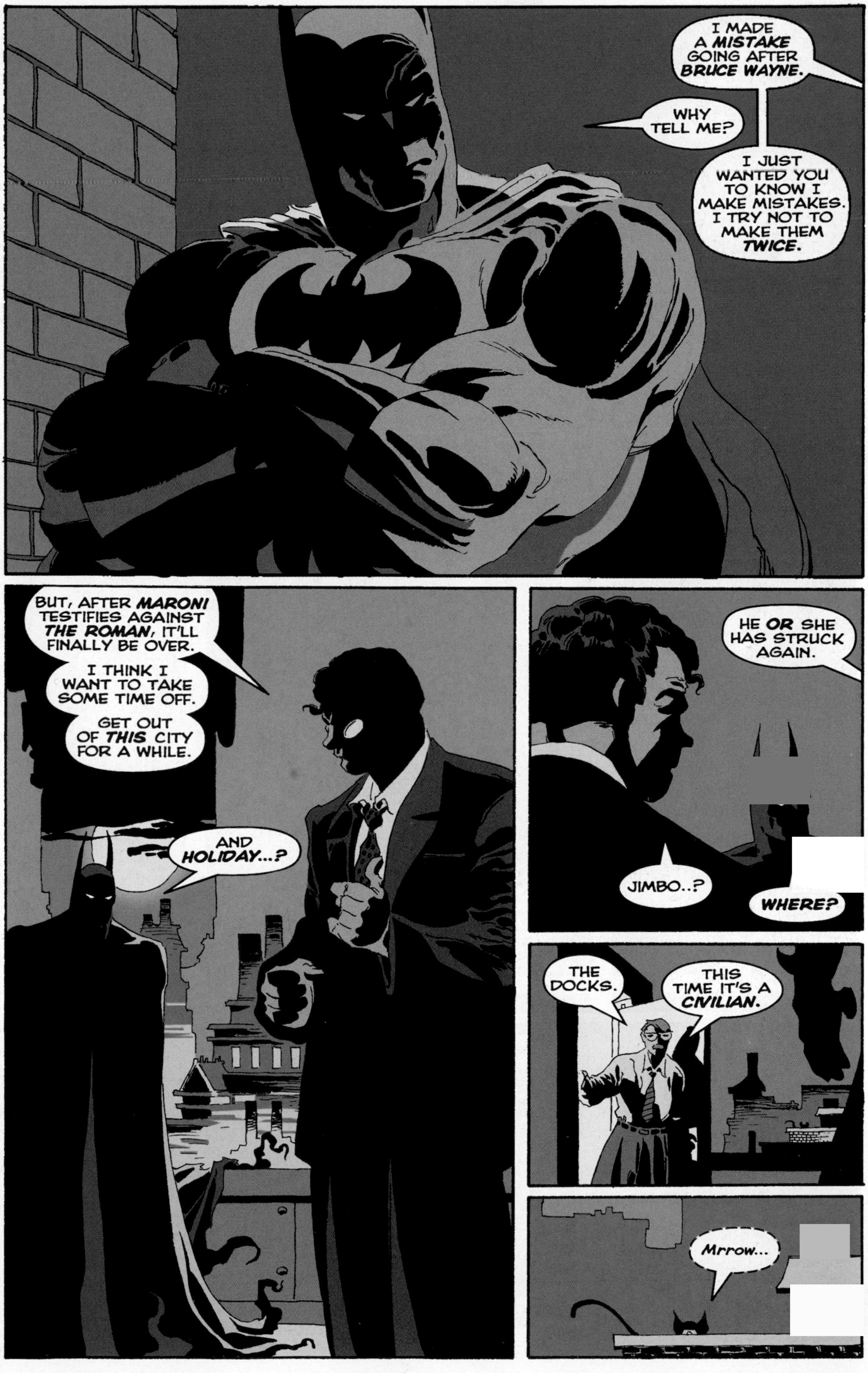

I MADE A MISTAKE GOING AFTER BRUCE WAYNE.
WHY TELL ME?
I JUST WANTED YOU TO KNOW I MAKE MISTAKES. I TRY NOT TO MAKE THEM TWICE.
BUT, AFTER MARONI TESTIFIES AGAINST THE ROMAN, IT'LL FINALLY BE OVER.
I THINK I WANT TO TAKE SOME TIME OFF.
GET OUT OF THIS CITY FOR A WHILE.
AND HOLIDAY...?
HE OR SHE HAS STRUCK AGAIN.
JIMBO..?
WHERE?
THE DOCKS.
THIS TIME IT'S A CIVILIAN.
Mrrow...

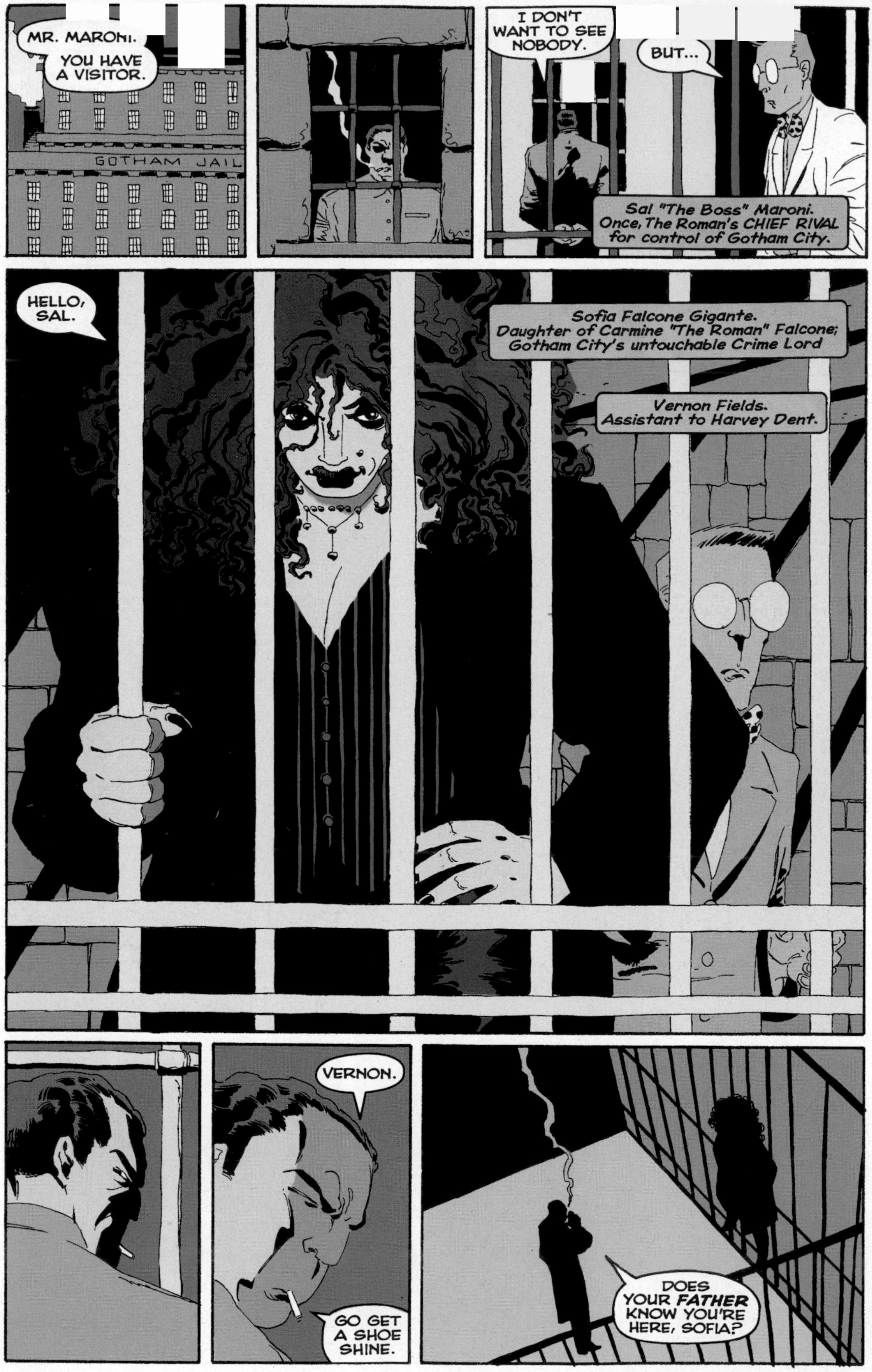
MR. MARONI.
YOU HAVE A VISITOR.
I DON'T WANT TO SEE NOBODY.
BUT...
Sal "The Boss" Maroni. Once, The Roman's CHIEF RIVAL for control of Gotham City.
HELLO, SAL.
Sofia Falcone Gigante. Daughter of Carmine "The Roman" Falcone; Gotham City's untouchable Crime Lord
Vernon Fields. Assistant to Harvey Dent.
VERNON.
GO GET A SHOE SHINE.
DOES YOUR FATHER KNOW YOU'RE HERE, SOFIA?

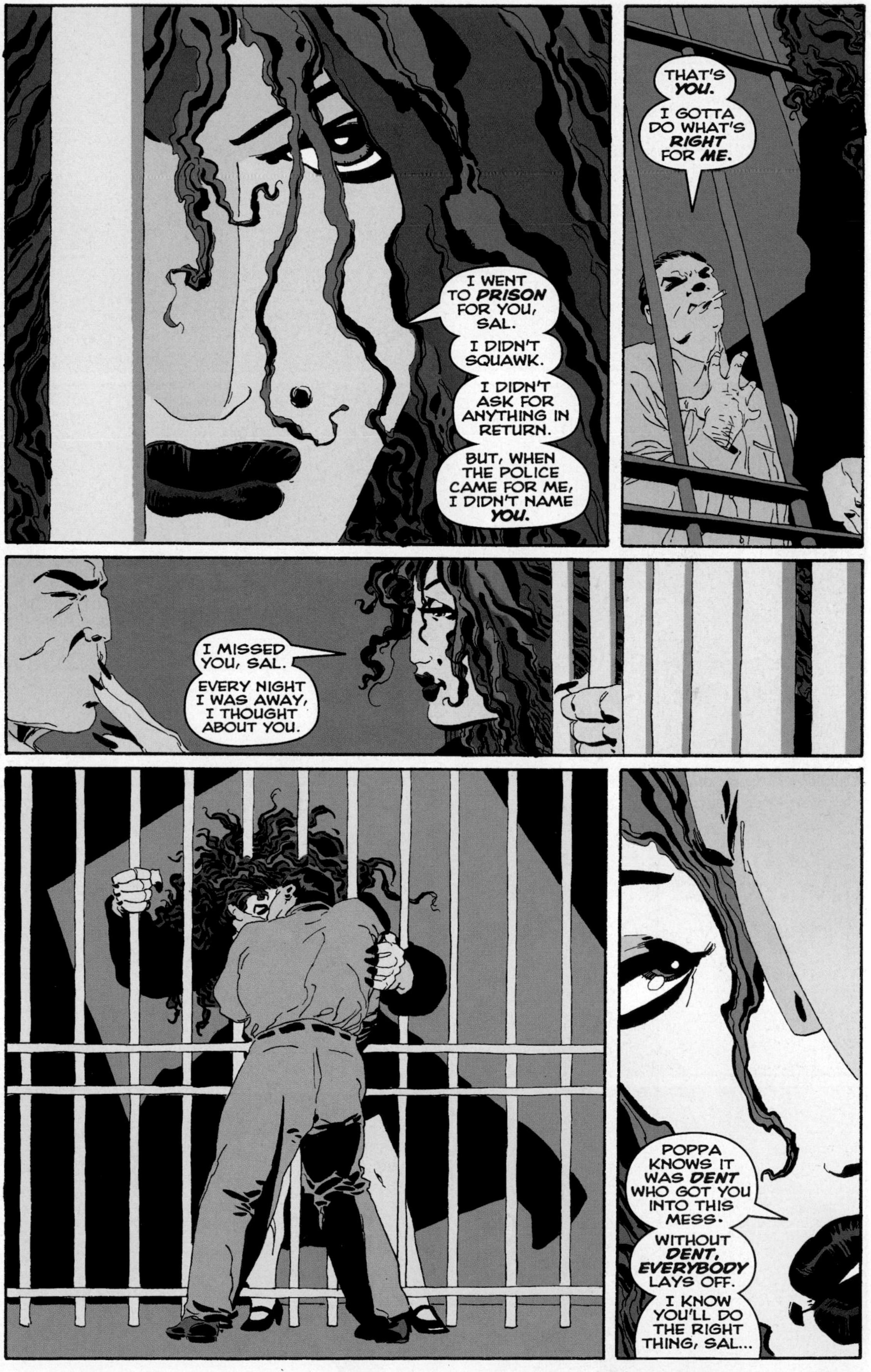
I WENT TO *PRISON* FOR YOU, SAL.
I DIDN'T SQUAWK.
I DIDN'T ASK FOR ANYTHING IN RETURN.
BUT, WHEN THE POLICE CAME FOR ME, I DIDN'T NAME *YOU.*
THAT'S *YOU.*
I GOTTA DO WHAT'S *RIGHT* FOR *ME.*
I MISSED YOU, SAL.
EVERY NIGHT I WAS AWAY, I THOUGHT ABOUT YOU.
POPPA KNOWS IT WAS *DENT* WHO GOT YOU INTO THIS MESS.
WITHOUT *DENT, EVERYBODY* LAYS OFF.
I KNOW YOU'LL DO THE RIGHT THING, SAL...

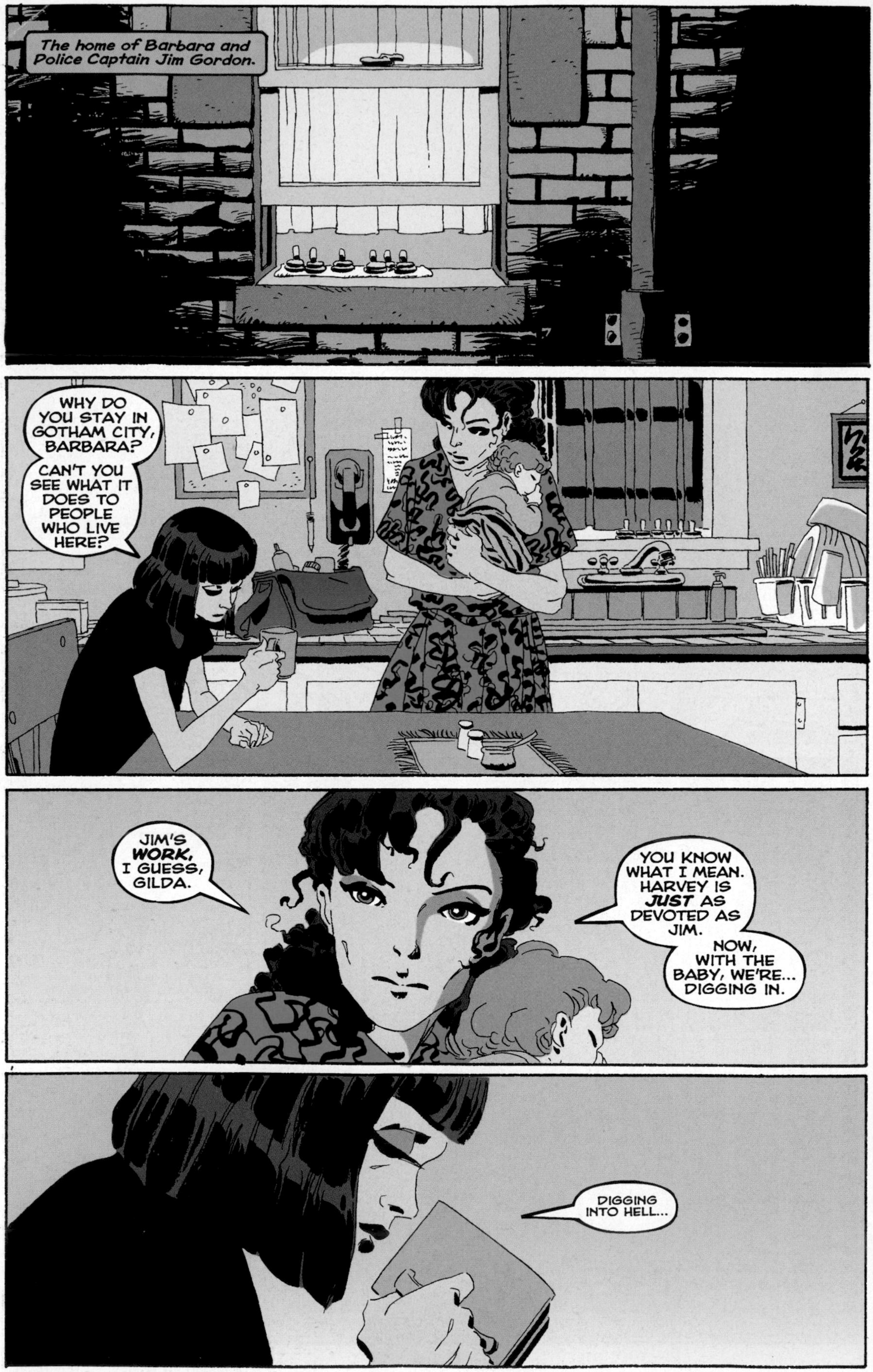

The home of Barbara and Police Captain Jim Gordon.
WHY DO YOU STAY IN GOTHAM CITY, BARBARA?
CAN'T YOU SEE WHAT IT DOES TO PEOPLE WHO LIVE HERE?
JIM'S **WORK,** I GUESS, GILDA.
YOU KNOW WHAT I MEAN. HARVEY IS ***JUST*** AS DEVOTED AS JIM.
NOW, WITH THE BABY, WE'RE... DIGGING IN.
DIGGING INTO HELL...

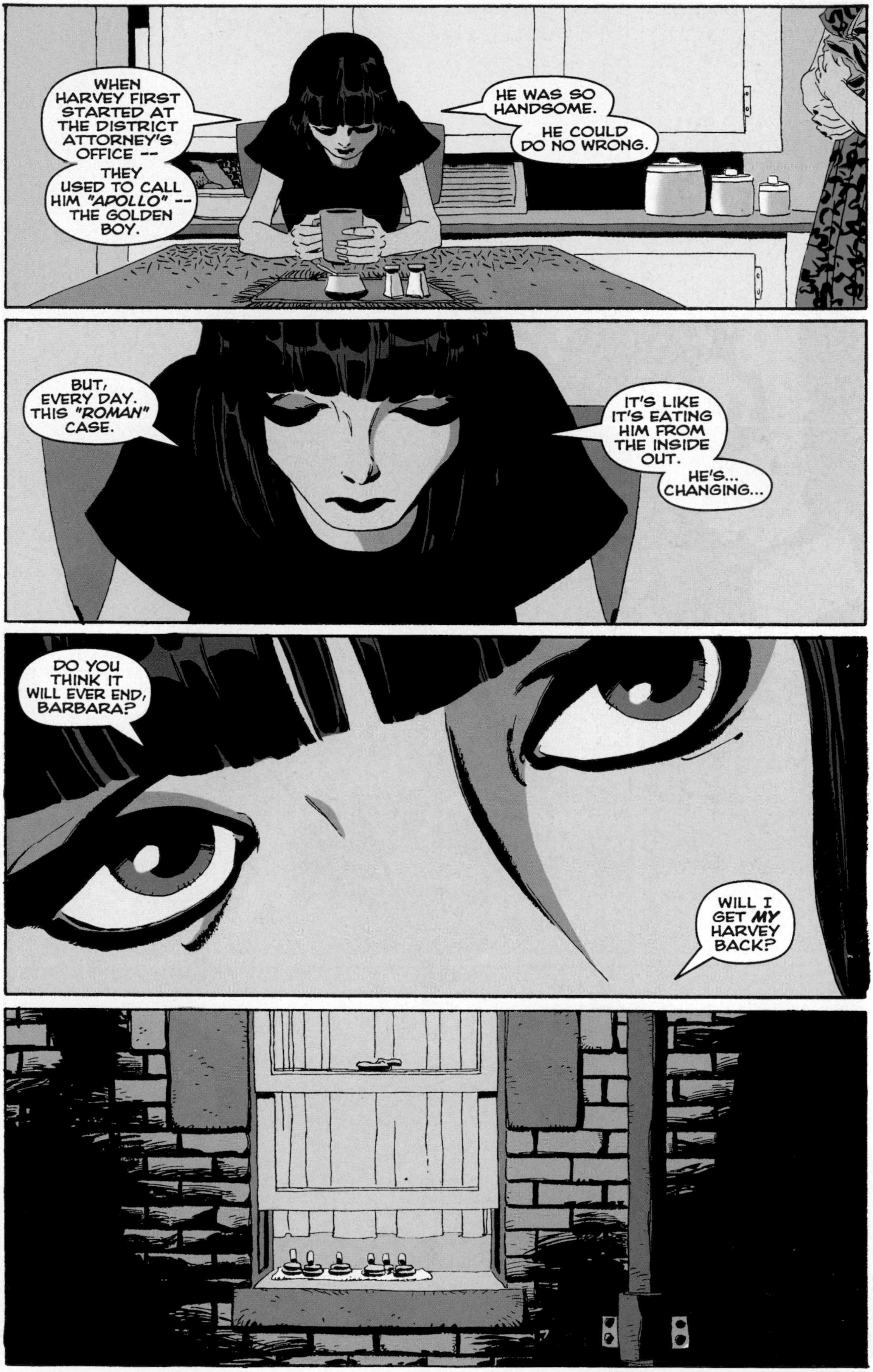
WHEN HARVEY FIRST STARTED AT THE DISTRICT ATTORNEY'S OFFICE --
THEY USED TO CALL HIM "APOLLO" -- THE GOLDEN BOY.
HE WAS SO HANDSOME.
HE COULD DO NO WRONG.
BUT, EVERY DAY. THIS "ROMAN" CASE.
IT'S LIKE IT'S EATING HIM FROM THE INSIDE OUT.
HE'S... CHANGING...
DO YOU THINK IT WILL EVER END, BARBARA?
WILL I GET MY HARVEY BACK?

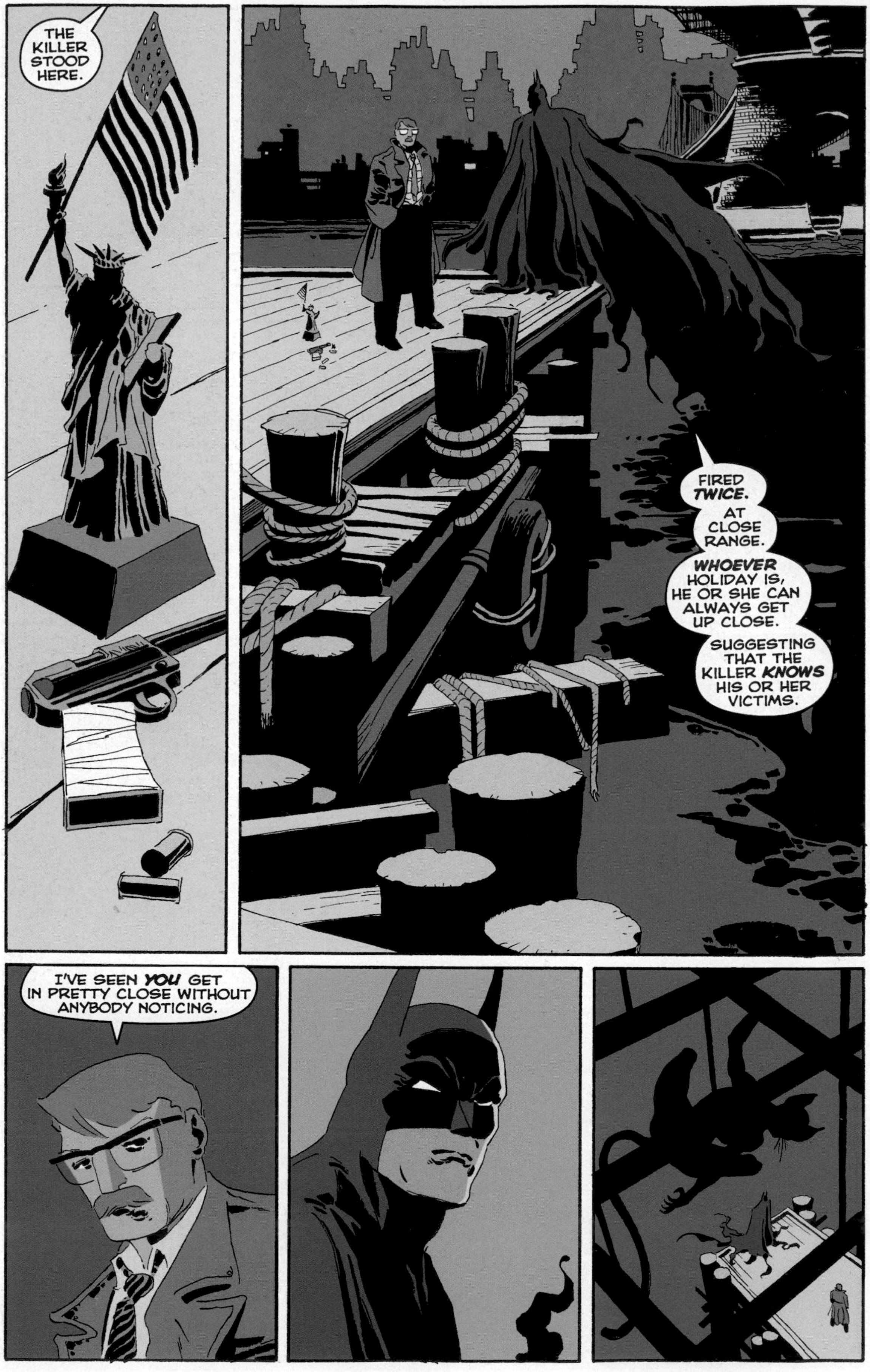
THE KILLER STOOD HERE.
FIRED TWICE. AT CLOSE RANGE.
WHOEVER HOLIDAY IS, HE OR SHE CAN ALWAYS GET UP CLOSE.
SUGGESTING THAT THE KILLER KNOWS HIS OR HER VICTIMS.
I'VE SEEN YOU GET IN PRETTY CLOSE WITHOUT ANYBODY NOTICING.

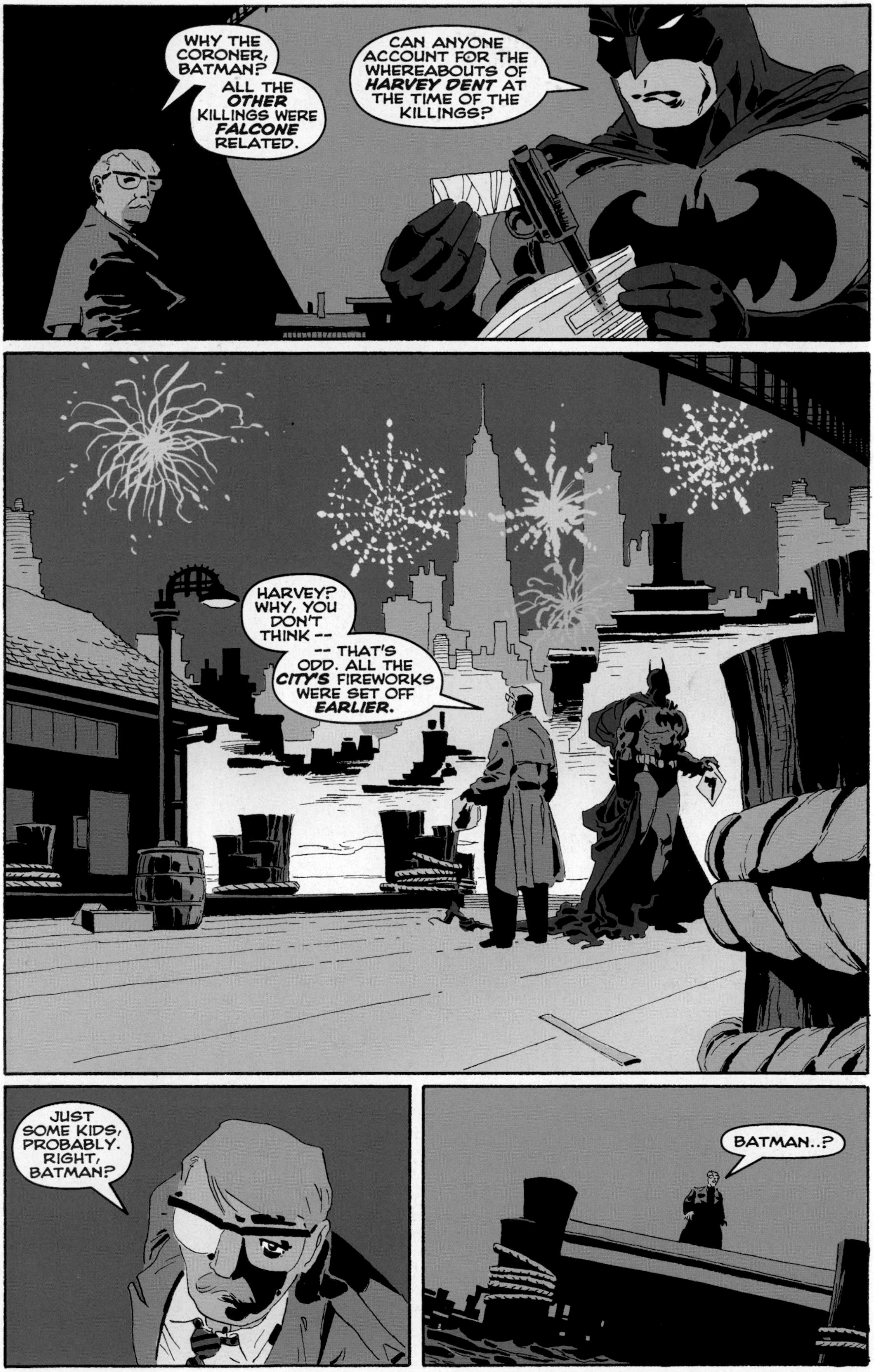
WHY THE CORONER, BATMAN?
ALL THE OTHER KILLINGS WERE FALCONE RELATED.
CAN ANYONE ACCOUNT FOR THE WHEREABOUTS OF HARVEY DENT AT THE TIME OF THE KILLINGS?
HARVEY? WHY, YOU DON'T THINK --
-- THAT'S ODD. ALL THE CITY'S FIREWORKS WERE SET OFF EARLIER.
JUST SOME KIDS, PROBABLY. RIGHT, BATMAN?
BATMAN..?

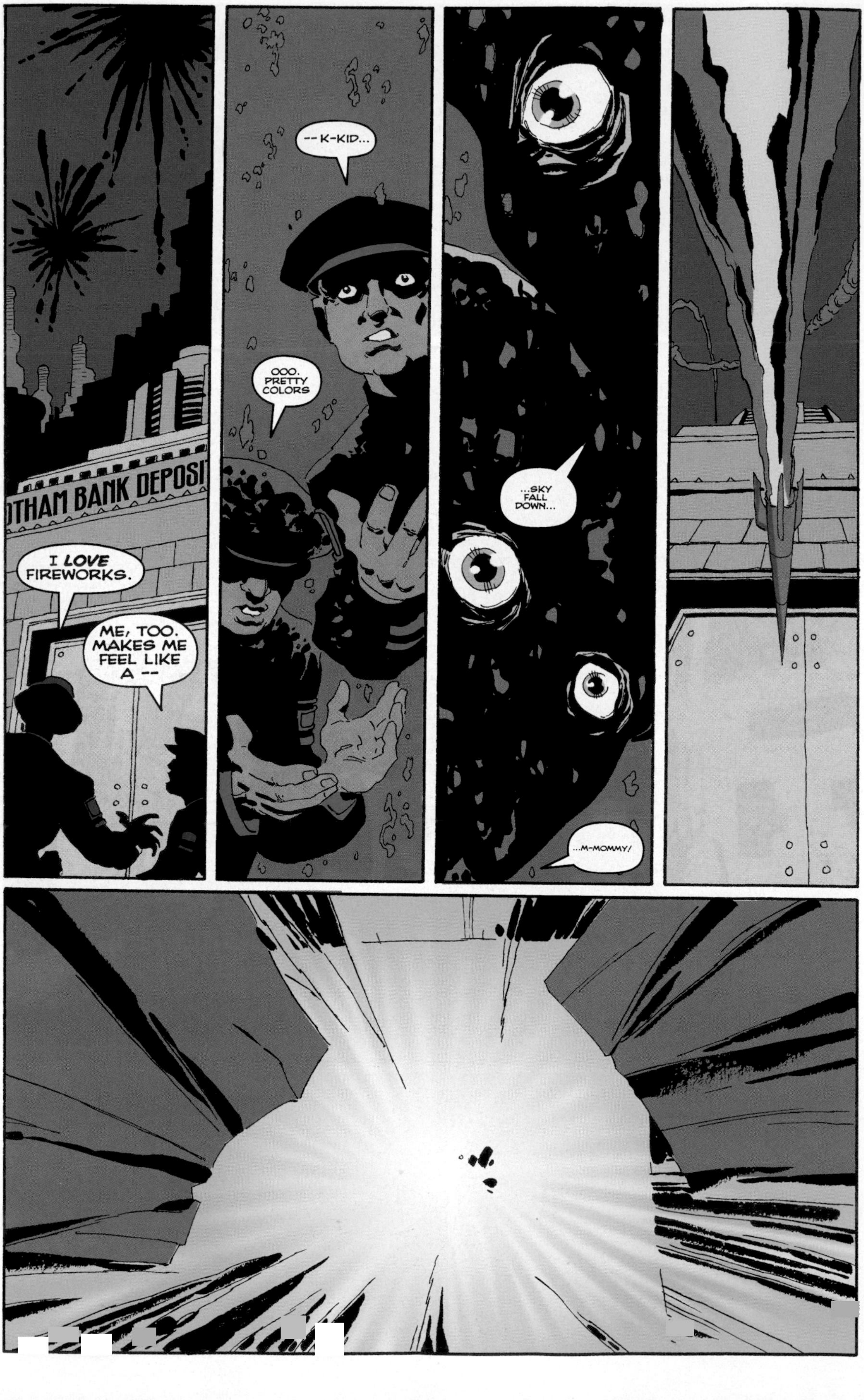
OTHAM BANK DEPOSI
I *LOVE* FIREWORKS.
ME, TOO. MAKES ME FEEL LIKE A --
--K-KID...
OOO. PRETTY COLORS
...SKY FALL DOWN...
...M-MOMMY!

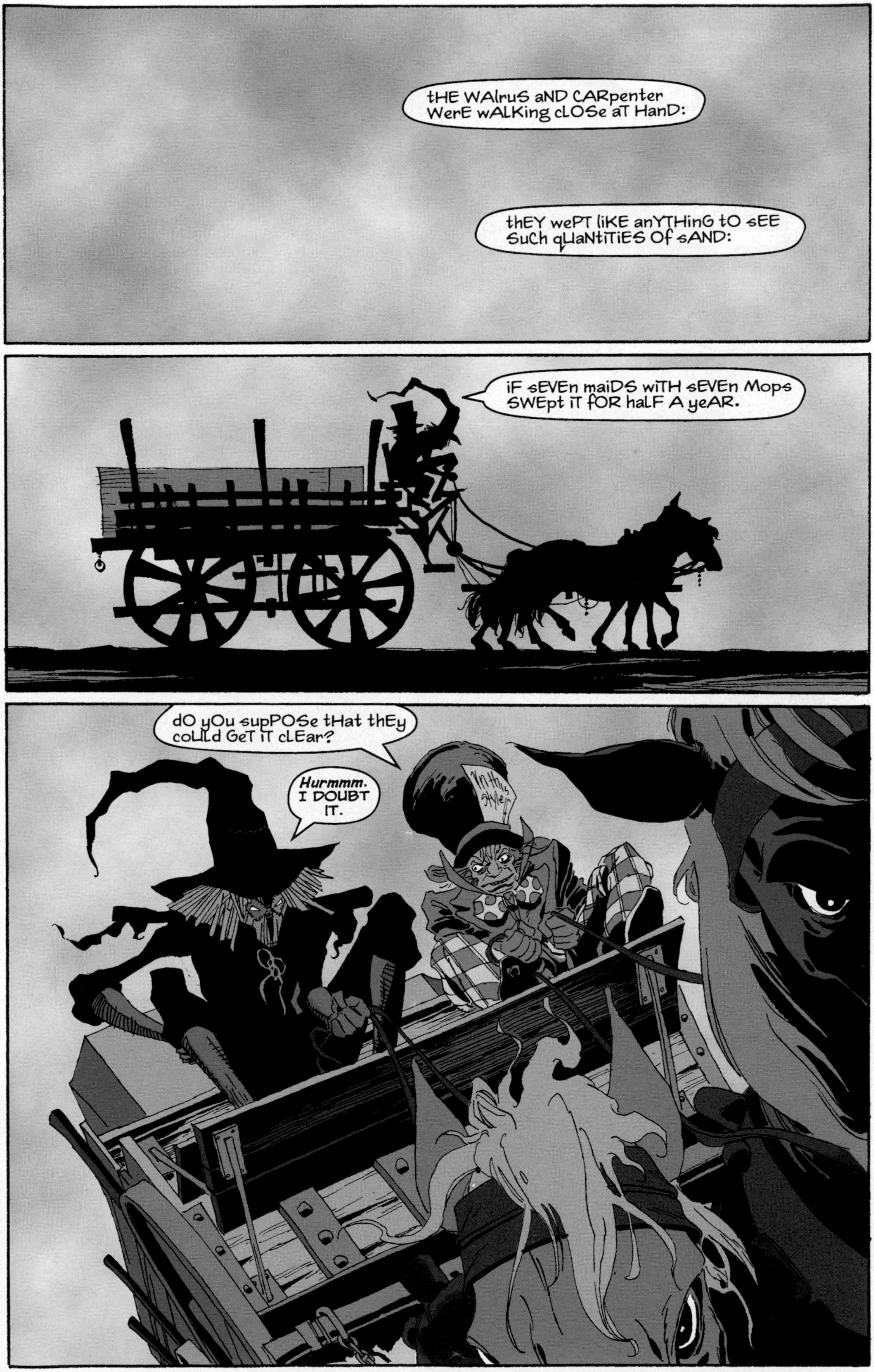
tHE WAlruS aND CARpenter WerE wALKing cLOSe aT HanD:
thEY wePT liKE anYTHinG tO sEE SuCh quANtiTiES Of sAND:
iF sEVEn maiDS wiTH sEVEn Mops SWEpt iT fOR halF A yeAR.
dO yOu supPOSe tHat thEy coULd GeT iT cLEar?
Hurmmm. I DOUBT IT.

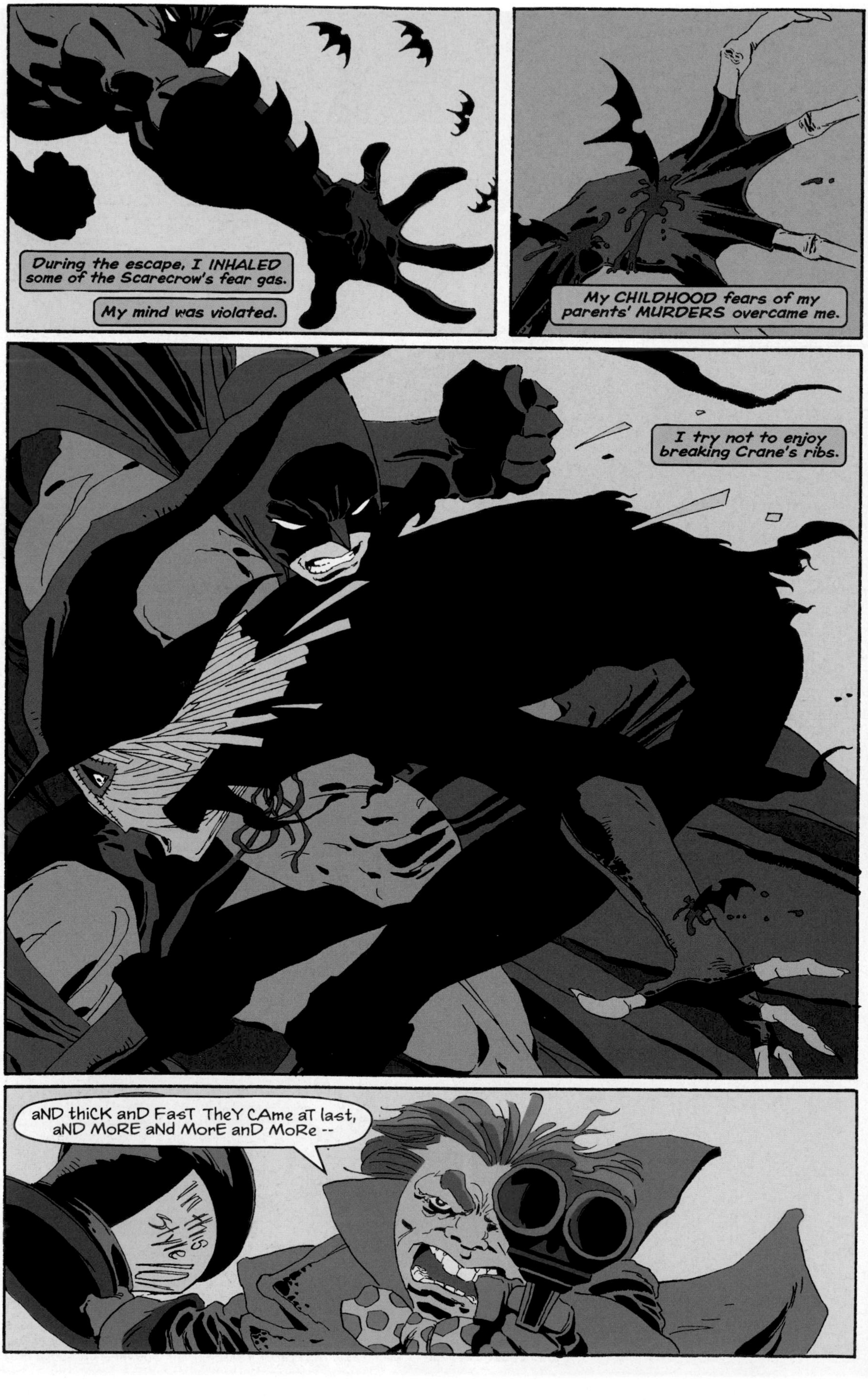
During the escape, I INHALED some of the Scarecrow's fear gas.
My mind was violated.
My CHILDHOOD fears of my parents' MURDERS overcame me.
I try not to enjoy breaking Crane's ribs.
aND thiCK anD FasT TheY CAme aT last, aND MoRE aNd MorE anD MoRe --
In this style

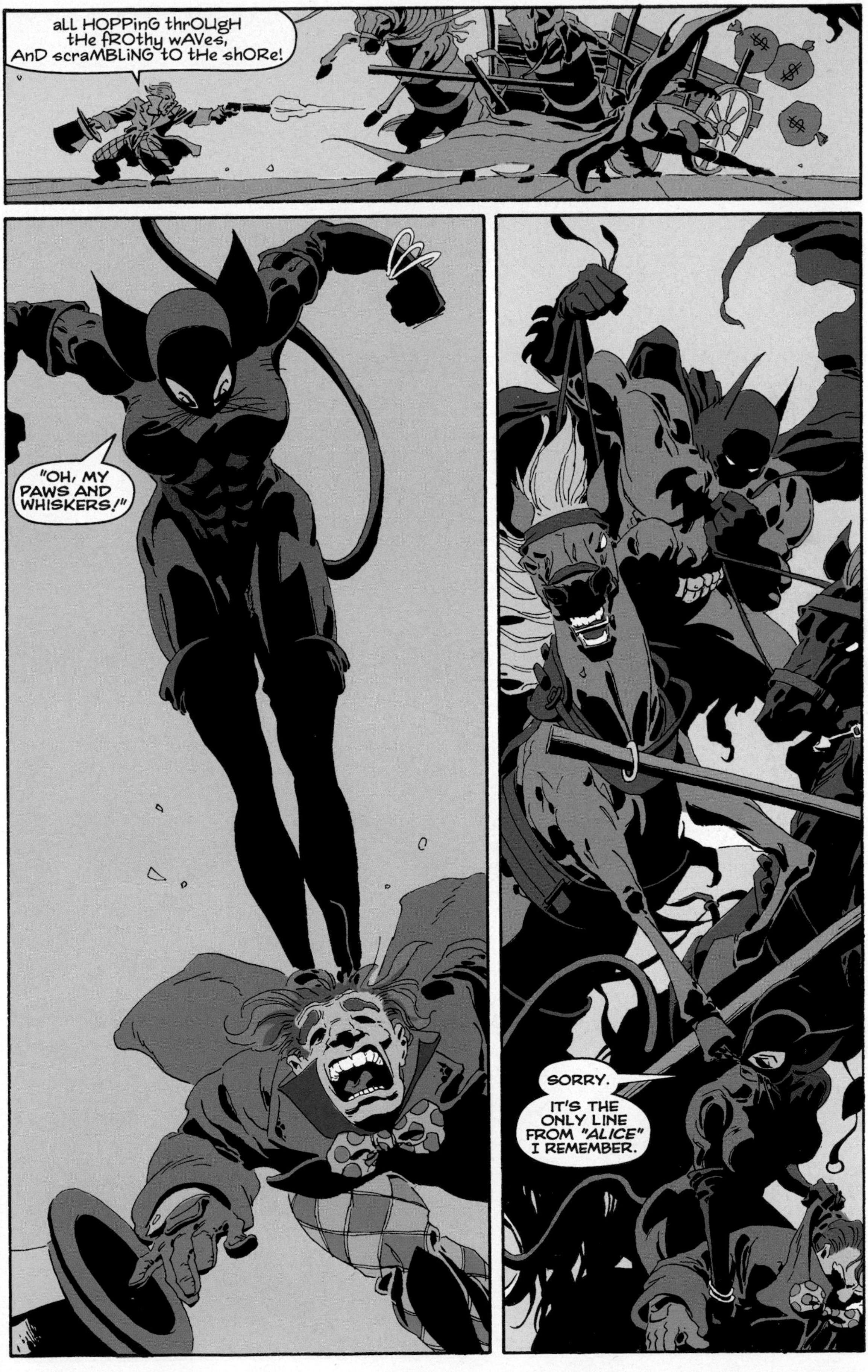
aLL HOPPinG thrOUgH tHe fROthy wAVes, AnD scraMBLinG TO tHe shORe!
"OH, MY PAWS AND WHISKERS!"
SORRY.
IT'S THE ONLY LINE FROM "ALICE" I REMEMBER.

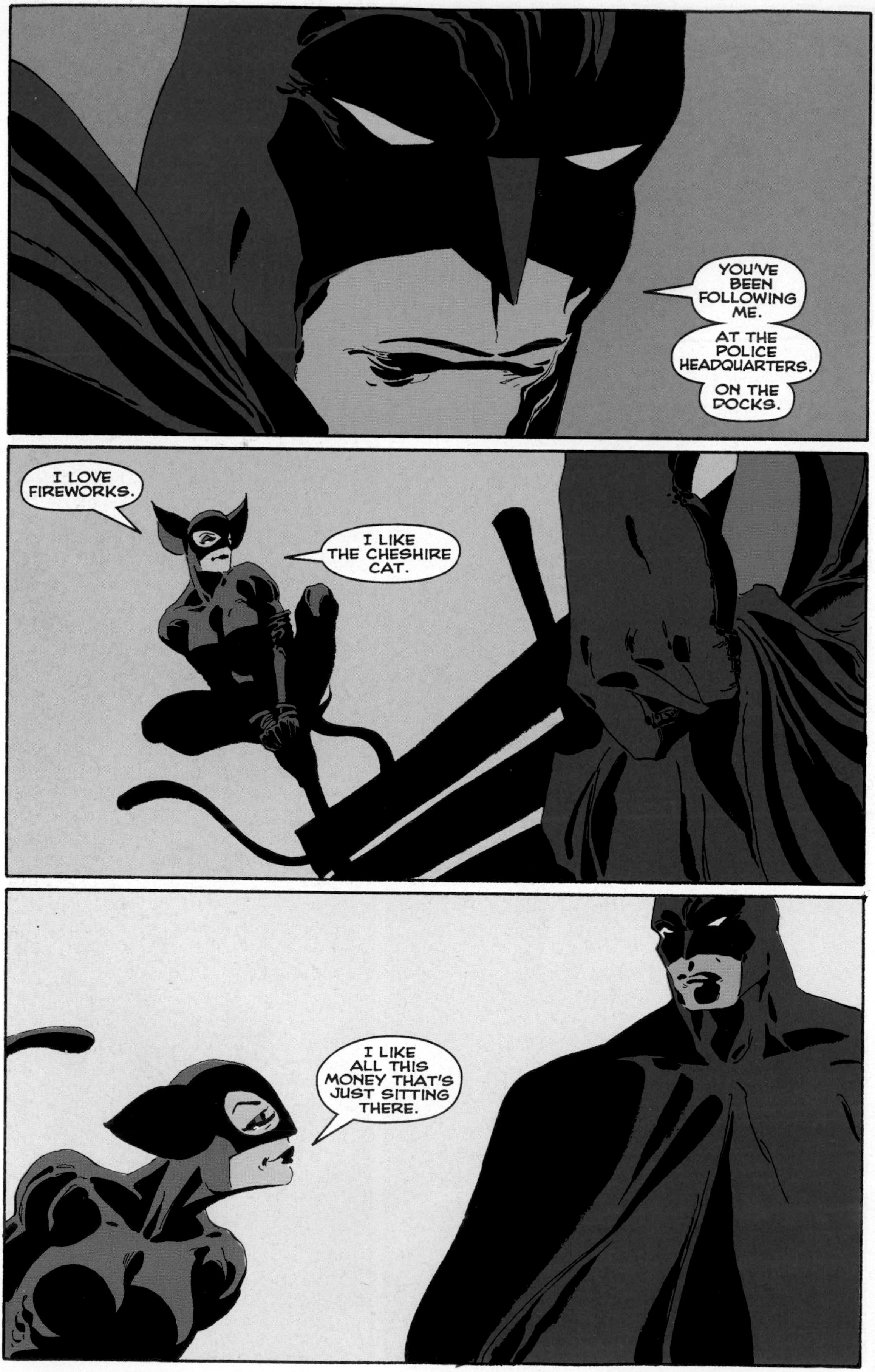
YOU'VE BEEN FOLLOWING ME.
AT THE POLICE HEADQUARTERS.
ON THE DOCKS.
I LOVE FIREWORKS.
I LIKE THE CHESHIRE CAT.
I LIKE ALL THIS MONEY THAT'S JUST SITTING THERE.

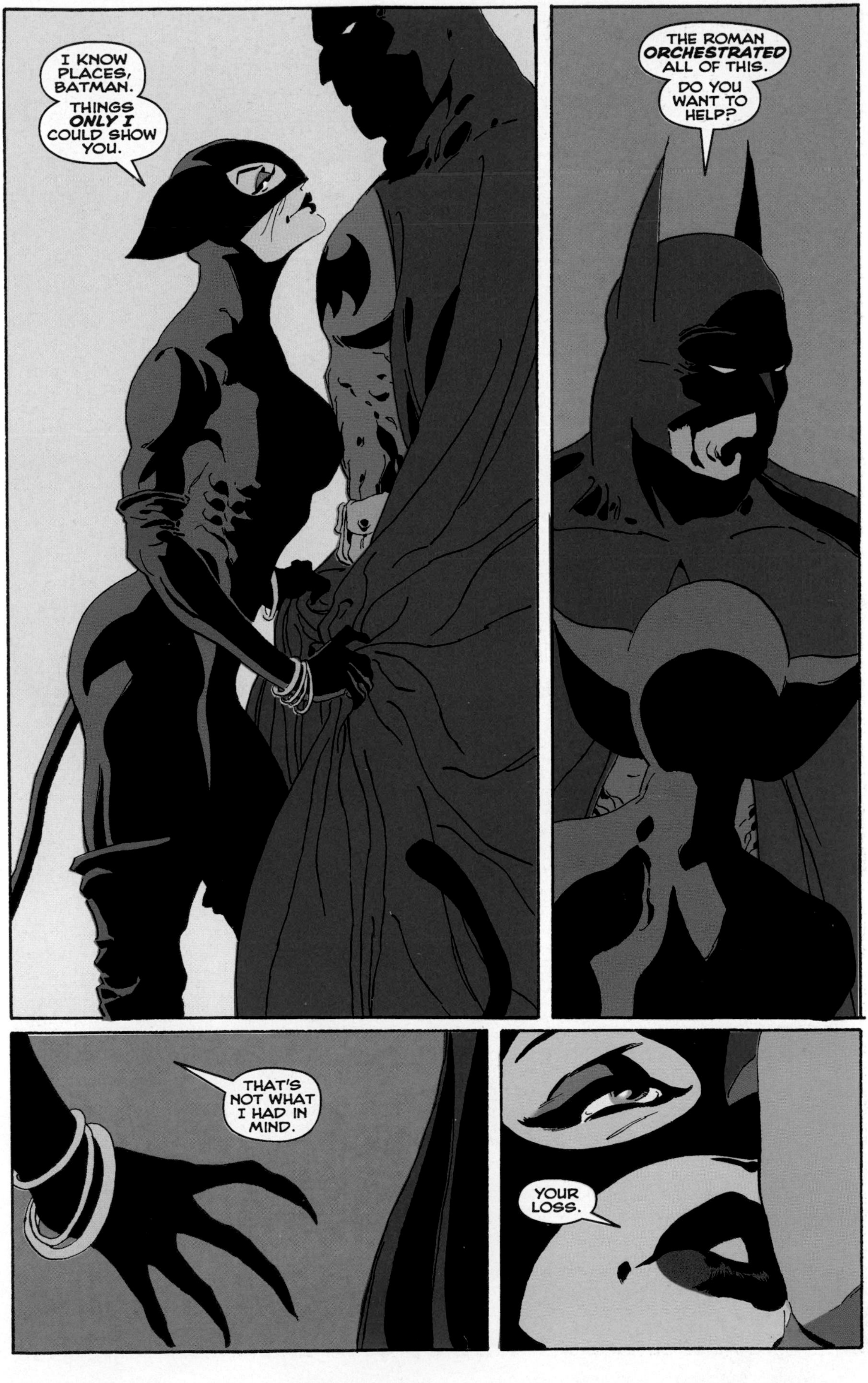

I KNOW PLACES, BATMAN.
THINGS ONLY I COULD SHOW YOU.
THE ROMAN ORCHESTRATED ALL OF THIS.
DO YOU WANT TO HELP?
THAT'S NOT WHAT I HAD IN MIND.
YOUR LOSS.

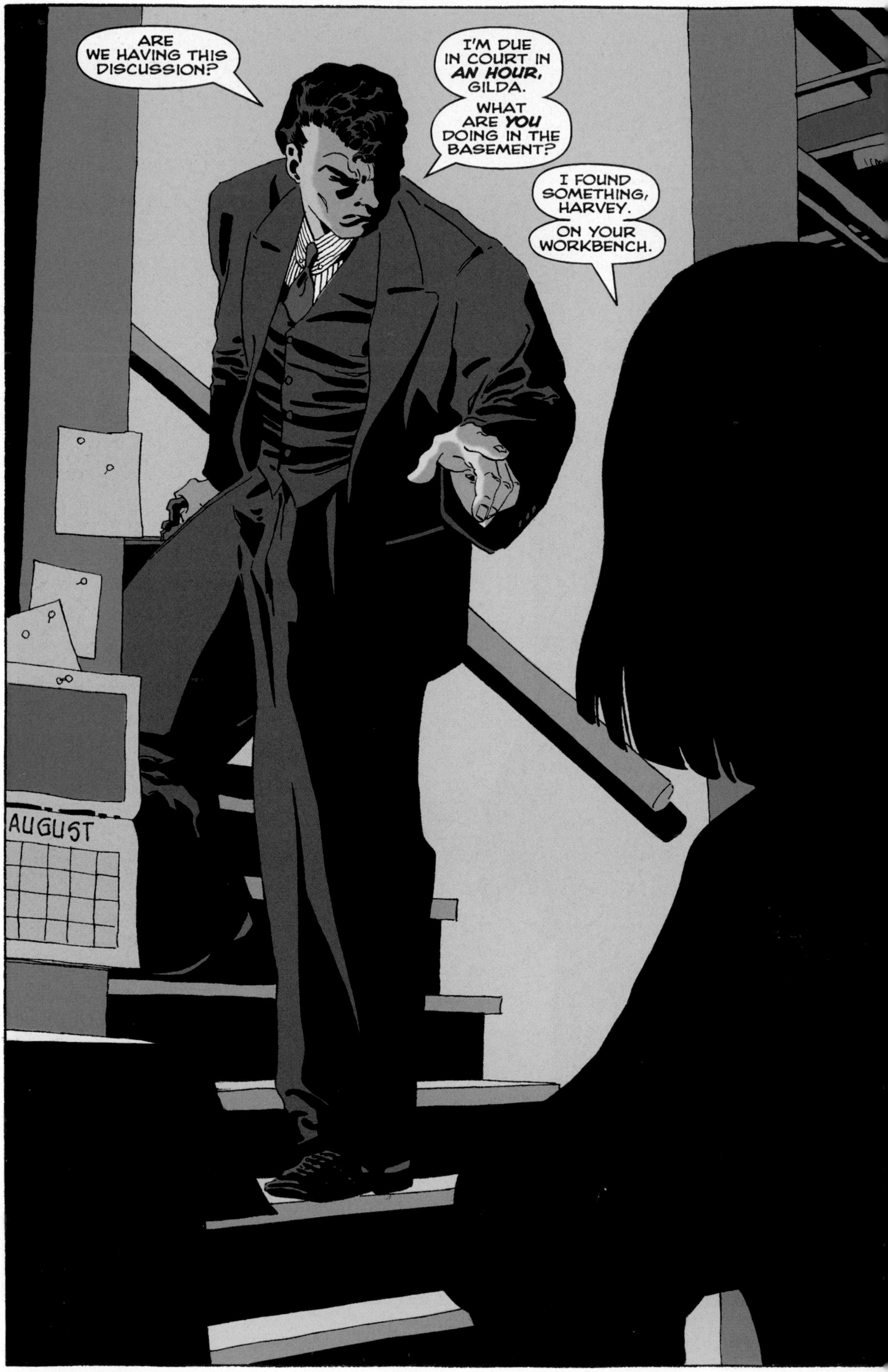
ARE WE HAVING THIS DISCUSSION?
I'M DUE IN COURT IN AN HOUR, GILDA.
WHAT ARE YOU DOING IN THE BASEMENT?
I FOUND SOMETHING, HARVEY.
ON YOUR WORKBENCH.
AUGUST

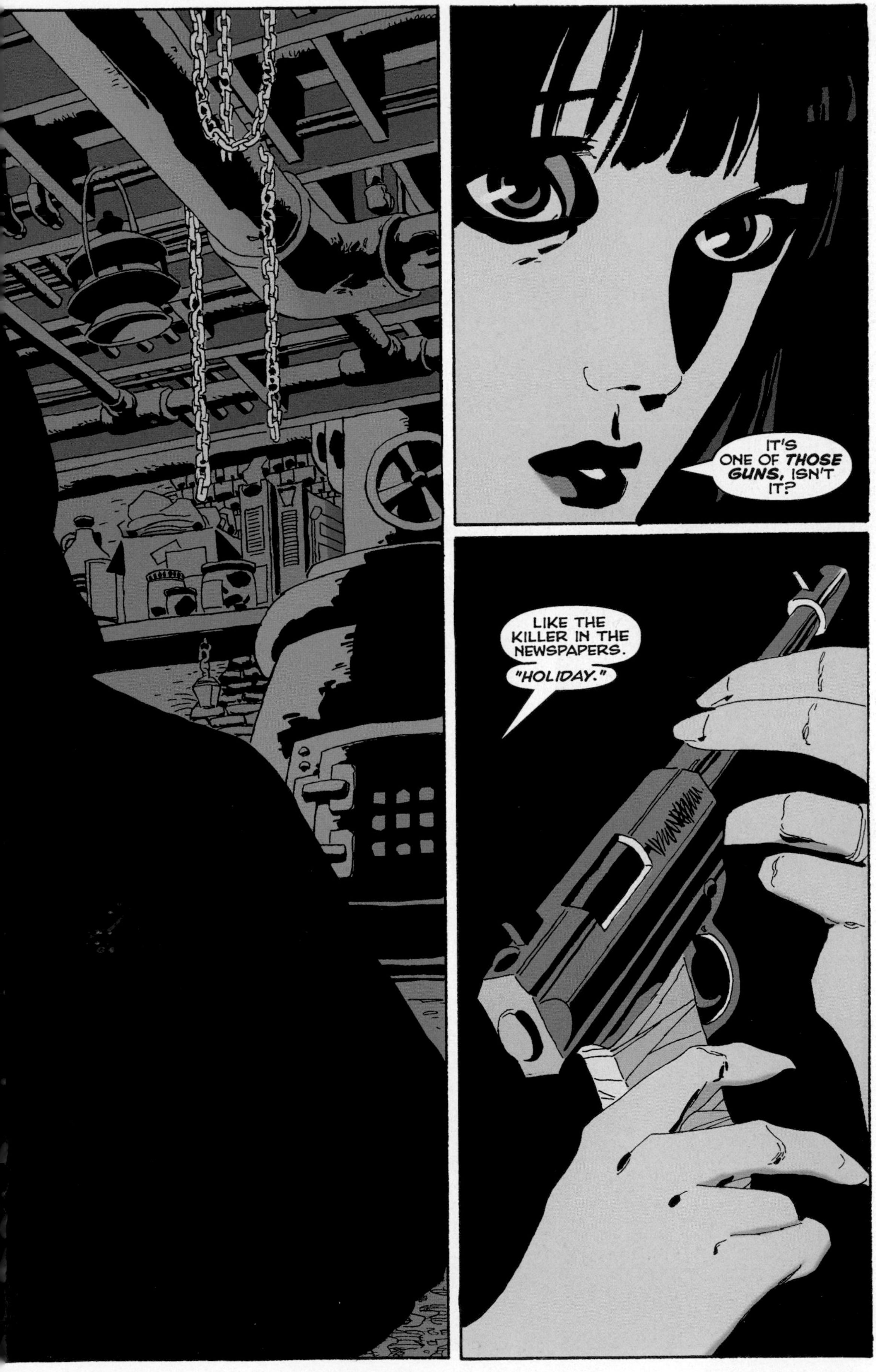
IT'S ONE OF *THOSE GUNS,* ISN'T IT?
LIKE THE KILLER IN THE NEWSPAPERS.
"HOLIDAY."

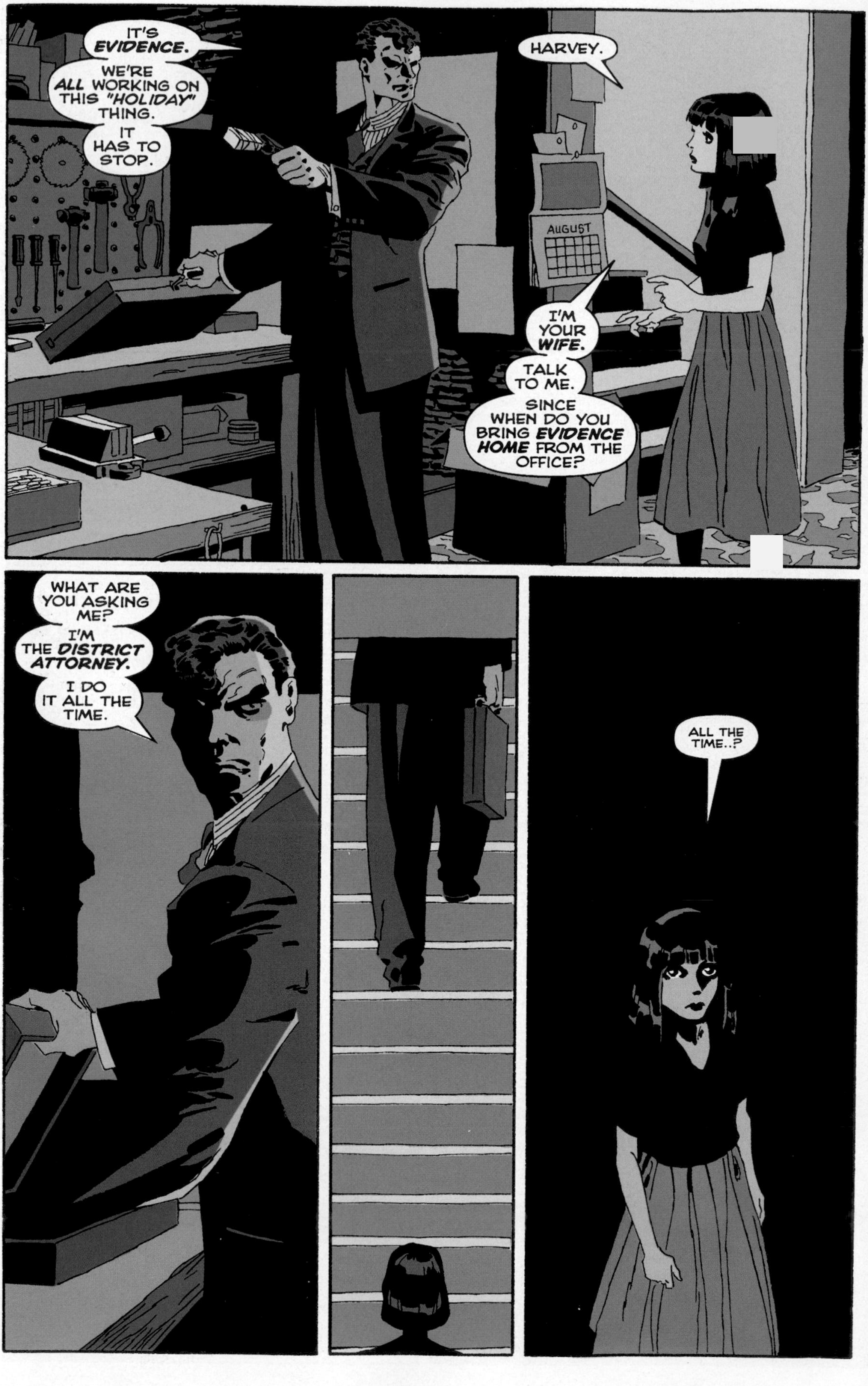
IT'S EVIDENCE.
WE'RE ALL WORKING ON THIS "HOLIDAY" THING.
IT HAS TO STOP.
HARVEY.
AUGUST
I'M YOUR WIFE.
TALK TO ME.
SINCE WHEN DO YOU BRING EVIDENCE HOME FROM THE OFFICE?
WHAT ARE YOU ASKING ME?
I'M THE DISTRICT ATTORNEY.
I DO IT ALL THE TIME.
ALL THE TIME..?

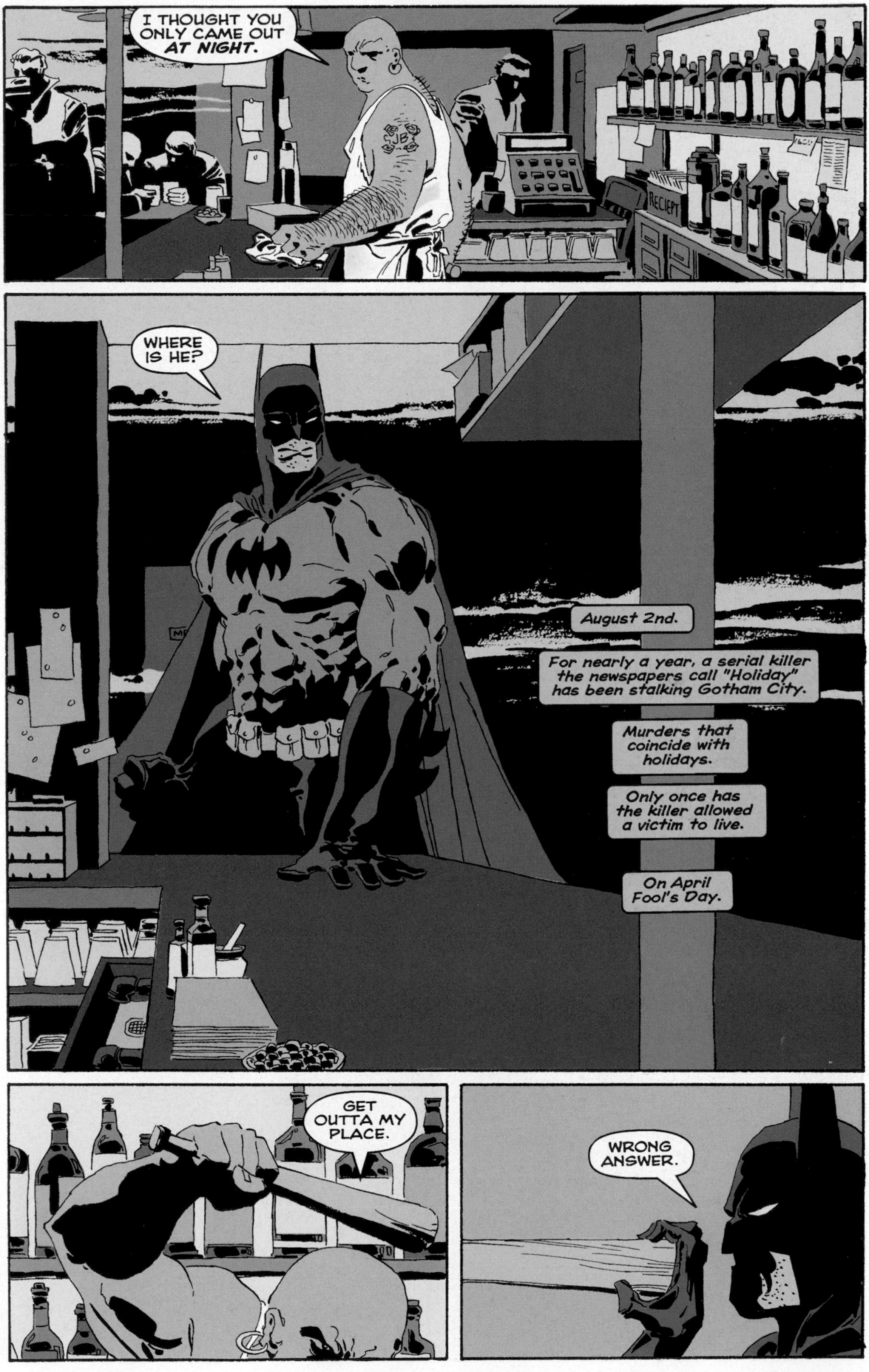
I THOUGHT YOU ONLY CAME OUT AT NIGHT.
WHERE IS HE?
August 2nd.
For nearly a year, a serial killer the newspapers call "Holiday" has been stalking Gotham City.
Murders that coincide with holidays.
Only once has the killer allowed a victim to live.
On April Fool's Day.
GET OUTTA MY PLACE.
WRONG ANSWER.

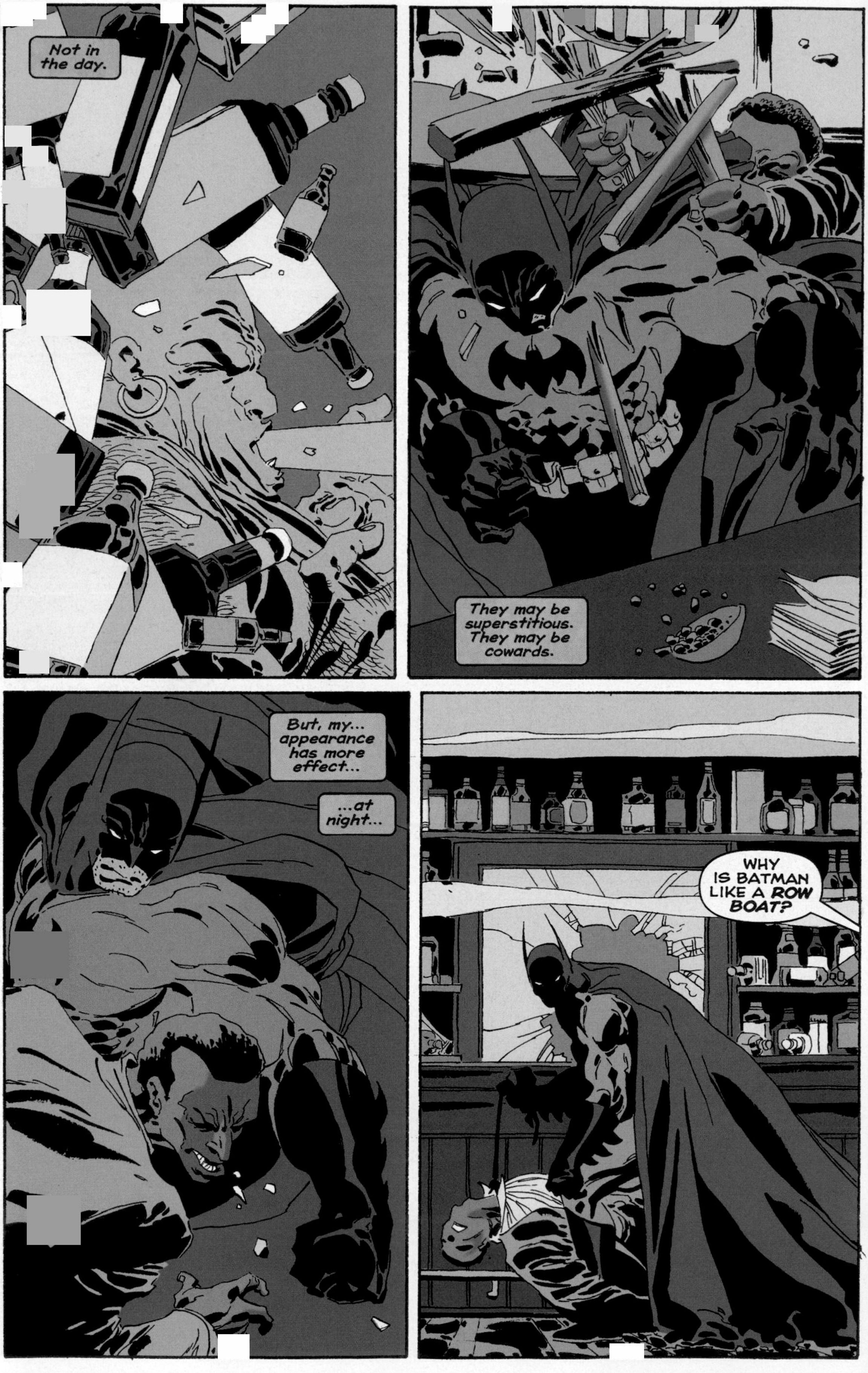

Not in the day.
They may be superstitious. They may be cowards.
But, my... appearance has more effect...
...at night...
WHY IS BATMAN LIKE A ROW BOAT?

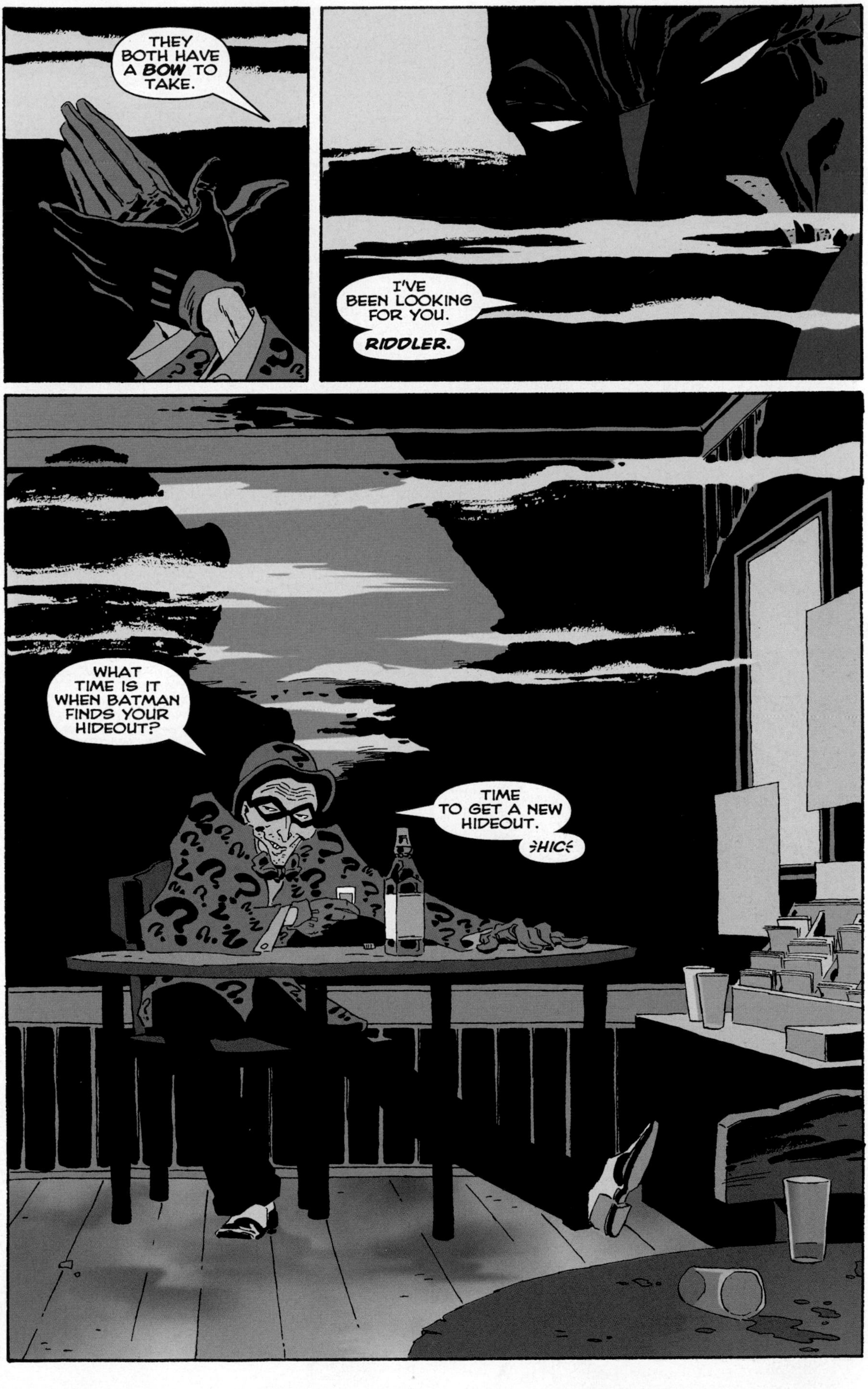
THEY BOTH HAVE A BOW TO TAKE.
I'VE BEEN LOOKING FOR YOU.
RIDDLER.
WHAT TIME IS IT WHEN BATMAN FINDS YOUR HIDEOUT?
TIME TO GET A NEW HIDEOUT.
HIC

ON APRIL FOOL'S DAY.

YOU SAW HIM, DIDN'T YOU?

YOU SAW "HOLIDAY."

He's scared. Not of me. But of something he knows.

YES. AND NO.

‡HIC‡

YOU WERE *OUTSIDE* THE ROMAN'S BUILDING. WHAT DID THE ROMAN WANT WITH YOU?

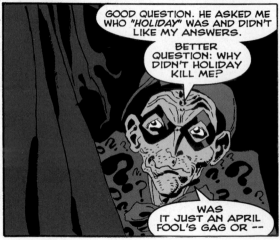

GOOD QUESTION. HE ASKED ME WHO "HOLIDAY" WAS AND DIDN'T LIKE MY ANSWERS.

BETTER QUESTION: WHY DIDN'T HOLIDAY KILL ME?

WAS IT JUST AN APRIL FOOL'S GAG OR --

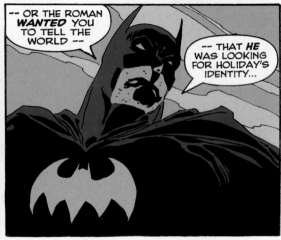

-- OR THE ROMAN *WANTED* YOU TO TELL THE WORLD --

-- THAT *HE* WAS LOOKING FOR HOLIDAY'S IDENTITY...

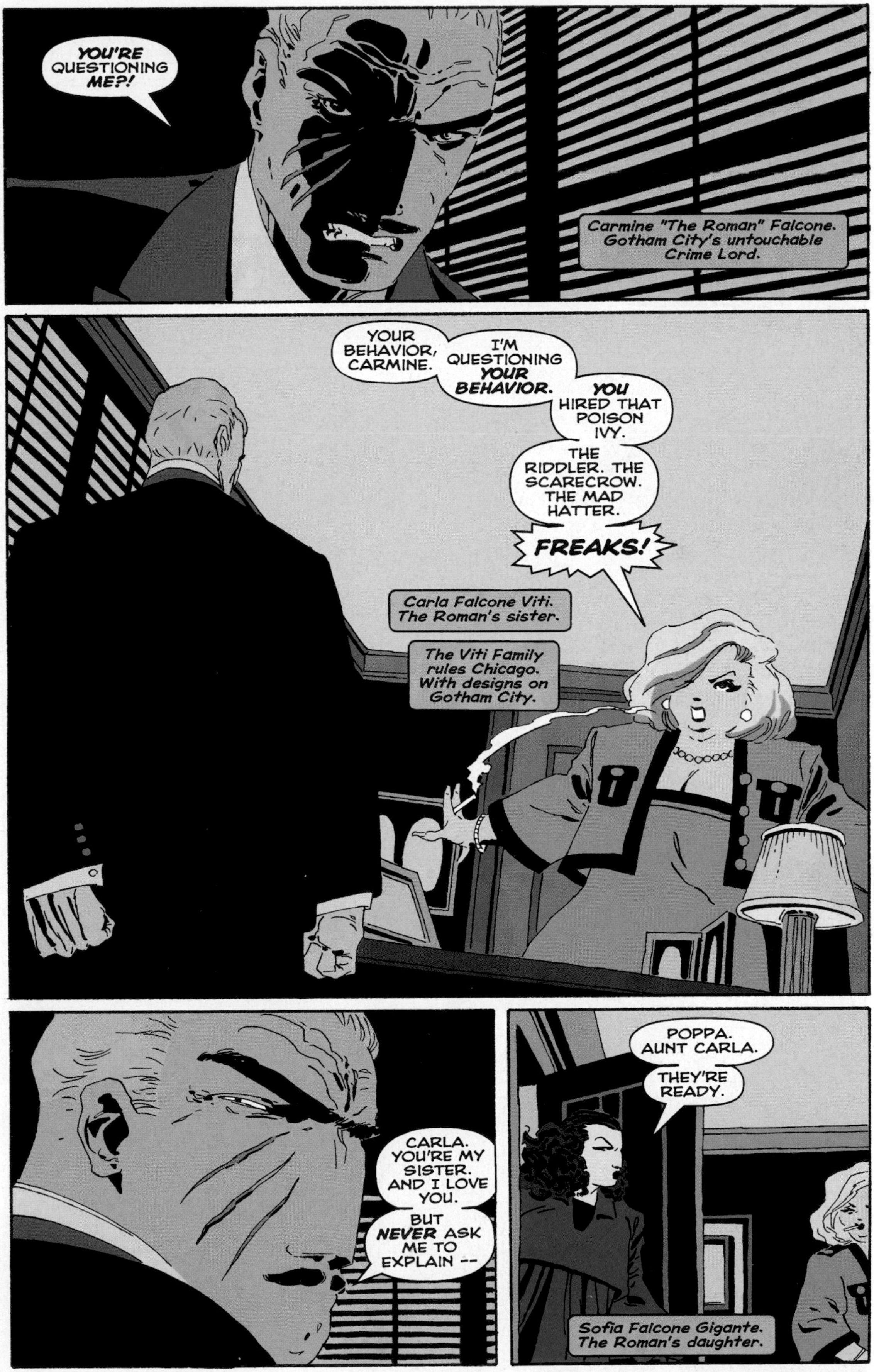
YOU'RE QUESTIONING ME?!
Carmine "The Roman" Falcone. Gotham City's untouchable Crime Lord.
YOUR BEHAVIOR, CARMINE.
I'M QUESTIONING YOUR BEHAVIOR.
YOU HIRED THAT POISON IVY.
THE RIDDLER. THE SCARECROW. THE MAD HATTER.
FREAKS!
Carla Falcone Viti. The Roman's sister.
The Viti Family rules Chicago. With designs on Gotham City.
CARLA. YOU'RE MY SISTER. AND I LOVE YOU.
BUT NEVER ASK ME TO EXPLAIN --
POPPA. AUNT CARLA.
THEY'RE READY.
Sofia Falcone Gigante. The Roman's daughter.

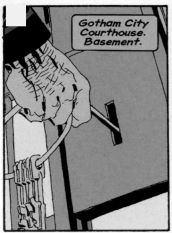

Gotham City Courthouse. Basement.

Sal "The Boss" Maroni. Once, The Roman's chief rival for control of Gotham City.

Now, the District Attorney's chief WITNESS against The Roman.

Captain Jim Gordon. An honest cop.

In Gotham City, he is unique.

WHAT'S THE MATTER, JIMMY?

DON'TCHA TRUST ME?

NO.

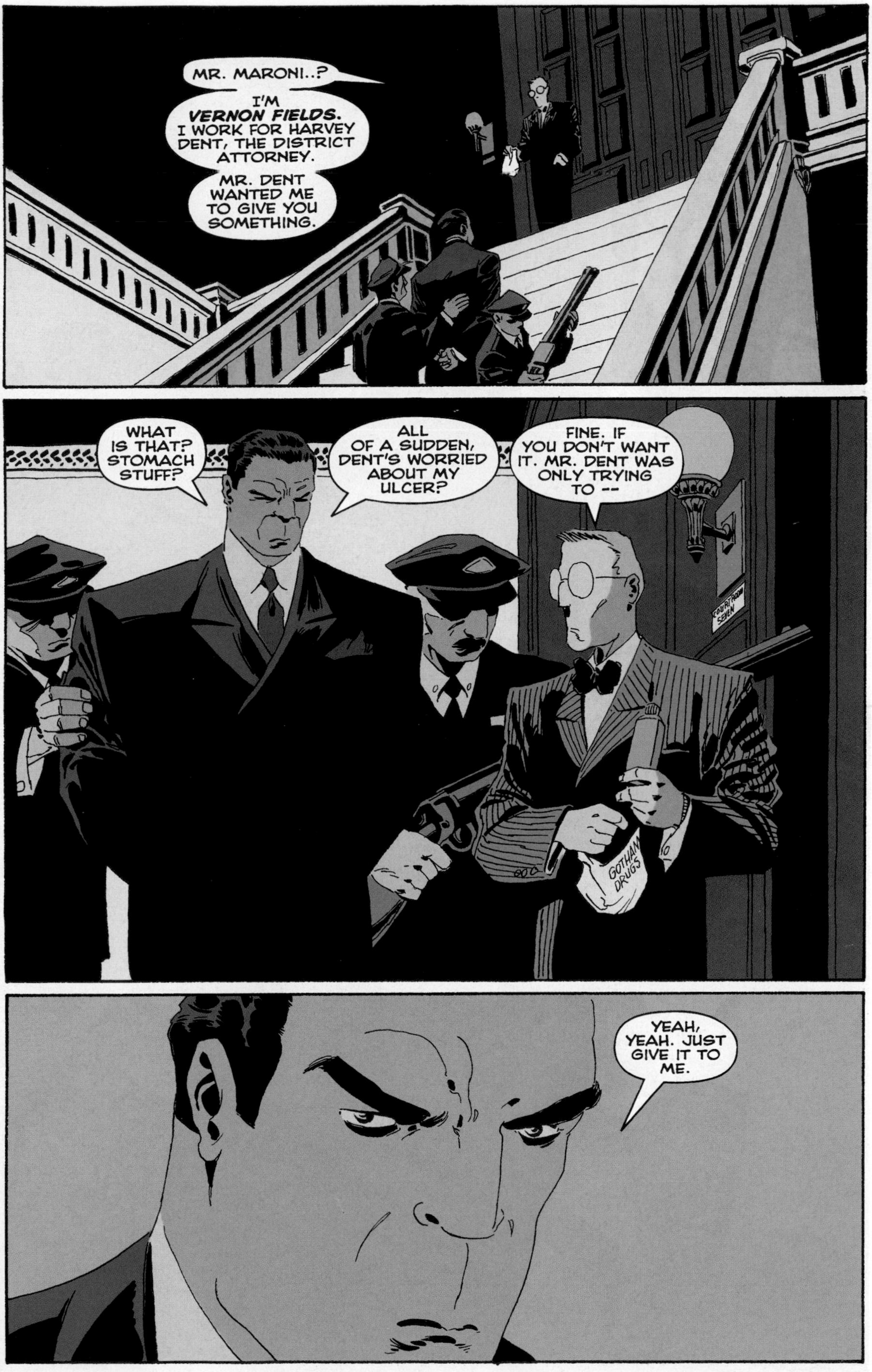
MR. MARONI..?
I'M VERNON FIELDS. I WORK FOR HARVEY DENT, THE DISTRICT ATTORNEY.
MR. DENT WANTED ME TO GIVE YOU SOMETHING.
WHAT IS THAT? STOMACH STUFF?
ALL OF A SUDDEN, DENT'S WORRIED ABOUT MY ULCER?
FINE. IF YOU DON'T WANT IT. MR. DENT WAS ONLY TRYING TO --
COURTROOM SEVEN
GOTHAM DRUGS
YEAH, YEAH. JUST GIVE IT TO ME.

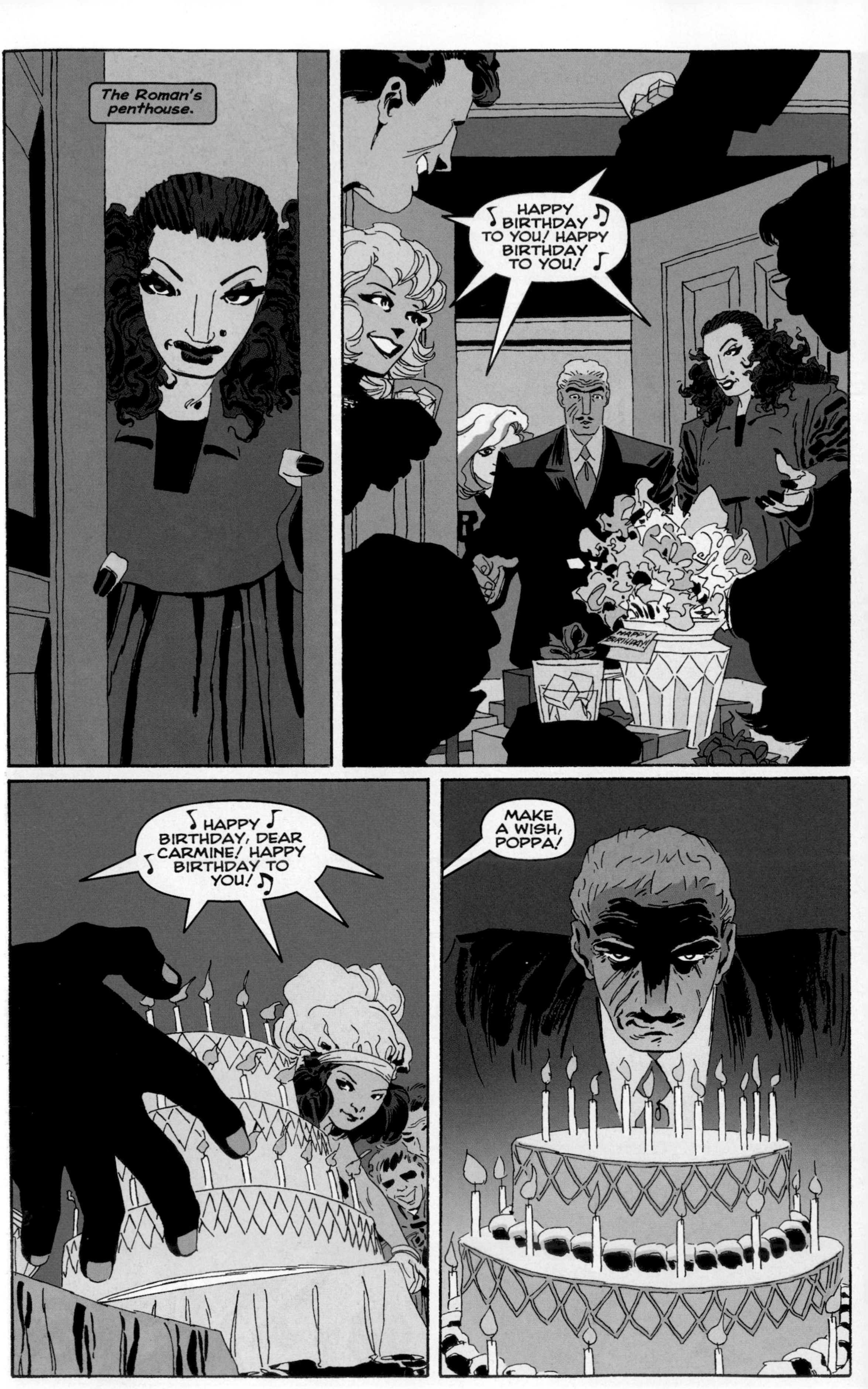

The Roman's penthouse.
HAPPY BIRTHDAY TO YOU! HAPPY BIRTHDAY TO YOU!
HAPPY BIRTHDAY!
HAPPY BIRTHDAY, DEAR CARMINE! HAPPY BIRTHDAY TO YOU!
MAKE A WISH, POPPA!

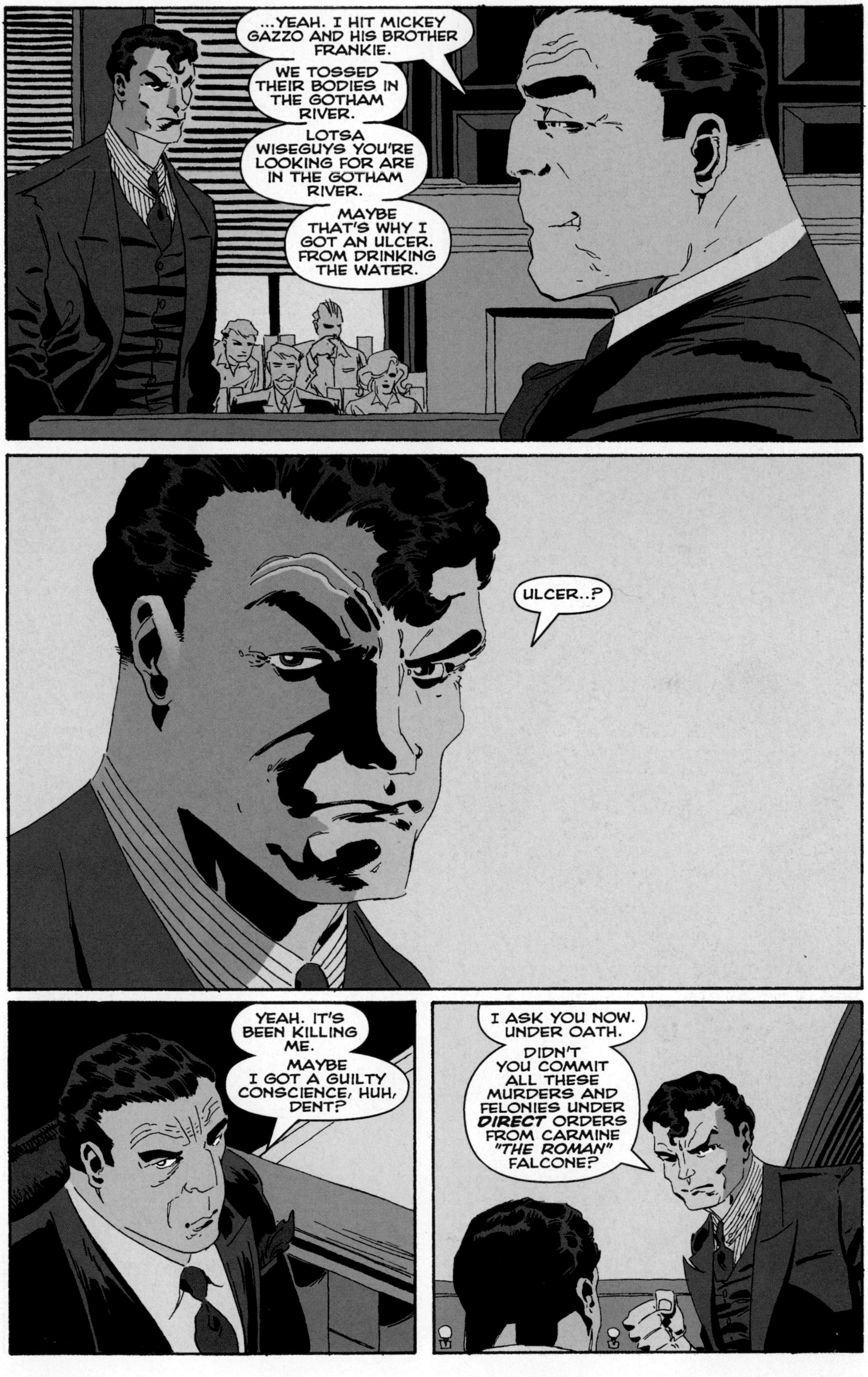
...YEAH. I HIT MICKEY GAZZO AND HIS BROTHER FRANKIE.
WE TOSSED THEIR BODIES IN THE GOTHAM RIVER.
LOTSA WISEGUYS YOU'RE LOOKING FOR ARE IN THE GOTHAM RIVER.
MAYBE THAT'S WHY I GOT AN ULCER. FROM DRINKING THE WATER.
ULCER..?
YEAH. IT'S BEEN KILLING ME.
MAYBE I GOT A GUILTY CONSCIENCE, HUH, DENT?
I ASK YOU NOW. UNDER OATH.
DIDN'T YOU COMMIT ALL THESE MURDERS AND FELONIES UNDER ***DIRECT*** ORDERS FROM CARMINE ***"THE ROMAN"*** FALCONE?

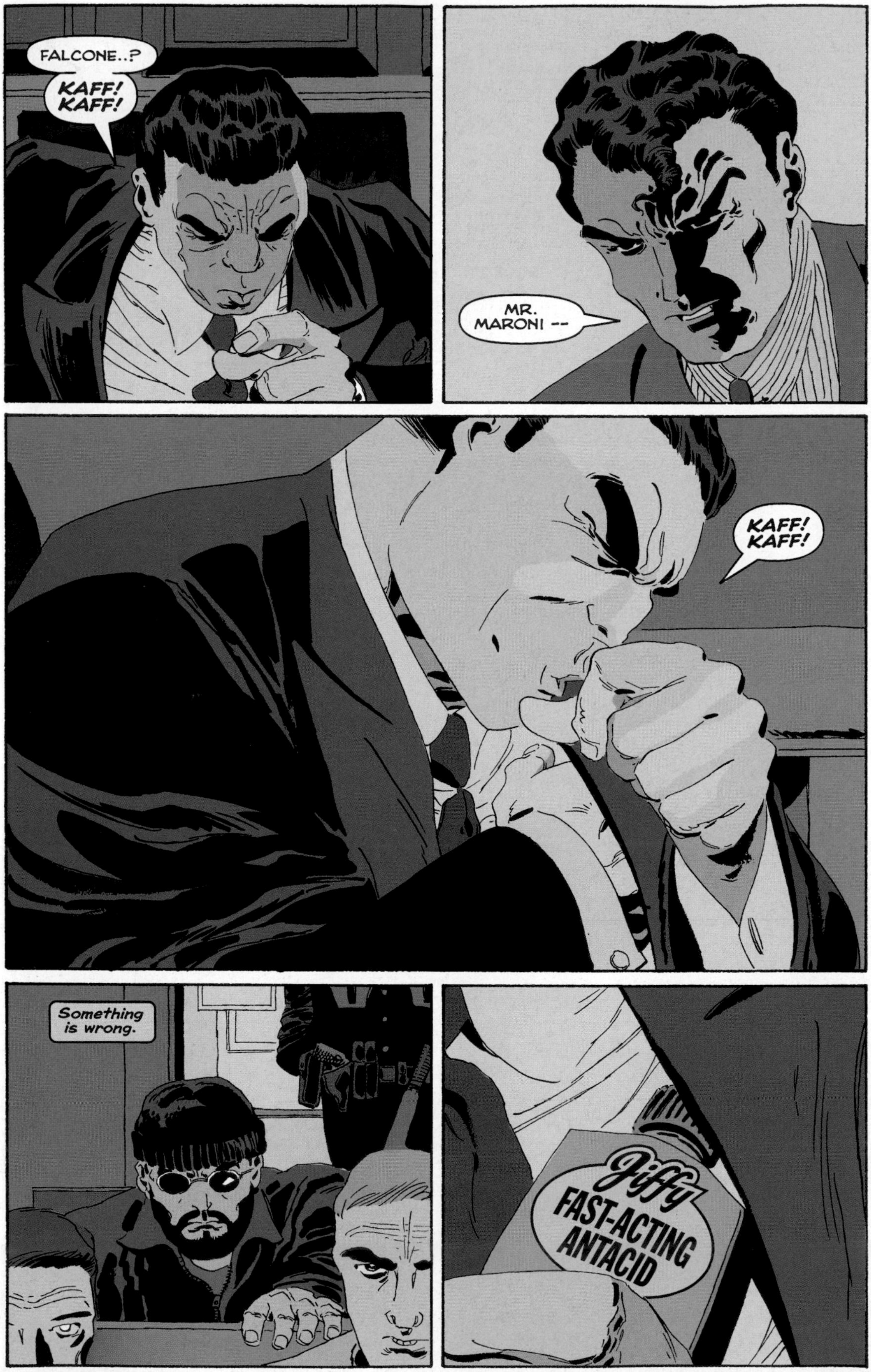
FALCONE..?
KAFF! KAFF!
MR. MARONI --
KAFF! KAFF!
Something is wrong.
Jiffy
FAST-ACTING ANTACID

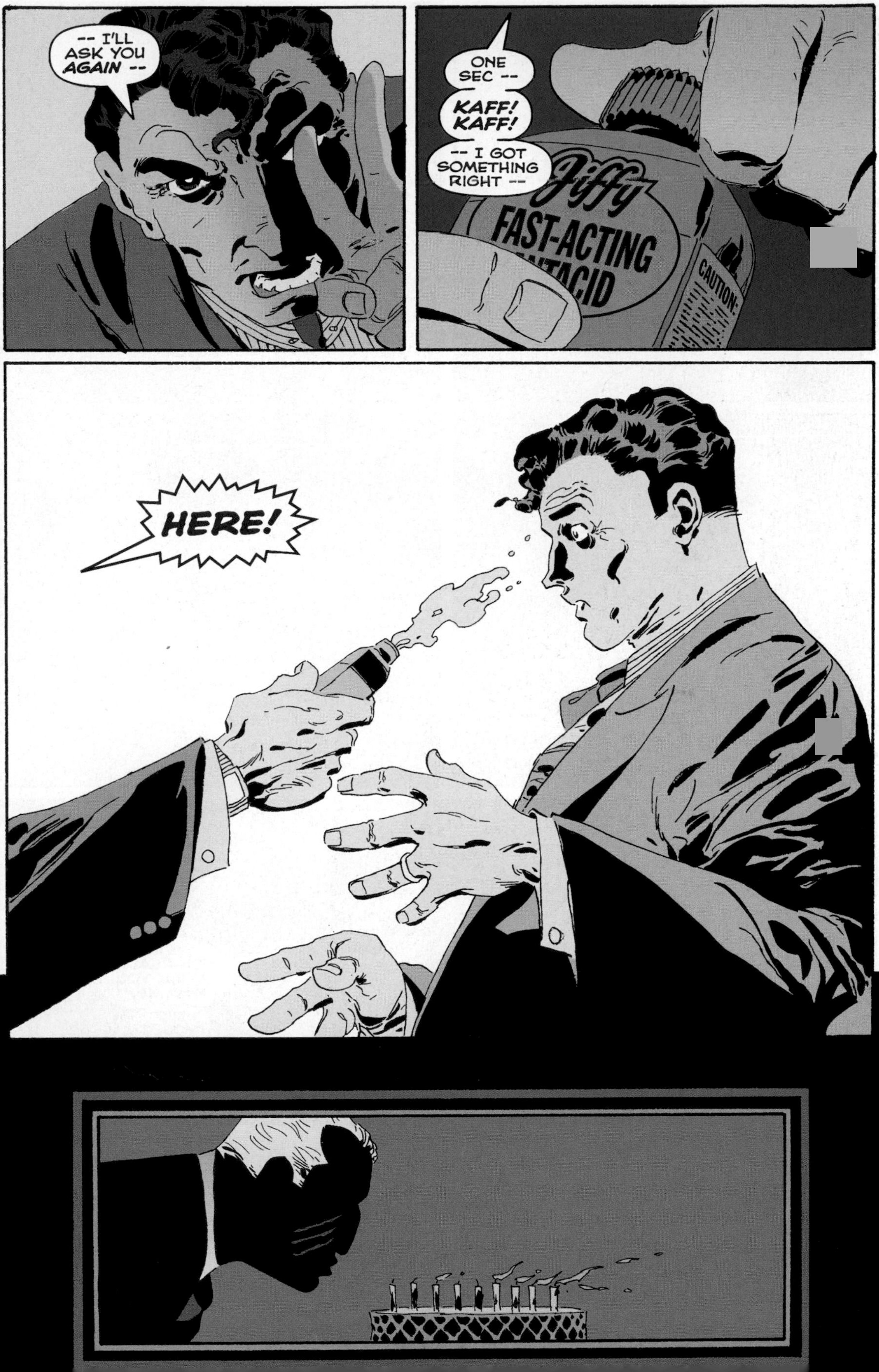
-- I'LL ASK YOU AGAIN --
ONE SEC --
KAFF! KAFF!
-- I GOT SOMETHING RIGHT --
Jiffy
FAST-ACTING
CAUTION:
HERE!

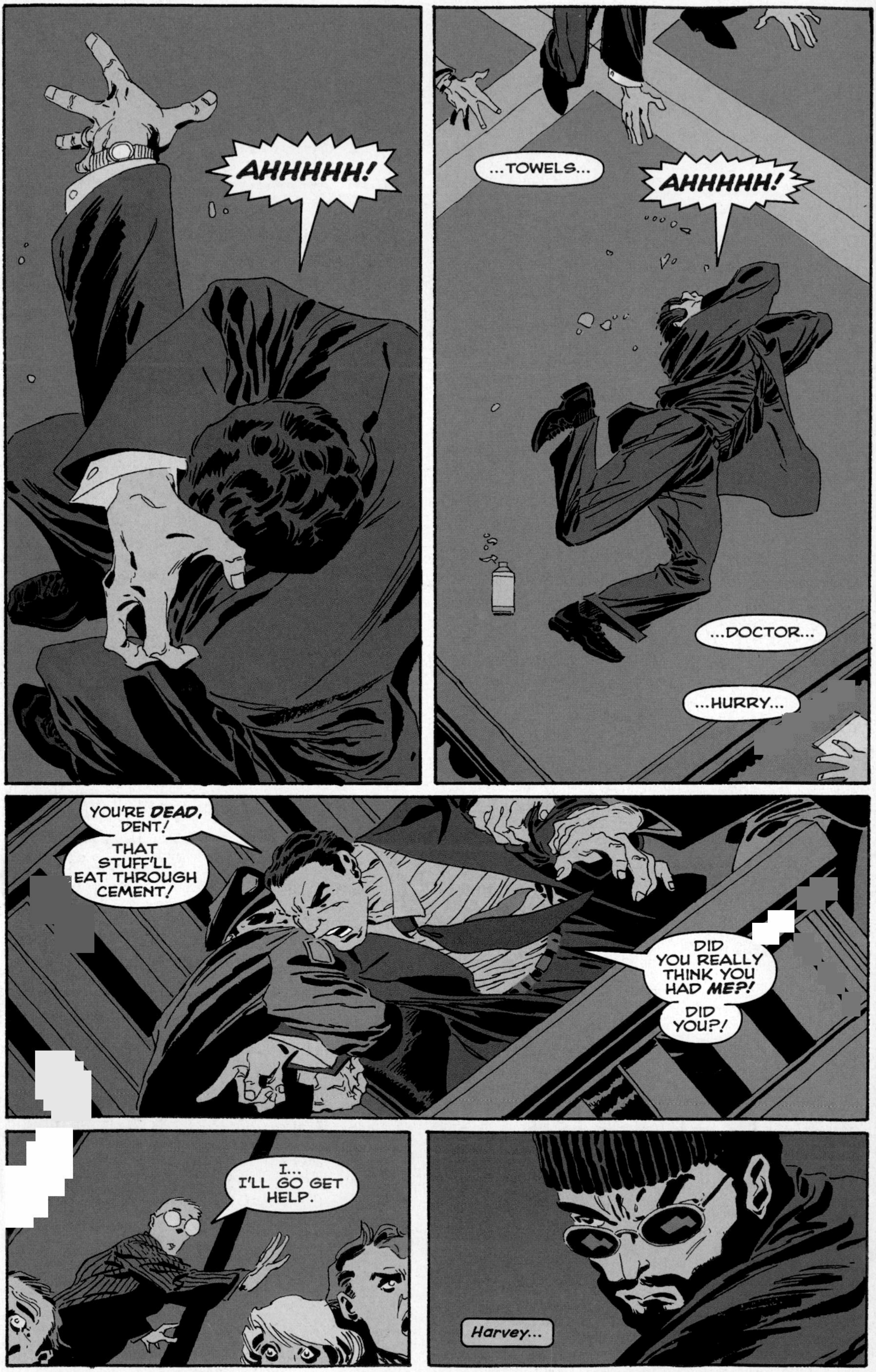
AHHHHH!
...TOWELS...
AHHHHH!
...DOCTOR...
...HURRY...
YOU'RE DEAD, DENT!
THAT STUFF'LL EAT THROUGH CEMENT!
DID YOU REALLY THINK YOU HAD ME?!
DID YOU?!
I... I'LL GO GET HELP.
Harvey...

I will never forget the sound of his screaming...

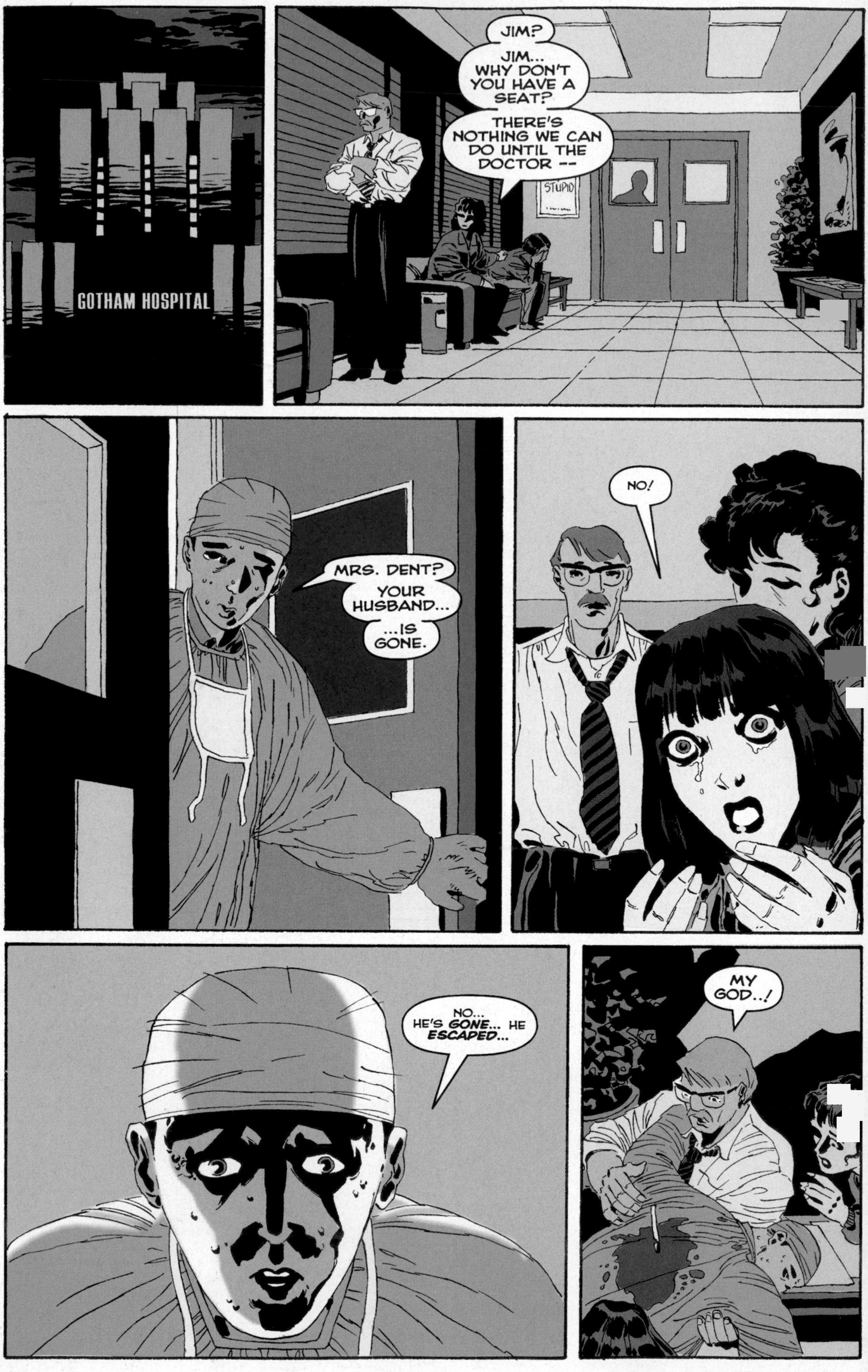
GOTHAM HOSPITAL
JIM?
JIM... WHY DON'T YOU HAVE A SEAT?
THERE'S NOTHING WE CAN DO UNTIL THE DOCTOR --
STUPID
MRS. DENT? YOUR HUSBAND...
...IS GONE.
NO!
NO... HE'S GONE... HE ESCAPED...
MY GOD..!

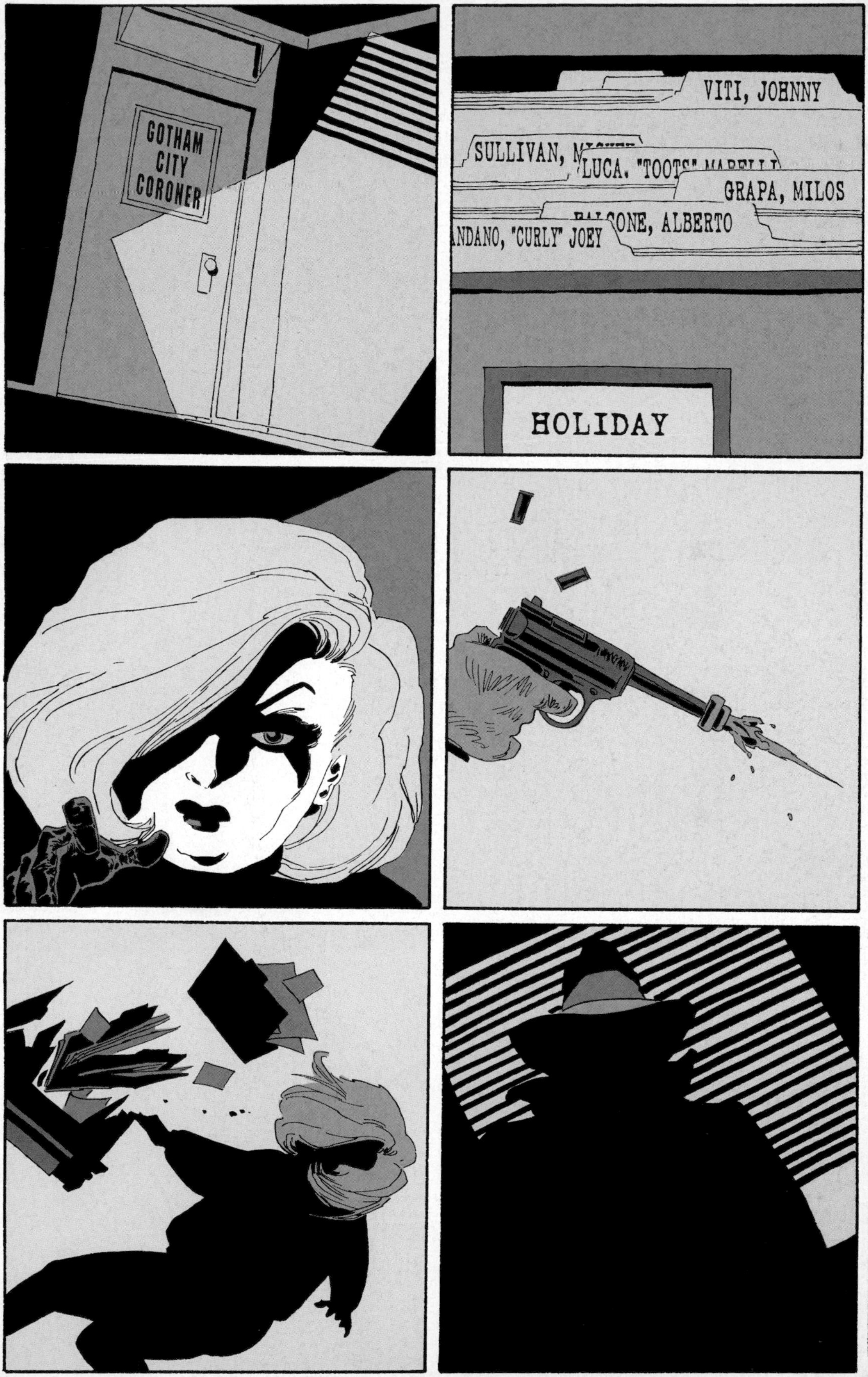
GOTHAM CITY CORONER
VITI, JOHNNY
SULLIVAN,
GRAPA, MILOS
HOLIDAY

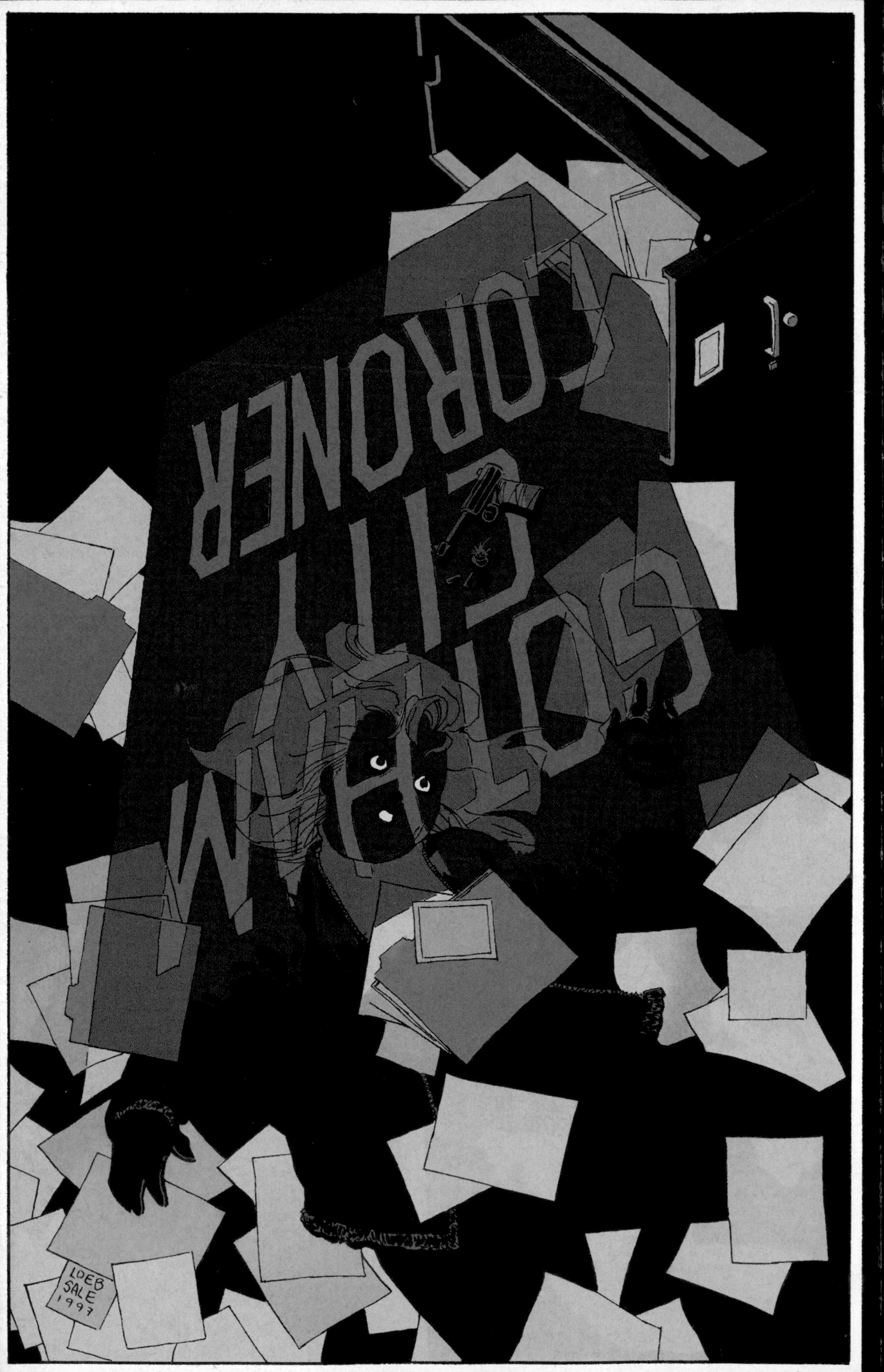
GOTHAM CITY CORONER
LOEB SALE 1997

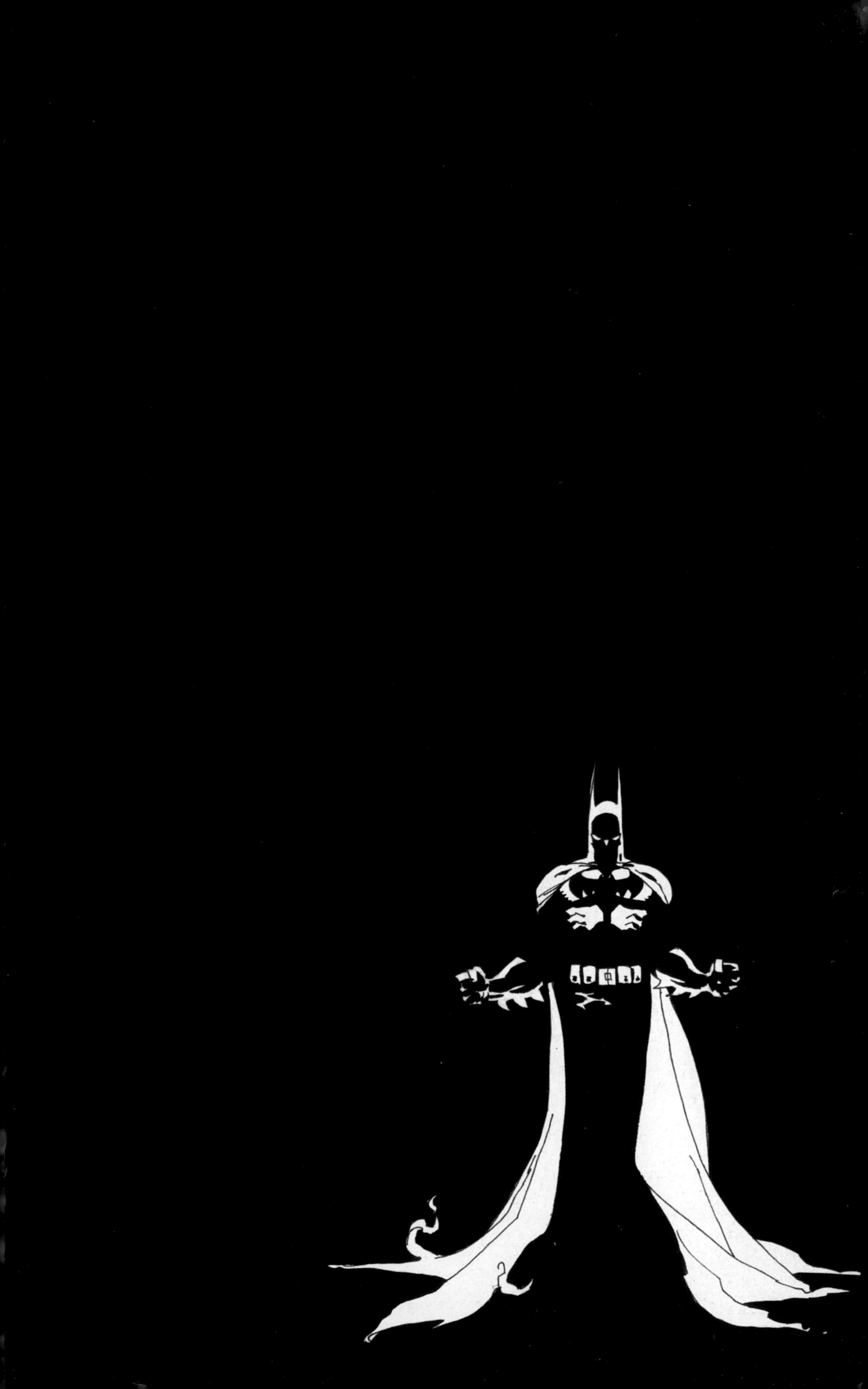

CHAPTER TWELVE
LABOR DAY

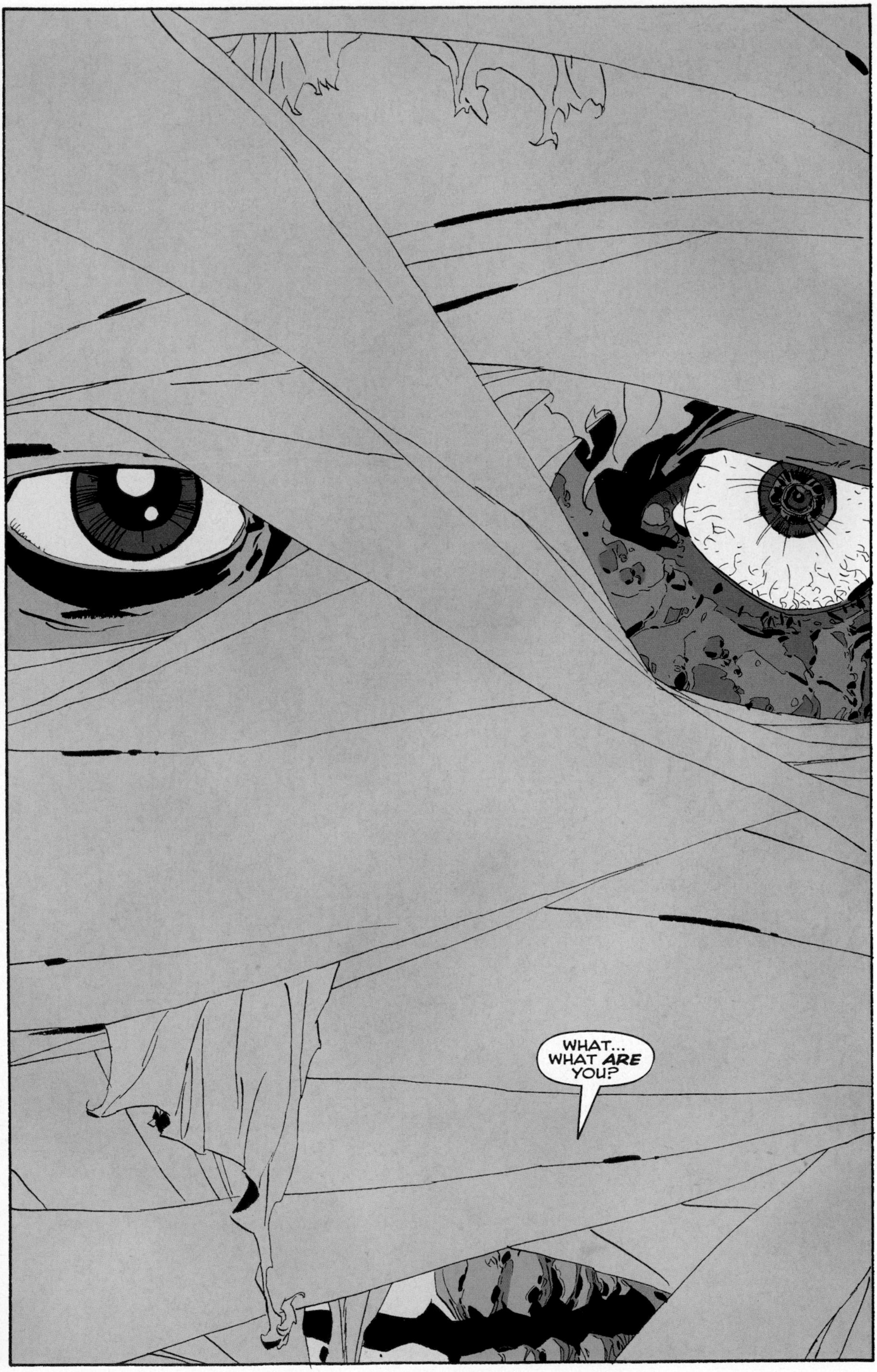
WHAT... WHAT ARE YOU?

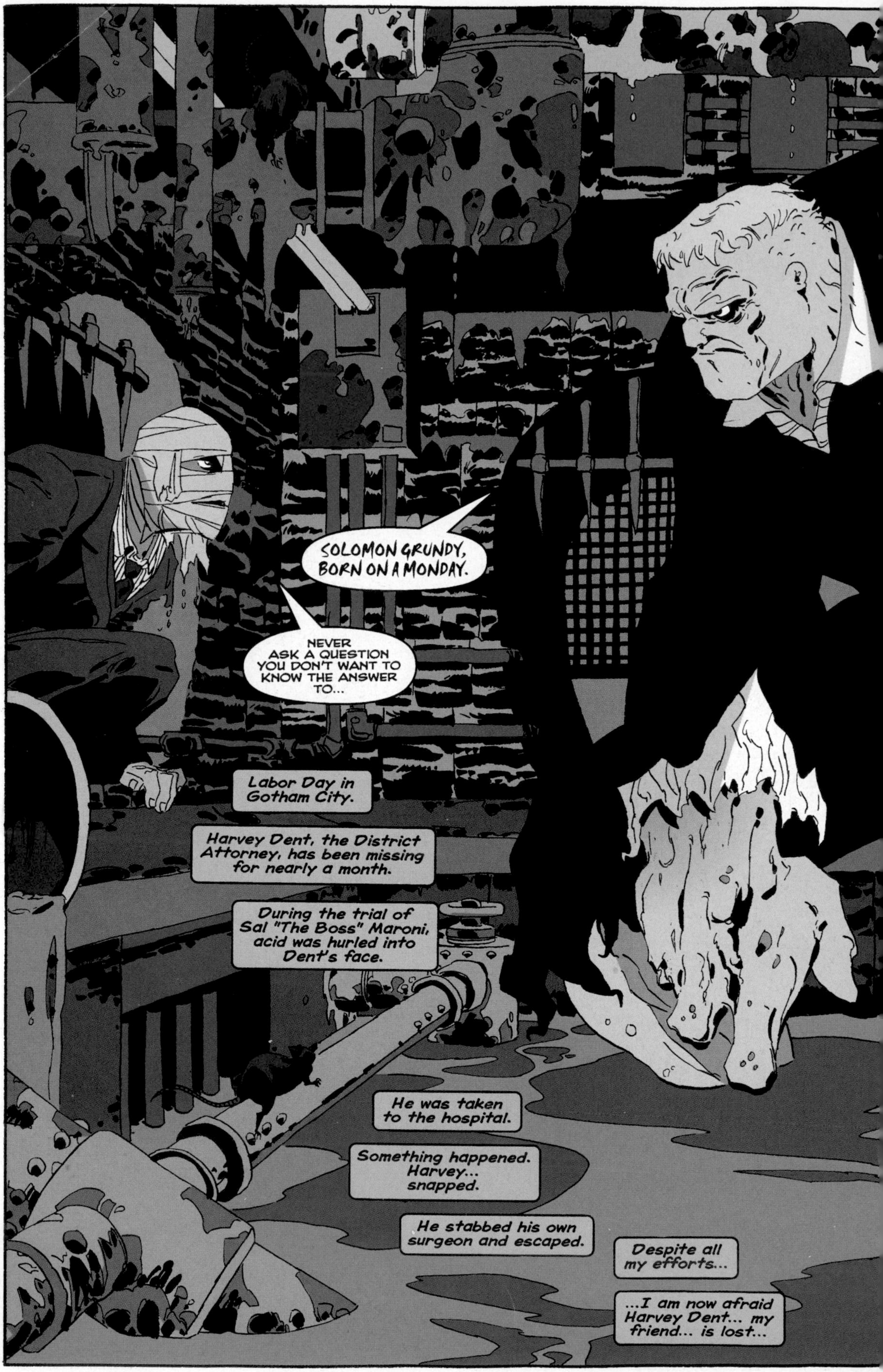
SOLOMON GRUNDY, BORN ON A MONDAY.
NEVER ASK A QUESTION YOU DON'T WANT TO KNOW THE ANSWER TO...
Labor Day in Gotham City.
Harvey Dent, the District Attorney, has been missing for nearly a month.
During the trial of Sal "The Boss" Maroni, acid was hurled into Dent's face.
He was taken to the hospital.
Something happened. Harvey... snapped.
He stabbed his own surgeon and escaped.
Despite all my efforts...
...I am now afraid Harvey Dent... my friend... is lost...

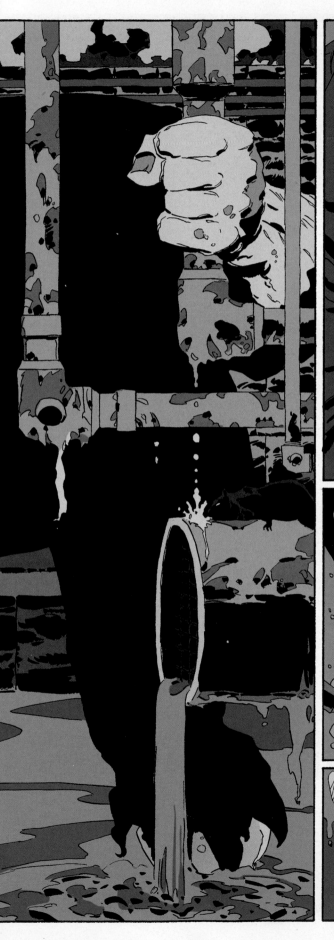

SOLOMON GRUNDY, BORN ON A MONDAY.

SOLOMON GRUNDY, BORN ON A MONDAY.

"CHRISTENED ON A *JACK* STARK AND STORMY TUESDAY..?"

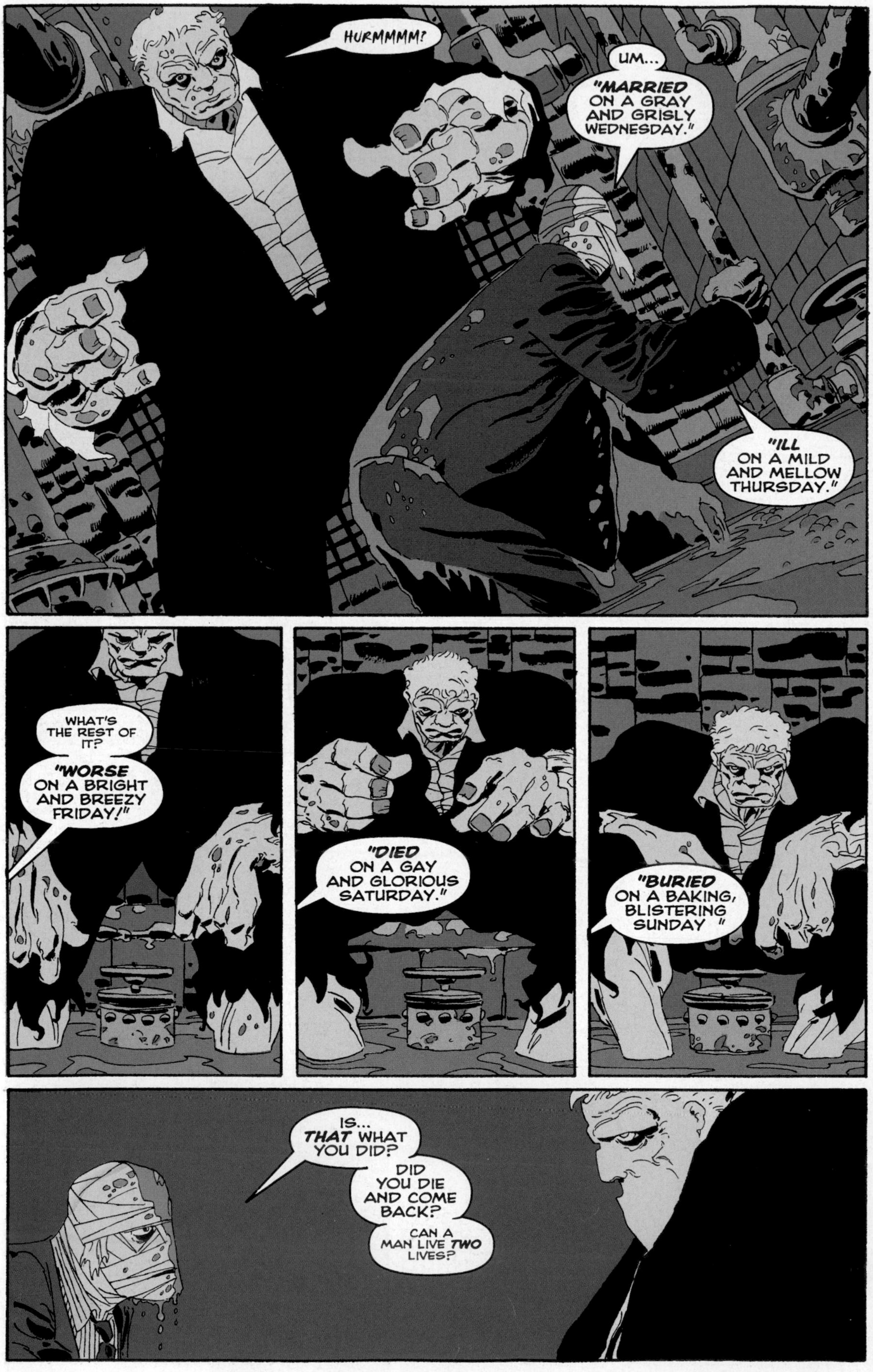
HURMMMM?
UM...
"MARRIED ON A GRAY AND GRISLY WEDNESDAY."
"ILL ON A MILD AND MELLOW THURSDAY."
WHAT'S THE REST OF IT?
"WORSE ON A BRIGHT AND BREEZY FRIDAY!"
"DIED ON A GAY AND GLORIOUS SATURDAY."
"BURIED ON A BAKING, BLISTERING SUNDAY "
IS... THAT WHAT YOU DID?
DID YOU DIE AND COME BACK?
CAN A MAN LIVE TWO LIVES?

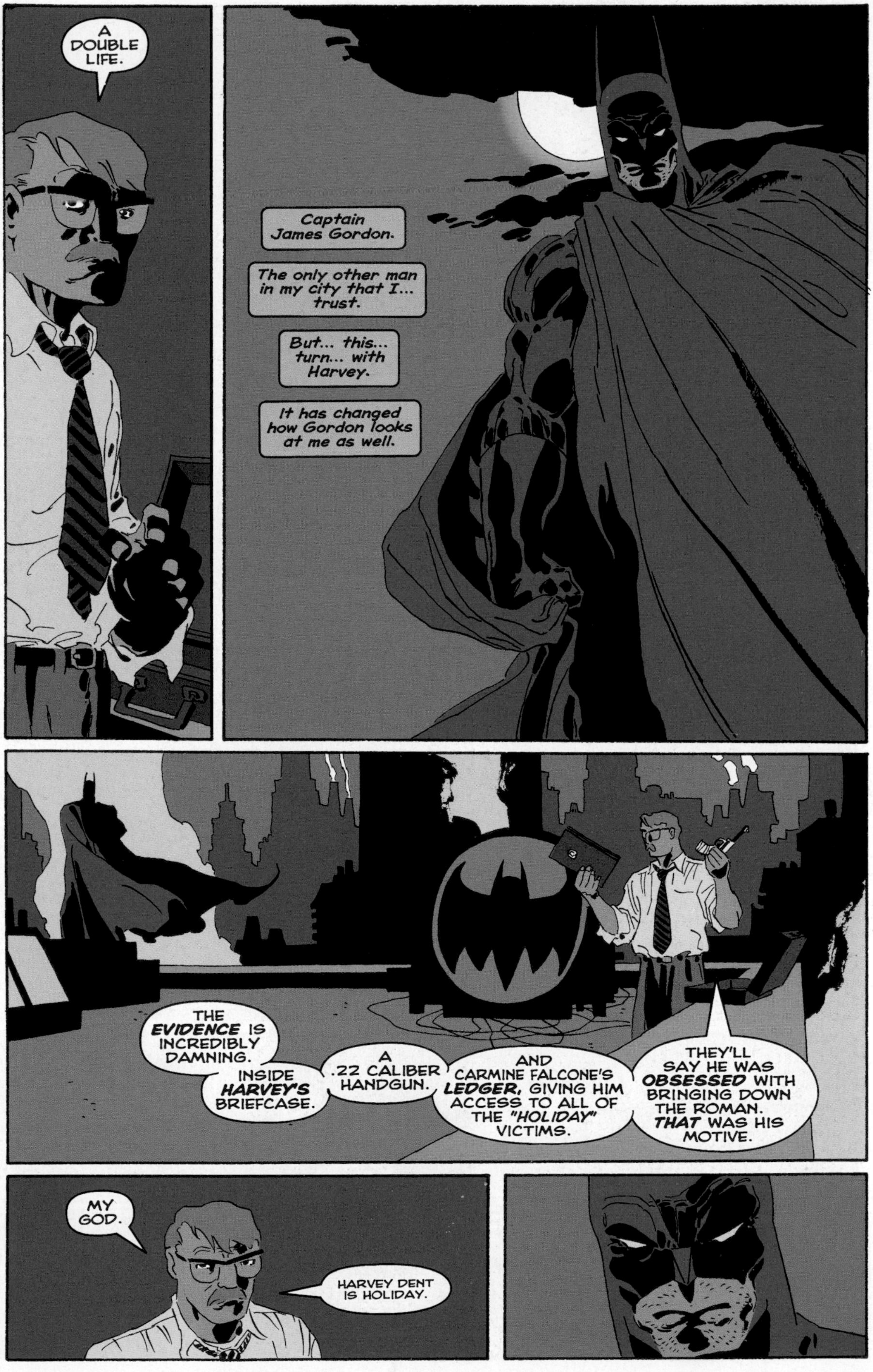
A DOUBLE LIFE.
Captain James Gordon.
The only other man in my city that I... trust.
But... this... turn... with Harvey.
It has changed how Gordon looks at me as well.
THE EVIDENCE IS INCREDIBLY DAMNING.
INSIDE HARVEY'S BRIEFCASE.
A .22 CALIBER HANDGUN.
AND CARMINE FALCONE'S LEDGER, GIVING HIM ACCESS TO ALL OF THE "HOLIDAY" VICTIMS.
THEY'LL SAY HE WAS OBSESSED WITH BRINGING DOWN THE ROMAN. THAT WAS HIS MOTIVE.
MY GOD.
HARVEY DENT IS HOLIDAY.

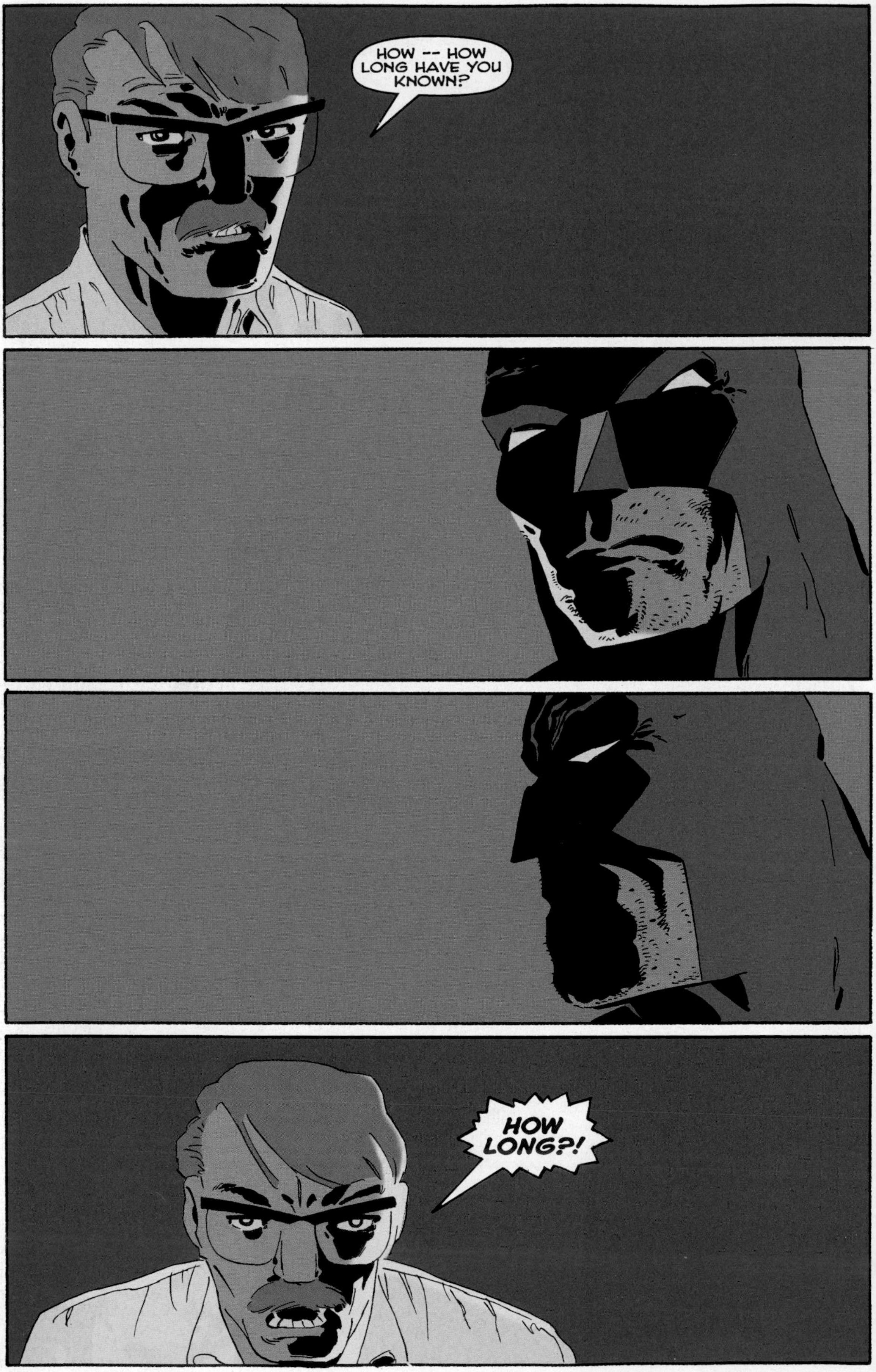
HOW -- HOW LONG HAVE YOU KNOWN?
HOW LONG?!

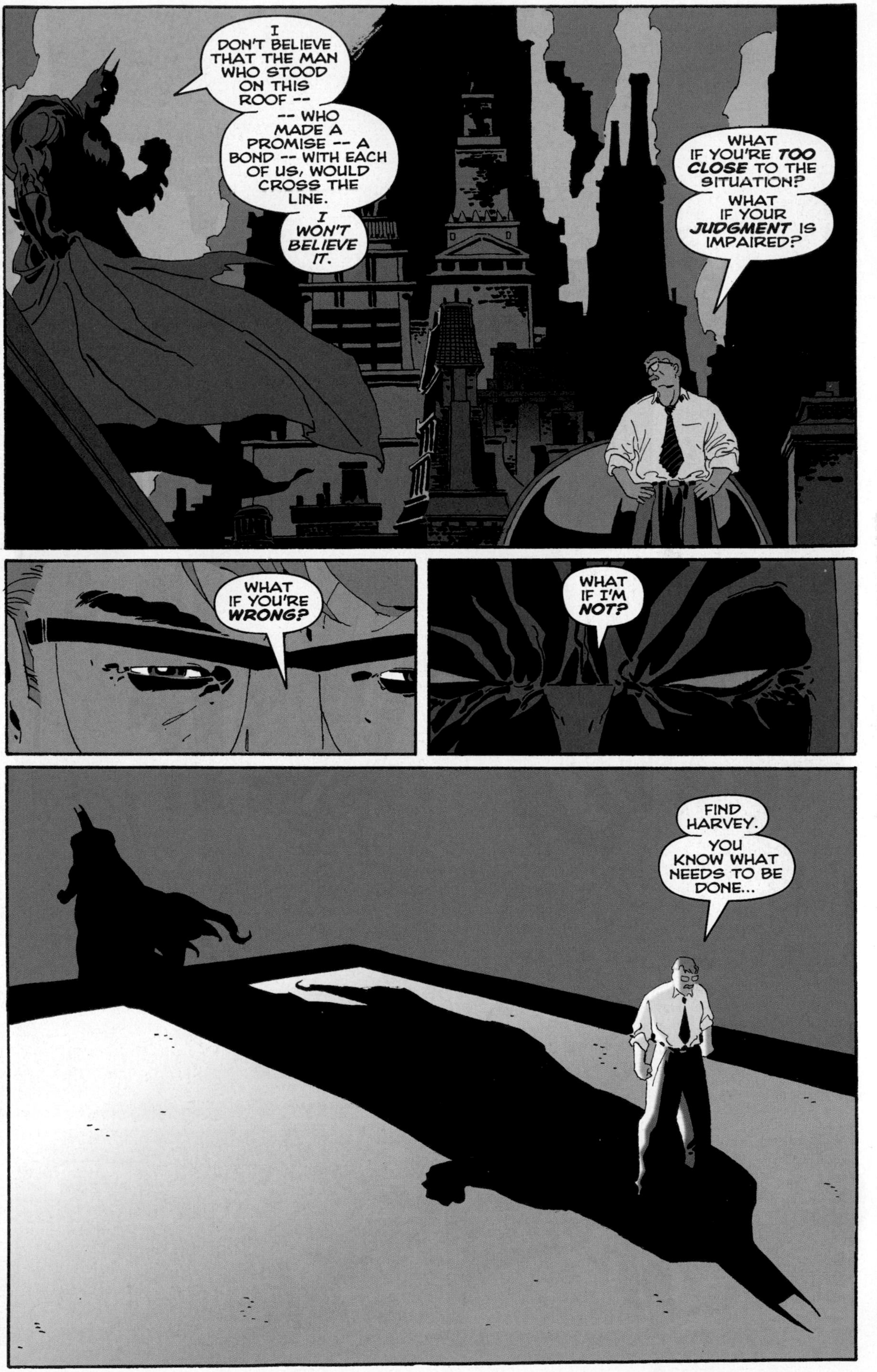
I DON'T BELIEVE THAT THE MAN WHO STOOD ON THIS ROOF --
-- WHO MADE A PROMISE -- A BOND -- WITH EACH OF US, WOULD CROSS THE LINE.
I WON'T BELIEVE IT.
WHAT IF YOU'RE TOO CLOSE TO THE SITUATION?
WHAT IF YOUR JUDGMENT IS IMPAIRED?
WHAT IF YOU'RE WRONG?
WHAT IF I'M NOT?
FIND HARVEY.
YOU KNOW WHAT NEEDS TO BE DONE...

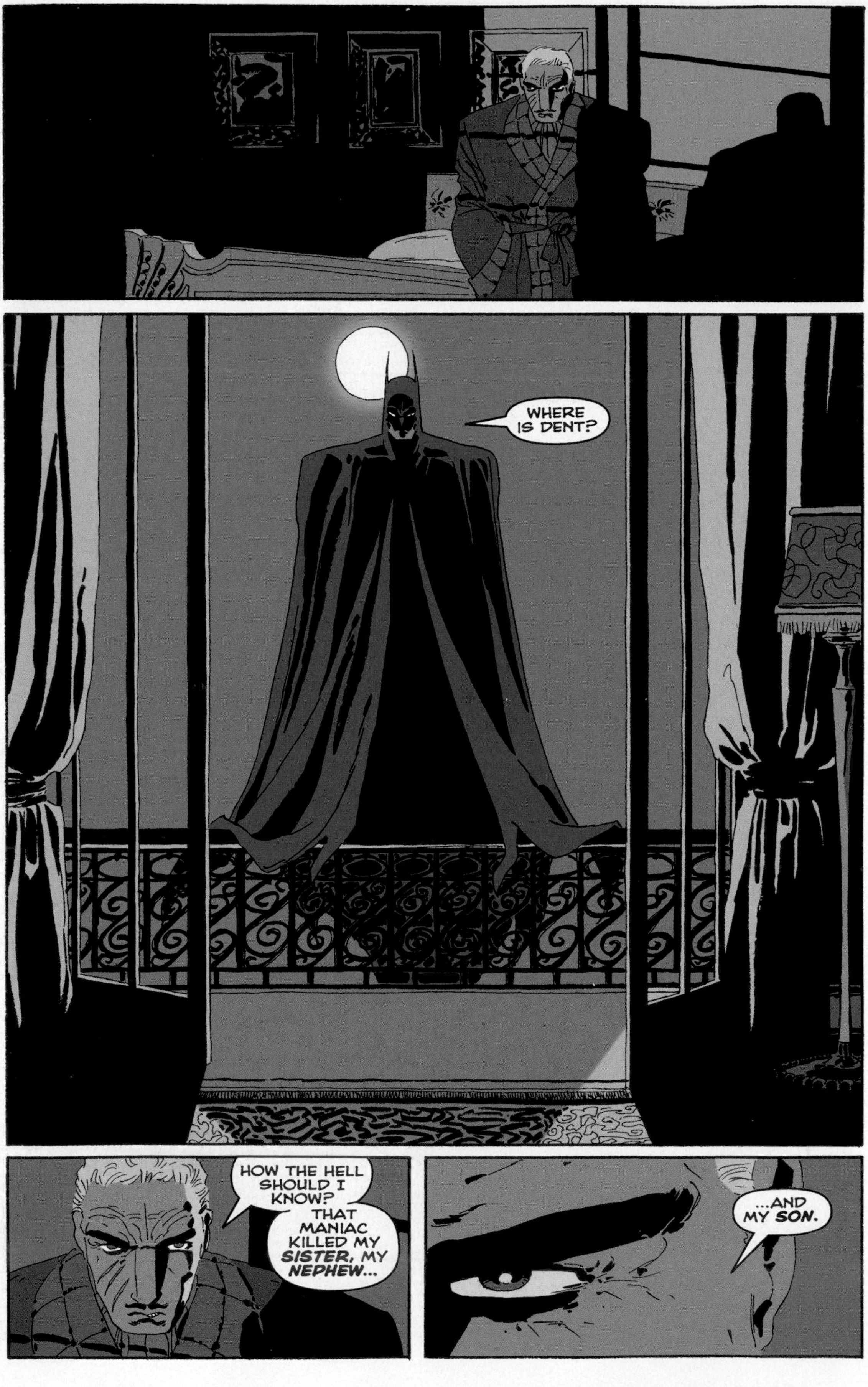
WHERE IS DENT?
HOW THE HELL SHOULD I KNOW?
THAT MANIAC KILLED MY SISTER, MY NEPHEW...
...AND MY SON.

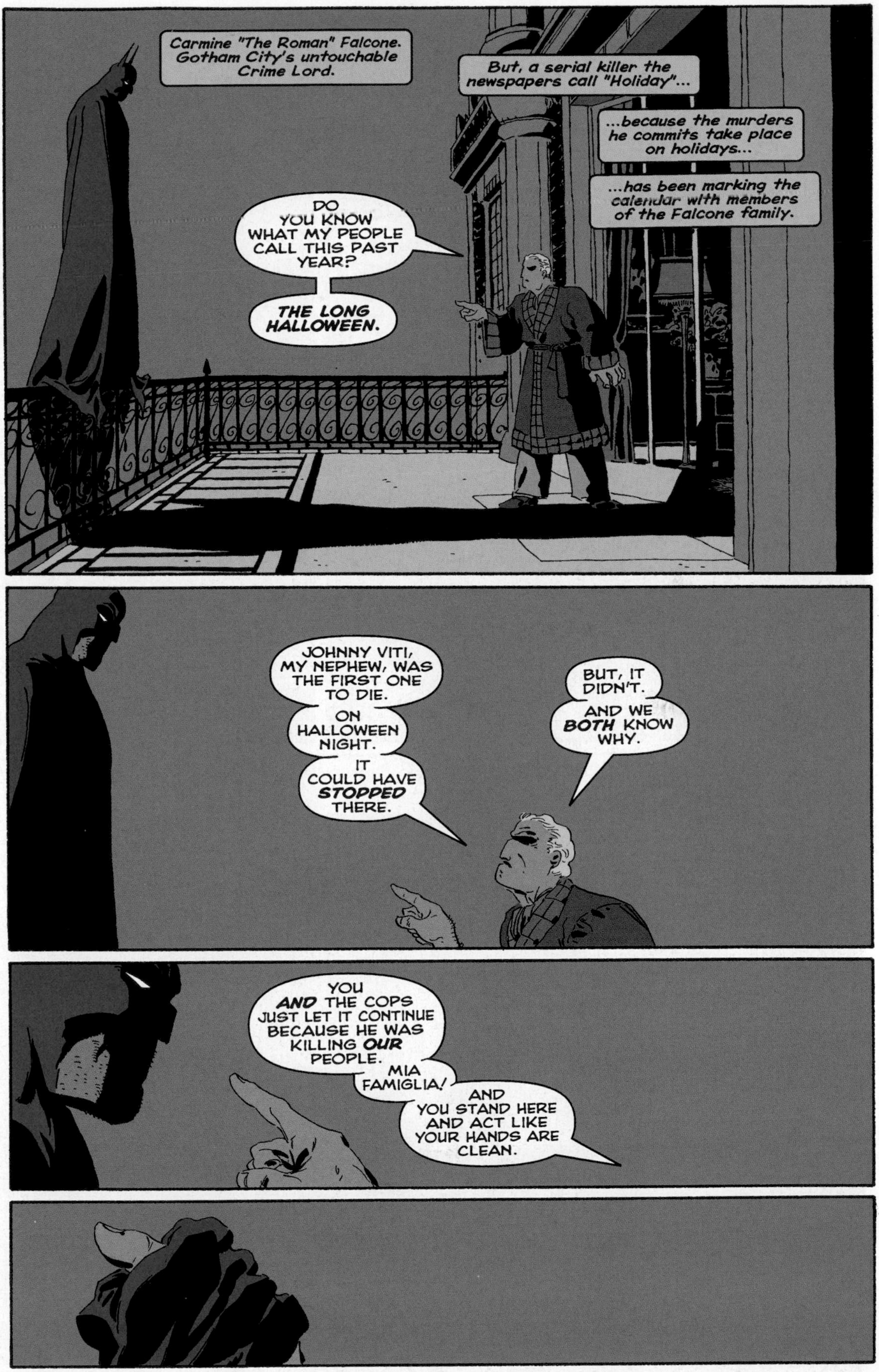
Carmine "The Roman" Falcone. Gotham City's untouchable Crime Lord.
But, a serial killer the newspapers call "Holiday"...
...because the murders he commits take place on holidays...
...has been marking the calendar with members of the Falcone family.
DO YOU KNOW WHAT MY PEOPLE CALL THIS PAST YEAR?
THE LONG HALLOWEEN.
JOHNNY VITI, MY NEPHEW, WAS THE FIRST ONE TO DIE.
ON HALLOWEEN NIGHT.
IT COULD HAVE STOPPED THERE.
BUT, IT DIDN'T.
AND WE BOTH KNOW WHY.
YOU AND THE COPS JUST LET IT CONTINUE BECAUSE HE WAS KILLING OUR PEOPLE.
MIA FAMIGLIA!
AND YOU STAND HERE AND ACT LIKE YOUR HANDS ARE CLEAN.

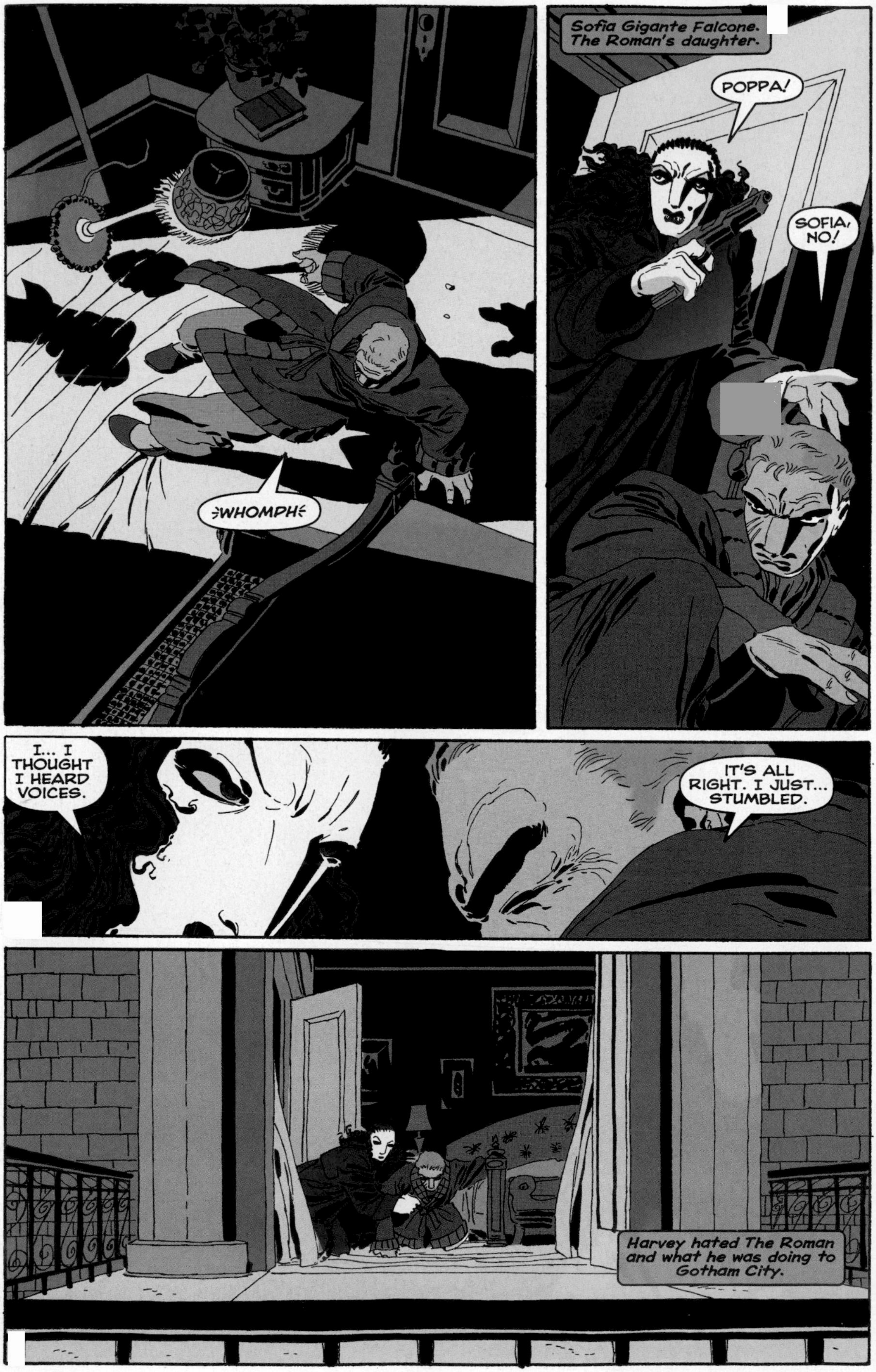
WHOMPH
Sofia Gigante Falcone. The Roman's daughter.
POPPA!
SOFIA, NO!
I... I THOUGHT I HEARD VOICES.
IT'S ALL RIGHT. I JUST... STUMBLED.
Harvey hated The Roman and what he was doing to Gotham City.

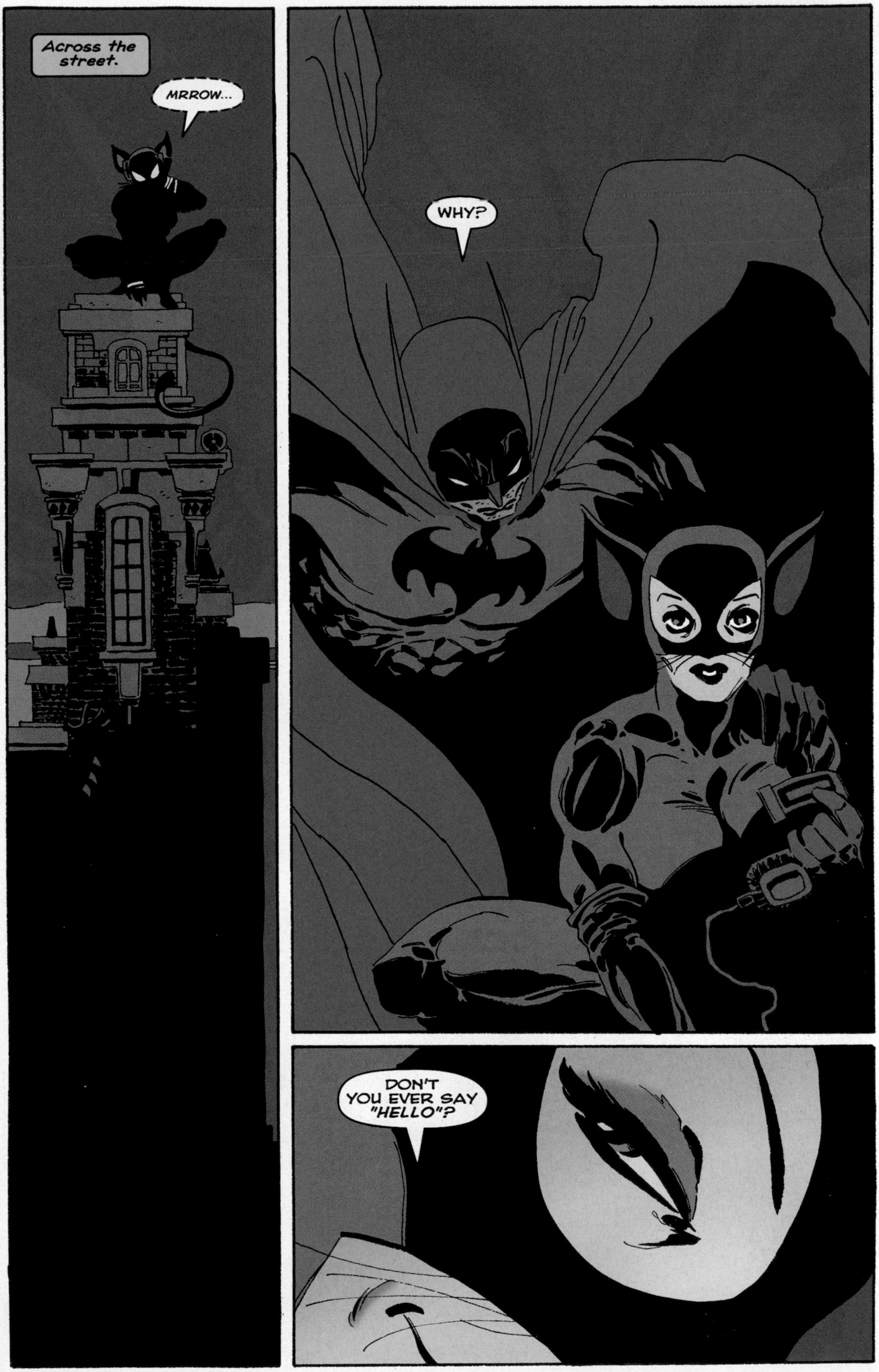
Across the street.
MRROW...
WHY?
DON'T YOU EVER SAY "HELLO"?

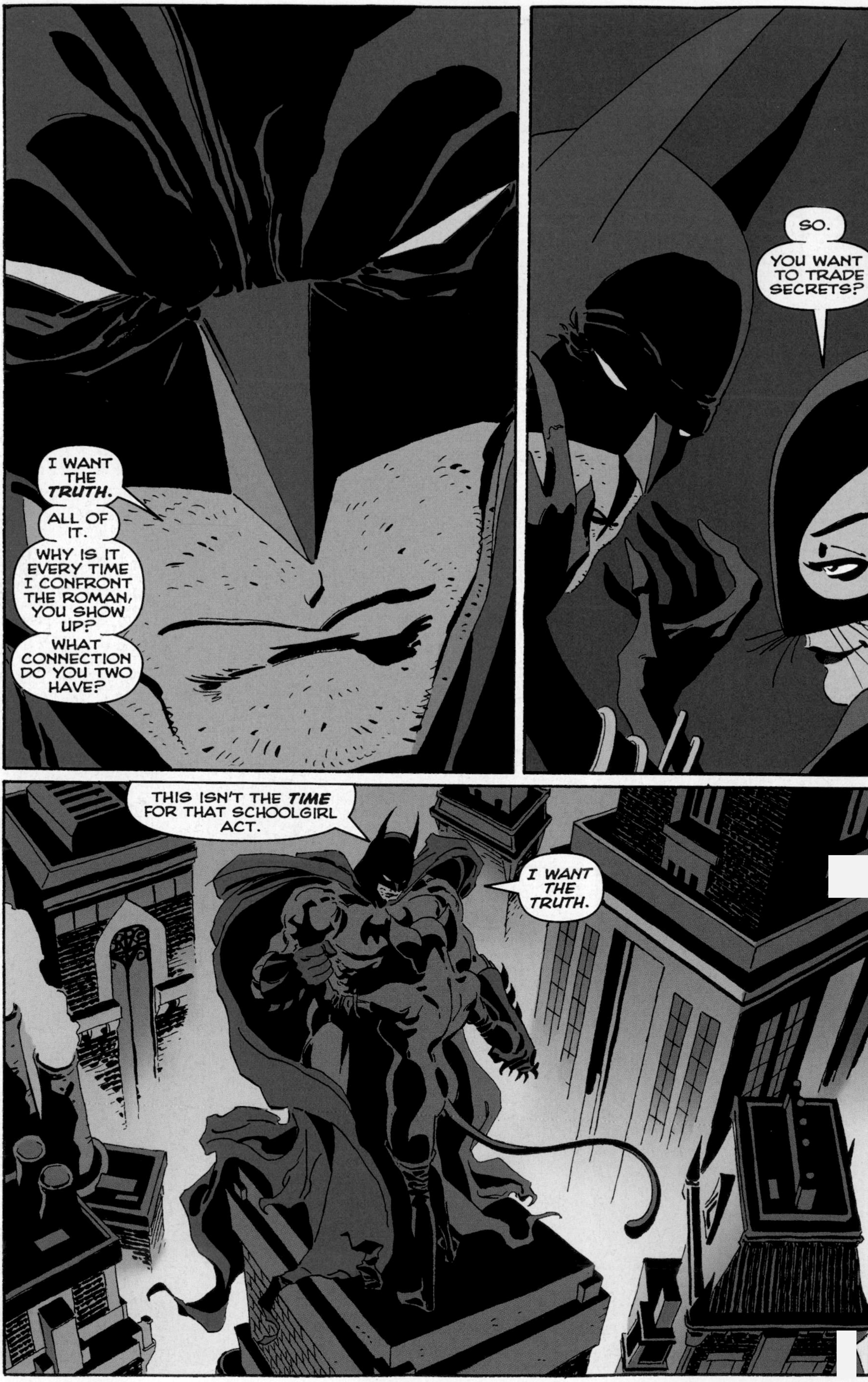

I WANT THE *TRUTH*.
ALL OF IT.
WHY IS IT EVERY TIME I CONFRONT THE ROMAN, YOU SHOW UP?
WHAT CONNECTION DO YOU TWO HAVE?
SO.
YOU WANT TO TRADE SECRETS?
THIS ISN'T THE *TIME* FOR THAT SCHOOLGIRL ACT.
I WANT THE TRUTH.

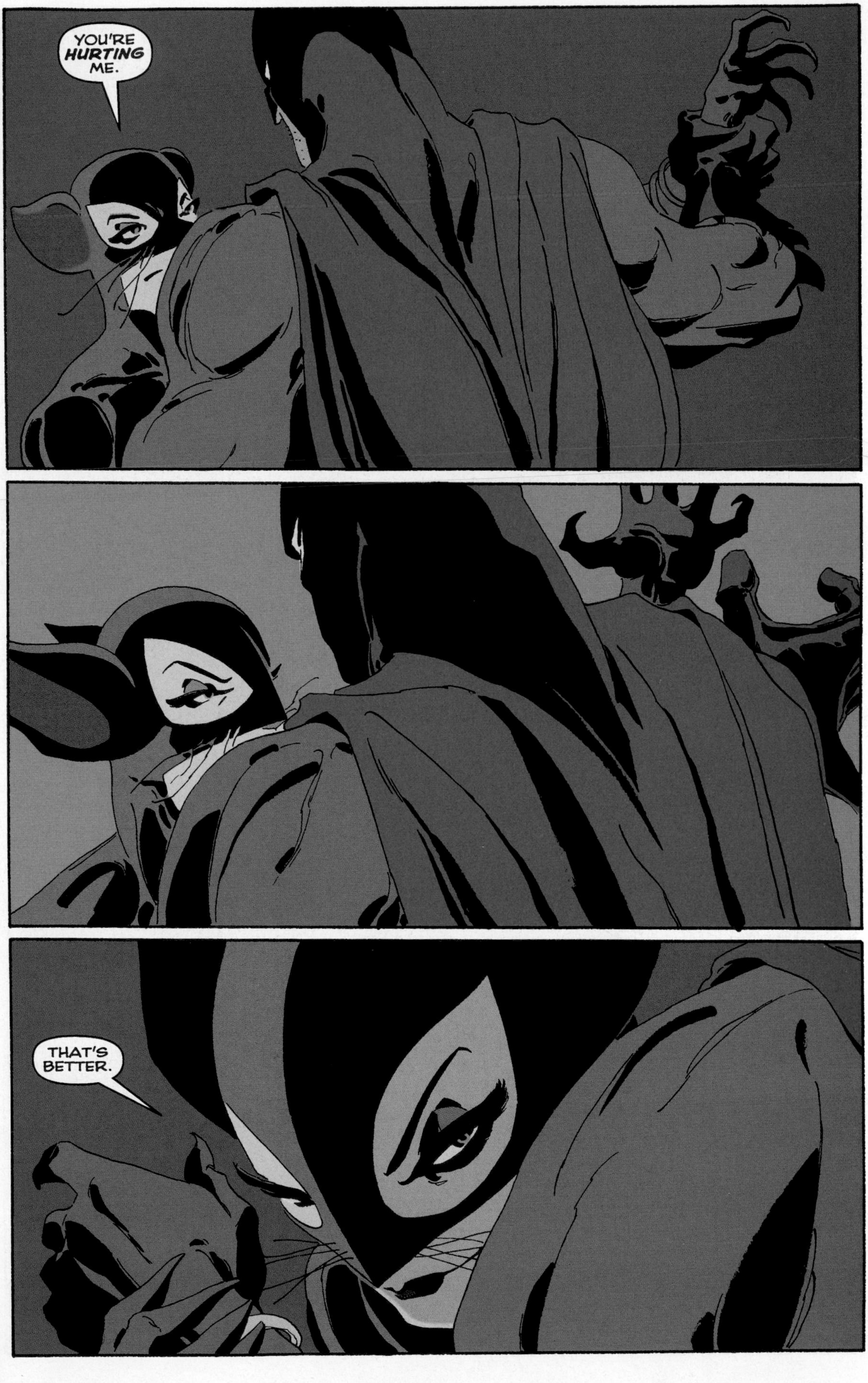
YOU'RE HURTING ME.
THAT'S BETTER.

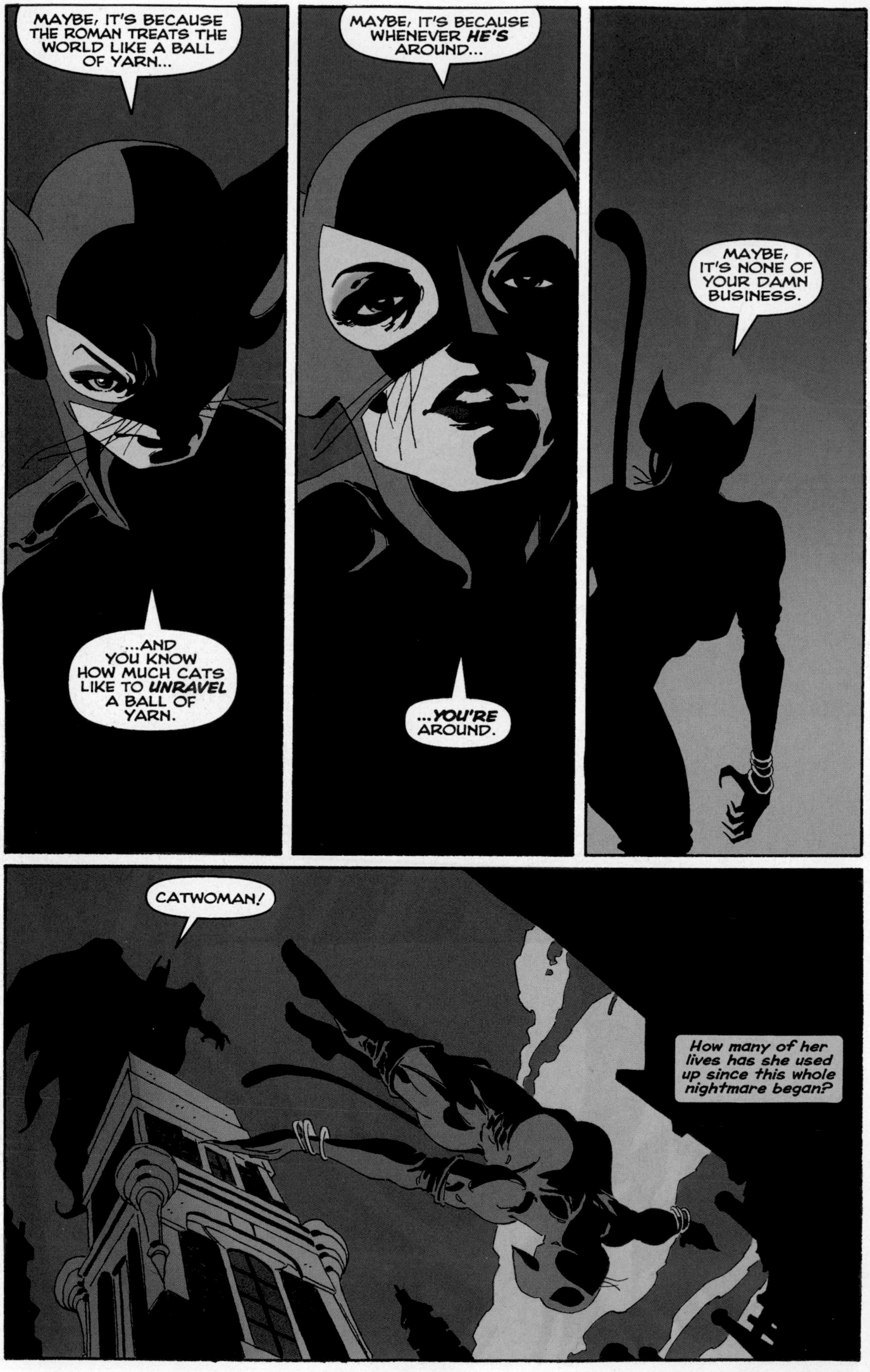
MAYBE, IT'S BECAUSE THE ROMAN TREATS THE WORLD LIKE A BALL OF YARN...
...AND YOU KNOW HOW MUCH CATS LIKE TO *UNRAVEL* A BALL OF YARN.
MAYBE, IT'S BECAUSE WHENEVER *HE'S* AROUND...
...*YOU'RE* AROUND.
MAYBE, IT'S NONE OF YOUR DAMN BUSINESS.
CATWOMAN!
How many of her lives has she used up since this whole nightmare began?

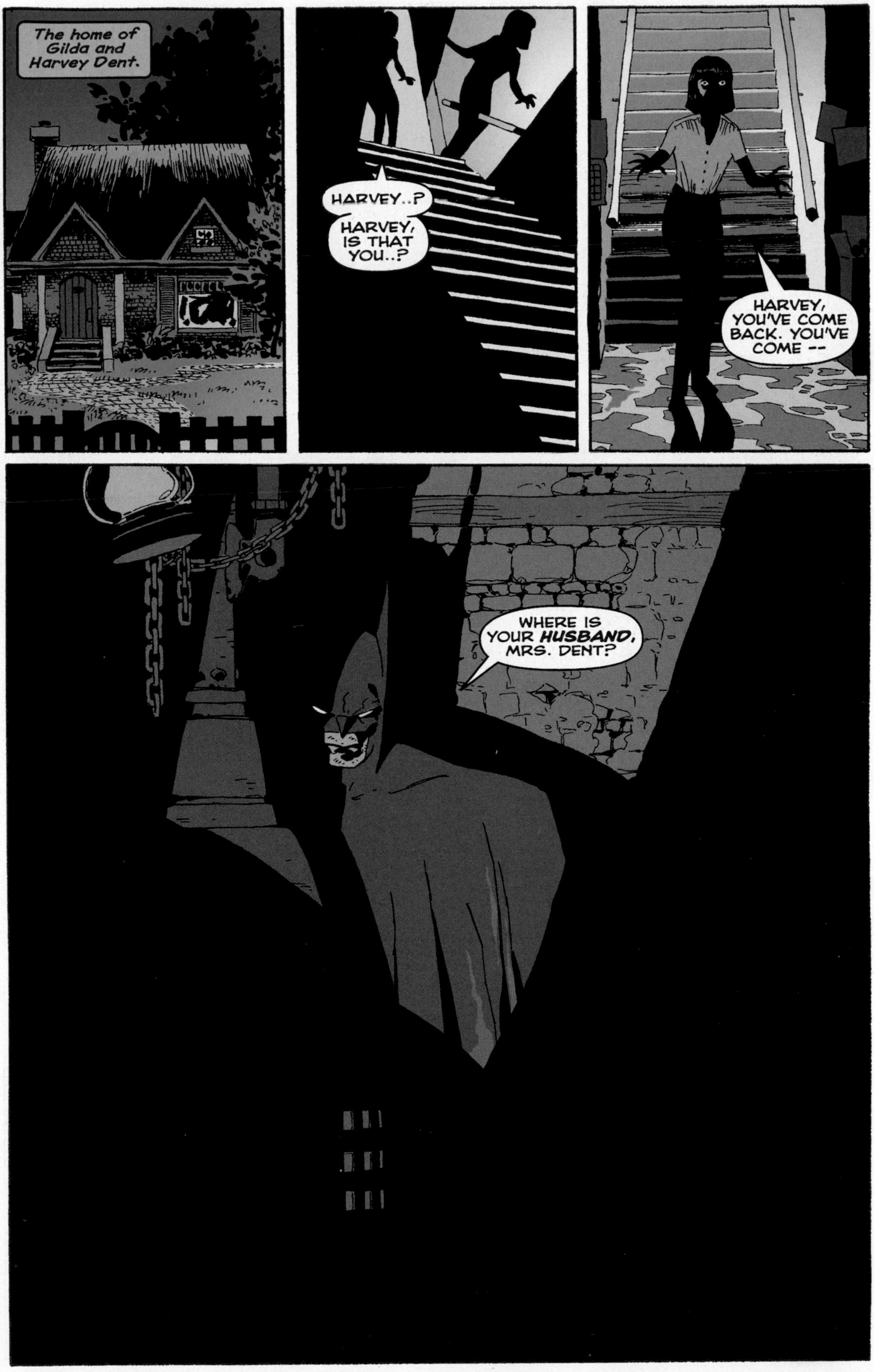
The home of Gilda and Harvey Dent.
HARVEY..?
HARVEY, IS THAT YOU..?
HARVEY, YOU'VE COME BACK. YOU'VE COME --
WHERE IS YOUR HUSBAND, MRS. DENT?

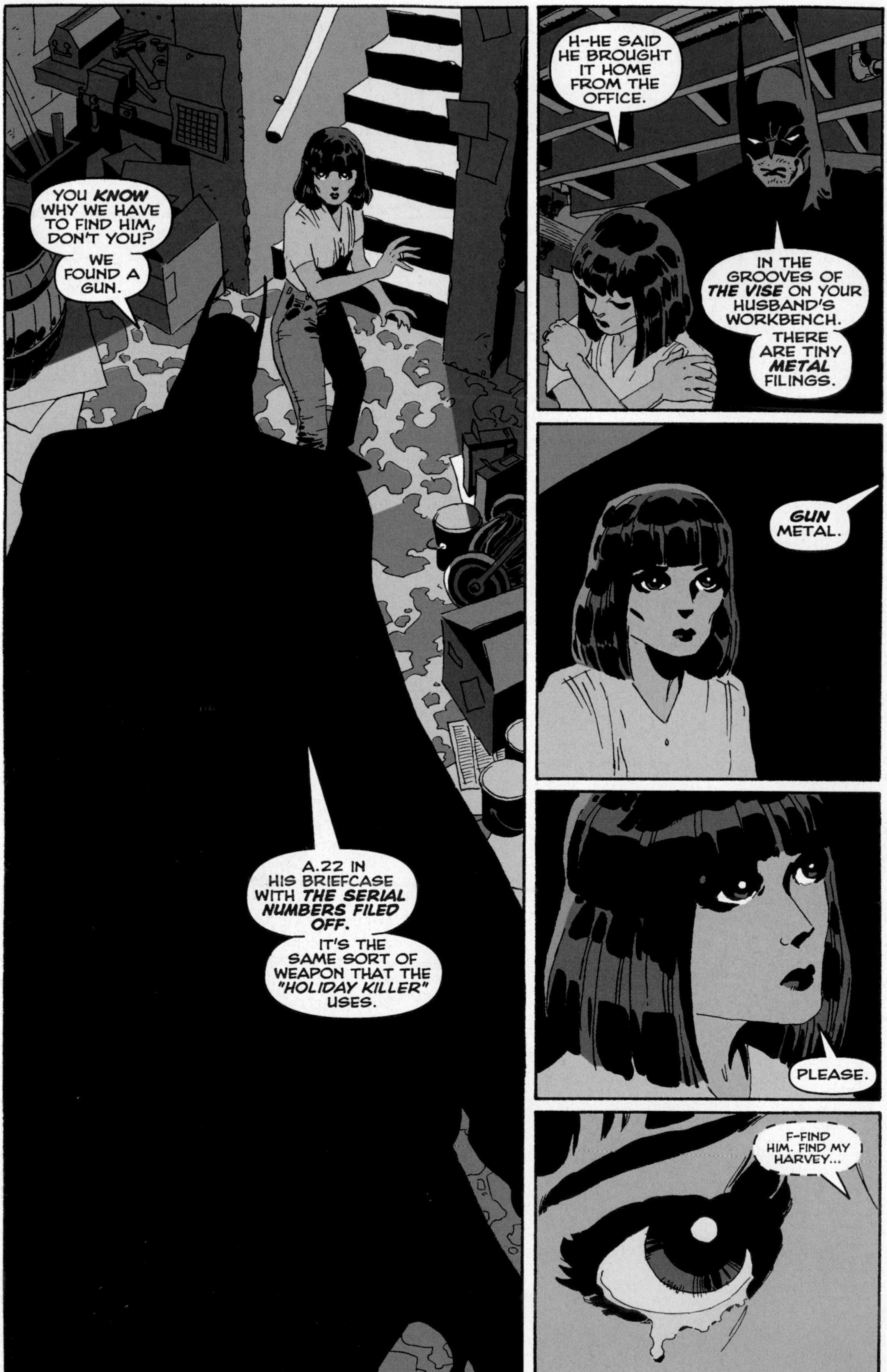
YOU KNOW WHY WE HAVE TO FIND HIM, DON'T YOU?
WE FOUND A GUN.
A.22 IN HIS BRIEFCASE WITH THE SERIAL NUMBERS FILED OFF.
IT'S THE SAME SORT OF WEAPON THAT THE "HOLIDAY KILLER" USES.
H-HE SAID HE BROUGHT IT HOME FROM THE OFFICE.
IN THE GROOVES OF THE VISE ON YOUR HUSBAND'S WORKBENCH.
THERE ARE TINY METAL FILINGS.
GUN METAL.
PLEASE.
F-FIND HIM. FIND MY HARVEY...

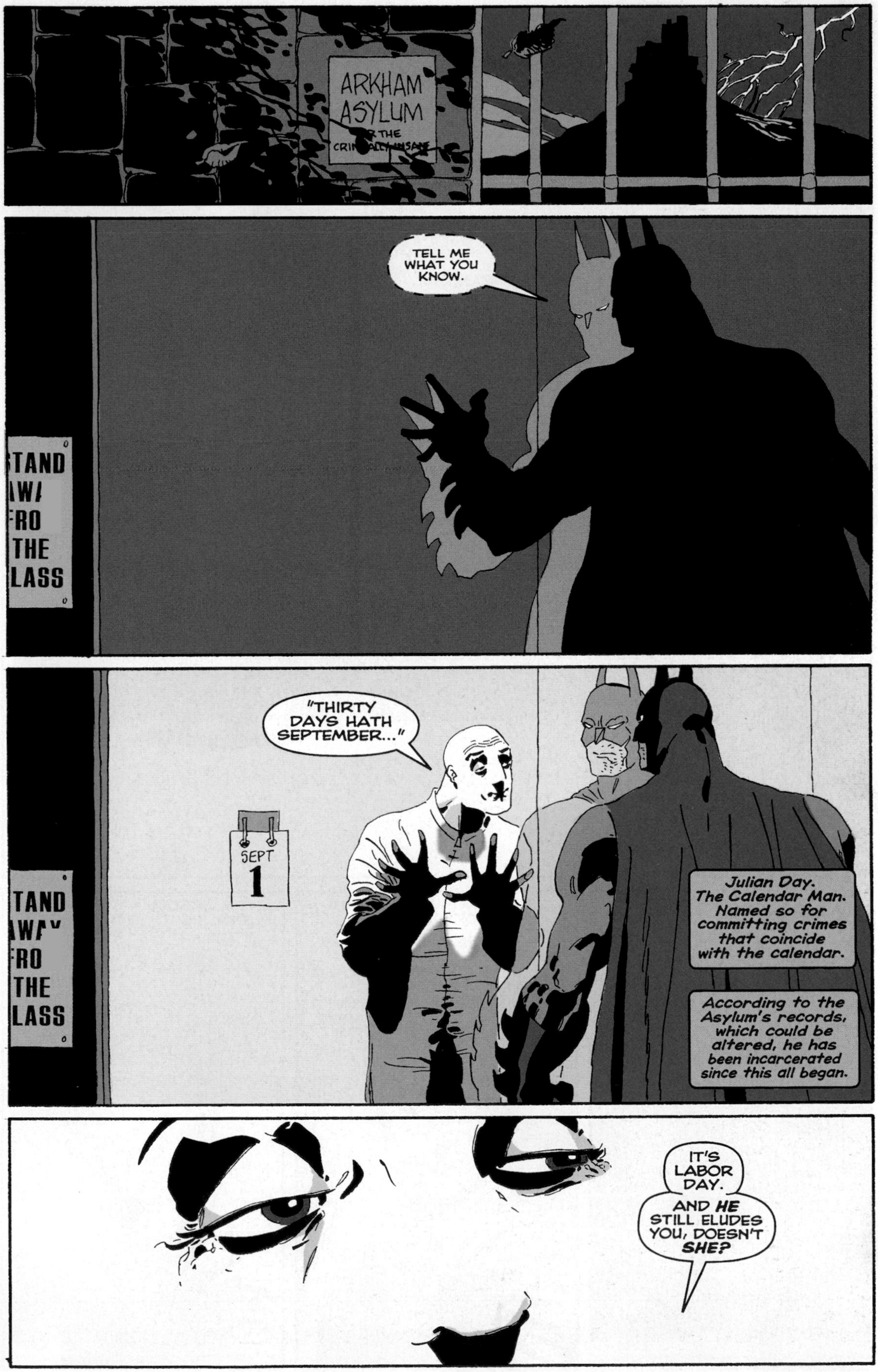
ARKHAM ASYLUM
TELL ME WHAT YOU KNOW.
"THIRTY DAYS HATH SEPTEMBER..."
SEPT 1
Julian Day. The Calendar Man. Named so for committing crimes that coincide with the calendar.
According to the Asylum's records, which could be altered, he has been incarcerated since this all began.
IT'S LABOR DAY.
AND HE STILL ELUDES YOU, DOESN'T SHE?

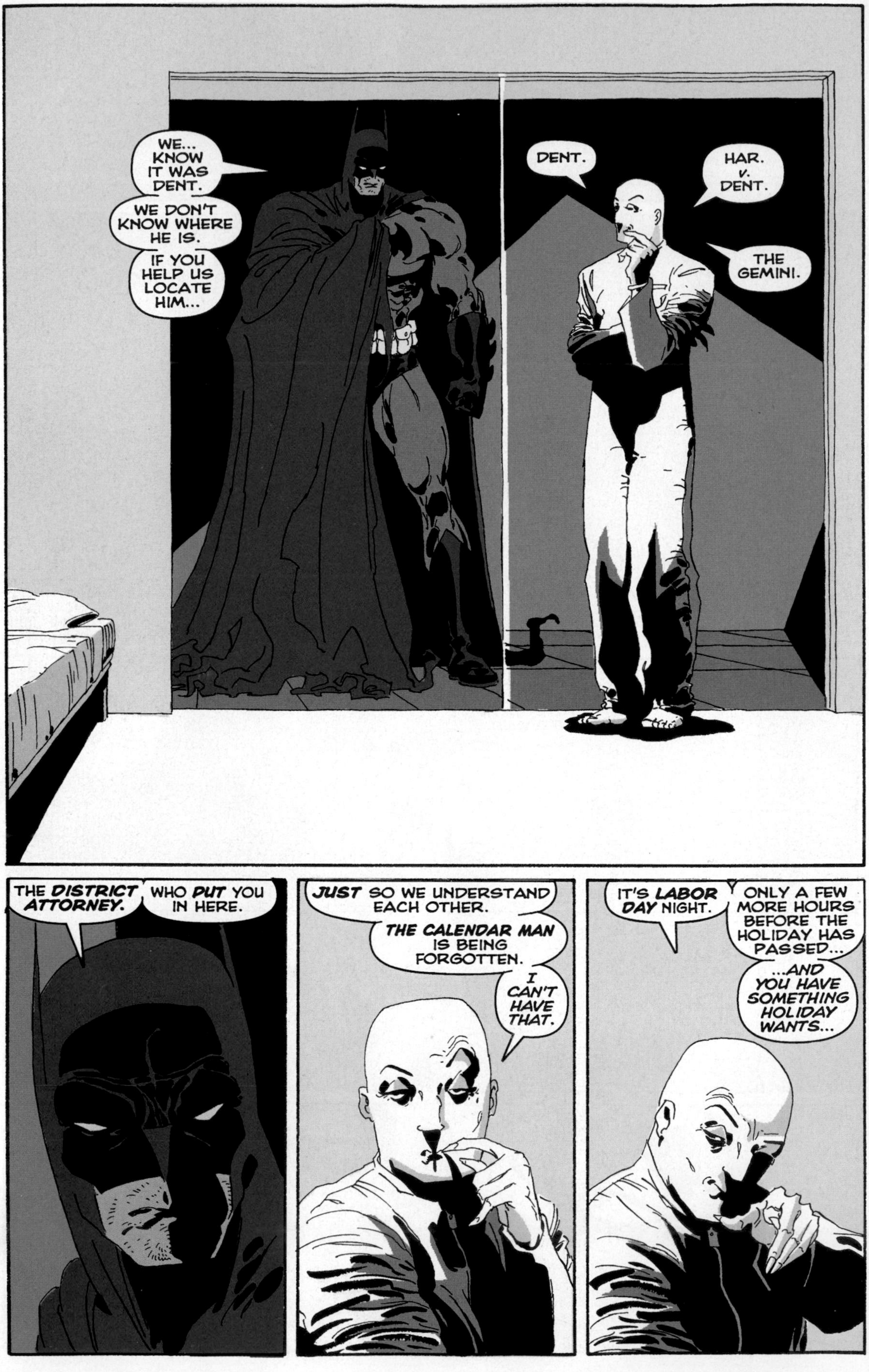
WE... KNOW IT WAS DENT.
WE DON'T KNOW WHERE HE IS.
IF YOU HELP US LOCATE HIM...
DENT.
HAR. v. DENT.
THE GEMINI.
THE DISTRICT ATTORNEY.
WHO PUT YOU IN HERE.
JUST SO WE UNDERSTAND EACH OTHER.
THE CALENDAR MAN IS BEING FORGOTTEN.
I CAN'T HAVE THAT.
IT'S LABOR DAY NIGHT.
ONLY A FEW MORE HOURS BEFORE THE HOLIDAY HAS PASSED...
...AND YOU HAVE SOMETHING HOLIDAY WANTS...

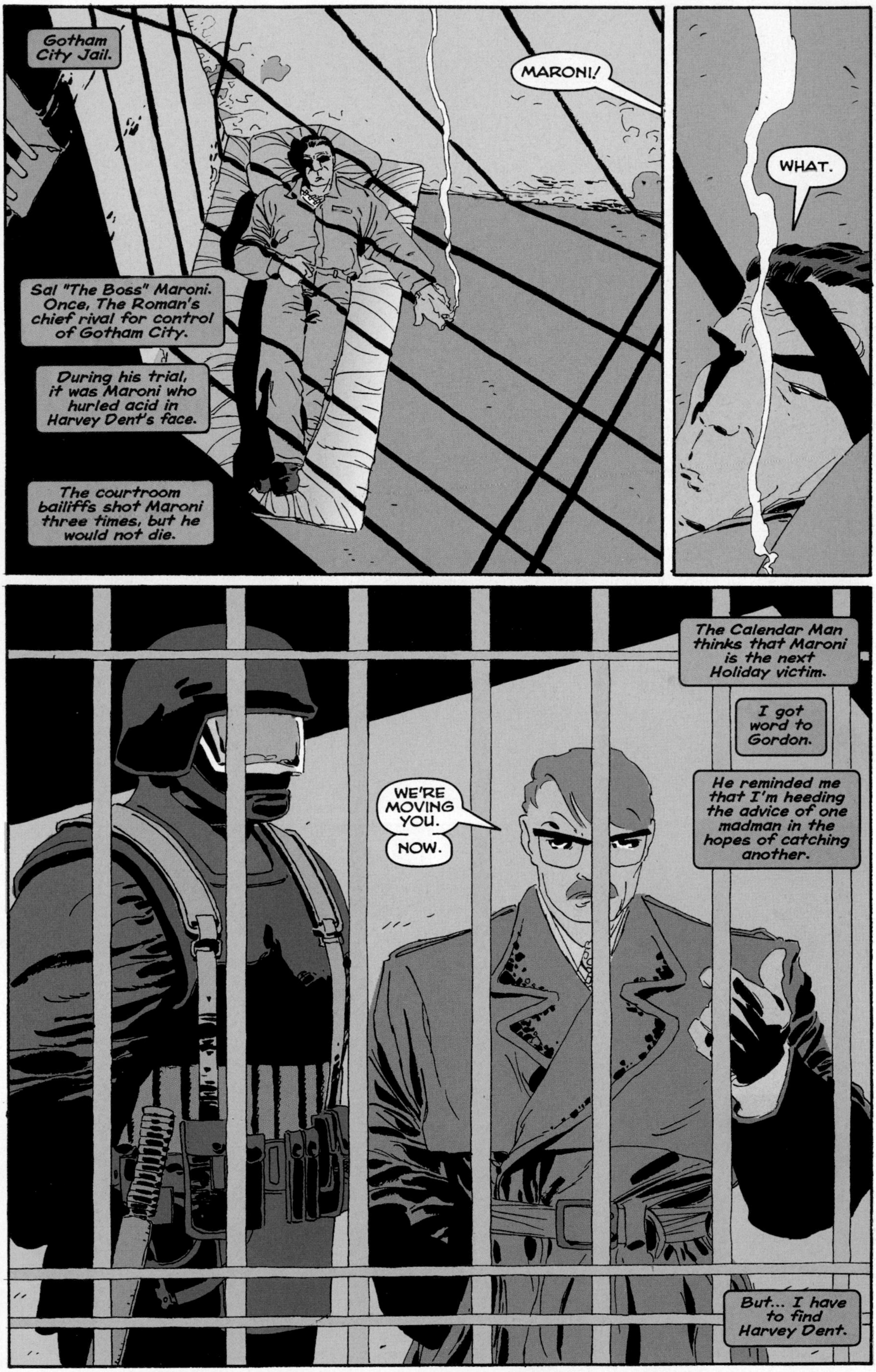
Gotham City Jail.
MARONI!
Sal "The Boss" Maroni. Once, The Roman's chief rival for control of Gotham City.
During his trial, it was Maroni who hurled acid in Harvey Dent's face.
The courtroom bailiffs shot Maroni three times, but he would not die.
WHAT.
The Calendar Man thinks that Maroni is the next Holiday victim.
I got word to Gordon.
WE'RE MOVING YOU.
NOW.
He reminded me that I'm heeding the advice of one madman in the hopes of catching another.
But... I have to find Harvey Dent.

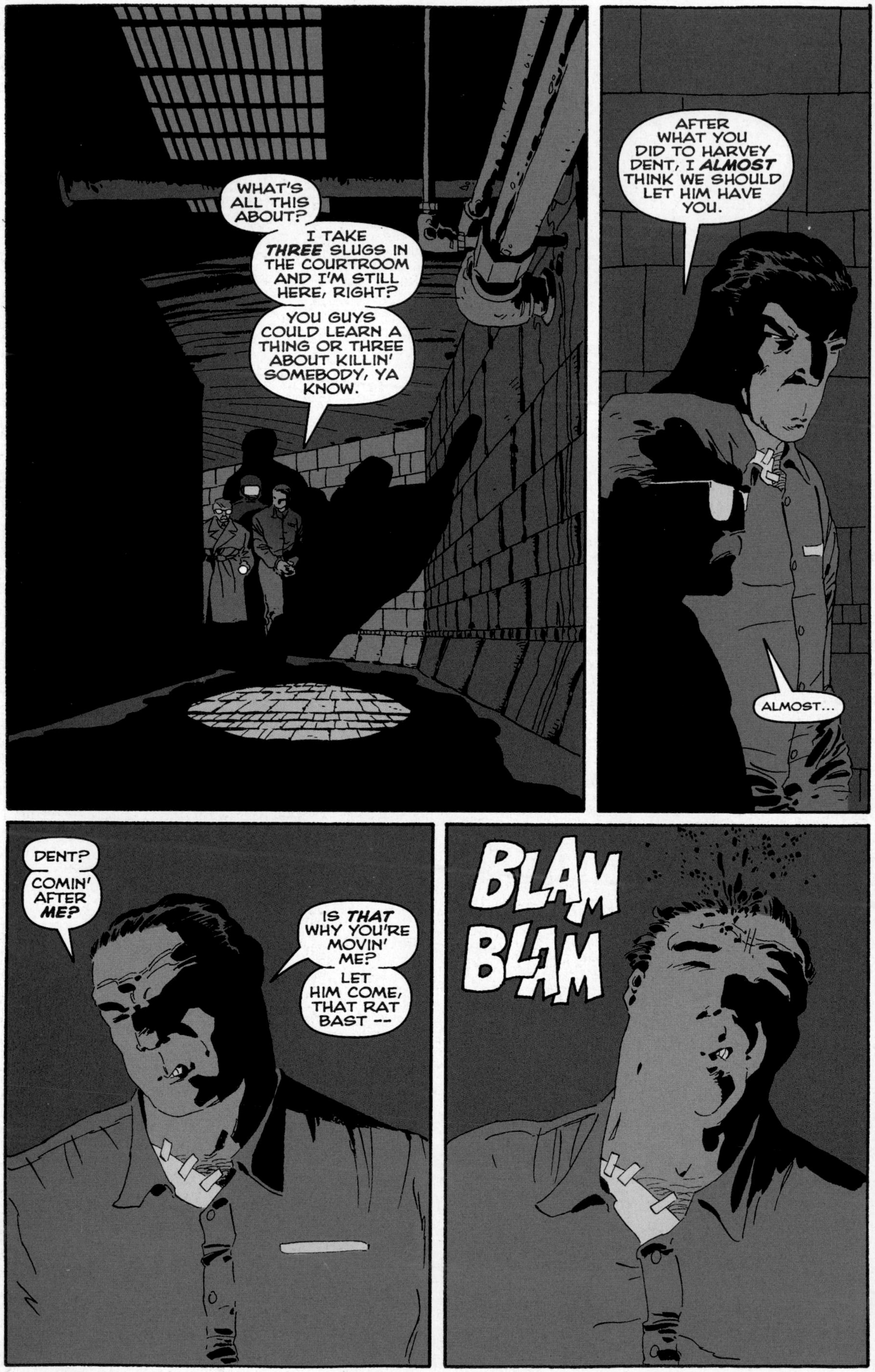
WHAT'S ALL THIS ABOUT?
I TAKE THREE SLUGS IN THE COURTROOM AND I'M STILL HERE, RIGHT?
YOU GUYS COULD LEARN A THING OR THREE ABOUT KILLIN' SOMEBODY, YA KNOW.
AFTER WHAT YOU DID TO HARVEY DENT, I ALMOST THINK WE SHOULD LET HIM HAVE YOU.
ALMOST...
DENT?
COMIN' AFTER ME?
IS THAT WHY YOU'RE MOVIN' ME?
LET HIM COME, THAT RAT BAST --
BLAM
BLAM

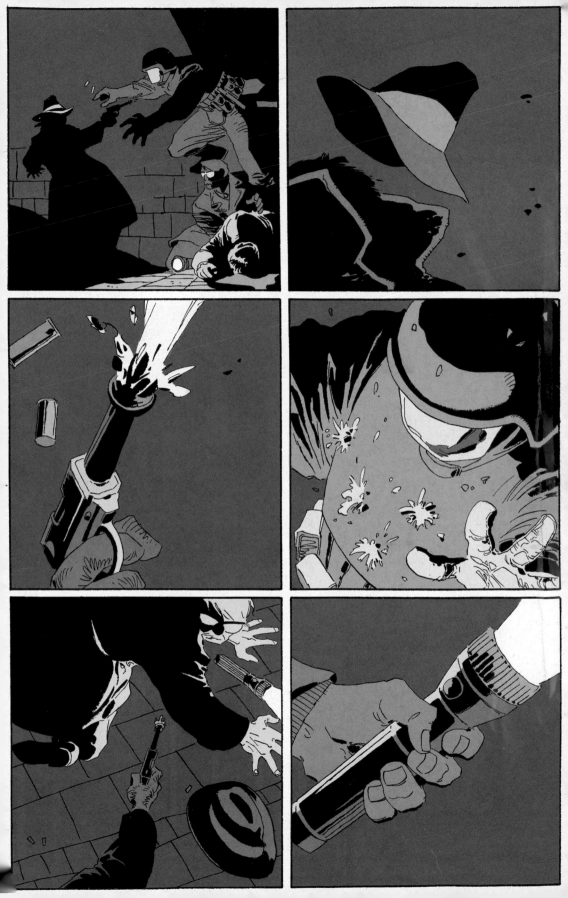

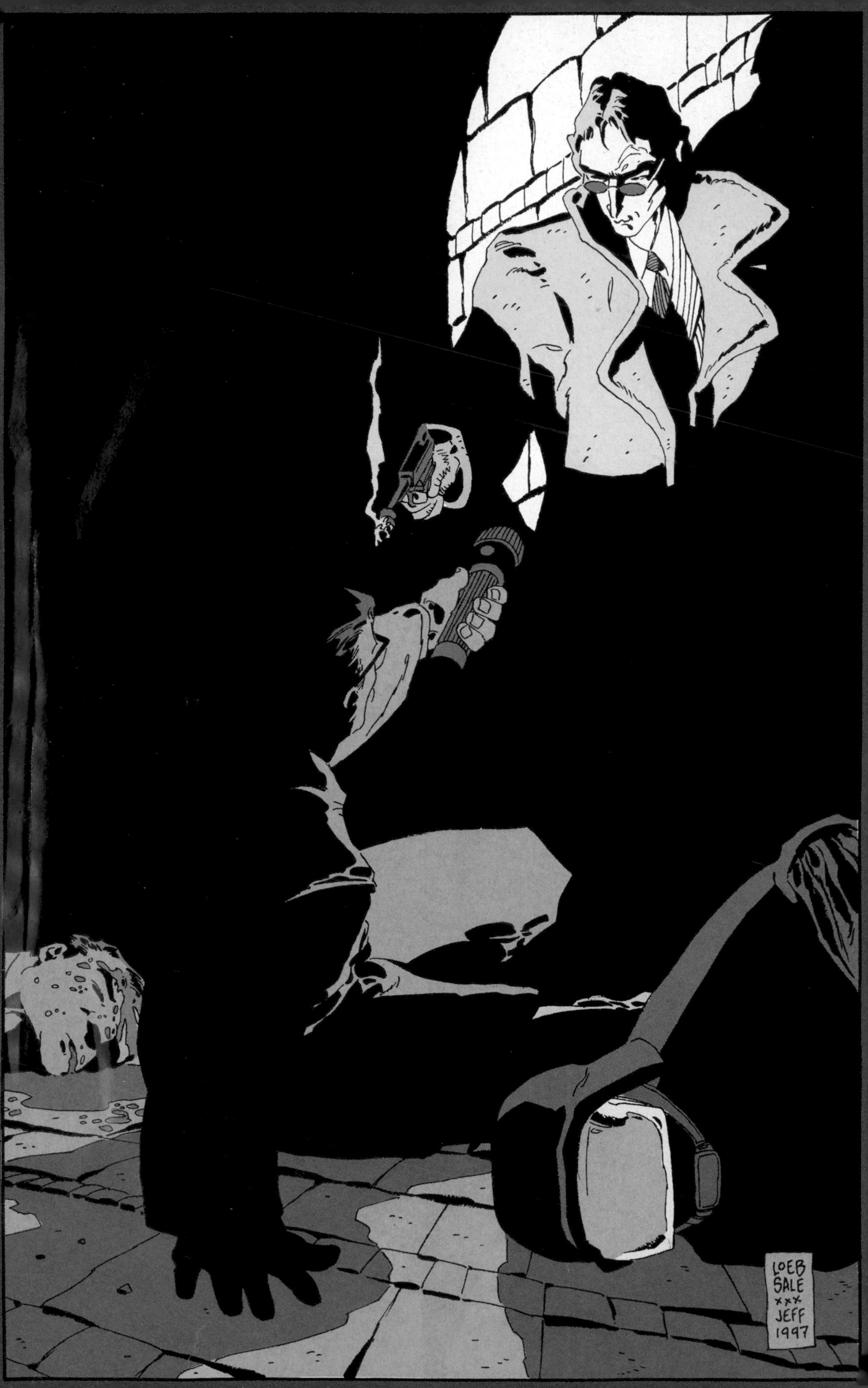
LOEB
SALE
xxx
JEFF
1997

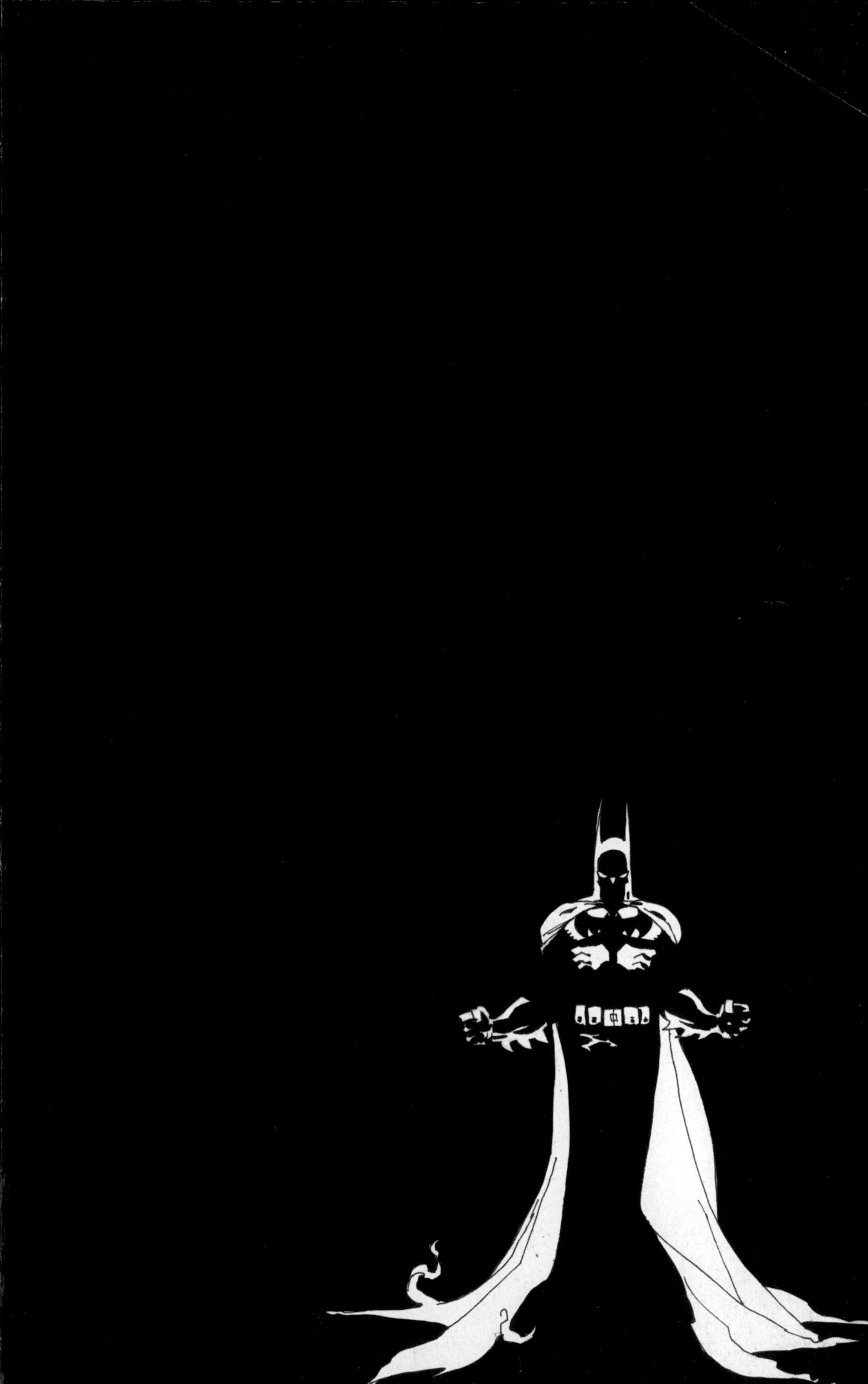

CHAPTER THIRTEEN

PUNISHMENT

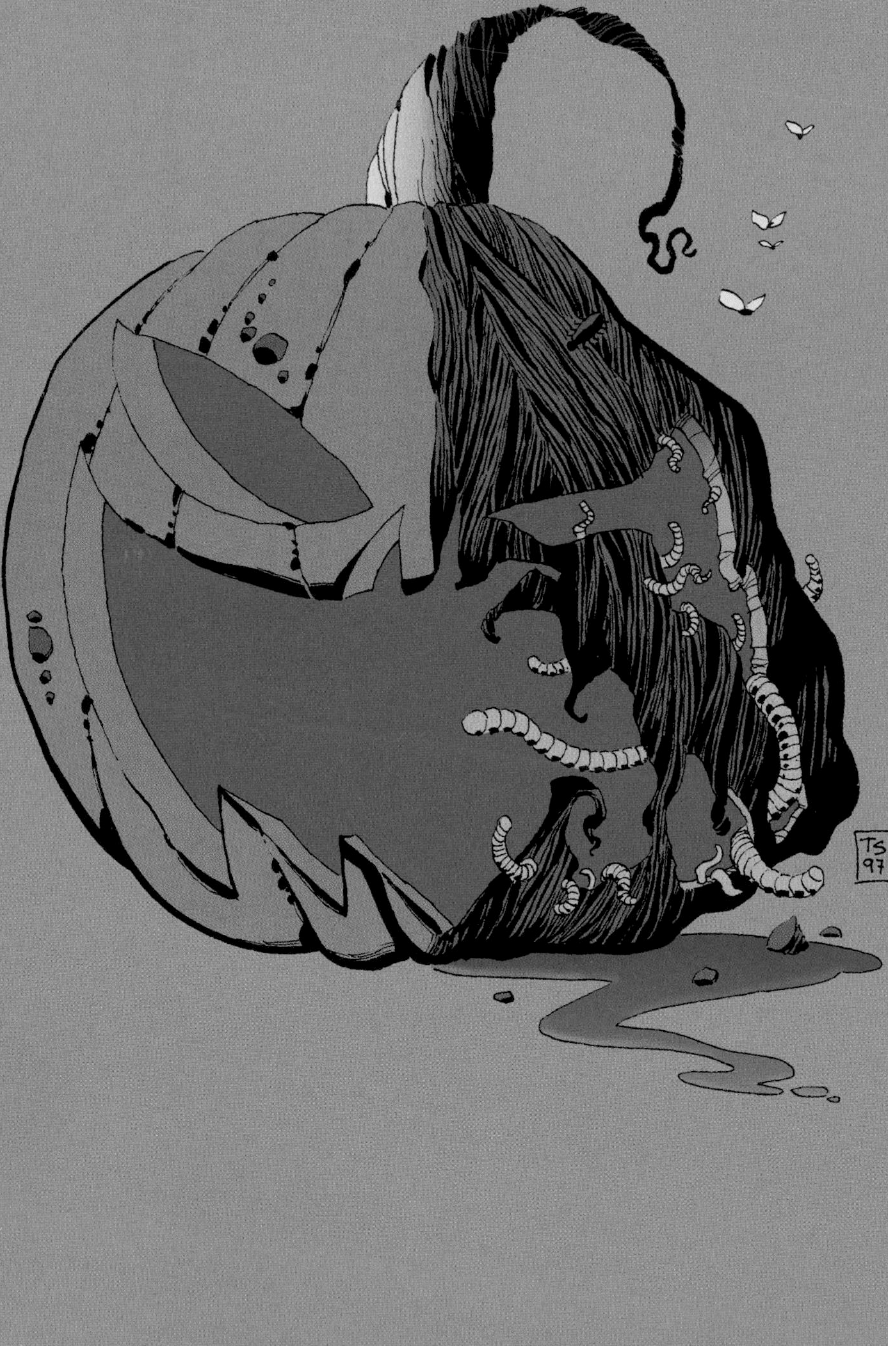
TS
97

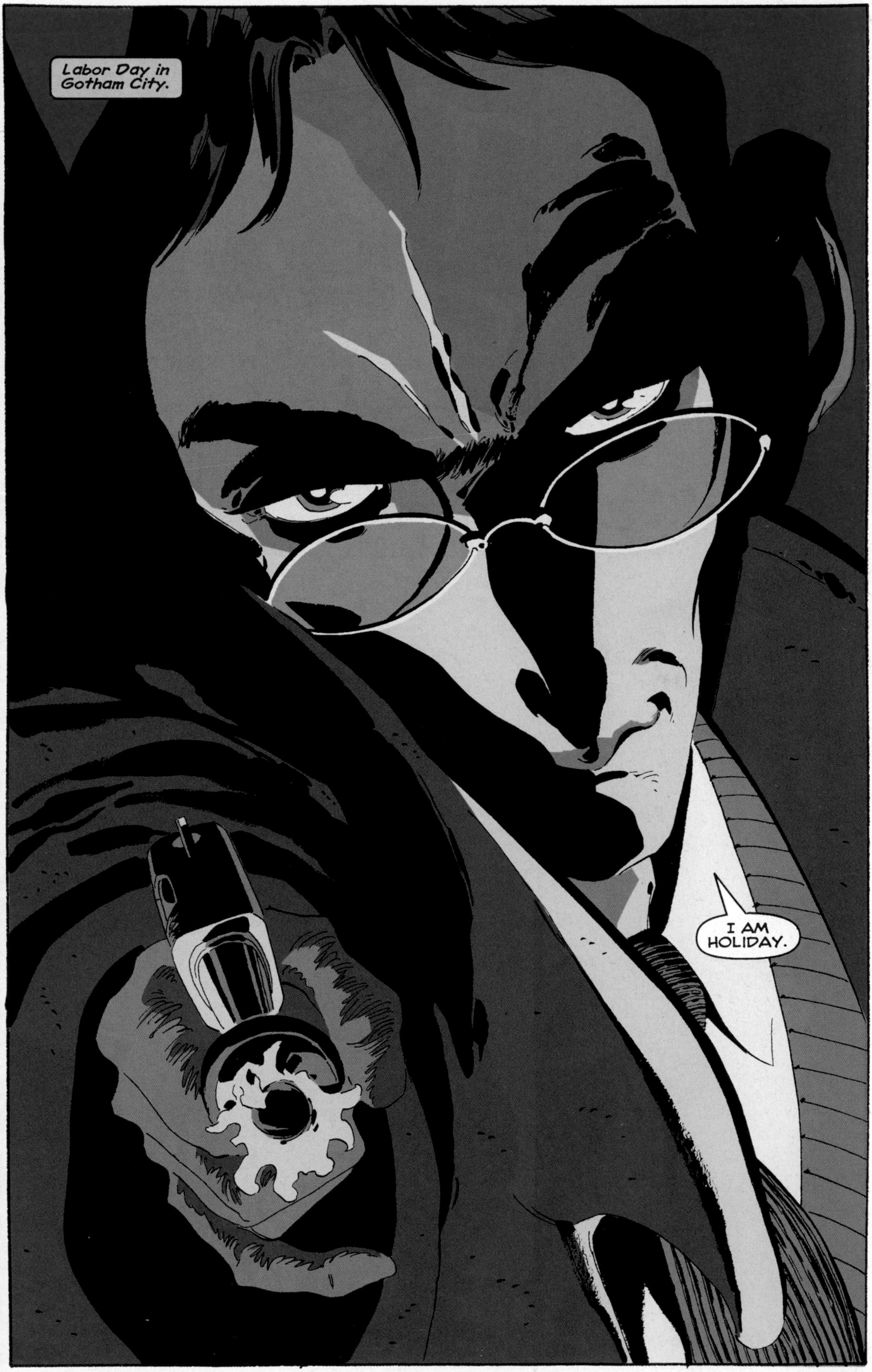
Labor Day in Gotham City.
I AM HOLIDAY.

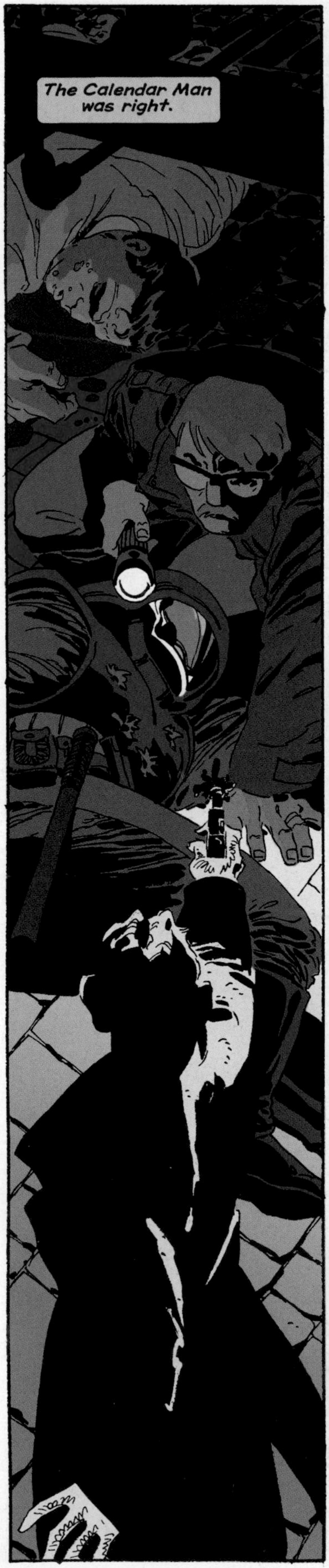
The Calendar Man was right.

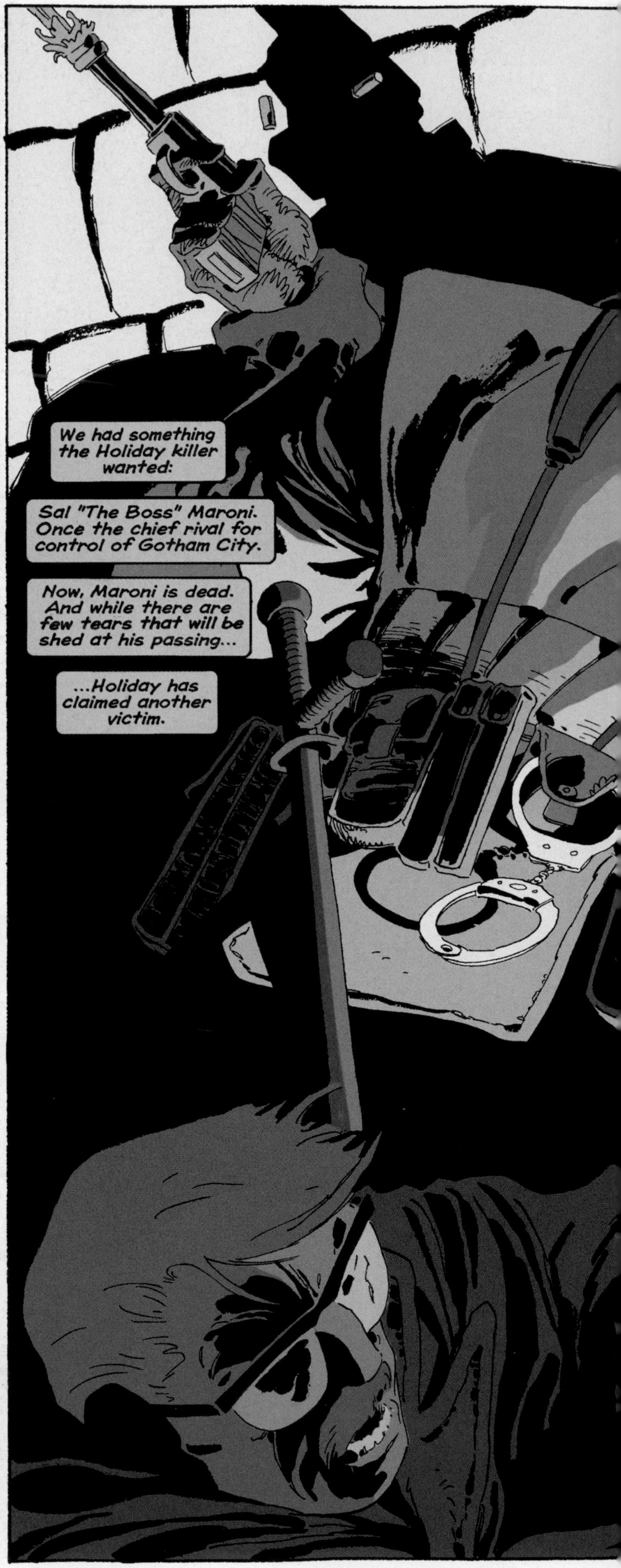
We had something the Holiday killer wanted:
Sal "The Boss" Maroni. Once the chief rival for control of Gotham City.
Now, Maroni is dead. And while there are few tears that will be shed at his passing...
...Holiday has claimed another victim.

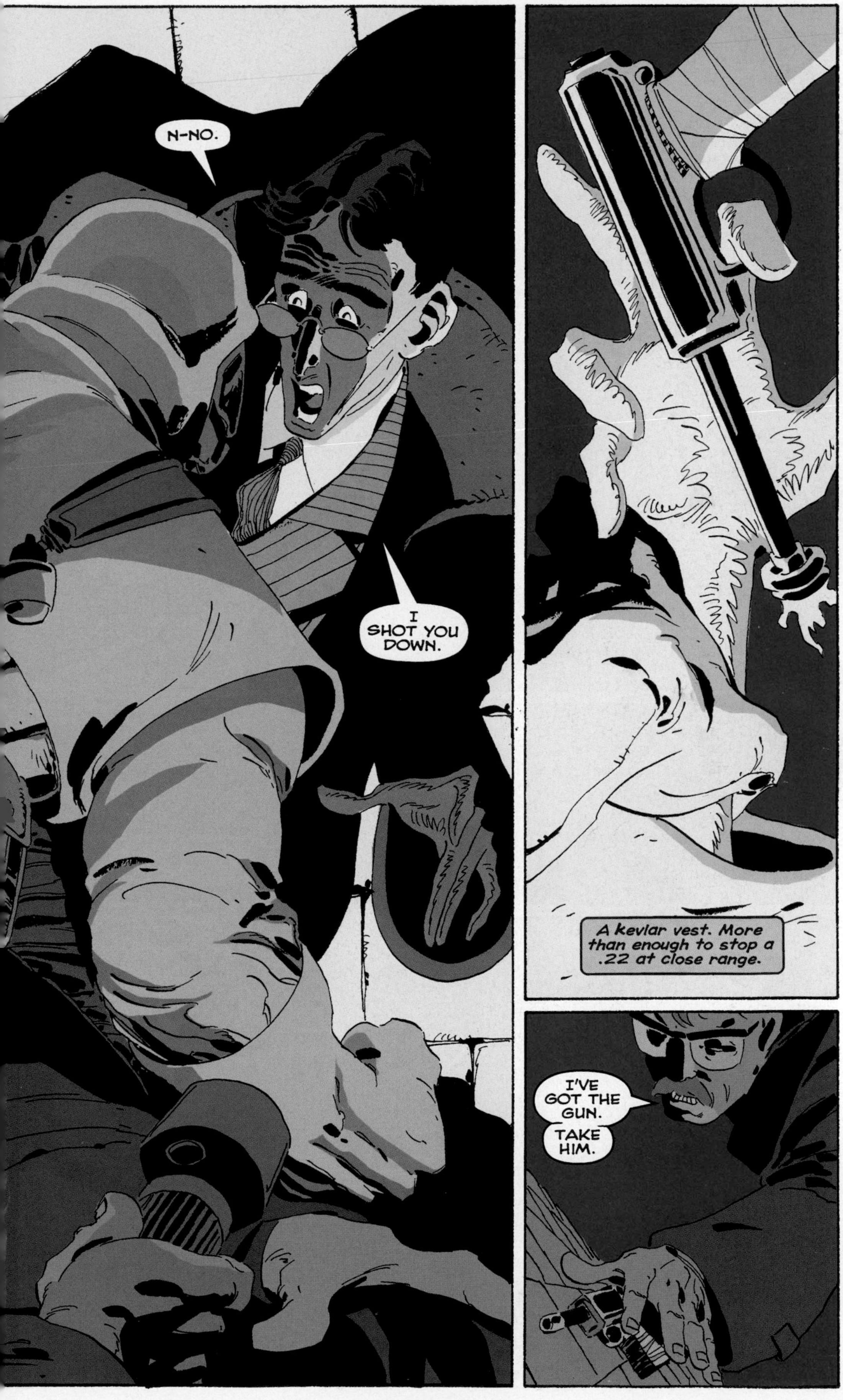
N-NO.
I SHOT YOU DOWN.
A kevlar vest. More than enough to stop a .22 at close range.
I'VE GOT THE GUN.
TAKE HIM.

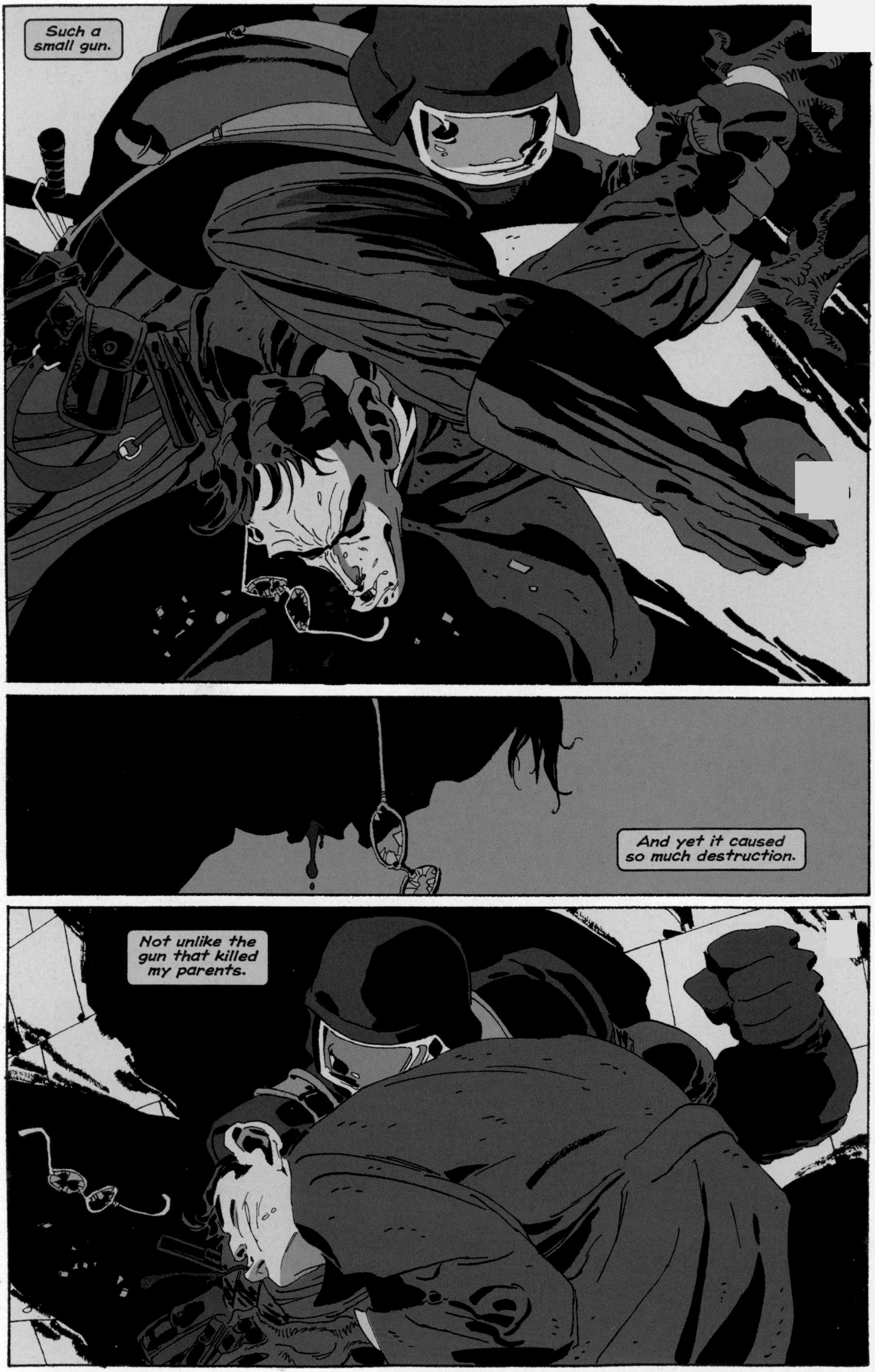
Such a small gun.
And yet it caused so much destruction.
Not unlike the gun that killed my parents.

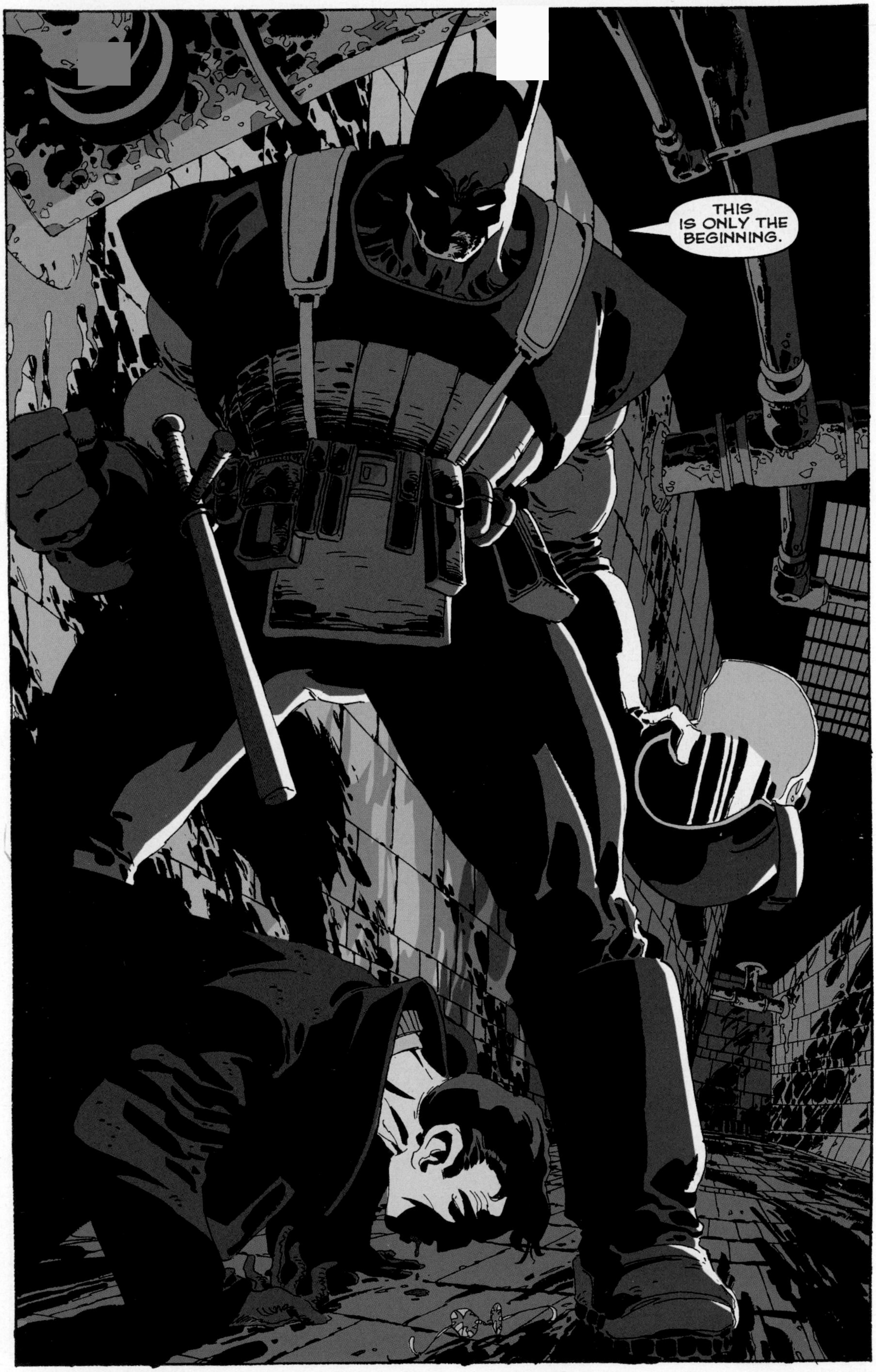
THIS IS ONLY THE BEGINNING.

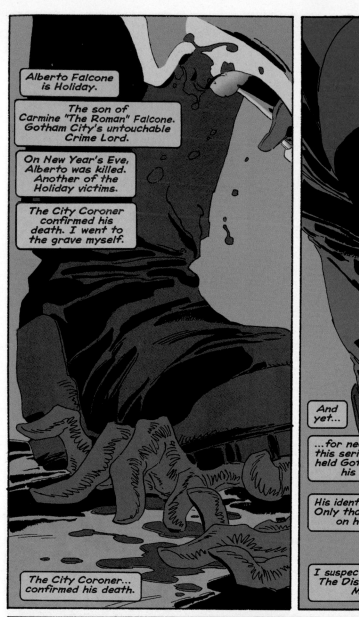

Alberto Falcone is Holiday.

The son of Carmine "The Roman" Falcone. Gotham City's untouchable Crime Lord.

On New Year's Eve, Alberto was killed. Another of the Holiday victims.

The City Coroner confirmed his death. I went to the grave myself.

The City Coroner... confirmed his death.

And yet...

...for nearly a year, this serial killer has held Gotham City in his grasp.

His identity unknown. Only that he struck on holidays.

I suspected Harvey Dent. The District Attorney. My friend.

I was wrong.

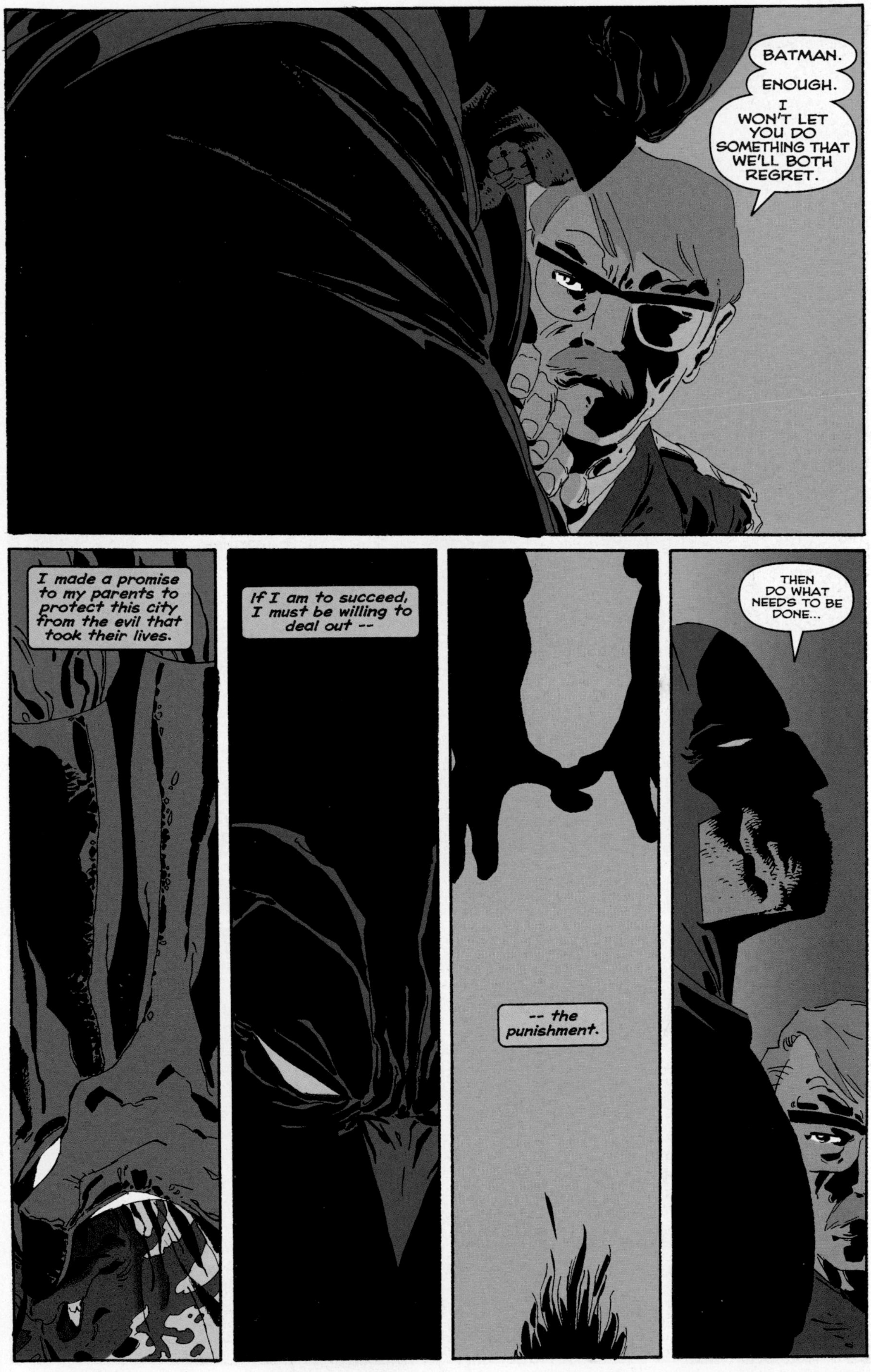
BATMAN.
ENOUGH.
I WON'T LET YOU DO SOMETHING THAT WE'LL BOTH REGRET.
I made a promise to my parents to protect this city from the evil that took their lives.
If I am to succeed, I must be willing to deal out --
-- the punishment.
THEN DO WHAT NEEDS TO BE DONE...

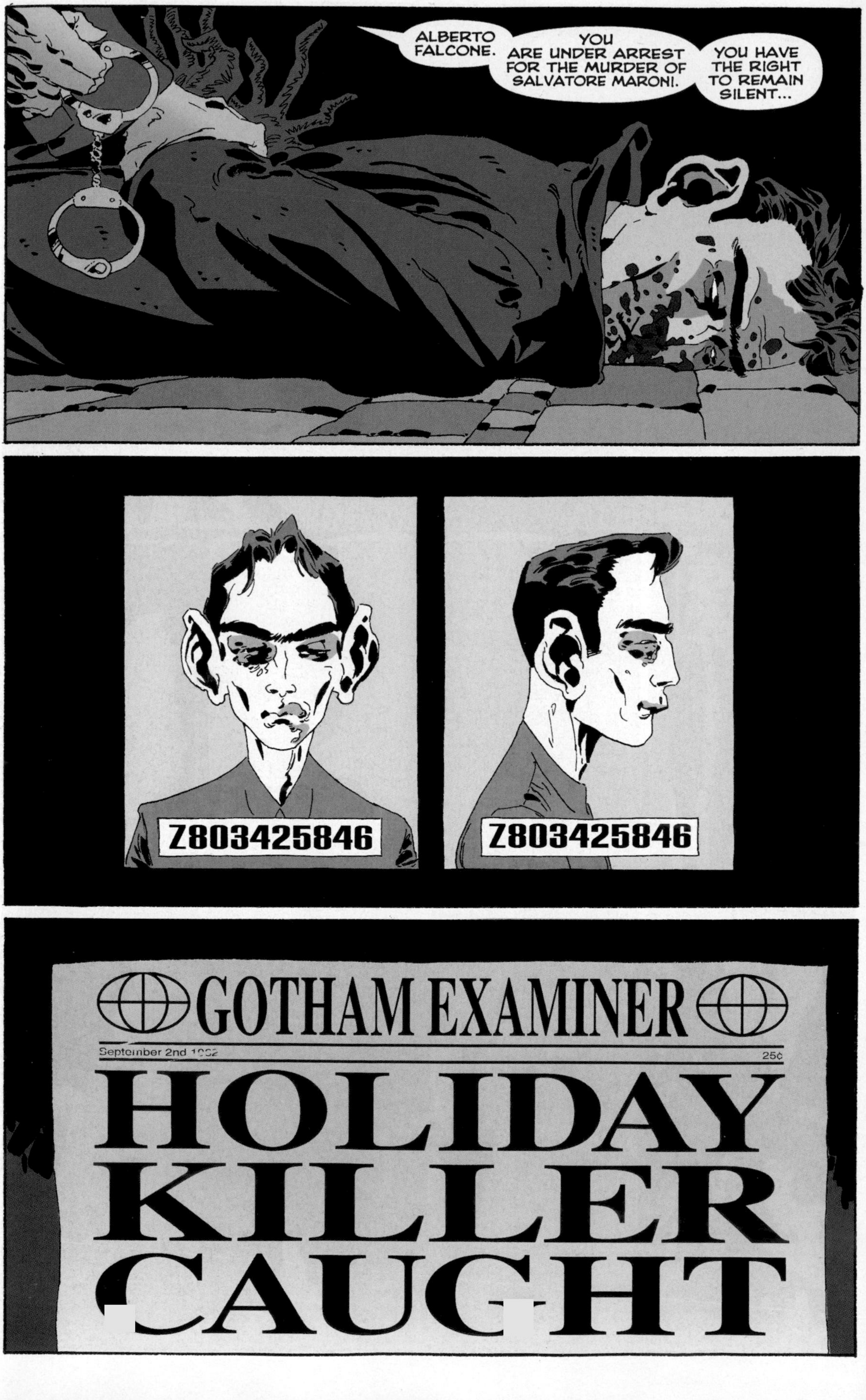
ALBERTO FALCONE.
YOU ARE UNDER ARREST FOR THE MURDER OF SALVATORE MARONI.
YOU HAVE THE RIGHT TO REMAIN SILENT...
Z803425846
Z803425846
GOTHAM EXAMINER
September 2nd
25¢
HOLIDAY KILLER CAUGHT

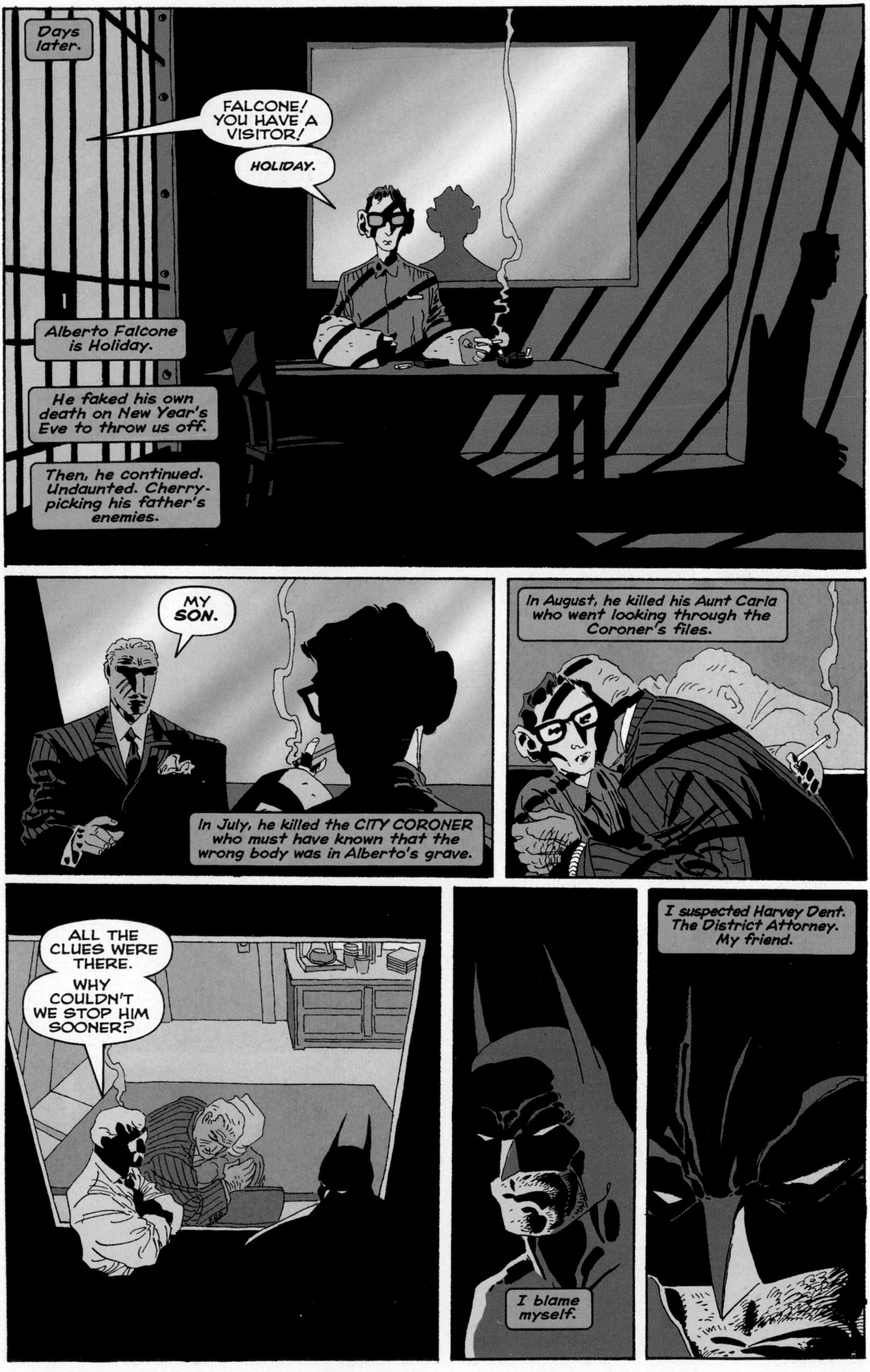
Days later.
FALCONE! YOU HAVE A VISITOR!
HOLIDAY.
Alberto Falcone is Holiday.
He faked his own death on New Year's Eve to throw us off.
Then, he continued. Undaunted. Cherry-picking his father's enemies.
MY SON.
In July, he killed the CITY CORONER who must have known that the wrong body was in Alberto's grave.
In August, he killed his Aunt Carla who went looking through the Coroner's files.
ALL THE CLUES WERE THERE.
WHY COULDN'T WE STOP HIM SOONER?
I blame myself.
I suspected Harvey Dent. The District Attorney. My friend.

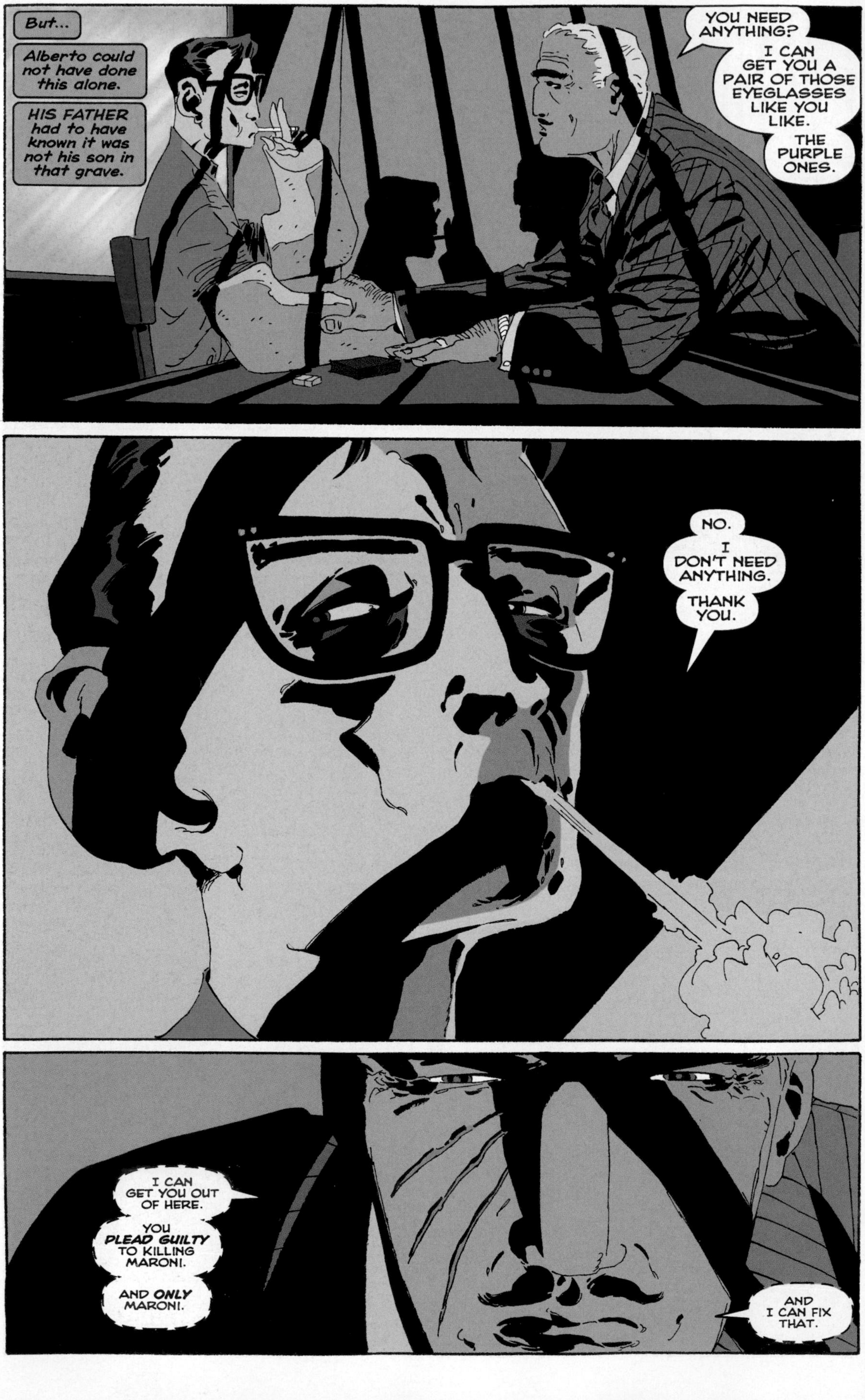
But...
Alberto could not have done this alone.
HIS FATHER had to have known it was not his son in that grave.
YOU NEED ANYTHING?
I CAN GET YOU A PAIR OF THOSE EYEGLASSES LIKE YOU LIKE.
THE PURPLE ONES.
NO.
I DON'T NEED ANYTHING.
THANK YOU.
I CAN GET YOU OUT OF HERE.
YOU PLEAD GUILTY TO KILLING MARONI.
AND ONLY MARONI.
AND I CAN FIX THAT.

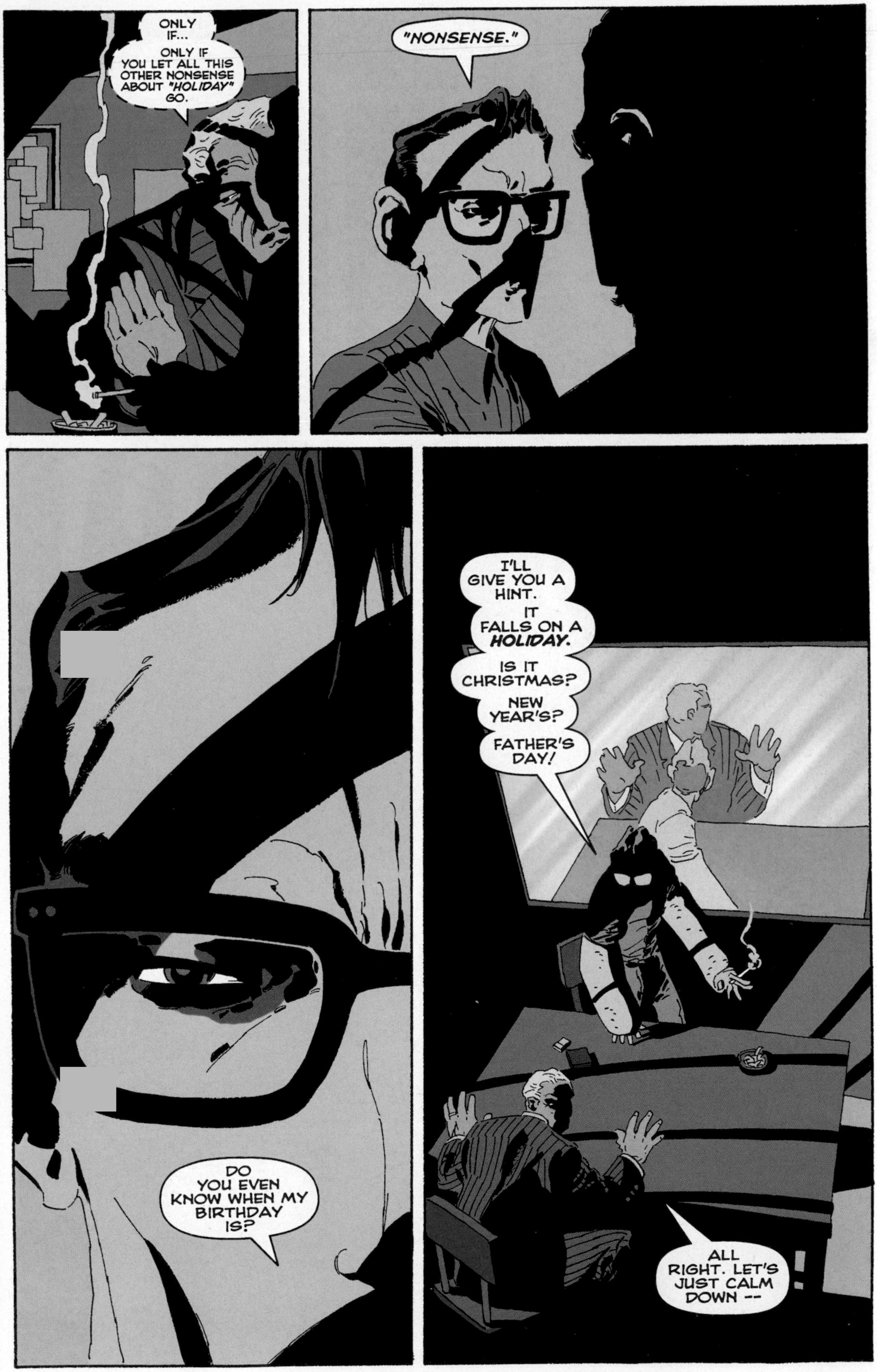
ONLY IF...
ONLY IF YOU LET ALL THIS OTHER NONSENSE ABOUT "HOLIDAY" GO.
"NONSENSE."
DO YOU EVEN KNOW WHEN MY BIRTHDAY IS?
I'LL GIVE YOU A HINT.
IT FALLS ON A HOLIDAY.
IS IT CHRISTMAS?
NEW YEAR'S?
FATHER'S DAY!
ALL RIGHT. LET'S JUST CALM DOWN --

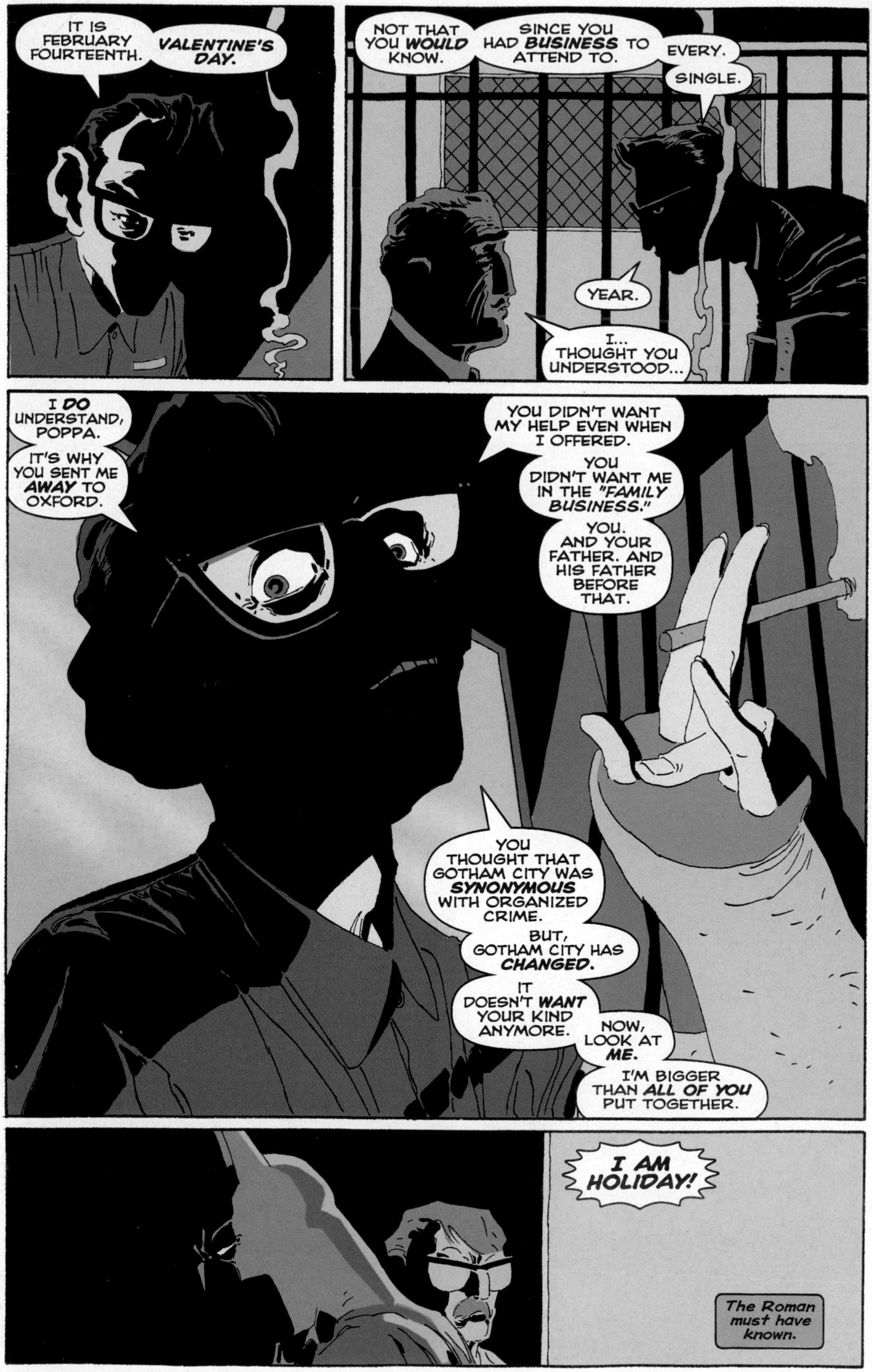
IT IS FEBRUARY FOURTEENTH.
VALENTINE'S DAY.
NOT THAT YOU WOULD KNOW.
SINCE YOU HAD BUSINESS TO ATTEND TO.
EVERY.
SINGLE.
YEAR.
I... THOUGHT YOU UNDERSTOOD...
I DO UNDERSTAND, POPPA.
IT'S WHY YOU SENT ME AWAY TO OXFORD.
YOU DIDN'T WANT MY HELP EVEN WHEN I OFFERED.
YOU DIDN'T WANT ME IN THE "FAMILY BUSINESS."
YOU. AND YOUR FATHER. AND HIS FATHER BEFORE THAT.
YOU THOUGHT THAT GOTHAM CITY WAS SYNONYMOUS WITH ORGANIZED CRIME.
BUT, GOTHAM CITY HAS CHANGED.
IT DOESN'T WANT YOUR KIND ANYMORE.
NOW, LOOK AT ME.
I'M BIGGER THAN ALL OF YOU PUT TOGETHER.
I AM HOLIDAY!
The Roman must have known.

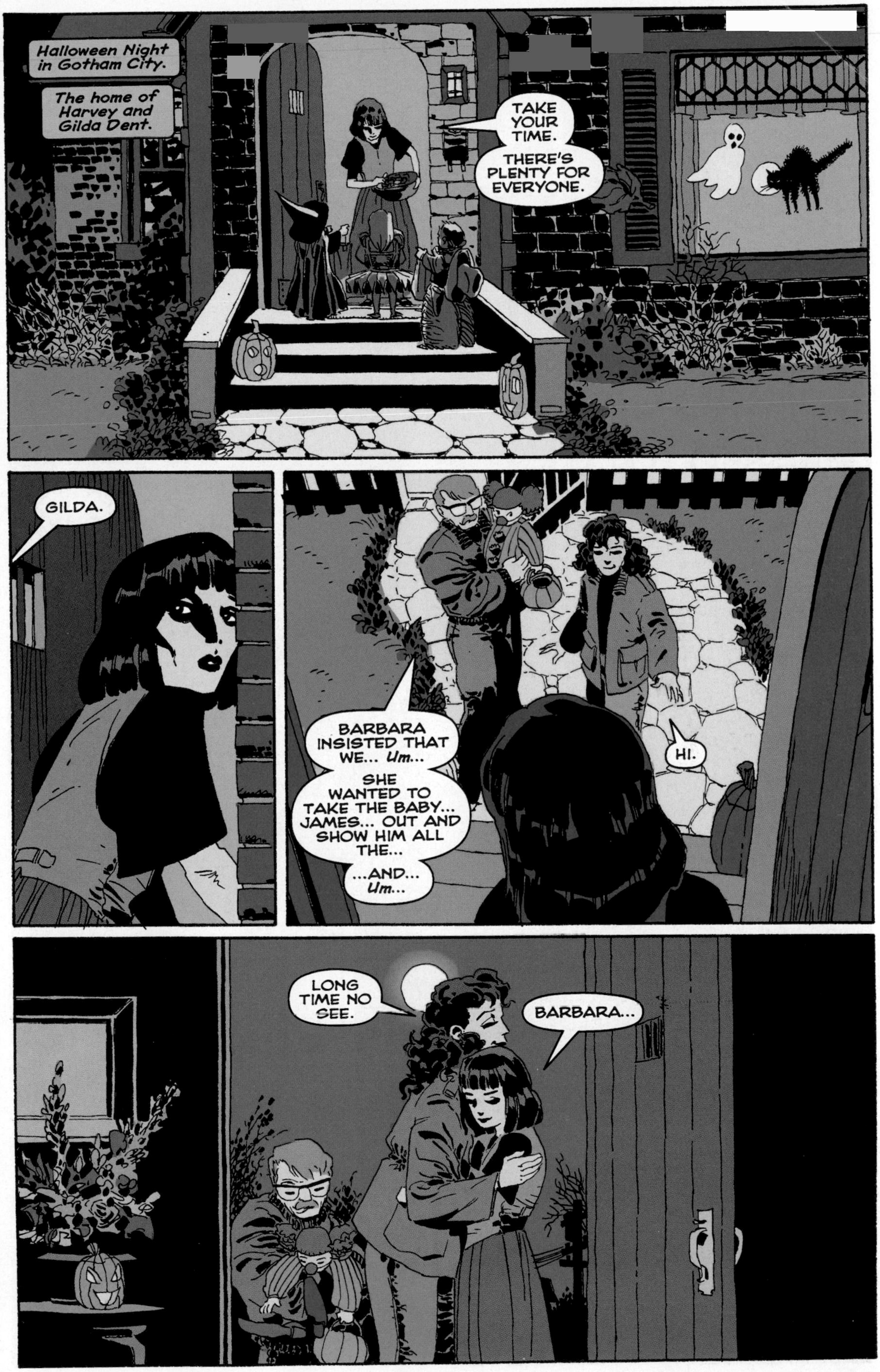

Halloween Night in Gotham City.
The home of Harvey and Gilda Dent.
TAKE YOUR TIME.
THERE'S PLENTY FOR EVERYONE.
GILDA.
BARBARA INSISTED THAT WE... Um...
SHE WANTED TO TAKE THE BABY... JAMES... OUT AND SHOW HIM ALL THE...
...AND... Um...
HI.
LONG TIME NO SEE.
BARBARA...

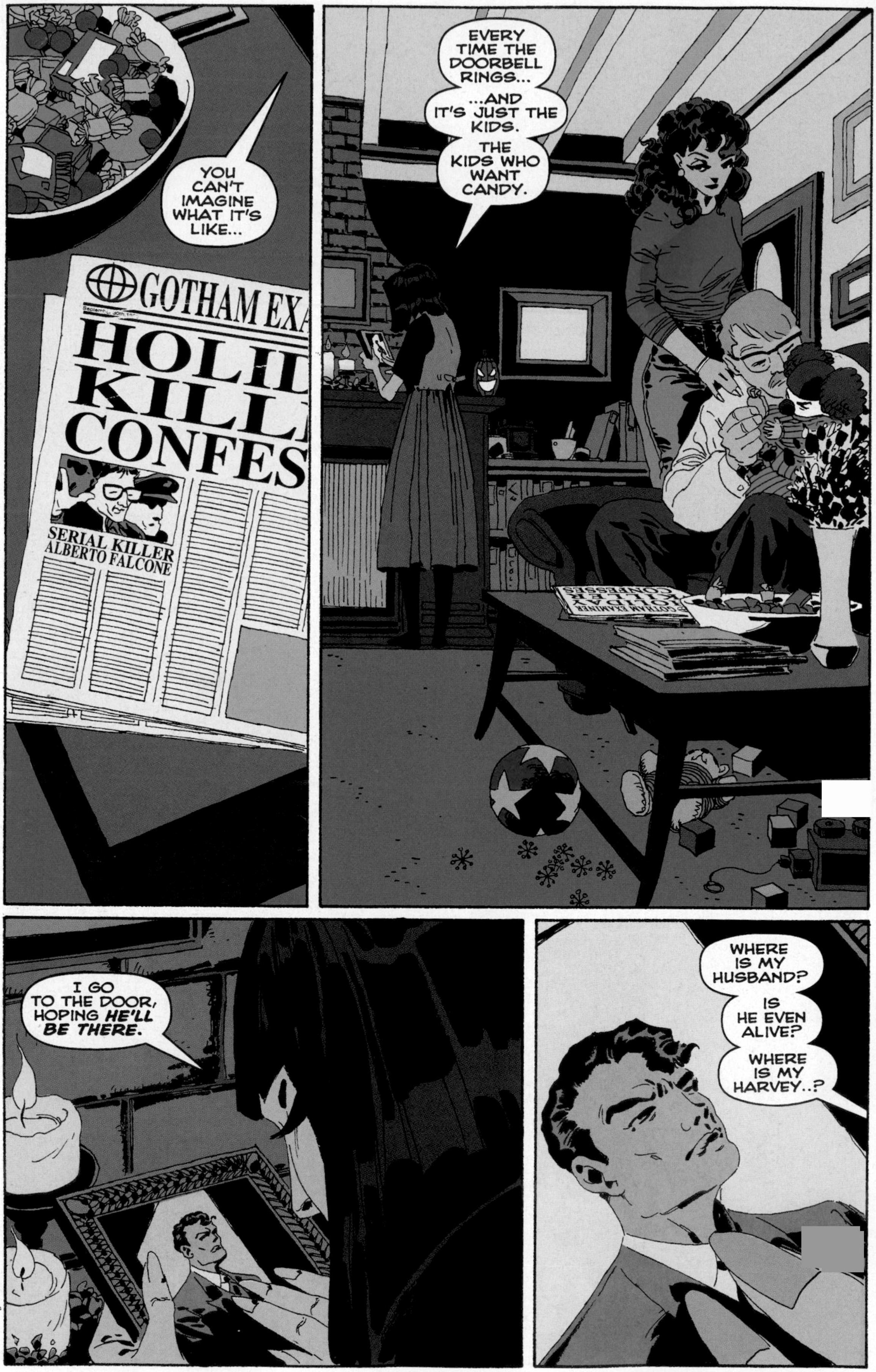
YOU CAN'T IMAGINE WHAT IT'S LIKE...
GOTHAM EXA
HOLID
KILLI
CONFES
SERIAL KILLER ALBERTO FALCONE
EVERY TIME THE DOORBELL RINGS...
...AND IT'S JUST THE KIDS.
THE KIDS WHO WANT CANDY.
I GO TO THE DOOR, HOPING HE'LL BE THERE.
WHERE IS MY HUSBAND?
IS HE EVEN ALIVE?
WHERE IS MY HARVEY..?

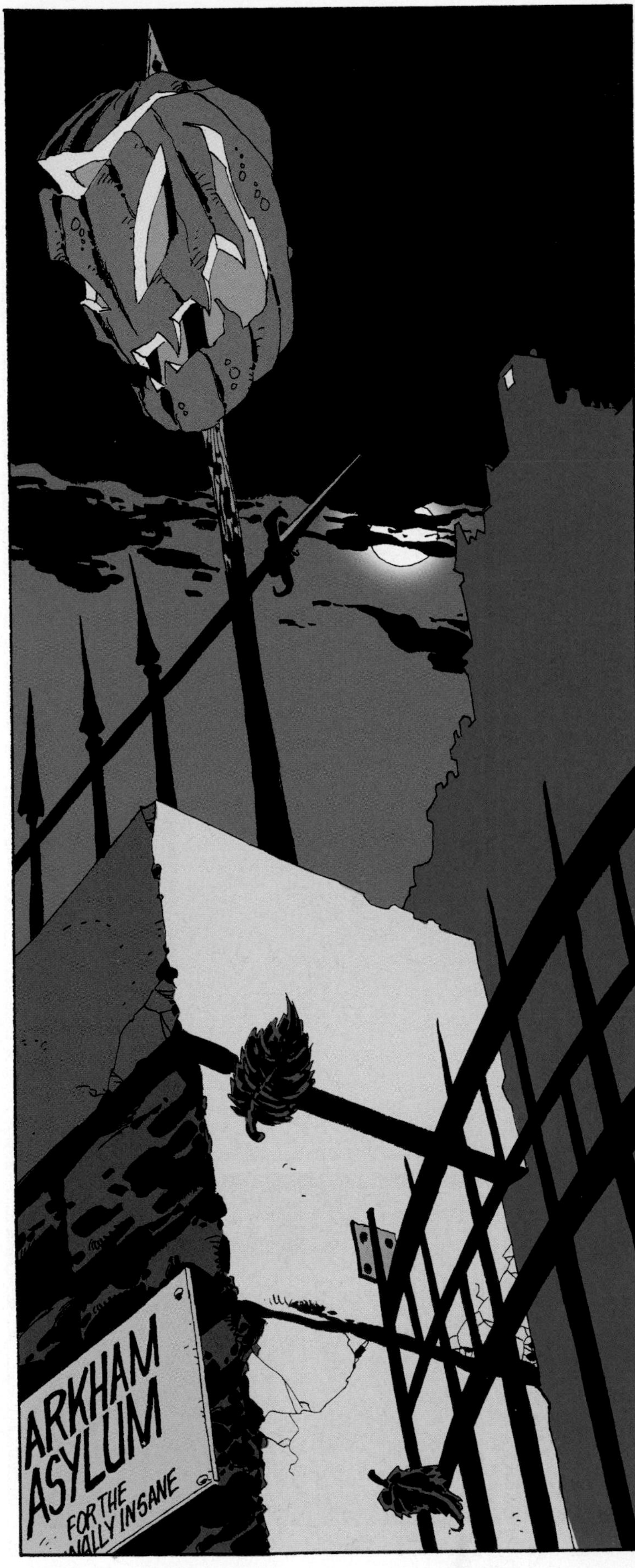
ARKHAM ASYLUM
FOR THE
WALLY INSANE
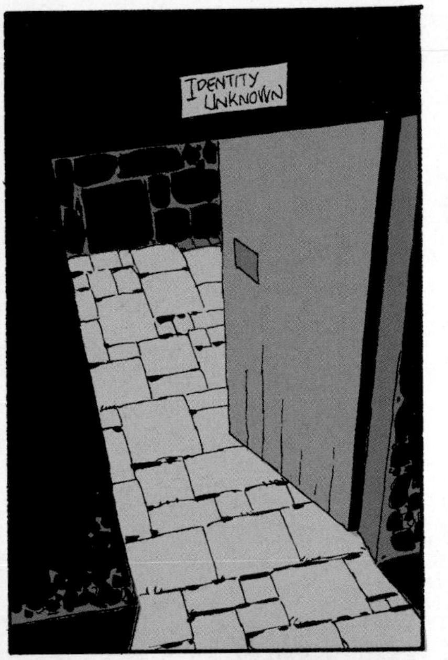
IDENTITY
UNKNOWN
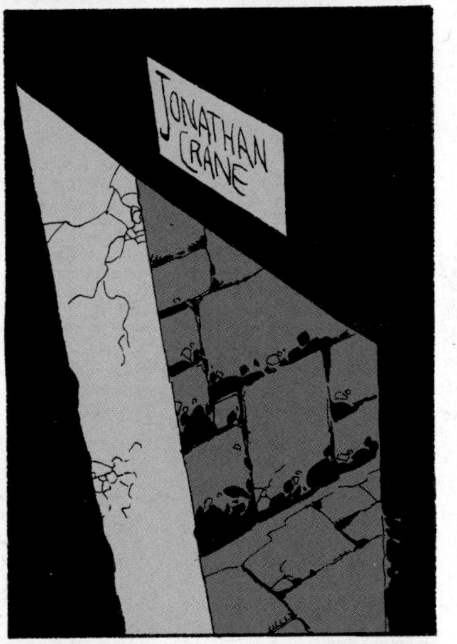
JONATHAN
CRANE
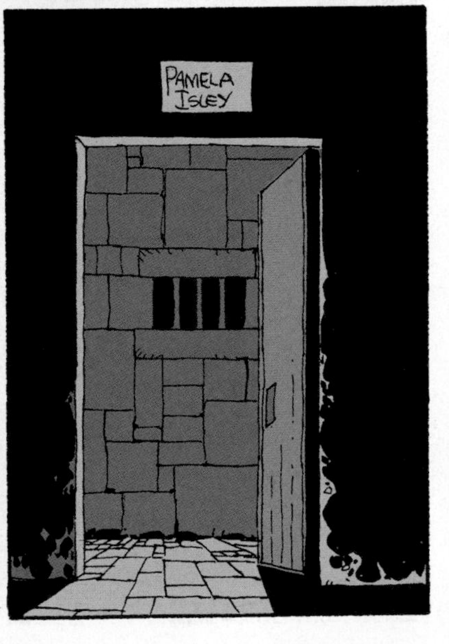
PAMELA
ISLEY

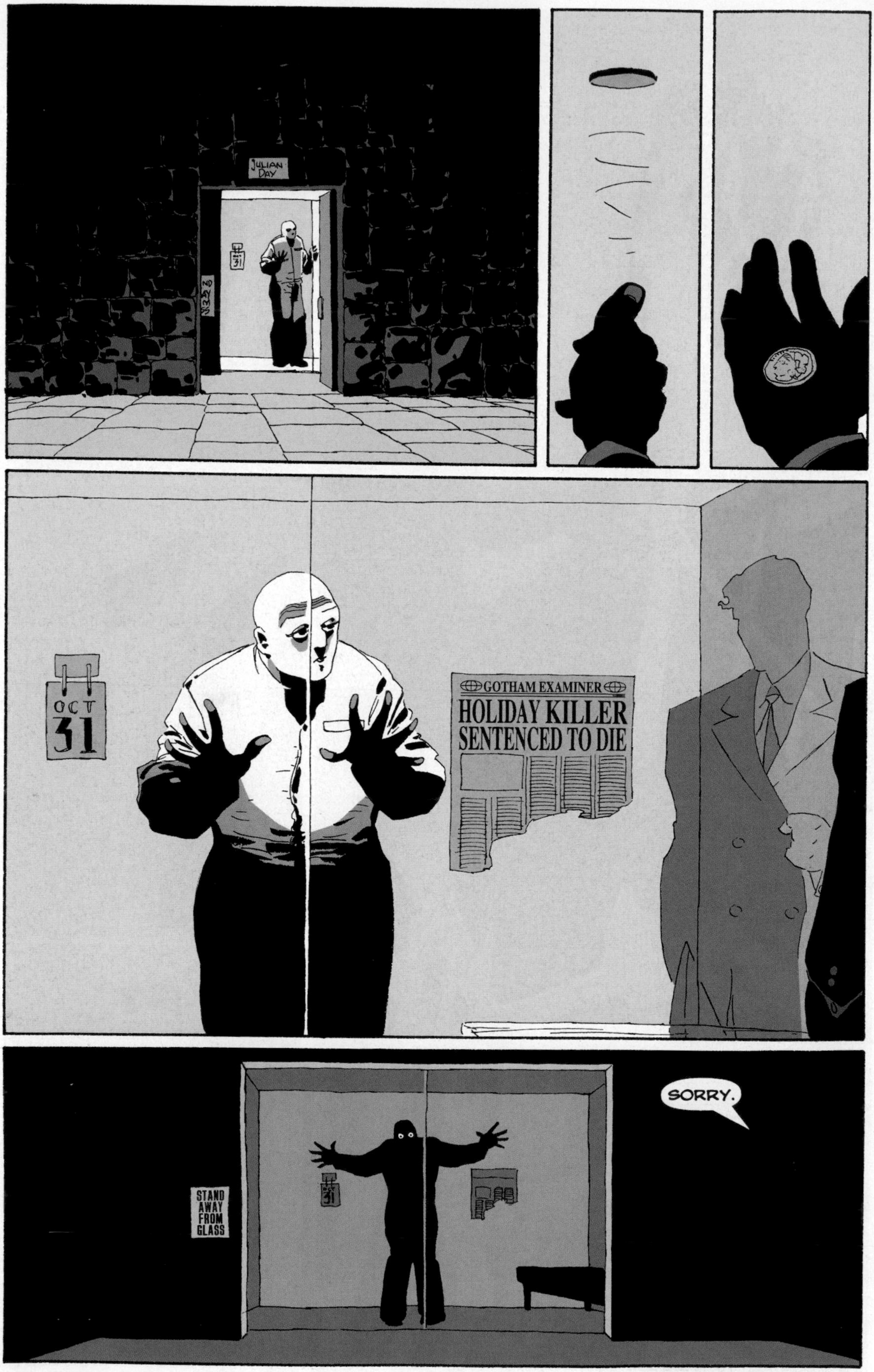
JULIAN DAY
OCT 31
GOTHAM EXAMINER
HOLIDAY KILLER SENTENCED TO DIE
SORRY.
STAND AWAY FROM GLASS

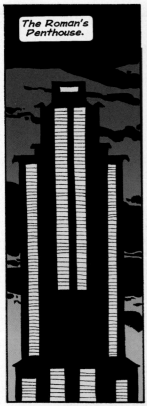

The Roman's Penthouse.

HOW DARE HE DEFY ME?!

MY OWN SON!

HE'S GOING TO THE GAS CHAMBER WHEN I COULD HAVE STOPPED THE WHOLE THING!

ALBERTO...

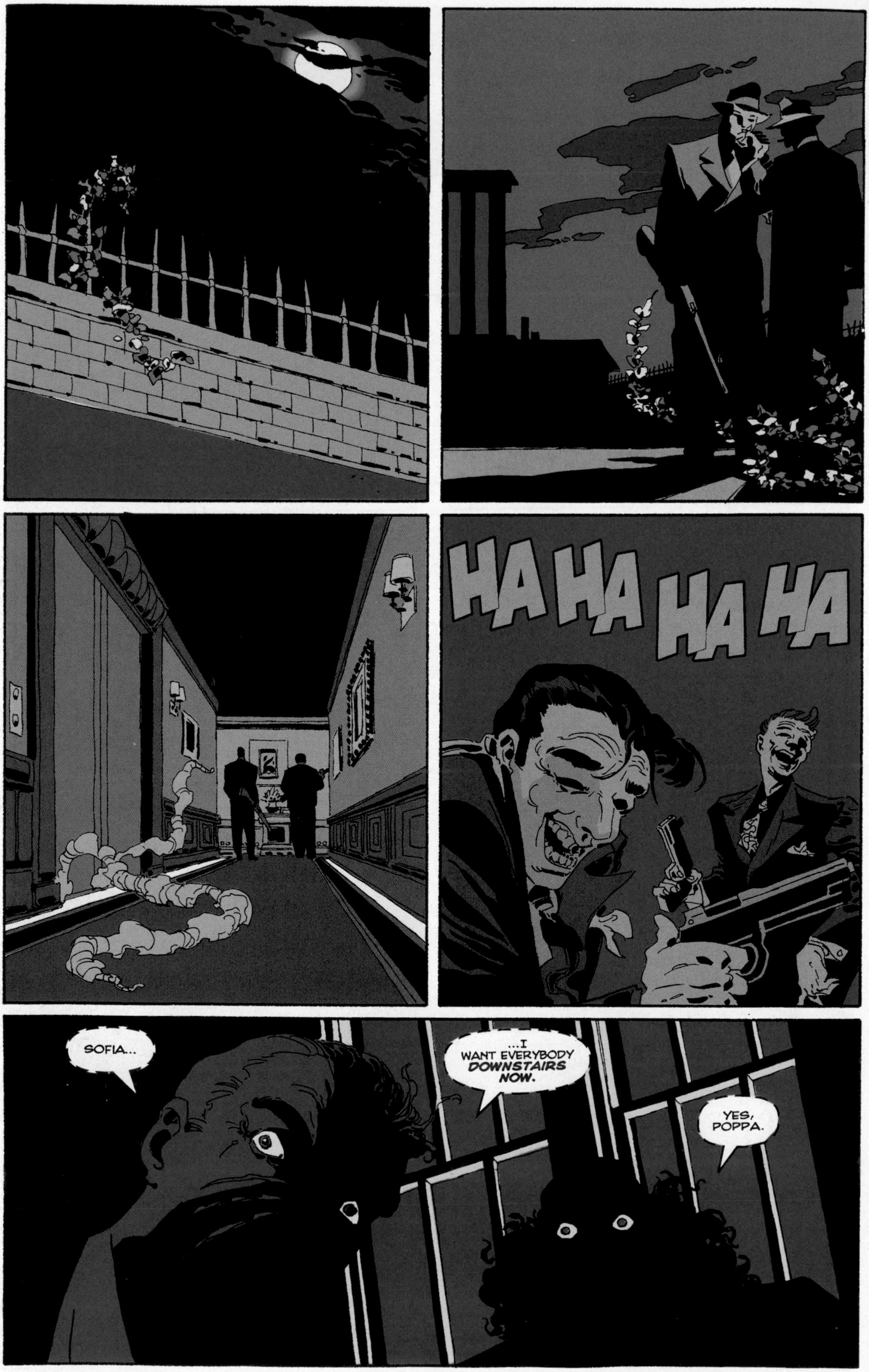
HA HA HA HA
SOFIA...
...I WANT EVERYBODY *DOWNSTAIRS NOW.*
YES, POPPA.

THIS IS BAD.

BAD.

VERY BAD.

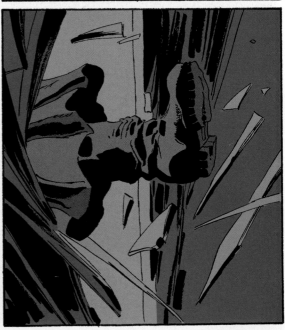

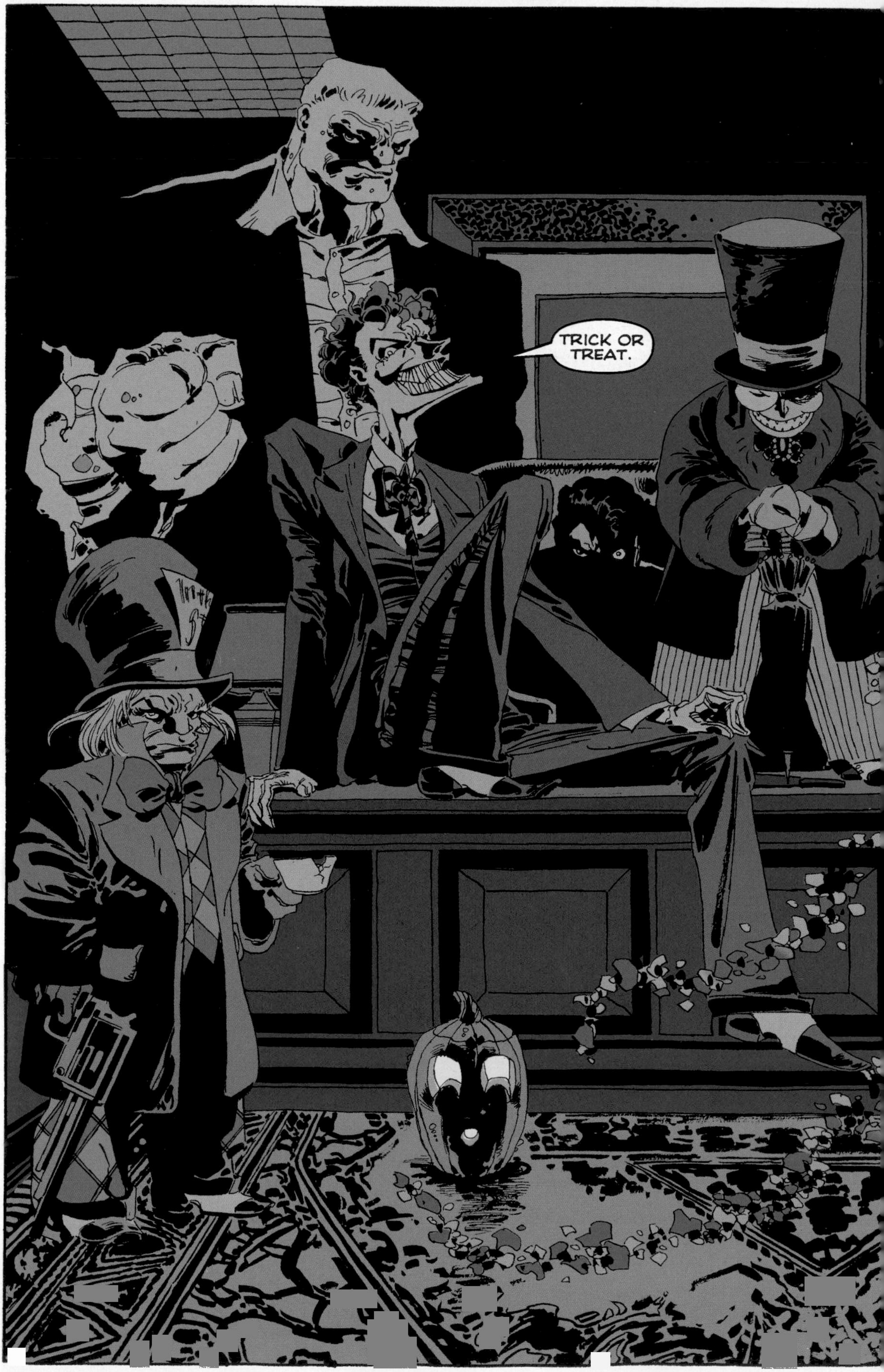
TRICK OR TREAT.

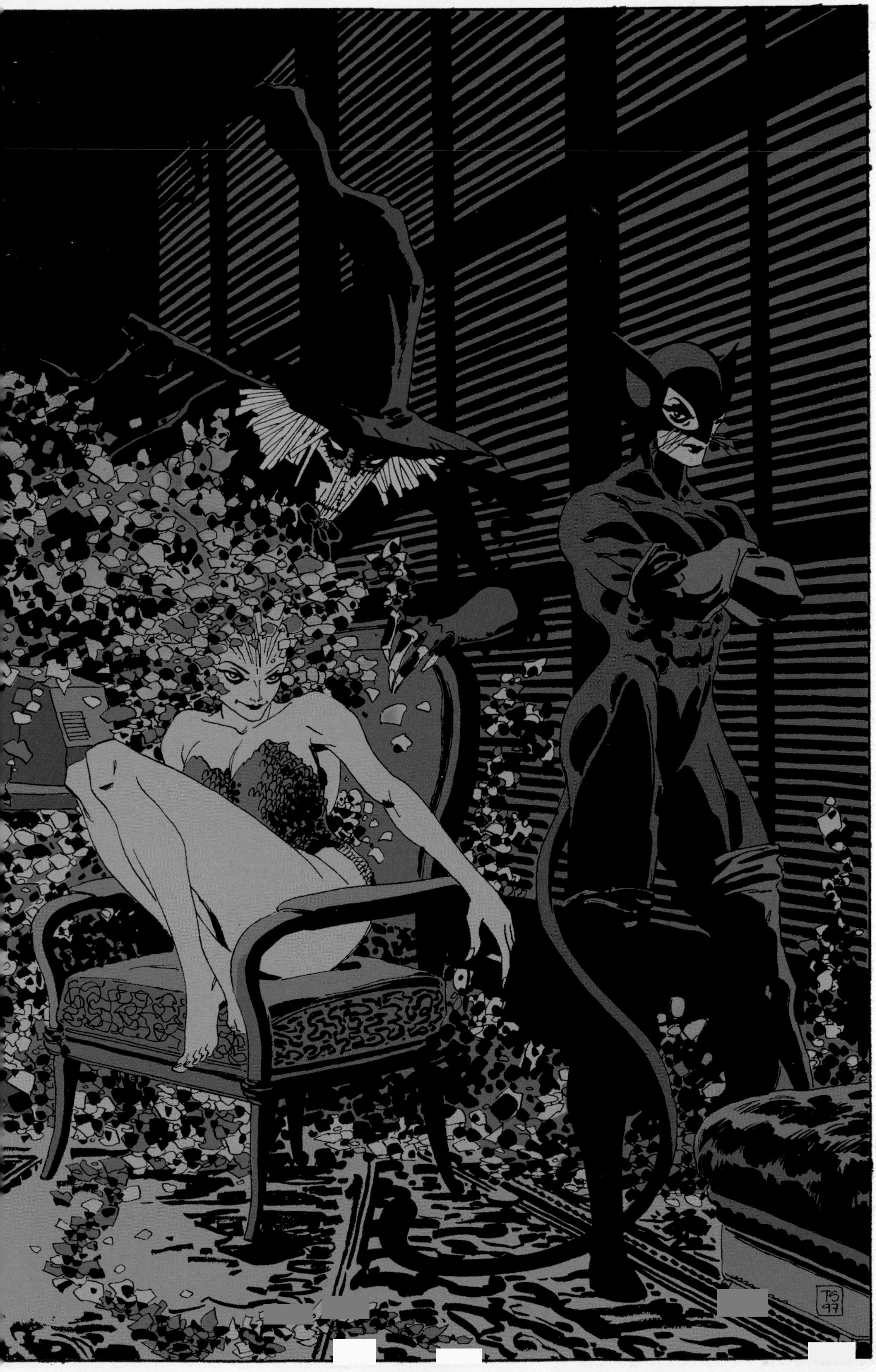

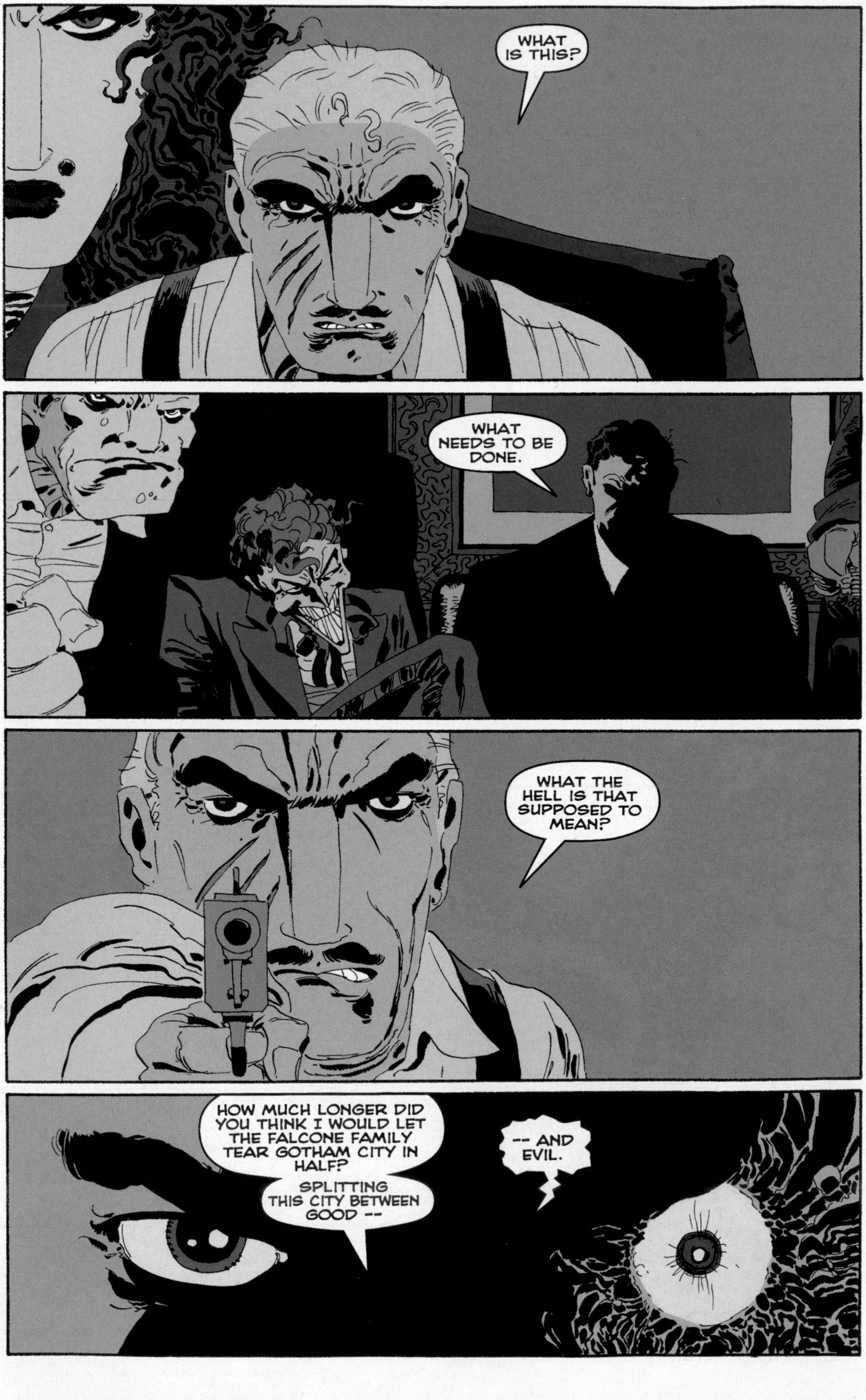
WHAT IS THIS?
WHAT NEEDS TO BE DONE.
WHAT THE HELL IS THAT SUPPOSED TO MEAN?
HOW MUCH LONGER DID YOU THINK I WOULD LET THE FALCONE FAMILY TEAR GOTHAM CITY IN HALF?
SPLITTING THIS CITY BETWEEN GOOD --
-- AND EVIL.

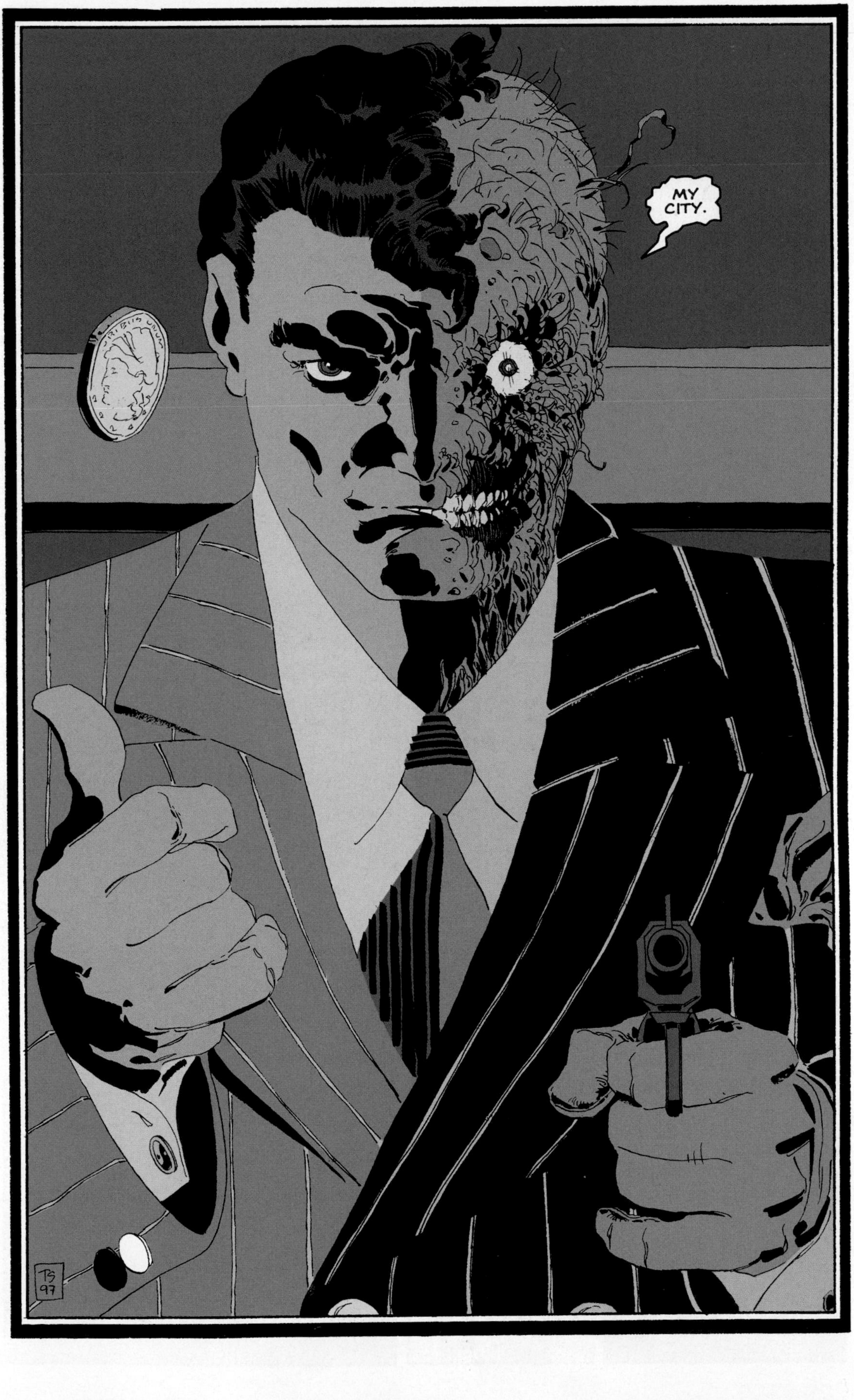
MY CITY.

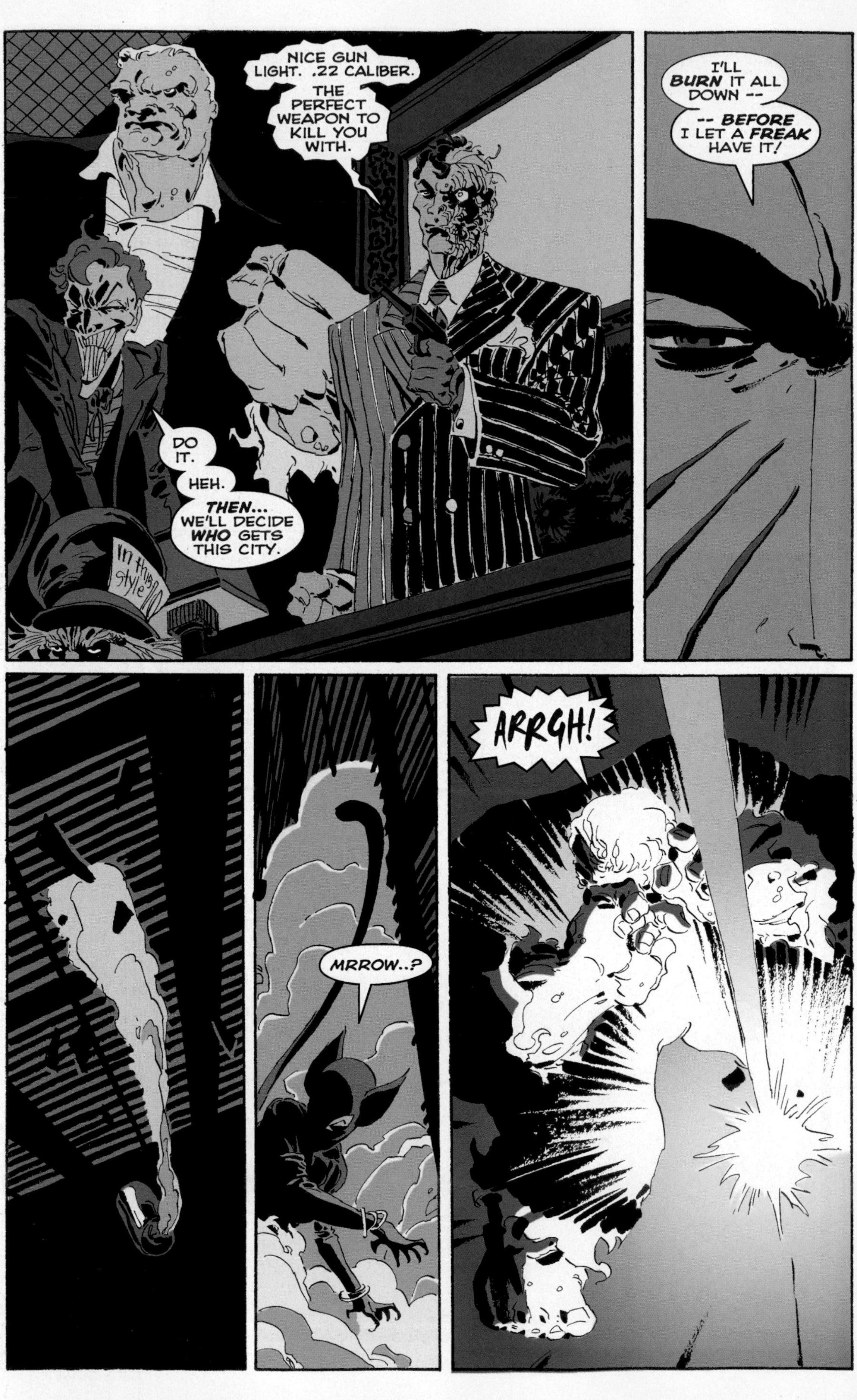

NICE GUN LIGHT. .22 CALIBER.
THE PERFECT WEAPON TO KILL YOU WITH.
DO IT.
HEH.
THEN... WE'LL DECIDE WHO GETS THIS CITY.
I'LL BURN IT ALL DOWN --
-- BEFORE I LET A FREAK HAVE IT!
MRROW..?
ARRGH!

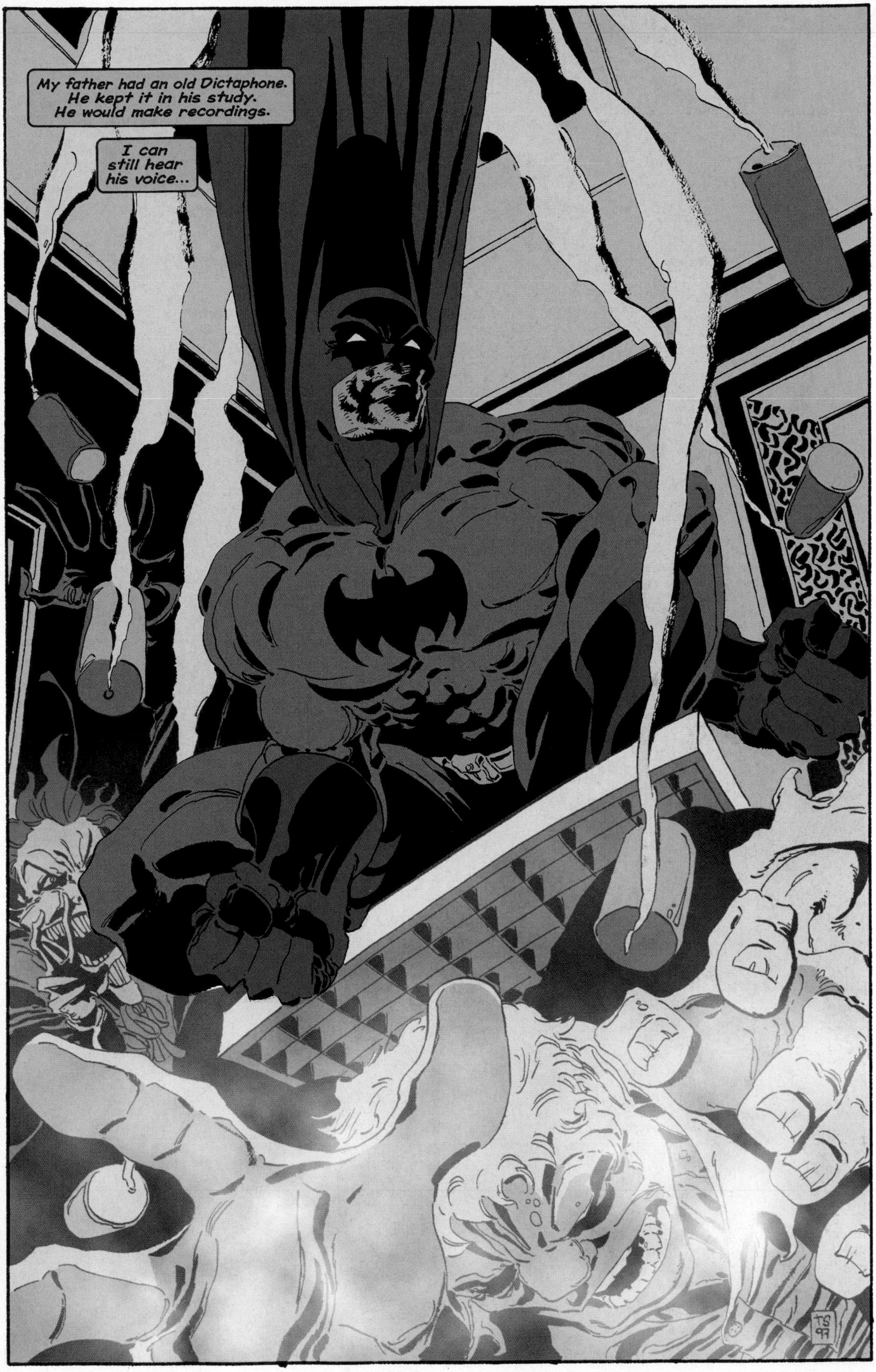
My father had an old Dictaphone. He kept it in his study. He would make recordings.
I can still hear his voice...

"When faced with a seemingly insurmountable problem..."

"...your only option is to act swiftly, some might even say, irrationally."

"Removing the most dangerous elements first.."

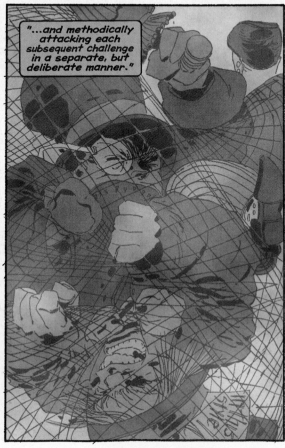

"...and methodically attacking each subsequent challenge in a separate, but deliberate manner."

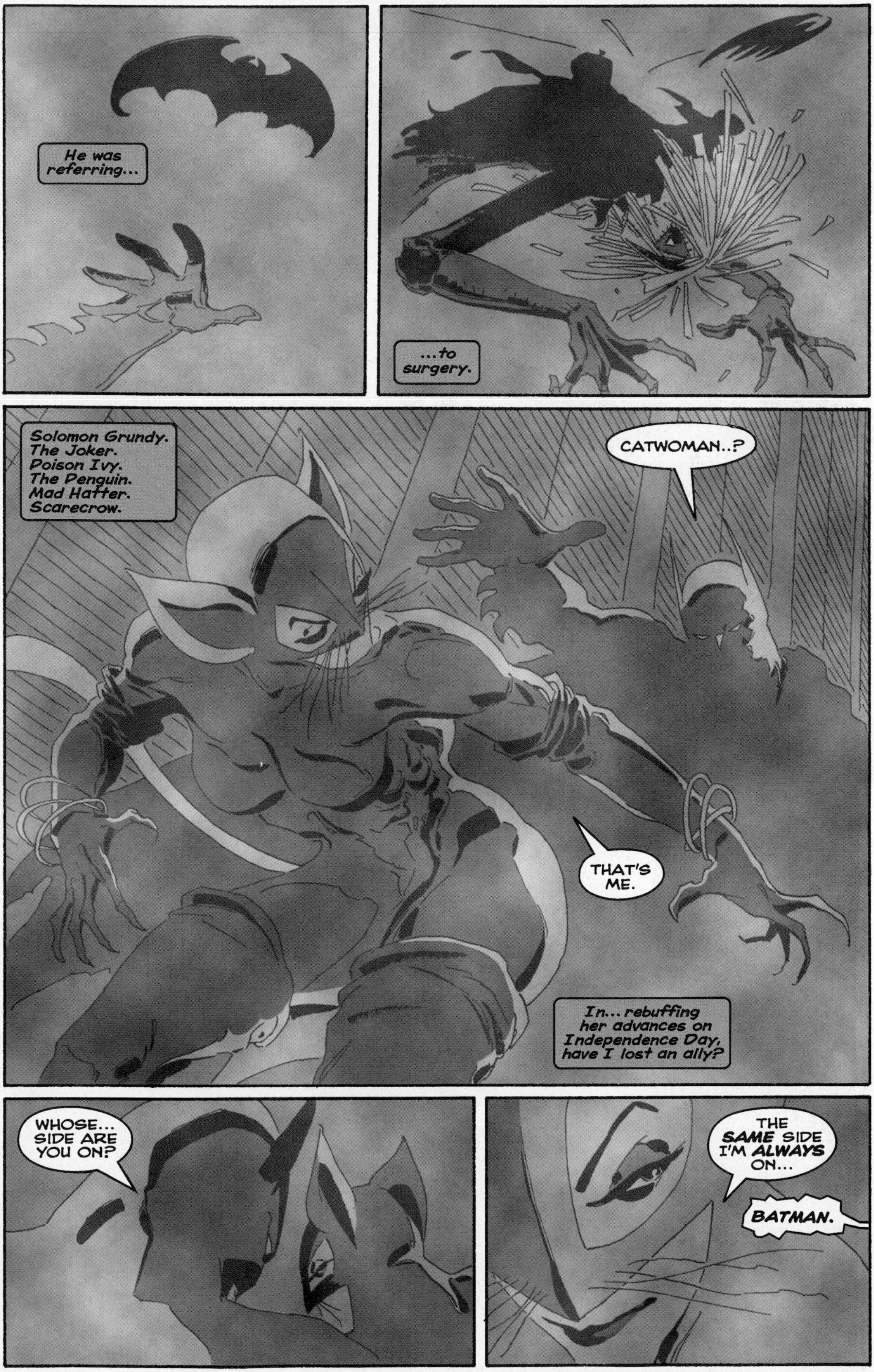
He was referring...
...to surgery.
Solomon Grundy.
The Joker.
Poison Ivy.
The Penguin.
Mad Hatter.
Scarecrow.
CATWOMAN..?
THAT'S ME.
In... rebuffing her advances on Independence Day, have I lost an ally?
WHOSE... SIDE ARE YOU ON?
THE SAME SIDE I'M ALWAYS ON...
BATMAN.

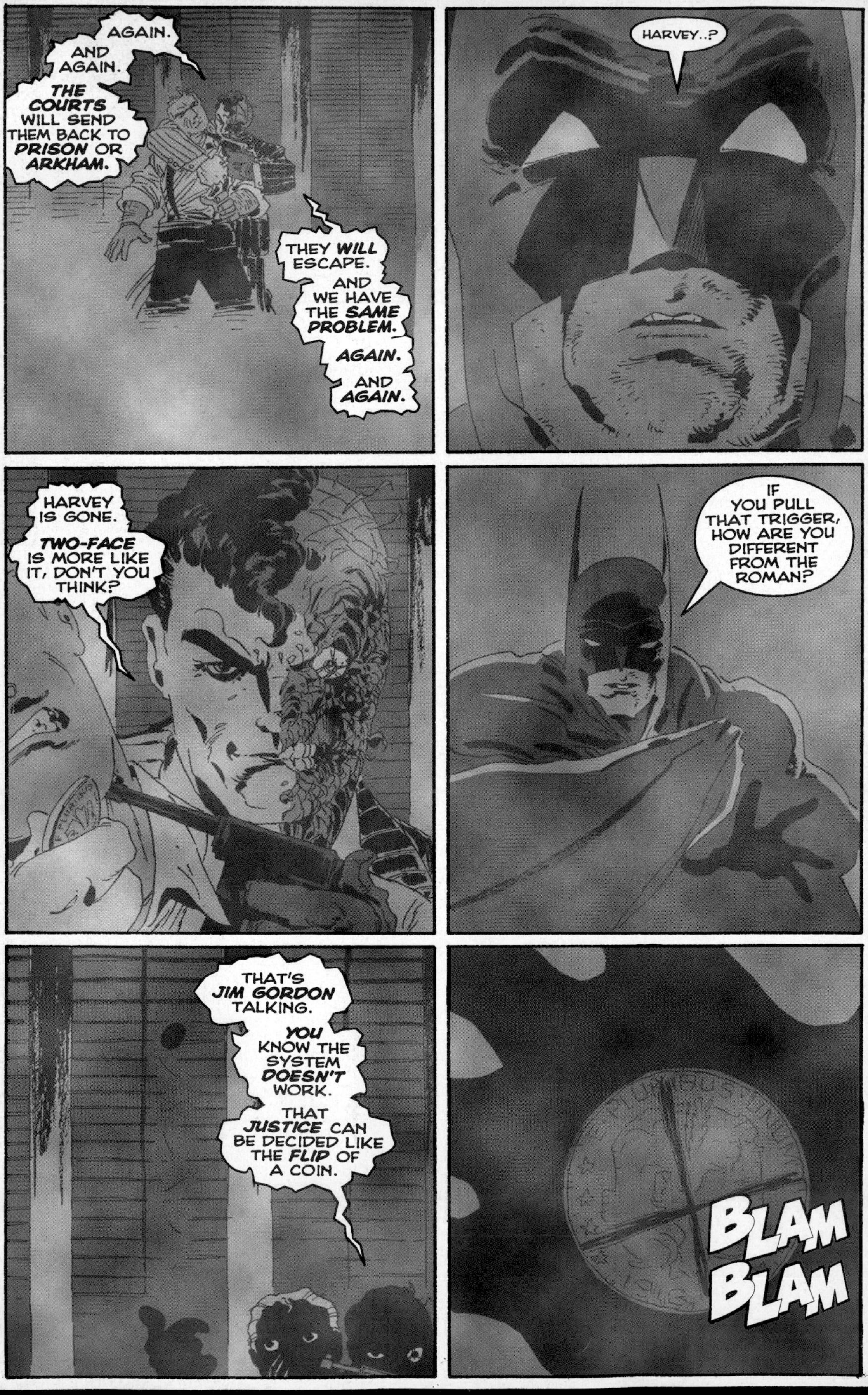

AGAIN.
AND AGAIN.
THE COURTS WILL SEND THEM BACK TO PRISON OR ARKHAM.
THEY WILL ESCAPE.
AND WE HAVE THE SAME PROBLEM.
AGAIN.
AND AGAIN.
HARVEY..?
HARVEY IS GONE.
TWO-FACE IS MORE LIKE IT, DON'T YOU THINK?
IF YOU PULL THAT TRIGGER, HOW ARE YOU DIFFERENT FROM THE ROMAN?
THAT'S JIM GORDON TALKING.
YOU KNOW THE SYSTEM DOESN'T WORK.
THAT JUSTICE CAN BE DECIDED LIKE THE FLIP OF A COIN.
BLAM
BLAM

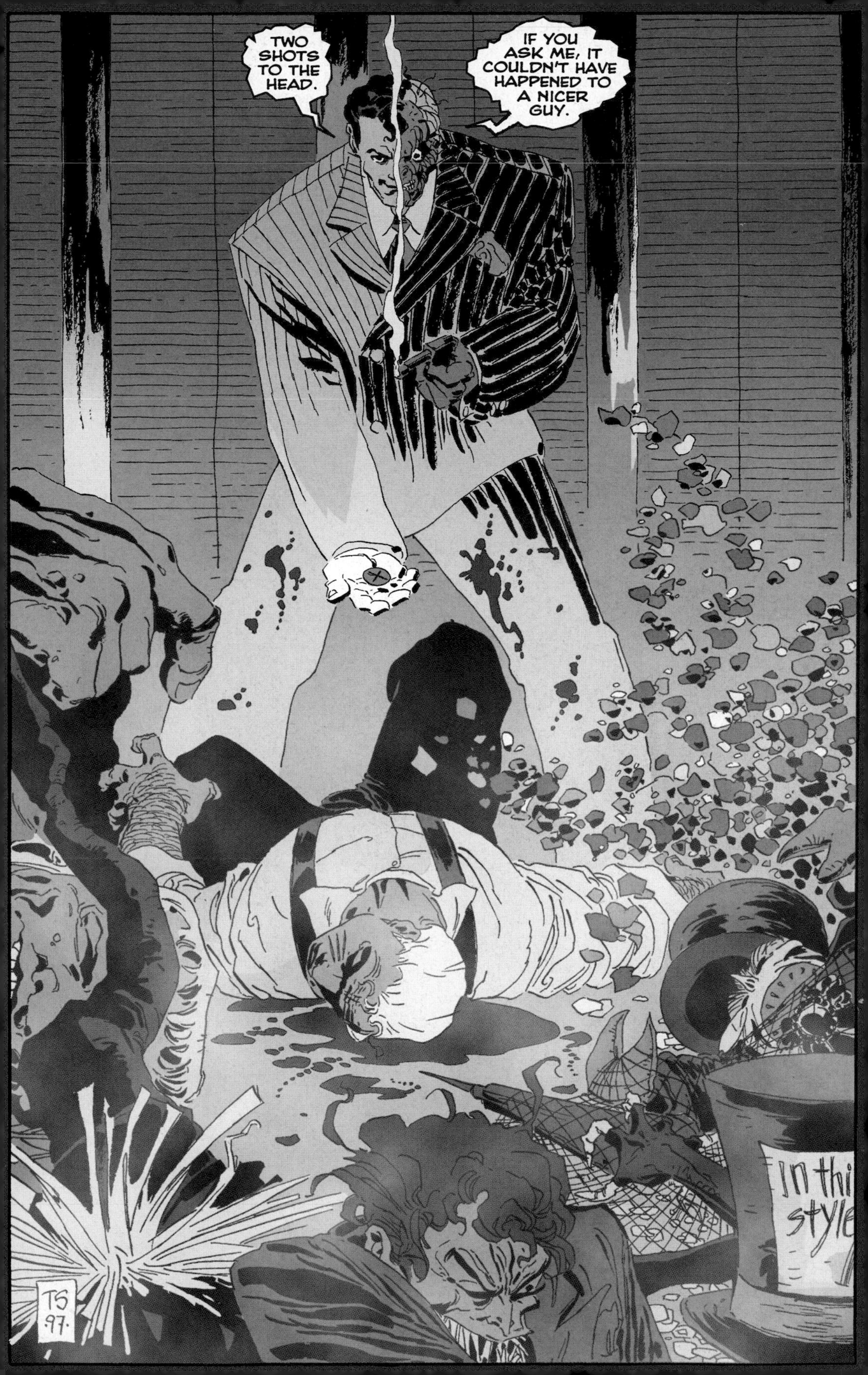
TWO SHOTS TO THE HEAD.
IF YOU ASK ME, IT COULDN'T HAVE HAPPENED TO A NICER GUY.

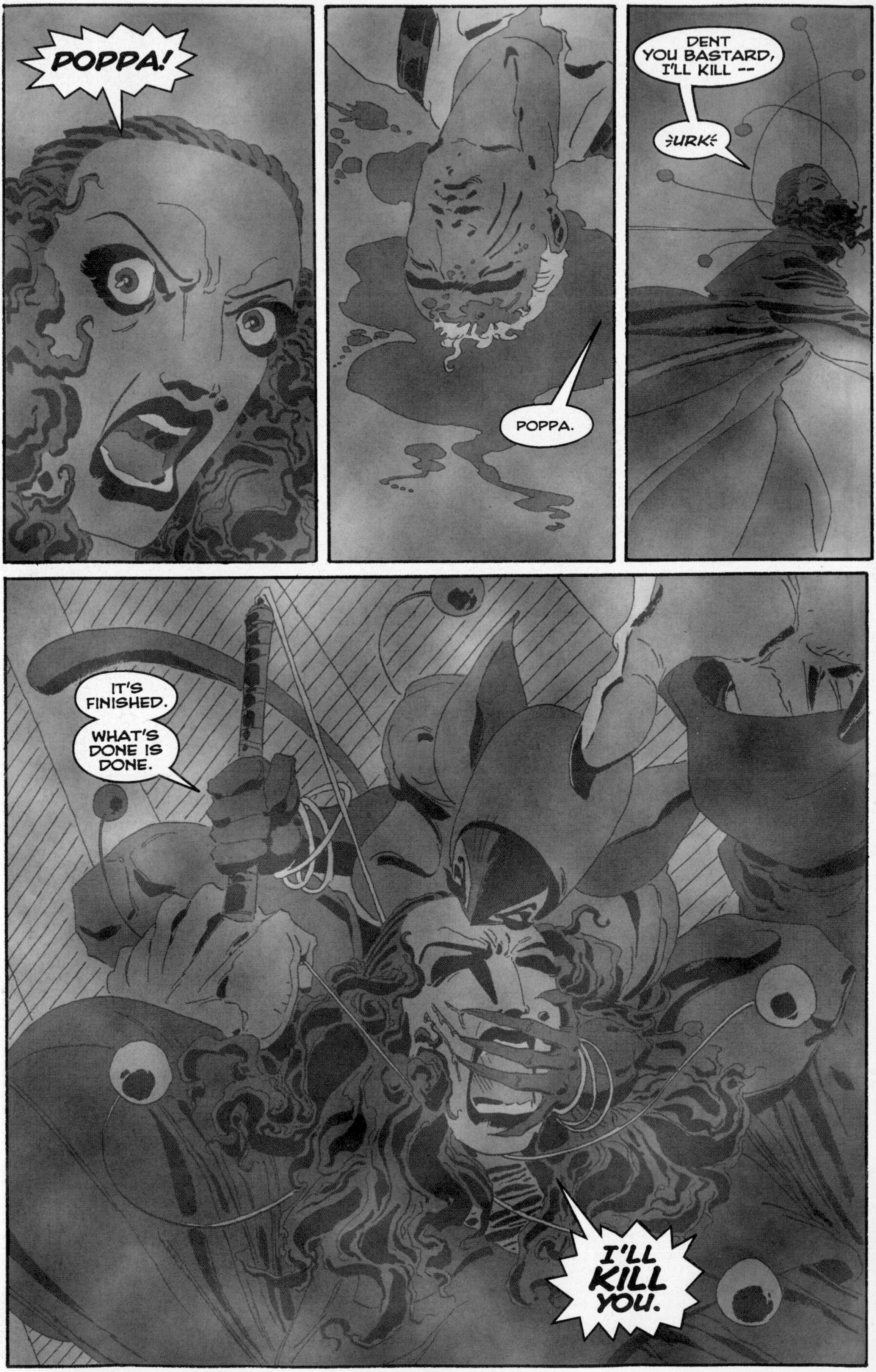
POPPA!
POPPA.
DENT YOU BASTARD, I'LL KILL --
URK
IT'S FINISHED.
WHAT'S DONE IS DONE.
I'LL KILL YOU.

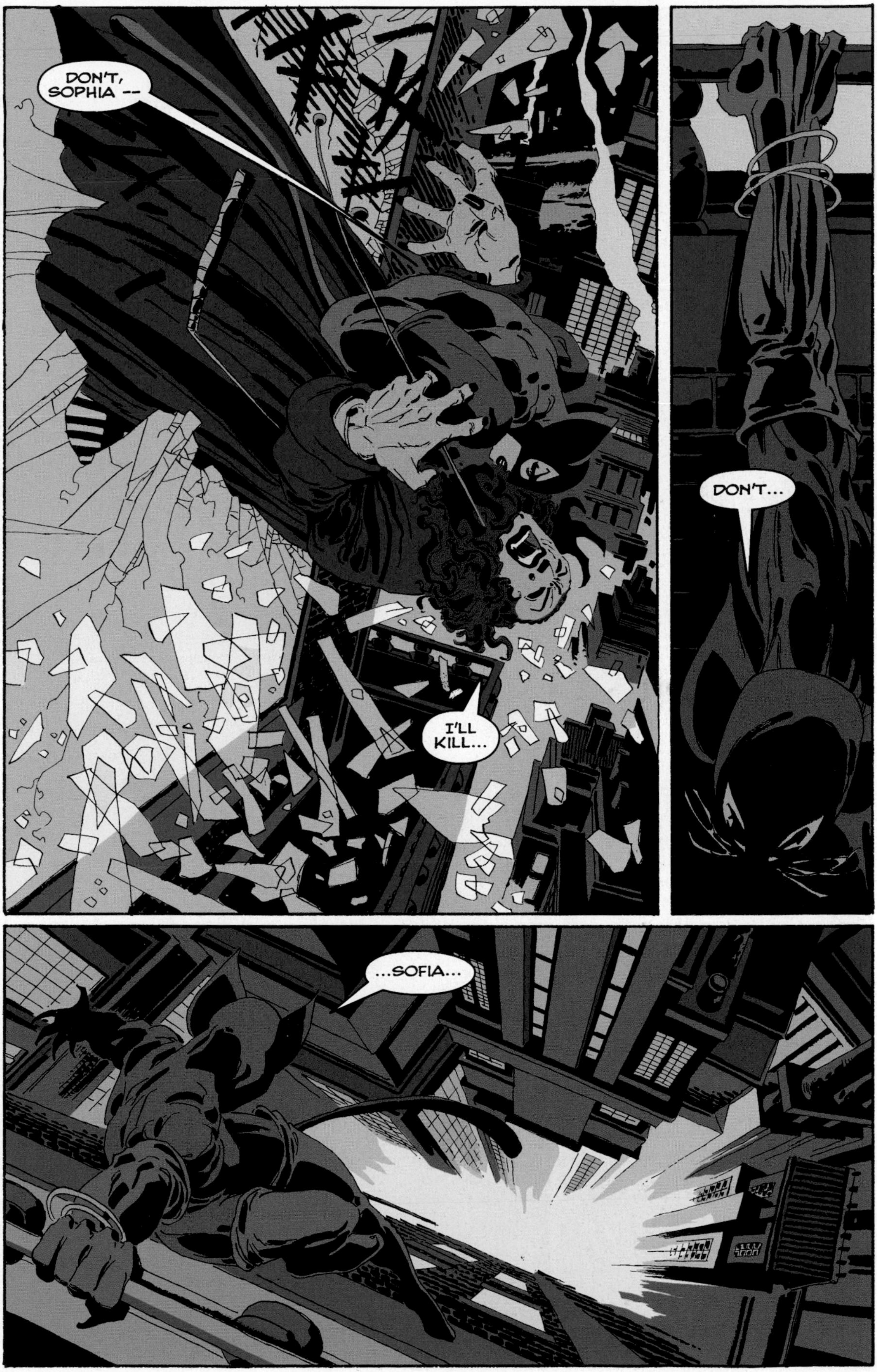
DON'T, SOPHIA --
I'LL KILL...
DON'T...
...SOFIA...

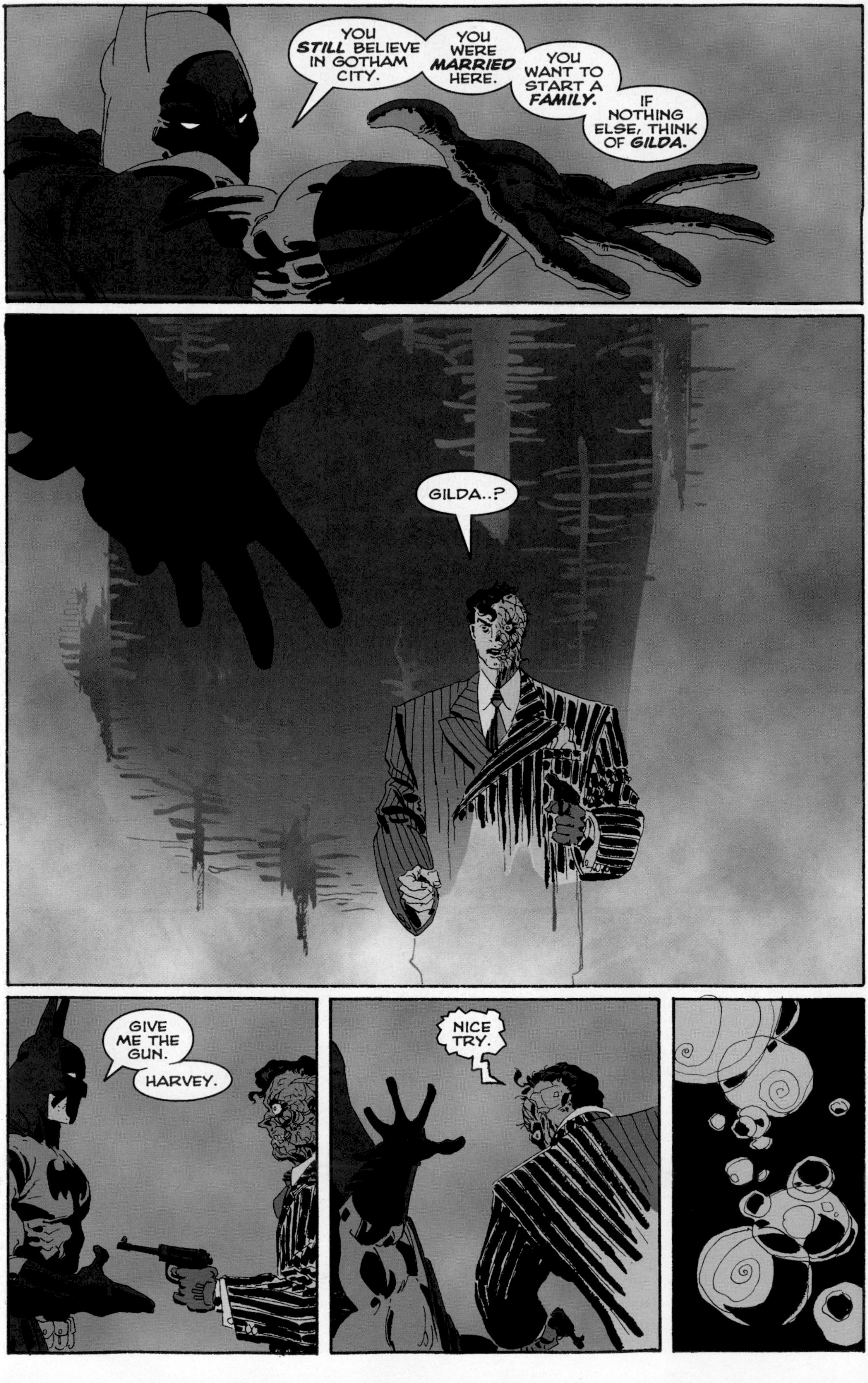

YOU STILL BELIEVE IN GOTHAM CITY.
YOU WERE MARRIED HERE.
YOU WANT TO START A FAMILY.
IF NOTHING ELSE, THINK OF GILDA.
GILDA..?
GIVE ME THE GUN.
HARVEY.
NICE TRY.

Across town. Soon.

WORKING LATE AGAIN, VERNON?

W-WHO..?

YOU HAVE TO ANSWER FOR *HARVEY DENT.*

SOMEBODY GAVE *MARONI* THE ACID TO THROW IN DENT'S FACE.

SOMEBODY WHO SAW MARONI *JUST BEFORE* HE ENTERED THE COURTROOM.

THAT SOMEBODY IS *YOU.* VERNON FIELDS. *ASSISTANT* TO DISTRICT ATTORNEY HARVEY DENT.

YOU BELIEVE IN THE JUSTICE SYSTEM, DON'T YOU, VERNON?

YOU DIDN'T SPEND *ALL THOSE YEARS* IN LAW SCHOOL FOR NOTHING, RIGHT?

THEN YOU KNOW, JUSTICE HAS *TWO SIDES.*

INNOCENT OR GUILTY.

LIKE THIS COIN.

ONE SIDE CLEAN. THE OTHER SIDE *SCARRED.*

HARVEY DENT
DISTRICT ATTORNEY

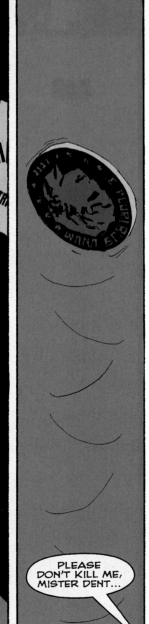

PLEASE DON'T KILL ME, MISTER DENT...

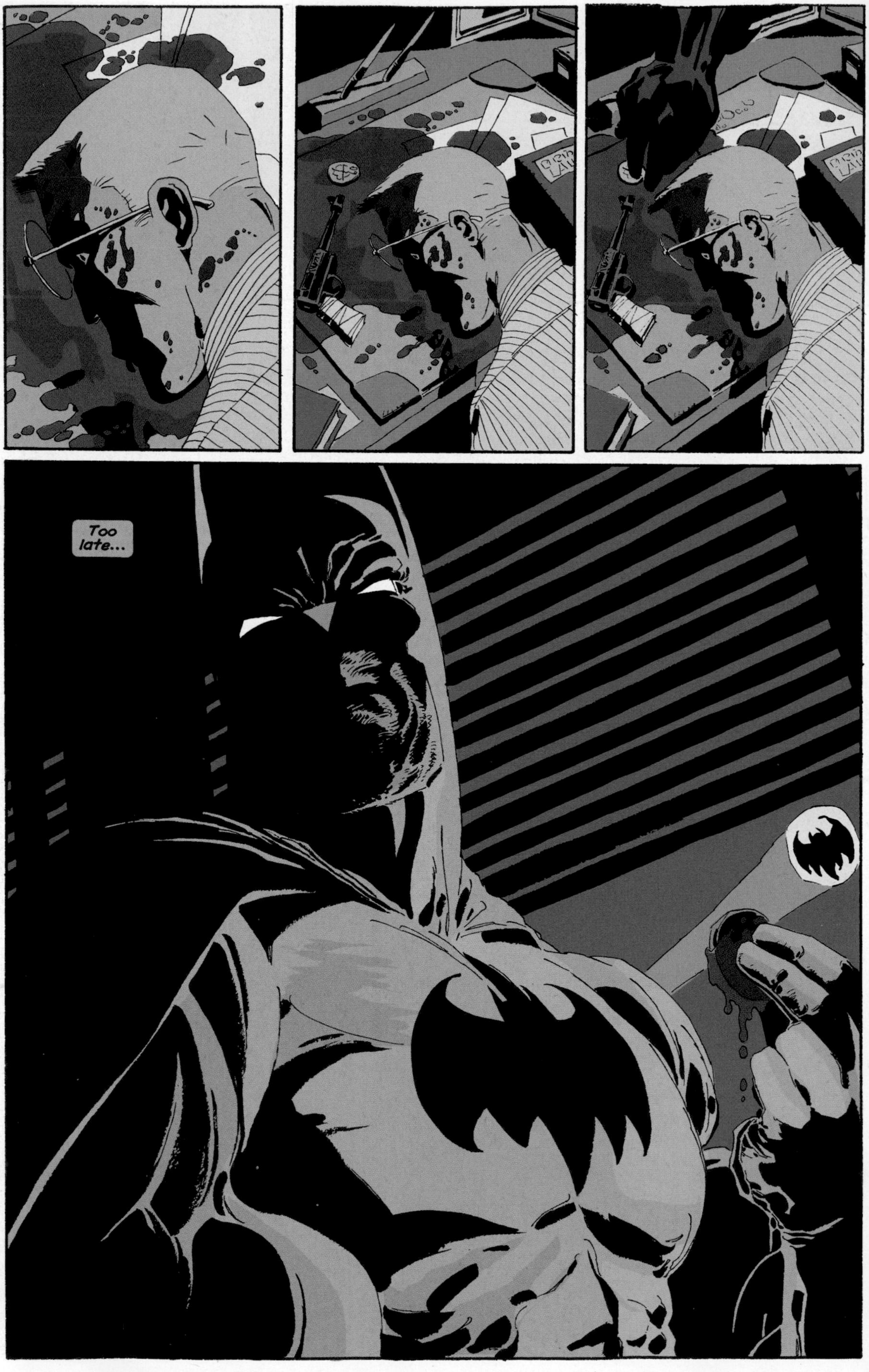
Too late...

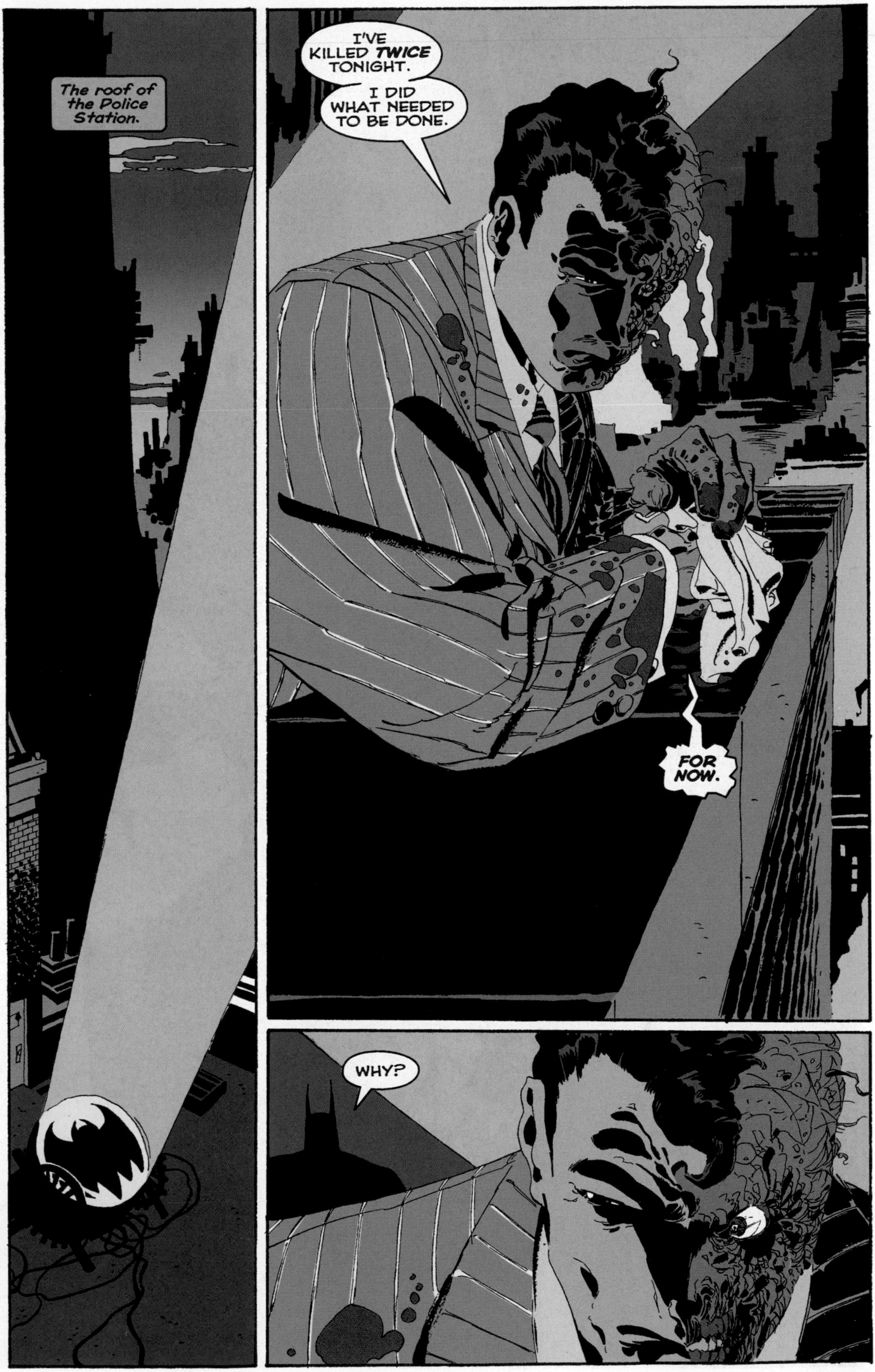
The roof of the Police Station.
I'VE KILLED TWICE TONIGHT.
I DID WHAT NEEDED TO BE DONE.
FOR NOW.
WHY?

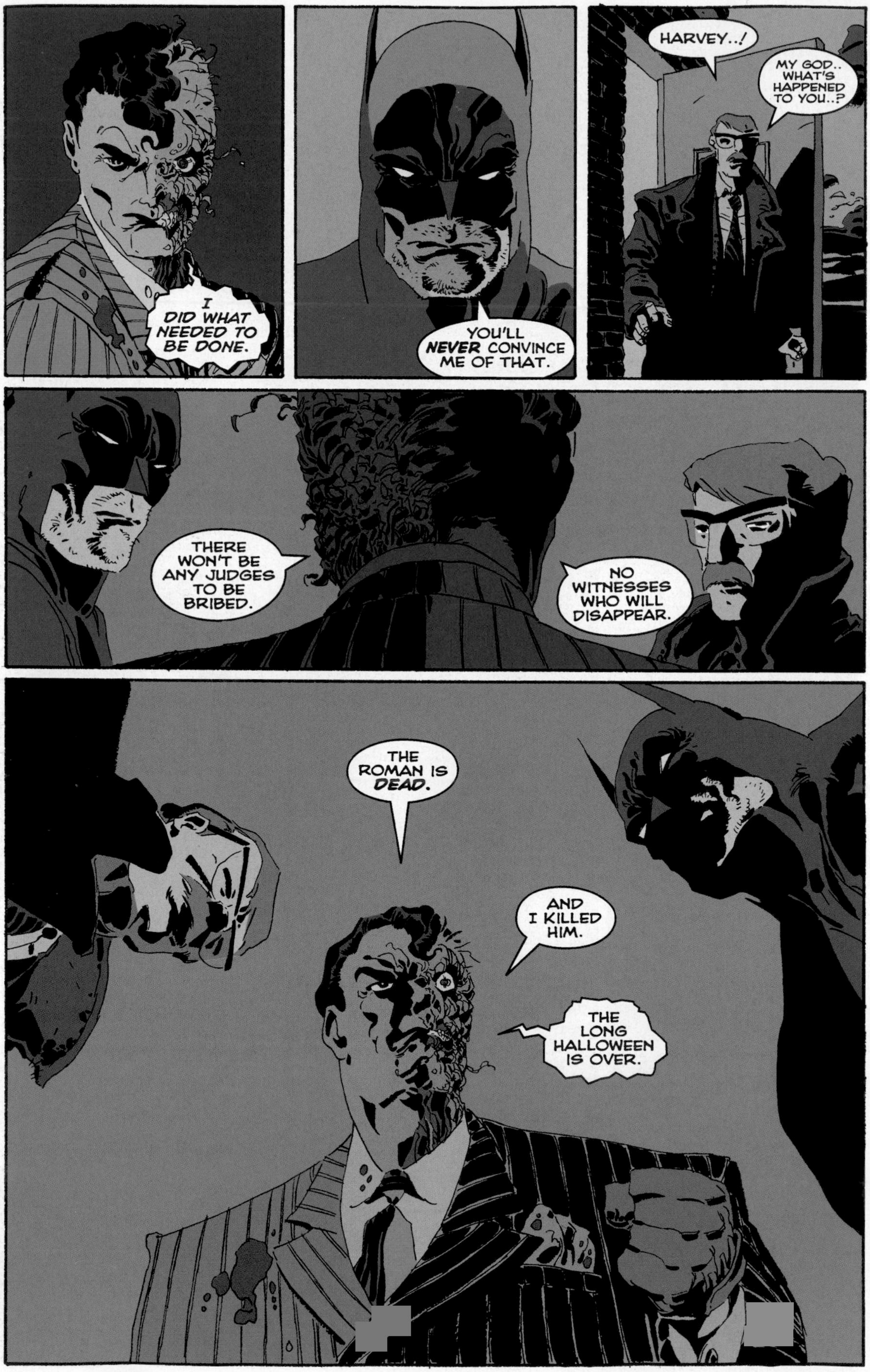
I DID WHAT NEEDED TO BE DONE.
YOU'LL NEVER CONVINCE ME OF THAT.
HARVEY..!
MY GOD.. WHAT'S HAPPENED TO YOU..?
THERE WON'T BE ANY JUDGES TO BE BRIBED.
NO WITNESSES WHO WILL DISAPPEAR.
THE ROMAN IS DEAD.
AND I KILLED HIM.
THE LONG HALLOWEEN IS OVER.

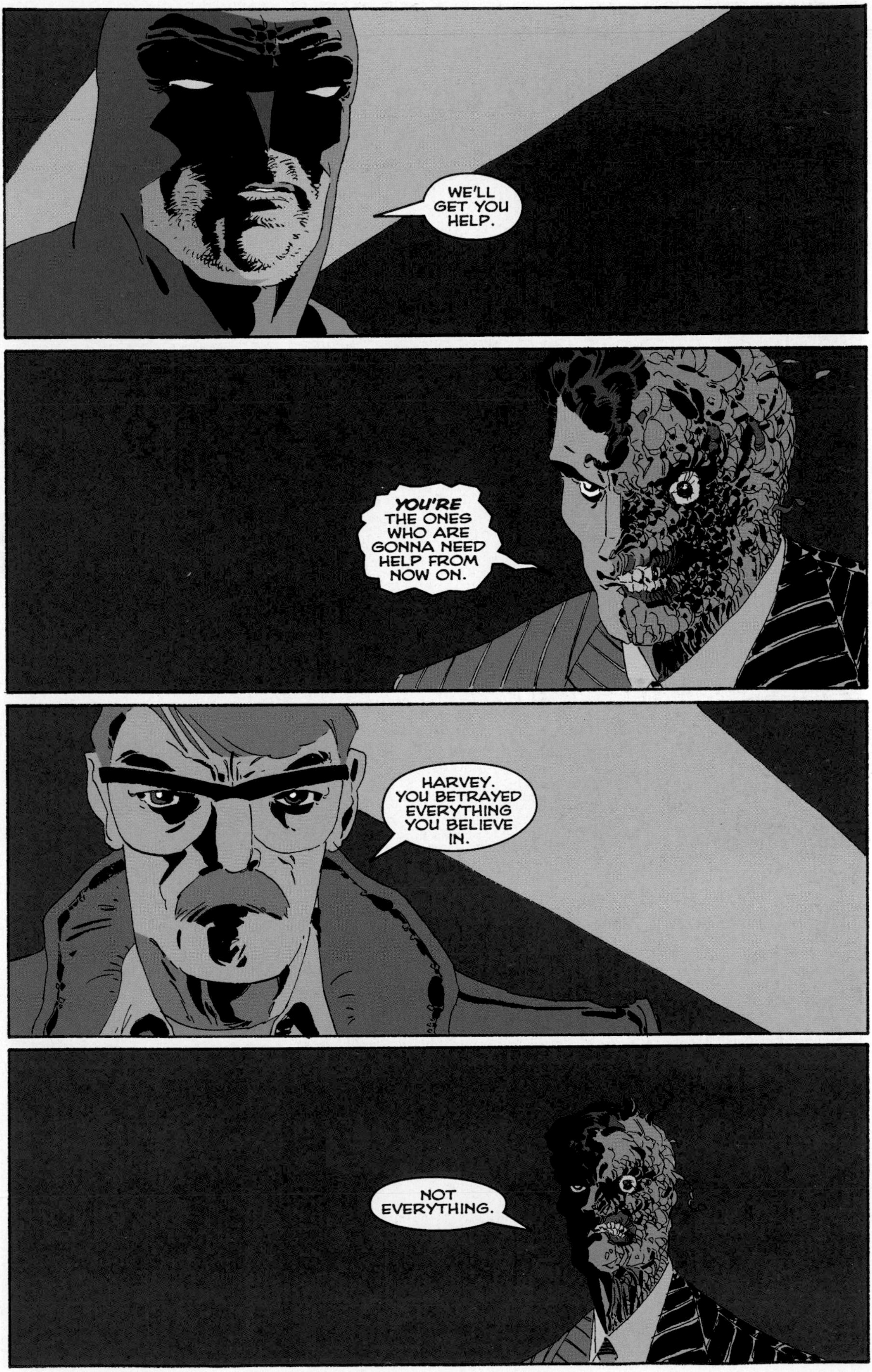
WE'LL GET YOU HELP.
YOU'RE THE ONES WHO ARE GONNA NEED HELP FROM NOW ON.
HARVEY. YOU BETRAYED EVERYTHING YOU BELIEVE IN.
NOT EVERYTHING.

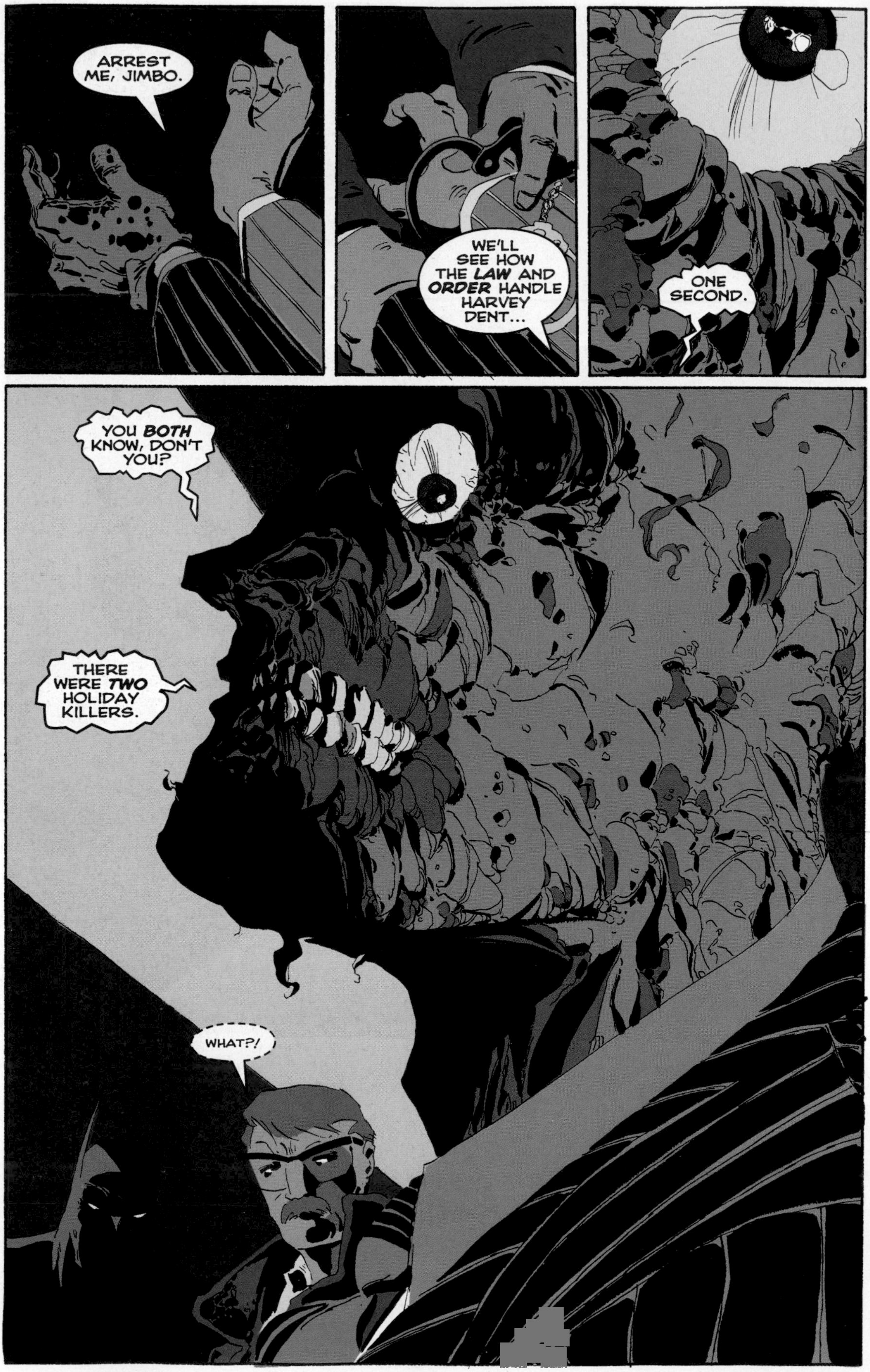
ARREST ME, JIMBO.
WE'LL SEE HOW THE LAW AND ORDER HANDLE HARVEY DENT...
ONE SECOND.
YOU BOTH KNOW, DON'T YOU?
THERE WERE TWO HOLIDAY KILLERS.
WHAT?!

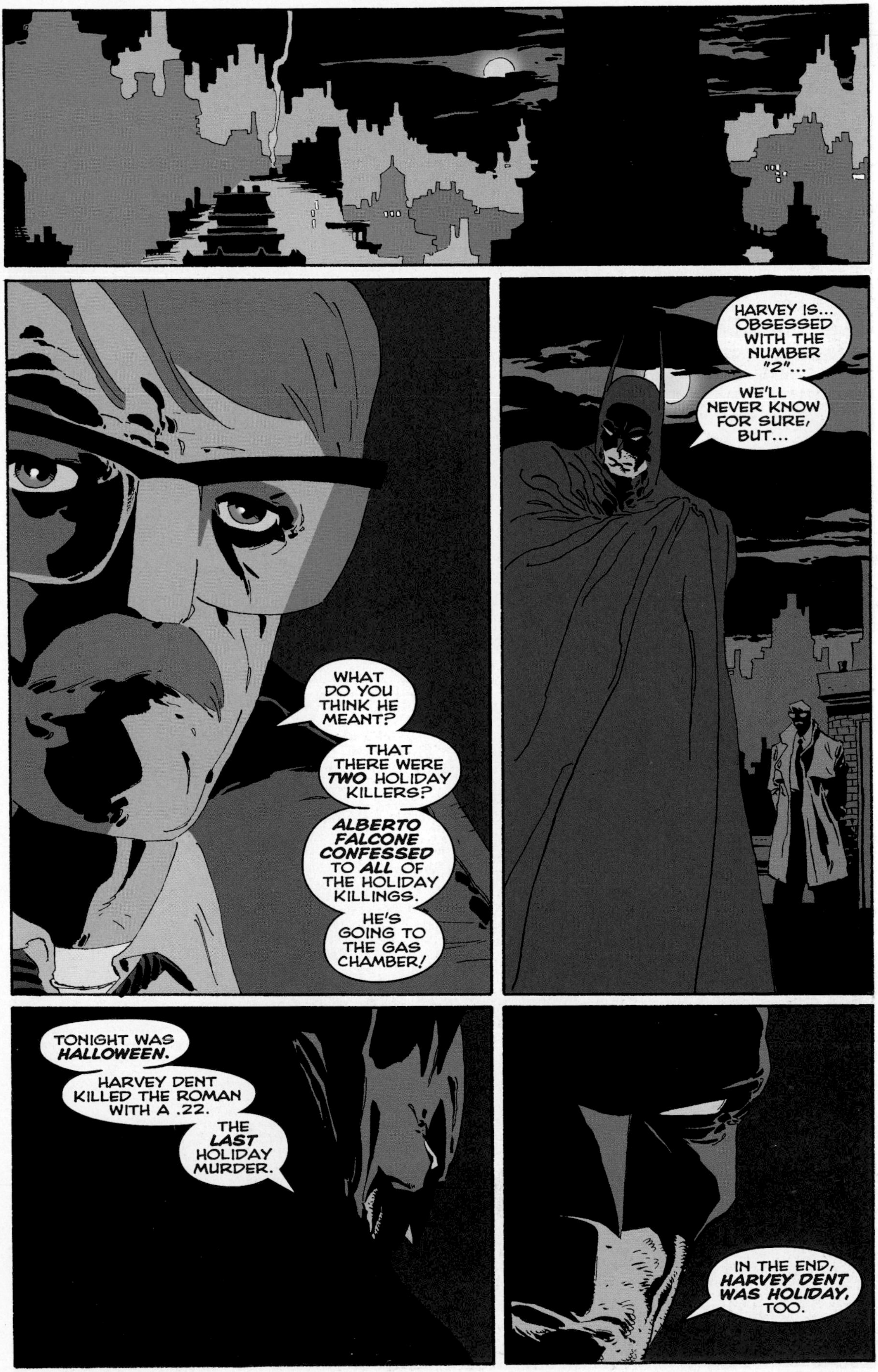

WHAT DO YOU THINK HE MEANT?
THAT THERE WERE TWO HOLIDAY KILLERS?
ALBERTO FALCONE CONFESSED TO ALL OF THE HOLIDAY KILLINGS.
HE'S GOING TO THE GAS CHAMBER!
HARVEY IS... OBSESSED WITH THE NUMBER "2"...
WE'LL NEVER KNOW FOR SURE, BUT...
TONIGHT WAS HALLOWEEN.
HARVEY DENT KILLED THE ROMAN WITH A .22.
THE LAST HOLIDAY MURDER.
IN THE END, HARVEY DENT WAS HOLIDAY, TOO.

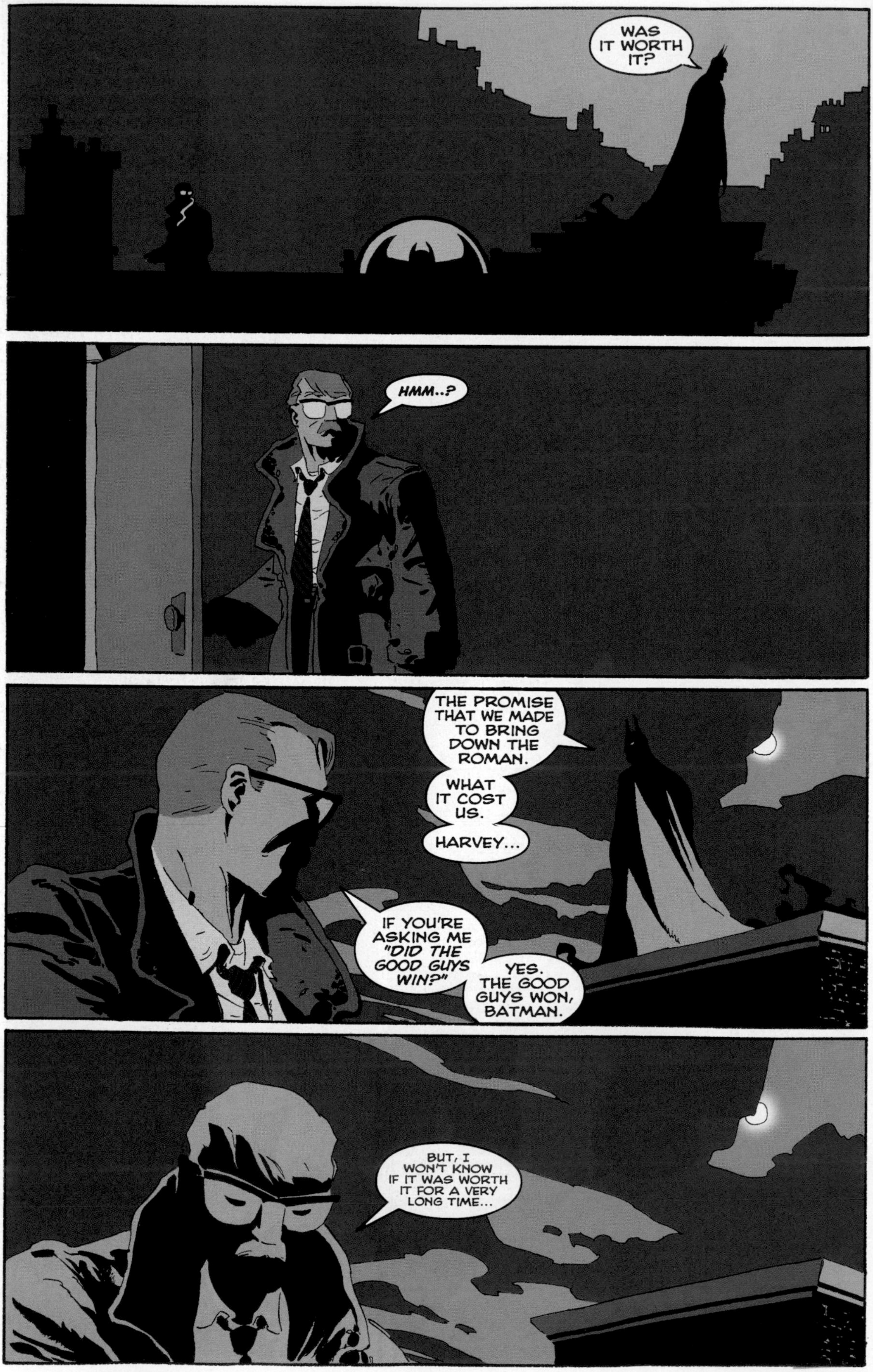
WAS IT WORTH IT?
HMM..?
THE PROMISE THAT WE MADE TO BRING DOWN THE ROMAN.
WHAT IT COST US.
HARVEY...
IF YOU'RE ASKING ME "DID THE GOOD GUYS WIN?"
YES. THE GOOD GUYS WON, BATMAN.
BUT, I WON'T KNOW IF IT WAS WORTH IT FOR A VERY LONG TIME...

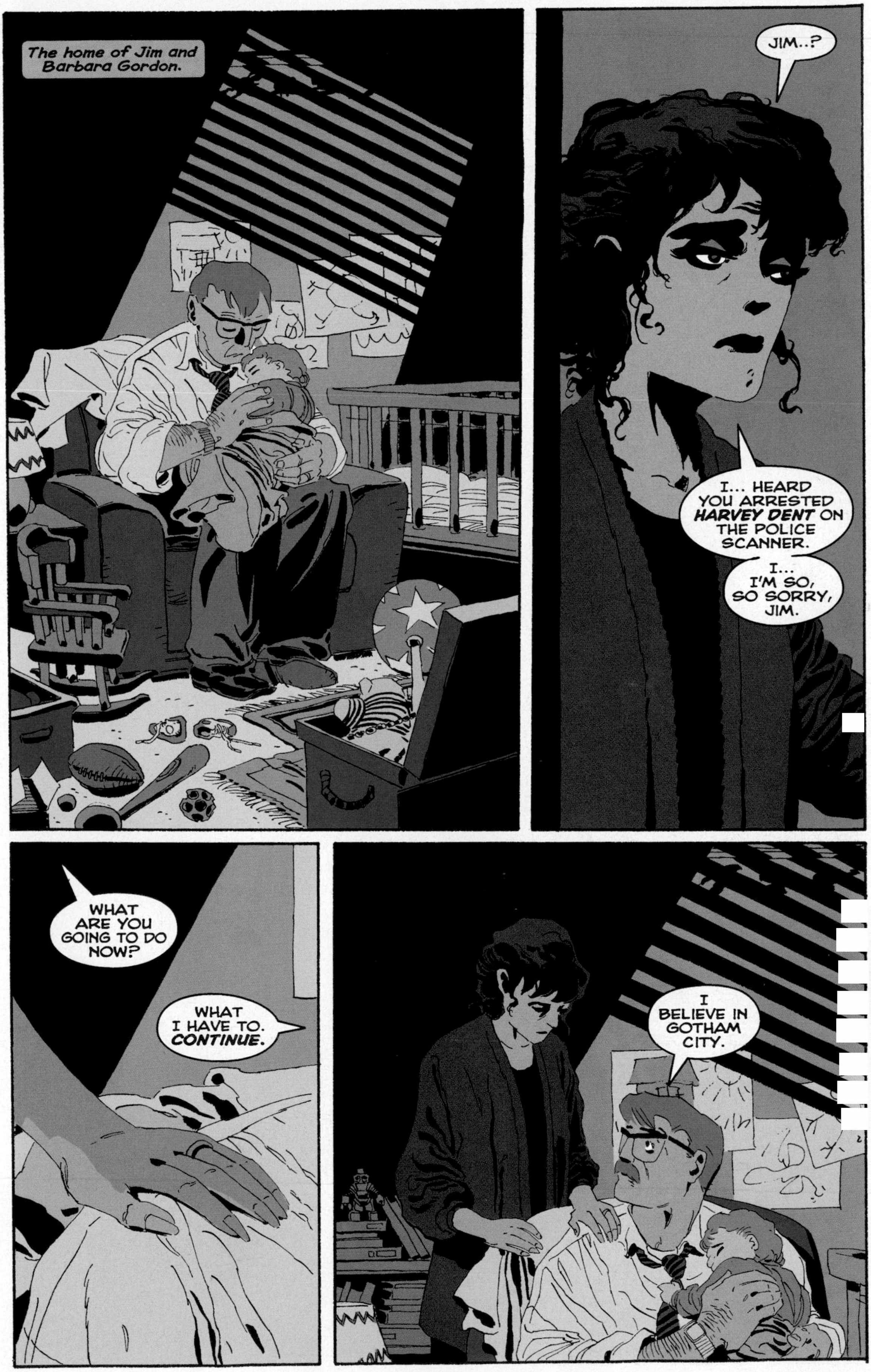
The home of Jim and Barbara Gordon.
JIM..?
I... HEARD YOU ARRESTED HARVEY DENT ON THE POLICE SCANNER.
I... I'M SO, SO SORRY, JIM.
WHAT ARE YOU GOING TO DO NOW?
WHAT I HAVE TO. CONTINUE.
I BELIEVE IN GOTHAM CITY.

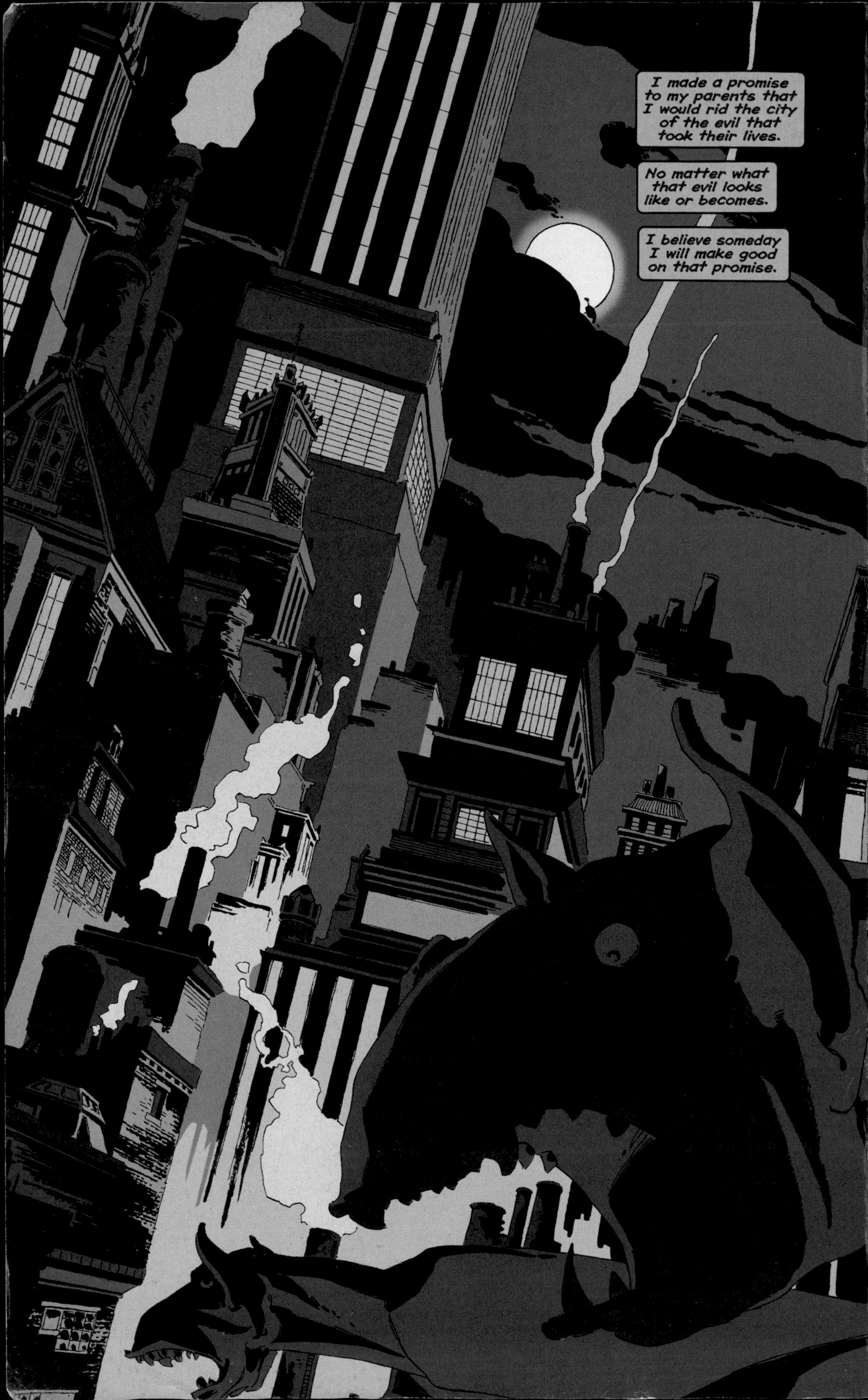
I made a promise to my parents that I would rid the city of the evil that took their lives.
No matter what that evil looks like or becomes.
I believe someday I will make good on that promise.

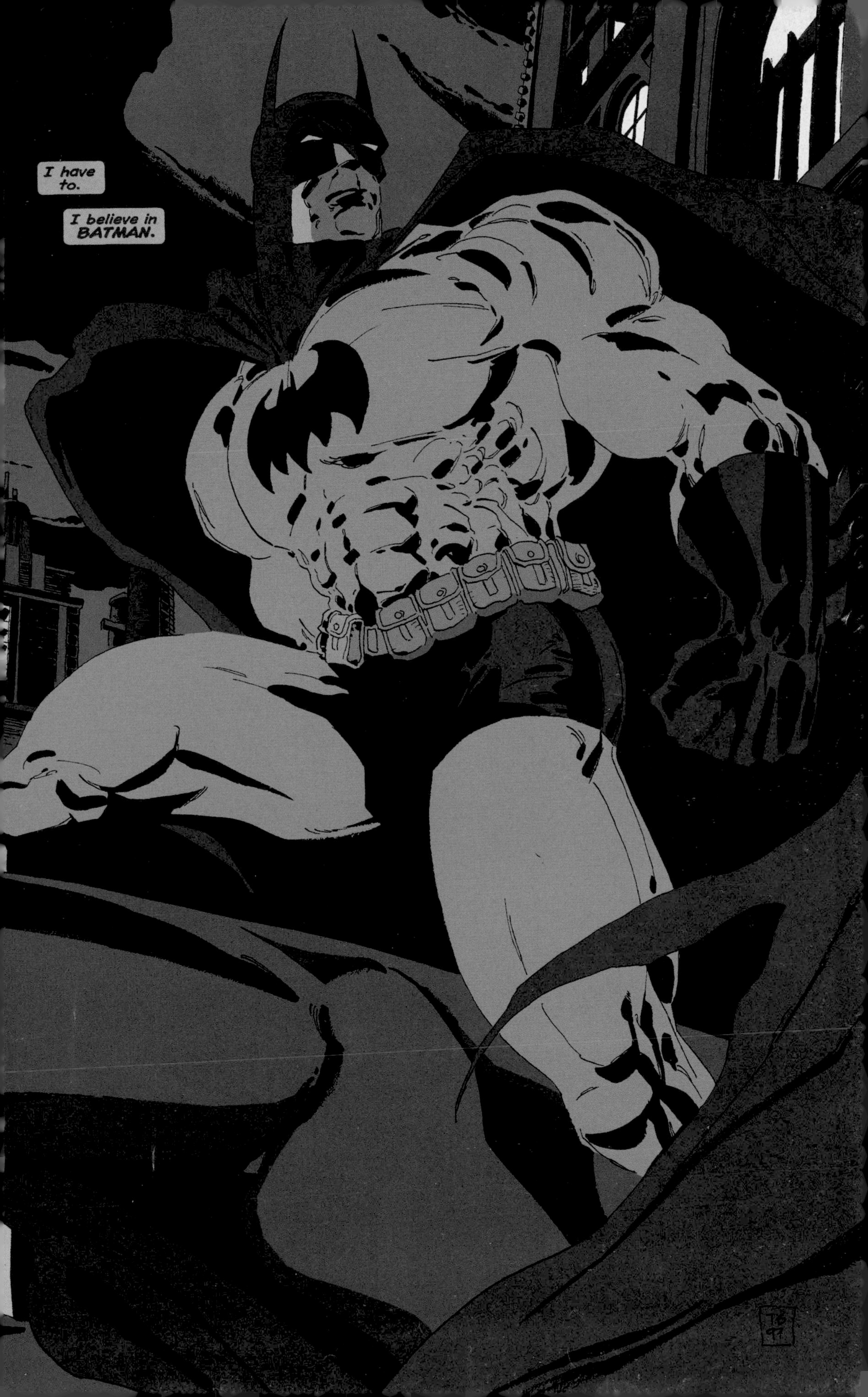
I have to.
I believe in BATMAN.

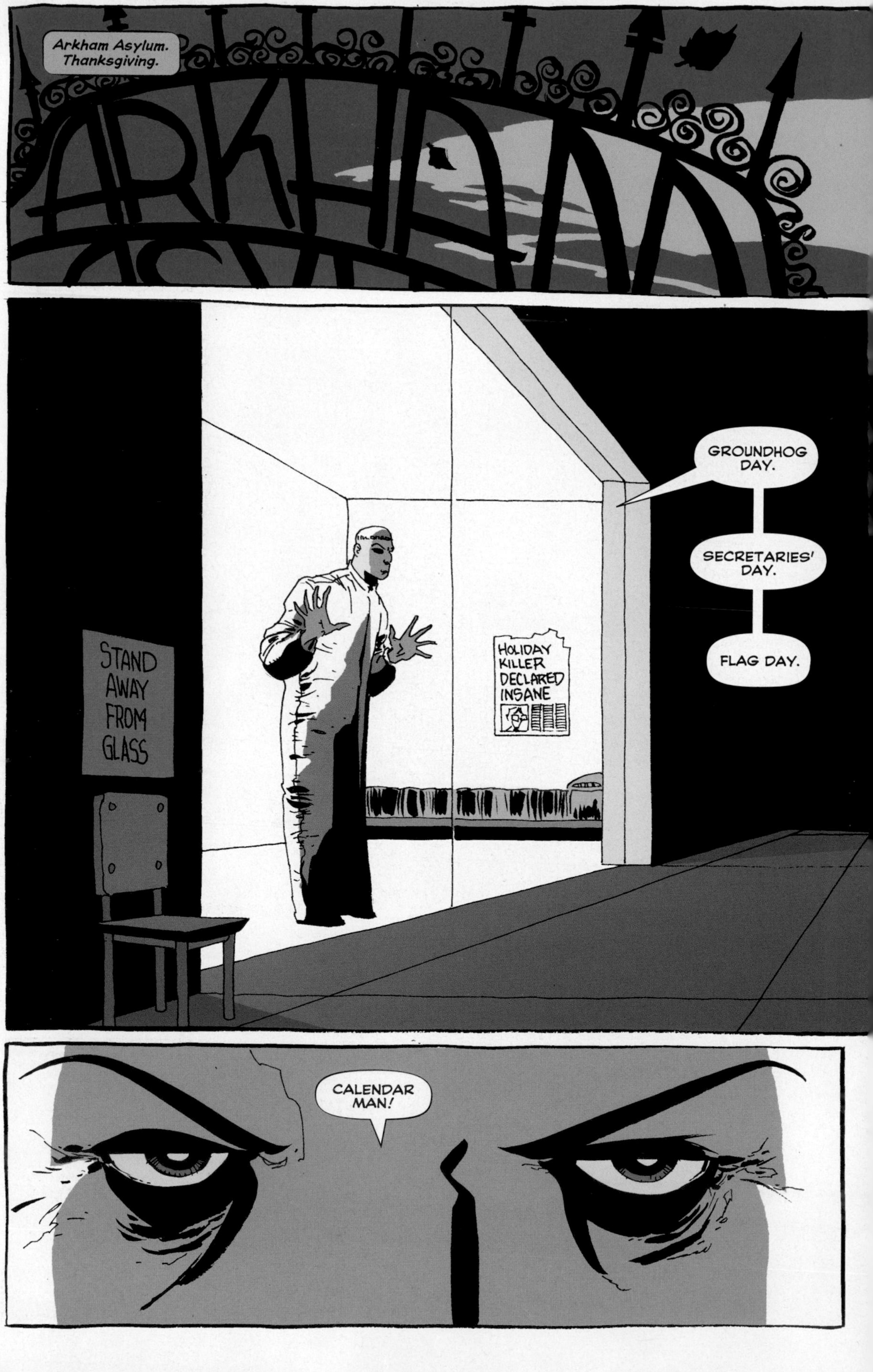
Arkham Asylum. Thanksgiving.
STAND AWAY FROM GLASS
HOLIDAY KILLER DECLARED INSANE
GROUNDHOG DAY.
SECRETARIES' DAY.
FLAG DAY.
CALENDAR MAN!

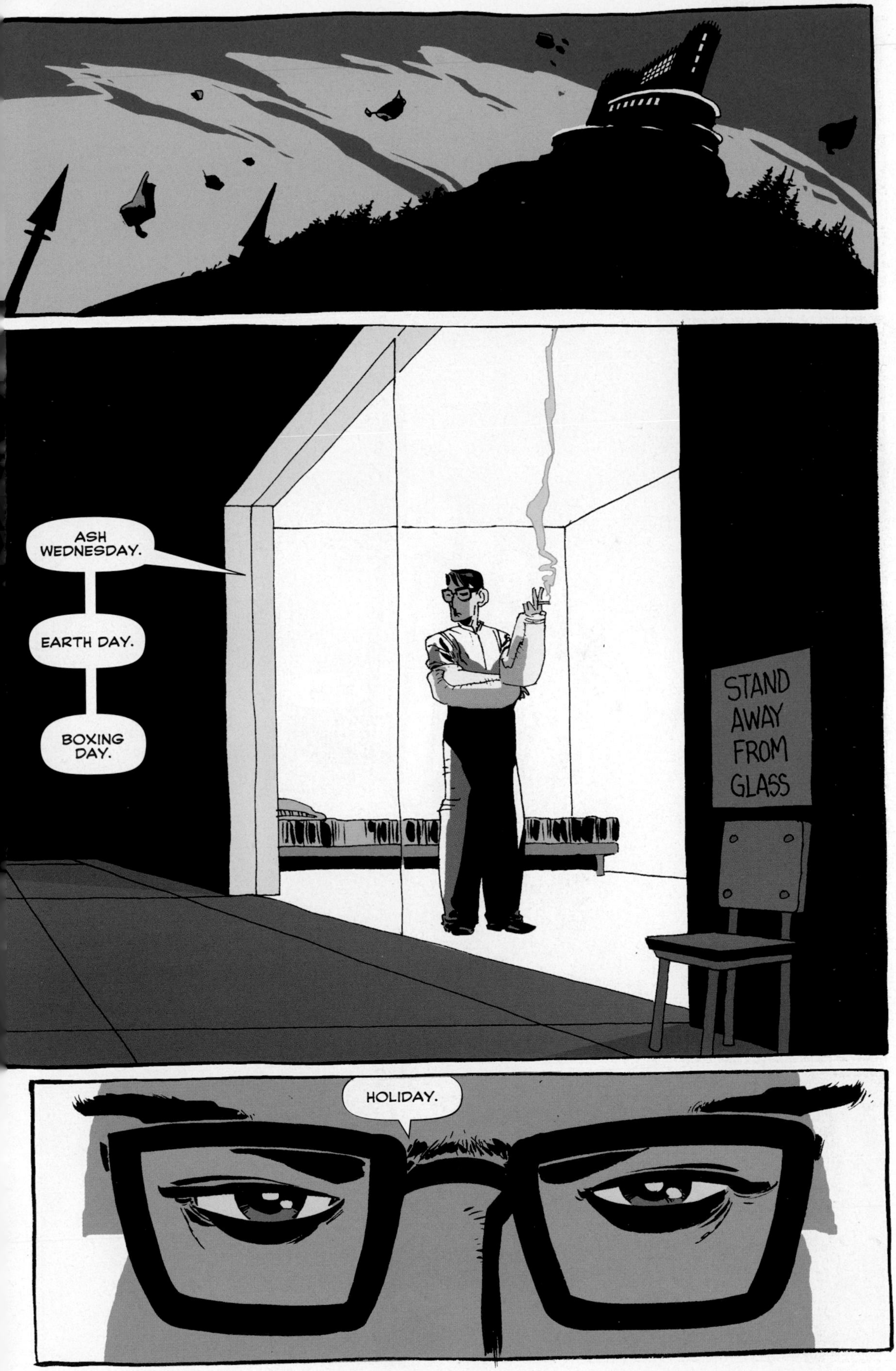
ASH WEDNESDAY.
EARTH DAY.
BOXING DAY.
STAND AWAY FROM GLASS
HOLIDAY.

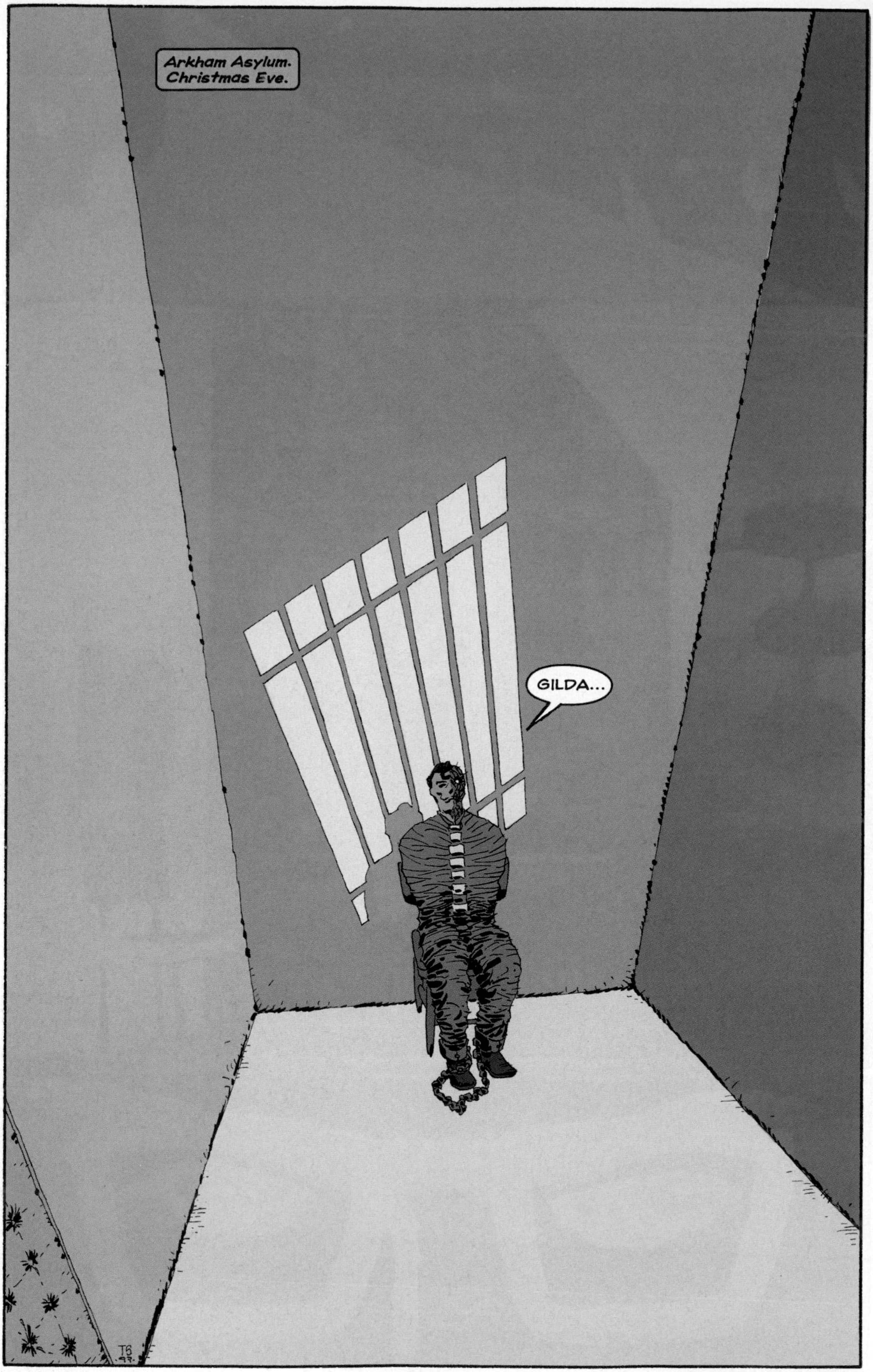
Arkham Asylum.
Christmas Eve.
GILDA...

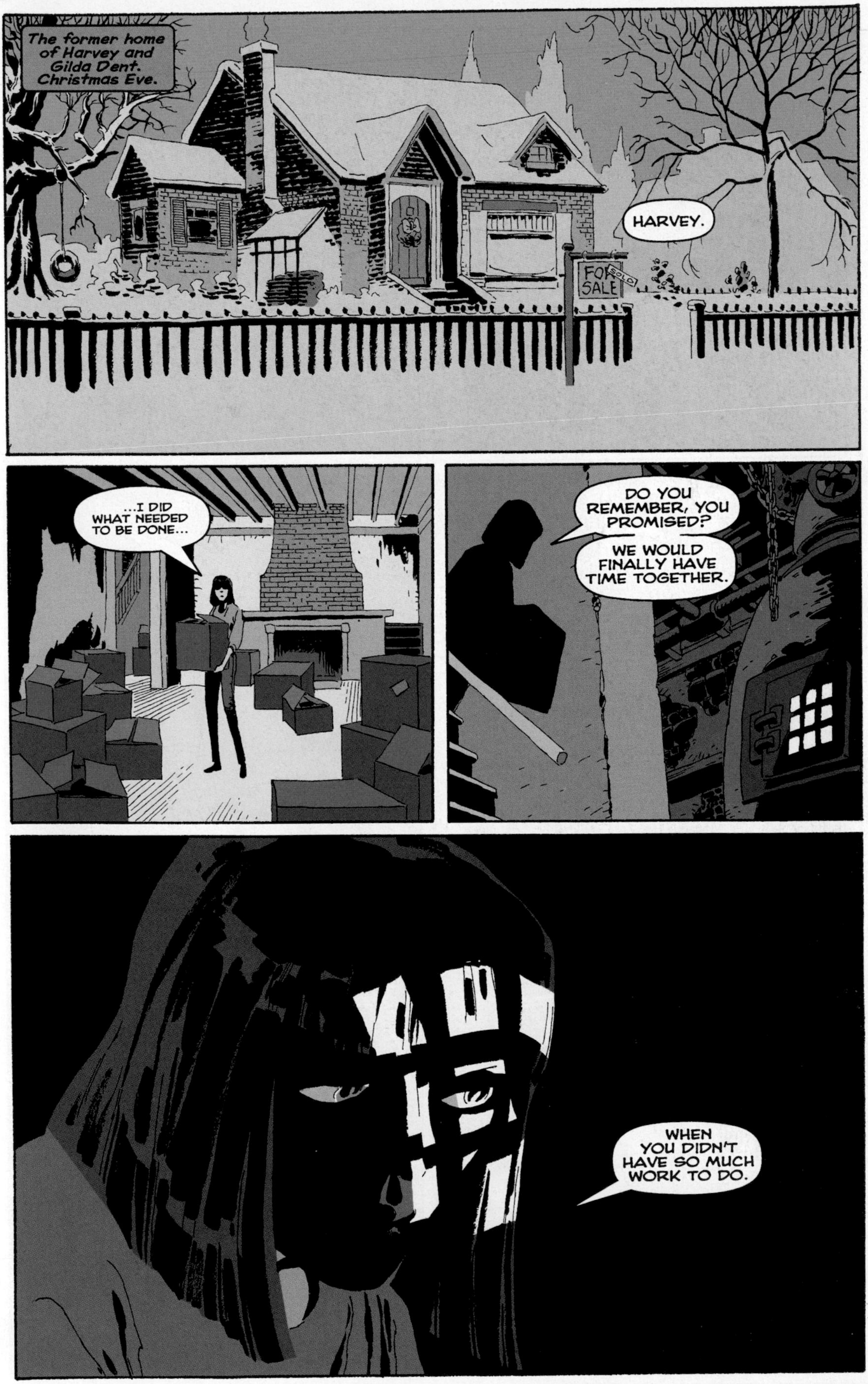
The former home of Harvey and Gilda Dent. Christmas Eve.
FOR SALE
SOLD
HARVEY.
...I DID WHAT NEEDED TO BE DONE...
DO YOU REMEMBER, YOU PROMISED?
WE WOULD FINALLY HAVE TIME TOGETHER.
WHEN YOU DIDN'T HAVE SO MUCH WORK TO DO.

I READ YOUR CASE FILES.

ABOUT TAKING SERIAL NUMBERS OFF GUNS AND...

...AND HOW A *BABY BOTTLE NIPPLE* WOULD MUFFLE THE SOUND.

HOW *CLUES* ARE LEFT AT MURDER SCENES.

AND I THOUGHT IF I DID *THAT*, BATMAN WOULD THINK IT WAS SOMEONE *EXTRAORDINARY* AND NOT ME.

NOT ME.

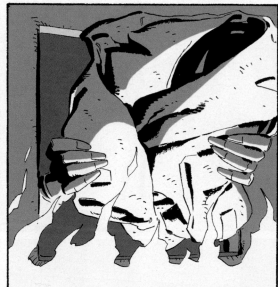

I USED YOUR HAT AND COAT FOR A DISGUISE AND LEFT THOSE... THINGS AT THE KILLINGS.

JOHNNY VITI WAS *THE FIRST*.

THEN, AGAIN, ON *THANKSGIVING*, I LEFT THE HOSPITAL WHILE YOU SLEPT.

AND AGAIN, ON *CHRISTMAS*.

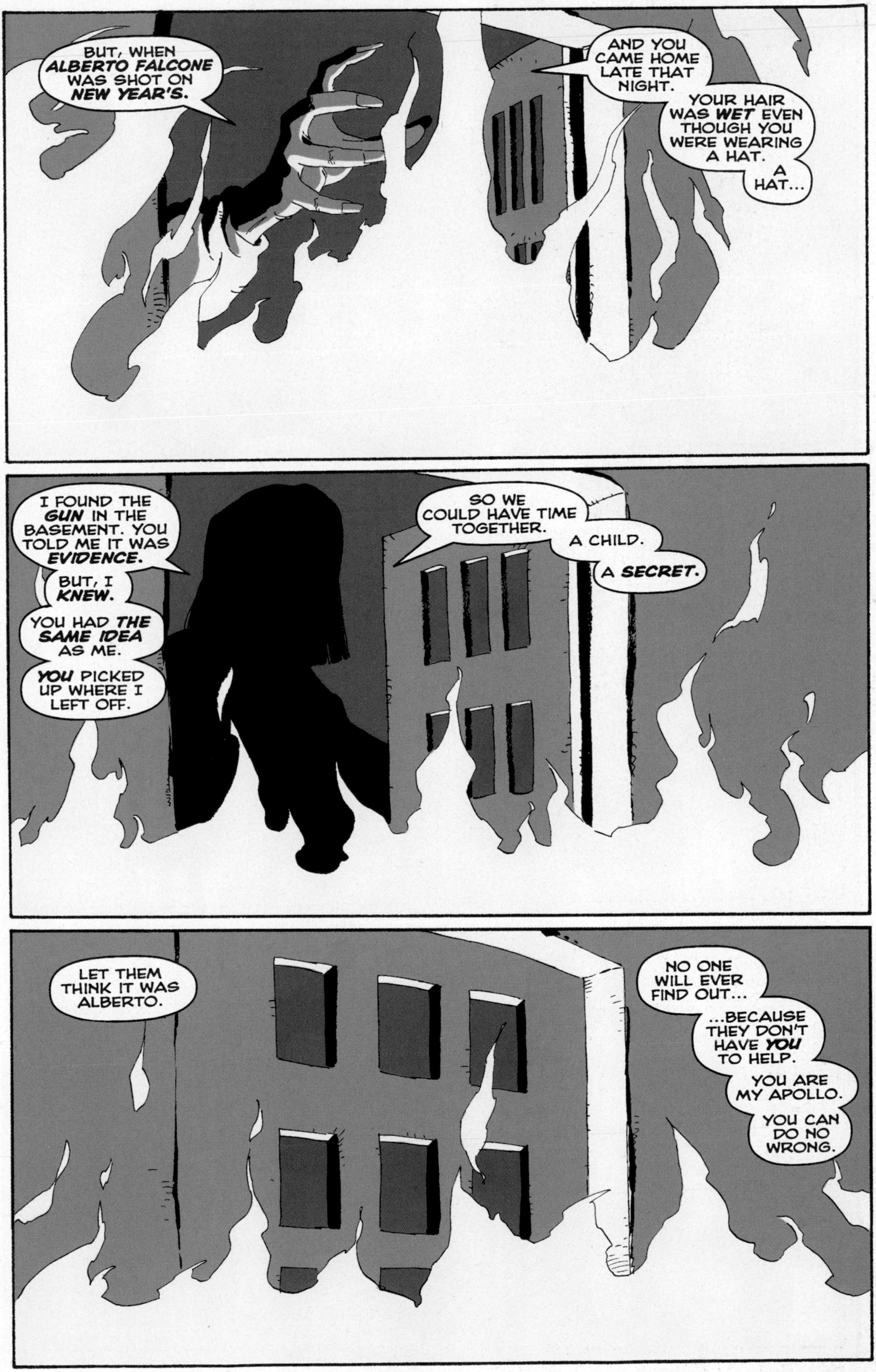
BUT, WHEN ALBERTO FALCONE WAS SHOT ON NEW YEAR'S.
AND YOU CAME HOME LATE THAT NIGHT.
YOUR HAIR WAS WET EVEN THOUGH YOU WERE WEARING A HAT.
A HAT...
I FOUND THE GUN IN THE BASEMENT. YOU TOLD ME IT WAS EVIDENCE.
BUT, I KNEW.
YOU HAD THE SAME IDEA AS ME.
YOU PICKED UP WHERE I LEFT OFF.
SO WE COULD HAVE TIME TOGETHER.
A CHILD.
A SECRET.
LET THEM THINK IT WAS ALBERTO.
NO ONE WILL EVER FIND OUT...
...BECAUSE THEY DON'T HAVE YOU TO HELP.
YOU ARE MY APOLLO.
YOU CAN DO NO WRONG.

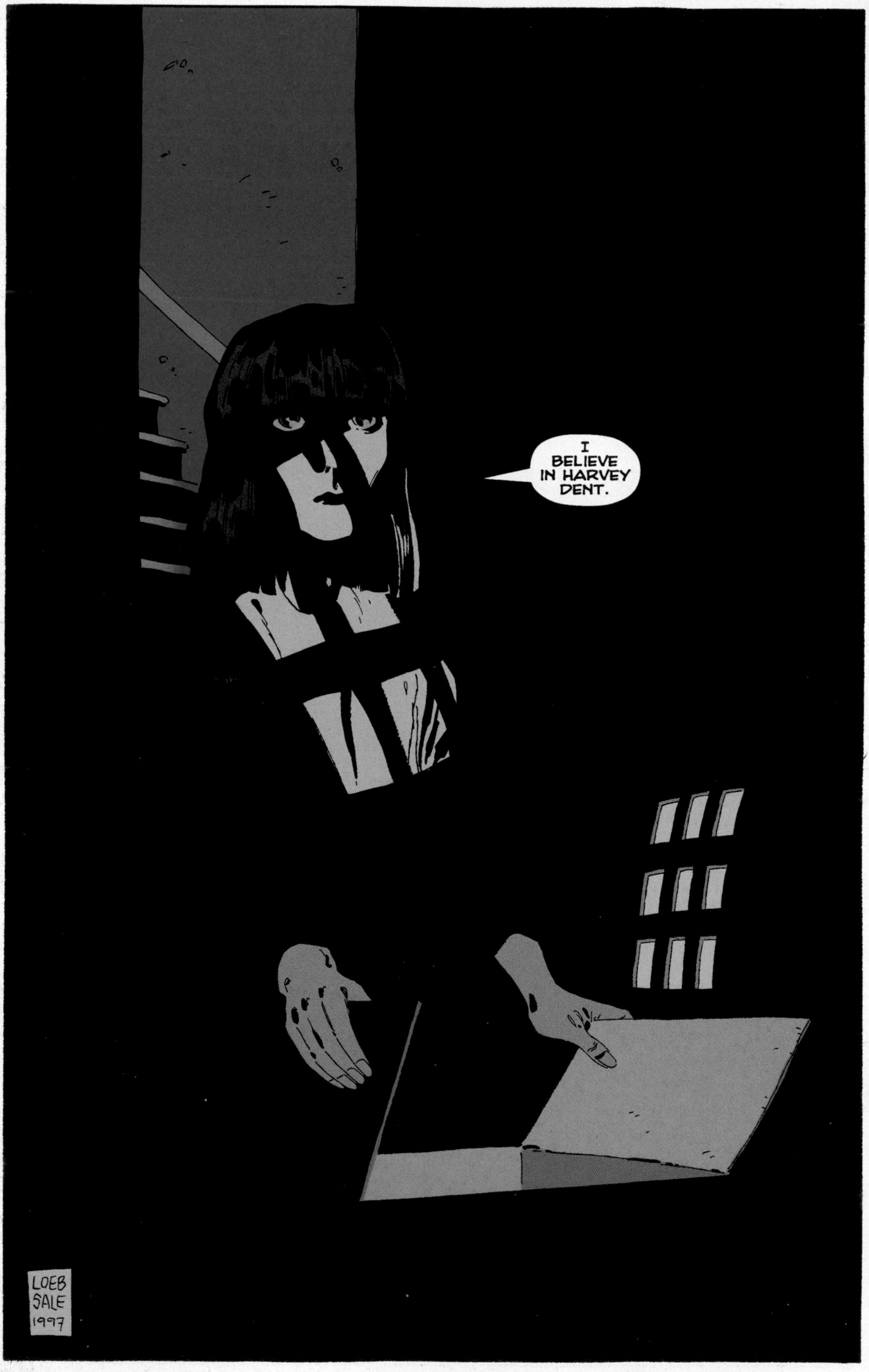
I BELIEVE IN HARVEY DENT.
LOEB SALE 1997

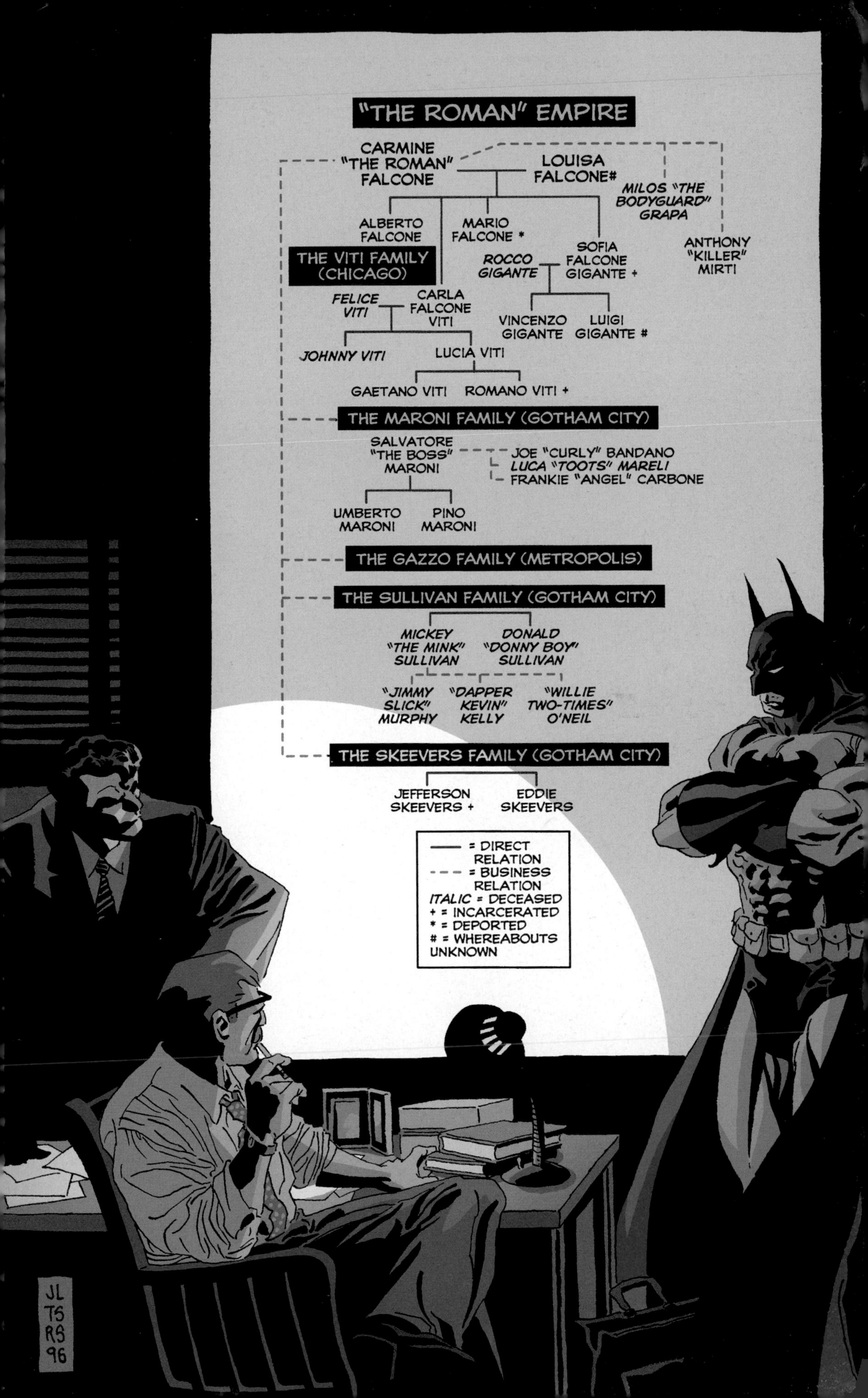
"THE ROMAN" EMPIRE
CARMINE "THE ROMAN" FALCONE
LOUISA FALCONE#
MILOS "THE BODYGUARD" GRAPA
ANTHONY "KILLER" MIRTI
ALBERTO FALCONE
MARIO FALCONE *
SOFIA FALCONE GIGANTE +
ROCCO GIGANTE
THE VITI FAMILY (CHICAGO)
FELICE VITI
CARLA FALCONE VITI
VINCENZO GIGANTE
LUIGI GIGANTE #
JOHNNY VITI
LUCIA VITI
GAETANO VITI
ROMANO VITI +
THE MARONI FAMILY (GOTHAM CITY)
SALVATORE "THE BOSS" MARONI
JOE "CURLY" BANDANO
LUCA "TOOTS" MARELI
FRANKIE "ANGEL" CARBONE
UMBERTO MARONI
PINO MARONI
THE GAZZO FAMILY (METROPOLIS)
THE SULLIVAN FAMILY (GOTHAM CITY)
MICKEY "THE MINK" SULLIVAN
DONALD "DONNY BOY" SULLIVAN
"JIMMY SLICK" MURPHY
"DAPPER KEVIN" KELLY
"WILLIE TWO-TIMES" O'NEIL
THE SKEEVERS FAMILY (GOTHAM CITY)
JEFFERSON SKEEVERS +
EDDIE SKEEVERS
— = DIRECT RELATION
- - - = BUSINESS RELATION
ITALIC = DECEASED
+ = INCARCERATED
* = DEPORTED
# = WHEREABOUTS UNKNOWN
JL TS RS 96

LONG HALLOWEEN HOLIDAY COVERS

TIM: With THE LONG HALLOWEEN, Jeph and I wanted to have a thematic cohesion to the covers, and Jeph came up with the idea of each cover depicting the villain of that month in a setting depicting the holiday highlighted in that issue.

JEPH: I really like the Valentine's Day with Catwoman, Batman, and Ivy. Oddly enough, Jim Lee would do a similarly themed idea on the second HUSH cover (BATMAN #609).

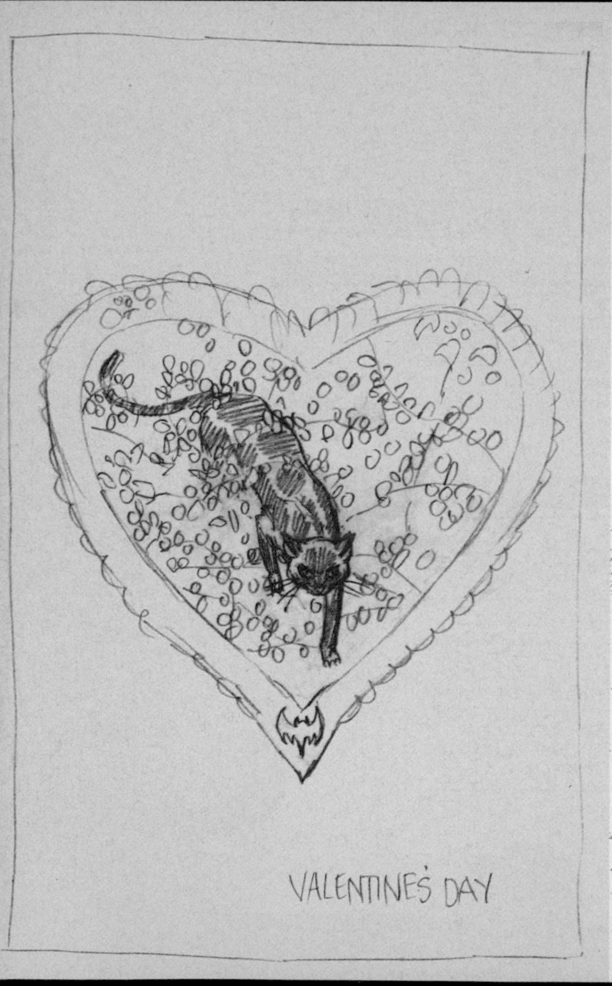
VALENTINE'S DAY

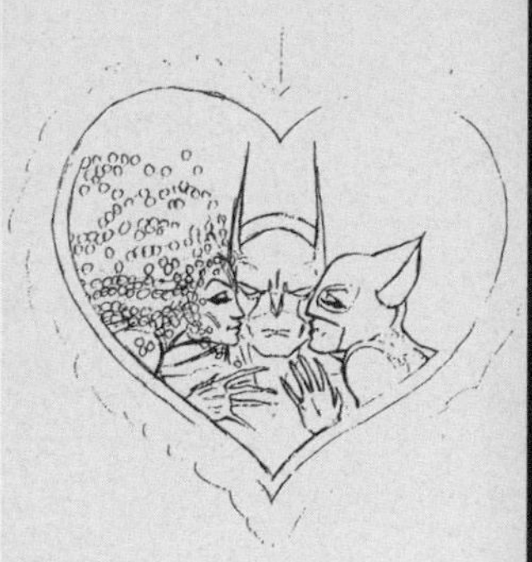

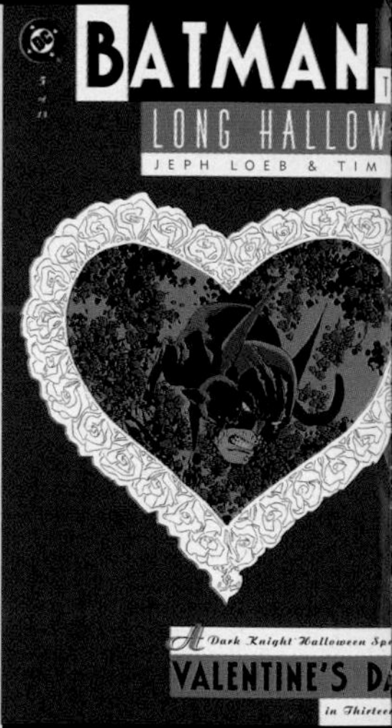
BATMAN
JEPH LOEB & TIM

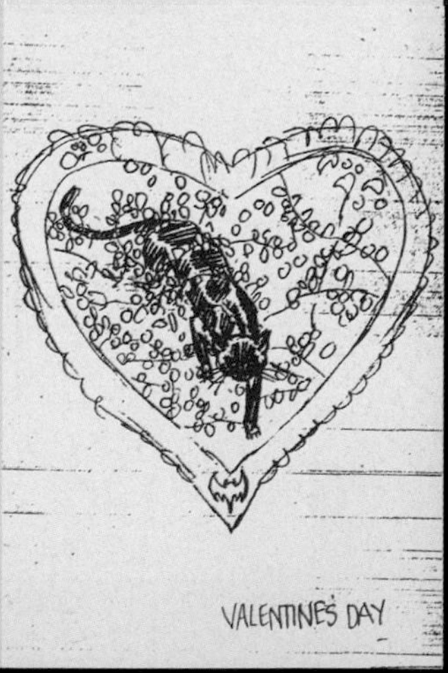
VALENTINE'S DAY

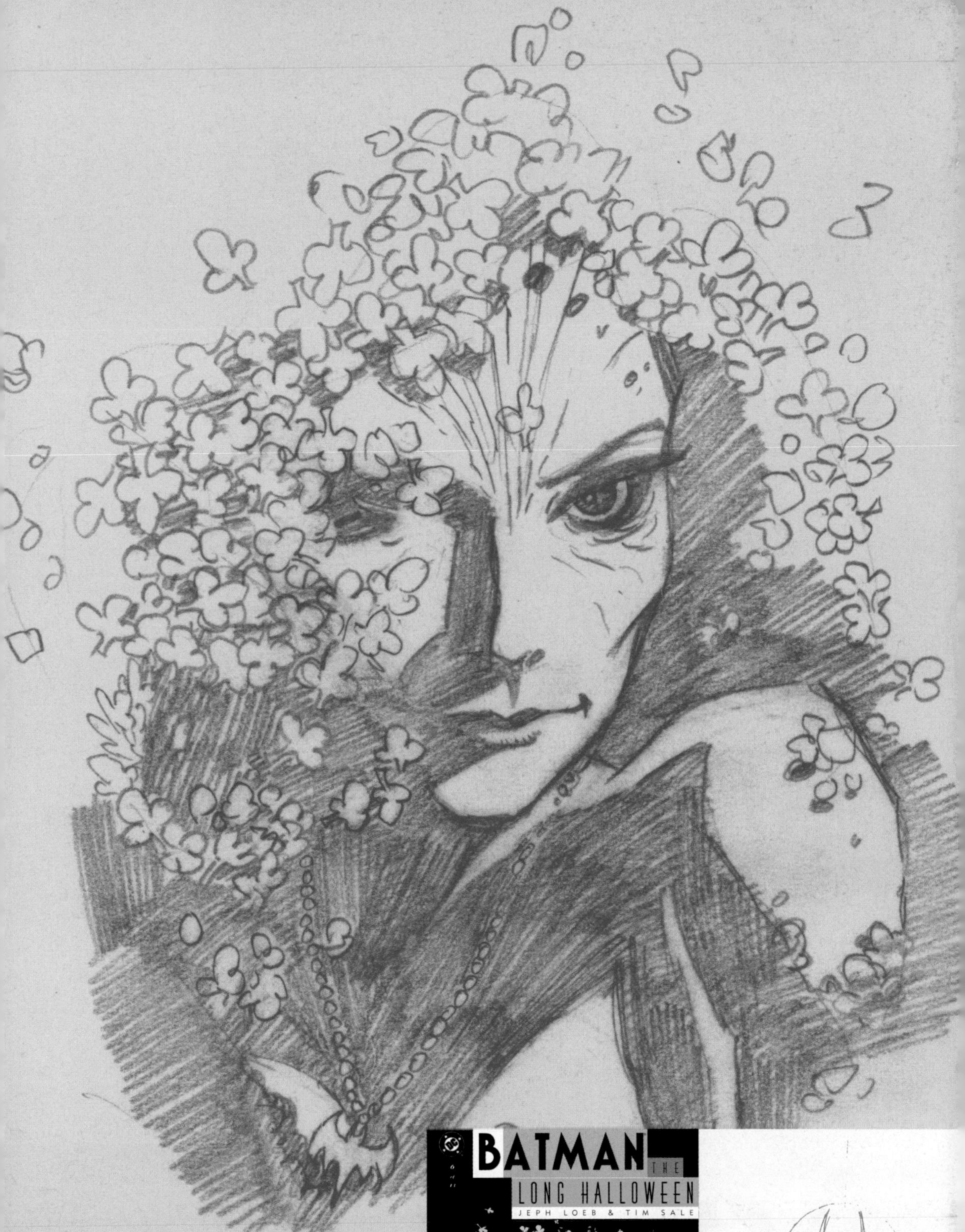

TIM: Other holidays were less clear, and required more work. I was happy to have Poison Ivy be the villain in March, otherwise my drawing of Batman drinking green beer would have made its debut.

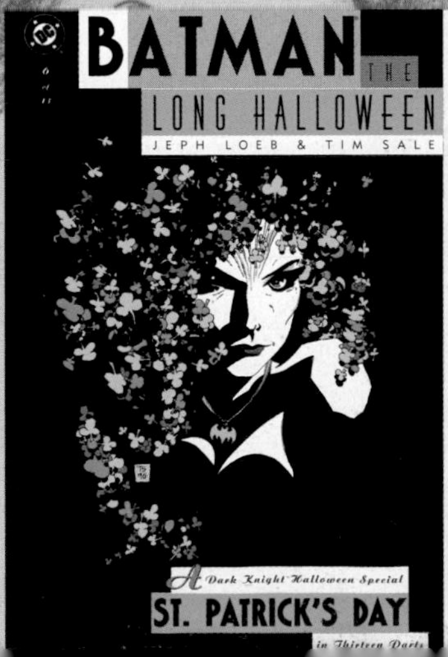
BATMAN
THE
LONG HALLOWEEN
JEPH LOEB & TIM SALE
A Dark Knight Halloween Special
ST. PATRICK'S DAY
in Thirteen Parts

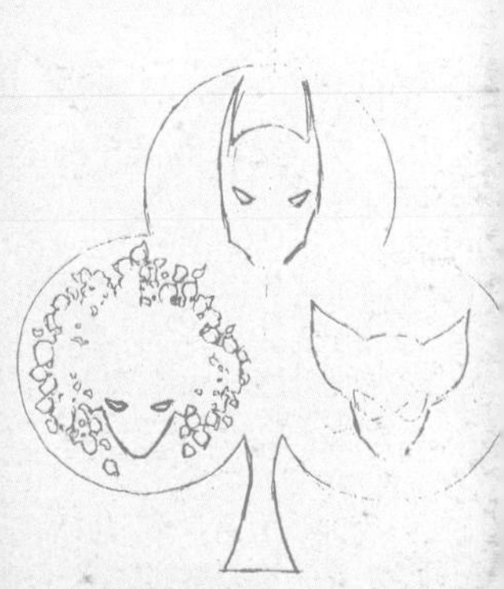

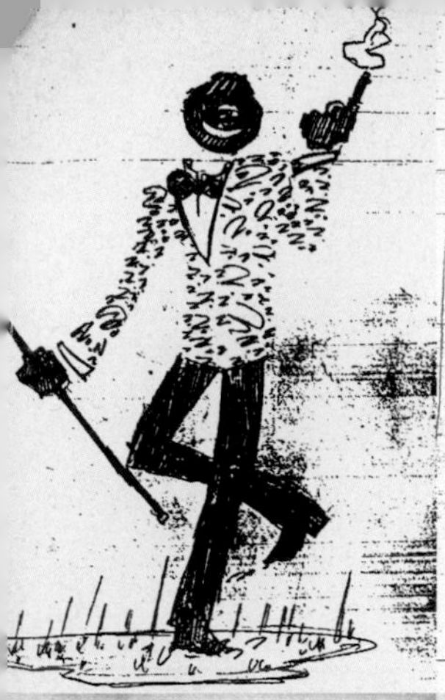

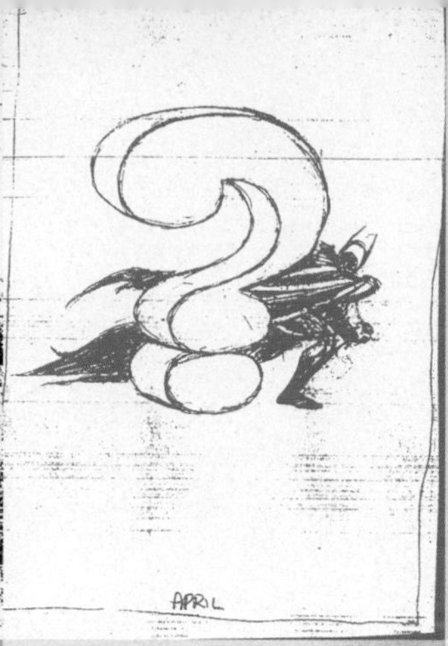
APRIL

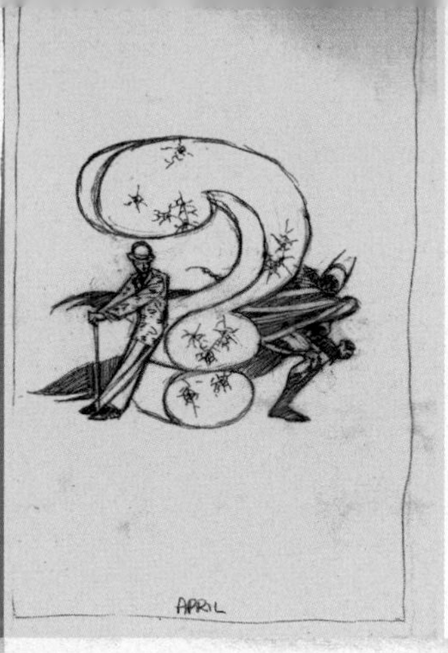
APRIL

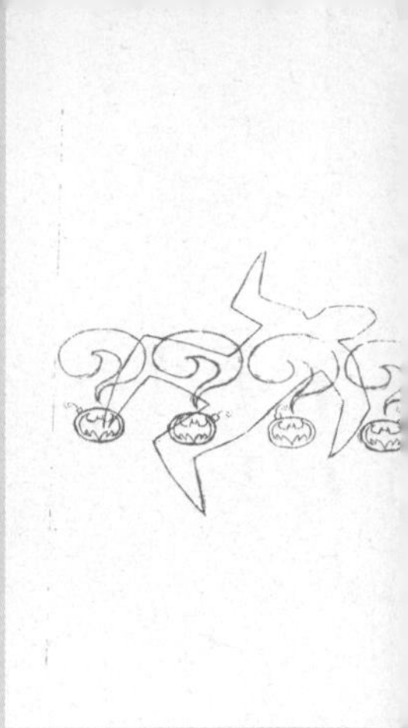

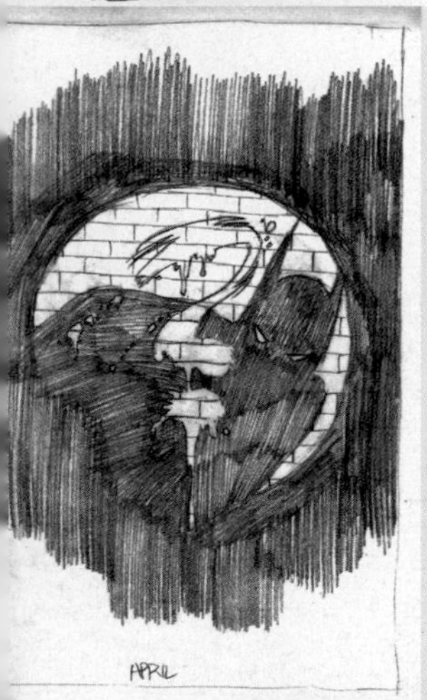
APRIL

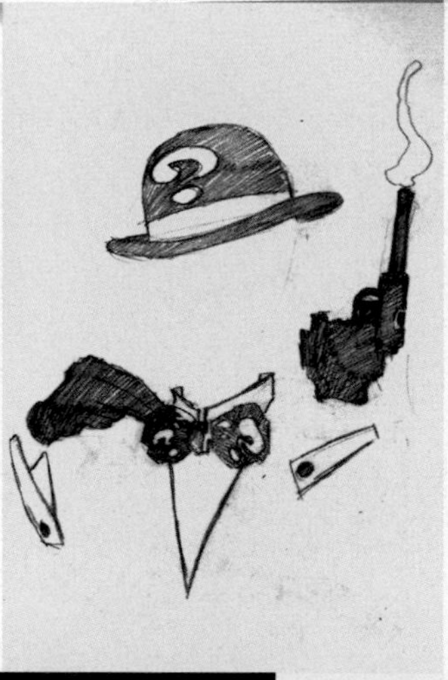

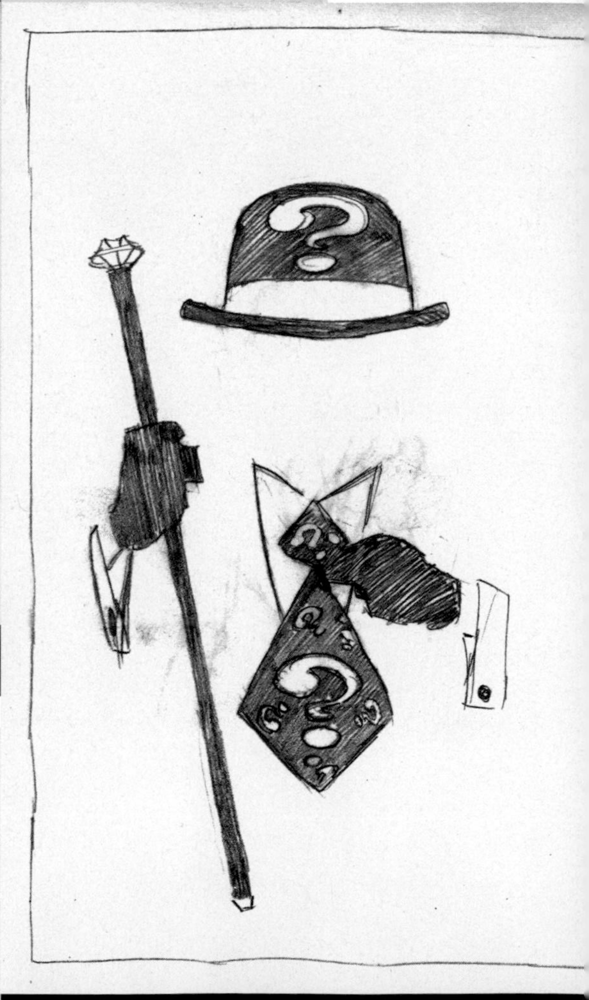

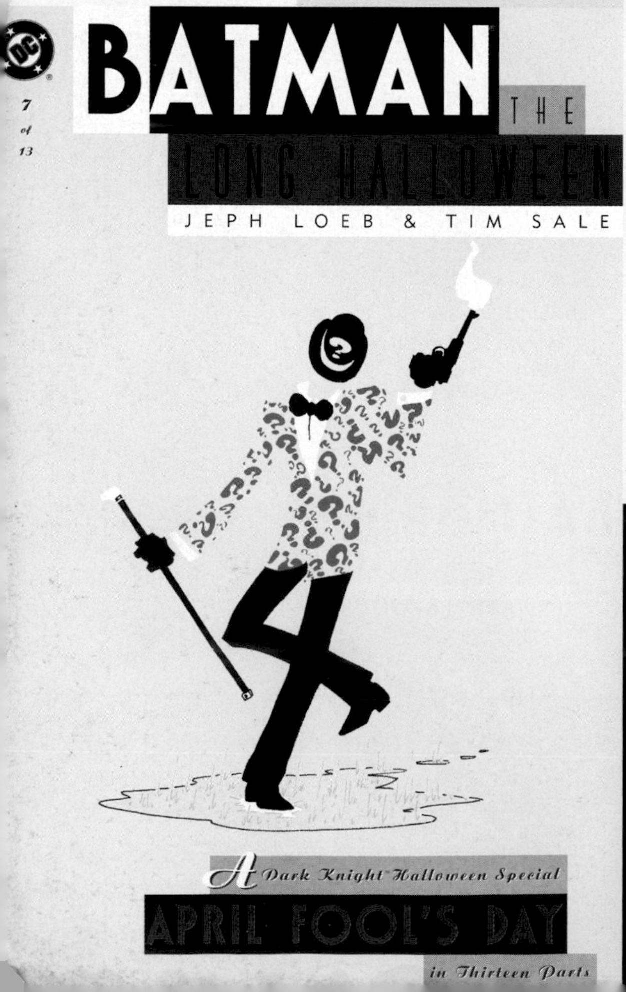
DC
BATMAN
THE
LONG HALLOWEEN
7
of
13
JEPH LOEB & TIM SALE
A Dark Knight Halloween Special
APRIL FOOL'S DAY
in Thirteen Parts

TIM: April also proved to be a challenge, although once I hit upon a design inspired by illustrator Coles Phillips' "fadeaway girl" look, I had my April Showers concept.

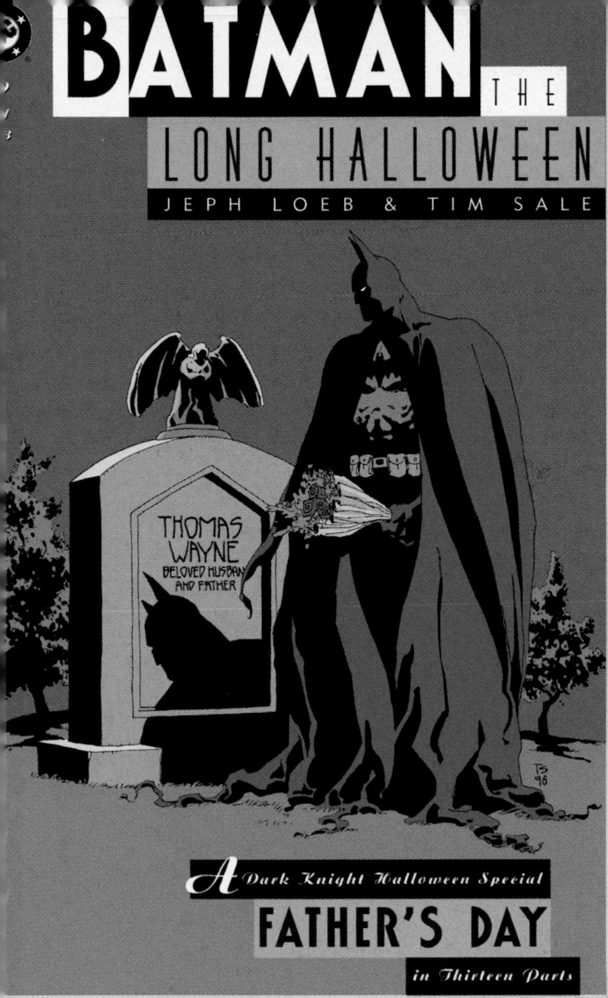
BATMAN
THE
LONG HALLOWEEN
JEPH LOEB & TIM SALE
THOMAS WAYNE
BELOVED HUSBAND AND FATHER
A Dark Knight Halloween Special
FATHER'S DAY
in Thirteen Parts

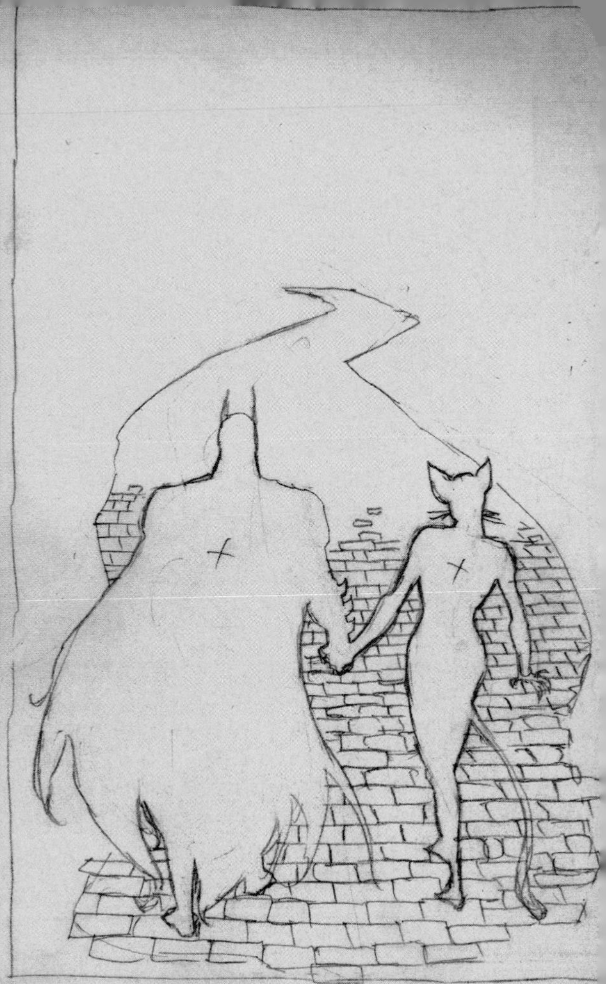

TIM: Mother's Day and Father's Day, Jeph wanted to mirror the young Bruce Wayne and the adult Batman.

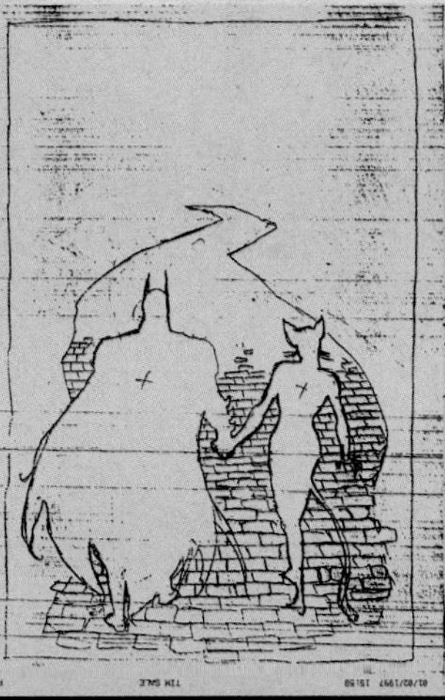

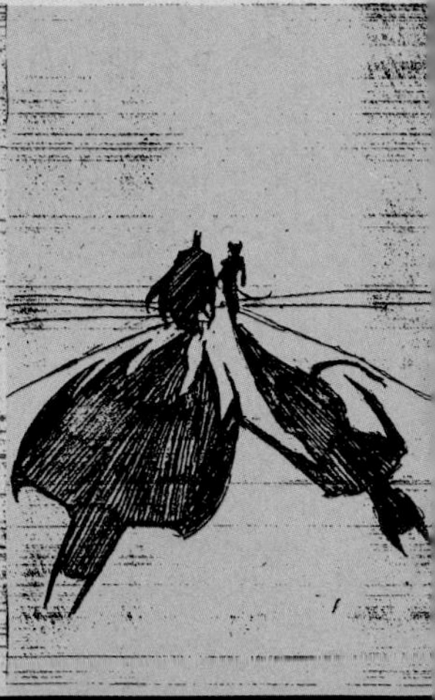

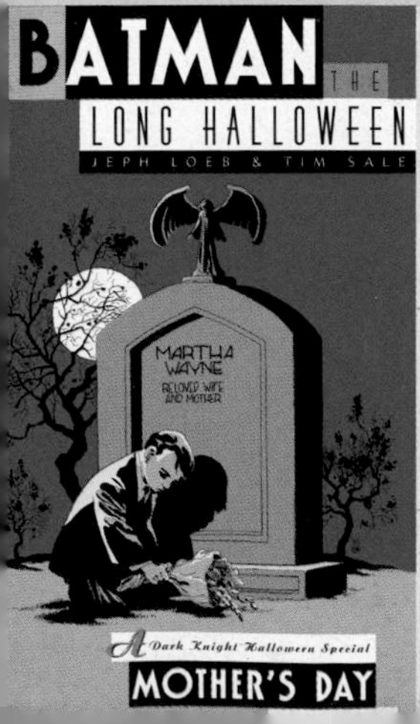
BATMAN
THE
LONG HALLOWEEN
JEPH LOEB & TIM SALE
MARTHA WAYNE
BELOVED WIFE AND MOTHER
A Dark Knight Halloween Special
MOTHER'S DAY

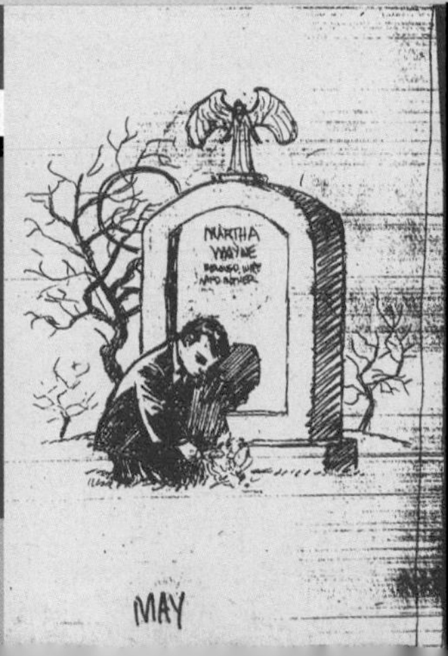
MAY

JEPH: (August) was the one without a holiday. But, my Dad's birthday was August 2nd (as a kid it was referred to as "the best day") so it was a smile to make the Roman's birthday the same day.

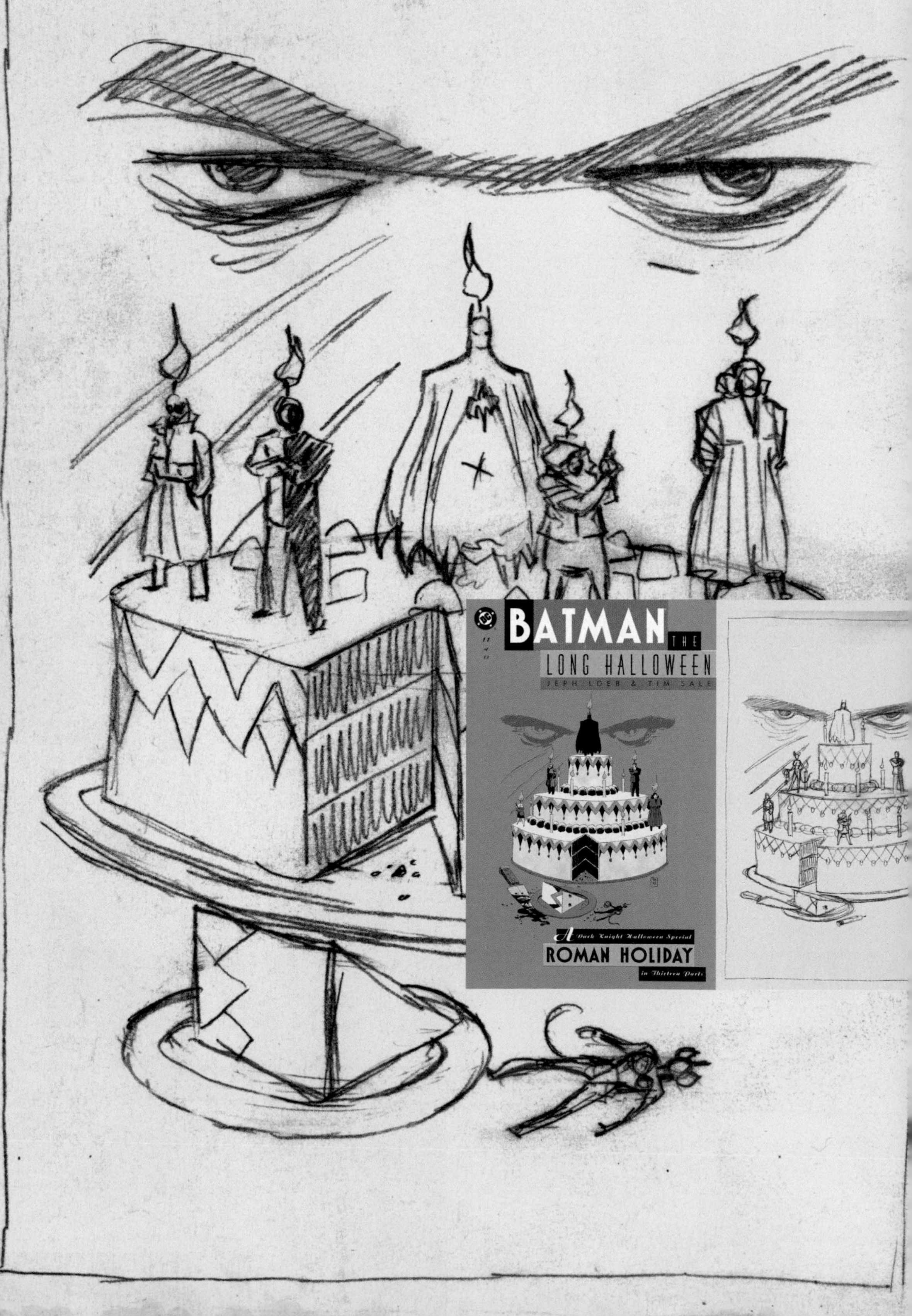
BATMAN
THE
LONG HALLOWEEN
JEPH LOEB & TIM SALE
A Dark Knight Halloween Special
ROMAN HOLIDAY
in Thirteen Parts

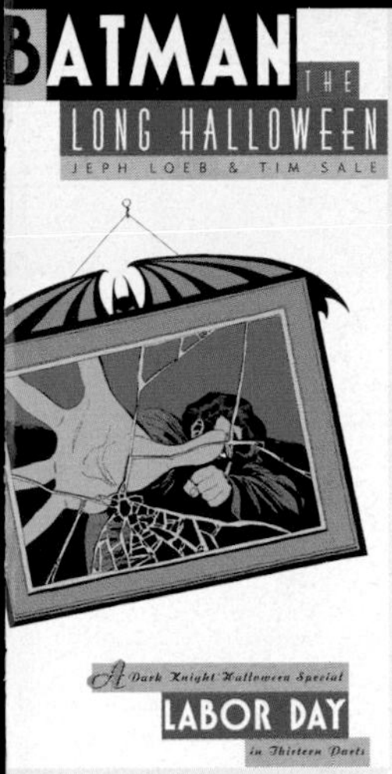
BATMAN THE
LONG HALLOWEEN
JEPH LOEB & TIM SALE
A Dark Knight Halloween Special
LABOR DAY
in Thirteen Parts

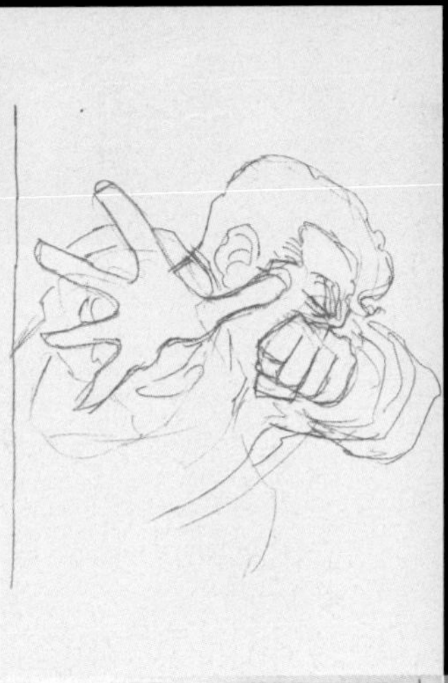

JEPH: This was, to my memory, the hardest one to come up with a concept. And we were close to the end and knew the Two-Face Pumpkin was in the bag for October. Archie Goodwin teased that we should have a pair of white sneakers and a hammer. He actually had to explain that there's a fashion no-no that you don't wear white after Labor Day.

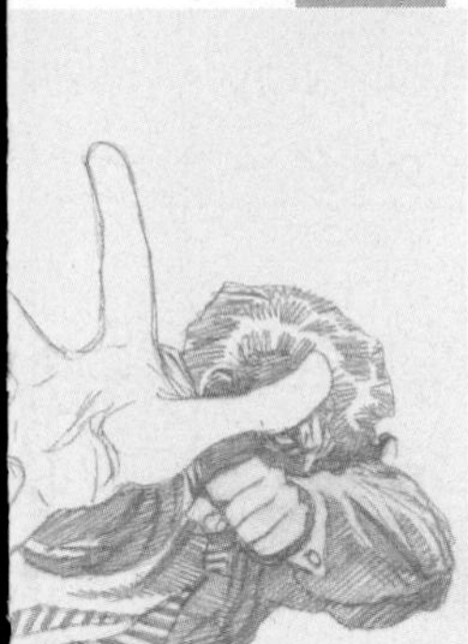

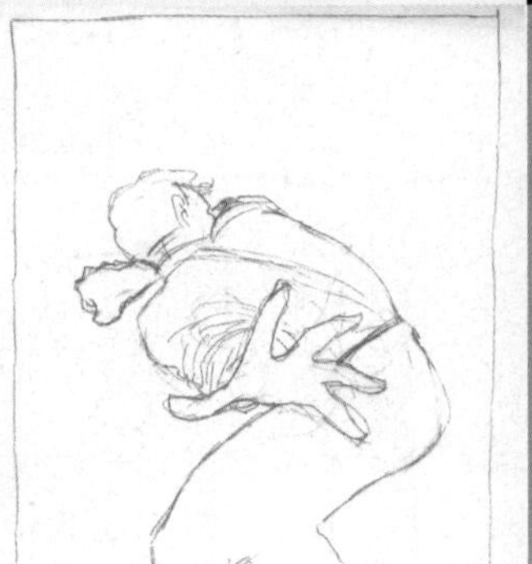

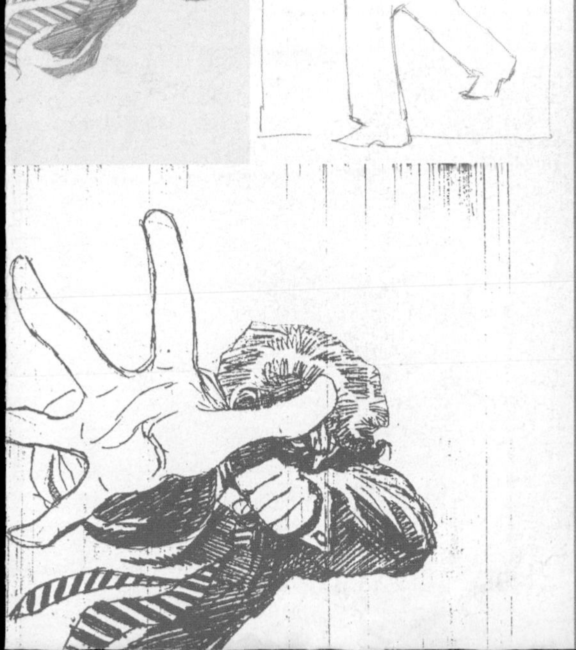

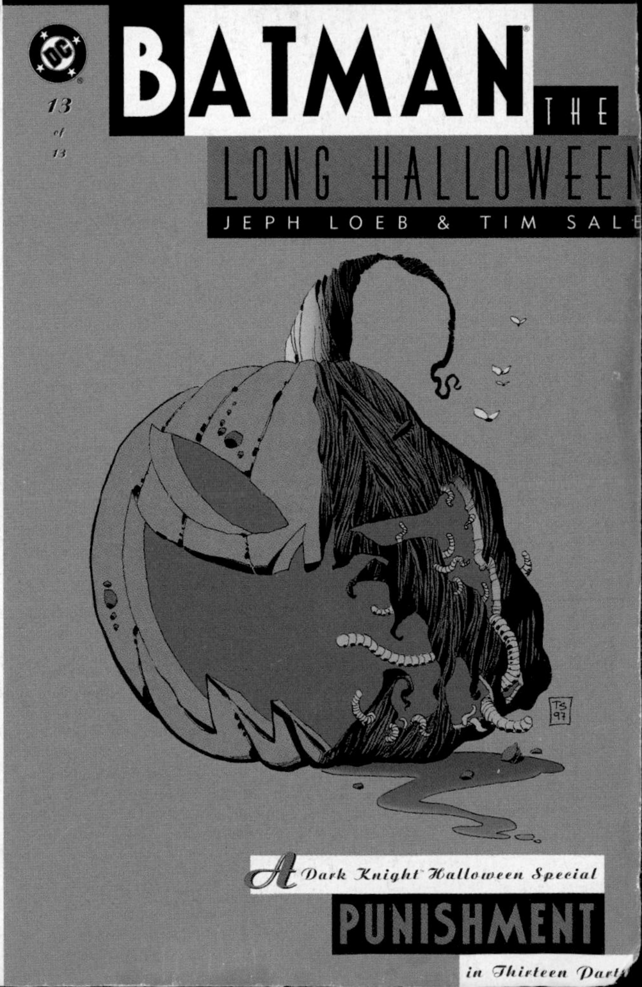
13
of
13
BATMAN THE
LONG HALLOWEEN
JEPH LOEB & TIM SAL
A Dark Knight Halloween Special
PUNISHMENT
in Thirteen Part

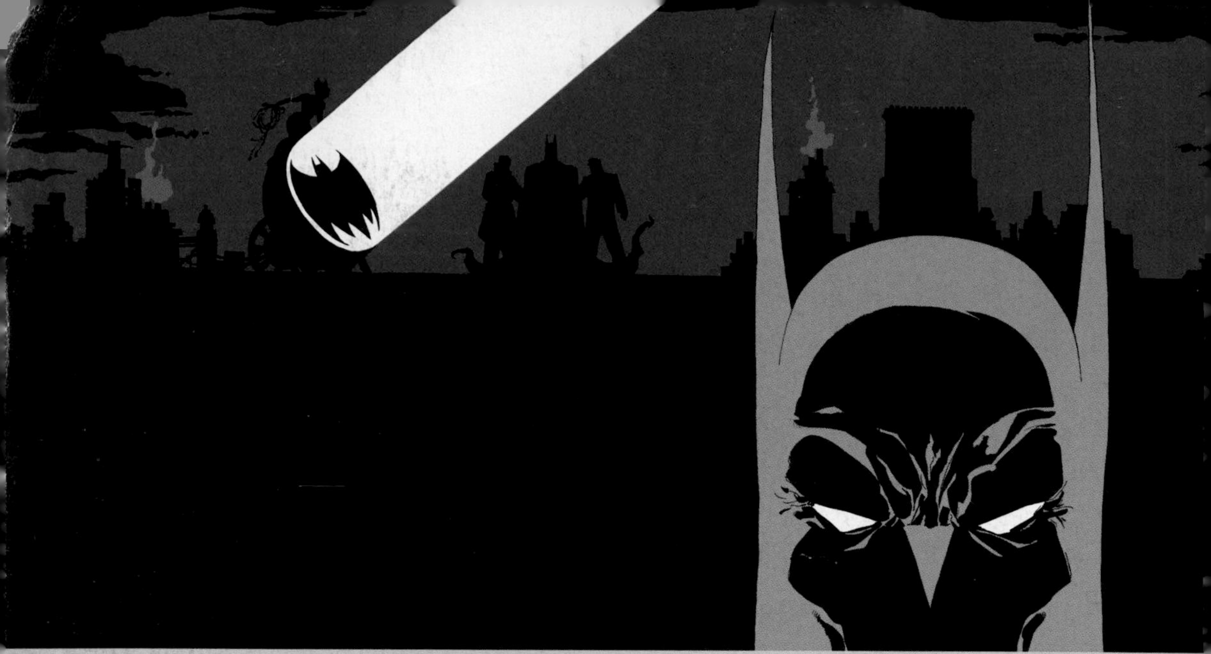

Wraparound cover art by Tim Sale from original hardcover collection of BATMAN: THE LONG HALLOWEEN.

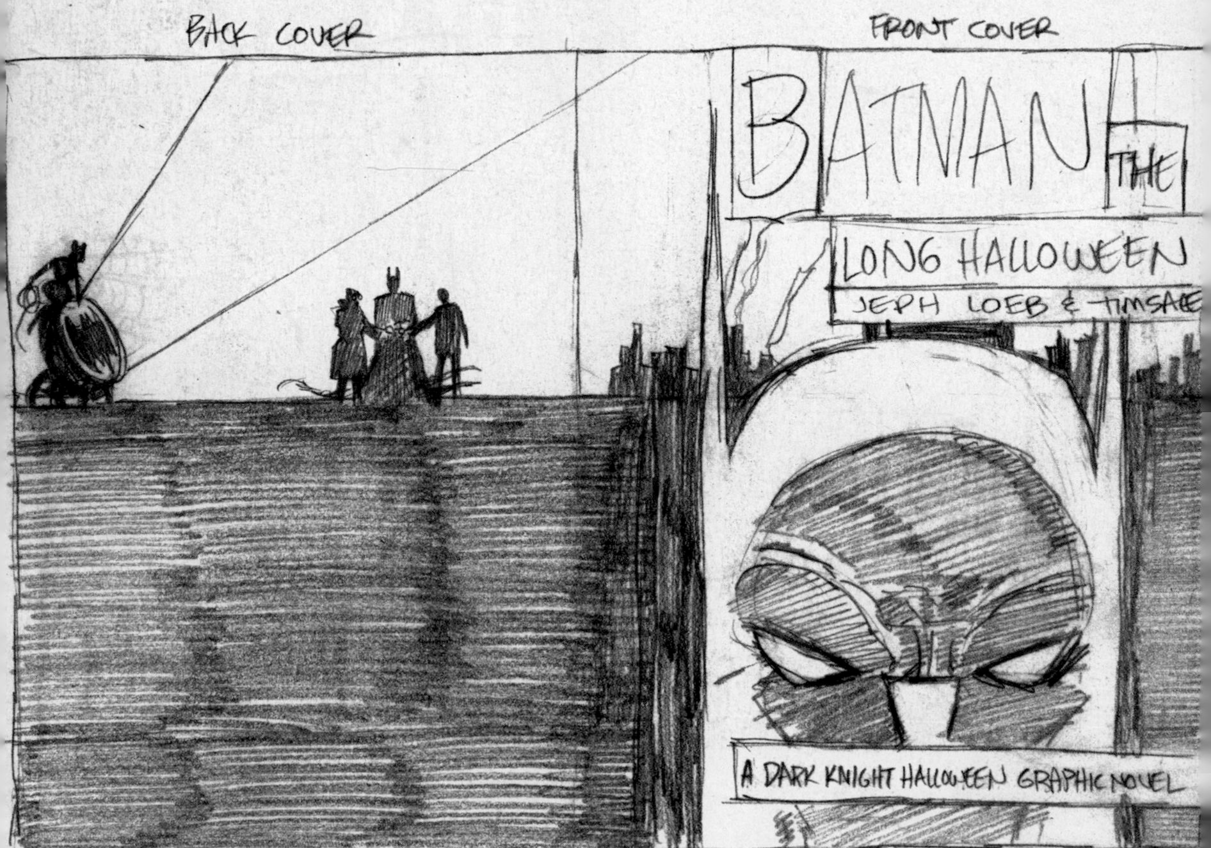

BACK COVER
FRONT COVER
BATMAN THE
LONG HALLOWEEN
JEPH LOEB & TIM SALE
A DARK KNIGHT HALLOWEEN GRAPHIC NOVEL

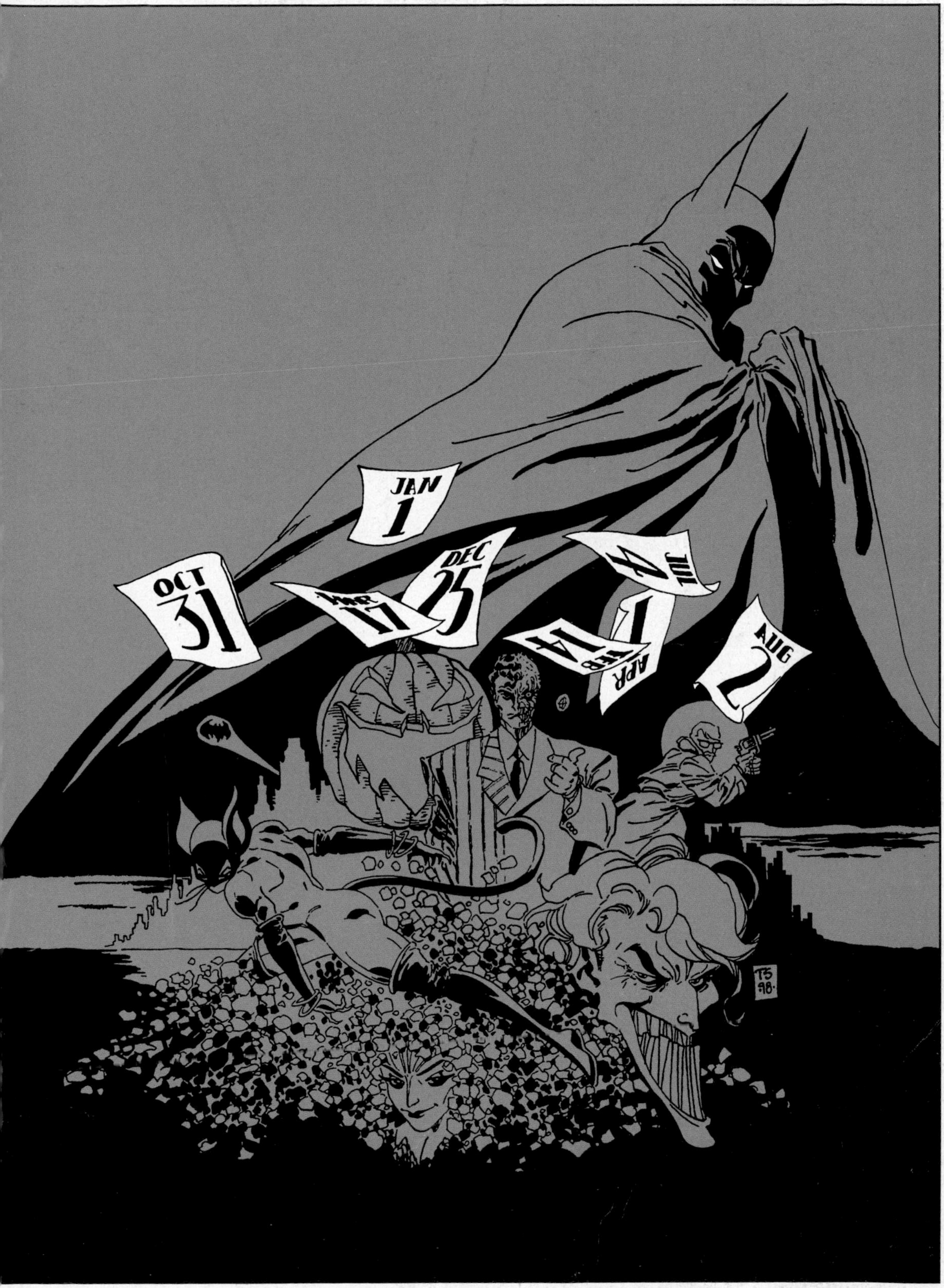
JAN 1
OCT 31
DEC 25
JUL 4
FEB 14
APR 1
AUG 2
TS 98.

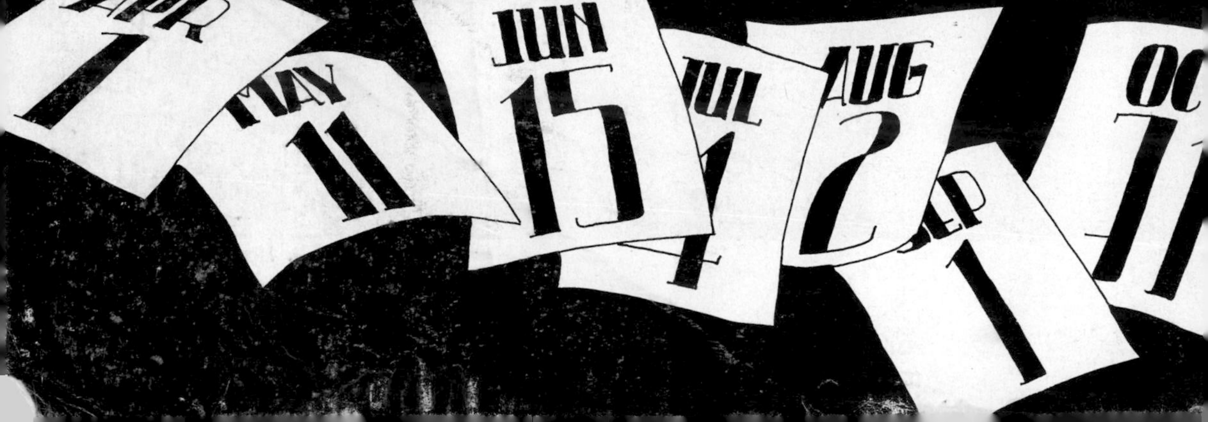
APR
1
MAY
11
JUN
15
AUG
2